GERALD DURRELL

Other biographies by the same author

Humboldt and the Cosmos
Hitler's Last General (with Ian Sayer)
Gavin Maxwell: A Life

GERALD DURRELL

THE AUTHORISED
BIOGRAPHY

Douglas Botting

HarperCollins*Publishers*

HarperCollins*Publishers*
77–85 Fulham Palace Road,
Hammersmith, London w6 8jb

Published by HarperCollins*Publishers* 1999
Copyright © Douglas Botting 1999

1 3 5 7 9 8 6 4 2
Douglas Botting asserts the moral right to
be identified as the author of this work

A catalogue record for this book is
available from the British Library

ISBN 0 00 255660 X

Set in PostScript Linotype Sabon by
Rowland Phototypesetting Ltd,
Bury St Edmunds, Suffolk

Printed and bound in Great Britain by
Caledonian International Book Manufacturing Ltd, Glasgow

Contents

Illustrations

Between pages 108 and 109

The marriage of Gerald Durrell's parents at Roorkee in North-West Province on 23 November 1910.

The Durrell family around 1923.

Gerald in his Indian babyhood.

Gerald as a toddler.

Gerald aged one at Brighton beach with Margo and Leslie during a visit to England in 1926.

Eight-year-old Gerald with his mother in Bournemouth before the Corfu adventure.

Gerald and Roger the dog soon after their arrival on Corfu in 1935.

On an enchanted evening near Pérama Gerald sits at the roadside overlooking an age-old view towards Mouse Island.

The Durrells on the balcony of the Daffodil-Yellow Villa in the winter of 1936.

Another group photo at the Daffodil-Yellow Villa.

Leslie on his boat in the summer of 1937.

Maria Condos, the Durrell family maid and later the mother of Leslie's child.

Dr Theo Stephanides, Gerald's mentor and natural history instructor.

The Snow-White Villa, last of the Durrells' three houses on Corfu.

Spiro and Gerald cooking a picnic dish of eels in red wine at a bay near the Lake of Lilies.

Gerald, aged eleven, with a pet barn owl.

Gerald and his faithful servant Pious in the Cameroons, 1948.

Second Cameroons expedition, 1949. Gerald and Ken Smith with African hunters and assorted monkeys.

Gerald's precious angwantibo.

Gerald at Liverpool Docks on his return from his second Cameroons expedition.

Ken Smith, Robert Lowes and Gerald getting the better of an eight-foot boa constrictor, British Guiana, 1950.

The most arduous part of any animal-collecting expedition: lecturing about it afterwards.

Gerald with iguana at a book fair in London in the 1950s.

Gerald at around the time he met Jacquie Rasen in Manchester.

Between pages 300 and 301

Gerald and Jacquie shortly after their marriage on 26 February 1951.

The attic room in Margaret's boarding house in Bournemouth where Gerald wrote his first best-selling books.

Book signing on publication day of *My Family and Other Animals*.

The Fon of Bafut. (*Howard Sochurek/Life Magazine Time Inc./ Katz*)

Jacquie dances the samba with the Fon, Bafut, 1957. (*Howard Sochurek/Life Magazine Time Inc./ Katz*)

One way of catching animals in the bush: doing it yourself. (*Howard Sochurek/ Life Magazine Time Inc./ Katz*)

Another way of catching animals: getting others to catch them for you. (*Howard Sochurek/Life Magazine Time Inc./ Katz*)

Gerald and Jacquie attend to their collection of Cameroons creatures in the back garden of Margaret's boarding house, 1957.

Les Augrès Manor, the sixteenth-century Jersey manor house that became the Durrell home and zoo headquarters in 1959.

Gerald with Claudius the tapir from Argentina.

Paula the cheetah taking Jeremy Mallinson for his morning run.

A young orang-utan quizzically pondering his human chum.

Chumley, Gerald and Lulu enjoying choir practice, 1959. (*BBC Natural History Unit*)

Gerald with Mai Zetterling and David Hughes.

Gerald and Lawrence with a rhesus monkey at the manor house, 1960.

Durrell family reunion, Christmas 1960.

Mother and son, Jersey, early 1960s.

Gerald and Jacquie, Jersey, 1969.

Gerald with albino emu, Australia, 1962.

Gerald and John Hartley during shooting of *Catch me a Colobus* in Sierra Leone, 1965. (*BBC Natural History Unit*)

A split-second of the formidable Durrell charm, 1966.

Between pages 492 and 493

Jambo, the silverback patriarch of the lowland gorillas at Jersey Zoo.

His son Assumbo, born 15 July 1973.

Jill Pook and Jeremy Usher-Smith with young captive-bred gorillas at Jersey Zoo in the 1970s.

Jambo stands guard over the unconscious body of five-year-old Levan Merritt, who had fallen into the gorilla enclosure. (*Peter De Sousa*)

Golden lion tamarin and young from Brazil.

Pigmy hog of Assam, the world's smallest pig.

Black and white ruffed lemur of Madagascar.

Right in the Hart of the Africn Jungel a small
wite man lives. Now there is one rather
xtrordenry fackt about him that is that he is the
frind of *all* animals.

From 'The Man of Animals' by Gerald Durrell, aged ten

Whoever saves one life,
Saves the world.

The Talmud

When you get to the Pearly Gates and St Peter
asks you, 'Well, what did you do?' if you can
say, 'I saved a species from extinction,' I think
he'll say, 'OK, well, come on in.'

John Cleese

Preface

I met Gerald Durrell only once in the flesh. It was in the early summer of 1989 at the London Butterfly House in Syon Park, where he and his wife Lee ceremonially launched an initiative called 'Programme for Belize' – intended to save for posterity a superb tract of tropical forest in the north-east of that country – by releasing newly hatched Belizean butterflies into the Butterfly House. Our encounter afterwards, as Durrell passed down a line of extended hands on his way out through the door, was brief, polite and perfunctory. At this meeting neither he nor I could have dreamed that biographer was meeting biographee. Had we known it, we would have had a lot to talk about. With better luck all round, we might have been talking still.

I thought no more about this until, one scorching late September noon in 1994, I found myself sitting with my elder daughter Kate on the terrace of the White House, Lawrence Durrell's old pre-war home at Kalami on the north-east coast of Corfu, watching the caïques coming in to the bay one by one, each with its complement of tourists on board. Across the water I could hear the running commentary of the Greek skippers. 'And now we enter beautiful Kalami Bay,' they intoned. 'On your left you will see the famous White House where Gerald Durrell once lived in Corfu and wrote his famous book, *My Family and Other Animals* . . .'

Gerald Durrell, of course, had done nothing of the kind. I turned to Kate. 'That's all wrong,' I said. 'Someone ought to do something to get it right. Come to think of it, someone ought to do something about writing a proper biography of Gerald Durrell.'

Kate, who was a Durrell fan, replied: 'Perhaps you ought to write it yourself.'

It was not a totally wild idea. I had already written two books about traveller-naturalists, and my recently published biography of the author-naturalist Gavin Maxwell had been well enough received for me to begin to think about writing some kind of sequel. I had read most of Gerald Durrell's books, I had even reviewed one or two for the national press, I felt I understood his world and mind-set, I had even – dammit! – shaken the man by the hand in the Butterfly House. As soon as I returned to England I phoned Gerald Durrell's personal assistant at Jersey Zoo, and on his advice wrote to Durrell's literary agent enclosing a copy of my latest book and, for good measure, proposing myself as her client's future biographer.

Within a few hours my book was in Durrell's hands in a London hospital ward, where he lay gravely ill after a major operation. He knew of Gavin Maxwell, of course, and had reviewed *Ring of Bright Water* for the *New York Times*. He opened the book and read the first lines of the preface: 'The sea in the little bay is still tonight and a full moon casts a wan pallor over the Sound and the hills of Skye. A driftwood fire crackles in the hearth of the croft on the beach, and through the open window I can hear all the sounds and ghosts of the night – the *kraak* of a solitary heron stalking fish in the moonlight at the edge of the shore, a seal singing softly in the bay, the plaintive child-like voice rising and falling like a lullaby in the dark . . .' Here in the noisy bedlam of the public ward, a world of bedpans, drips, catheters, trolleys and rubber sheets, of pain, squalor and despair, his weary head sunk deep into his hard starched pillow, his wild white hair strewn about him, he recognised at once a kind of mirror image of his own past life and dreams. He turned the page. 'A guru of the wilds among a whole generation, Gavin Maxwell was ranked with John Burroughs, W. H. Hudson and Gerald Durrell as one of the finest nature writers of the last hundred years . . .'

Durrell sat up a bit. For some time he had been putting together scattered fragments of his own autobiography. But lately, as the ceaseless cycle of fever and crisis, relapse and remission continued seemingly without end, he had put aside his notebook and pen. From time to time in recent years he had been approached by authors or would-be authors who had put themselves forward as his prospective biographer. Many of these had been wishful-thinkers and no-hopers, but one or two had been serious candidates. So long as he was well and active the story of his life was his own copy, and his alone. But now the situation had changed. He asked his wife Lee to read the book aloud to him, and as she read he began to feel that perhaps he had found his biographer. Henceforth the biography was a reality, something to aim at, a goal to achieve. In the highly adverse circumstances in which he found himself, it was to be one of the last preoccupations of his life.

Gerald was anxious to meet up with me in order to talk about the project face to face, and to come to a decision. But each time Lee called me with a date on which to visit the hospital she would have to ring back to reschedule, because Gerald was back in intensive care. Our meeting was not to be. Shortly after his death in January 1995, Lee authorised me to write a full and frank account of his life and work.

Over the next two years, I came to know more about Gerald Durrell than I did about myself. I thought I had got the measure of the man. Then one day I came upon an extraordinary, and utterly unexpected, sequence of private love letters. Here was a man moved by passion, joy, fear, romantic and erotic love, and by gratitude to the love of his life and to life itself and to the world. As I read, I inwardly sang and laughed and declaimed with him. And then I came to a letter written on 31 July 1978, and I fell silent:

> I have seen a thousand moons: harvest moons like golden coins, winter moons as white as ice chips, new moons like baby swans' feathers ... I have felt winds as tender and warm as a lover's breath, winds straight from the South Pole, bleak and wailing like a lost child ... I have known silence: the implacable stony silence of a deep cave; the silence when great music ends ... I have heard tree frogs in an orchestration as complicated as Bach singing in a forest lit by a million emerald fireflies. I have heard the cobweb squeak of the bat, wolves baying at a winter's moon ... I have seen hummingbirds flashing like opals round a tree of scarlet blooms. I have seen whales, black as tar, cushioned on a cornflower blue sea. I have lain in water warm as milk, soft as silk, while around me played a host of dolphins ... All this I did without you. This was my loss ...

As I read, I began to realise, first with disbelief and then with some degree of unease, that the voice inside my head was no longer my own. I had heard enough of Gerald Durrell's soft, beguiling, cultured English diction on tapes of interviews and radio and television broadcasts to be able to identify it with certainty. There was no doubt. The voice reading this impassioned love letter was Durrell's own. Not only had I got the measure of Gerald Durrell; Gerald Durrell, it seemed, had got the measure of me. I recalled something Sir David Attenborough had said at the farewell celebration of the man in London after his death: 'Gerald Durrell was magic.'

This, then, is the biography of Gerald Durrell – naturalist, traveller, raconteur, humorist, visionary, broadcaster, best-selling author, one of the great nature writers of the twentieth century, one of the great conservation leaders of the modern world, champion of the animal kingdom, founder and Honourary Director of Jersey Zoo and the Jersey Wildlife Preservation Trust, saviour of endangered species, champion of the lowly, the defenceless and the doomed.

I don't think it is hyperbole to say that though Gerald Durrell was not a particularly saintly man – his warts were several, and sometimes spectacular – he led a saintly life in pursuit of a saintly mission: simply put, to save animal species from extinction at the hands of man. In his way he was a latter-day St Francis, confronting a problem that St Francis could never have conceived in his worst nightmare. Since his struggle with that problem helped to kill him, it could be said that Gerald Durrell laid down his life for the animal kingdom and the world of nature he loved.

From the outset this biography was conceived as a full, searching and rounded portrait of the man, his life and his work. It was Lee Durrell's wish, when she authorised the book after her husband's death, that it should be so. In other words, though this book is described as the 'authorised' biography, I have had *carte blanche* in the writing of it, and the portrait of the man and the narrative of the life are mine and mine alone – though none of it could have been put together without the help of many others.

What 'authorised' actually means in this case is that I have been allowed exclusive access to the personal and professional archives of Gerald Durrell (which are voluminous) and to the files of the organisation he founded and directed, the Jersey Wildlife Preservation Trust (now renamed the Durrell Wildlife Conservation Trust). I also enjoyed unqualified freedom in approaching anybody involved in the Gerald Durrell story, of whom there are many.

I would particularly like to thank the following for their unstinting help and encouragement, and for their contributions to the story from its very centre: Dr Lee Durrell (Honorary Director of the Durrell Wildlife Conservation Trust), Jacquie Durrell, Margaret Duncan (*née* Durrell), Jeremy Mallinson OBE (Director of the Durrell Wildlife Conservation Trust), John Hartley (International Programme Director of the Trust), Simon Hicks (currently Development Director of the Trust) and Tony Allchurch (General Administrator, Jersey Zoo). I am also grateful to Peter Harrison, who between teaching assignments in Poland, Russia and the Gulf delved tirelessly into the Durrells' early years, introduced me to Gerald Durrell's Corfu and its *dramatis personae*, and produced a meticulous gloss on my first draft; John and Vivien Burton of the World Land Trust, for many valuable comments and insights; Anthony Smith, for his untiring advice in matters of science and zoology; and Sir David Attenborough, for critically important guidance. Thanks also to my publisher Richard Johnson and my editor Robert Lacey at HarperCollins for the care and support they have afforded this project, and my agent Andrew Hewson at John Johnson and Gerald Durrell's agent Anthea Morton-Saner at Curtis Brown for all their hands-on help and encouragement in bringing this huge task to fruition.

My thanks to Curtis Brown, acting on behalf of Mrs Lee Durrell, for permission to quote from published and unpublished works by Gerald Durrell.

Extracts from Jacquie Durrell's *Beasts in my Bed* (Collins, 1967) are reproduced by kind permission of the author; extracts from David Hughes's *Himself and Other Animals: A Portrait of Gerald Durrell* (Hutchinson, 1997) are reproduced by permission of the author and the publishers.

I would also like to thank Jill Adams; Michael Armstrong; Marie Aspioti; Michael Barrett; Quentin Bloxam (General Curator, Durrell Wildlife Conservation Trust); Kate and Anna Botting; Gordon Bowker; Gerry Breeze; Nicholas Breeze; Sarah Breeze; Tracy Breeze; Felicity Bryan; Rev. Geoffrey Carr; David Cobham; Philip Coffey; Anthony Condos; Menelaus Condos; Fleur Cowles; Sophie Danforth; Anthony Daniells; Eve Durrell; Mr and Mrs Alex Emmett; Doreen Evans; Dr Roger Evans (Manuscript Department, British Library); Tom Evans; W. Paterson Ferns; Bronwen Garth-Thornton; Bob Golding; Anna Grapes; Peter Grose; Lady Rhona Guthrie; Dr Jeremy Guyer; Jonathan Harris; Paula Harris; Gwen Hayball; E.C. (Teddy) Hodgkin; Penelope Hope (*née* Durrell); David Hughes; Dr Michael Hunter; The Earl of Jersey; Carl Jones; Colin Jones; Dorothy Keep; Sarah Kennedy; Françoise Kestsman; Patrick Leigh-Fermor; Vi Lort-Phillips; Thomas Lovejoy; Judy Mackrell; Odette Mallinson; Stephen Manessi; Dr Bob Martin; Alexandra Mayhew; Alexia Mercouri; Dr Desmond Morris; Lesley Norton; Richard Odgers; Dr Alan Ogden; Dr Guy O'Keeffe; Peter Olney; Eli Palatiano; Christopher Parsons OBE; Joss Pearson; Peggy Peel; Lucy Pendar; Julian Pettifer; Joan Porter; Tim R. Newell Price (Archivist, Leighton Park School); Betty Renouf; Dr Marielle Risse; Robin Rumboll; Tom Salmon; Peter Scott; Richard Scott-Simon; Dr Bula Senapati; Maree Shillingford; Trudy Smith; Mary Stephanides; Dr Ian Swingland; Dr Christopher Tibbs; Lesley Walden; Sam and Catha Weller; Edward Whitley; Celia Yeo.

Douglas Botting
14 December 1998

Prologue

The blue kingdom of the sea is a treasure-house of strange beasts which the boy longs to collect and observe. At first it is frustrating, for he can only peck along the shoreline like some forlorn seabird, capturing the small fry in the shallows and occasionally being tantalised by something mysterious and wonderful cast up on the shore. But now he has got a boat, and the whole kingdom is opened up for him, from the golden red castles of rock and their deep pools and underwater caves in the north to the long, glittering white sand dunes lying like snowdrifts in the south.

When he goes on any long expedition in the boat the boy always takes plenty of food and water in case he is blown off course and shipwrecked. If he has a full crew on board – three dogs, an owl, and sometimes a pigeon – and is carrying a full cargo – some two dozen containers full of seawater and specimens – it is a back-aching load to push through the water with the oars.

On this particular day the boy has decided to pay a visit to a small bay where a host of fascinating creatures dwell. His particular quarry is a peacock blenny, a curious-looking fish with a body shaped like an eel, and pop eyes and thick lips vaguely reminiscent of a hippopotamus. The boy is anxious to capture some of these colourful little fish, since it is their breeding season, and he is hoping to establish a colony of them in one of his aquariums so that he can watch their courtship.

After half an hour's stiff rowing he reaches the bay, which is rimmed with silvery olive groves and great tangles of broom that sends its heavy, musky scent out over the still, clear waters. He anchors the boat in two feet of water near the reef, and then, armed with his butterfly net and a wide-mouthed jar, he steps into the gin-clear sea which is as warm as a bath.

Everywhere there is such a profusion of life – sea slugs, sea urchins, chitons and top shells, hermit crabs and spider crabs – that it requires stern concentration for the boy not to be diverted from his task. Before long he catches a fine male blenny, brilliant and almost iridescent in its courting outfit of many colours, and by lunchtime he has also collected two green species of starfish which he has not seen previously.

The sun is now blisteringly hot, and most of the sea life has disappeared under rocks to lurk in the shade. The boy makes his way to the shore to sit under the olive trees and eat his lunch. The air is heavy with the scent of broom and full of the zinging cries of cicadas. Presently, after finishing his lunch, he loads up the boat, gets the dogs on board, and begins to row home so that he can settle the blennies in their aquarium.

When he gets up the next morning he finds, to his intense annoyance, that the blennies must have been active at dawn, for a number of eggs have been laid on the roof of the catching pot. Which female is responsible for this he does not know, but the male is a very protective and resolute father, attacking the boy's finger when he picks up the pot to look at the eggs.

The boy waits eagerly for the baby blennies to appear, but there must be something wrong with the aeration of the water, for only two of the eggs have hatched. One of the diminutive babies, to his horror, is eaten by its own mother, before his very eyes. Not wishing to have a double case of infanticide on his conscience, he puts the second baby in a jar and rows back down the coast to the bay where he caught its parents. Here he releases it, with his blessing, into the clear tepid water ringed with broom, hoping against hope that it will rear many multicoloured offspring of its own.

As a pioneer experiment in captive breeding, the blenny business is not an unqualified success. But it doesn't matter. The blenny is not an endangered species. The sea round Corfu is stuffed with blennies. And there is plenty of time, for the boy, Gerald Durrell, is still only twelve years old, a whole life with animals stretches before him, and the summer blazes on for eternity.

PART ONE

'The Boy's Mad . . . Snails in his Pockets!'

ONE

Landfall in Jamshedpur

India 1925–1928

Gerald Malcolm Durrell was born in Jamshedpur, Bihar Province, India, on 7 January 1925, the fourth surviving child of Louisa Florence Durrell (*née* Dixie), aged thirty-eight, and Lawrence Samuel Durrell, forty, a civil engineer.

When Gerald was older his mother told him something about the circumstances of his entry into the world. During the later stages of her pregnancy, it seems, she had swelled up to a prodigious degree, her enormous girth accentuated by her diminutive height, for she stood only five feet tall in her stockinged feet. Eventually she had grown so ashamed of her immense rotundity that she refused to leave the house. This annoyed her husband, who told her she ought to get out and about and go down to the Club, the social and recreational centre where all the local members of the British Raj used to congregate. 'I can't go to the Club looking like this,' she retorted. 'I look like an elephant.' Whereupon Gerald's father suggested building a howdah in which she could pass unnoticed, a flippancy which so annoyed her that she refused to speak to him for two days.

'As other women have cravings for coke or wood shavings or similar extraordinary foods when they are in this state,' Gerald was to record in an unpublished memoir about his Indian childhood, 'my mother's craving was for champagne, of which she drank an inordinate quantity until I was born. To this I attribute the fact that I have always drunk excessively, and especially champagne, whenever I could afford it.'

Gerald was by far the largest of his mother's babies, which might explain why she had grown so huge during her pregnancy, and when he was fully grown he would stand head and shoulders not only above her but above his sister and two brothers, who were all almost as small as their mother. But his birth, when it came, was simple. 'I slipped out of her like an otter into a pool,' he was to write, relating what his mother had told him. The staff from the household and from his father's firm gathered round to congratulate the sahib and memsahib on the arrival of their latest son. 'All the Indians agreed that I was a special baby, and that I had been born with a golden spoon in my mouth and that everything during my lifetime would be exactly as I wished it. Looking back at my life, I see that they were quite right.'

Both of Gerald's parents, as well as his grandfather on his mother's side, were Anglo-Indians in the old sense of the term (not Eurasians, but British whites with their family roots in India) who had been born and brought up in the India of the Raj. His father had been born in Dum Dum in Bengal on 23 September 1884, and his mother in Roorkee, North-West Province, on 16 January 1886. Her father too had been born in Roorkee, and was six years old when the Indian Mutiny polarised the subcontinent in 1857.

Gerald's family thus had little knowledge or experience of the distant but hallowed motherland of England. The depth of their association with India, which they regarded as their true home and native land, was such that when, many years later, Gerald's mother applied for a British passport, she was to declare: 'I am a citizen of India.' Though Gerald was not to live long in India, its influence on his sense of identity was palpable, and at no point in his life was he ever to feel himself entirely English, in terms of nationality, culture or behaviour. For his three older siblings, who lived a good deal longer in India – Lawrence George (not quite thirteen when Gerald was born, and at school in England), Leslie Stewart (seven, and also about to go to school in England) and Margaret Isabel Mabel (five) – the sense of dislocation was even stronger.

Gerald's mother was of pure Protestant Irish descent, the Dixies hailing from Cork in what is now the Irish Republic. It was to this Irish line that two of her sons, Gerald and Lawrence, were to attribute their gift of the gab and wilder ways. Louisa's father, George Dixie, who died before her marriage, had been head clerk and accountant at the Ganges Canal Foundry in Roorkee. It was in Roorkee that she first met Lawrence Samuel Durrell, then aged twenty-five, who was studying there, and in Roorkee that the couple married in November 1910. 'God-fearing, lusty, chapel-going Mutiny stock', was how Gerald's eldest brother Lawrence was to describe the family's Indian roots. 'My grandma sat up on the veranda of the house with a shotgun across her knees waiting for the mutiny gangs: but when they saw her they went the other way. Hence the family face . . . I'm one of the world's expatriates anyhow.'

Louisa Durrell was an endearing woman, rather shy and quietly humorous, and totally dedicated to her children. She was so protective towards her brood that she was for ever rushing home from parties and receptions to make sure they were safe and sound – not without reason, for India was a dangerous place for children: her second-born, Margery Ruth, had died of diphtheria in early infancy, and Lawrence and Leslie were often ill with one ailment or another. Her husband adored her, but forbade her from involving herself in most of the usual routines and duties of a wife and mother of her era (including the daily practicalities of running a home and family, all of which were attended to by the native servants) because he felt she should observe the proprieties of her status as a memsahib of the Raj.

But though she was utterly devoted to her dynamic, patriarchal and largely conventional husband, and seemingly compliant to his every wish, there lay behind Louisa's quiet, non-confrontational façade a highly individual and unusual woman, independent of spirit and not without fortitude, who unobtrusively went her own way in many things and quietly defied the rigid codes of conduct laid down for her sex in that era of high empire. As an Anglo-Indian, she was less mindful of her exalted status than the average white memsahib who passed her time in the subcontinent in a state of aloof exile. As a young woman she had defied convention and trained as a nurse, and had even scrubbed floors (unheard of for a white woman in India then). When her husband's work took him up-country or out into the wilds, his young wife, along with their children, would go with him and rough it without complaint. When he was back in town, and out at the office or on a construction site, she would spend hours in the heat and smoke of the kitchen learning from cook the art of curry-making, at which she became very adept, and developing a taste for gin at sundown, though Lawrence Samuel made sure she limited herself to no more than two chota-pegs a day. It was probably from his mother that Gerald (like his two brothers) inherited his humour and the alcohol gene. But it was from his father that he inherited his bright blue eyes and hair type (full and flopping over his eyes) and his height, exceptional in an otherwise very short family.

Physically minute, impractical, fey and seemingly somewhat bewildered as a person, Louisa was also in a way rather Oriental in her outlook and mindset – her son Lawrence was to describe her as a kind of born-again Buddhist. If Father was the respectable, uncomplicated patriarch, Mother was to a degree his opposite. 'My mother was the neurotic,' Lawrence Durrell once remarked. 'She provided the hysterical Irish parts of us and also the sensibility that goes with it. She's really to blame for us, I think – she should have been run in years ago.' Not altogether surprisingly, she had an interest in the paranormal. Perhaps it was the Irish in her, perhaps it was the miasma of India, but she had a fondness for ghosts, and felt no fear of them. In one of the family's Indian postings their house backed on to a wild forest, and the servants, shivering with fright, would complain to Louisa of the lonely spirit that cried there at night. She would then take a lantern – so the story goes – and set off into the depths of the forest on her own, with the servants trying to stop her, crying, 'Oh memsahib, oh memsahib,' until she was swallowed up by the trees and all they could hear was her voice calling out, 'Come on, come on,' as if trying to placate the lonely, desolate spirit.

Mother was to remain a hugely important figure in the lives of her offspring. 'I was the lucky little bastard that got all the attention,' Gerald was to recall years later. 'She was a most marvellous non-entity; a great mattress for her children.' But though Gerald was always the closest to his mother, it was Leslie who was her favourite, perhaps because she realised he might have the most need for her. Everyone loved Louisa – everyone, that is, except her eldest son Lawrence, who never forgave her for allowing him to be sent to England to complete his education, abandoned among the 'savages'.

Gerald's father, Lawrence Samuel Durrell, was, strictly speaking, not a Durrell at all. The facts of the matter are buried in a tangle of relationships involving his grandmother, Mahala Tye, in the depths of rural Suffolk in the early years of the Victorian era. After the suicide of her first husband, William Durrell, it seems that Mahala gave birth to an illegitimate son, whose biological father was a Suffolk farmer by the name of Samuel Stearne. Shortly afterwards Mahala married Henry Page, a labourer, who became the baby's stepfather and by whom she had five other children. Later in life the illegitimate son – the future grandfather of Gerald Durrell – sailed to India, and in Lucknow in 1883 he married for the second time, to Dora Johnstone, the twenty-one-year-old daughter of a sergeant-major in the Royal Horse Brigade, by whom he had eight children. Grandfather Durrell went on to serve with distinction in the Boxer Rebellion in China, rising eventually to the rank of major and dying in Portsmouth in 1914, shortly after volunteering for active service in the Great War at the age of sixty-three. The first of his children by his second wife was Gerald Durrell's father, Lawrence Samuel, elevated from birth by his illegitimate father's steady climb through the social scale from yokel stock to officer class.

Lawrence Samuel Durrell by all accounts was a decent but rather distant and often absent figure to his children, for his work as an engineer took him across the length and breadth of British India, from the Punjab and the Himalayas to Bengal, and as far away as the jungles of Burma. According to his eldest son, Lawrence, he was a good, serious, sincere man, deeply imbued with the Victorian faith in the overriding power of science to solve all things. He was not an imaginative man, nor was he particularly cultured, but though he was a straightforward servant of empire, he was not an entirely conventional one; he did not live like the British but like the Anglo-Indians, and he resigned from his club when an Oxford-educated Indian doctor he had proposed for membership was blackballed, even though he had saved his eldest son's life. This disregard for racial distinctions was shared by his wife.

Gerald's father was clearly a man of exceptional ability, determination and industry who rose from relatively modest beginnings to become a trail-blazing railway builder and civil engineer of the kind celebrated by the laureate of the Raj, Rudyard Kipling – an empire-builder in the classic mould. Dedicated to playing his part in laying down the infrastructure of a modern, industrialising India, from the construction of roads, railways, canals and bridges to the building of hospitals, factories and schools, Lawrence Samuel slogged away in monsoon and jungle, carting his family around with him like a band of privileged gypsies, and earning the highest commendations from his employers. 'A splendid man at his work,' went one report, 'full of energy and careful over details . . . With tact and gentle persuasion, Mr Durrell has managed his workmen splendidly.'

By 1918 Lawrence Samuel was Chief Engineer with the Darjeeling and Himalaya Railway on the India–Tibet border, leaving two years later to found his own company – Durrell & Co., Engineers and Contractors – in the new industrial boom town of Jamshedpur, planned and built as a 'garden city' by the giant Tata Iron and Steel Company, but in those days a raw-edged place in the middle of a hot, dusty plain. In the four years preceding Gerald's birth he became one of the fat cats of British India, successful, rich – and desperately overworked.

Most of the major construction projects that Durrell & Co. helped to build in Jamshedpur still stand today, among them extensions to the Tata works, the Tinplate Company of India, the Indian Cable Company, the Enamelled Ironware Company and much else beside, including 'Beldi', the home in which Gerald was born and in which he spent the first years of his life. 'Beldi' was a regulation D/6 type bungalow in European Town, Jamshedpur, a residence appropriate to Lawrence Samuel Durrell's status as a top engineer – a rung or two below the Army and the Indian Civil Service, a rung or two above the box-wallahs and commercials. It was not grand, but it was comfortable, with cool, shuttered rooms, a large veranda with bamboo screens against the heat of the sun, and a sizeable

garden of lawn, shrubs and trees, where Gerry the toddler took his first
steps.

Gerald was never much aware of his three older siblings during his
infant years in India. His elder brother Lawrence had already been packed
off to school in England by the time he was born, and Leslie (now back
in India) and Margaret (five years his senior), had advanced far beyond
baby talk and infant toys. He was even less aware of the outer fringes of
the Durrell family network – the army of aunts and his daunting paternal
grandmother, Dora, the overweight, doom-preaching, oppressive and
rather terrifying matriarch known as 'Big Granny', who circulated around
the family and was destined not to expire until 1943. For much of his
time Gerald was left in the company of his Indian surrogate mother, or
ayah. 'In those days children only saw their parents when they were
presented to them at four o'clock for the family tea,' Margaret was to
recall. 'So our lives revolved around the nursery and our Hindu ayah and
Catholic governess. Gerry would have had more to do with the ayah than
we older children did, so the biggest influence in his Indian years would
have been the Indian rather than the European part of the household.'

In later years Gerald claimed to remember a number of incidents from
his early life in Jamshedpur. One of the most vivid of these, often
recounted, was his first visit to a zoo, an experience so memorable that
he attributed to it the beginning of his lifelong passion for animals and
zoos. In fact there was no zoo in Jamshedpur in Gerald's day, though
there is one now. Even if there had been a zoo, it is highly unlikely that
Gerald could have remembered it, for when he was only a toddler of
fourteen months he left Jamshedpur with his father, mother, sister Margaret and Big Granny Dora, never to return. On 11 March 1926 the
Durrell party sailed from Bombay for England on board the P&O ship
SS *Ranchi*, and by April they were in London.

In the India of that time it was normal for British servants of the Raj
to take a furlough in Britain roughly every two years, but it seems that
the Durrells also had a mission to perform during their visit. Lawrence
Samuel was keen to find a property to buy in London, either as an invest-
ment or as a place to retire to, or both. As a successful engineer of empire
he had begun to amass a small fortune, and had already invested in a
large fruit farm in Tasmania, which he had purchased unseen. He was
now forty-two, and his workload was punishing. Many years later his
future (albeit posthumous) daughter-in-law Nancy, first wife of his eldest
son Lawrence, was to recall as she lay dying: 'Father decided he'd
had enough of this sort of life and wanted to go to England and live an
entirely different sort of life. His ambition was to go on the stage and

partner Evelyn Laye in the music hall.' Whether this was true (which seems improbable) or was one of Lawrence's numerous *canards* (which seems very possible), it appears that Father did intend to strike camp at some time, and leave an India where the clamour for self-rule was growing noticeably more vociferous and militant. But not yet. In due course he purchased a suitably grand eight-bedroomed house at 43 Alleyn Park in Dulwich, not far from Lawrence and Leslie's schools.

On 12 November 1926 Big Granny sailed back to Bombay on board the SS *Rawalpindi* after a six-month spell in England. A little later Louisa, Leslie, Margaret and Gerald followed her. They returned not to Jamshedpur but to Lahore, where Lawrence Samuel, who was engaged on contract work in the region, had established a new home in a substantial bungalow at 7 Davis Street. It was in Lahore that such memories as Gerald retained of his life in India were formed – though these were fragmentary and fleeting, and undoubtedly coloured by what his mother, brothers and sister later told him.

From an early age, it seems, Gerald was endowed (like his brother Lawrence) with a highly developed, almost photographic memory. He was to recall in an unpublished memoir:

> My handful of memories of this time were just little sharply etched vignettes in brilliant colour, with sight and sound and smell and taste added – the scarlet of the sunsets, for example, the harsh singing cries of a peacock, the smell of coriander and bananas, the tastes of different kinds of rice, especially the wonderful taste of my favourite breakfast, which was rice boiled in buffalo milk with sugar. I remember I used to wear little suits made out of tussore. I remember the lovely colour of it – a very pale biscuit brown – and the delicious soft silky feel of it and the rustling sound it made as my ayah dressed me in the morning. I remember my ayah refused to wake me in the morning unless it was to the strains of Harry Lauder on the gramophone, because otherwise I would be grumpy and morose and she couldn't do anything with me. The gramophone was a wind-up one and although it was very scratchy, like a lot of mice in a tin box, it was wonderful to my ears, and I would wake up with a beaming smile on my face, which made my ayah heave a sigh of relief.

It was in the India of his infancy that Gerald's intense sense of colour was born, but it was the young child's first glimpse of other life forms that was to have the profoundest impact on him. That glimpse was brief and unpromising, but for Gerald it was unforgettable, and from it all else was to follow. He was walking with his ayah, he remembered, and happened to wander to the edge of the road, where there was a shallow ditch.

> Here I found two enormous slugs, at least they appeared enormous to me, though they were probably not much more than three or four inches long. They were pale coffee colour with dark chocolate stripes and they were slowly sliding about over each other in a sort of dance and the slime from their bodies made them glitter as though they were freshly varnished. They were glutinous and beautiful and I thought they were the most marvellous creatures I had ever seen. When my ayah discovered I was slug-watching she pulled me away and told me that I must not touch or even watch such disgusting creatures as they were dirty and horrible. I could not understand, even at that age, that she could think such beautiful creatures could be dirty, and throughout my life I have met so many people who think things are disgusting or dirty or dangerous when they are nothing of the sort but miraculous pieces of nature.

Before long the infant Gerald really did set foot inside his first zoo, and his life was transformed for evermore. The zoo was in Lahore (not, as he was later to recall, in Jamshedpur), and the impact of this modest establishment was overwhelming. Gerald was to recall of this landmark in his life:

> The rich ammonia-like smell coming from the tiger and leopard cages, the incredible chatter and screams from the small group of monkeys and the melodious song of the various birds that inhabited the little zoo captivated me from the start. I remember the lovely black freckles on the leopard's skin, and the tiger, as he walked, looking like a rippling golden sea. The zoo was in fact very tiny and the cages minuscule and probably never cleaned out, and certainly if I saw the zoo today I would be the first to have it closed down, but as a child it was a magic place. Having been there once, nothing could keep me away.

According to his mother, 'zoo' was one of the first words Gerald ever uttered, and whenever he was asked where he wanted to go he would say 'zoo', loudly and belligerently. If he didn't go to the zoo his screams of frustration could be heard 'from the top of Everest to the Bay of Bengal'. Once, when he was too ill even to visit the zoo, Gerald was provided with a sort of substitute zoo of his own by the family butler, Jomen, who modelled a whole menagerie of animals – rhinocèros, lion, tiger, antelope – out of red laterite clay from the garden. Perhaps it was this collection of little mud replicas that gave Gerald the idea – that was to become an *idée fixe* by the time he was six – of having a real zoo of his own one day.

Other creatures that reinforced Gerald's love of animals made their appearance at this time:

> One day my Uncle John, Mother's favourite brother, a great shikar [hunter] who lived at Ranchi, and was employed by the government to shoot man-eating tigers and rogue elephants, sent us, in a moment of aberration, two fat Himalayan bear cubs. They were weaned but had come straight from the wild and no attempt had been made to tame them. They had very long, sharp claws and very sharp, white teeth and uttered a series of yarring cries of rage and frustration. They were housed temporarily under a big, dome-like basket on the back lawn and a man was detailed to look after them. Of course, having your own bears was a wonderful thing, even though they did smell very lavatorial. Unfortunately, at that age Margaret was ripe for any sort of mischief, and as soon as the bears' minder went off for some food she would overturn the bears' basket and then run screaming into the house, shouting, 'The bears are out! The bears are out!' After two or three days of this my mother's nerves could stand no more. She was terrified that the bears would escape and find me sitting on my rug and proceed to disembowel me. So the bears were packed up and sent down to the little zoo.

The long, golden days of Gerald's privileged infancy, with an army of servants and all the perks of an imperial elite, were to come to an abrupt stop in a tragedy of great consequence for all the Durrells.

Early in 1928 Gerald's father fell seriously ill. Though the illness was never satisfactorily diagnosed, the symptoms suggest a brain tumour of some kind. Margaret remembered her father suffering from severe head-aches, and talking and behaving in a very odd and frightening manner. One day, for example, she was dismayed to see him reach for the inkwell on his desk and drink its contents as if it were a glass of whisky or a cup of tea. Friends and relatives suggested it might help if the ailing man was taken up into the cool of the hills, away from the heat of the Lahore plains, and eventually he was transported to the hill station of Dalhousie, which at a height of nearly eight thousand feet crowned the most westerly shoulder of a magnificent snowy range of the lower Himalayas. Dalhousie had a small English cottage hospital looking out over the mountains, the air was crisp and the ambience calm.

Lawrence Samuel was made as comfortable as possible, but his condition continued to deteriorate. Louisa stayed at the hospital to be near him, while the younger children were billeted at a nearby house with their Irish governess. Sometimes the family would drive out into the surrounding hills, where in the cool pine forests, loud with the rustle of the trees, the throbbing chorus of birdsong and the bubbling of the shallow, brownwater streams, Gerald was given a broader vision of the world of nature. Occasionally he was given rides on his father's large bay horse, surrounded by a ring of servants in case he fell off. Not even the death of the horse, which fell down a cliff when Gerald suddenly startled it as it grazed with its feet tethered near the edge one day, could wean him off his burgeoning passion for the animal world.

On 16 April 1928, when Gerald was three years and three months of age, his father died of a suspected cerebral haemorrhage, and was buried the next day at the English cemetery at Dalhousie. Neither Gerald nor Margaret attended the funeral. Mother was entirely shattered.

Within the family there was a general feeling that Father's premature death, at the age of forty-three, was brought on by worry and overwork. He had made a fortune as a railway-builder, but had fared less well when he turned to road construction, on one occasion undertaking to build a highway on a fixed-price contact, only to find that the subsoil was solid rock. His sister Elsie believed he had 'worked himself to death', and was told that at the moment he was taken ill he was 'out in the heat of the midday sun supervising a critical piece of work on a bridge'. According to Nancy Durrell (who would have got it from her husband Lawrence), her father-in-law had quarrelled with the Indian partners in his business. 'They apparently turned a bit nasty, and there was a very gruelling lawsuit, which he handled all by himself, he wouldn't have a lawyer. But he got overexcited, and what exactly happened I don't know, but in the end he had a sort of brainstorm, and he died rather quickly.'

In July 1928 Lawrence Samuel's will was granted probate, and Louisa, now embarking on almost half a lifetime of widowhood, was left the sum of 246,217 rupees, the equivalent of £18,500 at the exchange rate of the time, or more than half a million pounds in today's money. Financially enriched but emotionally beggared, she was left bereft: grieving, alone and helpless. So great was her despair that years later she was to confess she had contemplated suicide. It was only the thought of abandoning Gerry, still totally dependent on her love and care, that restrained her. Mother and child were thus bound together for ever in a relationship of mutual debt and devotion, for each, in their different ways, had given the other the gift of life.

'When my father died,' Gerald was to recall, 'my mother was as ill-prepared to face life as a newly hatched sparrow. Dad had been the completely Edwardian husband and father. He handled all the business matters and was in complete control of all finances. Thus my mother, never having to worry where the next anna was coming from, treated money as a useful commodity that grew on trees.'

Gerald himself was seemingly unscathed by the family tragedy:

I must confess my father's demise had little or no effect upon me, since he was a remote figure. I would see him twice a day for half an hour and he would tell me stories about the three bears. I knew he was my daddy, but I was on much greater terms of intimacy with Mother and my ayah than with my father. The moment he died I was whisked away by my ayah to stay with nearby friends, leaving my mother, heartbroken, with the task of reorganising our lives. At first she told me her inclination was to stay in India, but then she listened to the advice of the Raj colony. She had four young children in need of education – the fact that there were perfectly good educational facilities in India was ignored, they were not English educational facilities, to get a proper education one must go 'home'. So mother sold up the house and had everything, including the furniture, shipped off ahead, and we headed for 'home'.

Mother, Margaret and Gerald took a train that bore them across half the breadth of India to Bombay, where they were to stay with relatives while they waited for the passenger liner that was to carry them, first class, to England. So Gerald sailed away from the land of his birth, not to return till almost half a century had gone by and he was white-haired and bushy-bearded. Like most of the other children on board, he was a good sailor – unlike the grown-ups. 'Two days out,' he wrote in his unpublished memoir, 'we were struck by a tumultuous storm. Huge grey-green waves battered the ship and she ground and shuddered. All the mothers immediately succumbed to sea-sickness, to be followed very shortly by the ayahs, who turned from a lovely biscuit brown to a leaden jade green. The sound of retching was like a chorus of frogs and the stifling hot air was filled with the smell of vomit.'

The reluctant crew were forced to take charge of a dozen or more children of around Gerald's age. Twice a day the children were linked together by rope like a chain gang, so that none of them could fall overboard, and taken up on deck for some fresh air, before being taken back down again to play blind man's buff and grandmother's footsteps in the heaving, yawing dining saloon. One of the crew had a cine projector and a lot of 'Felix the Cat' cartoon films, and these were shown in the club room as a way of diverting the children during the long haul to Aden and Suez.

'I was riveted,' Gerald remembered. 'I knew about pictures but I had not realised that pictures could move. Felix, of course, was a very simplistic, stick-like animal, but his antics kept us all enthralled. We were provided with bits of paper and pencils to scribble with, and while the others were scribbling I was trying to draw Felix, who had become my hero. I was infuriated because I could not get him right, simple a drawing though he was. When I finally succeeded, I was even more infuriated because, of course, he would not move.'

Whether it was a real live creature, or an animated image, or a drawing on a page, the child brought with him a passion and a tenderness for animals so innate it was as if it was embedded in his genes. In the years to follow, come hell or high water, this affinity was not to be denied.

So young Gerald came to a new home in a new country – and a new life without a father. The loss of the family's patriarch was to have a profound effect on the lives of all the Durrell siblings, for, deprived of paternal authority, they grew up free to 'do their own thing', decades before the expression came into vogue.

TWO

'The Most Ignorant Boy in the School'

England 1928–1935

The house at 43 Alleyn Park, in the prosperous and leafy south London suburb of Dulwich, now became the Durrell family home. It was a substantial house, befitting the family of a servant of empire who had made his pile, with large rooms on three floors and a big garden enclosing it. Before long Mother had installed Gerald's Aunt Prudence, a butler and a huge mastiff guard dog that chased the tradesmen and according to Gerald devoured two little dogs a day. But the new house was vast, expensive to run, and haunted: one evening Mother saw the ghost of her late husband, as plain as day, smoking a cigarette in a chair – or so Gerald claimed.

Early in 1930, therefore, when Gerald was five, the family took over a large flat at 10 Queen's Court, an annexe of the sprawling Queen's Hotel, a Victorian pile stuck in the faded south London suburb of Upper Norwood. Mother's cousin Fan lived here, along with other marooned refugees from the Indian Army and Civil Service, so for her the place felt almost like home. The family's new abode was a strange, elongated flat in the hotel grounds. The entrance was through the hotel, but there was a side door which allowed access to the extensive garden, with its lawns, trees and pond. 'The flat itself consisted of a big dining room cum drawing room,' Gerald recalled, 'a room opposite which was for Larry, then a small room in which I kept my toys, then a minuscule bathroom and kitchen, and finally Mother's spacious bedroom. Lying in bed in her room, you could look down the whole length of the flat to the front door.'

Mother's susceptibility to the paranormal showed no signs of abating, for this place too turned out to be haunted, one ghost being visible, two others audible. The first took the form of a woman who appeared at the foot of Mother's bed when she woke from a siesta one day. The woman smiled at Mother, then faded slowly away. She appeared again a few weeks later, this time witnessed by Gerald's cousins Molly and Phyllis, who came running into the kitchen shouting, 'Auntie, Auntie, there's a strange lady in your room.'

The second ghost took the form of a voice that kept telling Mother to put her head in the gas oven, and the third manifested itself in Larry's room one night when he was playing in a jazz band up in town. In Larry's room reposed the great teak roll-top desk that his father had had built to his own design. When the roll-top was raised or lowered the noise, Gerald recalled, was indescribable. That night, while Mother lay smoking in bed, waiting anxiously for Larry's return, she heard the unmistakable racket of the roll-top opening and closing. 'Taking me firmly by the hand,' Gerald was to recount, 'we went down the length of the flat, listening to the constant clatter of the lid being pulled shut and then opened again, but the moment we opened the door and looked into the room there was nothing to be seen.'

It was in the garden of the Queen's Hotel, while he was trying to catch birds by putting salt on their tails, that Gerald first came face to face with the more sensual side of life, in the form of a beautiful young woman called Tabitha. 'She had big, melting brown eyes,' he recalled, 'brown and glossy as new horse chestnuts, a wide smile, brown hair bobbed and with a fringe like a Christmas cracker.' Before long Tabitha was looking after him in her tiny flat whenever Mother went off house-hunting. She had a cat called Cuthbert and two goldfish called Mr Jenkins and Clara Butt, as well as a lot of gentlemen friends who came and went and seemed to spend a shorter or longer time in her bedroom – to talk business, she told her young friend.

'I loved the days I spent with Tabitha,' Gerald wrote in his private memoir:

> In fact I loved Tabitha very much. She was so gentle and gay, her smile engulfed you with love. She smelt gorgeous too, which was important to me, since Mother smelt gorgeous as well. She was not only very sweet and kind but very funny. She had a squeaky wind-up gramophone and a pile of records of Harry Lauder and Jack Buchanan, so we would clear away the furniture and Tabitha would teach me how to do the Charleston and the waltz. At times we went round and round so fast that eventually we would collapse on the sofa, she with peals of laughter and me giggling like a hysteric. Tabitha also taught me lots of songs, including one which enchanted me:

Iz 'e an Aussie, iz 'e, Lizzie?
Iz 'e an Aussie, iz 'e, eh?
Iz it because 'e iz an Aussie
That 'e makes you feel this way?

But alas, somehow or other Mother got to hear of Tabitha's business associates and my visits to her flat were ended. So Tabitha's lovely brown eyes and wonderful smell disappeared from my world, and I mourned the fact that I could no longer waltz and Charleston and sing silly songs with this enchanting girl.

Looking back in later years, it struck Gerald as odd that Mother should have been so prim. 'After all,' he noted, 'she was rearing a brood of offspring who became sexually precocious and pursued their own interests with the relentlessness of dynamos. Still, her fledglings managed to erode her Victorian attitudes and train her into more broad-minded ways, so that when, at the age of twenty-one, I went home one weekend with a girlfriend, I found a note from my mother which said: "I have made up two beds, dear, and the double bed, since you didn't tell me whether you are sleeping together or not. The sheets are aired and the gin is in the dining room cupboard."'

It was while living at the Queen's Hotel annexe that Mother got to know the Brown family – a matriarchy of English provenance who had recently come over from America, consisting of Granny Richardson, her daughter Mrs Brown, and Mrs Brown's young daughter Dorothy. Like the Durrells, the Browns had a garden flat at the hotel, and the two mothers soon became good friends, for both were exiles who had returned to a foreign motherland. Dorothy Brown was eleven when she first encountered Gerald, who had just turned five. 'He was a bright little spark,' she recalled, 'and even then he was very fond of animals. When our cat had kittens he was always there on the doorstep, clamouring to see them. He was very much a mother's boy and always terribly fond of her. As far as he was concerned she could do no wrong.'

Like Louisa Durrell, the Browns were looking for a house to buy, and finally settled on Bournemouth, a salubrious seaside resort on the south coast, stuffed with decaying ex-members of His Majesty's Forces and genteel ladies eking out modest pensions, but warmer and sunnier than most towns in England, and surrounded by beautiful countryside. Mother decided to follow her friends' example and move to Bournemouth, and early in 1931 the family became the proud possessors of Berridge House, at 6 Spur Hill, Parkstone, complete with a butler, a housekeeper and two servants. This marked the beginning of the Durrells' close association with Bournemouth, which has lasted to the present day.

Berridge House was a huge Victorian mansion standing in four acres of grounds, part woodland, part orchard, with a lawn on which two games of tennis could be played at once and a herbaceous border which was, Gerald remembered, 'slightly wider than the Nile and home to nearly every known weed, with the exception of Mandrake'. When Mother was asked if the house was not a trifle large for a widowed lady and a six-year-old boy – Margaret was now at Malvern, Leslie at Dulwich and Larry at a crammer's – she answered, rather vaguely, that she had to have room for her children's friends. To the young Gerald the place looked like a gigantic dolls' house, with a bewildering quantity of bedrooms, bathrooms and attic rooms, a huge drawing room, dining room and kitchen, a cellar and a parquet-floored basement ballroom that ran the length and width of the house. On rainy days this vast ballroom was his playroom, where he could indulge in ingenuity and uproar without knocking anything over or disturbing anyone upstairs.

To celebrate the move Mother bought Gerald a Cocker spaniel, the first dog of his very own. It arrived in a cardboard box, and when Gerald opened it the creature inside took his breath away – 'a dog all soft and squidgy, with hair the colour of ripe corn and big brown eyes and a loving disposition'. Gerald named the dog Simon, and from the moment he lifted him from his cardboard box he became his devoted companion.

There was no comparable companion for Mother, however, and the reality of her lonely state began to take its toll of her. 'The difficulties of living in a great, echoing, empty house with only a small boy as a companion began to tell on Mother's nerves,' Gerry was to write in his memoir. She devoted herself to her cooking and teaching Gerald how to cook, and to tending the herbaceous borders in the garden, but then came the evening, and solitude. 'She was lonely,' Gerald wrote, 'and she took to mourning the death of my father in earnest with the aid of the Demon Drink, resorting to the bottle more and more frequently.'

It helped, perhaps, that Gerald shared her bed with her. 'At the end of the day I would have my bath and then, with a clothes brush, I would climb into the bed that I shared with Mother and dust it carefully to make sure there was not a speck of dust anywhere. Then Mother would come to bed and I would curl up against her warm body in its silk nightgown and frequently I would wake to find myself pressed up against her in a state of arousal.' For many years to come, mother and child were to remain closer to one another than to any other human beings.

Eventually, matters reached a crisis. 'Mother departed,' Gerald remembered, 'to have what in those days was called a "nervous break-down" and Miss Burroughs entered my life.' Miss Burroughs was Gerald's first and last English governess. 'She had a face,' he recalled, 'which disappointment had crumpled, and embedded in it were two eyes, grey and sharp as flints.' Miss Burroughs had never had to deal with a small boy before. Terrified for some reason that Gerald might be kidnapped, she instituted a regime of locked doors, as though he were a dangerous prisoner. 'I was locked in the kitchen, the drawing room and the dining room, but the worst thing was that she banished Simon from my bedroom, saying that dogs were full of germs, and locked me in at night, so that by morning my bladder was bursting, and as I didn't dare wet the bed I had to lift a corner of the carpet to relieve myself.'

Miss Burroughs' cooking left a lot – indeed, 'virtually everything' – to be desired. She was, Gerald recollected, the only person he had ever met who put sago in the gruel she called soup – 'like drinking frog-spawn'. If the weather was bad, he was confined to the ballroom, where he and Simon invented their own games. Boy and dog built up an astonishing rapport, understanding completely how each other's human and canine imaginations were working.

'Sometimes, miraculously, Simon would become a pride of lions,' Gerald was to record, 'and I a lone Christian in an arena. As I prepared to strangle him, he would behave in the most un-lionlike way, slobbering over me with his moist, velvet-soft mouth and crooning endearments. At other times I would change into a dog and follow him round the ballroom on all fours, panting when he panted, scratching when he scratched and flinging myself down in abandoned attitudes as he did.'

Simon, Gerald noticed, was basically a coward, for whom 'a lawn-mower was a machine from hell', and sadly it was his cowardice, which should have saved his life, that was to cause his death. Startled by a chimneysweep driving away from the house on a motorcycle and sidecar, he turned and fled down the drive, into the road and under the wheel of a car, which, Gerald was to lament, 'neatly crushed Simon's skull, killing him instantly'.

Gerald was left as alone as his mother, now returned from her cure and, for the moment, recovered from her addiction. It was high time, she decided, for him to begin some kind of formal education and to mix with other children. Down the hill from Berridge House was a kindergarten called The Birches, run by a large old lady called Auntie and a dapper, kindly, intelligent woman called Miss Squire, better known to the children as Squig. Gerald remembered The Birches with fondness. It was the only school he ever attended where he completed the course.

Gerald loved The Birches because both Auntie and Miss Squire knew exactly how to teach and treat young people. Every morning he would take a tribute of slugs, snails, earwigs and other creepy-crawlies down to Squig, sometimes in matchboxes and sometimes in his pocket, thus forming a zoo of a kind. 'The boy's mad!' exclaimed brother Lawrence when he learnt of this. 'Snails in his pockets . . . !'

'Aren't they lovely?' Gerald would tell Squig.

'Oh, yes dear, quite beautiful,' Squig would reply, 'but I think they would probably be happier in the garden.'

Noticing the interest that Gerald's wrigglies aroused in his fellow pupils, Squig bought and installed an aquarium with some goldfish and pond snails in it, and they would all watch the antics of these creatures absolutely enthralled. It was about this time that Gerald, still only six, announced to his mother his wish to have a zoo of his own one day. He had kept a collection of small toy animals made of lead – camel, penguin, elephant, two tigers – in a wooden orange-box at the Queen's Hotel, but one day as he walked along the Bournemouth promenade with his mother he described to her his blueprint for a collection of real creatures, listing the species, the kinds of cages they would be housed in, and the cottage in which he and his mother would live at his zoo.

In 1932 the family moved a short distance to a brand new house at 18 Wimborne Road, Bournemouth, which Mother named Dixie Lodge in honour of her family. Though still substantial, it was a rather smaller property than Berridge House, in less extensive grounds, and so easier and cheaper to run. In Gerald's view it was a pleasanter place altogether, and the garden contained a number of climbable trees which were home to all sorts of strange insects. Here he settled down – 'quite happily', he said, 'under the raucous but benign influence of Lottie, the Swiss maid'.

But then, when he was eight, disaster struck out of a clear blue sky:

> Mother did something so terrible that I was bereft of words. She enrolled me in the local school. Not a pleasant kindergarten like The Birches, where you made things out of plasticine and drew pictures, but a real school. Wychwood School was a prep school where they expected you to learn things like algebra and history – and things that were even greater anathema to me, like sports. As both my scholastic achievements and interest in sports were nil, I was, not unnaturally, somewhat of a dullard.

Football and cricket were an utter bore for Gerald, gym and swimming lessons an absolute torture, bullying a constant menace. The only part of the curriculum that appealed to him was the one and a half hours per week devoted to natural history. 'This was taken by the gym mistress, Miss Allard,' he remembered, 'a tall blonde lady with protuberant blue eyes. As soon as she realised my genuine interest in natural history, she went out of her way to take a lot of trouble with me and so she became my heroine.'

Gerald came to hate the school so vehemently that it was all Louisa could do to keep him there at all. 'He used to be taken to school by his mother in the morning,' recalled a visitor to Dixie Lodge; 'at any rate she tried to take him – and he would cling onto the railings on the way, screaming, and then he'd have to be taken home, and then he'd get a temperature and the doctor would say, it's no good, you'll have to keep him away from school.' Eventually the GP diagnosed Gerald's recurring condition as a chronic form of what he called 'school pain' – a psychosomatic reaction which prevented the boy from ever completing his prep school education.

Soon after the Durrells moved into Dixie Lodge, Lawrence (who lived there off and on, as did Leslie and Margaret) had struck up a friendship with Alan Thomas, the assistant manager at Bournemouth's famous Commin's bookshop, a young man of about Lawrence's age who shared many of his intellectual and literary interests. Enormously tall, thin, bearded and 'spider-like', Alan lived in nearby Boscombe, and soon got to know the family well, becoming a kind of extra brother to the boys and a lifelong friend. It was not long after Gerald had joined the unhappy ranks of Wychwood that Alan happened to spot the headmaster browsing in his shop.

'I believe you have the brother of a friend of mine at your school,' said Alan.

'Oh?' said the headmaster. 'What's his name?'

'Durrell. Gerald Durrell,' Alan replied.

'The most ignorant boy in the school,' snapped the headmaster, and stalked out of the shop.

Gerald stumbled with difficulty through his lessons, until one day, falsely accused of a misdemeanour by the school sneak and given six of the best on his bare bottom by the headmaster, his mother took the mortified boy away from the school for good, thus terminating his formal schooling for ever at the age of nine.

To help Gerald get over the trauma of his beating, Mother decided to buy him a present, and took him down on the tram to Bournemouth town centre to choose a dog at the pet shop. Gerald recalled:

There was a whole litter of curly-headed black puppies in the window and I stood for a long time wondering which one I should buy. At length I decided on the smallest one, the one that was getting the most bullying from the others, and he was purchased for the noble sum of ten shillings. I carried him home in triumph and christened him Roger and he turned out to be one of the most intelligent, brave and lovely dogs that I have ever had. He grew rapidly into something resembling a small Airedale covered with the sort of curls you find on a poodle. He was very intelligent and soon mastered several tricks, such as dying for King and Country.

Roger was destined one day to become famous – and, in a sense, immortal.

Relieved of the intolerable burden of schooling, Gerald reverted to his normal cheerful, engaging self, exploring the garden, climbing the trees, playing with his dog, roaming around the house with his pockets full of slugs and snails, dreaming up pranks. It was Gerald, Dorothy Brown recalled, who would put stink-bombs in the coal scuttle when he came over with the family for Christmas. Mother presided over the moveable feast that was life at Dixie Lodge. 'No one was ever turned away from her table,' Dorothy remembered, 'and all her children's friends were always welcome. "How many of you can come round tonight?" she would ask, and they would all sit down, young and old together. Mother was very small but she had a very big heart. She was very friendly and a good mixer and she was a wonderful cook.'

The delicious aromas that drifted out of Mother's kitchen, the range and quality of the dishes she brought to the dining table, and the enthusiasm, good cheer and riotous conversation enjoyed by the company that sat down at that table had a deep and permanent impact on her youngest child. Gerald emerged into maturity as if he had been born a gourmet and a gourmand. Much of her cooking Louisa had learned from her mother, the rest from her Indian cooks in the kitchens of her various homes, where she would secretly spend hours behind her disapproving husband's back. When she returned to England she brought with her the cookbooks and notebooks she had carted around the subcontinent during her itinerant life there. Some of Louisa's favourite recipes – English, Anglo-Indian and Indian – had been copied out in a perfect Victorian copperplate by her mother: 'Chappatis', 'Toffy', 'A Cake', 'Milk Punch', 'German Puffs', 'Jew Pickle' (prunes, chillies, dates, mango and green ginger). Most, though, were in her own hand, and embraced the cuisine of the world, from 'Afghan Cauliflower', 'Indian Budgees' and 'American Way of Frying Chicken' to 'Dutch Apple Pudding', 'Indian Plum Cake', 'Russian Sweet', 'All Purpose Cake', 'Spiral Socks' (a mysterious entry) and 'Baby's Knitted

Cap' (another). But Indian cookery was her *tour de force* and alcoholic concoctions her hobby: dandelion wine, raisin wine, ginger wine (requiring six bottles of rum) and daisy wine (four quarts of daisy blossoms, yeast, lemons, mangoes and sugar).

Not surprisingly, Alan Thomas was soon spending almost every evening and weekend with the family. They were, he quickly realised, a most extraordinary bunch:

> There never was more generous hospitality. Nobody who has known the family at all well can deny that their company is 'life-enhancing'. All six members of the family were remarkable in themselves, but in lively reaction to each other the whole was greater than the sum of the parts. Amid the gales of Rabelaisian laughter, the wit, Larry's songs accompanied by piano or guitar, the furious arguments and animated conversation going on long into the night, I felt that life had taken on a new dimension.

At this time Lawrence was writing, Margaret rebelling about returning to school, and Leslie 'crooning, like a devoted mother, over his new collection of firearms'. As for Gerald, though he was still tender in years he was already a great animal collector, and every washbasin in the house was filled with newts, tadpoles and the like.

'While one could hardly say that Mrs Durrell was in control of the family,' Alan recalled, 'it was her warm-hearted character, her amused but loving tolerance that held them together; even during the occasional flare-ups of Irish temper. I remember Gerry, furious with Larry who, wanting to wash, pulled the plug out of a basin full of marine life. Spluttering with ungovernable rage, almost incoherent, searching for the most damaging insult in his vocabulary: "You, you (pause), you AUTHOR, YOU."'

But the boy Gerald owed much to his big brother's selfless and unstinting support: 'Years ago when I was six or seven years old and Larry was a struggling and unknown writer, he would encourage me to write. Spurred on by his support, I wrote a fair bit of doggerel in those days and Larry always treated these effusions with as much respect as if they had just come from the pen of T.S. Eliot. He would always stop whatever work he was engaged upon to type my jingles out for me and so it was from Larry's typewriter that I first saw my name, as it were, in print.'

Near the end of his life, with more than half the family now dead, Gerald looked back with fondness and frankness at the turmoil of his childhood days, scribbling a fleeting insight in a shaky hand on a yellow restaurant paper napkin: 'My family was an omelette of rages and laughter entwined with a curious love – an amalgam of stupidity and love.'

At about the time Mother bought Dixie Lodge, Lawrence met Nancy Myers, an art student at the Slade, slightly younger than him and very like Greta Garbo to look at – tall, slim, blonde, blue-eyed. Just turned twenty, Lawrence was living a dedicatedly Bohemian, aspiringly artistic existence in London, playing jazz piano in the Blue Peter nightclub, scribbling poetry, grappling with his first novel and reading voraciously under the great dome of the British Library. 'My so-called upbringing was quite an uproar,' he was to recall. 'I have always broken stable when I was unhappy. I hymned and whored in London. I met Nancy in an equally precarious position and we struck up an incongruous partnership.' Soon he and Nancy were sharing a bedsit in Guilford Street, near Russell Square. 'Well, we did a bit of drinking and dying. Ran a photographic studio together. It crashed. Tried posters, short stories, journalism – everything short of selling our bottoms to clergymen. I wrote a cheap novel. Sold it – well that altered things. Here was a stable profession for me to follow. Art for money's sake.'

Before long Lawrence decided it was time Nancy was given her baptism of fire and shown off to the family. Many years later, Nancy vividly remembered her introduction to that unforgettable *ménage*.

We drove down in the car for the weekend. I was fascinated to be meeting this family, because Larry dramatised everything – *mad* mother, *ridiculous* children, mother drunk, throwing their fortune to the winds, getting rid of everything . . . *hellish*, *foolish*, stupid woman. I mean, it's wonderful to hear anybody talking about their family like that, and I was very thrilled.

The house had no architectural merit at all, but the rooms were a fair size, and they had a certain amount of comfort – a rather *disarray* sort of comfort. I mean, they had a few easy chairs and a sofa in the sitting-room and the floors were carpeted and things. It all seemed a little bit makeshift somehow. But I remember I loved the house – the sort of craziness of it, people sort of playing at keeping house rather than really keeping house. You felt they weren't forced into any *mould* like people usually are – every sort of meal was at a different time, and everybody was shouting at everybody else, no control anywhere.

Really it was the first time I'd *been* in a family – in a jolly family – and the first time that I'd been able to say what I liked – there was nothing forbidden to say. It was a great opening-up experience for me, hearing everybody saying 'You bloody fool!' to everybody else, and getting away with it. It was marvellous. So I really fell in love with the family.

Gerry was six or seven at the time – a very slender, very delicate, very charming little boy who looked a bit like Christopher Robin and was too sensitive to go to school. Even at that time there was quite a lot of friction between Larry and Leslie, and Larry used to tease his brother mercilessly. Leslie was never very quick-witted, and Larry would make him look a fool any time he liked, and any time Leslie crossed him he used to absolutely flay him, which Leslie minded very much.

But my first visit ended in disaster. On our first morning Larry came into my room and hopped into bed with me, and then Gerry came along and hopped into bed too, so we were all sort of cosy under the blankets, cuddled together, the three of us, and this was too much for Mother. She came in and said she'd never been so disgusted in her life. 'What a way to behave!' she said, shouting. '*Out* you go, *out* you go this minute, out you *both* go, five minutes and you must get out, I'm not having Gerry corrupted!' She could have histrionics when she wanted to.

I was a bit abashed, feeling terrible about it, but Larry said, 'Oh, the silly woman, she'll get over it. Come on, we'll go. She'll get over it in a day and be pleased to have us back. Silly nothing – just like a stupid woman. Don't be such a fool, Mother . . .'

So we sort of tiptoed out of the house – but within a fortnight or so we were welcomed back, and you know, Mother closed her eyes to whatever we were doing from then onwards. And she was terribly sweet to me. I mean, I always felt rather like a goose among ducklings – they were all so small and I was so long and thin. But they couldn't have been sweeter. After that first moment Mother was always clucking over me. She thought I looked consumptive and used to give me lots of gold-top milk and butter and fill me up with cream and Weetabix and whatever was going. And she was a marvellous cook; she did most of the cooking, a lot of hot stuff, curries, Indian cooking . . .

I just loved the whole craziness of it. Mother used to drink a lot of gin at that time, and she used to retire to bed when Gerry went to bed – Gerry wouldn't go to bed without her, he was afraid of being on his own, I think – and she'd take her gin bottle up with her when she went. So then we *all* used to retire up there, carrying a gin bottle up to bed. She had a large double bed, and an enormous silver tea-tray with lots of silver teapots and things on it, and we'd carry on the evening sitting on the bed, drinking gin and tea and chatting, while Gerry was asleep in his own bed in the same room. I think he must have been able to go to sleep if there was a noise going on. It was all very cosy.

Though friends might adore the Durrells, the wider family – the cohort of aunts and grannies – disapproved mightily. They were appalled at Mother's incompetence and extravagance when it came to money, dismayed that she would not help her cousin Fan out of her penury, and scandalised at the way she was bringing up her children – her lack of control; their wild, undisciplined ways; the outrageous Bohemian ambience of her household, as they saw it, doubly shocking in the deathly polite context of suburban Bournemouth. Leslie especially was a cause for concern. One cousin, Molly Briggs, the daughter of Gerald's father's sister Elsie, remembered:

Leslie drove Aunt Lou mad at this time, staying in bed till midday and slouching about. He never settled to anything, never saw anything through. As children my sister and I didn't like him very much. Sometimes he would condescend to play with us, but you never knew from one minute to the next how he would behave. He would suddenly turn nasty for no reason at all. Both Gerry and Leslie ran rings round Aunt Lou and were quite unmanageable, But Gerry was a beautiful little boy, really, and great fun. He used to shin up a tree where he had a secret place we didn't dare follow him to. And he used to play with three slow worms, fondling them and winding them around his hands. We had been brought up in Ceylon to fear snakes, so were terrified of Gerry's pets and wouldn't touch them. I remember we learned to ride a bike with Gerry on a sunken lawn surrounded by heather banks. We were terribly noisy and shrieked with laughter whenever we fell over, which was very often, so eventually Larry, who was probably composing something, leaned out of an upstairs window and shouted: 'Stop that bloody row!'

'It's curious – something one didn't realise at the time – but my mother allowed us to *be*,' Gerald recalled.

She worried over us, she advised (when we asked) and the advice always ended with, 'But anyway, dear, you must do what you think best.' It was, I suppose, a form of indoctrination, a form of guidance. She opened new doors on problems that allowed new explorations of ways in which you might – or might not – deal with them – simple things now ingrained in me without a recollection of how they got there. I was never lectured, never scolded.

Lawrence and Nancy had been living for a year with their friends George and Pam Wilkinson in a cottage at Loxwood in Sussex, where Lawrence wrote his first novel, a novice work called *Pied Piper of Lovers*, which was published in 1935. At the end of 1934 the Wilkinsons had struck camp and moved on, emigrating to the Greek island of Corfu, where the climate was good, the exchange rate favourable and the living cheap and easy. Lawrence and Nancy, meanwhile, moved in with the family at Dixie Lodge. From time to time a letter would arrive from George Wilkinson describing the idyllic life they were leading on their beautiful, verdant and as yet unspoilt island, and gradually the idea began to grow – in Lawrence's mind first – that perhaps that was where he and Nancy should live and have their being, a perfect retreat for a young aspiring writer and a young aspiring painter, both of them keen to learn what they could of ancient Greek art and archaeology. There was nothing to keep Lawrence in England. It was not the land of his birth, he had no roots there, and there was much about the place and the English outlook and way of life – 'the English way of death', he called it – that he had detested from the moment he set foot there as a lonely, bewildered boy of eleven, exiled from his native India to begin his formal education at 'home'. 'Pudding Island' was his dismissive term for Britain. 'That mean, shabby little island,' he was to tell a friend much later, 'wrung my guts out of me and tried to destroy anything singular and unique in me.' Its dismal climate alone was reason enough to move on. 'Alan,' he had remarked to Alan Thomas after receiving a letter from George Wilkinson describing the orange groves surrounding his villa, 'think of the times in England when *everybody you know* has a cold.' Though the running was made by Lawrence, the idea of moving to Corfu soon took hold of the whole family.

While his mother was still alive, Gerald's version of events described a kind of mass migration to the sun dreamed up and pushed through by his eldest brother. It had all begun, he was to relate in a famous passage, on a day of a leaden August sky. 'A sharp, stinging drizzle fell,' he wrote, 'billowing into opaque grey sheets when the wind caught it. Along the Bournemouth seafront the beach-huts turned blank wooden faces towards a greeny-grey, froth-chained sea that leapt eagerly at the cement bulwark of the shore. The gulls had been tumbled inland over the town, and they now drifted above the housetops on taut wings, whining peevishly. It was the sort of weather calculated to try anyone's endurance.'

At Dixie Lodge the family were assembled – 'not a very prepossessing sight that afternoon'. For Gerald the weather had brought on catarrh, and he was forced to breath 'stertorously' through open mouth. For Leslie it had inflamed his ears so that they bled. For Margaret it had brought a fresh blotch of acne. For Mother it had generated a bubbling cold and a twinge of rheumatism. Only Larry was as yet unscathed, and as the afternoon wore on his irritation grew till he was forced to declaim: 'Why do we stand this bloody climate? Look at it! And, if it comes to that, look at us ... Really, it's time something was done. I can't be expected to produce deathless prose in an atmosphere of doom and eucalyptus ... Why don't we pack up and go to Greece?'

After his mother's death Gerald was to give an alternative – or perhaps additional – motive for the idea. Mother, it seems, had found some grown-up consolation and companionship at Dixie Lodge, in the company of Lottie, the family's Swiss maid. But then Lottie's husband fell ill – Gerald thought with cancer – and Lottie had no option but to leave Mother's employ in order to help look after her husband. 'So back to square one,' Gerald wrote in his unpublished memoir:

> Lonely evenings, where Mother had only myself, aged nine, as company. So loneliness, of course, nudged Mother closer and closer to the Demon Drink. Larry, recognising the pitfalls, decided that decisive action must be taken and told Mother he thought we ought to up sticks and go and join George in Corfu. Mother, as usual, was hesitant.
>
> 'What am I supposed to do with the house?' she asked.
>
> 'Sell it before it gets into a disreputable state,' said Larry. 'I think it is essential that we make this move.'

Larry himself gave a third, perhaps more cogent reason for emigrating, which he explained in a note to George Wilkinson out in Corfu: 'The days are so dun and gloomy that we pant for the sun,' he wrote. 'My mother has gotten herself into a really good financial mess and has decided to cut and run for it. Being too timid to tackle foreign landscapes herself, she wants to be shown around the Mediterranean by us. She wants to scout Corfu. If she likes it I have no doubt but that she'll buy the place ...'

It is very likely that all three pressures – booze, money and sun – played their part in the final decision. But Mother did not need a great deal of persuading. She always hated to say no, Lawrence said, and in any case there was not much to keep her in England. In fact there wasn't much to keep any of them there, for they were all exiles from Mother India, and none of them had sunk many roots in the Land of Hope and

Glory. 'It was a romantic idea and a mammoth decision,' Margaret was to relate. 'I should have been going back to school at Malvern but I said, "I'm not going to be left out!" and Mother, being a bit like that about everything, agreed."'

So the decision was made. The whole family would go – Larry and Nancy, Mother, Leslie (who would be eighteen by the time they sailed), Margaret (fifteen) and Gerald (ten). When Larry replied to George Wilkinson's invitation to move to Corfu, he asked about schooling for Gerry. A little alarmed, Wilkinson replied: 'D'you all intend coming(!) and how many is all?' But it was all or none. The house was put up for sale and goods and chattels crated up and shipped out ahead to Corfu.

The fate of the animals of the household presented a major headache, especially for Gerald, to whom they all belonged. The white mice were given to the baker's son, the wigged canary to the man next door, Pluto the spaniel to Dr Macdonald, the family GP, and Billie the tortoise to Lottie in Brighton, who twenty-seven years later, when Gerald was famous, wrote to ask if he wanted it back, adding: 'You have always loved animals, even the very smallest of them, so at least I know you couldn't be anything but kind.' Only Roger the dog would be going off with the family, complete with an enormous dog passport bearing a huge red seal.

Lawrence and Nancy were due to go out as the vanguard early in 1935. While they were living in Dixie Lodge prior to departure they decided to marry in secret – perhaps to keep the news from Nancy's parents, who may have disapproved of such a raffish and Bohemian husband for their beautiful daughter. The marriage took place on 22 January at Bournemouth Register Office. Alan Thomas was sworn to secrecy and asked to act as witness. There was some anxiety before the wedding that because Alan and Nancy were so tall and Lawrence so short, the registrar might marry the wrong pair without realising it. 'With a view to avoiding any such contingency,' recalled Alan, 'we approached a couple of midgets, then appearing in a freak-show at the local fun-fair, and asked them to appear as witnesses; but their employer refused to allow such valuable assets out of his sight.'

On 2 March 1935 Lawrence and Nancy set sail from Tilbury on board the P&O liner SS *Oronsay*, bound for Naples on the first stage of their journey to Corfu. Within the week the rest of the family were also *en route*. On 6 March they checked into the Russell Hotel in London, from where, the following day, Leslie sent Alan Thomas a postcard: 'We are going to catch the boat this evening (with luck). P.S. Note the address – we are getting up in the world – 12/6 a night bed and etc!!!!'

In his published account of the family's Corfu adventure, Gerald gives the impression they travelled overland across France, Switzerland and Italy. In fact Mother, Leslie, Margaret, Gerald and Roger the dog sailed from Tilbury, travelling second class on board a Japanese cargo boat, the SS *Hakone Maru* of the NYK Line, bound for Naples. Leslie seems to have been the only Durrell on board who was up to writing, and his postcards and other missives constitute virtually his last recorded utterance in this history. Chugging through the Dover Straits he told Alan Thomas on 8 March: 'So far I have a cabin of my own. The people in the Second Class are quite nice and very jolly. The ship's rolling a bit but the Durrells are all fine.'

Two days later, butting their way across the Bay of Biscay, the adventure was hotting up nicely. 'We had a heavy snow storm this morning,' wrote Leslie, 'and we had to go up to the top deck where the lifeboats are and give that ******* dog some exercise. *God* what a time we had, what with the dog piddling all over the place, the snow coming down, the old wind blowing like *HELL* – *God what a trip*! No one seemed to know what to do at lifeboat drill, so if anything goes wrong it will only be with the *Grace of God* (if there is one) if any of us see the dear coast of Old England again.'

By 15 March, after a trip ashore at Gibraltar – 'none of the Durrells sick so far, not even that ******* dog,' reported Leslie – they had reached Marseilles. Next stop Naples, the train to Brindisi and the ferry to Corfu, 130 miles away across the Strait of Otranto and the Ionian Sea

It was an overnight run. 'The tiny ship throbbed away from the heel of Italy,' Gerald recalled of that fateful crossing, 'out into the twilit sea, and as we slept in our stuffy cabins, somewhere in that tract of moon-polished water we passed the invisible dividing-line and entered the bright, looking-glass world of Greece. Slowly this sense of change seeped down to us, and so, at dawn, we awoke restless and went on deck.' For a long time the island was just a chocolate-brown smudge of land, huddled in mist on the starboard bow.

Then suddenly the sun shifted over the horizon and the sky turned the smooth enamelled blue of a jay's eye ... The mist lifted in quick, lithe ribbons, and before us lay the island, the mountains sleeping as though beneath a crumpled blanket of brown, the folds stained with the green of olive-groves. Along the shore curved beaches as white as tusks among tottering cities of brilliant gold, red, and white rocks ... Rounding the cape we left the mountains, and the island sloped gently down, blurred with silver and green iridescence of olives, with here and there an admonishing finger of black cypress against the sky. The shallow sea in the bays was butterfly blue, and even above the sound of the ship's engines we could hear, faintly ringing from the shore like a chorus of tiny voices, the shrill, triumphant cries of the cicadas.

Decades later, old and sick and near the verge of death, Gerald Durrell was to recall that magic landfall that was to transform his life with all the pain and longing of remembered youth. 'It was like being allowed back into Paradise,' he whispered. 'Our arrival in Corfu was like being born for the first time.'

THREE

The Gates of Paradise

Corfu 1935–1936

A few hours later the Durrells disembarked at the quay in Corfu town, Gerald clutching his butterfly net and a jam-jar full of caterpillars, Mother – 'looking like a tiny, harassed missionary in an uprising' – holding on tightly to a dog desperate to find a lamp-post. Two horse-drawn cabs, one for the family and one for the luggage, conveyed the party through the narrow, sun-bright streets of the island's elegant, faintly rundown capital, and after a short ride they reached the first stop in their island adventure, the Pension Suisse, not far from the Platia, the town's main square, where they were reunited with Lawrence and Nancy. 'The family crawled ashore today,' Lawrence reported to Alan Thomas, 'and took us in bed so to speak ... The scenic tricks of this paragon of places are highly improbable, and I don't quite believe my eyes yet.'

Next morning Mother and her brood were taken house-hunting by the hotel guide, driving round the surrounding countryside in a cloud of dust to inspect villas of all sorts and situations. But Mother shook her head at everything she saw, for not one of the properties had an essential requirement – a bathroom. In the meantime the whole family hung on at the Pension Suisse. On 29 March Leslie wrote to Alan asking him to send various newspapers and magazines – the *Daily Mirror* and the overseas edition of any other newspaper; *Puck* and *Crackers* for Gerry; *Stitchcraft* and *Good Housekeeping* for Mother; and *The American Rifleman* and *Game and Gun* for Leslie. At the end of the letter Mother added a post-script suggesting Corfu had so far fallen some way below her expectations.

> We are still in the hotel and hope some day to be settled. Don't believe a word they say about this smelly island. The country around is beautiful, I will admit, but as for the town – the less said about it the better. However, if you ever feel like coming out we

will give you a corner. You might have to sleep with Leslie or Gerry – but one gets used to anything in Corfu.

Mother had good reason to feel dejected. They all did. They were stranded in a strange country, whose language they did not speak and whose manners they did not understand, not knowing what they were doing or where they were going, and feeling confused, anxious and querulous. Worse, the bank in London hadn't sent any money, so they were penniless, and Lawrence's and Nancy's baggage hadn't turned up, so Lawrence was shirtless and bookless. Stuck in the stuffy recesses of the Pension Suisse, they survived by borrowing from the proprietor. Margaret, or Margo, as she was always known on Corfu, was homesick and cried; and Gerry howled in unison. Only the colours in the streets, he recalled, and the look of the sea down by the old fort gave any promise or hope.

It was below the old fort during those early limbo days in Corfu town that Gerald made a crucial breakthrough in his island life, and finally entered a new dimension of existence, by learning to swim. During his brief time at prep school swimming lessons had filled him with dread and taught him nothing but a profound fear of drowning. But all that suddenly changed when he reached the island.

'Mother and I,' he recalled,

accompanied by a bustling Roger, would go down to a small rocky cove beneath the great sandcastle-like Venetian fort that dominated the town. It was here that I learnt for the first time what a delicious, magical element water was. At first I was up to my knees, then up to my armpits and then, incredibly, I was swimming in the blue, warm, silky blanket, tasting the wonderful rind of salt on my lips, buoyed up by the water and rid of my fear. Soon I was swimming so far out in this liquid glass that Mother used to get alarmed and run up and down the shore like a distraught Sandpiper, imploring me to come back into the shallows.

While the rest of the family hung about in the town, Lawrence and Nancy were soon fixed up with a small house on a hill near the Villa Agazini, the home of their friends the Wilkinsons at Pérama, along the coast to the south. From the hill they could look down on the great sweep of the sea and the comings and goings on the dirt road below them. A fortnight or so after moving Lawrence wrote to Alan Thomas:

I've told you how unique it is up here, stuck on the hillside, haven't I? Well, multiply that by four. Today we rose to a gorgeous sunlight and breakfasted in it. Our breakfast table looks out plumb over the sea, and fishing boats go swirling past the window. There is a faint mist over Albania today but here the heat is paralysing. Bees and lizards and tortoises are making hay . . . God the Sun.

Shortly afterwards, while Mother was still scouting for a place to settle, Lawrence wrote again to Alan, unable to contain his enthusiasm for his new island home.

I'd like to tell you how many million smells and sounds and colours this place is. As I sit, for instance. Window. Light. Blue grey. Two baby cypress lulling very slightly in the sirocco. Pointed and perky like girls' breasts. The sea all crawling round in a bend as the coast curves away to Lefkimo with one sailing boat on it. In the road . . . the peasants are passing on donkeys. Raving, swearing, crashing colours, scarves and head-dresses. To the north nothing. Ahead Epirus and Albania with a snuggle of creamy cloud clotted on them. South mists and the mystery of the other islands lying out there, invisible, on the water.

Mother meanwhile had decided to hire a car so that she and Leslie, Margo and Gerald could go and view a house in Pérama owned by the proprietor of the Pension Suisse. It was thus that the family came face to face with an outsize character who was to change their life on the island, or at any rate greatly facilitate the way they conducted it. Jostled and harassed at the taxi-rank in the main square by a crowd of grumpy taxi drivers who spoke only Greek, they were suddenly startled by a deep, vibrant, booming voice – 'the sort of voice you would expect a volcano to have', Gerald recalled – speaking in English, or at any rate a sort of English.

'Hoy! Whys donts yous have someones who can talks your own language?'

'Turning, we saw an ancient Dodge parked by the kerb,' Gerald was to write, 'and behind the wheel sat a short barrel-bodied individual, with ham-like hands and a great leathery, scowling face surmounted by a jauntily-tilted peaked cap.'

'Thems bastards would swindles their own mothers,' he roared. 'Wheres you wants to gos?'

This was the family's first glimpse of Spyros Chalikiopoulos, better known as Spiro Americano on account of the eight years he had spent working in Chicago making enough money to come home, a great fire-eating fury of a man with a heart of gold who was to become the family's fixer, philosopher and friend on a virtually permanent basis. To Gerald he was a 'great brown ugly angel ... a great suntanned gargoyle'; to Lawrence he resembled a 'great drop of olive oil'.

'Bathrooms?' Spiro brooded. 'Yous wants a bathrooms? Oh, I knows a villa with a bathrooms.'

Seated in Spiro's Dodge, they shot off through the maze of streets and out along the dusty white prickly-pear-lined road into a countryside of vineyards and olive groves.

'Yous English?' Spiro bawled, swivelling round to address the family in the back as his Dodge swayed from one side of the road to the other. 'Thought so ... English always wants bathrooms ... I likes the English ... Honest to Gods, if I wasn't Greek I'd likes to be English.' Spiro, it seems, was an anglophile to his very guts. 'Honest to Gods, Mrs Durrell,' he informed Mother later, 'you cuts me opes you find the Union Jack inside.'

They bowled along the edge of the sea, then sped up a hill. Suddenly Spiro jammed his foot on the brake and the car juddered to a halt in a thick cloud of dust.

'Theres you ares,' he said, jabbing with a stubby finger; 'that's the villa with the bathrooms, likes you wanted.'

They saw a small, square, single-storeyed, strawberry-pink villa, situated only a stroll away from Larry and Nancy's place. It stood in its own minuscule garden, guarded by a group of slim, gently swaying cypresses, with a sea of olive trees filling the valley and lapping up the hill all around. The tiny balcony at the front was overgrown with a rampant bougainvillaea and the shutters had been faded by the sun to a delicate, cracked green. They loved the place, instantly and totally. 'The warm air was thick with the scent of a hundred dying flowers,' Gerald recalled, 'full of the gentle, soothing whisper and murmur of insects. As soon as we saw it, we wanted to live there – it was as though the villa had been standing there waiting for our arrival. We felt we had come home.'

Moving day came, and the family's baggage was carted up the hill, the shutters opened, floors swept, linen aired, beds made, charcoal fire lit in the kitchen, pots and pans arrayed, a home slowly formed amid much babble and commotion. To keep out of the way Gerald absconded to the garden, a strange garden with tiny flowerbeds laid out in complicated geometrical patterns of stars, half-moons, triangles and circles. That garden was a revelation – 'a magic land,' he remembered, 'through which roamed creatures I had never seen before.' Never had he seen such fecundity in nature. Under every stone he found twenty different creatures, on every plant stem twenty more: ladybirds, carpenter bees, hummingbird hawk-moths, giant ants, lacewing-flies that laid eggs on stilts, crab-spiders that changed colour like chameleons. Bewildered by the profusion of life on his doorstep, he wandered round the garden in a daze, then spent hours squatting on his heels watching the private lives of the creatures around him. 'It wasn't until we moved into that first villa,' Gerald was to tell a friend years later, 'that suddenly we realised we had been transported into paradise . . . For me it was like being pushed off the Bournemouth cliffs into heaven. From then onwards, just like that, I was home.'

So the family settled in, with the thunderous Spiro attending to their every need. It was Spiro who took them shopping down in the town, bargaining fiercely over the smallest purchase. It was Spiro who chivvied and harassed the bank manager about Mother's missing funds and hectored the customs officials over confiscated baggage. It was Spiro who, 'bull-voiced and scowling', advised them on everything they needed to know about day-to-day life on the island and tended to their smallest whim. Mother he adored, hovering over her like a guardian angel, and he was horrified one day when Leslie told him: 'She's really not much good as a mother, you know.' Spiro leapt instantly to her defence. 'Donts says that!' he roared. 'Honest to Gods, if I hads a mother like yours I'd gos down every mornings and kisses her feets.'

Each member of the Durrell family adapted to their new environment according to their temperament and needs. Margo's adaptation was the quickest. Short, blonde and attractive, by simply donning a revolutionary two-piece swimsuit and sunbathing in the olive groves she soon attracted an admiring band of peasant youths who appeared 'like magic' out of an apparently empty countryside. Or so Gerald was to claim in the bestselling account of Corfu he wrote twenty years later, *My Family and Other Animals*, a book which gives much of the essence of the Durrells' years on Corfu, though only the barest outline of the chronology. Margo saw herself differently. 'Gerald thought of me as a totally idiotic girl who was only interested in boys,' she complained years later. 'Gerry never saw the real me, the depth of character I consider I have. Looking back, I see myself as having been a romantic, sensitive person who wanted to understand the spirit of the Greeks. I'm the one who got to grips with the reality of Corfu.'

Leslie's acclimatisation was the noisiest. The moment he arrived he unpacked his guns, cleaned, oiled and loaded them, then blazed away at an old tin-can from his bedroom window. Mother meanwhile pottered about all day in the kitchen, tending the bubbling pots on the charcoal fires amid an aroma of garlic and herbs. 'Mother Durrell and I had a lot of fun cooking,' Nancy recalled. 'She was very keen on making tremendously hot things that nobody else could really eat. We made all kinds of lime chutneys, and tomato jam and marrow jam, and we ate loquats in the season, and lots of prickly pears.'

As for Lawrence, he was, Gerald recorded later, 'designed by Providence to go through life like a small, blond firework, exploding ideas in other people's minds, and then curling up with cat-like unctuousness and refusing to take any blame for the consequences'. Though *My Family and Other Animals* gives the impression that Lawrence shared the same house as the rest of the family, in fact he and Nancy lived under a separate roof for most of their time on Corfu. Equally, though Lawrence liked to declare publicly that he never saw the family on the island except at Christmas, in fact he and Nancy saw them a great deal. This was easy in the first months, when they were near neighbours at Pérama, but relatively more difficult when they moved to the north of the island later. Nancy was to recall her association with the family all too clearly.

> Larry used to needle Leslie *mercilessly*, telling him what a fool he was, how he'd wrecked his life, slapping him down all the time. Leslie had three or four different sorts of guns and when he got angry with Larry he used to point one at him and threaten to shoot him. I really thought he possibly would, and sometimes he used to take my side – used to rush in and point his gun at Larry when Larry and I were quarrelling. Poor old Leslie, he just marched across the fields with the field police, a very low category of person, with rifles over their shoulders. He had a pierced eardrum, so he didn't enjoy all the swimming and things we did. It wasn't much of an existence for a nineteen-year-old boy.

The villa only had three bedrooms, so though Gerald no longer passed his nights curled up in the same bed as his mother, he still had to share a room with her, squeezing into a cot in the corner. To Lawrence fell the role of father figure, then and for ever more. Lawrence was old enough to appear to the boy as someone from an earlier, more fatherly than brotherly generation, and he was all-knowing and authoritarian enough to fulfil the boy's expectations of a father substitute.

Gradually the family came to grips with the fact that, Spiro apart, virtually nobody they ever encountered spoke to them in an intelligible tongue. Greek was not an easy language to learn, and the Durrells' struggle to master it was long and dogged. For the younger members of the family it was a struggle slowly but surely won, less by a process of formal learning than a kind of osmosis, so that gradually they turned – linguistically speaking – into Corfiot peasant Greeks, retaining the language more or less intact till the end of their lives. 'Gradually I came to understand them,' Gerald remembered. 'What had at first been a confused babble became a series of recognisable separate sounds. Then suddenly, they took on meaning, and slowly and haltingly I started to use them myself.'

Corfu was arguably the most beautiful of all the Mediterranean islands, and in the Durrells' time it was virtually untouched by modern development. It was also one of the most sophisticated regions of Greece, and successive rulers of the island, including the Venetians, the French and the British, had all made contributions of one sort or another to how it looked and how its people lived. The Venetians had contributed an island aristocracy, much of Corfu town and many of the finest buildings, while the British, who had departed in 1864, had introduced ginger beer, a postal service and the game of cricket. It helped the Durrells hugely that the British were highly regarded by the islanders, who still believed that every Britisher they met was a lord and a paragon of all civilised virtues. Gerald was often greeted as 'the little English lord' by the local peasantry, and all doors were almost always open to him.

But like all unspoiled Edens, the island had its drawbacks. 'The peasants are incorrigible thieves and liars,' Lawrence noted soon after his arrival at Pérama, 'but make up for it by having the dandiest arse-action when they walk. This is due to always carrying huge weights on their heads.' Lawrence soon changed his opinion of the Corfiots, and the family grew very close to many of them. But the Corfiot world took some getting used to, as Gerald was later to explain:

> Corfu was wonderful because it was so lunatic, so insane. When a man in a shop said, with the Corfiot's gentle charm, he would have a thing ready for you tomorrow, he was working in a world that would have mystified Einstein. The word tomorrow might mean half an hour later or two weeks or two months hence or, indeed, never. The word tomorrow had no normal meaning. It became yesterday, last month, the year after next. It was an Alice in Wonderland world.

Greece was not a mass holiday destination in those days – too far, too rough – and the few tourists who could afford to go abroad tended to make for Italy. Greece, therefore, remained a primitive backwater by European standards, and a foreigner contemplating setting up residence there confronted some hefty practical problems, even on Corfu.

Corfu before the discovery of DDT, Lawrence was later to point out, was 'one large flea – one enormous hairy gnashing flea – and several kinds of bedbug as well, mostly elephant-sized'. In some ways, he reckoned, the island was almost as primitive as Africa, what with the insects, the malaria, the heat in summer and the rough going underfoot. In a remote Greek village a visitor was deep in the Middle Ages as far as medical matters were concerned, and if you fell ill it was up to the local 'good women' – masseuses, cuppers, bonesetters and specialists in herbal cures – to pull you round. Though there were qualified medics in the more civilised parts, going to see a Greek doctor, Gerald was to recall later, was 'like going over Niagara in a barrel'. Roads were few, mostly dirt and caked in three inches of white dust; those that led up to the north were hard going even in summer and sometimes washed away in winter. Transport to the remoter parts of the island's coast was best left to the passenger fishing boats called caïques, but in winter if the sea was rough the caïques stopped sailing.

For the Durrells, living a short car ride from Corfu town, life was less primitive. Fruit and vegetables – potatoes, corn, carrots, tomatoes, green peppers, aubergines – were cheap and abundant in season, and there was a rich variety of fresh fish to be had every day. But even at the best of times there was no butter, and the milk was goats' milk. Chickens were thin and scrawny, beef was non-existent, though there was always good lamb and sometimes pork. Almost the only tinned food was peas and tomato paste, and the bread was heavy, grey, coarse and sour. There was no gas, electricity or coal. Heating for cooking was mostly charcoal, so that it took twenty minutes to boil a kettle for a cup of tea, and the ironing was done by maids using huge black charcoal irons. Light came from oil lamps, which filled the room with their distinctive smell, and oil stoves were used in winter to warm the rooms, along with wood fires. On special occasions the family would buy huge church candles for the veranda and garden, and set hollowed-out tangerines on the dining table with a little wick in oil inside. There were no refrigerators on Corfu, but Mother had an icebox which Spiro would refill with a huge block of ice he brought from town. Otherwise the best place to keep foodstuffs cool was the bottom of a deep well, or failing that a sea cave. 'Sometimes it was so hot,' Lawrence recalled, 'that we carried our dinner table out into the bay and set it down in the water. It was cool enough if you sat with the water up to your waist while you dined. The water was so still and clear that the candles hardly moved on such summer nights. And the bronze moon was huge.'

Corfu's compensations enormously outweighed any drawbacks. Their rent was cheap (£2 a month for a large house overlooking the sea), and so was food. 'There is a good peasant wine,' Lawrence reported to Alan Thomas, 'which tastes and looks like iced blood. It costs 6 drachs – 3d per bottle. What more does one want? In England I couldn't buy a bottle of horse-piss for 3d. Yesterday we dined very royally on red mullet – as you know a most epicurean dish – it cost 1od.' Clothes were casual for the most part. Gerry wore shorts throughout his time on the island, and usually kept his hair very long, as he hated going to the barber in town. When an admirer gave Margo a large silk shawl she did not care for, Gerald appropriated it and pinned it round his neck like a cloak when he went out riding on the village pony. The shawl had a pattern in gold, green, red and purple, and a long red fringe. 'I thought I cut a hell of a dash,' he recalled, 'as I galloped round the countryside.'

Generally the Durrell abodes on Corfu were sparsely furnished. All the rooms had bare floorboards which were scrubbed once a week in rotation and holystoned, and all the bedclothes were hung out of the windows each day to air. The furniture was mostly simple, rural and Greek, with the addition of a few exotic Indian items that Mother had brought out from England – deep blue curtains with huge peacocks on them; ornate round brass tables, intricately embossed and standing on elaborately carved teak legs; ashtrays decorated with peacocks and dragons.

At a domestic level the family's life on Corfu was simple, uncluttered, unhurried, unpressured. At a more exalted level, the island was gloriously beautiful, utterly unspoilt, a paradise on earth surrounded by an unpolluted crystalline sea. For Gerald, it was a revelation:

> Gradually the magic of the island settled over us as gently and clingingly as pollen. Each day had a tranquillity, a timelessness about it, so that you wished it would never end ... In those days I lived a curious sort of triple life. I dwelt in three worlds. One was the family, one was our eccentric friends, and the third was the peasant community. Through these three worlds I passed unobserved but observing.

For Gerald, Corfu was a kind of Mediterranean Congo peopled with natives and crawling with wildlife, where every foray was a venture into the interior, and every bend in the track and view through the trees portended something utterly new, unexpected and absorbing.

The family had decided on a six-month trial period to see if they liked Corfu and wanted to stay. Gerald remembered this as a time of pure freedom, a total holiday – no lessons, no duties, no set hours, just *carte blanche* to roam at will, exploring the wonders of his paradise island. As the weeks of that first enchanted summer of exploration and discovery went by he increased the range of his excursions away from the Strawberry-Pink Villa.

Every day began with the rising sun striking the shutters of his bedroom windows, followed soon after by the smell of a charcoal fire in the kitchen, cock-crows, yapping dogs, goats' bells clanging as the flocks wended their way to their grazing grounds. After a breakfast of coffee, toast and eggs under the tangerine trees Gerald would put on his wellington boots – Mother, having been brought up to dread snakes in India, insisted he wore these in the early days – and saunter forth in the cool of the morning, his butterfly net in his hand, empty matchboxes in his pockets, following the black, bouncing form of Roger the dog, his constant and dearly beloved companion on all his forays.

Within a six-mile radius of the villa Gerald became the local equivalent of the town crier, or a sort of itinerant human newspaper. In those days some of the peasant communities would only see each other once or twice a year at fiestas. So, travelling around as he did, it was Gerald who brought the news from village to village – how Maria had died and how Spiro's potato crop had failed (that was Spiro with the blind donkey, not Spiro with the Dodge convertible). '*Po! Po! Po!*' the villagers would cry in horror – 'and he has the whole winter stretching before him, potatoless. St Spiridion preserve him.'

It was in these early outings that Gerald got to know the Corfiot peasants of the locality, many of whom became his friends. There was the cheerful simpleton, an amiable but retarded youth with a face as round as a puffball and a bowler hat without a brim. There was rotund, cheerful old Agathi, past seventy but with hair still glossy and black, spinning wool outside her tumbledown cottage and singing the haunting peasant songs of the island, including her favourite, 'The Almond Tree', which began '*Kay kitaxay tine anthismeni amigdalia . . .*'. Then there was Yani, the toothless old shepherd, with hooked nose and great bandit moustache, who plied the ten-year-old Gerald with olives and figs and the thick red wine of the region (well-watered to a rosy pink).

And then there was the Rose-beetle man, one of the most extraordinary characters of the island, a wandering peddler of the most extreme eccentricity. When Gerald first encountered him in the hills, playing a shepherd's pipe, the Rose-beetle Man was fantastically garbed, wearing a battered hat that sprouted a forest of fluttering feathers of owl, hoopoe, kingfisher, cockerel and swan, and a coat whose pockets bulged with trinkets, balloons and coloured pictures of the saints. On his back he carried bamboo cages full of pigeons and young chickens, together with several mysterious sacks, and a large bunch of fresh green leeks. 'With one hand he held his pipe to his mouth, and in the other a number of lengths of cotton, to each of which was tied an almond-size rose-beetle, glittering golden green in the sun, all of them flying round his hat with desperate deep buzzings.' The beetles, the man mimed – for he was dumb as well as strange – were substitute toy aeroplanes for the village children.

One of the Rose-beetle Man's sacks was full of tortoises, and one in particular struck the boy's fancy – a sprightly kind of tortoise, with a brighter eye than most, and possessed (so Gerald was to claim) of a peculiar sense of humour. Gerald named him Achilles. 'He was undoubtedly the finest tortoise I had ever seen, and worth, in my opinion, at least twice what I had paid for him. I patted his scaly head with my finger and placed him carefully in my pocket.' But before setting off down the hill he glanced back. 'The Rose-beetle Man was still in the same place in the road, but he was doing a little jig, prancing and swaying, while in the road at his feet the tortoises ambled to and fro, dimly and heavily.'

From the Rose-beetle Man Gerald obtained several other small creatures that took up residence in the Strawberry-Pink Villa, including a frog, a sparrow with a broken leg, and the man's entire stock of rosebeetles, which infested the house for days, crawling into the beds and plopping into people's laps 'like emeralds'. Perhaps the most idiosyncratic of these creatures was a revolting-looking young pigeon which refused to learn to fly and insisted on sleeping at the foot of Margo's bed. So repulsive and obese was the bird that Larry suggested calling it Quasimodo. It was Larry who first noticed that Quasimodo was partial to dancing around the gramophone when a waltz was being played, and stomping up and down with puffed-up chest when the record was a march by Sousa. Eventually Quasimodo surprised everybody by laying an egg, whereupon she grew wilder and wilder, abjured the gramophone, and finally, suddenly endowed with the gift of flight, flew out of the door to take up residence in a tree with a large cock bird.

With Gerald rapidly turning into part of the fauna of Corfu, Mother decided it was time he had some sort of education. George Wilkinson was hired for this thankless task. Every morning he would come striding through the olive groves, a lean, lanky, bearded, bespectacled, disjointed figure in shorts and sandals, clutching bundles of books from his own small library, anything from the *Pears Cyclopaedia* to works by Wilde and Gibbon. 'Gerry really did everything he could to escape lessons,' Nancy recalled. 'He was utterly bored with lessons and with George as a tutor.' The only way George could gain his attention was to introduce animals into everything he taught, from history ('Good heavens, look. A jaguar,' remarked Christopher Columbus as he stepped ashore in America for the first time) to mathematics ('If it took two caterpillars a week to eat eight leaves, how long would it take four caterpillars?'). It was George who persuaded Gerald to start a nature diary, meticulously noting everything he saw and did every day in a set of fat blue-lined notebooks – a compilation sadly later lost.

Gerald was never at his best within the confines of a room, but outside – whether in a herbaceous border in the garden or a swamp full of snakes – he was a person transformed. Quickly realising this, George instituted a programme of *al fresco* lessons, out in the olive groves or down by the little beach at the foot of the hill overlooking Pondikonissi (Mouse Island). There, while discussing in a desultory way the historic role played by Nelson's egg collection at the Battle of Trafalgar, they would float gently out into the shallow bay, and Gerald would pursue his real studies – the flora and fauna of the seabed, the black ribbon-weed, the hermit crabs, the sea-slugs slowly rolling on the sandy bottom, sucking in seawater at one end and passing it out at the other. 'The sea was like a warm, silky coverlet,' wrote Gerald later, 'that moved my body gently to and fro. There were no waves, only this gentle underwater movement, the pulse of the sea, rocking me softly.'

George Wilkinson was an aspiring novelist, but Gerald was so bored by his English lessons that one day he suggested he should write a story of his own, just like his brother Larry (then busy on his second novel, *The Black Book*). Entitled 'The Man of Animals' and written in a wobbly and erratic hand and eccentric, nursery school spelling, the story relates, with uncanny prescience, the adventures of a man who was remarkably like the one Gerald would become:

Right in the Hart of the Africn Jungel a small wite man lives. Now there is one rather xtrordenry fackt about him that is that he is the frind of *all* animals. Now he lives on Hearbs and Bearis, both of which he nos, and soemtimes, not unles he is prakticly starvyng, he shoot with a bow and arrow a Bird of some sort, for you see he dos not like killing his frinds even wene he is so week that he cann hardly walk!

One of his favreret pets is a Big gray baboon, wich he named 'Sotine'. Now there are surten words this Big cretcher nows, for intenes if his master was to say 'Sotine I want a stick to mack a Bow, will you get me one?' then the Big ting with a nod of his Hede would trot of into the Jungel to get a bamboo fo the Bow and Arrow. But before Brracking it he would bend it so as to now that it would be all right, then breacking it of he would trot back to his master and give it to him and wight for prase, and nedless to say his master would give him a lot . . .

So far, so good. But now, obviously not averse to experimental writing, the youthful author suddenly switches from the third to the first person, and the adventure continues not from the narrator's but from the Man of Animals' point of view.

> One day wile I was warking in frount of my porters in Africa a Huge Hariy Hand caught my sholder and I was dragged of into the Jungel by this unseen figer. At last I was put down (not to gently) and I found my self looking into the eyes of a great baboon. 'Holy mackrarel,' I egeackted, 'what the devel made you carry me of like this, ay?' I saw the Baboon start at my words and then it walked over to the ege of the clearing, beckning me with a Big Hairy Hand ...

As well as writing extended narratives in those early Corfu days, Gerald was also trying his hand at verse. At first this shared the simplicity – and the spelling – of his more ambitious works, but combined his passion for natural history with the conventions of pastoral verse:

> That coulerd brid of incect land
> floating on the waves of light
> atractd by the throbing hart
> and pulsing viens
> this winged buaty
> hovers then swops down
> siting on the downey pettles
> sucking the honey greedly
> while the pollen
> fall softly
> on its red and yelow wings
> its hunger qunched
> it cralls up the slipry dome
> and flys away
> to its home
> in the skelaton
> of a liveing tree!

It was the discovery of a series of mysterious small silken trapdoors set into the floor of a neighbouring olive grove, each about the size of an old shilling piece, that led to an encounter that was to change for ever the direction of Gerald's life. Puzzled by the trapdoors, he made his way to George Wilkinson's villa to seek his advice. George was not alone. 'Seated in a chair was a figure which, at first glance, I thought must be

George's brother,' Gerald remembered, 'for he also wore a beard. He was, however, immaculately dressed in a grey flannel suit with waistcoat, a spotless white shirt, a tasteful but sombre tie, and large, solid, highly polished boots.'

'Gerry, this is Dr Theodore Stephanides,' said George. 'He is an expert on practically everything you care to mention. And what you don't mention, he does. He, like you, is an eccentric nature-lover. Theodore, this is Gerry Durrell.'

Gerald described the tiny trapdoors in the olive grove and Dr Stephanides listened gravely. Perhaps, he suggested, they could go together to look at this phenomenon, since the olive grove lay on a roundabout route back to his home near Corfu town. 'As we walked along I studied him covertly. He had a straight, well-shaped nose; a humorous mouth lurking in the ash-blond beard; straight, rather bushy eyebrows under which his eyes, keen but with a twinkle in them and laughter-wrinkles at the corners, surveyed the world. He strode along energetically, humming to himself.'

A quick inspection revealed that each trapdoor concealed the entrance to a burrow from which a spider emerged to catch passing prey. The mystery solved, Dr Stephanides shook Gerald's hand and prepared to go on his way. 'He turned and stumped off down the hill, swinging his stick, staring about him with observant eyes. I was at once confused and amazed by Theodore. He was the only person I had met until now who seemed to share my enthusiasm for zoology. I was extremely flattered to find that he treated me and talked to me exactly as though I was his own age. Theodore not only talked to me as though I was grown up, but also as though I was as knowledgeable as he.'

Gerald did not expect to meet the man again, but clearly his enthusiasm, high seriousness and powers of observation had made an impression on Theodore, for two days later Leslie came back from town carrying a parcel addressed to Gerald. Inside was a small box and a letter.

> My dear Gerry Durrell,
> I wondered, after our conversation the other day, if it might not assist your investigations of the local natural history to have some form of magnifying instrument. I am therefore sending you this pocket microscope, in the hope that it will be of some use to you. It is, of course, not of very high magnification, but you will find it sufficient for *field* work.
> With best wishes,
> Yours sincerely,
> Theo. Stephanides

P.S. If you have nothing better to do on Thursday, perhaps you would care to come to tea, and I could show you some of my microscope slides.

With the doctor and naturalist Theo Stephanides as his mentor, Gerald was to journey through a world of unfamiliar yet strangely intimate forces and phenomena, entering the orbit of Zatopec the poet and the ex-King of Greece's butler, the microscopic world of the scarlet mite and the one-eyed cyclops bug, the natural profligacy of the tortoise hills, the lake of lilies, the phosphorescent porpoise sea. In the course of his travels he was to become transformed, learning the language and gestures of rural Greece, absorbing its music and folklore, drinking its wine, singing its songs, and shedding his thin veneer of Englishness, so that in mind-set and social behaviour he was never to grow up a true Englishman – a handicap which, like his lack of a formal education, was to prove a tremendous boon in later years.

Theodore Stephanides had just passed forty when Gerald first encountered him. Though the Stephanides family originated from Thessaly in Greece, Theo (like Gerald) was born in India, thus qualifying him for British as well as Greek nationality. At home in Bombay he and his family spoke only English, and it was not until his father retired to Corfu in 1907, when Theo was eleven, that he began to learn Greek properly. After serving in the Greek army in Macedonia in World War One and in Asia Minor in the ensuing war against the Turks, Theo went to Paris to study medicine, later returning to Corfu, where he established the island's first x-ray unit in 1929, and shortly afterwards married Mary Alexander, a young woman of English and Greek parentage and the granddaughter of a former British Consul on Corfu. Though Theo was a doctor he was never well off, mainly because much of his work he did free of charge, and he and his wife lived in the same rented house in Corfu town throughout the period of their stay on the island.

Theo was a man of immense integrity and courtesy, behaving in the same way to old and young, friends and strangers. He was shy socially, except with close friends, but he had a highly developed sense of humour and loved cracking a good joke, or even a really silly one, at which he would chuckle mightily. He loved Greek dances, and would sometimes perform a *kalamatianos* by himself. He travelled all over Corfu in his spare time, by car where there were roads and on foot where there were not, singing almost every inch of the way. Whenever Gerald was with him he sang a nonsense song of which he was very fond, in a kind of pantomime English:

There was an old man who lived in Jerusalem
Glory Halleluiah, Hi-ero-jerum.
He wore a top hat and he looked very sprucelum
Glory Halleluiah, Hi-ero-jerum.
Skinermer rinki doodle dum, skinermer rinki doodle dum
Glory Halleluiah, Hi-ero-jerum . . .

'It had a rousing tune,' Gerald recalled, 'that gave a new life to tired feet, and Theodore's baritone voice and my shrill treble would ring out gaily through the gloomy trees.'

Theo held views on ecological matters that were very advanced for their time, particularly in Greece, and these planted the germs of a way of thinking in young Gerald's head that was to stand him in valuable stead in future years. If Theo went for a drive in the country he would throw tree seeds out of the window, in the hope that a few would take root, and he took time off to teach the peasants how to avoid soil erosion when they were tilling the ground, and to persuade them to restrain the goats from devouring everything that grew. As a good doctor he did his best to improve public health on the island, encouraging the villagers to stock their wells with a species of minnow which fed on mosquito larvae and thus helped eradicate malaria.

For Gerald, being tutored by Theo was like going straight to Oxford or Harvard without the usual intermediary steps of primary and secondary schools in between. Theo was a walking, talking fount of knowledge, not only breathtakingly wide-ranging, but deep, detailed and exact. Born before the age of ultra-specialisation, he knew something – sometimes a great deal – about everything. In the course of a day he could engage the young Gerald in an advanced tutorial that would hop effortlessly through the fields of anthropology, ethnology, musicology, cosmology, ecology, biology, parasitology, biochemistry, medicine, history and much else. 'I had few books to guide and explain,' Gerald was to write, 'and Theodore was for me a sort of walking, hirsute encyclopaedia.'

Theo was no mere pedant, with a kleptomaniac gift for collecting sterile, unrelated facts. He was a true polymath, who related the phenomena of past and present existence in a master synthesis, a grand vision which had its feet firmly planted in science but its head peering speculatively among the clouds. 'Although the classroom basics of biology were a closed book to me,' Gerald admitted to a friend in his middle age, 'walks with Theo contained discussions of everything from life on Mars to the humblest beetle, and I knew they were all part and parcel, all interlocked.'

On top of all this, Theo Stephanides bestrode the iron curtain between art and science, for he was not only a doctor and a biologist, but a poet whose friends included some of Greece's leading poets. 'If I had the power of magic,' Gerald once remarked, 'I would confer two gifts on every child – the enchanted childhood I had on the island of Corfu, and to be guided and befriended by Theodore Stephanides.' Under Theo's tutelage Gerald became more than a juvenile version of a naturalist in the classic nineteenth-century mould, more even than a straightforward zoologist of the kind turned out by the British universities of the era – though that was what he was to put as his profession in his passport. For Theo not only taught him what biological life was and how it worked, but imbued him with two principles regarding the role of man in the scheme of things. The first was that life without human intervention maintained its own checks and balances. The second was that the proper role of mankind among living things was omniscience with humility – and the greater of these two was humility.

'Not many young naturalists have the privilege of having their footsteps guided by a sort of omnipotent, benign and humorous Greek god,' Gerald would recall. 'Theodore had all the very best qualities of the early Victorian naturalists, an insatiable interest in the world he inhabited and the ability to illuminate any topic with his observations and thoughts. His wide interests are summed up by the fact that (in this day and age) he was a man who had a microscopic water crustacean named after him, as well as a crater on the moon.'

From 1935 to 1939 Theo and his wife Mary visited the Durrells once a week, arriving after lunch and leaving after dinner. Their young daughter Alexia, often ailing, was usually left at home with her French nanny, because Theo was jealous of his afternoons with Gerald, who was like a son to him. For if Gerald was fortunate to have encountered such a gifted tutor in such a place at such a time in his life, Theodore was no less fortunate to have found an acolyte so innately endowed with responsive gifts of his own. Quite apart from his boundless energy and enthusiasm, his inexhaustible spirit of enquiry – remarkable for one so young, noted Theo – the boy had all the essential qualities of a naturalist. Patience, for a start. He could remain perched in a tree for hours on end, utterly still, utterly enthralled, as he watched the comings and goings of some small creature. Even Nancy, no naturalist, saw this special quality in him: 'He had an *enormous* patience when he was very young. He used to make lassoes for catching lizards – lassoes of grass – and he would stay hours crouched in front of a little hole where he knew the lizard was, and then he would pull the noose tight and lasso it.'

Theo also discerned that Gerald lacked the arrogance that most human beings brought to their encounters with animals. Animals, Gerald felt by instinct, were his equals, no matter how small, or ugly, or undistinguished; they were, at a level beyond the merely sentimental, his friends and companions – often his only ones, for he had no great rapport with other children. And the animals, in their turn, sensed this, and responded accordingly, not just when he was a boy on Corfu but throughout all the years of his life.

By corollary, it followed in Gerald's mind that it was a fundamental moral law that all species had an equal right to exist, this at a time when most human societies observed no ethical principles applicable to living things outside of humankind. It also followed that he had difficulty pursuing the study of natural history in the way that was the common practice of the period: that is by snuffing the life out of living things in order to examine, classify and dissect them in death. 'Live with living things, I say,' he was later to declare, 'don't just peer at them in a pool of alcohol.' Gerald, in other words, was a behavioural zoologist (or ethologist) from the very start, and natural history for him was the study of living things – all too evidently living, as his family were to find out soon enough.

The family's first winter came, coolish and very wet. By now Larry and Nancy, seeking the wilder, lonelier shores of the island, had moved up to Kalami, a remote hamlet on the north-east coast of Corfu, where they took a single-storey, whitewashed fisherman's house – the White House – on the edge of the sea overlooking a small bay, with the barren hills of Albania only a couple of miles away across the straits. The winter rain in Corfu was almost tropical in density, the sea pounded on the rocks below the house, and the only heating was some smouldering logs in the middle of the room.

When nineteen-year-old Alex Emmett, a family friend who had been at school with Leslie, arrived to join the Durrells for their first Christmas at the Strawberry-Pink Villa, he found Mother still downing gin, Leslie an aimless, rootless, mother-fixated castaway, and Gerry utterly absorbed in his trapdoor spiders and his natural history lessons with Theo Stephanides. But for Theo, Emmett reckoned, young Gerry might easily have become a drifter like Leslie.

Having arrived for Christmas, Emmett stayed on for the family's first full-blown spring on Corfu. It was to prove a season of singular magic. Gerald observed it through eyes round with wonder. The whole island was 'flower-filled, scented and a-flutter with new leaves'. The cypress trees were now covered with a misty coat of greenish-white cones. Waxy yellow crocuses tumbled down the banks and blue day-irises filled the oak thickets. Gerald recorded: 'It was no half-hearted spring, this; the whole island vibrated with it as though a great, ringing chord had been struck. Everything and everyone heard it and responded. It was apparent in the gleam of flower-petals, the flash of bird wings and the sparkle in the dark, liquid eyes of the peasant girls.'

The family responded to the spring in their different ways. Leslie blazed away at turtle-doves with his guns. Lawrence bought a guitar and a large barrel of strong red wine and sang Elizabethan love songs which induced a mood of melancholy. Margo perked up, bathed frequently and took an interest in a good-looking but boring young Turk – not a popular choice on a Greek island.

Gerald's excursions took on an even greater range and interest when, in the summer of 1936, the family moved to another villa on the far side of Corfu town. According to Gerald, it was Larry who provoked the move. He had invited some friends to come to stay on Corfu – Zatopec the poet (an Albanian whose real name was Zarian), three artists called Jonquil, Durant and Michael, and the bald-headed Melanie, Countess of Torro – and he wanted Mother to put them up in the Strawberry-Pink Villa. Since the villa was barely big enough for the family, let alone an untold number of guests, Mother's circuitous logic decided that the easiest solution was to find a bigger place. In any case, the Strawberry-Pink Villa never had a bathroom worthy of the name, only a separate washroom and a primitive toilet in the grounds, which alone was a compelling enough reason to move on.

The new house, which Gerald was to dub the Daffodil-Yellow Villa, was a huge Venetian mansion called Villa Anemoyanni, after the family who had owned it until recently. It stood on a modest eminence set back from the sea at a place called Sotoriotissa, near Kondokali, overlooking Gouvia Bay to the north of Corfu town. From the attic the children could watch the once-weekly Imperial Airways flying-boat splash down in the bay below. The house had stood empty for three years; it had faded green shutters and yellow walls, and was surrounded by neglected olive groves and untended orchards of lemon and orange trees. Gerald recalled:

The whole place had an atmosphere of ancient melancholy about it, the house with its cracked and peeling walls, the tremendous echoing rooms, its verandas piled high with drifts of last year's leaves and so overgrown with creepers and vines that the lower rooms were in a perpetual green twilight ... The house and land were gently, sadly decaying, lying forgotten on the hillside over-looking the shining sea and dark, eroded hills of Albania.

It was Spiro who found the villa, and Spiro who organised the move – the long line of handcarts piled high with the family's possessions heading north in the now familiar cloud of white dust. But even after they had moved everything in, the house remained vast and echoing, mainly because much of the decrepit antique furniture that came with it disintegrated at the first touch of a human hand (or bottom). It was big enough for Gerald to be allocated a large room of his own on the first floor – his study, he called it, though to the rest of the family it was known as the Bug House. The Bug House was Gerald's first true den and centre of operations:

> This room smelt pleasantly of ether and methylated spirits. It was here I kept my natural history books, my diary, microscope, dissecting instruments, nets, collecting bags, and other important items. Large cardboard boxes housed my birds' eggs, beetle, butterfly and dragon-fly collections, while on the shelves above were a fine range of bottles full of methylated spirit in which were preserved such interesting items as a four-legged chicken, various lizards and snakes, frog-spawn in different stages of growth, a baby octopus, three half-grown brown rats (a contribution from Roger), and a minute tortoise, newly hatched, that had been unable to survive the winter. The walls were sparsely, but tastefully, decorated with a slab slate containing the fossilised remains of a fish, a photograph of myself shaking hands with a chimpanzee, and a stuffed bat. I had prepared the bat myself, without assistance, and I was extremely proud of the result.

For Gerald the winter was enlivened by his tea-time natural history lessons every Thursday in Theo's wonderful study in his flat in Corfu town. The room was packed with books, notebooks, x-ray plates, jars and bottles full of minute freshwater fauna, a telescope pointing at the sky, and a microscope table laden with instruments and slides, where Gerald would sit for hours on end peering transfixed at the mouth-parts of the rat flea, the egg-sacs of the one-eyed cyclops bug, the spinnerets of the cross or garden spider. When the weather improved they ventured out. Theo would come over to the Daffodil-Yellow Villa on foot, followed by his wife Mary and sometimes his young daughter Alexia in Spiro's taxi; together he and Gerry would sally forth to explore the surrounding countryside, striding out side by side, singing at the top of their voices.

Alan Thomas, on a visit to Corfu, witnessed them setting out on an expedition, Theo in an immaculate white suit and a homburg that would have been a credit to Edward VII, Gerry running alongside, almost dancing with happiness, both of them strapped around with collecting equipment. 'I turned to Larry,' Thomas recalled, 'and I said: "It's wonderful for Gerry to have Theodore." And Larry replied: "Yes, Theodore is Gerry's *hero*."' They always carried a bottle of fresh lemonade and biscuits or sandwiches on these excursions, together with dipping nets and knapsacks and canvas bags full of collecting bottles and boxes and a few clumps of damp moss, for as Theodore explained: 'Both Gerald and I were more interested in studying *live* creatures and kept our collection of preserved specimens to a minimum.'

Exploring the countryside with the close concentration of watchmenders, they left no stick or stone unturned, no puddle unexamined. 'Every water-filled ditch was, to us, a teeming and unexplored jungle,' Gerald recalled, with the minute cyclops and water-fleas, green and coral pink, suspended like birds among the underwater branches, while on the muddy bottom the tigers of the pool would prowl: the leeches and the dragonfly larvae. Every hollow tree had to be scrutinised in case it should contain a tiny pool of water in which mosquito-larvae were living, every mossy rock had to be overturned to find out what lay beneath it, and every rotten log had to be dissected. On their return they ransacked Mother's kitchen for soup plates and teaspoons, which they used to sort out their finds before accommodating them in the gravel-bottomed, weed-aired jam jars and sweet bottles that would be their home. Before long, Theo was to recall, they had assembled a 'whole army corps of aquaria'.

Soon Gerald was setting off from the Daffodil-Yellow Villa and exploring in every direction – always dressed, at his mother's insistence, in very brightly coloured pullovers so that he could be easily spotted even when he strayed some distance from home. A myrtle-covered hill behind the house was covered with tortoises newly awakened from their winter's hibernation, and Gerald would spend hours watching their romantic urges revive in the sun. 'The actual sexual act,' he was to record, 'was the most awkward and fumbling thing I have ever seen. The incredibly heavy-handed and inexpert way the male would attempt to hoist himself on to the female shell, overbalancing and almost overturning, was extremely painful to watch; the urge to go and assist the poor creature was almost overwhelming.' No less intriguing to the twelve-year-old was the sex life of the mantises, and he would stare in horror as the female slowly munched her way through her partner's head while he proceeded to fertilise her with what was left of his body: a beautifully simple demonstration of the two purposes of life – feeding to ensure the survival of the individual, and copulation to ensure the survival of the species – neatly combined in a single event.

Sometimes Gerald would go out bat-hunting at night, an altogether different adventure in a world metamorphosed by silence and moonlight, where the creatures of the darkness – jackals, foxes, squirrel dormice, nightjars – slipped silently in an out of vision like shadows. Once he found a young Scops owl covered in baby down and took it home, naming him Ulysses. Ulysses was a bird of great strength of character, Gerald noted, and not to be trifled with, so when he grew up he was given the freedom of the Bug House, flying out through the window at night and riding on Roger the dog's back when Gerald went down to the sea for a late-evening swim.

Gerald now began to collect creatures on a grand scale, and before long his room was so full that he had to house them in various nooks and crannies throughout the villa. This led to some embarrassing, not to say fractious situations, for the rest of the family did not share his affection for the island's wildlife, and positively objected if they encountered it in the wrong place. For a while the house was infested with giant mosquitoes, whose provenance remained obscure until Theo realised that what Gerald thought were tadpoles in his aquarium were in fact the inch-long, pot-bellied larvae of *Theobaldia longeareolata*, the largest mosquito on the island. Gerald had been puzzled by the fact that, instead of turning into frogs, they had seemingly been vanishing into thin air. But worse was to follow.

Gerald had long been fascinated by the black scorpion, a particularly venomous version of a species which had a fearsome reputation – as Yani the shepherd once explained, its sting could kill, especially if it managed to crawl into your ear, as had happened to one of Yani's friends, a young shepherd who died in unspeakable agony. Gerald was never deterred by dangerous animals, however, and in the crumbling wall surrounding the sunken garden of the Daffodil-Yellow Villa he was delighted to discover a whole battalion of black scorpions, each about an inch long. 'They were weird-looking things,' he was to write, 'with their flattened, oval bodies, crooked legs, the enormous crab-like claws, bulbous and neatly jointed as armour, and the tail like a string of brown beads ending in a sting like a rose-thorn.' At night he would go out with a torch and watch the scorpions' wonderful courtship dances, claw in claw, tails entwined. 'I grew very fond of these scorpions. I found them to be pleasant, unassuming creatures with, on the whole, most charming habits.' Their cannibalism apart.

One day Gerald found a fat female scorpion in the wall, with a mass of tiny babies clinging to her back. Enraptured, he carefully put mother and babies into one of his empty matchboxes, intending to smuggle them into the Bug House where he could watch the babies grow up. Unfortunately, lunch was served just as he went into the house, so he put the matchbox on the drawing room mantelpiece for temporary safekeeping, and joined the rest of the family. The meal passed affably, then Lawrence rose and went to fetch his cigarettes from the drawing room, picking up the matchbox he found conveniently ready on the mantelpiece.

Gerald watched as, 'still talking glibly', Lawrence opened the matchbox. In a flash the mother scorpion was out of the box and on to the back of his hand, sting curved up and at the ready, babies still clinging on grimly. Lawrence let out a roar of fright, and with an instinctive flick of his hand sent the scorpion scooting down the table, shedding babies to left and right. Pandemonium ensued. Lugaretzia dropped the plates, Roger the dog began barking madly, Leslie leapt from his chair, and Margo threw a glass of water at the creature, but missed and drenched Mother.

'It's that bloody boy again,' Lawrence could be heard bawling above the universal turmoil. Roger, deciding Lugaretzia was to blame for the brouhaha, promptly bit her in the leg.

'It's that bloody boy,' bellowed Lawrence again. 'He'll kill the lot of us. Look at the table ... knee-deep in scorpions ...'

Soon the scorpions had hidden themselves under the crockery and cutlery, and a temporary lull descended.

'That bloody boy ...' Lawrence reiterated, almost speechless. 'Every matchbox in the house is a death trap.'

In another potentially heart-stopping incident, it was Leslie's turn to undergo trial by terror. One hot day in September, seeing that his water snakes were wilting in the heat, Gerald took them into the house and put them in a bath full of cool water. Not long afterwards, Leslie returned from a shooting expedition and decided to have a bath to freshen up. Suddenly there was a tremendous bellow from the direction of the bathroom, and Leslie emerged on to the veranda wearing nothing but a small towel.

'Gerry!' he roared, his face flushed with anger. 'Where's that boy?'

'Now, *now*, dear,' said Mother soothingly, 'whatever's the matter?'

'Snakes,' snarled Leslie, 'that's what's the matter ... That bloody *boy's* filled the soddin' *bath* full of bleeding *snakes*, that's what's the matter ... Damn great things like *hosepipes* ... It's a wonder I wasn't bitten.'

Gerald removed the snakes from the bath and put them into a saucepan from the kitchen, returning in time to hear Lawrence holding forth to the lunch party on the veranda, 'I assure you the house is a death trap. Every conceivable nook and cranny is stuffed with malignant faunae waiting to pounce. How I have escaped being maimed for life is beyond me . . .'

One day Gerald and Theo came back with a jar full of medicinal leeches – gruesome red-and-green-striped bloodsuckers, all of three inches long. Even today Lake Scotini, the only permanent freshwater lakelet on Corfu and a favourite hunting ground for the indomitable pair, swarms with such creatures. Due to a mishap the jar was knocked off a table, and the leeches vanished. For nights Lawrence lay awake in terror, expecting to find the creatures feeding on his body and the sheets soaked in blood. It was, he felt, the ultimate nightmare visitation, the apotheosis of all Gerry's wildlife horrors.

Lawrence's estimation of his youngest brother, which had been sinking lower with each daily delivery of centipedes, scorpions or toads into the family home, rallied somewhat when one day, to his intense surprise, he heard the bug-happy boy whistling part of the first movement of Beethoven's Eighth Symphony. But the years did not mellow him when it came to the matter of Gerald's life-threatening proclivities on Corfu. 'As a small boy he was impossible,' he told a friend many years later. 'A terrible nuisance. He has recounted the worst of himself as well as the best in that *Family* book. Oh, it was matchboxes full of scorpions all the time, I didn't dare to sit down anywhere in the house, and of course Mother was there to defend him – the slightest criticism and she would snarl like a bear, and meanwhile there were beetles in the soup. No, he was intolerable, he needed to be thrashed.'

Since the family was so dismayed by many of Gerald's strange pets, Theo's affirmation of the boy's ruling passion was like a papal benediction for him. Later Gerald was to relate how, when the rains began to fill the ponds and ditches, he and Theo would prowl among them, 'as alert as fishing herons':

> I was seeking the terrapin, the frog, toad or snake to add to my menagerie, while Theo, his little net with bottle on the end, would seek the smaller fauna, some almost invisible to the eye.
>
> 'Ah ha!' he would exclaim when, having swept his net through the water, he lifted the little bottle to his eye. 'Now this is – er, um – *most* interesting. I haven't seen one of these since I was in Epir . . .'
>
> 'Look, Theo,' I would say, lifting a baby snake towards him.
>
> 'Um – er – yes,' Theo would reply. 'Pretty thing.'
>
> To hear an adult call a snake a pretty thing was music to my ears.

FOUR

The Garden of the Gods

Corfu 1937–1939

So the bug-happy boy wandered about his paradise island while conventional education passed him by. For a time Mother endeavoured to stop him turning completely wild by sending him off for daily French lessons with the Belgian Consul, another of Corfu's great eccentrics. The Consul lived at the top of a tall, rickety building in the centre of the Jewish quarter of Corfu town, an exotic and colourful area of narrow alleys full of open-air stalls, bawling vendors, laden donkeys, clucking hens – and a multitude of stray and starving cats. He was a kindly little man, with gold teeth and a wonderful three-pointed beard, and dressed at all times in formal attire appropriate to his official status, complete with silk cravat, shiny top hat and spats.

Gerald acquired little French from his lessons, but his boredom was alleviated by a curious obsession of his tutor's. It turned out that the Consul was as compulsive a gunman as Gerald's brother Leslie, and every so often during the morning lessons he would leap out of his chair, load a powerful air rifle, take careful aim out of the window and blaze away at the street outside. At first Gerald's hopes were raised by the possibility that the Consul was mixed up in some deadly family feud, though he was puzzled why no one ever fired back, and why, after firing his gun, the Consul would be so upset, muttering dolefully, with tears in his eyes: 'Ah, ze poor lizzle fellow . . .' Finally Gerald discovered that the Consul, a devoted cat lover, was shooting the hungriest and most wretched of the strays. 'I cannot feed zem all,' he explained, 'so I like to make zem happiness by zooting zem. Zey are bezzer so, but iz makes me feel so zad.' And he would leap up again to take another potshot out of the window.

The Belgian Consul fared no better than any of Gerald's other hired tutors, totally failing to strike a spark from the boy's obdurate flint. It was his brother Larry's educative influence that complemented that of

Theo Stephanides, firing him with what he called a 'sort of verbal tonic'. 'He has the most extraordinary ability for giving people faith in them- selves,' he was to write of his eldest brother. 'Throughout my life he has provided me with more enthusiastic encouragement than anyone else, and any success I have achieved is due, in no small measure, to his backing.' Not long after the family had settled down on Corfu, Lawrence began to take his youngest brother's literary education in hand. It was under his eclectic but inspired guidance that Gerald was introduced to the world of reading and the basics of writing – above all to the world of Lawrence's vivid, ever-fermenting imagination.

'My brother Larry was a kind of god for me,' Gerald recalled, 'and therefore I tried to imitate him. Larry had people like Henry Miller staying with him in Corfu and I had access to his very varied library.' Larry would throw books at him, he remembered, with a brief word about why they were interesting, and if Gerald thought he was right he'd read them. 'Good heavens, I was omnivorous! I read anything from Darwin to the unexpurgated *Lady Chatterley's Lover*. I adored books by W.H. Hudson, Gilbert White and Bates' *A Naturalist on the River Amazons*. I believe that all children should be surrounded by books and animals.' It was Lawrence who gave his young brother copies of Henri Fabre's classic works *Insect Life: Souvenirs of a Naturalist* and *The Life and Love of the Insects*, with their accounts of wasps, bees, ants, gnats, spiders, scorpions – books which Gerald was later to claim 'set me off on Corfu', and which remained an inspiration throughout his life on account of the simplicity and clarity with which they were written and the stimulation they provided the imagination. He was to write:

> If someone had presented me with the touchstone that turns every- thing to gold, I could not have been more delighted. From that moment Fabre became my personal friend. He unravelled the many mysteries that surrounded me and showed me miracles and how they were performed. Through his entrancing prose I became the hunting wasp, the paralysed spider, the cicada, the burly, burnished scarab beetle, and a host of other creatures as well.

Ironically, though, it was a publication that Gerald borrowed from his highly unliterary, gun-slinging brother Leslie that was to sound the clearest call to action for his future life. This was a copy of a popular adventure magazine called *Wide World*, which serialised a refreshingly humorous account by an American zoologist, Ivan Sanderson, about a recent animal-collecting expedition, led by Percy Sladen, in the wilds of the Cameroons in West Africa. Sanderson's beguiling tale planted a dream inside Gerald's young skull, a dream which hardened into a youthful vow of intent that one day he too would combine his love of animals with his yearning for adventure and brave the African wilds in search of rare animals – animals which he would bring back alive, not trapped, shot and stuffed like Percy Sladen's.

Lawrence's greatest gift to Gerald was not printed books but language itself, especially language at its most evocative and illuminating, in the form of simile and metaphor. Judging by the progression from Gerald's earliest literary offerings to those that followed, the impact of his brother's tuition was electrifying. It was as if Gerald had grown up in a year, emerging by the summer of 1936, when he was eleven, with the perception of someone three times his age. If his next poem, 'Death', was not written by Lawrence, the influence of Lawrence totally dominates it, from the subject to the prosody. And the transformation in Gerald's spelling is suspiciously miraculous.

> on a mound a boy lay
> as a stream went tinkling by:
> mauve irises stood around him as if to
> shade him from the eye of death which
> was always taking people unawares
> and making them till his ground
> rhododendrons peeped
> at the boy counting sheep
> the horror is spread
> the boy is dead
>
> BUT DEATH HIMSELF IS NOT SEEN

Lawrence was so impressed by the poem that he sent a copy of it to his friend Henry Miller in America, naming his younger brother as the author. 'He has written the following poem,' he wrote. 'And I am envious.' Later he included the poem in the November 1937 issue of the *Booster*, the controversial literary magazine of the American Country Club near Paris, which he edited with Miller, Alfred Perlès and William Saroyan.

By now Mother had found Gerald a new tutor to take the place of George Wilkinson, who had remained at Pérama. He was a twenty-two-year-old friend of Lawrence's by the name of Pat Evans, 'a tall, handsome young man,' Gerald noted, 'fresh from Oxford.' Evans entertained serious ambitions of actually educating his young pupil, an aim Gerald himself found 'rather trying' and did his best to subvert. He need not have worried, however, for soon the island began to work its languorous magic on the new arrival, and all talk of fractions and adverbs and suchlike was abandoned in favour of a more outdoor kind of teaching, like floating about in the sea while chatting in a desultory way about the effects of warm ocean currents and the origins of coastline geology. Evans had a keen interest in natural history and biology, and he passed on his enthusiasm to his young pupil in a casual, unobtrusive way, 'walking around, just looking at bugs', as Margo recalled.

Gerald persuaded Pat Evans to let him write a book as a substitute for English lessons, and soon he was busy scribbling away at a narrative he was to describe as 'a stirring tale of a voyage round the world capturing animals with my family', a work Lawrence called 'his great novel of the flora and fauna of the world' – a story written very much in the style of the *Boy's Own Paper*, with one chapter ending with Mother being attacked by a jaguar and another with Larry caught in the coils of a giant anaconda. Unfortunately, the manuscript was inadvertently left behind in a tin trunk when the family finally left the island, and was probably impounded (so Gerald reckoned) by a bunch of Nazi illiterates during the war and thus lost to posterity for ever.

One fragment of Gerald's early writing that did survive was a remarkable prose poem, 'In the Theatre', which Lawrence also published in the *Booster* – it was, indeed, Gerald's first published work. It was clear from 'In the Theatre' that Gerald shared with his eldest brother an aptitude for vivid, concrete imagery and the instinct for simile and metaphor which lies at the heart of all poetic vision – much of it drawn from the wildlife the boy had been observing at first hand in his rambles around Corfu.

They brought him in on a stretcher, starched and white, every stitch of it showing hospital work. They slid him on to the cold stone table. He was dressed in pyjamas and jacket, his face looked as if it was carved out of cuttlefish. A student fidgeted, someone coughed, huskily, uneasily. The doctor looked up sharply at the new nurse: she was white as marble, twisting a blue lace handkerchief in her butterfly-like hands.

The scalpel whispered as if it were cutting silk, showing the intestines coiled up neatly like watchsprings. The doctor's hands moved with the speed of a striking snake, cutting, fastening, probing. At last, a pinkish-grey thing like a sausage came out in the scorpion-like grip of the pincers. Then the sewing-up, the needle burying itself in the soft depth and appearing on the other side of the abyss, drawing the skin together like a magnet. The stretcher groaned at the sudden weight.

When Lawrence first read this prose-poem with his eleven-year-old brother's name appended to it, he thought it must have been his tutor Pat Evans who had really written it. But Evans denied any involvement. 'Do you suppose,' he told Lawrence, 'that if I could write as well as that I would waste my time on being a tutor?'

But Pat Evans clearly was an inciting agent of some sort in Gerald's literary development, for later in the year Gerald wrote to Alan Thomas enclosing a copy of his most recent poetic concoction:

> I send you my latest opus. Pat and I set each other subjects to write poems in each week. This is my first homework [sic].
> NIGHT-CLUB.
>
> > Spoon on, swoon on to death. The mood is blue.
> > Croon me a stave as sexless as the plants,
> > Deathless as platinum, cynical as love.
> > My mood is indigo, my dance is bones.
> > If there were any limbo it were here.
> > Dancing dactyls, piston-man and pony
> > To dewey negroes played by saxophones . . .
> > Sodom, swoon on, and wag the deathless boddom.
> > I love your sagging undertones of snot.
> > Love shall prevail – and coupling in cloakrooms
> > When none shall care whether it prevail or not.
>
> Much love to you. Nancy is drawing a bookplate for you. Why?
> Gerry Durrell

Did the eleven-year-old boy with his simple, innocent passion for blennies and trapdoor spiders really write this unbelievably precocious piece of desperately straining and contrived *Weltschmerz*? Not only the subject, but the existentialist mind-set, the mood, the vocabulary, the startling and often far-fetched imagery, the compulsive desire to shock, all reek of the influence of Larry the poet, not to mention Larry the uncompromising, anarchic novelist then wrestling with his first major work of fiction, his seriously black – and blue – *Black Book*. Did Larry actually write it? If not, it can only be seen as a pastiche of Larry, and as such quite stunning for one so young – bizarrely sophisticated nonsense work that nonetheless makes a kind of sense.

A later poem by Gerald entitled 'An African Dialogue' was later published, with Lawrence's help, in a fringe literary periodical called *Seven* in the summer of 1939. As the final verse indicates, it is remarkable for the cryptic compression of its metaphysical conceit.

She went to the house and lit a candle.
The candle cried: 'I am being killed.'
The flame: 'I am killing you.'
The maid answered: 'It is true, true.
For I see your white blood.'

Meanwhile, family life *chez* the Durrells was beginning to disintegrate into riot and pandemonium. 'We've got so lax,' Larry wrote to Alan Thomas, 'what with Leslie farting at meals, and us nearly naked all day on the point, bathing.' Nancy agreed. Mother could keep no kind of order at all. 'Even Gerry could have done better with a little more discipline,' she complained. 'I mean he did grow up with really no discipline at all.' Nancy and Larry were glad of the seclusion and tranquillity of their whitewashed fisherman's house at Kalami, far from the uproarious family. 'Ten miles south,' Larry reported to Thomas, 'the family brawls and caterwauls and screams in the cavernous new Ypso villa.'

At a cost of £43.10s. the Durrell splinter party had had a top storey added to their house, with a balcony from which they could look over the sea and the hills towards the dying day. For them at least, and later for Gerald and the rest of the family on their forays north, the island entered a new dimension of enchantment.

'The peace of those evenings on the balcony before the lighting of the lamps was something we shall never discover again,' Lawrence was to write; 'the stillness of objects reflected in the mirror of the bay . . . It was the kind of hush you get in a Chinese water-colour.' As they sat there, sea and sky merging into a single veil, a shepherd would start playing his flute somewhere under an arbutus out of sight.

Across the bay would slide the smooth, icy notes of the flute; little liquid flourishes, and sleepy squibbles. Sitting on the balcony, wrapped by the airs, we would listen without speaking. Presently the moon appeared – not the white, pulpy spectre of a moon that you see in Egypt – but a Greek moon, friendly, not incalculable or chilling . . . We walked in our bare feet through the dark rooms, feeling the cool tiles under us, and down on to the rock. In that enormous silence we walked into the water, so as not to splash, and swam out into the silver bar. We didn't speak because a voice on that water sounded unearthly. We swam till we were tired and then came back to the white rock and wrapped ourselves in towels and ate grapes.

'This is Homer's country pure,' Lawrence scribbled enthusiastically, if not entirely accurately, to Alan Thomas. 'A few 100 yards from us is where Ulysses landed ...' The diet, he said, was a bit wild. 'Bread and cheese and Greek champagne ... Figs and grapes if they're in ... But in compensation the finest bathing and scenery in the world – and ISLANDS!'

It was inevitable that sooner or later, looking out every day over such an incomparably mesmeric expanse of sea, the family should eventually take to the water. Leslie was the leading spirit in this foray. Before he came to Corfu he had badly wanted to join the Merchant Navy, but his local doctor deemed his constitution wasn't strong enough. In Corfu he acquired a small boat, the *Sea Cow*, which he first rowed, then, following the addition of an outboard engine, motored up and down the coast, often alone, sometimes with the rest of the family.

'You should see us,' Leslie wrote in one of his infrequent missives home, 'the whole bloody crowd at sea, it would make you laugh.

> One day Larry and Nan came here and I said I would take them home in the boat – Mother, Pat, Gerry, Larry, Nan and myself all in the motor boat. We started off and ran into quite a rough sea. Pat lying on the deck and holding on for all he was worth was dripping in about 5 minutes. Larry, Nan, Mother and Gerry crawled under a blanket – most unseamanlike. The blanket was wet and so was everyone under it. This went on for a bit and things got worse, when suddenly the boat did a beautiful roll and sent gallons of sea water over us. This was enough for Mother and we had to turn back. When Larry, Nan and Pat had had some whiskey and dry clothes they went home in a car.

Sometimes, on dead-still moonlight nights with a glassy sea, Lawrence and Nancy would row across to the Albanian coast for a midnight picnic and then row back, an adventure out of dreamland, pure phantasmagoria. Soon he had bought a boat of his own, a black and brown twenty-two-foot sailing boat called the *Van Norden* – 'a dream, my black devil' – in which they could sail to remoter coasts and islands. Leslie acquired for £3 another small boat, soon to bear the proud name of the *Bootle-Bumtrinket*, which he and Pat Evans fixed up for Gerald as a birthday present. The boat they produced was, according to Gerald, a genuine oddity in the history of marine construction. The *Bootle-Bumtrinket* was seven feet long, flat-bottomed and almost circular in shape, painted green and white inside, with black, white and orange stripes outside. Leslie had cut a remarkably long cypress pole for a mast, and proposed raising this at the ceremonial launch and maiden voyage from the jetty in the bay in front of the villa. All did not go according to plan, however, for the moment the mast was inserted in its socket, the *Bootle-Bumtrinket* – 'with a speed remarkable for a craft of her circumference,' Gerald observed – turned turtle, taking Pat Evans with it.

It took a little while for Leslie to redo his calculations, and when he finally sawed the mast down to what he estimated to be the correct length, it turned out to be a mere three feet high, which was insufficient to support a sail. So for the time being the vessel remained a rowing boat, a tub which bobbed upright on the surface of the sea 'with the placid buoyancy of a celluloid duck'. Gerald made his maiden voyage on a summer's dawn of perfect calm, with just the faintest breeze. He pushed off from the shore and rowed and drifted down the coast, in and out of the little bays and around the tiny islets of the offshore archipelago, rich in shallow-water marine life. 'The joy of having a boat of your own!' he was to remember. 'There was nothing to compare with that very first voyage.'

Lying side by side with Roger the dog in the bow of the boat as it drifted in towards the shallows, he peered down through a fathom of crystal water at the tapestry of the seabed passing beneath him – the gaping clams stuck upright in the silver sand, the serpulas with their feathery orange-gold and blue petals, 'like an orchid on a mushroom stem', the pouting blennies in the holes of the reefs, the anemones waving on the rocks, the scuttling spider-crabs camouflaged with coats of weeds and sponges, the caravans of coloured top shells moving everywhere. Eventually, as the sun sank lower, he began to row for home, his glass jars and collecting tubes full of marine specimens of all kinds. 'The sun gleamed like a coin behind the olive trees,' he was to write, 'and the sea was striped with gold and silver when the *Bootle-Bumtrinket* brought her round behind bumping gently against the jetty. Hungry, thirsty, tired, with my head buzzing full of the colours and shapes I had seen, I carried my precious specimens slowly up the hill to the villa . . .'

Sometimes in the summer, if the moon was full, the family went bathing at night, when the sea was cooler than in the heat of the day. They would take the *Sea Cow* out into deep water and plunge over the side, the water wobbling bright in the moonlight. On one such night, when Gerald had floated out some distance from both shore and boat, he was overtaken by a shoal of porpoises, heaving and sighing, rising and diving all around him. For a short while he swam with them, overjoyed at their beautiful, exuberant presence; but then, as if at a signal, they turned and headed out of the bay towards the distant coast of Albania. 'I trod water and watched them go,' he remembered, 'swimming up the white chain of moonlight, backs aglow as they rose and plunged with heavy ecstasy in the water as warm as fresh milk. Behind them they left a trail of great bubbles that rocked and shone briefly like miniature moons before vanishing under the ripples.'

Soon the family discovered other marvels of the Corfu night – the phosphorescence in the sea and the flickering of the fireflies in the olive groves along the shore, both better seen when there was no moon. On the memorable night that Mother took to the water for the first time in her home-made bathing suit, the porpoises, the fireflies and the phosphorescence coincided in a single breathtaking display. Gerald was to write:

> Never had we seen so many fireflies congregated in one spot. They flicked through the trees in swarms, they crawled on the grass, the bushes and the olive trunks, they drifted in swarms over our heads and landed on the rugs, like green embers. Glittering streams of them flew out over the bay, swirling over the water, and then, right on cue, the porpoises appeared, swimming in line into the bay, rocking rhythmically through the water, their backs as if painted with phosphorous ... With the fireflies above and the illuminated porpoises below it was a fantastic sight. We could even see the luminous trails beneath the surface where the porpoises swam in fiery patterns across the sandy bottom, and when they leapt high in the air the drops of emerald glowing water flicked from them, and you could not tell if it was phosphorescence or fireflies you were looking at. For an hour or so we watched this pageant, and then slowly the fireflies drifted back inland and further down the coast. Then the porpoises lined up and sped out to sea, leaving a flaming path behind them that flickered and glowed, and then died slowly, like a glowing branch laid across the bay.

The motorboat gave the Durrells a greater freedom to roam round the island than ever before. At first it was Leslie who did the trail-blazing, mainly because of the rich opportunities for hunting and shooting provided by the wilder country to the north. Sometimes he picked up Lawrence and Nancy on the way, since Kalami lay on his passage north from Kondokali. 'A week or 2 ago,' Lawrence wrote to Alan Thomas, 'we went up to a death-swamp lake in the north, Les and Nancy and me for a shoot. Tropical. Huge slime covered tracts, bubbled in hot marsh-gas and the roots of trees. Snakes and tortoises swimming quietly above and toads below. A ring of emerald slime thick with scarlet dragon-flies and mosquitoes. It's called ANTINIOTISSA (enemy of youth).'

Before long Lawrence had become almost as obsessive a hunter as Leslie. It is extraordinary that Gerald was able to nurture his passion and love for the animal world while his two older brothers seemed hell-bent on blasting the wildlife of the island to pieces. But he did, conniving in the slaughter to the extent of helping to fill Leslie's cartridges for him and sometimes accompanying him on pigeon shoots, looking on when, out of compassion, Leslie shot the stray and starving dogs that followed the family on their picnics.

Lawrence was largely indifferent to the natural world, except as spectacle, and his expeditions with Leslie to the north of the island revealed a killer streak. 'I'm queer about shooting,' he wrote to Alan Thomas. 'So far I've prohibited herons. But duck is a different matter. Just a personified motor-horn, flying ham with a honk. No personality, nothing. And to bring them down is the most glorious feeling. THUD. Like breaking glass balls at a range. I could slaughter hundreds without a qualm.' As for octopus, which he learned to hunt with a stick with a hook like the Greeks, they were 'altogether filthy . . . utterly foul'.

Larry began to revise his opinion of Leslie somewhat after a few shooting trips with him in the north. 'You wouldn't recognise Leslie I swear,' he wrote to Alan Thomas in the summer of 1936. 'His personality is really amazingly strong now, and he can chatter away in company like Doctor Johnson himself. It's done him a world of good, strutting about with a gun under each arm and one behind his ear, shooting peasants right and left.' Leslie saw himself as a tough guy in a tough guy's world, the fastest gun on the island – 'dirty, unshaven,' his kid brother said, 'and smelling of gun-oil and blood'.

The family had a Kodak camera, and from time to time snapped family groups and memorable outings. Many of the photographs were taken by Leslie, who had an eye for a picture – and a handsome woman. On the back of a snap of Maria, the family's maid, he jotted a caption full of portent: 'Maria our maid (jolly nice)'.

Towards the end of the summer of 1936 Mother decided to dispense with the services of Gerald's tutor, Pat Evans – according to Gerald, on the grounds that he was getting far too fond of Margo, and Margo of him. So departed one of the staunchest supporters of Gerald's budding natural history and literary endeavours. Banished for ever from the family, the disconsolate Evans found his way to mainland Greece, where during the war he became a local hero, fighting behind the lines as a British SOE agent in Nazi-occupied Macedonia. A rather shy and diffident loner, Evans was, Margo recalled, 'very, very attractive', and she had become deeply infatuated with him. She took the news of his dismissal badly, and shut herself away in the attic, eating hugely. 'This was the period when Margaret was in a very bad way,' Nancy remembered. 'She began to get very fat, I mean she really did get *awfully* fat, and she got so ashamed of herself that she wouldn't even appear – wouldn't come down to meals or anything.' It was neither gluttony nor a broken heart that was the cause of Margo's weight problem, however, for according to reports it later turned out that she had a glandular condition that was causing her to put on a pound a day.

A new tutor was found, a Polish exile with French and English ancestry by the name of Krajewsky, whom Gerald in his book was to call Kralefsky. A gnome-like humpback, his redeeming virtue, as far as Gerald was concerned, was the huge collection of finches and other birds he kept on the top floor of the mouldering mansion on the edge of town where he lived with his ancient, witch-like mother ('a ravaged old queen').

His lessons, however, were old-fashioned and boring – history was lists of dates and geography lists of towns – so it came as a relief to the wearied boy when he discovered that his tutor possessed another virtue. For Krajewsky was a fantasist, and often conjured up an imaginary world in which his past life was presented as a series of wild adventures – a shipwreck on a voyage to Murmansk, an attack by bandits in the Syrian desert, a spot of derring-do in the Secret Service in World War One, an incident in Hyde Park when he strangled a killer bulldog with his bare hands – all of them in the company of 'a Lady'. Henceforth lessons passed in a more agreeable fashion, with Gerald's imagination and grasp of story-telling stimulated at the expense of the acquisition of new knowledge.

'Like everything else in Corfu,' Gerald was to reflect, 'it was singularly lucky, this string of outlandish professors who taught me nothing that would be remotely useful in making me conform and succeed and flourish, but who gave me the right kind of wealth, who showed me life.' And not only life, but freedom, pleasure, the sheer brilliance and sensuality of Corfu.

Gerald was growing up. In January 1937 he celebrated his twelfth birthday by throwing a party. To all the guests he sent an invitation in verse, decorated with a self-portrait of himself disguised as a Bacchanalian figure sporting a wild beard and looking uncannily like the man he was to become in later life:

> Oh! Hail to you my fellow friends.
> Will you yourselves to us lend?
> We're giving a party on 7th of Jan.
> Do please come if you possibly can.
> The doors are open at half-past three.
> Mind you drop in and make whoopee with me.

One of those invited was the Reverend Geoffrey Carr, then Chaplain of the Holy Trinity Church that served the British community living on Corfu, and a good friend of Theo Stephanides and his seven-year-old daughter Alexia.

It was, Carr recalled, a splendid party, with Theo and Spiro and the Belgian Consul and a whole host of Corfu friends in attendance, and Leslie, Theo and the ex-King of Greece's butler dancing the *kalamatianos*, and all the pets behaving badly, including the birthday present puppies, who were promptly christened Widdle and Puke, with good reason. A huge home-made cracker, constructed by Margo out of red paper, was suspended from the ceiling. It was eight feet long and three feet in diameter, and was stuffed with confetti, small toys and gifts of food and sweets for the local peasant children (who were sometimes nearly as hungry as the dogs). Disembowelled by Theo using a First World War bayonet belonging to Leslie, the cracker's demise was the climax of the party, with a scrum of children scrabbling around for the gifts and sweets scattered about all over the floor.

Leslie and Lawrence had already carried out a reconnaissance of Antiniotissa, the large lake at the northern end of the island, and the rest of the family soon followed. The lake was an elongated sheet of shallow water about a mile long, bordered by a dense zariba of cane and reed and closed off from the sea at one end by a broad dune of fine white sand. The best time to visit it was at the season when the sand lilies buried in the dune pushed up their thick green leaves and white blooms, so that the dune became, as Gerald put it, 'a glacier of flowers'. One warm summer dawn they all set off for Antiniotissa, Theodore and Spiro included, two boat-loads full, with the *Sea Cow* towing the *Bootle-Bumtrinket*. As the engine died and the boats slid slowly towards the shore, the scent of the lilies wafted out to greet them – 'a rich, heavy scent that was the distilled essence of summer, a warm sweetness that made you breathe deeply time and again in an effort to retain it within you'.

After establishing their picnic encampment among the lilies on the dune, the family did whatever came naturally to them. Leslie shot. Margo sunbathed. Mother wandered off with a trowel and basket. Spiro – 'clad only in his underpants and looking like some dark hairy prehistoric man' – stabbed at fish with his trident. Gerald and Theo pottered among the pools with their test tubes and collecting bottles looking for minuter forms of fauna. 'What a heavenly place,' murmured Larry. 'I should like to lie here for ever. Eventually, of course, over the centuries, by breathing deeply and evenly I should embalm myself with this scent.' Lunch came, then tea. Gerald and Theo returned to the edge of the lake to continue their search for insufficiently known organisms. Daylight faded as Spiro grilled a fish or an eel on the fire, and before long it grew dark – a still, hushed, magic dark, fireflies rising, fire spitting. This was a special place, Gerald knew, and he absorbed its balm through every sense.

> The moon rose above the mountains, turning the lilies to silver except where the flickering flames illuminated them with a flush of pink. The tiny ripples sped over the moonlit sea and breathed with relief as they reached the shore at last. Owls started to chime in the trees, and in the gloomy shadows fireflies gleamed as they flew, their jade-green, misty lights pulsing on and off.
>
> Eventually, yawning and stretching, we carried our things down to the boat. We rowed out to the mouth of the bay, and then in the pause while Leslie fiddled with the engine, we looked back at Antiniotissa. The lilies were like a snow-field under the moon, and the dark backcloth of olives was pricked with the lights of fireflies. The fire we had built, stamped and ground underfoot before we left, glowed like a patch of garnets at the edge of the flowers.

Towards the end of 1937 Mother, Margo, Leslie and Gerald moved to another villa, their third, smaller and handier than the cavernous mansion at Kondokali, but in many ways more desirable and elegant, in spite of its decrepit state. It was a beautiful Georgian house built in 1824 at a spot called Criseda as the weekend retreat, in the days when the British ruled Corfu, of the Governor of the British Protectorate of the Ionian Islands. The new house was perched on a hill not so very far from the Strawberry-Pink Villa, and it was dubbed the Snow-White Villa. A broad, vine-covered veranda ran along its front, and beyond lay a tiny, tangled garden, deeply shaded by a great magnolia and a copse of cypress and olive trees. Lawrence and Nancy would sometimes come over for a few days when Kalami became too lonely for them, for as Lawrence put it: 'You can have a little too much even of Paradise and a little taste of Hell now and then is good for my work – keeps my brain from stagnating. You can trust Gerry to provide the Hell.'

From the back the villa looked out over a great vista of hills and valleys, fields and olive-woods, promising endless days of exploration and a ceaseless quest for creatures great and small – from giant toads and baby magpies to geckoes and mantises. From the front, the villa faced the sea and the long, shallow, almost landlocked lagoon called Lake Halikiopoulou, along whose nearest edge lay the flatlands Gerald was to call the Chessboard Fields. Here the Venetians had dug a network of narrow irrigation canals to channel the salty waters of the lagoon into salt pans, and these ditches now provided a haven for marine life and a protective barrier for nesting birds. On the seaward side of the maze of canals lay the flat sands of the tide's edge, the haunt of snipe, oyster-catchers, dunlins and terns. On the landward side lay a checkerboard patchwork of small square fields yielding rich crops of grapes, maize, melons and vegetables. All this was Gerald's hunting ground, where he could roam at will in the orbit of seabird and waterfowl, terrapin and water snake. Here he was to stalk a wily and ancient terrapin he called Old Plop to his heart's content, and in a roundabout way acquire a favourite pet bird, a black-backed gull called Alecko – Lawrence called it 'that bloody albatross' – which he claimed to have got from a convicted murderer on a weekend's leave from the local gaol.

Gerald was in an ancient rural Arcadia here. There was no airport runway across the lake (unlike today), no busy road at the foot of the hill, no tourist developments, no mini-markets, next to no cars. One old monk still lived alone in the monastery on Mouse Island across the water, and there were still fisher families in the cottages there (now razed). Sometimes Gerald and Margo would go down to the beach at the foot of the hill and swim across the shallow channel to Mouse Island. There Gerald would search for little animals while Margo would sunbathe in her two-piece bathing costume – invariably the old monk would come down and shake his fist at the attractive, pale English girl and yell, 'You white witch!' The north European preoccupation with near nudity and sunburn was rather shocking to the devout, straitlaced Greeks.

Not long after Gerald's thirteenth birthday in January 1938, his idyllic life on Corfu was given a severe jolt when his tutor and mentor Theo Stephanides decided to leave the island to take up an appointment with an anti-malarial unit founded by the Rockefeller Foundation in Cyprus. His departure was to mark the beginning of the end of the Durrell family's utopian dream.

Leslie had begun to go native, drinking and brawling with the Greek peasant men whenever the opportunity offered. Larry and Nancy had kept themselves busy making improvements to their house in Kalami, but it was not enough. Holed up in the solitude of the north, the young couple had turned upon themselves, rowing vehemently and sometimes violently. It had not helped that in the summer of 1936 Nancy had become pregnant, and had had an abortion arranged by Theo, not something taken lightly in the moral climate of that place and time. Mother had been shocked to the core when she found out about it. The family edifice had begun to crack after that, and Lawrence had started to grow restless and bored in the narrow confines of paradise. When two young English dancers of his acquaintance came to stay, he slept between them on the beach at night, telling Nancy to find somewhere else to sleep. 'He was going through a stage when he was tired of being an old married man,' Nancy recalled with bitterness, 'and so he tried to push me out of it, and snub me all the time, and was being rather beastly.' Finally Lawrence had decided they should recharge their creative batteries in Paris and London, and leave the island for a while. Margo, now twenty, decided it was time she made her own way in the 'real world', and returned to England.

As for Gerald, such childish innocence as he may have brought to the island – not much, doubtless, but some – was blown away with the onset of puberty, when other interests began to conflict with his earlier enthusiasm for non-human forms of life. From time to time he would play 'mothers and fathers' with a young female counterpart – an activity that was seen as a natural part of the curiosity of a highly intelligent boy – and in middle age he was to confide to a friend: 'Before you knew where you were, the knickers were off and you were away.'

Though the remaining Durrells seemed content to drift aimlessly into the future on their paradise island, the world beyond Corfu's shores had other plans. War was looming in Europe. In the north, Hitler's Germany was preparing to march. In the south, Mussolini was loudly braying Italy's claims to dominion over Albania and to territorial rights over Greece, Corfu included.

Lawrence and Leslie had always sworn to help defend the island against the Italians, but they were overtaken by events. By April 1939 Mary Stephanides and her daughter Alexia had already left Corfu to live in England. Gerald was sorry to see the young girl go, for she had become his best and closest playmate. As war in Europe grew more inevitable by the day, Louisa began to think it might be unwise to linger. In *My Family* Gerald was to claim that it was her concern for his future education that prompted Mother to leave Corfu. By now he was fourteen years old, and was, as Mary Stephanides recalled, 'quite independent of adult control. Lawrence tried to be a father to him at times, but he was seldom living in the same home, and was in any case too indulgent towards his small brother. And Gerald always got his own way with his mother. Only Theodore maintained any form of control over him, and that was only once a week. So even if war had not started in 1939, the Corfu days of Gerald Durrell were by then strictly numbered.'

It was Grindlays Bank, Mother's financial advisers in London, who gave the final push, warning her that when war came her funds might be cut off, and she would be stranded in Greece for the duration without any means of support. In June 1939, therefore, she left the island with Gerald, Leslie and the thirty-year-old Corfiot family maid, Maria Condos.

'As the ship drew across the sea and Corfu sank shimmering into the pearly heat haze on the horizon,' Gerald was to write of that decisive farewell, 'a black depression settled on us, which lasted all the way back to England.' From Brindisi the train bore the party – consisting of four humans, three dogs, two toads, two tortoises, six canaries, four gold-finches, two greenfinches, a linnet, two magpies, a seagull, a pigeon and an owl – northward to Switzerland.

At the Swiss frontier our passports were examined by a disgrace-fully efficient official. He handed them back to Mother, together with a small slip of paper, bowed unsmilingly, and left us to our gloom. Some moments later Mother glanced at the form the official had filled in, and as she read it, she stiffened.

'Just look what he's put,' she exclaimed indignantly, 'imperti-nent man.'

On the little card, in the column headed *Description of Passengers* had been written, in neat capitals: ONE TRAVELLING CIRCUS AND STAFF.

Now only Lawrence and Nancy were left – or so it seemed – clinging on in the White House on the edge of Kalami bay as the late summer sun burned down on them and the Germans marched into Czechoslovakia and the Italians occupied Albania, only a few miles across the water. But there was one last twist in the family's Corfu saga, for one day Margo suddenly reappeared, having decided that the island was where her true home and friends were. She holed up in a peasant hut with a tin roof on the Condos family patch at Pérama, sleeping in the same big old wooden bed as her peasant friends Katerina and Renee, washing in a little basin outside the door, and hoping that she could sit out the war on her beloved island disguised as a peasant girl herself.

Lawrence and Nancy lingered a little longer, in some trepidation as to what the future would bring. The confusion of impending war had lapped as far as the north of Corfu now, and it was time to decide whether to go or to be marooned on the island. Margo received a secret note from Spiro, still loyally guarding the family's interests: 'Dear Missy Margo, This is to tell you that war has been declared. Don't tell a soul.' Lawrence recalled the day war was declared with anguish. 'Standing on the balcony over the sea,' he wrote to his friend Anne Ridler in October, 'it seemed like the end of the world ... It was the most mournful period of my life those dark masses murmuring by the lapping water like the Jews in Babylon; such passionate farewells, so many tears, so much language ...'

Every able-bodied man and every horse had been mobilised. Corfu town was swarming with people looking for a way to escape, and huge naphtha flares burned on the boats that were unloading bullets and flour at the docks. In Kalami children were weeping in the garden, and Cretan infantry were marching about, 'smelling like hell, but with great morale'. The local commander was planning to rig up torpedo tubes outside the White House and to mine the straits. Then all the men of the village were sent inland to a secret arms dump, including Anastassiou, 'our suave, cool, beautiful landlord, too feminine and hysterical to handle a gun'. Only the women were left, weeping around the wells, and the uncomprehending children. 'I had nothing to say goodbye to except the island,' Lawrence wrote. 'I ached for them all.'

Frantically Lawrence and Nancy prepared to leave, destroying papers and drawings, packing the few books they could carry. The little black and brown *Van Norden* would have to be left behind, and Nancy's paintings – 'lazy pleasant paintings of our peasant friends' that hung on every wall. In weird, autumnal weather, clouds piled high over Albania, the narrow straits like a black sheet, the thin rain falling 'like stardust', they boarded a smoky little Athens-bound steamer at Corfu quay and fled the island. 'I remembered it all,' he was to write, 'with a regret so deep that it did not stir the emotions ... We never ever speak of it any more, having escaped.'

Only Margo was left. Before his departure Lawrence had advised her that, should trouble come, she should sail the *Van Norden* down the Ionian Sea and into the Aegean to Athens – no mean voyage, especially as she had never handled a boat in her life. But she had no fears for her future: 'I was young, and when you're young you're not frightened of anything.' She had taken to going into Corfu town to hear the news reports and war bulletins relayed to the populace in the Platia, the central square. There, over a coffee or iced drink, she sometimes met up with the Imperial Airways flying-boat crews who were still operating the Mediterranean leg of the Karachi–UK air link. The airmen were aghast at her plan to ride out the war in the Corfu hills, and urged her to leave before the island was invaded and all communications with the outside world were cut. She became friendly with one officer in particular, a dashing young flight engineer by the name of Jack Breeze, and it was he who finally persuaded her to pull out and provided her with the means of doing so. Shortly after Christmas Margo was packed on to one of the last British aircraft flying out of Corfu, and left the island of her young womanhood for ever.

In October 1940 Italian forces entered Greece, and the following year they occupied Corfu. The White House at Kalami lay abandoned, and Larry's little cutter sunk. Below the Strawberry-Pink Villa, where the boy Gerald had first strode out to explore the wild interior, the Italians built a huge tented camp, where they kept their ration store and marched their soldiers up and down. Later the Germans moved in, strafing the causeway and the chessboard fields of the Venetian lagoon where Gerald had once stalked Old Plop the terrapin, and bombing the old town, killing Theo Stephanides's parents and Gerald's tutor Krajewsky and his mad mother and all his birds. What fate befell the boy Gerald's great manuscript novel of the flora and fauna of the world will never be known.

The Durrell family had been driven from Eden, swept away by the fury and folly of war. All they were left with from their island years were a few crumpled photographs and the memories of a magic life that for long afterwards continued to burn in their minds as vivid and bright as the sun itself.

It was in large part Corfu that made Gerald the person he was to be. But on the island he had known only love and affection, happiness and ease. As a result he was to be ill-equipped Gerald for the vicissitudes of real life, which one day would do their best to cut him off at the knees.

Looking back from the hard world beyond the walls of that enchanted garden, Lawrence was to observe many years later: 'In Corfu, you see, we reconstituted the Indian period which we all missed. The island exploded into another open-air time of our lives, because one lived virtually naked in the sun. Without Corfu I don't think Gerry would have managed to drag himself together and do all he has achieved . . . I reckon I too got born in Corfu. It was really the spell between the wars that was – you can only say paradise.'

FIVE

Gerald in Wartime

England 1939–1945

Mother, Leslie and Gerald were back in England before war was declared on 3 September 1939. The dogs were put in quarantine the moment they landed, and the rest of the animals Gerald had brought back from Corfu, plus a marmoset and some magpies he had acquired in England, were housed on the top-floor landing of a London lodging house which Mother rented while she looked around for a more permanent home. Before long they had moved to a flat in a terraced house off Kensington High Street. Mother hankered to return to Bournemouth, where at least she had roots of a kind, and whenever she went off on one of her many forays into various part of the countryside in search of a house, the fourteen-year-old Gerald – now wearing his first pair of long trousers – was free to explore the capital. 'I found London, at that time, fascinating,' he would later recall. 'After all, the biggest metropolis I was used to was the town of Corfu, which was about the size of a small English market town, and so the great sprawling mass of London had hundreds of exciting things for me to discover.'

Sometimes he would spend the afternoon in the Coronet cinema round the corner, absorbed in the illusory adventure and romance on the silver screen before him – a lifelong passion. At other times he would go to the Natural History Museum or the zoo, which only strengthened his belief that working in a zoo was the only real vocation for anyone.

It was in the London of the so-called 'Phoney War' – no air raids as yet, no nights spent in cellars or bomb shelters – that Gerald started his first job, as junior assistant in a pet shop called The Aquarium, not far from where he was living. It was a remarkably well-stocked shop, with rows of great tanks full of brilliant tropical fish, and glass-fronted boxes containing grass snakes, pine snakes, big green lizards, tortoises, newts with frilled tails like pennants and gulping, bulbous-eyed frogs. His job was to feed all these creatures and clean out their tanks and cages, but it soon became clear that he knew a great deal more about their needs and habits than the shop's owner, who was astonished by the boy's detailed knowledge and instinctive feeling for the animals' welfare.

Before long Gerald had introduced a change in the creatures' previously unvarying diet, forgoing his lunchtime sausage and mash in order to collect woodlice in Kensington Park for the reptiles and amphibians, and tipping pots of little water fleas into the fishtanks as a change from the fishes' usual fare of tubifex worms. Then he began to improve the animals' living conditions, putting clumps of wet moss into the cages of the large leopard toads so that they had some damp and shade, bathing their raw feet with olive oil and treating their sore eyes with Golden Eye ointment. But his *pièce de résistance* was the redecoration of the big tank in the shop window, which contained a large collection of wonderfully coloured fish in what looked like an underwater blasted heath.

I worked on that giant tank with all the dedication of a marine Capability Brown. I built rolling sand dunes and great towering cliffs of lovely granite. And then, through the valleys between the granite mountains, I planted forests of Vallisneria and other, more delicate, weedy ferns. And on the surface of the water I floated the tiny little white flowers that look so like miniature water-lilies. When I had finally finished it and replaced the shiny black mollies, the silver hatchet fish, the brilliant Piccadilly-like neon-tetras, and stepped back to admire my handiwork, I found myself deeply impressed with my own genius.

So was the owner. 'Exquisite! Exquisite!' he exclaimed. 'Simply exquisite.' Gerald was promptly promoted to more responsible tasks. Periodically he was sent off to the East End of London to collect fresh supplies of reptiles, amphibians and snakes. 'In gloomy, cavernous stores in back streets,' he remembered, 'I would find great crates of lizards, basketfuls of tortoises and dripping tanks green with algae full of newts and frogs and salamanders . . . and a crate full of iguanas, bright green and frilled and dewlapped like any fairytale dragon.' On one such jaunt 150 baby painted terrapins escaped from the box in which he was carrying them on the top of a double-decker bus. But for the help of a Blimpish, monocled colonel who also happened to be on the bus and who crawled up and down the aisle 'heading the bounders off', Gerald would have experienced the first catastrophe of his professional career. 'By George!' cried the colonel. 'A painted terrapin! *Chrysemys picta*! Haven't seen one for years. There's one going under the seat there. Tally-ho! Bang! Bang!'

By the time Mother had found what she was looking for, a family-sized house at 52 St Alban's Avenue in the Bournemouth suburb of Charminster, much of the family was dispersed to the four winds. Lawrence and Nancy were in Athens, where their daughter Penelope was born in April 1940. Early that year Lawrence got word that his sister Margaret had married her flier, Jack Breeze, in Bournemouth, with Leslie (who was living in the house in St Alban's Avenue) giving the bride away. When Jack was posted to South Africa with Imperial Airways, Margaret went with him, and she was to spend the whole of the war in Africa, moving gradually north, first to Mozambique and then to Ethiopia, till, like Larry, she ended up in Egypt.

When the German armies crossed the Greek border and rolled south towards Athens in April 1941, the king and government left the capital for Crete, and Lawrence and Nancy followed their example. It was a perilous and close-run thing. They escaped from the Peleponnesus by caïque one day before the Germans invaded, and after six nightmare weeks under German air attack in Crete they left on almost the last passenger ship to get out, arriving in Alexandria two days before Greece fell. Lawrence soon got a job as foreign press officer at the British Embassy in Cairo, and was to remain in Egypt for the rest of the war, but in July 1942, with the Egyptian cities under threat from the advancing Germans, Nancy and Penelope were evacuated to Palestine, a parting which effectively marked the end of the marriage. A year later Lawrence fell in love with an Alexandrian girl, Eve Cohen, who was eventually to become his second wife.

For Mother, the move back to England, with its blackouts, gasmasks and ration books, was just one more in a series of upheavals that had punctuated her life ever since, far away and long ago, she had married her much-loved and much-missed husband in India, the land of her birth. To this latest uprooting she responded as she had always done – without complaint, without fuss, making do, always there. But after the cheap living and favourable exchange rate of the Corfu years, the move back to England was a backward step financially, and leaner times now loomed. Much of the money her husband had left to her had been dissipated in imprudent disbursements before the war, and when in due course the Japanese overran Burma a substantial proportion of her remaining assets, which were invested in Burmah Oil, were lost for ever. The steady decline in the family's standard of living in Bournemouth during the war was barely perceptible to friends and relatives who saw them on a regular basis, but to Lawrence, who was away for all of that time, its extent was quite shocking when he saw it for himself on his return.

For all that, Louisa continued to cluck and fuss over her remaining brood, an unfailing (if faintly vague) source of culinary aromas and mother love for the two sons still in her care. But for Leslie, sadly, the return to England marked a big step in his gradual descent into waste and oblivion. At the outbreak of hostilities he had hoped to join the Royal Air Force, which had both glamour and guns galore. But he had loosed off one shotgun too many in his time on Corfu, and a military medical board declared that his hearing was defective, and that he was unfit for military service. Barred from doing his bit with the RAF, Leslie was condemned to spend the war toiling away at inglorious, menial tasks in the local aircraft factory.

As for Gerald, now fifteen, the retreat to Blighty – from a sun-drenched Mediterranean island to whose human and animal fauna he had closely related, to a mist-shrouded North Sea island to which he barely related at all – was more than just a migration from one kind of habitat to another: it was like a flight into limbo, an existential near-void about which he was to say little in future years, and to write next to nothing till near the very end. The shock was palpable, and considerable adjustments were required for him to adapt to his new physical and cultural environment.

Gerald was no longer a boy, but an adolescent, with all that that turbulent transitional phase of development entailed. He was also, as a result of his upbringing on Corfu, part Greek in manners and outlook. More, he had no education – none, at any rate, that the authorities in the United Kingdom would recognise as such. Nor was he ever likely to receive any, for he was now almost past the statutory age of compulsory education in Britain. Not only had he long ago parted company with any school syllabus worthy of the name, but he stood no chance of passing any exam of any sort anywhere at any time.

Not that Mother didn't give his education one last try, taking him along to a minor public school outside Bournemouth in the hope that the place might fire his enthusiasm. The visit was only a partial success. The headmaster chose to test the boy's scholastic potential by asking him to write out the Lord's Prayer, but Gerald could only remember the first six words, and invented the rest. A visit to the labs with the biology master was more promising – the man turned out to have once spent a holiday in Greece – but Gerald was rated no higher than 'backward but bright'. Not that it mattered much, for Gerald had no wish to go to any school.

Believing, as always, that her children knew what was best for them, his mother tried a private tutor instead. Harold Binns was a neat, quiet man, with a face scarred by shrapnel in the Great War. He had written a study of the English poets, and was oddly addicted to eau de Cologne, often popping into the toilet to give himself a quick squirt. Mr Binns bestowed two great gifts upon his ill-educated student – how to unlock the treasures contained within the British public library system, and how to appreciate to the full the words of the English language in all their associations and assonances, nuances and overtones. His method was to teach Gerald for an hour, then fetch a volume of verse from his bookshelf for Gerald to browse through on his own. In an unpublished autobiographical fragment written in the last year of his life, Gerald recalled Mr Binns and the excitement he generated for the music and the magic of the language.

He would burst into the room in a tidal wave of eau de Cologne. 'Now, dear boy,' he would say, eyes raised to Heaven, hands outstretched. 'Time to remove the cobwebs from the mind, eh? Leave that geometry which appears insoluble to you and let's have a look at Swinburne. You know Swinburne? I think you'll find he has something in common with you – yes – um – yes – um – this for a start.'

He would thrust a book into my hands and gallop out of the room trailing eau de Cologne like a bride's train behind him.

A little later, bustling back into the room, he would ask: 'Did you like him?'

'I think the poetry is fascinating,' I said, 'and I love alliteration.'

'So do I,' he said fervently. 'The whole poem is an example of what poetry should be. So few modern poets chime in the ear like a seashell whispering mysteries. At least he conjures up lantanas in your mind, illuminating your brain with fabulous words . . .'

All this was a revelation to Gerald, and would greatly influence him, as brother Larry had previously done, in his approach to his own writing.

While Mr Binns endowed Gerald with access to knowledge and reinforced the love of words Lawrence had encouraged on Corfu, there was no one to teach him the biology which fascinated him. Working his way at random through the textbooks in the Bournemouth public library and elsewhere, Gerald taught himself as best he could. There were advantages to this eclectic exploration of the subject, for it allowed him to approach it from eccentrically revelatory angles. But there were enormous disadvantages too, great gaps in his knowledge, and his grasp of the science could hardly be said to rest on sound foundations.

He was always conscious of this, especially when he became a high-profile practitioner and spokesman of the very science he had never been formally taught. Much later, he was to say:

> Yes, a degree might have helped – but would it? In the long run it might have killed the other side of me. Because of no job, which was because of no degree, only the need to write for a living compelled me to write at all. Also, the degree idea is waved about like a flag to such an extent that one thinks one needs it – when it's only society needing it. These absolute dolts in my own field have the application to store knowledge like a squirrel and regurgitate it all over ruled paper at the right moment. That shows a sense of inferiority on my part, doesn't it?

More than compensating for his lack of formal qualifications, Gerald was endowed with a highly developed and inventive intelligence. His Corfu childhood under the tutelage of Theo Stephanides had provided him with a superlative insight into the phenomena of natural life, an education in hands-on biology largely denied to his peers in the United Kingdom, and his brother Lawrence had instilled in him the principles of creative literature in a way no classroom lessons could have done. The rest of the family, his mother especially, also contributed. 'She encouraged us in everything we wanted to do,' he was to recall. 'She would say, "Well, try it, dear," and if it failed, it failed. I was allowed to read anything I wanted to. Every question I asked was answered absolutely honestly, if it could be answered. In a funny way, I got a unique education which included dealing with an endless procession of eccentrics – so now, nothing a human being does surprises me.'

But his grasp of the mainstream of schoolboy learning – sums and stinks and 1066 and the rest – was patchy and uncertain. Gerald was therefore a highly unorthodox teenager in the Britain of his time. The familiar routine of morning assemblies and school games and end of term exams had passed him by. His primary education was fragmentary, his secondary education nil, his chances of higher education non-existent. For a youth with such an apparently oddball background there was only one option in wartime Bournemouth – to get a job, probably a mundane and lowly one, until he was old enough to be called up and have his head shot off in the war.

The only job that Gerald could imagine tolerating was working with animals. Though it doesn't sound much, for Gerald a day spent in a pet shop in the company of white rats was not a day wasted. He had managed to run an aviary and keep a few adders in the garden at home during these years, but the largest animal he had to cope with was a fallow deer which was given to him by a boy who lived in the New Forest and was moving to Southampton. The boy had described it as a 'baby' and a 'household pet', but when it arrived it turned out to be a petulant creature at least four years old – far from the submissive, friendly fawn Gerald had been promised. With much patience he eventually learned how to pacify the deer, which he named Hortense, by scratching the base of its antlers, but in the end he had to give way to family pressure, and Hortense was exiled to a nearby farm.

As for the war, though a few stray bombs did land on Bournemouth, one of them rocking the treasurehouse of Commin's bookshop, Gerald admitted that he did not really know what war was, nor care very much about it.

> We used to see Southampton get a pasting, eagerly enjoying the eastern sky aflame, and there were plenty of jolly dogfights upstairs – but on the whole we had a cushy war. The entire family did. We were pinned to the nine o'clock news, cheering for victory, and I followed daily the progress of the battles on whatever front it was ... but only selfishly. I wanted to get the war over as fast as possible and do something interesting, like return to Greece and see how the Germans had behaved to the swallowtails and trapdoor spiders. Even so, I spent every moment out of doors – aged fifteen to twenty – risking death at the hands of the bombers on the way to Coventry or somewhere that really copped it. I helped with the harvest. I went out – not on a donkey now, but a bicycle – looking for nests and animals, rediscovering the local fauna with more patience and a maturer knowledge, like waiting for the bird to return to her nest to make sure of the species, at any hour of day or night, because I was used on Corfu to regarding the villa merely as a dormitory. The outside was home. Two hundred yards from the house I had the woods to keep an eye on, and then at the end of the road the golf links, beyond which the country started. The real country. Bournemouth in my time was a country town. It was ideal from my point of view – though of course it wasn't Corfu.

The 'real country' was the moorlands of the Purbecks, the wilder woodlands of the New Forest, the broad sweep of shore and water around Poole Harbour. Once he went much further afield, on a bird-watching holiday to the outlying Scilly Isles, beyond the western tip of Cornwall.

Gerald found England stiff and starchy after the relaxed lifestyle of his Mediterranean island, especially when it came to sex and girls. He had reached puberty on Corfu, and with a little help from a young local girl he had discovered sex – or at least its preliminaries – without suffering any of the inhibitions and sense of guilt that tormented so many of his contemporaries in England. On Corfu sex had seemed something pure and natural – a romp and a tumble in the olive woods and myrtle groves, a giggle and a tangle of limbs.

On Corfu all his tutors had taught him about sex, and it was discussed quite freely at home. In England, by contrast, it was Presbyterian black and sin-laden. 'I couldn't understand why in England boys of my age found something dirty and furtive about it. And I was soon to realise with girlfriends in Bournemouth that I couldn't treat them with quite the same gay abandon in case they thought me naughty and wicked. In some confusion I was forced to retreat to a chaste and stolen kiss on the brow. It was like being suddenly flung out of Rabelais into William Morris.'

Gerald was a good-looking youth, with an attractive, open face and engaging manner. His good looks were almost to prove his undoing when a local girl was raped, strangled and mutilated, and her body found under the rhododendrons in one of the local beauty spots called the Chines. The *Bournemouth Echo* reported that the police were anxious to interview a tall, fair young man with blue eyes and a charming personality – Gerald to a tee. Mother, of course, immediately saw the hempen rope being adjusted around her son's neck.

'You're not to go out, dear,' she warned Gerald. 'You might be arrested as the murderer. You're to stay at home. You know what the police are like. Once they've arrested you they'll never stop till they've hung you. And hanging's no laughing matter.'

Within a day or two, a couple of detectives did indeed call at the house in order to eliminate the young naturalist from their inquiries. Satisfied with Gerald's answers to their questioning, they left without even taking his fingerprints. When they had gone, Mother reappeared.

'Now, tell me what you said, dear,' she insisted. 'It's very important to get our stories to match when we're in court.'

In some ways Gerald at this time was almost feminine in his looks. But he did his best to disguise it, partly because he had found, to his embarrassment, that he was becoming attractive to homosexual men. This sometimes got him into difficulties, and was all the more galling because he was totally heterosexual himself. 'In those days I used to plaster my pale blond hair with vaseline,' he recalled, 'hoping it would become a manly dark brown and thus attract all the ladies who would otherwise have thought me too weak and pretty. Little did I know that this treatment plaited my long locks into something closely resembling an eel migration of some magnitude and only the kindliest and ugliest of girls would consent to be seen with me.'

This phase didn't last long, and soon Gerald's interest in girls was matched by his ability to arouse their interest in him. 'I've always had a fair amount of attraction for women,' he said, 'but I hope I've never used it – except to seduce them, of course.' He was, he reckoned, a consummate seducer, though never a cynical or dishonest one: 'I treated women as human beings, which is of course fatal.' In the early days of what he would later refer to as his sexual career it was all pretty much hit and miss anyway: 'I must admit that at the age of sixteen I was still of the opinion that the idea was "to get the girl aboard the lugger" and that was the end of it.'

As well as appreciating their physical allure, Gerald genuinely liked and respected the opposite sex. Perhaps because, unlike most English boys of his class and generation, he had not been to boarding school, he felt at ease in the company of women and at home with the feminine side of human nature. Indeed, he preferred the company of women to that of men, though on the whole he trusted animals more than either. He could admire, and sometimes even adore, individuals of the opposite sex, but he never entirely lost his head over them. In any case, he was continually reminded of the fact that women could be as flawed and clay-footed as the rest of the human species, as an incident towards the end of the war years forcibly reminded him:

Dark hair, huge glistening eyes, like chestnuts newly polished, a face composed and gently supported by bone structure as beautiful as a coral reef. A mouth moist, wide and gentle, a loving mouth. A body as eloquent as a teenage birch tree. Brown hands like starfish, which when they moved illuminated what she was saying, as a conductor to an orchestra. She was a girl who not only filled your eye and heart but made you stop and listen to the magic of her voice and the tapestry of what she said. Her wonderful head carefully positioned on a neck as slender and beautiful as Nefertiti's. I longed to know her, to have the privilege of taking her into a secret garden full of night jasmine, tangerine and flowering creatures that would attempt to emulate her beauty but could only enhance it. She was the pure Garden of Eden for which Adam sacrificed his navel. For her I would have sacrificed much more. The waiter brought the bill and I paid. As I passed the table of this lovely, delicate paragon I heard her say – loud as a conch shell being blown – 'You stupid, sodding twit, I can't think why I married you. Your balls are as big as warm eggs and as much use.' I have never felt the same about women since.

In his early manhood Gerald's sex appeal was so overt and palpable that it was assumed by those who did not know him that he was a ladykiller. In his maturer years his tendency to flirt with every woman in the room led many to believe he was a womaniser. In his old age he told so many stories about the intimate encounters of his youth that he gave the impression his bachelor years had been one long serial orgy. All this probably exaggerates his sexual propensities. 'He wasn't a *particularly* sexy man,' Margaret remembered. 'I mean, I don't think he was a *highly* sexed man, to be honest – not like Larry – and though he gave the impression that he was to some people, and sometimes even said he was, it was really just flirting, purely harmless. In fact I would say Gerry was more mother-orientated than sex-orientated. Sex was probably the dream but I honestly don't think it was his scene. Basically he didn't like to be on his own. He always liked to have a woman around, even if she was only messing about in the kitchen.' In his later years Gerald was to confirm his sister's view: 'I wasn't too preoccupied with sex, because I had too many other matters to absorb me ... I wouldn't worry if nothing happened.'

Among the other matters that absorbed the young Gerald was his dedicated self-education. He spent a lot more time with books than he ever did with girls. Books were his entrée into another world, a world of boundless knowledge and endless diversion, an alternative world of the imagination, a real world of science and fact. He worked the public library system for all it was worth, and when he could afford it he bought books at Commin's in Bournemouth town centre. Later he was to say: 'I believe that books are an essential of life. To be surrounded by them, to read and re-read them gives you a carapace of knowledge so that you can lumber through life, as a tortoise does, carrying a library in your skull. Books surround you like a womb of knowledge.'

In idle moments in later years he found it fun to beachcomb through his memory for the flotsam of books he remembered reading in his youth. These ranged from children's classics to Victorian adventure books for boys and on to more ambitious literary works like Shakespeare, Rabelais, the Bible, Lamb's *Essays of Elia* and the novels of Rudyard Kipling and D.H. Lawrence, as well as the books of comic writers such as Edward Lear, Jerome K. Jerome, P.G. Wodehouse, James Thurber and Patrick Campbell. He even set about gnawing his way through those two daunting paper megaliths, *Larousse* and the *Encyclopaedia Britannica*. His reading in works of natural history was even more voracious and wide-ranging, with a broad base of classics – Charles Darwin, Alfred Wallace, Henry Bates, Henri Fabre, Gilbert White, Richard Jefferies, W.H. Hudson – and a broad trawl of more contemporary works, from the popular nature books of 'Romany' (who preached the gospel of 'the balance of nature') to Julian Huxley and H.G. Wells' comprehensive biological overview *The Science of Life*.

In many ways it is probable that his lack of a formal education was the making of Gerald Durrell. It left his innate, highly original intelligence unfettered and unchannelled, free to roam at will, to explore far and wide, to make connections outside the orthodoxy of the teaching of the time, develop new trajectories of thought and pioneer new lines of progression that could not have emerged, except with difficulty, from an institutionalised mind indoctrinated within the conventions of a traditional education. Gerald believed this himself: 'I think the set routine of an average school kills the imagination in a child. Whereas the way I was brought up, the imagination was allowed to grow, to blossom. It taught me a lot of things which you're not normally taught in school and this proved very valuable to me in dealing with animals and as a writer. My eccentric upbringing has been of great value to me.'

By way of example, it was his lack of a conventionally programmed education that enabled him, very early on, to stumble on the matter of declining animal populations (he was particularly struck by the parlous state of the black-footed ferret of the Great Plains of North America). He was barely out of his teens when he began to compile his own 'rather shaky and amateurish' version of a Red Data Book of endangered species*– one of the earliest compilations of its sort in the United Kingdom. If he had gone to university to read zoology, he would have come away with a thorough grasp of comparative anatomy and the Linnaean order of species, but it is doubtful if the world at large would ever have had reason to know his name

So Gerald's adolescence passed. Towards the end of 1942, when the tide of war had just begun to turn in the Allies' favour – though years of bloody slaughter still remained – he received his call-up papers. Now nearly eighteen, he reported for his army medical in Southampton. First he and his fellows were marshalled – 'rather like cattle in a slaughter house' – and told to strip. Then they were each given a beaker and told

* Red Data Books, regularly compiled by the International Union for the Conservation of Nature and Natural Resources (IUCN), list all known endangered or extinct species worldwide.

to pee in it. Gerald had drunk several pints of beer beforehand to make sure he had a full bladder, but unfortunately he had overdone it. The beaker filled up and slopped over. ''Ere!' cried the orderly. 'Slopped all over the place. I 'opes you ain't got no infectious bleeding diseases.' In an unpublished account, Gerald recalled:

My next nerve-shattering encounter was with a small, fat doctor, who looked exactly like one of the less prepossessing garden gnomes. He peered in my mouth, peered in my ears and finally placed a stubby finger on the end of my nose.

'Follow my finger,' he said, as he drew it away, so I followed it. I remember wondering at the time what subtle medical trick this was to expose the mechanism of your body.

'I don't mean follow my finger,' he snapped.

'But you just told me to,' I said, bewildered.

'I don't mean *follow* my finger, I mean follow my finger,' he said irritably.

'But that's what I was doing,' I said.

'I don't mean follow it with your whole body.'

I was beginning to doubt the mental stability of this man.

'I can't follow your finger without my body,' I explained patiently.

'I don't want your whole body, I just want your eyes,' he snapped.

I began to wonder which lunatic asylum he had escaped from and should I tell the other doctors about his condition. I decided to be patient and calming.

'But you can't have my eyes without my body,' I explained, 'they're attached to it, so if you want my eyes you have to have the body too.'

His face went the colour of an old brick wall.

'Are you an idiot?' he enquired simmeringly.

'I don't think so, sir,' I said placatingly. 'I just don't see how you can have my eyes without the body thrown in, as it were.'

'I don't want your Goddamed eyes,' he shouted. 'All I want you to do is follow my finger.'

'But I did, sir, and then you got angry.'

'Follow it with your eyes, you imbecile,' he bellowed, 'with your Goddam bloody eyes.'

'Oh, I see, sir,' I said, although to tell the truth I didn't.

I wandered off to the next member of the medical profession, who was a dismal man with greasy hair, and looked somewhat like a failed Maitre d'Hôtel on the verge of suicide. He examined me minutely from stem to stern, humming to himself gently like an unhappy bear sucking its paw. He smelt of cinnamon and his eyes were violet coloured, very striking and beautiful.

'And now,' he said, 'I want to look up your nose, so we'll draw the curtains and be in the dark.'

Here, I thought to myself, we have another lunatic.

'Wouldn't you see it better in daylight, sir?' I asked.

'No, no, darkness, because I've got to stick something into your mouth,' he explained.

'What sort of thing?' I asked, determined to guard my honour to the last redoubt.

'A torch,' he said. 'It won't hurt, I assure you.'

So the curtains were drawn and a slim pencil torch was inserted in my mouth and switched on.

'Damn,' he said, 'the batteries have gone.'

He removed the torch, which shone as brightly as a bonfire.

'That's funny,' he said and stuck the torch back into my mouth.

'What,' he said ominously, 'have you stuffed up your nose?'

'Nothing,' I said truthfully.

'Well, why can't I see the light? I can't see the light,' he said querulously. 'I should be able to see your sinuses, but there's nothing there.'

'They've been mucking about with my nose for years, sir,' I explained, 'and it never seems to do any good.'

'My God!' he explained. 'You must go and see a specialist. I'm not taking responsibility for this. Why, your sinuses look like – look like – well, they look like the Black Hole of Calcutta!'

Gerald was sent to see Dr Magillicuddy, a sinus specialist, who stood no nonsense.

Sitting behind a huge desk he read my medical report carefully, darting fierce glances at me from opal-blue eyes.

'Come over here,' he said gruffly, his Scottish r's rolling out of his mouth like bumble bees.

He stuck a torch in my mouth. There was silence for a moment and then he let out a long, marvelling sigh.

'Hoots, mon,' he said. 'I've never seen sinuses like yours. It's like gazing at a bit of Edinburgh Castle. If anyone wanted to clean that up they'd have to excavate your skull with a pickaxe.'

He went back to his desk, sat down, laced his fingers and gazed across them at me.

'Tell me truly, laddie,' he said, 'you don't want to go into the army, navy or air force, do you?'

This was the moment when I realised truth was the only answer.

'No, sir,' I said.

'Are you a coward?' he asked.

'Yes, sir,' I answered.

'So am I,' he said. 'But I don't think they'll want a coward with sinuses like the Cheddar Gorge. Off you go, young man.'

'Thank you, sir,' I said, and as I got to the door he barked –

'Dinna underestimate yourself – it takes courage for a man to admit he's a coward. Good luck to you.'

Eventually Gerald received a letter informing him that he was unfit for military service, but would have to do something to aid the war effort. He had two choices. He could work in a munitions factory or on the land. Unsurprisingly, he plumped for the latter. 'Does it matter what sort of farm?' he asked the clerk at the Labour Office, for he preferred the idea of a farm with sheep and cows to one growing cabbages and corn. 'Personally,' sniffed the clerk, 'I don't care which sort of farm. They're all shit and smell to me.'

So Gerald set off on his bicycle in search of the ideal farm. His luck was in. He found Brown's, a riding school at Longham, to the north of Bournemouth, that kept a few cows. Mr Brown was a short, round, ruddy-faced man with a treble voice who lived with his mother and never wore anything but hacking jacket, jodhpurs and flat cap. With this jolly fellow – 'like a gigantic choir boy' – Gerald struck a bargain. In return for his mucking out and grooming the twenty-two horses in the stables and leading people around on half a dozen rides a day, Mr Brown would assure the authorities he was helping to run a farm. And this Gerald did till the end of the war, congenially occupied in giving riding lessons to horsy local ladies and American GIs with cowboy delusions stationed in the vicinity.

Looking back on that aimless but idyllic limbo time, Gerald recalled with exquisite nostalgia (and perhaps a degree of romantic mythomania) his amorous entanglements with some of the more beautiful women who came to him for lessons. This had less to do with his own attractiveness or powers of seduction, he reckoned, than with the headily romantic context in which they found themselves, the seclusion and magic of the woods they rode through, alone in a world of their own. They were like shipboard affairs, these erotic rides – amorous adventures that were permissible because they were so far from the routines and obligations of port and home (or so, for a few hours, it seemed). Longer-lasting were the girls who were his friends, like Jean Martin, a nice country type who also worked at Brown's stables, and of whom he was very fond, though he never even bestowed a kiss upon her, let alone any promises of eternal love.

Before long Gerald had a horse of his own, called Rumba, and on his days off he would ride out alone down the silent glades of the pine woods. He formed a very close relationship with his horse, and would spend hours in the saddle, letting his mind wander, making up poetry, breathing deeply of the very breath of nature. Often the horse, a creature of habit, bore him, dreaming, to his favourite pub in the forest, and refused to budge until he had finished off a pint of ale 'for the road'.

So the months passed in this agreeable fashion. Gerald did not believe he was ducking his wartime duty, or letting the side down. What side? He did not feel that England was his country, even by adoption, and so was moved by no great stirrings of patriotic fervour. His grasp of the nature of the war was too tenuous for him to realise that England was not fighting for England alone.

At last, in May 1945, the guns in Europe fell silent. Gerald's obligation to contribute to the war effort came to an end, and within a few weeks he had taken his first step towards his true life goal. By his own account he had long ago – as far back as Corfu, even – worked out what he wanted to do in life. First he would travel the world collecting animals for zoos, then he would establish a zoo of his own. Both objectives were highly unusual and extraordinarily difficult, and both required an expertise he did not possess in 1945. 'I realised,' he was to record later, 'that if I wanted to achieve my ambitions, it was necessary for me to have experience with creatures larger than scorpions and sea horses.' There seemed to be only one thing he could do – get a job in a zoo.

> Having decided this, I sat down and wrote what seemed to me an extremely humble letter to the Zoological Society of London, which, in spite of the war, still maintained the largest collection of living creatures on one spot. Blissfully unaware of the enormity of my ambition, I outlined my plans for the future, hinted that I was just the sort of person they had always been longing to employ, and more or less asked them on what day I should take up my duties.
>
> Normally, such a letter as this would have ended up where it

deserved – in the waste-paper basket. But my luck was in, for it arrived on the desk of a most kindly and civilised man, one Geoffrey Vevers, the Superintendent of the London Zoo. I suppose something about the sheer audacity of my letter must have intrigued him for, to my delight, he wrote and asked me to attend an interview in London. At the interview, spurred on by Geoffrey Vevers' gentle charm, I prattled on interminably about animals, animal collecting and my own zoo. A lesser man would have crushed my enthusiasm by pointing out the wild impracticability of my schemes but Vevers listened with great patience and tact, commended my line of approach to the problem, and said he would give the matter of my future some thought. I left him even more enthusiastic than before.

A few weeks later Gerald received a courteous letter informing him that unfortunately there were no vacancies for junior staff at London Zoo, but if he wished he could have a position as relief keeper at Whipsnade, the Zoological Society's country zoo.

As a relief keeper, Gerald would be the lowest of the low. But since he was clearly a special case, and not at all typical of the usual recruit to the ranks of zoo keepers, Geoffrey Vevers thought up the grandiose title of 'student keeper' for him. 'If he had written offering me a breeding pair of snow leopards,' Gerald recalled, 'I could not have been more delighted.'

A few days later – 'wildly excited' – Gerald set off for Whipsnade. He had two suitcases with him, one full of old clothes, the other containing natural history books and many fat notebooks in which he intended to jot down everything he observed of his animal charges and everything he learnt from his fellow keepers. On 30 July 1945 he began his lifelong involvement with zoos. If his adolescent reading had provided his secondary education, Whipsnade was to be his university.

SIX

Odd-Beast Boy

Whipsnade 1945–1946

Gerald's first port of call at Whipsnade was the office of the zoo's super-intendent, Captain William Beal, a former army veterinary officer from the Gold Coast (now Ghana). Gerald found him sitting behind a large desk in his shirtsleeves, sporting handsome striped braces:

> As the captain stood up, I saw that he was a man of immense height and girth. He came lumbering round the desk and stared at me, breathing heavily through his nose.
> 'Durrell?' he boomed interrogatively. 'Durrell?'
> He had a deep voice and he spoke in a sort of muted roar.
> 'Think you'll like it here?' asked Captain Beal so suddenly and so loudly that I jumped.
> 'Er . . . yes, sir, I'm sure I shall,' I said.
> 'You've never done any of this sort of work before?'
> 'No, sir,' I replied, 'but I've kept a lot of animals at one time or another.'
> 'Ha!' he said, almost sneeringly. 'Guinea pigs, rabbits, goldfish – that sort of thing. Well, you'll find it a bit different here.'

Shortly afterwards, Gerald was told he was to start work straight away next morning – on the lions.

Whipsnade village, Gerald discovered, was a tiny place with one pub and a handful of cottages scattered among valleys full of hazel copses. His digs turned out to be an oak-beamed room in one of the cottages, the bee-loud, flower-bowered home of Charlie Bailey, who worked with the elephants up at the zoo, and his wife. Gerald was a rather surprising lodger for this modest couple, for with his upper-class accent and sophisti-cated ways he was more like a toff than a lowly trainee keeper.

'What made you come to Whipsnade, Gerry?' asked Charlie, not unreasonably, over a huge supper of country fare.

'Well,' Gerald replied, 'I've always been interested in animals, and I want to become an animal collector – you know, go out to Africa and places like that and bring back animals for zoos. I want to get experience with some of the bigger things. You know, you can't keep big things down in Bournemouth. I mean, you can't have a herd of deer in a suburban garden, can you?'

'Ah,' Charlie agreed. 'No, I see that.'

Eventually, stuffed with food, Gerald made his way up to his room. 'I climbed into bed,' he recalled, 'and heaved a great sigh of triumph. I had arrived. I was here at Whipsnade. Gloating over this thought I fell asleep.'

He could not have been more fortunate in his place of work experience, for Whipsnade was a very special kind of zoo. Occupying five hundred acres of a former farm estate perched high on the Dunstable Downs in Bedfordshire, thirty-five miles north-west of London, Whipsnade had been opened in 1931. From the outset it had been conceived as a country zoo park – the first public one in Britain – where all the animals could, as far as possible, live in natural surroundings instead of in the barren and insanitary cages that were their lot in most of the zoos around the globe. The idea was not new: the great German animal dealer Karl Hagenbeck had created the first modern zoological garden in Hamburg back in the middle of the nineteenth century. But Whipsnade went far beyond the confines of the zoological garden. As an open-plan zoo park, lions and tigers could roam through Whipsnade's dells, zebra and antelope could graze freely in the great rolling paddocks, and wolves could wander in a pack through the woods. Gerald noted that it was 'the nearest approach to going on safari that one could attempt at that time'.

But the purpose of Whipsnade was not simply to display animals to the public in ideal surroundings. It was also intended as a place for preserving some of the world's dwindling natural resource of wild animals, and it soon became internationally renowned for its success in the captive breeding of endangered species, from the nearly extinct white Chartley cattle and Przewalski's Mongolian wild horse to the American bison, the musk ox and Père David's deer. With unerring good fortune, Gerald Durrell had pitched up at a more than passable combination zoo and propagation centre, not perhaps up to the standards of the San Diego Wild Animal Park or New York's World of Birds, but doing its best to cope in wartime. Its influence on his future life and career was to prove immeasurable.

Jill Johnson, an eighteen-year-old girl who looked after the huskies and Shetland ponies at the zoo, remembered encountering Gerald on his first working morning at Whipsnade. 'I was called down to meet a new boy,' she recalled:

> I went down to the office and there stood a fair-haired boy with a nice, open, friendly face, wearing an open-necked white shirt with the sleeves rolled up. He was taller than me, about five foot eight or so, and he had bright blue eyes, I remember. I said: 'What's your name?' and he said: 'You can call me Gerry or Durrell.' So I said: 'Gerry will do. Get a bike and follow me.' As we rode along I asked him: 'Why aren't you in the forces?' and he explained that he was a Greek citizen and that he wanted to be a big animal collector one day, which I treated with a pinch of salt. I took him to see the huskies and showed him around and after that we became good friends and got to know each other very well.

Though Gerald was officially described as a 'student keeper', his real role was that of 'odd-beast boy', at the very bottom of the heap in terms of status. But by dint of his personality he defied all conventional classification among his friends and colleagues at the zoo. The odd-beast boy was at everyone's disposal, and could be assigned to any task with any creature, big or little, docile or lethal. In terms of learning the ropes at a premier zoo – the hands-on care of large and dangerous animals (including lions and tigers, bears and buffalo), daily routine and standard zoo practice – the job was exactly what Gerald wanted. But he wanted to learn more than that.

Gerald continued his voracious reading, but now he focused his interest much more on zoo business. Almost without exception, he realised, most of the world's zoos since Victorian times had served merely as peep-shows, places of public entertainment, where people went to be amused in much the same spirit that their ancestors used to visit lunatic asylums. Scientific research at most zoos was virtually nil, and if an animal died it was simply replaced from what was taken to be Nature's unending bounty. Before long, it dawned on Gerald that this bounty was in fact being rapidly exhausted:

> As I pursued my reading, I began to learn with horror of man's rapacious encroachment upon the world and the terrible devastation that he was producing among animal life. I read of the dodo, flightless and harmless, discovered and exterminated in almost the same breath. I read of the passenger pigeon in North America,

whose vast numbers darkened the sky, who were so numerous that their nesting colonies measured several hundred square miles. They were good to eat; the last one died in Cincinnati Zoo in 1914. The quagga, that strange half horse, half zebra once so common in South Africa, was harried to extinction by the Boer farmers; the last one died in London Zoo in 1909. It seemed incredible, almost impossible, that people in charge of zoos should have been so ignorant that they did not realise that these animals were tottering on the border of extinction and that they did not do something about it. Surely this was one of the true functions of a zoological garden, to help animals that were being pushed towards extinction?

Jill Johnson remembered Gerald saying, 'A lot of animals are going to become extinct. Wouldn't it be wonderful if one could breed these animals and put them back where they came from?' But then he would have doubts, and remark: 'Perhaps they're becoming extinct because they're meant to, because the world is changing. Perhaps they're becoming extinct like the sabre-toothed tiger became extinct, because it's in the order of things, because they're meant to be replaced by something else.' But was it in the order of things for one species to commit biocide against all the others? For man to take it into his own hands to speed half the animal kingdom to extinction? Sixty million buffalo once trampled the Great Plains of America – the greatest animal congregation that ever existed on earth. Then the white man came and began to kill them off at the rate of a million a year, so that by the 1880s there were just twenty left in the whole USA. A man could ride a thousand miles across the plains and never be out of sight of a dead buffalo and never in sight of a living one. Was that in the order of things? Nothing in Gerald's life so far gave him greater insight into the acuteness of this problem, and its potential solution, than his encounter with Père David's deer.

Père David's deer had provided the world with a classic case of near-extinction and captive breeding undertaken by default. A distant relative of the red deer, it was once widespread in China, but by the end of the nineteenth century it had been hunted almost to extinction, and during the Boxer Rebellion in 1900 the few that remained were killed in the emperor's garden in Peking. Or so it seemed. As it happened, before their total extinction in their natural homeland a few specimens had been sent to Woburn Park, not far from Whipsnade, by an English aristocrat, the Duke of Bedford. From this small group the numbers of the almost vanished species were increased by haphazard natural breeding in captivity to a point where Père David's deer can now be found all over the world.

Gerald was well aware of this extraordinary story, and he was fascinated when four newborn specimens of the famous deer – still rare at that time – were sent to Whipsnade to be hand-reared:

> They were delightful little things with long gangling limbs over which they had no control, and strange slanted eyes that gave them a distinctly oriental appearance . . . They had to be fed once during the night, at midnight, and again at dawn . . . I must say I rather enjoyed the night duties. To pick one's way through the moonlit park towards the stable where the baby deer were kept, you had to pass several of the cages and paddocks, and the occupants were always on the move. The bears, looking twice as big in the half light, would be snorting to each other as they shambled heavily through the riot of brambles in their cage. At one point the path led through the wolf wood, with the moonlight silvering the trunks and laying dark shadows along the ground through which the wolf pack danced on swift, silent feet, like a strange black tide, swirling and twisting among the trunks.
>
> Then you'd reach the stable and light the lantern. The baby deer would start moving restlessly in their straw beds, bleating tremulously. As you opened the door they'd rush forward, wobbling on their unsteady legs, sucking frantically at your fingers or the edge of your coat, and butting you suddenly in the legs with their heads, so that you were almost knocked down. Then came the exquisite moment when the teat was pushed into their mouths and they sucked frantically at the warm milk, their eyes staring, bubbles gathering like a moustache at the corners of their mouths. In the flickering light of the lantern, while the deer sucked and slobbered over the bottles, I was very conscious of the fact that they were the last of their kind, animal refugees living a precarious existence on the edge of extermination, dependent for their existence on the charity of a handful of human beings.

Jill Johnson was Gerald's partner in this operation. She recalled:

> I used to milk the goats, and Gerry used to take the bottle of goat milk to feed the deer. But it was a bit of a nuisance doing it this way, because the deer kept swallowing the teats. So one day we decided to take the nanny goat in to the deer so that they could suck from her direct. This worked pretty well when the deer were small, but eventually they grew bigger than the nanny and would

butt under her and lift her up in the air, legs sprawling, and feed from her like that . . .

After that venture we moved on to looking after sick and orphaned animals, and were even allowed to help with operations by the vet. But the Père David's deer may well have given Gerry his first glimpse into the possibilities of captive breeding. We used to talk about them perhaps breeding in the Park and then being reintroduced into China. It was just a dream then, but later it did happen.

At Whipsnade Gerald continued to compile his own list of animals in danger of extinction. He was moved, he later confided to a friend, by a mixture of horror, despair, determination and love, quoting Cecil Rhodes' alleged dying words, 'So much to do, so little done.'

Jill Johnson thought Gerald must have been rather a lonely soul at Whipsnade, his class and intelligence distancing him from his fellow keepers. His family never visited him, as far as she could tell. Eventually he moved out of the Baileys' house and into a room in a bleak and chilly place called the Bothy – he referred to it as the Brothel – a huddle of four or five keepers' cottages opposite a pub called Chequers at the bottom of the zoo. Sometimes he was invited for a curry (West African style with lots of chilli peppers) at the home of Captain and Mrs Beal – 'So hot,' he told Jill, 'it makes me sweat like a fever.'

Among Gerald's friends at Whipsnade was Guinea Pig Gus. 'As a romantic figure,' he recalled, 'Gus had little to commend him.' His skull sloped back from his nose like a Neanderthal's. His nose looked like some fungus squashed on his face. He suffered acutely from acne, had adenoids and bit his nails. 'He was quite the most unattractive human being I had ever encountered,' Gerald wrote in his autobiographical jottings years later, 'yet he had the kindest of hearts.' It was Gus who walked all the way to Dunstable and back to get patches and glue when Gerald punctured his bicycle tyres. It was Gus who brought him half a bottle of whisky – 'God knows from where, for at that time a bottle of whisky was as valuable as the Koh-i-noor diamond' – when he had pleurisy and thought he was going to die. It was Gus who took Gerald's shoes to be soled and heeled so that he didn't have to do it on his day off.

Gus's heart belonged to the guinea pig, and all his spare cash went towards materials for the palace he was planning to build for these favoured creatures. When it became clear to Gerald that Gus would never have enough money to finish it, he decided it was time to repay him for all his past kindness, and to break his vow to live on his meagre salary by hook or by crook and never to write home for funds. 'I wrote to my mother,' he recorded, 'explaining about Gus and his guinea pigs. By return came a letter containing ten crisp pound notes. In her letter, my mother said: "Don't hurt his feelings, dear. Tell him an uncle who liked guinea pigs died and left it to you."'

So the Guinea Pig Palace was completed, and the grand opening day arrived. 'It was a splendid occasion,' Gerald recalled, 'attended by no lesser personages than Gus's mother and father, his dog, his cat, me, his goldfish, his frog, and the girl from next door, as exciting as a dumpling. The Guinea Pigs took the move from their old home with great aplomb and dignity. Three jugs of beer from the pub and some elderberry wine and the party got so convivial that Gus's mother fell into the goldfish pond and Gus at last succeeded in kissing the girl next door.'

The Guinea Pig Palace, which also contained other species of rodents, became the place where Gerald took his girlfriends. It was, he reckoned, the most romantic spot available. Not all the girls agreed. Gerald recalled:

The first one, a town girl, suddenly said: ''Ere, you're paying more attention to them rats than wot you are to me. I can tell, your eyes get all unfocused like.' I felt this was unfair, since most of her clothing was scattered about the hazel grove, but I must admit the dormice were enchanting, and enchanted by us.

At last I met an adorable girl with a Devonshire accent like cream out of a jug and dark blue-grey eyes fringed with eyelashes as long as hollyhocks. She loved dormice, but this was the trouble.

'No, don't, not now,' she would say. 'You'll disturb them, dear wee mites. And anyway – you never know – they might be watching.'

Gerald finally struck lucky with a policeman's daughter – 'buxom, blonde and willing' – who ran Pets' Corner. Her office was in a wooden hut which was often locked from the inside at lunchtime. 'We were poking the living daylights out of each other at every opportunity,' Gerald later confided to a friend. 'I thought I would marry her in the end.' Gerald took her home to Bournemouth to meet the family once or twice. 'Really she was quite hefty and rotund,' his sister Margaret recalled. 'Gerry was very keen on her at the time. But then, what young man *isn't* very keen at the time?' It was not to last, though, as the policeman's daughter turned out to have another boyfriend hovering in the wings.

How Gerald Durrell saw himself in his leisure hours at Whipsnade – a Lothario among the paddocks – was not quite how others saw him. Jill Johnson recalled:

The waitresses in the cafeteria said he looked like a Greek god, but really he was not the most handsome, though he had a nice face. He wasn't particularly macho, either, but nor was he the opposite. To tell you the truth, I don't remember him having any close girlfriends at all. If anyone went out with him it was me, but I was only a friend who happened to be a girl. We were close, but we never had a romance. Neither of us was interested in boyfriends and girlfriends, we were interested in learning as much as we could about the animals. There wasn't much to do in the evenings, nowhere much to go, no TV in those days. We used to go out for bike rides in the evening, and sometimes he'd take me up into the hay barn. You'd think we were up to something, but we weren't. He'd say: 'Sshh ... be quiet ... they won't know where we are. I'm going to read some Housman; see if you like him.' And he'd read out loud to me, in his beautiful voice:

> Oh, when I was in love with you,
> Then I was clean and brave,
> And miles around the wonder grew
> How well did I behave ...

Gerry would provide much more intelligent conversation than any of the keepers who used to go down to the pub in the evening. He was quite a deep thinker, but he was fun too. Sometimes, sitting up in the dark, watching over a sick animal, he'd tell the most wonderful stories – some of them really quite rude. He did have a special way of treating women – rather cosmopolitan, a bit Latin perhaps. One day I was with another girl in the office and he came rushing in, and he got down on one knee in front of this other girl and made a most elaborate and passionate speech to her. 'There is a question I have got to ask you,' he said, 'but I don't know how to put it.' We both thought he was going to ask her to marry him. Then he burst out: 'Can you tell me where the gentlemen's lavatory is?' So he was great fun, very lively, very bright, very special, a nice, kind, unusual person to know.

Lucy Pendar, the teenage daughter of the resident engineer at Whipsnade, remembered Gerald less as a ladykiller than as a generous and supportive young man with a highly developed, rather bawdy sense of humour:

Gerry's stay at Whipsnade brought a new dimension to our lives. A slim young man with unusual blue eyes, his long fair hair fell over his eyes and he wore suede shoes. To me, he looked more like a poet than a keeper! His burning ambition was to be a wild animal collector. We'd heard of Wilfred Frost and Cecil Webb, the Great White Hunters, but this was our first encounter with anyone aspiring to such a dangerous and thrilling occupation! What a captivated audience we were as this new person in our midst told us about his early life. He related splendid stories as we sat, spellbound, on the oatsacks or on the grass. He expounded, at length, his pet theories on the care of animals in captivity, many of which he subsequently put into practice. The slim, aesthetic young man was a great deal tougher than he looked. None of us had any doubts that he would ultimately achieve anything he set his sights on.

Gerry was enormous fun, Lucy Pendar remembered. He was always bursting into lusty renderings of 'The Lincolnshire Poacher' or 'The Last Rose of Summer', or piping up with ribald verses like 'Little Mary'.

> Little Mary, in the glen,
> Poked herself with a fountain pen.
> The top came off, the ink ran wild
> And she gave birth to a blue black child.
> And they called the bastard Stephen ...
> They called the bastard Stephen ...
> They called the bastard Stephen ...
> 'Cos that was the name of the ink.

When Lucy fell ill, it was Gerry who read to her. When she had doubts, it was he who encouraged her to stick at it. When she tripped him up during a romp at a VJ-Day party, so that he sprawled headfirst into a cow pat – 'I always lay claim to fertilising that brain,' she joked later – he took it in good part. 'It is unbelievable the influence one person can have upon another in so short a time,' Lucy Pendar was to reflect, 'but he was ever after indelibly imprinted on my memory. A wonderful man. We had the faith in him the adults did not, and we were right.'

At Whipsnade Gerald learned that zoo keeping, like many jobs, was not quite as romantic as it sounded. Most of a keeper's time was spent on routine work such as feeding and cleaning. Gerald worked in a number of sections, each of which took its name from its principal animals. The lion section, for example, where he started, also included wombats, Arctic foxes, tigers and polar bears, which could be very dangerous if sufficiently annoyed. From 'lions' he moved on to 'bears', where there were also wolves, warthogs, zebras and gnus. But though Gerald enjoyed his work at Whipsnade, and was able to find time to learn more about the animals in his charge, it sometimes seemed to him that the only knowledge he had acquired was how to muck out and how to avoid a goring. The most dangerous animals, he discovered, were not necessarily the ones with the most fearsome reputations. Even a velvet-eyed zebra could be transformed into a raging demon that would treat one's behind like a kettle drum given half a chance, while the much-feared wolf did not deserve its terrible notoriety at all.

Gerald was acquiring a priceless grounding in the daily running of a first-class, up-to-date zoo. But there were some minuses. He was disappointed at the lack of scientific expertise at Whipsnade, and at the reluctance of his fellow keepers, fearful for their jobs, to impart their knowhow to him. He was also alarmed by certain aspects of the animal management procedures, and convinced that some of the keepers were putting his life in danger. Gerald had a wonderful way with animals, but he was no fool. Most of the animals at Whipsnade were half wild. Some of the keepers thought they knew the ways of the creatures in their charge, but they didn't, and one day, Gerald was sure, there would be an accident. Often the keepers asked him to do things which he was reluctant to do because he knew he could be injured. One day he was asked to fetch a baby water buffalo from its mother, a nearly suicidal undertaking. He managed to get hold of the baby and make a run for it, but the enraged mother caught up with him and rammed him with her horns, smashing his hand against the metal bars of the paddock and breaking several bones.

One exception among the keepers was a new man, recently discharged from the RAF, by the name of Ken Smith. Early on Gerald had struck up a rapport with Smith, who was then in charge of the Père David's deer, and this friendship was to continue for many years, with great significance for the careers of both men.

On 7 January 1946 Gerald celebrated his twenty-first birthday and came into his inheritance – a sum of £3000 (worth over £60,000 in today's money) which had been set aside for him in his father's will. Suddenly Gerald – who until now could barely afford the price of half a pint of watery bitter or a packet of Woodbines – was a man of means. He had already decided to leave Whipsnade some months before. His ambition was still to go animal collecting and start his own zoo one day, and he knew he was not going to further either ambition if he stayed where he was.

Every evening he would sit in his little cell-like room in the cold, echoing Bothy, writing painstaking letters to any animal collectors who were still in business asking if they would take him on one of their expeditions if he paid his own expenses. These fearless, resourceful frontiersmen were a legendary breed of men. But their replies all said the same thing – as he had no collecting experience, they could not take him with them. If he ever managed to acquire some experience, then he should by all means write again.

'It was at this point in my life, depressed and frustrated, that I had a brilliant idea,' Gerald recalled. 'If I used some of my inheritance to finance an expedition of my own, then I could honestly claim to have had experience and then one of these great men might not only take me on an expedition but actually pay me a salary. The prospects were mouthwatering.'

This, he decided, was what he would do. He would try his hand as a freelance animal-catcher, paying his way on his own expedition collecting animals for zoos. He now had capital, and this was how he proposed to invest it. Though the war had largely put an end to the animal-catchers' unusual way of earning a living, with the coming of peace many zoos needed to restock their dwindling collections, and for the rarer and more exotic animals the demand was considerable and prices high.

At Gerald's farewell curry dinner at Whipsnade, however, Captain Beal was less than enthusiastic. 'No money in it,' he warned in doleful tones. 'You'll be chuckin' money away, mark my words.'

'And watch out,' warned a keeper called Jesse. 'It's one thing to have a lion in a cage and another to have the bugger creeping up behind you, see?'

The next morning, Gerald went the rounds saying goodbye to the animals. 'I was sad,' he recalled, 'for I had been happy working at Whipsnade but, as I went round, each animal represented a place I wanted to see, each was a sort of geographical signpost encouraging me on my way. Everywhere the animals beckoned me and strengthened my decision.'

On 17 May 1946 Gerald Durrell left Whipsnade in pursuit of his dream. His time there had taught him many valuable and practical things about the profession upon which he was now embarked. No less importantly, his experience at Whipsnade had crystallised his thinking about zoos in general, and the ideal zoo in particular. He later wrote:

When I left Whipsnade I was still determined to have a zoo of my own, but I was equally determined that if I ever achieved this ambition my zoo would have to fulfil three functions in order to justify its existence.

Firstly, it would have to act as an aid to the education of people so that they could realise how fascinating and how important the other forms of life in the world were, so that they would stop being quite so arrogant and self-important and appreciate the fact that the other forms of life had just as much right to existence as they had.

Secondly, research into the behaviour of animals would be undertaken so that by this means one could not only learn more about the behaviour of human beings but also be in a better position to help animals in their wild state, for unless you know the needs of the various species of animal you cannot practise conservation successfully.

Thirdly – and this seemed to me to be of the utmost urgency – the zoo would have to be a reservoir of animal life, a sanctuary for threatened species, keeping and breeding them so that they would not vanish from the earth for ever as the dodo, the quagga and the passenger pigeon had done.

All that lay in the future. For the moment he had the more immediate problems of his first – his great – expedition to grapple with. As the weeks went by he became obsessed with the adventure and romance of the idea. Lacking the gift of hindsight, his ambition at this stage was unclouded by any doubts as to the ethics of what he was proposing. At an early age Gerald had set himself a dual agenda for his working life – first, collecting animals in the wild for the world's zoos, and later establishing a zoo of his own. These two components may have had animals in common, but they had paradoxically contrasting effects: while the zoo of Gerald's dreams might save species from extinction, the practice of collecting often condemned individual animals to death – an outcome Gerald did not clearly foresee and never fully acknowledged, even to himself, though the poacher would turn gamekeeper soon enough.

SEVEN

Planning for Adventure

1946–1947

Gerald went home to Bournemouth to make preparations for his expedition. Only one cloud darkened the family reunion – the erratic behaviour of Leslie, who had been giving cause for concern.

Leslie had always been the enigma of the family, the cracked bell who was always striking a dud note. Corfu, he once said, was 'the dangerous corner in my life, five golden, drifting, ultimately destructive years'. Larry used to have a go at Mother sometimes: 'We must put Leslie to something,' he'd tell her. But she would say, 'Leave him alone, he'll be all right.' But, unlike his brothers, he wasn't. The rest of the Durrells had always rallied loyally around whenever Leslie stepped out of line, for he was basically well-intentioned, and never malicious. But years later he was to remark to an interviewer: 'It's a funny thing, you know – however hard I try, nothing seems to go right for me. I've got a sort of jinx on me, I think.'

He put all of his inheritance into a fishing boat, which sank before it had even got out of Poole Harbour. Next he tried market gardening, but that failed too. Unable to settle to anything, drifting and shiftless and convinced the world owed him a living, Leslie passed himself off for a while as 'Major-General Durrell', trying to develop various ambitious scams, including one involving luxury yachts and motorboats, till Margaret warned him he could end up in prison for fraudulent impersonation if he didn't watch out. He 'helped' his mother get through a lot of money – not having a clue herself, she always took Leslie's advice on financial matters, for he had always been her favourite child.

Nothing much worked for Leslie. Though he was a talented painter – Gerald once described some of his work as 'astonishingly beautiful' – he practised his gift in a most desultory way, and never made a penny from it. In the end, Lawrence and Gerald gave up on him. Gerald was to confide years later, 'Though my elder brother and I frequently tried to help him, he would always end up doing something that would make us lose patience with him.'

All through the war, while he toiled ingloriously in the aircraft factory, Leslie had been living in Bournemouth with his mother, Gerald (till he went to Whipsnade) and the family's Greek maid Maria Condos. By 1945 he was twenty-seven, and he and Maria, some ten years his senior, had begun a liaison – one of several for Leslie, the love of her life for Maria. Margaret, who was closest to the drama, recalled:

> I walked right into the Maria furore when I got back from North Africa to have my second baby early in 1945, and of course, as in all these family crises, it was always me who had to be the strong one, because there was nobody else around to deal with things.
>
> Mother, of course – being Mother – hadn't noticed anything going on. So I told her: 'Maria's pregnant.' Then I had to rush around trying to find an unmarried mothers' home for her to go to, and when the baby was born in September she kept marching up and down the street with the baby in a pram, telling all and sundry it was a Durrell baby, another Bournemouth Durrell boy, which was rather embarrassing for the family. Leslie saw him first when he was a babe in arms, but neither Gerry nor Larry ever set eyes on the child at that time. They were adamant Leslie shouldn't marry the girl. Not that he intended to, because he was also going out with Doris by now, the manageress of the local off-licence who had kept Mother in gin during the war and who employed Leslie to make the beer deliveries after it. They were odd characters, you know, Gerry and Larry. Though they could both be very unconventional and wild, they could also be very prudish and correct, surprising though that may sound.

The child, named Anthony Condos, had early recollections of the house in St Alban's Avenue. His mother slept in a cot in the kitchen, and he remembered 'monkeys climbing over the furniture and snakes in chests of drawers'. Since Leslie took no interest in either the baby or Maria, Mother paid up as usual and Maria went and got a job in a laundry in Christchurch, and then a council house, and brought the baby up on her own. 'After my mother and I left the folds of the family,' Tony Condos recalled, 'we lived in various places, moving from flat to flat and room to room around Bournemouth. I think that Margaret, another woman, may have felt sympathy for my mother. My mother kept up a good relationship with her for many years and we were always kindly received at her house at number 51. But mother had to work incredibly hard to

raise me and had a very difficult life.' Maria remained very much in love
with Leslie, Margaret was to say: 'Years later she'd still remember him
adoringly as "my *roula-mou*" – that's Greek for "darling" – in fact deeper,
more tender than darling.'

Tony Condos grew up never knowing if his father was dead or alive.
'Though my mother obviously loved him very much,' he was to reflect,
'her feelings towards him oscillated between love and hate, and it made
me very confused in my younger days. My main regret in life is that I
never knew my father. For many years I felt extreme animosity towards
him and the rest of the family. But as I grew older I started to appreciate
the situation that the whole Durrell family must have been in with regard
to my mother and me. Now I have only sadness that I was not one of
them, the family ... And oddly enough, I am *proud* of being a Durrell,
albeit nameless.'

Gerald, meanwhile, was grappling with a small nightmare of his own.
For a novice, an animal collecting expedition in the wilds of a distant
continent represented a daunting challenge. How should he set about it?
Where should he go? What should he catch? How much would it cost?
There was no apprenticeship, no one to help him, and a mountainous
number of bureaucratic restrictions to overcome. In the aftermath of the
war, much of the world remained difficult of access, and some countries
were still off-limits.

Months went by while Gerald struggled with a host of imponderables
to produce a plan of action. He had long cherished a dream to see Africa,
and within that continent one country stood out as a prime target for
any would-be animal collector – the undeveloped and little-visited territory known as the British Cameroons, a remote, narrow backwater of
empire on the eastern frontier of Nigeria, unsurpassed not only for
the wild beauty of its high mountains and tropical forests but for the
spectacular richness of its wildlife, from the gorilla, the pangolin and the
rare angwantibo to the hairy frog, giant water shrew and giant hawk
eagle.

Having settled the problem of where, Gerald turned his attention to
other pressing questions – when, how, with whom and for what. The
details took months to work out. Foreign travel was still an exotic pastime
in 1946, beyond the reach of all but a privileged few, and information
was scant. His plans took a leap forward when he made contact with a
collector naturalist by the name of John Yealland, a highly regarded
aviculturist and ornithologist almost twice his age but with interests close
to his own. A few months after Gerald left Whipsnade, Yealland had
helped Peter Scott found the nucleus of his Wildfowl Trust at Slimbridge,

on the edge of the Severn mudflats in Gloucestershire, and later he was to become Curator of Birds at the London Zoo. Gerald told Yealland of his ambition to collect rare animals in the Cameroons, and Yealland responded with encouraging enthusiasm. They agreed to pool their talents and see the thing through together.

So now there was a team. And before long there would be a plan, a schedule, an itinerary – even a departure date. But not much else. As one newspaper was to report: 'Their bring-'em-back-alive expedition was their first safari into the jungle. No one knew where they were going, no one placed any orders with them, and no one in the Cameroons knew they were arriving.' In fact five zoos – London, Bristol, Chester, Belle Vue (Manchester) and Paignton – had expressed an interest in seeing anything that the expedition brought back, and had even quoted prices for the rarer species, though none was prepared to put money up front.

The Durrell family were first surprised, then excited by Gerald's ambitious plans. As far as they were concerned his life to date – for all his lively enthusiasm and quirky originality – had seemed about as unpromising as his brother Leslie's.

During 1947 Gerald was increasingly drawn to London. The capital had many advantages for the intending expeditionary, including a world-class zoo and museums to visit, experts to consult, specialist dealers to advise about a legion of purchases, libraries to bone up in and bookshops to buy from. London also had, at that time, Peter Scott, the only son of Scott of the Antarctic, a war hero, portrait painter and successful painter of wildfowl who was already making a name for himself as a naturalist and pioneer conservationist in a world still largely oblivious of conservation and all it stood for.

Though there were a number of things Gerald did not have in common with Scott (background and personality being but two), they overlapped in two essential regards. Scott's trail-blazing Wildfowl Trust at Slimbridge on the Severn marshes, which had been set up the previous year, was a model of the type of conservation establishment Gerald himself dreamed of founding one day. And Scott's reverence for animal life was very close to Gerald's own as yet unarticulated view. 'My interest in the processes of evolution,' Scott was to write, 'has produced in me a kind of reverence for every species of flora and fauna, which have as much right to their place on earth as does *homo sapiens*. The prospect of extinction of any existing species then appears as a potential disaster which man's conscience should urge him to avert.' The destruction of nature and its living forms was, Scott felt, 'a crime against an undefined but immutable law of the universe'.

Scott was living at the time in Edwardes Square, Kensington, and it is likely that the young Gerald Durrell went there to seek the advice of the older, more established professional. But though Gerald was a relative ingenu, Scott was aware that he already had enough clout to persuade John Yealland, Scott's own first curator at Slimbridge, to go off to the wilds of the Cameroons with him.

Besides all its resources and experts, London also had women. Between the age of sixteen and twenty-two, a number of girls had drifted in and out of Gerald's life. But though he was far from virginal, he was still a *naïf* in his relations with the opposite sex. This was now to change.

It was at lunch in a Greek restaurant in the West End, where he had gathered with Larry and a bunch of fawning failed poets, that Gerald met the woman who was to indoctrinate him into the deeper mysteries of love. He called her Juliet, but whether that was her real name may never be known. She was in her late twenties, six or seven years older than Gerald, married (but separated) with two young children. Gerald fell for her almost at once. She was not pretty, but she had a memorable face and beautiful eyes, and besides, she looked pale and sad, so that Gerald felt protective as well as drawn towards her.

'What do you do?' he asked.

'I paint horses,' she said.

Gerald had some problem with this. 'I could not believe it – the mind boggled,' he was to recall, 'but surrounded by Greeks anything was possible.'

'You mean you take a shire horse and a bucket of paint and accost him with it?' he asked her.

'No,' she said. 'I paint pictures of them – for their owners. Pedigree horses, of course.'

'Of course,' said Gerald gravely, adding tentatively: 'Can I come and see your etchings some time?'

'Yes,' she replied. 'How about tomorrow? Come and have lunch.'

So the tryst was made. Gerald caught a bus to Juliet's, clutching a dozen gulls' eggs for lunch in the hope that they would prove an efficacious aphrodisiac. Her house, he recalled, smelled of coffee and oil paints having a bath together. She showed him her paintings – 'she wasn't as good as Stubbs,' he recalled, 'but damned near it' – and he stayed so long that they went out to dinner. Within a few days he had moved out of his Aunt Prue's house in Drayton Gardens, Chelsea, which had been his base in town, and installed himself and his baggage at Juliet's. 'She was,' he sighed with nostalgia for lost love, 'the most wonderful woman in the world.'

'Juliet was Gerry's first real affair, his first complete realisation of love and sex and all that,' his sister Margaret remembered. 'She really opened his eyes to it. Not that he saw much future to it.'

The affair lingered on and off for two years, punctuated by Gerald's long absences abroad. He took it seriously enough to have thoughts of marrying the woman, which looking back he reckoned would have been a disaster. But there *was* no future to it. One morning he popped down to Bournemouth on some business or other and returned that evening to find a letter from Juliet waiting for him on the dressing table. It was, he recalled, 'a note in the traditional manner, using all the trite phrases out of the novels we secretly enjoy but pretend are bad, like "we're growing too fond of each other" and this sort of crap'. Distraught at this unexpected turn of events, Gerald got wildly drunk, and then cracked up. He had deeply cared for the woman after all. Eventually, in sadness and anger, he gathered his books together, packed his bags and sloped back to Aunt Prue's with his tail between his legs. Not that it mattered much in the end. The wild world beckoned, and before long he would again be off to bigger and more challenging horizons.

In the meantime, Gerald concentrated on the real matter in hand. As the boxes of traps, guns, lanterns, socks, salt, suet, fish-hooks, maps, field guides and medicines began to clutter up the family home, word got about in Bournemouth that young Gerry, the former pet shop assistant and riding instructor, had turned into a naturalist and explorer, and was about to set off to Darkest Africa in search of pythons and apes. Earlier in the year his brother Lawrence had thought his career was tending in an entirely different direction, writing to Henry Miller from Rhodes: 'My younger brother Gerry's emerging as a poet. He is rather an iconoclast at present – feels he has to assert his individuality – thinks you a bad writer and me a *terribly* bad writer.' In April 1947 Lawrence had to revise his opinion. After visiting Bournemouth with his new Egyptian wife Eve – the first time the whole family had been together since the Corfu days before the war – he wrote to Miller: 'Gerald has turned out as a zoologist as he wanted and is leaving for Nigeria in September.' Margaret, who now had two young sons, was soon to divorce her airman, Jack Breeze, and would use her legacy from her father to buy a large house across the road from Mother, while Leslie moved in with Doris Hall, a laughing, booming divorcee with a son of her own. Substantially older and bigger than Leslie, Doris still ran the off-licence half a mile down the road.

Gerald's preparations were gathering momentum. At last the byzantine negotiations with the bureaucracies responsible for export, import, animal and gun licences were resolved. A cabin and cargo space were booked on a cargo vessel bound for Victoria in the Cameroons. Late in September

1947 Gerald collected a new passport. It described him as a zoologist, domiciled in Bournemouth, eyes blue, hair brown, and five feet seven in height.

Cargo ships are notoriously erratic when it comes to schedules. The boat on which Gerald hoped to sail was due to depart from London, and he stayed at Aunt Prue's while he waited – interminably – for the boat to arrive. One day he happened to bump into Larry emerging from a bookshop carrying a large parcel of books.

'Oh, hullo,' said Larry in surprise. 'What are you doing in London?'

'Waiting for a boat,' replied Gerald.

'A boat? Ah, yes, London docks and so on. Down to the sea in shops. Well, ships in my experience are notoriously tardy. Either they don't sail at all or else they sink, which gives you time for a drink.'

Larry suggested that to while away the time Gerald should look up an old friend and champion of his, a Sinologist and poet by the name of Hugh Gordon Porteus. Interesting chap, Larry told him. Lived in a cellar in Chelsea, played the organ and lived off horsemeat. 'Knows a lot about Chinese poetry,' Larry continued. 'I think you'd like him – unless you're too bloody English to eat horse.'

Hugh Porteus's menage was every bit as eccentric as Gerald had been led to expect. A gaggle of nubile young women were gathered in the sitting room while Porteus stirred soup in a tin bidet (a trophy from one of the best brothels in Paris) on the gas ring.

'I gazed on the scene,' Gerald recorded in his notebook later. 'Most of the girls were wearing very little else but diaphanous dressing gowns and bras and exciting lace panties underneath. The soup bubbled in the bidet. The horse steaks were lying in a row on the top of the bookcase.' At seven o'clock sharp Porteus looked at his watch, pulled a miniature organ out of a cupboard, and called for silence. An infirm old lady by the name of Mrs Honeydew lived in the room above, and it was Porteus's custom to play her a few tunes on his organ while she listened through the floorboards as she had her beef tea.

'All right for sound, Mrs Honeydew?' he shouted.

A walking stick could be heard rapping sharply on the ceiling, and Porteus settled himself more firmly on his stool.

'The next minute we were engulfed in the *Blue Danube*,' Gerald recalled. 'Everything in that enclosed space danced to the magnificent waltz. The girls' breasts wobbled, the horse steaks on the bookcase quivered, the bidet trembled on the gas-ring, and a book by a sixth century traveller in China fell out of the bookcase. One of the girls suddenly put her warm hands in mine, drew me aloft as it were, pressed her warm and

An Anglo-Indian wedding in the heyday of the Raj – the marriage of Gerald Durrell's mother, Louisa Florence Dixie, and his father, Lawrence Samuel Durrell, at Roorkee in North-West Province on 23 November 1910.

The Durrell family around 1923. With Mother and Father are Leslie (left), Margaret and Lawrence. Gerald's arrival is still a year or two in the future.

Gerald Durrell in his Indian babyhood. The first word he uttered was reputedly 'zoo'.

Gerald as a toddler.

Gerald (centre) aged one at Brighton beach with Margo and Leslie during a family visit to England in 1926.

Eight-year-old Gerald with his mother in Bournemouth before the Corfu adventure.

Gerald and Roger the dog soon after their arrival on Corfu in 1935. In the early days his mother made him wear wellington boots as a protection against poisonous snakes.

The idyll begins. On an enchanted evening near Pérama Gerald sits at the roadside overlooking an age-old view towards Mouse Island.

Above: The Durrells photographed by Leslie on the balcony of the Daffodil-Yellow Villa in the winter of 1936. Left to right: Margo, Nancy, Lawrence, Gerald and Mother.

Below: Another group photo at the Daffodil-Yellow Villa. Leslie, Spiro, Lawrence, Gerald's tutor Pat Evans, Mother, Nancy.

Above: Leslie on his boat in the summer of 1937.

Above right: Maria Condos, the Durrell family maid and later the mother of Leslie's child. She was twenty-eight when Leslie took this photo. On the back he wrote: 'Maria our maid (jolly nice)'.

Dr Theo Stephanides, Gerald's mentor and natural history instructor, in uncharacteristic garb minus suit, tie and homburg hat.

Right: The Snow-White Villa, last of the Durrells' three houses in Corfu, built at Criseda as the weekend retreat of the British Governor of the Ionian Islands in 1824.

Above: Spiro and Gerald cooking a picnic dish of eels in red wine at a bay near the Lake of Lilies. Spiro's celebrated Dodge taxi is parked on the beach.

Gerald, aged eleven, with a pet barn owl.

Right: Gerald and his faithful servant Pious in the Cameroons, 1948.

Below: Second Cameroons expedition, 1949. Gerald on the left, Ken Smith (sticking plaster over tropical ulcer on leg) on the right, with African hunters and assorted monkeys.

Right: Gerald's precious angwantibo eating a grape. This was his prize catch in the Cameroons, and was only the second ever brought back to Europe alive.

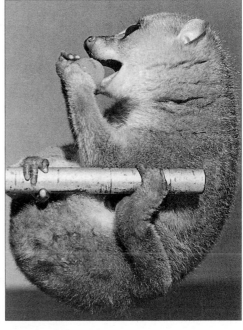

Left: Gerald at Liverpool Docks on his return from his second Cameroons expedition. The curious creature on his shoulder is a guenon monkey.

Ken Smith, Robert Lowes and Gerald (at the sharp end) getting the better of an eight-foot boa constrictor, British Guiana, 1950.

The most arduous part of any animal-collecting expedition – lecturing about it afterwards. A popular feature of Gerald's public lectures was his lightning sketches of the animals he encountered on his travels.

Gerald (second from right) with iguana at a book fair in London in the 1950s. Throughout his life he sought to fire the young with a respect for animal life.

mobile mouth against mine, pressed herself to me and started to waltz.'

At this point Theodore Stephanides arrived. Now resident in London and working as a radiologist at Lambeth Hospital, Theo knew the Porters through Larry. Still every inch the Edwardian gentleman, he wore a tweed suit, 1908 waistcoat, highly polished boots and a staunch trilby, and sported a perky beard and moustache and a neat new steel-grey haircut. 'Even I,' noted Gerald, 'who had known Theodore since the age of ten, would have been appalled at the idea of inserting him into such a milieu.' The girls had never set eyes on a human being such as this before, and to the dismay of both Porteus and Gerald they greeted the new arrival with effusive admiration:

> They cooed around him like doves round a fountain. They pressed olives on him and cheese biscuits. They sat round him in a ring of delicious fragrance, palpitating at each word he spoke. Theodore sat there like an ultra benevolent Father Christmas, delving into his considerable memory for jokes that *Punch* thought hilarious in 1898.
>
> 'There is this – um – you know – a sort of tongue twister. I don't know if you've heard it,' ventured Theodore. "What noise annoys an oyster most – er – um – ha! A noisy noise annoys an oyster most.'
>
> The girls rippled with liquid laughter, crowding closer to Theodore's feet. This was the kind of humour they had not encountered before and to them it was as marvellous as finding a fully working spinning wheel in the attic.

So the frustrating evening wore on. Gerald and Porteus sat together disconsolate, ignored by the girls, who pressed round the scholarly, stuttering Theo. He reminisced about a friend of his in Paris, a freshwater biologist who kept a most interesting collection of crustacea in a complex system of fourteen interconnecting bidets in his room. Dipping into his mushroom soup, he expounded at length on the lethal potential of this kind of dish – some 2841 different kinds of fungi, he said, and more than two thousand of them poisonous or deadly. 'Gold, green, blue, hazel and olive-black eyes,' Gerald recalled, 'regarded Theo like a group of children who are being told the true story of Bluebeard.'

'Did you know,' later confided a wide-eyed girl whom Gerald particularly fancied, 'that the gorilla has a brain capacity almost that of a man?'

'I knew that,' growled Gerald morosely, 'when I was seven.'

At length Gerald received news that a vessel bound for the Cameroons was loading up in Liverpool – a banana boat in the form of an old German rustbucket seized by the British as war booty and due to sail at the beginning of December. He took the first train north, and secured his passage. Now at last, it seemed, he was on his way. Within a day or two Yealland had joined him, the expedition stores had been safely stowed in the hold and the personal baggage packed in the cabin. The good luck telegrams were delivered, the last goodbyes said and the gangway drawn up. And the ship refused to budge an inch from the dock.

On 2 December 1947, after three days on board, with the ship still defiantly tied up to the jetty, Gerald unpacked his portable typewriter and started his first missive to Mother – the first lengthy, coherent narrative he had written in his life.

> Dear Mother,
> We are still at Garston Docks in Liverpool. The bloody boat being a German one, no one seems to know anything about the inside of her. Something in the engines has given out, and so hordes of sweaty men are messing about in pools of oil. We have however had three days board and lodging at the expense of the firm, so that's not too bad. What we object to is the view from our porthole: a very dirty length of jetty with a pile of rotting bananas on it. John says it might be rather pretty in the spring, if we stay long enough . . .

Their cabin was large and well-appointed, but what really staggered Gerald, long accustomed to rationed austerity in post-war Britain, was the food. 'For breakfast,' he crooned, 'I had rolled oats (lots of milk and sugar) followed by kidneys and bacon with potatoes, toast and marmalade and butter (in a dish as big as a soup plate) and coffee.' Even better, the booze was stunningly cheap, and flowed like water: 'Beer (pre-war quality) costs us ten pence, whiskey and gin a shilling (two fingers), and we get fifty cigarettes for three shillings.' The captain, Gerald noted, was 'a stupid, pompous idiot of the worst kind', but the rest of the officers were 'sweet'. As for the other passengers, they were a 'very queer lot'. But all were charming to the two young animal catchers, and were reassuringly encouraging about the abundance of animals there.

> Don't worry about us, as we are having a wonderful time. We spend most of the day screaming with laughter. We hope to leave tomorrow morning, with luck this evening.
> Love
> Gerry

But it was not until 14 December, a full fortnight after the pair had first clambered on board, and with their laughter worn a little thin by the interminable wait, that the ship finally cast off, eased out of the docks, turned left at the mouth of the Mersey and butted its way south down the Irish Sea, throbbing along towards the equator and the sun and the blue.

PART TWO

Promise Fulfilled

EIGHT

To the Back of Beyond

First Cameroons Expedition 1947–1948

The ship broke down three more times, and in the Bay of Biscay the sea was so rough that Gerald and Yealland were thrown out of their bunks, along with all their kit. The weather hotted up by the time they reached the Canaries, and they watched entranced as the warm-water creatures of the ocean began to make their appearance around the ship, along with exotic insect stragglers – butterflies, dragonflies and a solitary orange ladybird – from the unseen African shore beyond the eastern horizon.

'We have seen a great number of Flying fish,' Gerald wrote to his mother. 'Porpoise and Dolphin have been playing round the ship, and yesterday we saw three Whales blowing about fifty feet off the ship. Also there have been a lot of Portuguese Man of War, a kind of jellyfish which puts up a small sail and goes whizzing about on the surface carried by the wind. These sails are vivid magenta in colour, and when there are several dotted about on the blue sea they look beautiful.'

What with the breakdowns and delays, the ship was still at sea, some forty miles off the Senegal coast, on Christmas Eve. The occasion was celebrated with bacchanalian fervour. First there was a huge dinner in the dining room, followed by lashings of whisky in the second officer's cabin, and then a carol-singing party in the smoking room. By this time Gerald was well into his first recorded binge. Though he was too far gone to remember anything himself next morning, Yealland duly noted it all down in his diary:

Such is the strength of the intoxicants on board that Gerry, who had formerly held the little holy man and his wife in considerable detestation, waxed more and more friendly towards him. They retired rather early, but when he came back to get a book he had left behind, Gerald seized him round the neck, stuffed a cigarette into his mouth, and speaking French with unheard-of fluency implored 'mon très cher ami' to have a drink. Just then the holy one's wife came in with her hair down and saved him from a fate worse than death, and on catching sight of her Gerry exclaimed: 'Voilà! La femme de moi!'

A few days later they finally reached their African landfall. For Gerald it was a moment of overwhelming magic:

> The ship nosed its way through the morning mist across a sea as smooth as silk. A faint and exciting smell came to us from the invisible shore, the smell of flowers, damp vegetation, palm oil, and a thousand other intoxicating scents drawn up from the earth by the rising sun, a pale, moist-looking nimbus of sun seen dimly through the mists. As it rose higher and higher, the heat of its rays loosened the hold the mist had on land and sea, and gradually the bay and the coastline came into view and gave me my first glimpse of Africa.

Ahead, across the glittering waters, he could see a scatter of jungly islands, and behind them the coastlands that rose in forested waves upwards to where Mount Cameroon loomed, 'dim and gigantic', in the early morning light. Across the islands flocks of grey parrots were making their way towards the forested shore, the air full of their clownish excited screams and whistles. Astern, in the glistening wake of the ship, Gerald saw a fish eagle swoop out of the dispersing mist, and two brown kites circling overhead, scavenging for scraps. And then he smelled that magic smell again – 'stronger, richer, intoxicating with its promise of deep forest, of lush reedy swamps, and wide magical rivers under a canopy of trees' – the smell of Africa. 'We landed,' he recalled, 'as in a dream.'

Years later, remembering that first landfall with aching nostalgia, he confided to a friend: 'It had such a powerful impact that I was drugged for hours, even days, afterwards. One glass of beer that morning and I was as high as an eagle. To sit there, drink a beer, watch a lizard, vivid orange and swimming-pool blue, just nodding his head on the balcony. It's there for ever in my mind, much more than reality, because it was alive and I was alive.'

For Gerald and his friend John Yealland every minute of those first few days in Africa – every sight, every sound, every face, every creature, every plant – was a source of wonder and delight. It was as if they had been born again – nothing was familiar, nothing expected. Hither and thither they went, ecstatic and bemused, like men in a mescaline trance.

'On the very first night,' Gerald recalled, 'we had dinner and drifted down to the little botanical gardens there. The British always had a habit of making botanical gardens, like country clubs, wherever they went. And with torches we walked down a tiny stream with all this lush undergrowth. And like a couple of schoolkids we picked up whatever we found, tree frogs, woodlice, centipedes, anything, carted it all back to the rest house in jars and boxes, and oohed and gooed over them all until three in the morning.'

From the little white rest house on top of a hill in the flower-filled little capital town of Victoria (population a meagre 3500), Gerald wrote to his mother in the first paroxysm of enthusiasm: 'The country around here is simply beautiful, and John and I go round gasping at the birds and flowers.' Wherever they turned they found a myriad of exotic creatures. On a palm nut plantation a little out of town they discovered giant millipedes – 'our first catch, six inches long and as thick as a sausage'. Down on the beach they were amazed to find a strange species of crab – 'purple in colour, with one huge claw and one small' – and a score of mud skippers, 'a small fish with a head like a hippo'. 'If everything is as plentiful,' Gerald wrote home, 'we should make a fortune in no time.'

Often they had to enlist the help of local Africans, communicating as best they could in pidgin English – a genuine *lingua franca* at which Gerald soon became highly adept. To his mother he described a typical encounter.

ME: Goodmorning. (Very British)
NATIVE: Goodmorning, sah. (Taking off filthy rag which is his hat)
ME: We look for small beef.*You have small beef here?
NATIVE: Sah?
ME: Small beef . . . SMALL BEEF.
NATIVE: Ah! Small beef, sah? Yes, we hab plenty, sah, plenty.
ME: (In Victorian tones) Where dis small beef, ay?
(Native now makes remark which I can't understand, and points)
ME: (Pretending to understand) Ah ah! Dis place far far?
NATIVE: No, sah, you walker walker for fibe minutes, sah.
ME: (With lordly wave of hand) Good, you show me.

And so the procession started: the two natives in front, John and I behind, feeling like a Hollywood film set. We marched like this for half a mile, and then we found the two natives arguing on the

* In pidgin all animals are called 'beef'. There are four kinds: 'small', 'big', 'bad' and 'bery bad' beef.

banks of a very fast river. I asked one of them how we were supposed to get across, and he said he would carry us. Thinking we would have to get used to this sort of thing, I uttered a short prayer and got on his back. How he got across I don't know: the water was up to his thighs, and the river bed was made up of these huge boulders. To my surprise he got me over safely and returned for John. I have never seen anything so funny – John clutching his topee, with one arm round the native's neck and a huge bag of specimen boxes slung on his back. When they reached the middle of the stream, the most difficult part, John started to laugh, and this started the native off. They both stood there, swaying in the middle of the stream, hooting with laughter, and I expected at any moment to see them fall into the water and all my valuable speci-mens floating down stream.

Emerging from the river adventure safe and sound and laden with 'small beef', but dripping with sweat and very hot, the Englishmen asked if there were any coconuts about – coconut milk being the only safe thing to drink in these parts.

We punched holes in the nuts and sat by the side of the road drinking. About half a mile down from us they were pruning the tall palms, and we could see the men high up in the trees, sitting in the grass rope seats, chopping the great fronds off. Each time one fell it made a loud swish, and then a big thonk as it hit the ground. The workers were singing to each other as they worked, and it was most attractive to listen to. They make up a short verse about anything that takes their fancy and each verse ends with a prolonged wail like: Eoooo Eoooo. When the D.O. came along in his car they sang: 'The D.O. is here in his car . . . eooooo eoooo.' Then there was a short pause, and another one would sing out: 'He is going to Bemanda to get milk . . . eoooo eoooo.' And so on. What with the birds singing, the crickets shouting, the swish of the falling fronds, and this curious wailing song echoing through the trees, it was a wonderful experience. John sat there with sweat dripping down his face, his topee tilted back, swigging at his coco-nut and ejaculating at intervals: 'Bloody marvellous, boy!'

Victoria was merely a curtain-raiser to the real show, and 'small beef' were small beer compared to the 'big, big beef' they hoped to find in the wild interior. Much of the first week was spent sorting themselves out and stocking up with supplies for the six months of adventures that lay ahead. Their immediate plan was to drive two hundred miles to the small up-country town of Mamfe, which would be their springboard to the wilder country of the primeval rainforest that stretched all around.

On Monday, 5 January 1948, they finally set off in a manner to which they were soon to become accustomed. For a start, the lorry turned up four hours late and turned out to be crowded with the driver's relatives, whom Gerald had to clear out, along with their household goods and livestock. The driver himself did not inspire much confidence, for as he was turning the lorry for loading he twice backed into the rest house wall and once into the hibiscus hedge. The expedition's baggage was tossed into the back with such wild abandon that Gerald wondered if any of it would arrive intact in Mamfe. 'I need not have worried,' he noted later. 'It turned out that only the most indispensable and irreplaceable things got broken.' The name of the lorry – 'The Godspeed' – was painted in large white letters above the windscreen. 'It was not until later,' Gerald was to write, 'that we discovered what a euphemism the name really was.'

So the great adventure began. Gerald's letters to Mother (never published before) provide a raw and spontaneous day-by-day account of its gradual unfolding.

> Eventually we were ready to start, and John and I got in the front, and sat there looking as regal as circumstances would let us. We whizzed out of Victoria and had got about five miles down the road, the lorry making a most impressive roaring noise, when there was a terrific gurk and the engine stopped. We got out of the lorry, and while the driver, with the rest of the staff, probed into the bowels of the engine, Pious (the steward) put cushions at the side of the road, poured out beer, and fanned the flies away from our recumbent forms. After half an hour everything was ready, and once again we set off, tearing madly along at about 15 m.p.h. Ten miles further on the damn thing broke down again, and the same process was repeated. Before we reached Kumba (the place where we had arranged to spend the night) we had broken down four times.
>
> About ten miles out of Victoria the palm nut plantations gave place to forest proper, and John and I just sat with our mouths open, in a sort of daze. You have no idea how beautiful it was: giant trees, hundreds of feet high, leaned over the road, each one festooned with tree ferns, long strands of grey moss, and lianas as thick as my body. On the solitary telegraph wire sat lots of kingfishers, each no bigger than a sparrow, orange and blue in colour.

In the trees flocks of hornbills were feeding, and on the rocks along the sides of the road there were lots of a very beautiful kind of lizard, with orange head, bright Prussian blue body and tail, and splashed with red and yellow and grass-green all over. They are unbelievably bright in the sun. Once there was a great shout from the back of the lorry and we pulled up quickly under the impression that the cook had fallen out and been killed. It turned out they had seen a Nile monitor (a lizard about three feet long – John thought nearer to four feet) by the side of the road. We all rushed back and spread out in a circle. We closed in on it and it made a dash at the driver, who, thinking that discretion was the better part of valour, ran like hell. The last we saw of it was a tail going into the bush.

The country is very hilly, and all thickly forested. Each hill we went up we had to put up with the frightful noise made by the driver with his gear box. Every time we came down the other side we had to cross a river in a deep ravine, spanned by what John calls a 'death trap' – four planks with a few rotten beams, no railings or anything pansy like that. After about the fourth we got quite used to them and we could open our eyes a bit.

At around five o'clock, much to their surprise, they reached Kumba, where they stayed the night at the house of the local medic – 'a charming fat little Scotsman and a keen ornithologist' – who had assembled a prodigious collection of bird skins. At dawn they were off again for another day of death traps and breakdowns, arriving in the late afternoon at a place called Bakebe, where they were to stay for three days till the rest house at Mamfe became free.

It was wonderful at Bakebe because we were right in the heart of the forest. I engaged a hunter the next day, and two boys, and armed with a shotgun sallied into the jungle, à la Frank Buck. In the depths of the forest itself there is a sort of green twilight, with huge termite nests, each built like a mushroom, and an extraordinary white butterfly which flits among the trees like a whisp of white lace. In the sunny clearings there were many other sorts of insect life, including some black ants an inch and a half long. Unfortunately they discovered me before I saw them, and it was very painful. I was dancing around while the hunters were plucking the ants off, all saying 'Sorry Sah' loudly, as though they had put them there. When you trip over a root you hear about three voices behind you saying 'Sorry Sah.' We saw several monkeys feeding in the trees, and tracks of Duikers, small rats, and Leopard. Then we discovered the tracks of a Red River hog and followed them up. We walked for about four miles and stumbled right into a herd of them. One baby broke only about twenty feet from me.

The collecting business now began to gather momentum. The next day Gerald went back into the forest, and among other things caught a creature that in the fullness of time and in the most indirect way was to prove pivotal to his future career. This was the hairy frog – 'a large frog,' he explained in his letter home, 'with curious filaments like hairs on its legs and the sides of its body.' But most of the growing list of animal acquisitions were caught or donated by others. The United Africa Company agent at Bakebe presented his pet dog-faced baboon, the doctor at Kumba sent two baby giant kingfishers, a DO who lived a hundred miles out in the sticks proposed giving them his three-year-old chimpanzee, a local boy brought in 'a lovely rat with red fur and a yellow tummy', and a man from a nearby village turned up dragging along a baby drill (today one of the most endangered monkey species in Africa) on a bit of string.

The Drill is the sweetest little thing, standing about a foot high. He is very young, and the pink patches on his behind only the size of a shilling. He was very wild the first day, but is quite tame now, and when I return from a trip into the forest he comes running to meet me, uttering loud screams, and climbs up my leg and then wraps his arms round my waist and clings there making little crooning noises. I am sure I shall not want to part with him when the time comes.

There is no doubt that Gerald loved the country he had come to. He was held in thrall by the stillness and grandeur of the primeval forest, and adored the birds he saw flying free and the animals running wild no less than the curious assortment of creatures that came into his care. But it is clear from his letters and field notes that the Gerald Durrell of up-country Cameroons in 1948 was not yet the Gerald Durrell the world was to come to know in later years; and in one important respect the unreformed twenty-three-year-old might have dumbfounded his future fans. The young man of 1948, though he dearly loved animals, was fully prepared to slaughter them if there was a good enough reason to do so. He had brought to the Cameroons a rifle and a shotgun he had borrowed from his brother Leslie, and he knew how to use these weapons and was prepared to do so. Partly this was standard practice. No self-respecting expedition to the African interior in those days would have dreamed of setting off without guns of some sort – to shoot game to supplement their rations and feed the carnivores they collected. But the young Gerald Durrell sometimes succumbed to the hunting instinct in a way that would have dismayed the man of later years.

Only a day or two after his arrival at Bakebe, for example, he had tried to shoot a red river hog, thinking it would make good eating (forgetting the £150 – some £3000 in today's money – he could get for a live specimen back in England). On 7 January, his twenty-third birthday, he shot a black kite that had been stealing chickens, spectacularly blasting the bird out of the air with his shotgun in the middle of a juju dance in the village street, winning uproarious acclaim from the populace. 'I was swept down the main street by the mob,' he recorded, 'surrounded by yelling and capering juju dancers. I presented the corpse to the chief, and there was much bowing and exchange of compliments. I felt like a scene out of a Tarzan film and departed secure in the knowledge that the White Man's Prestige had been upheld.'

On Saturday, 10 January, the expedition prepared to set off for Mamfe at last. Its troubled procession north now turned from penance to pantomime, as Gerald reported:

The morning we moved from Bakebe to Mamfe was the funniest thing to date. The scene was indescribable. Our stuff was piled six feet high, boxes full of birds, rats, insects and frogs, and squatting about were Pious the steward, Fillup the cook, Emanuel, Daniel and Edward, the hunters, the carpenter and his wife and child, the hunter's wife and child, the chief's wife and the U.A.C. man's three children, all hoping for a lift to Mamfe, plus about fifty relatives who had come to see them off. It was now twelve and the lorry should have been there at eight and by this time I was nearly mental. At last the lorry arrived, and thank God it was a large one – the driver had brought six relatives along for the joy ride. How we got everything on to the lorry I shall never know. There were about sixty people in a solid wedge around the back of the lorry, all shouting at once and endeavouring to climb on, the air full of whirling bundles full of sweet potatoes, yams and bananas. I was overwhelmed by a fighting horde of natives, my feet were trodden on, also my hand. When they had all piled on I remounted the lorry, and pointing to the crates of birds and animals explained that if one was dead or injured when we reached Mamfe they would all go before the D.O. After that they sat like mice, and must have been damn stiff when we reached Mamfe.

Mamfe was situated at the highest navigable point of the Cross River, on the edge of a vast swathe of uninhabited country – a pestilential place where malaria was rife and leprosy common. Gerald and John spent a little over a week there, often dining with the local DO, a helpful Englishman by the name of Robin, whose house was situated on a steep hill four hundred feet above the river. Gerald was profoundly enchanted by this spot, deep in the untamed heart of Africa, far, far from anywhere, and yet surrounded by all the comforts of privilege.

The house overlooks the place where two rivers meet. It forms a wide stretch of water like a lake. On each side is the jungle, and in the centre a dazzling white sandbar. Sitting on the terrace in the evening, you can see a herd of five hippo which live here, swimming about. Then, when it grows dark, you can hear them blowing and snorting and roaring below you. The two rivers flow through steep rocky gorges, and are spanned by so-called suspension bridges. The termites have had a wonderful time with these for the past twenty years, and the planks rattle and groan when you walk over them, a hundred and twenty feet above rocks and water. Down below you can see kingfishers and red and blue swallows nesting, and in the trees you can see monkeys in the evening.

There were few pleasures and interests to divert the scattering of European expatriates who lived in this land other than those which age-old Africa could provide. There were no hotels, no restaurants, no shops, no cinemas, no libraries, next to no electricity and – Gerald made a particular note of this – next to no white girls. By way of compensation however, the stranded Brits could avail themselves of a lifestyle little changed since the high noon of Empire. Gerald took to this sybaritic life like a duck to water, and could not resist writing home to let his family know of the contrast with the austerity Britain he had left only a few weeks ago.

Apart from the hard work we have to do with the animals, our lives are like those of the upper-classes in pre-war Britain: real luxury. Think of being able to change your shirt five times a day if you want to. Writing this letter I am taking half an hour off: I am sitting in a deck chair, a glass of beer at my elbow, and Pious the Steward is standing behind my chair ready to refill my glass when it is empty and give me another fag when I have finished the one I am smoking. Pious is only sixteen, but he is simply wonderful. It's he that has got the whole rest house in order, beds up, table laid for a meal, bath water ready, and so on. Now the table is laid for lunch and a fragrant smell is wafted towards me – the cooking is very fine. A chicken costs three shillings in a place like this, bananas are a penny a hand (about twelve). We are rationed to four bottles of whiskey a month, but I get it all as John does not like it. We smoke cigars (5/- for 50) at dinner in the evening. Our staff now consists of two cooks, two stewards and a washboy – and the carpenter whom we pay two shillings a day. In fact it is collecting in luxury.

It is clear from Gerald's frank, unguarded letters to his mother that within a very short time of setting foot in Africa he had adapted both to the country and to the lifestyle as to the manner born. This was his first experience of the world outside Europe (early infancy apart), and it was essentially a colonial experience, and an old-fashioned one at that. By virtue of his race and nationality he had automatically joined an élite caste – that of the British imperium – from the moment he arrived in the Cameroons. Indeed, in his attitude to the African underclass and his perception of his own status and authority among them, he quickly became more colonial than the colonials, a kind of super DO, peerless and fearless in his dealings with both man and beast. From time to time in his letters he even refers to himself, not altogether jokingly, as 'Empire Builder', 'Sanders of the River' and 'the Great White Master'.

Having cast himself in this imperious role, the accounts he wrote home of his behaviour on trek in the Cameroons sometimes make embarrassing reading. One especially trying morning in Mamfe, for example, he was told a hunter had just brought in a particularly rare bird to sell.

I found the hunter sitting down on the ground, hat on the back of his head, cigarette in his mouth, explaining to the crowd how clever he had been to capture this creature. He said good morning without bothering to get up, remove his hat, or take the cigarette out of his mouth. By this time I was quite angry with everyone and every-thing. 'Get up, take your hat off, take that thing out of your mouth and then say good morning properly!' I snarled in my best Sanders of the River voice. He obeyed like a naughty schoolboy.

Fifty years on, this sort of thing can make uncomfortable reading. Yet in the context of the time and place it was a normal, even a prescribed, adaptation to the colonial ambience – the 'remember you're British' syndrome. For a tyro colonial boy like Gerald there was no other model – apart from 'going native' – and any departure from the unwritten rules of the imperial game would have been looked on as letting the side down.

What was different in Gerald's case was the impact of instant privilege and power on his own personality. He was a charismatic young man of great self-assurance and persuasiveness, but as with many young men, his self-confidence could turn into arrogance, his egotism into selfishness, and his ebullience into boorishness. In a word, his was a big personality, full of charm, leavened by a tremendous sense of comedy and fun, but veering to temper and contempt when frustrated, and tending to dominance when given his head. In the polite, inhibited middle-class society of the Home Counties England of the forties such an original and spirited, not to say eccentric, personality was in large measure restrained by the mores of his *milieu*. But out here in Africa, a fully-paid-up member of the white man's club, let loose in the dark interior, Gerald blossomed. It was as if, here in the depths of the rainforest, a genie had popped out of a bottle. If it was not always a totally admirable genie, it was a genie nonetheless; and in the course of time, a Gerald Durrell broadly recognisable as the persona of his maturer future would step tentatively on to the stage, and the overpowering ego of his youth would be replaced by the wisdom and compassion of the man who would take on some of the cares and responsibilities of the wider world beyond.

The two Englishmen now decided to split up: John Yealland to establish a main base at Bakebe, which he reckoned would be a good place for birds; Gerald to set up a subsidiary camp at Eshobi, a tiny village on the edge of a huge swathe of equatorial forest that stretched hundreds of miles northwards to the mountains where the gorilla had its stronghold – virgin territory for collecting animals and reptiles.

On Wednesday, 18 January 1948, Gerald's party left the comforts of Mamfe for the dubious pleasures of Eshobi. In the environs of this distant village, from all reports, there was plenty of 'stuff', as Gerald and John termed the animals they sought – but not much else. As there was no motorable track, the party had to travel on foot, with carriers to shoulder the stores in time-hallowed style. It was to prove an even more vexing departure than normal, for driver ants had caused havoc in the night, and a mêlée of Africans swarmed about the compound.

In the middle of all this my ten carriers arrived for their loads. They were such a band of cut-throats that John said I would be eaten three miles out of Mamfe. I thought that I had better have my hair cut before plunging into the unknown, so hot on the heels of the carriers came the village barber.

The scene in the compound beggars description. There was the staff leaping about trying to get the ants out of the stores, the carriers leaping about fighting as to who should have the smallest load, John leaping about imploring someone to get fish for his kingfishers, and in the middle of all this there sat I enthroned on a rickety chair, snarling at the barber and stamping my feet to keep the ants from crawling up . . .

At last the party was ready to start. The loads were lifted on to the heads of the carriers, the staff shuffled into Indian file, and at a word from Gerald the column lurched off down the road and into the forest in the direction of Eshobi. Clinging to Gerald's waist were two baby baboons, and in his hand a baby crocodile wrapped in a blanket. 'My ten evil-looking carriers marched ahead with the loads,' he wrote, 'and on either side of me, guard of honour, marched Pious and the cook, while behind marched my personal smallboy, Dan, carrying my money-bag and field-glasses. We passed over two suspension bridges in great style, looking like Stanley looking for Livingstone.' John Yealland accompanied them as far as the rusting suspension bridge that spanned the Cross River. At the other side of the bridge Gerald looked back and waved to his companion, then turned and was swallowed up by the forest.

He was to describe the track to Eshobi as 'the worst bush path I know' – convoluting course, one-in-three gradient, six-inch width, six-mile length, but feeling like sixty. He wrote in a letter home:

Sometimes it's there and sometimes it isn't. You spend most of your time leaping up huge boulders about six foot high, crawling under or over fallen trees, and tripping over creepers. The baby baboons were awfully good; they clung on by themselves without my having to hold on to them, occasionally making little wailing noises to show me they were still there. After the first hour they went to sleep, and then I had to put my hand under their bottoms or they would have fallen off. When we stopped for a rest and a drink of beer, Amos [the baby drill] seized the chance to do a wee-wee all over me, but as I was already soaked in sweat it didn't matter much. Just before we reached the village we came to a stream, which had the usual supply of dangerous stepping stones. I reached the last one with a cry of triumph and leapt on to the bank. Here I found I had landed on a slide of clay, and my feet shot up and I fell heavily into about two foot of dirty water. The baboons uttered wild cries of fright and scrambled up on to my head. I was helped out, dripping, by Pious and the cook in a perfect gale of 'Sorry Sah's', and so we reached the village at last.

Gerald was now at the sharp end of the bushwhacking life. He reached Eshobi drenched in sweat, tired, thirsty and querulous. A few days ago he had sent a government messenger ahead to make prior arrangements and prepare a base camp. Gerald took one look at the camp site and (as he informed Mother) 'nearly fainted'. This was no Hollywood-style safari encampment, but a shanty pitched on a midden that had once been a banana patch. He rounded on the messenger and ordered him to summon labour from the village at once to level the site and make a proper camp.

'The labour brigade turned up,' he wrote to Mother, 'and appeared to consist entirely of quite the most ugly set of old women I had ever seen. They were clad only in dirty bits of cloth round their waists, and all were smoking short black pipes.' After half an hour he decided to retire to the village for some beer. 'Pious made the owner of the only chair and table in the place produce them, somewhat reluctantly, and I was enthroned in state under the only tree in the middle of the village street.'

In Eshobi Gerald came face to face with the reality of tribal life out in the bush for the first time – the destitution, deprivation and sickness. 'All around me stood the population in a solid wedge, giving a wonderful display of disease ranging from yaws to leprosy. Even little kids of four and five were covered from head to foot with the huge sores, all mattering and fly-covered, of yaws. One female had the entire heel of one foot eaten away. Another delightful man had no nose and half his fingers missing.' Gerald drank his beer with an effort and returned to the camp site, dismayed and a little chastened, hardly guessing that before many weeks were out he too would be among the diseased and ailing of this unhealthy place.

At the camp the ground had now been cleared, a kitchen built, the tent erected more or less upright. A start had been made on a house for the staff and another – the 'Beef House' – for the animals. The village chief paid a courtesy visit, the staff settled down to their bush routine, and Gerald's first real stint as an animal collector in the wilds began.

It did not begin very well. During the first night a great thunderstorm broke over Eshobi, the rain fell in torrents, the tent leaked, and by morning everything was sodden – bed, books, Gerald, everything. He noted in his diary for 22 January:

Woke up wet and cold after a filthy night and drank some neat whiskey with my tea. Found after this that death was not so near, so got up and shaved. The croc bite on my finger has gone septic, so must do something about it. In the middle of the morning I found Pious sick. He had fever, though his pulse was normal. Having no medicines at all I dosed him with whiskey and aspirin, covered him with all the blankets I could get hold of and left him to sweat. By three o'clock he was OK again and after another shot of whiskey resumed work. Must get the birds out of the beef box, as it is most unsuitable for them. If John could see them he'd have a fit, dear old ostrich.

Almost immediately the animals started pouring in. He sent Mother a list of his acquisitions:

Four Bush-tailed Porcupine (five shillings each); one Mongoose (two shillings); one Fruit Bat (one shilling); four baby Crocodiles (five bob each – the longest is four foot long); two Pangolin (five bob each); nine Tortoises (one shilling each); ten rats for two shillings (these are green with bright rufous bottoms and noses); one full-grown Yellow Baboon for two quid; and one Red-eared Monkey for two bob.

It was difficult for even Gerald Durrell to relate to some of these species, but one or two particularly took his fancy, none more than the yellow baboon and the red-eared monkey.

The Yellow Baboon (whom I have called George) was brought to me all the way from the French Congo (some five hundred miles away). You see how the news spreads – they even know in the French Congo that I am buying animals. He stands about two feet high and is as tame as a kitten. When you tickle him under the armpits he lies on his back and screeches with laughter. The staff were very afraid of him at first, but now they love him and he spends most of his time wreaking havoc in the kitchen. If dinner is late it is always due to George having upset the soup or something.

The Red-eared Monkey is simply sweet. Its back is brindled green, its legs and arms lovely slate grey, white cheeks, red ear tufts and a red tail about two feet long. Bright red. It has the largest eyes I have ever seen in a monkey, light brown. It makes a delightful twittering noise like a bird. Its fingers are long and boney like an old man's and it looks so sweet when you give it a handful of grasshoppers, it sits there cramming its mouth, twittering, and examining its fingers carefully to make sure it hasn't missed any.

Before long the impact of Gerald's collecting expedition on the impoverished economy of the locality had turned into something like an oil strike, relatively speaking. The inhabitants of the area would come in at all times of day and night from miles around, with a range of creatures so motley and diverse that any zoologist would have been seriously challenged to identify half of them. One of the joys of the business was that it was impossible to know what kind of animal would turn up next – large or small, rare or common, dangerous or docile.

At two o'clock one night, for example, Gerald was woken by a trembling watchnight (the local term for a night watchman) who informed him that a man was on his way with a large python. Gerald got out of bed expecting to see some backwoodsman with a snake about two feet long. 'Instead of which,' he recorded, 'a crowd, as always, roared into the compound with hurricane lamps and in their midst were four carriers on whose shoulders was an enormous wicker basket about six foot long. They dumped the thing outside my tent and I found it contained a twelve foot python. Next came the jolly task of getting the bloody thing out of the basket and into the box.' When it proved impossible to shake the snake out, Gerald tried to pull it out by the tail, and when that failed he grabbed it by the head and pulled. When this didn't work either, he had no alternative but to cut the basket clean away and shake like mad. 'He went into the box with an angry hiss and a bump, and I went into the tent and had a quick whiskey, as it had all been rather nerve-wracking. I am now Number One Juju Man in the village, because I touched the head and tail of the python and still remain alive.'

Most of the animals brought into camp were of the commoner varieties. To obtain the rarer species Gerald had to go out and find them himself. And so he entered the mysterious depths of the rainforest for the first time, and was bewildered and enchanted and for ever won over by the sights and the sounds and the scents of this almost holy wilderness.

'The leafmould alone,' he was to write of his first day in the forest,

contained hundreds of insects I had never seen or heard of before. Roll over any rotting log and I found a world as bizarre as anything dreamed up by science fiction. Each hollow tree was an apartment block containing anything from snakes to bats, from owls to flying mice. Every forest stream was an orchestra of frogs, a ballet of tiny fish, and from the canopy above came a constant rain of fruit, twigs and pirouetting blossoms thrown down by the great army of creatures – mammals, birds, reptiles and insects – that inhabit this high, sunlit, flower-scented realm. I did not know where to look next. Every leaf, flower, liana, every insect, fish, frog or bird was a lifetime's study in itself, and I knew that there was another hidden, secretive army of creatures that would emerge at night to take over. As any naturalist knows, there is nothing like a rainforest for replacing arrogance with awe.

Gerald felt his own sense of life echoing back to him from the surrounding jungle. 'In the Cameroons I was walking in a cathedral,' he recalled, 'staring endlessly upwards, only just able to glimpse the frescoes on the ceiling. That was rainforest for me. As a naturalist you have no idea, until you've experienced the tropical forest, how complex, astonishing and differentiated it is. When I first read Darwin's outpourings in *The Voyage of the Beagle* I thought they were poetic licence – only to discover, in Africa, that he was grossly understating it.'

Hunting in this primordial world was an arduous and occasionally perilous task at which Gerald rapidly became highly expert. Not that he ever felt afraid during these forays. In pursuit of the most sought-after prizes, he clearly believed that the ends justified the means.

I have been doing something very illegal, hunting at night with lights. The lights are carbon-burning ones like the miners use. You wear them on your forehead and with the terrific beam they throw out you can see the animals' eyes reflected, and it dazzles them so that you can get close enough to catch them. I have been going out every other night with seven hunters, combing the forest for a very rare Lemur called an angwantibo. If I can get one my stock with London Zoo will rocket to heaven. So far no luck.

The other night we went out and had the best night yet. We walked for miles without seeing a thing, and then we came to a river. This was not very wide, but fast running, and the bed was composed of slabs of grey sandstone. The water had worn away the stone into channels, so you got a sort of canal about three feet wide and two feet deep. The sides were choked with vegetation, mostly ferns. I had only two hunters with me. These two are really very funny. Elias is short and fat, with a face like an ex-boxer and a funny waddling walk. His taste runs to highly coloured sarongs with blue and orange flowers plastered all over them. The other is called Andrai,* and he is tall and willowy, with an extraordinary face and very long fingers. He has a wonderful swaying walk, uses

---

* Spelt 'Andraia' in Gerald's later book. The correct spelling is 'Andreas', and the man is still alive.

his hands like a Greek, and wears sarongs of pale pastel shades. The other member of our Band of Hope was a boy whose job it was to carry all the nets and bags and was as near as makes no matter to being a half-wit.

We waded up miles of these channels, Elias first, me next, followed by Andrai and the half-wit, who made as much noise as a herd of frightened elephants. Elias said that we might see a crocodile, and had cut me a forked stick to deal with such an eventuality should it arise. I thought the possibility was very remote, so I dropped the stick when no one was looking, and no sooner had I done this than Elias came to a sudden standstill, and groped behind me, imploring me to hand him the stick. I replied that I had lost it, and he uttered a cry of pain, drew his machete and crept forward. I strained my eyes to see what it was he was trying to catch. Suddenly I saw it, something dark which glinted in the light, the same shape and size as a baby croc. Elias made a dive at it with his knife, but it wiggled through his legs and swam at great speed down the channel towards me. I made a grab, missed and fell into the water, yelling to Andrai that it was coming. Andrai leapt into the fray and was neatly tripped by the bagboy. I saw the thing swim out of the narrow channel into a broad one. Here, I thought, we had lost it for ever. However, the bagboy had got his half wit working and had noted the stone under which it had gone to ground.

We all rushed down there, making a tidal wave of water and foam, and clustered round the rock. Andrai insinuated a long arm into the hole and then withdrew it again with a shrill cry of anguish, his forefinger dripping blood.

'This beef can bite man,' explained Elias, with the proud air of having made a discovery.

Andrai was at last persuaded to put his hand back inside the hole after some argument and cries of 'Go on!' and 'Cowardy-cowardy-custard!' in the local dialect. He lay on his tummy in about six inches of water, his arm in the bowels of the earth, explaining to everyone how very brave he was to do this. There was a short silence, broken only by grunts from Andrai as he tried to reach the beef. Then he let out a yell of triumph and stood up holding the thing by the tail. When I saw it I nearly fainted, because instead of the baby croc I expected he was holding a Giant Water Shrew – one of the rarest animals in the whole of West Africa.

The Water Shrew soon got tired of hanging by its tail, so turned and climbed up its own body and buried its teeth in Andrai's thumb. He leapt about three feet in the air, and let out an ear-piercing scream of pain.

'OW ... OW ... OW!' he screeched. 'Oh, Elias, Elias, get it off. OW ... MY JESUSCRI ... it done kill me ... OW OW OW ... Elias, quickly ...'

Elias and I struggled with the animal, but I was laughing so much I was not much use. At last we got it off and pushed it wiggling and hissing into the bag. Andrai had to rest on the bank, moaning softy and tut-tutting over the mud on his pale mauve sarong. When he was quite sure he was not going to die we moved on, and further down the river we caught two crocs, so altogether it was a very good night.

There was no denying the courage, perseverance and expertise demonstrated by Gerald – and by his African companions, with whom he now began to relate more closely and sympathetically – in such difficult and challenging circumstances. It was as though he had been cut out for this unusual task from the cradle. His energy and enthusiasm were inexhaustible, his sense of humour rarely flagged, he delighted in the adventure and sheer unpredictability of it all, never knowing what the next hour would bring. Night after night and day after day he marched off into the forest, rarely emerging empty-handed. And as his collection of birds and animals grew, so did the workload of looking after them. He wrote to his mother:

The day goes something like this. Six o'clock, Pious appears in the tent, beaming, with tea. After three cups I feel I might live, so go down in my dressing gown to feed the birds and see what has escaped or died during the night. By the time I have done this my hot water is ready and I wash. After this I dash into my clothes and take the monkeys out of their sleeping boxes and tie them up to their poles. By this time my breakfast is ready: pawpaw, two eggs, toast, coffee. I have this and a fag and then start the real work of the day.

First, there are about four little boys with cages of birds to look at. I pick out the worthwhile ones to keep for John and pick out the ones that are almost dead to feed to the animals that eat meat. After this I repair to the Beef House, where Dan, my ten-year-old assistant, is awaiting orders. I clean out the birds, about ten cages, while he washes out the food and water dishes and refills them.

Then we start on the animals. The Mongoose has to be given a dead bird to chew so that I can get my hand inside to clean him out without getting bitten. Then the three cages of Brush-tailed Porcupine. Of these I have one full-grown pair which stink to high heaven, one full-grown female, and one tiny baby. The latter is very sweet and in the evening goes all skittish, leaping and gambolling like a rabbit. When he is frightened he stamps his feet and rattles his spines like knitting needles. Then it's the turn of the Fruit Bats. Eating pawpaw and bananas all night their cage is always in the most frightful stinking mess. Then the monkeys have to be fed, and while this is going on you can't hear yourself think.

Then come the reptiles. The chameleons have to be sprayed with water and given grasshoppers. The tortoises have to have fruit and greenstuff. And the crocs have to be washed (very difficult, this).

Then it's lunch-time: soup, chicken with sweet potatoes and green pawpaw, fresh fruit, coffee, cigar. The hardship of collecting! After this, if I have been out all the previous night hunting, I sleep until tea-time; or I plunge into the forest with the hunters. After tea we start all over again: porcupine food, bat food, rat food, monkey milk, mongoose meat, water, etc. etc. I retire about seven, feeling shattered, to my bath, taken in the open before a group of fascinated villagers. Then dinner: duck or deer or porcupine meat, peas, potatoes, sweet, coffee, cigar. Three quick whiskeys, a short stroll round to see everything is alright, and so to bed.

There is so much to tell you about that I could sit down and write ten thousand words if I had time. How a crowd of tiny toddlers appears each day clutching tins, bottles and gourds full of grasshoppers. How a villager tried to strangle his wife down by the river and how the staff and I had to rush down, lay the man out and throw the mother-in-law into the river.

Gerald had now been in Eshobi for many weeks, and the animal collection had grown to such an extent that the Beef House was virtually full. Gerald had learnt the ways of the forest and its wild creatures – and of the Africans among whom he was living. His affection and respect for them – poor people, but brave, big-hearted, loyal and talented in many different ways – had grown, as had theirs for him. Though he was still the 'Master', he no longer felt as alien and insecure as he had when he first arrived, and he no longer insisted on the deference he had once thought befitted his status. Indeed, Sanders of the River was even showing signs of going native. 'Sometimes in the evenings,' he told Mother, 'I would go and sit in the kitchen with the staff and discuss such thrilling topics as "Home Rule for the Cameroons" and "Did God Make the World in Seven Days?"' His departure, when it came, was a matter of some emotion on both sides.

When we were ready to leave Eshobi the village threw a dance in my honour and I was escorted to the main square by the staff and all the village elders and enthroned in state in the front row. Everyone had on their best clothes, ranging from cheap print dresses to shorts made out of old flour bags. Elias, my hunter, was the M.C., clad in a green shirt and pinstripe trousers – God knows where he got them. He had an enormous watch-chain with a huge whistle on it, which he blew loudly to restore order. They do the most curious dances, which are a mixture of nearly every known dance, with the barn dance predominating. Elias, wagging his bottom in the centre, roared the instructions to the dancers: 'ADvance!! . . . right turn . . . meet and waltz . . . let we set . . . all move . . . back we set again . . . ADvance . . . right turn . . . meet and waltz . . . conduct for yourself . . . etc. etc.' When the dance was over the chief made a speech to me. It was really rather funny, because he stood in the centre of the square and so the poor boy who acted as interpreter had to keep running about twenty yards to tell me what he was saying and then run back to hear the next sentence. The speech went something like this:

'People of Eshobi! You know why we are here tonight . . . to say goodbye to the Master who has been with us so long. Never in the whole history of Eshobi have we had such a Master . . . money has flowed as freely from him as water in the river-bed. Those who had the power went to bush and caught beef, for which they were paid handsomely. Those who were weak, the women and children, could obtain money and salt by bringing white ants and grasshoppers. We, the elders of the village, would like the Master to settle here. We would give him land and build him a fine house. We can only hope that he tells all the people in his country how we, the people of Eshobi, tried to help him, and to hope that on his next tour he will come back here and stay even longer.'

This was followed by loud and prolonged cheers, under cover of which the interpreter fainted into the arms of a friend. Then the band, consisting of three flutes and four drums and a triangle, struck up a red-hot version of 'God Save the King', and the party broke up.

So, very nearly, did Gerald himself. By now he was in a fairly exhausted condition. He had given his all in an unhealthy and enormously demanding environment. He had been bitten and stabbed by an extraordinary variety of fangs, spines, teeth, beaks, probosces, claws and jaws. He had had jiggers in his toes, ants in his pants, lice in his hair, bugs in his bed, and rats in his tent. He had reckoned on staying up all night packing, so as to be able to leave Eshobi before dawn and get to Mamfe around ten, before the sun got too hot for the animals. But after supper he began to feel very out of sorts, and by nine o'clock he was staggering about as though he was drunk. By ten he could barely walk, and had to be carried out to the latrine by Pious and George, the washboy. He collapsed on his bed, leaving it to the staff to pack up camp. Every five minutes Pious would creep in and peer down at him, making a solicitous 'tch tch' noise. Once George came in and tried to cheer him up, telling him that if he died they would never be able to find another Master like him.

'This was the beginning of the best bout of sandfly fever I've had to date,' Gerald wrote reassuringly to Mother. 'It's bloody awful: it doesn't kill you, or harm you in any way, but while you've got it you feel quite sure you're going to die. You walk as though you are dead drunk, and everything further away than ten feet is blurred and out of focus. You sweat like Hell and your head feels about four times normal size.'

In this condition Gerald now faced the prospect of a five-hour trek through the bush under the blazing equatorial sun. Leaning on the faithful Pious, and tap-tapping along with the aid of a stick, the ailing young white man shuffled along behind a column of sixty black carriers, half of them women. At the first small river he came to he had to be carried across by an elder who had come along to say goodbye. 'Nearly I cried when I see you carried,' Pious told him. 'I make sure you going to die then.' The track steepened after that, running up a hill at a gradient of one and three, and Gerald had to be half-dragged and carried up by Pious. The main column marched on till it was out of sight. 'Every two hundred yards we would stop for five minutes,' Gerald recalled, 'while I sank down on the path and sweated like a hero in a film and Pious fanned me with a hat.'

One way or another, Gerald got to Mamfe by half-past ten, and by two he was eating lunch with John Yealland at Bakebe. The reunion was heartfelt. Gerald had formed a high opinion of John's qualities as an ornithologist and a man, relishing his slow drawl and dry humour, his wisdom and kindness. It was a pleasure to be with a fellow-countryman again, to speak plain English, swap the news of the last few months, and inspect each other's impressive collections of birds and animals.

After three days' rest at Bakebe, Gerald began to feel much better, only suffering from the disappointment of not having got an angwantibo. This disappointment was to be short-lived. One day, not long after his return to Bakebe, Gerald set off for a reconnaissance of the nearby mountain N'da Ali, which had almost sheer sides thickly covered with forest. Gerald's aim was to find a camp site and to spend ten days or so trying to catch some of the large numbers of chimpanzees reputed to live there. He wrote home:

> I set off early one morning on a borrowed bike, a small boy on the crossbar with a bag of beer and other nourishment, to meet the hunter who was going to lead me up. We had gone about four miles, and I was just wondering if my legs were going to hold out, when in the distance I saw a man marching along with a bag made out of palm leaves in his hand. Thinking it was yet another Pouched Rat or Brush-tailed Porcupine, I dismounted and waited for him. When he got near I saw to my surprise that he was one of my ex-hunters from Eshobi. When he got to within hailing distance I asked him what he had got, and he replied that it was small beef. I regret to say that on peering into the basket the only sound I could produce was a sort of strangled 'Arrrrr . . .' Then I loaded the hunter with my gear, threw the boy off the crossbar, and hanging the Angwantibo round my neck fled frantically back home again.

Gerald had obtained his first angwantibo in the nick of time, for shortly afterwards there came word from England – a tip-off from his Whipsnade friend Ken Smith – that the legendary collector Cecil Webb of the London Zoo had set sail for the Cameroons with the express intention of catching angwantibo. A veteran of expeditions all over the world, Webb regarded Durrell and Yealland as novices and upstarts. For their part, they saw him as an irritating rival who was over the hill.

Eventually, Webb caught up with them. 'He is a huge, lanky man (six foot six, I believe),' Gerald reported to Mother, 'with a protruding jaw and faded blue eyes. We found him clad in faded blue jeans and an enormous sort of straw sun-bonnet which made me want to giggle. He asked, with a careless air that almost strangled him, if we had still got the Angwantibo, to which we replied that it was thriving. I am going up to Bemenda in a few days time and will pass through Mamfe, where he is now. I shall then take great pleasure in telling him that we have now got three (3) Angwantibo!!!!!!!!'

Webb did not go away empty-handed, however, for Gerald was duty bound to hand over to him for delivery to London Zoo the most remarkable animal in his collection – Cholmondeley (pronounced Chumley) the chimpanzee. Gerald had acquired Cholmondeley from a District Officer who had asked him if he could find a home for a chimp at London Zoo. Gerald had agreed, imagining that the creature would be about a year old and around eighteen inches high. He was amazed when a lorry arrived with a large crate in the back containing a full-grown chimpanzee of eight or nine years of age, with huge arms, a bald head, a massive, hairy chest that measured at least twice the size of Gerald's, and bad tooth growth that made him look like an unsuccessful prize-fighter.

> I opened the crate with some trepidation. Cholmondeley gave a little hoot of pleasure, gathered up the long chain which was attached to a collar round his neck, hung the loops daintily over his arm, and stepped down. Here he paused briefly to shake my hand in the most regal and dignified manner before walking into the house as if he owned it. He gazed around the living room of our humble grass hut with the air of a middle-European monarch inspecting a hotel bedroom suspected of containing bed bugs. Then, apparently satisfied, he ambled over to the table, drew out a chair and sat down, crossing his legs and staring at me expectantly.

We stared at each other for a bit, and then I got out my cigarettes. Immediately Cholmondeley became animated. It was quite obvious that after his long journey he wanted a cigarette. I handed him the packet, and he removed a cigarette, carefully put it in his mouth, and then replaced the packet on the table. I handed him a box of matches, thinking this might possibly fool him, but he slid the box open, took out a match, lit the cigarette, and threw the matches back on the table. He crossed his legs again and lay back in his chair inhaling thankfully and blowing great clouds of smoke out of his nose.

> Cholmondeley had other predilections. Hot, sweet tea was one. He would drink it out of a battered mug the size of a tankard, balancing it on his nose to drain the last dregs of syrupy sugar at the bottom. Then he would either hold out the mug for more or hurl it as far away as he could. He had also developed a fondness for beer, though Gerald only proffered it to him once, when he drank a whole bottle very quickly, with much lip-smacking and delight, till he was covered in froth and began to turn somersaults. After that he was given nothing stronger than lemonade or tea. Gerald parted with this extraordinary character with much regret, though he was destined to meet up with him again soon enough.

At last, in July, the time came to wind down operations and pack up the expedition. The rains were beginning, and Gerald had run out of money. He had spent heavily on stores, staff and accommodation, but especially on the birds, animals and reptiles which made up his huge collection. The situation was dire enough for him to swallow his pride and telegraph home for a loan, receiving by return the sum of £250 (more than £5000 in today's money) from Leslie's girlfriend Doris, the off-licence manageress.

The remaining camp stores were sold off, as John Yealland recorded in his diary:

> Gerald started to sell up the home this evening and did a brisk trade with his topee and umbrella and my oilskin, along with two sacks of maize, half a sack of coconuts, crockery, pots and pans and some spare cartridges. Such was Gerald's salesmanship that he even sold an alarm clock which never lost less than one and a half hours in twenty-four for 15 shillings. He also sold a watch which he dropped on a concrete floor at Victoria and which still ticks though it doesn't move its hands. So now we dine off cracked plates, but at least we have some money for cables to Belle Vue and Chester Zoos.

Gerald and John had originally planned to sail on 24 June, but their collection had grown so huge that the crates and boxes – five hundred cubic feet in volume – would not fit into the hold of the ship they had booked, and it sailed without them. Eventually they were able to secure berths and cargo space on a banana boat, the SS *Tetela*, sailing from the port of Tiko a whole month later, on 25 July, and began to prepare for their departure.

'You cannot just climb aboard a ship with your animals,' Gerald pointed out, 'and expect the cook to feed them.' A vast hoard of foodstuffs had to be got together, gathered from all over the country, and soon the expedition hut at Kumba resembled a market, with bananas, pawpaws, pineapples, oranges, eggs, sacks of corn, potatoes and beans, and the carcass of a whole bullock strewn across the floor.

It was at this point that Gerald went down with malaria, and lay feverish and ill with a temperature of 103 for a week. The plan was to drive down to Tiko during the night of 24 July, arriving at dawn on the day the ship was due to sail. But when the doctor called on the day before their departure, he was aghast at the idea of Gerald going anywhere. 'You should be kept in bed for at least a fortnight,' he thundered. 'You can't travel on that ship.' Otherwise, he bluntly informed the ailing Englishman, he would die.

But Gerald went, alternately sweating and shivering in the cab of the lorry as it ploughed down the mud road through the first rains of the season. A torrential downpour half-drowned the animals as they were being loaded on board at the docks, and though he felt like death Gerald insisted on drying the sodden creatures and giving them their night feed. Then the steward poured him a whisky which, he recalled, 'could have knocked out a horse', and he lay down in his cabin convinced he was going to die.

But he didn't. He was lucky with the weather on the voyage home, and soon began to revive with the fresh sea air. The crew found a playpen for Sue the chimpanzee, and titbits and blankets for any monkey with a sniff or a cough. The only casualty was a mongoose that staged a breakout and jumped overboard.

At 4 p.m. on Tuesday, 10 August 1948, the *Tetela* tied up at Garston Docks, Liverpool, and Gerald Durrell and John Yealland stepped back on to dry land at the end of their African adventure. They had been away more than seven months, and had brought back nearly two hundred creatures all told – among them ninety-five mammals (including the three angwantibo, forty monkeys, a baby chimp and a giant white mongoose), twelve reptiles and ninety-three rare birds. This cargo was sufficiently exotic to attract the attention of the national press. 'Awantibos, ahoy!' cried the headlines. 'The Awantibo is here today . . . only once seen alive in a European zoo!'

'Eventually,' Gerald was to recall, 'the last cage was towed away, and the vans bumped their way across the docks through the fine, drifting rain, carrying the animals away to a new life, and carrying us towards the preparations for a new trip.'

The expedition had been an enormous challenge, and had turned out a considerable triumph, putting Gerald Durrell and John Yealland in the front rank of British zoo collectors and field workers, and marking the definitive starting point of Gerald's spectacular career.

NINE

In the Land of the Fon

Second Cameroons Expedition 1948–1949

With the African animals finally settled in their English zoos, and a bit of profit jingling in his pocket, Gerald was free to go home to Bournemouth. He was greeted as if he had come home from the moon, and his residual malaria, diagnosed by Alan Ogden, the family doctor, as the particularly severe strain *plasmodium falciparum*, was viewed like a badge of courage brought back from some distant battlefield. Leslie was living with Doris nearby, and Margaret and her children were still in residence at Mother's house. At Christmas Larry and Eve returned from Argentina and temporarily rejoined the fold.

Gerald was already a very good story-teller, and he held the house in St Alban's Avenue in thrall with tales of his extraordinary adventures. In the comforting ambience of kith and kin he began to ease up after the strenuous travails of the last year. Slowly – perhaps not so slowly – his mind turned to the long-lost local girlfriends of that far-off pre-Cameroons era of the year before, whose company he had been deprived of for so long during the chaste jungle months. He even thought of taking a holiday – a proposal that provoked an odd reaction. 'Nothing annoys a collector more,' he was to recall, 'than to return after six months of bites, scratches, trouble and toil and to announce to one's friends that one is thinking of taking a short holiday, only to be told – "But you've just *had* one!"'

It was during Gerald's brief hometown visit that he encountered a young woman whose equivocal charms were to alternately intrigue and appall him for a long time to come. Her real name was Diane, but he was later to bequeath her the unforgettable *nom d'amour* of Ursula Pendragon White. His subsequent account of this flawed paragon is intricate and involved, but there is no doubting his fascination with her divine looks and her less than divine language, and the spell cast over him by both. 'I found,' he was to recall, 'that she was the only one who could arouse feelings in me that ranged from alarm and despondency to breathless admiration and sheer horror.'

Ursula was an ex-public school young woman from Canford Cliffs, at the posh end of Bournemouth (though later, to disguise her identity, Gerald was to say she was from Lymington in the New Forest). Gerald first set eyes on her on the top of a double-decker bus in Bournemouth town centre, his attention initially drawn by her 'dulcet Roedean accents, as penetrating and all-pervading as the song of a roller canary'.

Gerald's sister Margaret remembered Ursula as 'a young dolly bird with long blonde hair who sat around in a droopish fashion which was very irritating to the rest of us'. According to Gerald's later description, though (again, perhaps to disguise her identity), Ursula had dark, curly hair. Her eyes were huge, fringed with long dark lashes and set under very dark eyebrows. 'Her mouth,' he recalled, 'was of the texture and quality that should never, under any circumstances, be used for eating kippers or frogs' legs or black pudding.'

When Ursula stood up to get off the bus, Gerald saw that she was tall, with long, beautifully shaped legs and 'one of those willowy, coltish figures that turn young men's thoughts to lechery'. He reckoned, sighing, that it was unlikely he would ever set eyes on her again. But within three days she was back in his life, and remained so off and on for the next five years.

Encountering her again at a friend's birthday party, where she greeted him effusively as 'the bug boy', Gerald, by his own account, 'gazed at her and was lost'. It was not just her looks that infatuated him, it was also the sounds she made – 'her grim, determined, unremitting battle with the English language'. For this svelte and spirited beauty suffered from a sort of oral dyslexia, and was for ever forcing words and phrases to do her bidding, expressing meanings they were never meant to express. There was no guessing what fantastical imagery she would conjure up next. She would speak excitedly of 'Mozart's archipelagoes', of having bulls 'castigated', and of 'ablutions' to prevent 'illiterate babies'. In Ursula's world there was never fire without smoke, and rolling moss gathered no stones. In the prim confines of Bournemouth society 'she dropped bricks at the rate of an unskilled navvy helping at a building site'.

There began a lengthy (and possibly unconsummated – the evidence is unclear) game of romantic cat and mouse. To give Ursula the impression that he was her equal in wealth, class and breeding, Gerald persuaded Margaret's ex-husband Jack Breeze to drive him to his rendezvous with her in the vintage Rolls-Royce Jack owned at the time, with Jack smartly turned out in his BOAC officer's uniform, for all the world like some pasha's personal chauffeur. Ferried around in style, Gerald took Ursula to dinner at the Grill Room ('She has the appetite of a rapacious python,' he was warned, 'and no sense of money'); to a symphony concert at the Pavilion (where her Pekinese puppy jumped out of its basket and created havoc in the auditorium); and into the country for gin and shove ha'penny at the ancient Square and Compass pub, where the aged yokels were mesmerised by her unique brand of English ('A fine young woman, sir,' commented one pickled veteran, 'even though she's a foreigner'). Gerry never got on terribly well with his girlfriends' fathers in those days, and Ursula's, stuffy and well-heeled, was conventional enough to brandish a horse-whip one night when he brought her home late, threatening to thrash him within an inch of his life if it ever happened again.

But while Ursula was Gerald's distraction, it was the animal wilds of Africa that were his obsession, and she was convinced that sooner rather than later her beloved would end up tied in knots by a gorilla, or devoured by a lion before breakfast. One day she telephoned him. Her voice was so penetrating that he had to hold the receiver away from his ear.

'Darling,' she cried, 'I'm *engaged*!'

'I confess that my heart felt a sudden pang,' Gerald was to write of this poignant moment, 'and a loneliness spread over me. It was not that I was in love with Ursula; it was not that I wanted to marry her – God forbid! – but suddenly I realised that I was being deprived of somebody who could always lighten my gloom.'

Ursula duly married her intended. A long time later, she and Gerald met one last time, at a smart but stuffy old Edwardian café called the Cadena, among the elderly seaside gentry. As she came through the door it was obvious she was far gone with her second child.

'Darling!' she screamed. 'Darling! *Darling*!'

'She flung her arms round me,' Gerald remembered, 'and gave me a prolonged kiss of the variety that is generally cut out of French films by the English censor. She made humming noises as she kissed, like a hive of sex-mad bees. She thrust her body against mine to extract the full flavour of the embrace and to show that she cared, really and truly. Several elderly ladies, and what appeared to be a brigadier who had been preserved (like a plum in port) stared at us with fascinated repulsion.'

'I thought you were married,' said Gerald, tearing himself from her with an effort.

'I *am*, darling,' replied Ursula. 'Don't you think my kissing's improved?'

They sat down at their table.

'I don't suppose you'd like me now,' Ursula said wistfully. 'I've reformed. I've become very dull.'

'Do you think so?' asked a still-infatuated Gerald.

'Oh, yes,' she said, looking at him solemnly with her great blue eyes. 'I'm afraid I'm now what they call one of the petty beaujolais.'

Gerald did not intend to linger long in England. Partly the spell of Africa had got into his blood. Partly there was nothing for him to do in Britain. No longer a novice, but a fully-fledged old hand, he planned a second Cameroons expedition, aiming for bigger and infinitely more profitable 'stuff' this time round, including gorilla, hippo and elephant, all valued by British zoos at up to £1000 per animal (around £20,000 in today's money). His ambition to collect the really big game was not based entirely on greed, but also on the imperatives of personal survival. His first expedition had cost him roughly half his inheritance. The second was likely to cost the same, possibly more. He had to succeed – or go under.

It was an enormous fillip that Herbert Whitley, the wealthy owner of a large private collection of rare animals at Paignton, which later became the basis of Paignton Zoo, had agreed to buy half his collection on his return, plus any animals that London Zoo did not want. Gerald found Whitley highly eccentric – he was so shy that if anyone came to see him he would run through the house locking the doors, then flee in a special lift – but he was to have more than a passing influence on the young Gerald, for he was at the forefront of captive breeding. 'He tried to breed an alligator and an all-yellow salamander for a while,' Gerald was to recall. 'He had a particular obsession for breeding blue things. Part of this was to confound experts. He bred blue pigeons, blue Great Danes, blue ducks.'

John Yealland was not available to accompany Gerald back to the Cameroons, so in his place Gerald invited the experienced Ken Smith, a near neighbour in Bournemouth whom he had first met at Whipsnade. Smith was senior to Gerald both in terms of age (he was thirty-seven) and status (he was to be superintendent of Paignton Zoo) – but in Gerald's eyes his role made him the junior partner. Though physically Smith was hardly cast in the Tarzan mould, and was rather less gung-ho than his younger friend in face-to-face encounters with the larger and more fearsome beasts of the jungle, he knew his business, and was to prove a loyal and tireless companion in the long slog that lay ahead.

With Smith's help Gerald began to assemble a more sophisticated and better targeted range of expedition stores, including bigger and better guns, folding cages, a gallon of cod liver oil and twelve dozen babies' teats for the younger animals, several roll-neck pullovers 'to keep a gorilla warm on the ship back' and a splendid wedding marquee to house the animals at the base camp in the bush.

The second expedition was not intended simply to be a rerun of the first, for though Gerald would again work the rainforest around Mamfe, he also proposed to strike north into new territory – the high grassland region of central Cameroons, which offered a completely different range of fauna.

Early in January 1949, a few days before his twenty-fifth birthday, Gerald boarded the cargo boat MV *Reventazon* at Liverpool docks, together with his companion and all the paraphernalia of a major African collecting expedition. The press, who had witnessed his return from the first trip six months before, were back to witness his departure on the second, for his unusual way of earning a living had begun to attract some popular interest. 'He's off to Darkest Africa', went one headline. 'Mr Durrell, who is a bachelor, will journey inland for about 500 miles by lorry, then begin an eight-day safari. He is after gorilla and may also have a shot at capturing a buffalo or even a hippopotamus. "We shall try to get the gorillas in a sort of giant mousetrap," he said. "They can be very nasty."'

The ship sailed on time, and the voyage out was uneventful. Only Smith provided Gerald with much diversion. 'He wakes in the morning,' Gerald wrote to his mother, 'and tells me that he has been dreaming about catching Gorilla with the help of the stewardess and the Liverpool representative of Grindlays Bank. The other night he was reading a bit about Buffalo. That of course set him off and about twelve o'clock he fought with his bedclothes for about an hour and a half, sweat pouring down his face, uttering wild cries.'

On 10 February the ship nudged in towards the coast of Cameroons and Gerald noted in his diary: 'We were on deck about six, a bit unsteady after the farewell party last night. The islands in the bay loomed up through the mist, overloaded with vegetation ... It's wonderful to be back again.' Then, in case he forgot the reason he was there, he added: 'I am going to make a packet on this trip. I feel it in my bones, and Smith feels it in his varicose veins.'

The magic of Africa overwhelmed him once more – every crack in the wall a menagerie, every tree jam-packed with a hierarchy of species, the road at sundown paved with nightjars, the woods loud with the cry of the touracou, the songs of the bulbul and currichane thrush on the mountain 'sweet and liquid like the English blackbird and song thrush'. Gerald wrote home: 'Victoria is as beautiful as ever. Now all the trees are in bloom, and every one of them is covered in huge waxy flowers of every colour: yellow, blue, mauve, and scarlet. Hibiscus hedges are simply aflame with flower, and huge masses of bougainvillaea and canna lilies are everywhere. Ken has been walking around in a daze, with his mouth so wide open that I am afraid his teeth will drop out.'

'Everyone seems to remember me,' he wrote in his diary on his second day, 'and everyone is most charming and so very helpful.' The word went out on the bush telegraph that the animal collectors were back, and within a few days the pace of events accelerated dramatically. 'Now for some extraordinary news,' Gerald wrote excitedly to his mother on the fourteenth. 'We have started our collection with a bang by obtaining a young male Chimpanzee!! A planter and his wife have him and are willing to give him to us. He is a dear little chap, and when I picked him up he pushed out his lips and kissed me.'

Gerald's growing reputation for eccentricity was enhanced when he brought the chimpanzee, Charlie by name, to Victoria on the back of a bike, the chimp hanging round his neck 'hooting with joy and occasionally sticking his fingers in my eyes, so that I narrowly missed running over several members of the Victoria populace'. Both Gerald and Ken Smith were regarded as slightly mad, and were known as the 'animal maniacs' to the white community and as the 'beef masters' to the black. But whereas Gerald was regarded as largely unconventional, Smith was entirely comical, not least to his younger companion. While going for a swim in an up-country river, for example, he earned a thunderous round of applause from a large crowd of watching villagers when he suddenly sneezed, projecting his dentures some distance into the water.

Gerald already knew that animal collecting was a business which required some odd, exotic qualities in its practitioners. He later wrote:

Most people's idea of an animal collector is a brawny, Tarzan-like kind of bloke, but in fact most animal collectors look half dead from birth. To be successful at his job it's best if a collector is born a bit mental and grows up with a highly developed sense of humour and no sense of smell (I mean, have you ever smelled a monkey cage first thing in the morning?). It's also helpful if he has a private income, so it doesn't matter so much if he doesn't make a penny from the business. Of course, there are all sorts of ways of catching animals – traps, nets, smoking out caves and hollow trees, hunting with dogs, hunting at night (very good for reptiles) – but contrary to popular belief, collecting wild animals is not particularly dangerous – or at any rate only as dangerous as the collector is stupid.

Really it's not catching the animals that is so difficult, it's keeping them once you've caught them. Having a collection of animals is like having two or three hundred pernickety babies with stomachs as delicate as debutantes, all with different likes and dislikes. Naturally when life is spent in close proximity with these creatures you get involved in many embarrassing and irritating matters, particularly their lavatorial habits. For example, I had a hyrax that would only go to the toilet in the DO's hat, and a pouched rat that would only do big jobs in its drinking bowl. Sometimes a collector has to share his bed with a baby animal for warmth, and this can lead to all sorts of strange experiences, especially if the creature in question is a porcupine.

The plan was to establish the marquee base camp at a suitable site overlooking the river near Mamfe, and for this to be used as the central depository for all the animals coming in from the surrounding area and from further afield. Ken Smith would be more or less permanently billeted at the Mamfe base as keeper-*cum*-vet, while Gerald roamed far and wide in the neighbouring forests and the mountain grasslands to the north, hunting for creatures on the wanted list which would then be despatched back to Mamfe.

On 18 February the little party headed off for the interior, overnighting at Kumba on their way to Mamfe. 'We started fairly early this morning,' Gerald noted in his diary, 'and made Kumba in good time. The ride was wonderful and it was lovely to feel we were at last heading for bush.' Two days later they reached Mamfe, and in due course, with the help of thirty panting labourers and to the amazement and delight of a surging crowd of villagers, the great canvas mass of the English wedding marquee was hauled and pulled into position till it stood, four-square and proud as a medieval tented pavilion, on the bank of the slow brown river at the edge of the primeval forest.

There was still another week of preparations – cages to be erected, ponds dug, food supplies laid on, chiefs propositioned with lists of wanted animals, a hundred and one things – before systematic collecting could start. By the beginning of March they were all set, and Gerald ventured forth into the surrounding wilds on his second great quest in search of rare 'beef'. From this point forward he was to be subject to a life of such relentless physical endeavour and such sensory richness and intensity that his diary reads like the breathless log of some inter-galactic voyager, every day a new adventure, every minute a mind-blowing revelation. It is difficult to do justice here to the extraordinary document he typed with two fingers and a thumb every evening in the yellow circle of light from the hurricane lamp in his jungle camp, exhausted almost to the point of collapse; but various important features emerge from it.

The first is that the Gerald Durrell who is thinking aloud, so to speak, in the 1949 diary, seems quite a different young man from the one who had first arrived in the country the year before. Gone are all the imperial pretensions and colonial posturings. Now he responds to the phenomena of Africa and the Africans in his own way. Though still inclined to paternalism now and then, he finally seems to have perceived that the bush Africans with whom he was to spend most of the seven months to come were individuals every bit as eccentric, engaging, irritating, talented or flawed as the rest of the animal species known as man – himself and Ken Smith included. He also knew that without the help and support of the local Africans the entire enterprise would fail, for virtually everything depended on them, from collecting to cooking. And in the course of this second expedition he would grow so close to the people of the Cameroons that he would become almost a blood brother to one of them, with whom his name would be associated for the rest of his life.

Another feature that emerges powerfully from Gerald's diary is his sense of the overwhelming prodigality of the Africa through which he travelled – an ancient Africa still largely virgin, still largely wild, still host to a nature as beautiful as it was cruel – an Africa where the concept of 'extinction' seemed to bear little relation to the seemingly endless procession of flying, running, hopping, crawling, slithering, swimming species that daily crossed the traveller's line of sight or range of hearing.

Yet another feature of the diary is Gerald's growing appreciation of the beauty and preciousness of this primordial world, his mounting sense of wonder and awe. Every patch of sky, every bend in the river, every clearing in the forest held some surprise and joy for him. Increasingly, as the weeks went by, all his hard-bitten, tough-guy posturing began to melt away, and in its place emerged a rather less hearty, more sensitive and reflective young man, increasingly aware of the immense privilege of being where he was and seeing what he saw.

Finally, the diary reveals Gerald's dawning gift for literary expression. As he strove to put into words his simple yet subtle reactions to the wonders all around, his powers of observation grew sharper, his sense of comedy more incisive, his story-telling more practised, and his handling of language more fluent and expressive. In his diary entry for 3 March, for example, describing a foray by dugout canoe down the Mamfe River, one can begin to detect a real writer in the making, trying hard to find an authentic voice:

Really, even if one does not capture anything of real value on these jaunts, the experience itself is worth while. It is wonderful to walk along knee-deep in the brown, slowly moving water, with the great glittering sandbanks like huge white ribs in the river, each having on it the carcasses of giant forest trees that have been uprooted in the rains and are now left high and dry. On either bank the forest climbs upwards, an almost solid mat of lianas, ferns, and a thousand variety of plants. The only sound, apart from the cries of the insects, is the faint swish of your movements through the blood-warm water. Suddenly a Wattled plover will flap off the bank before you, with shrill and twittering cries, or a Fishing eagle will fly over on silent wings, or a foolish Hornbill threshing the air, honking wildly. If you sit on the smooth slopes of grey stone in the evening you will see the monkeys coming down to drink, leaping from tree to tree in a crash and rustle of branches. There seems to be no *time* here: you lose all sense of it: it may be ten or two for all you know, for the forest has no time. When it's dark the day has finished, when it's light the day has begun. All the time you are only aware of the present, the everlasting Now.

Nothing Gerald ever wrote gives quite such a raw, moment-by-moment impression of the sheer excitement of animal collecting and the demands made on the stamina and ingenuity of the collector as his diary account of his pursuit of the rare *Anomalurus* (flying squirrel) and *Idiurus* (pigmy flying squirrel) in the rainforest around Eshobi between 4 and 8 March. These animals had never been seen in any zoo anywhere in the world, and were of great exhibition value and scientific interest. To get them safely back to Britain would be a tremendous coup.

The walk to Eshobi was as abominable as it had been the previous year, but Gerald was given a warm welcome when he arrived, the whole village turning out to greet their long-lost white friend and much-missed moneybags. That evening he met up with the hunters and gave them all a pep talk about the importance of catching *Idiurus* and *Anomalurus* the next day. 'They said they all fit try, and that by God Power we should get them, on which happy note the party broke up and we all went to bed.'

At first light the next day Gerald set off with his hunters to find the tree where he had seen an *Anomalurus* the previous year. To his amazement the animal was still there, though there was no easy way of catching it.

The diary continued:

As we were blundering about the base of the tree, the thing inside took fright at the sound of our voices and shot out of the top. It left the tree as if it had been catapulted and soared through the air, giving me my first sight of a Flying Squirrel in action. It was a breathtakingly beautiful sight. It had about forty feet to go before it reached the nearest tree, and it hurtled through the air with the straight swoop of a glider, the membranes on the sides of its body curved out like umbrellas with the rush of air. Just before it reached the next tree it straightened up, and then as it was just about to touch the bark it turned completely upright, standing, as it were, in mid-air. Then it landed and proceeded to scuttle upwards, hunching its body like a huge caterpillar. I then did a thing which I have regretted ever since: I lifted the gun and fired. It dropped like a stone, and I rushed forwards, tripping through the undergrowth shouting to the hunters to keep the dogs off, and praying that it would only be slightly wounded. Of course the poor thing was dead, and as I picked it up I could have cried, it was such a very beautiful creature . . .

The next day Gerald and the hunters set out at dawn and smoked ten trees. Nothing much came out of the first nine, apart from a few bats, millipedes and scorpions.

We came to the last tree, but by then I was so tired and my lungs so full of smoke that I just sat down and couldn't have cared less what was produced. So I thought. The net was hung, the fire lit, and green leaves (for smoke) put on it. Then we just sat and waited, while I dug thorns out of my hands and wished that I was in bed and asleep. At last I gave the order that the net was to be taken down, as it was obvious that nothing was inside. James the wash-boy started to take the net down, and then I saw him pick something up from inside the tree. He came forward holding it by its tail. 'Master want this kind of beef?' he inquired with an engaging smile. I took one look at it and shot to my feet with a yelp, for there, dangling by its curious feathery tail, its sides heaving and its eyes closed, was a small brownish mouse-like creature: a real live *Idiurus macrotis*. 'Quick, quick,' I snarled to the small boy, 'bring box for this beef . . . no, not that one you bloody fool, a good one . . . that's it . . . now put small leaf for inside . . . small leaf, not half a tree . . . there!' And *Idiurus* was placed reverently inside. It lay there quite unconscious from the smoke, its tiny sides heaving and its little pink paws twitching, and I gathered a bunch of leaves and fanned him thoroughly. Slowly he started to come round, and then I put the lid on the box and we made tracks for home. When we got back it was quite dark and by bush light I had to sit down and make a cage for the *Idiurus*, then, keeping awake only with a very liberal application of White Horse, I skinned the bats and cleaned the gun, then fell into bed and slept like a log. The *Idiurus* is the most curious little beast, looking not unlike an English dormouse, but more greyish in colour. The speed it can travel up wood is really extraordinary. It runs like a dog, unlike the Anomalurus, which has to hunch itself like a caterpillar.

The next day was a real red-letter day. Deep in the forest the hunting party found a hollow tree 150 feet high, and when Gerald crawled inside its base and looked up he was stunned to discover that it was swarming with *Idiurus*. Fortunately there was a small tree growing alongside, which enabled one of the hunters to climb it and hoist a net over the main tree, and when a fire was lit at its base the smoke drove the *Idiurus* out into it. Altogether eight *Idiurus* were caught in this way, along with three extraordinary-looking bats which Gerald was convinced were a new species. 'I killed them with great care to avoid damage,' he wrote in his diary, 'and packed them in cotton wool.'

Though he was by now exhausted, he decided take the *Idiurus* into Mamfe that night, since at least there was a proper cage for them there. 'As the little chaps jumped out of the tin and started to scurry up the walls of the cage,' he noted in his diary, 'Smith was screeching with excitement and fluttering round the tent like an elderly will-o'-the-wisp. I was dead beat but very happy, hearing the *Idiurus* squeaking and rustling in their cage.'

It turned out that James the wash-boy had found a way of climbing the unclimbable *Idiurus* tree of the previous day, and next afternoon he arrived with a carrier who brought a huge cage covered with banana leaves into the Mamfe camp. 'What a sight met our popping eyes: it was crammed like the Black Hole with *Idiurus* of all ages and sexes to the tune of thirty-five! Smith and I nearly went mad. If we get the whole colony back alive we will shake the zoological world to its foundations!'

To his mother he wrote excitedly later that day:

Let me tell you the really great news. In the corner of the marquee stands a six foot tall cage, and it now houses about thirty of the rarest animals in West Africa – Pigmy Flying Squirrels. These are known only by a few skins in museums, and not more than a dozen people have ever seen them alive in the jungle, let alone caged in Europe. They will be, if we can get them back alive, the zoological event of the year, and coming on my Awantibo will just raise me to heights unknown. However, I mustn't speak too soon, as the little buggers have only been with us twenty-four hours and are as nervous as old ladies on a dark common, and very tricky about their food.

It had always been part of Gerald's plan on this expedition to travel north to the mountains, where the forest gave way to the great grasslands – a completely different world, with a cooler climate, strange vegetation and fauna quite unlike that of the steamy forests of the lowlands. A British District Officer had suggested that the most fruitful area of the grasslands might be Bafut, a region the size of Wales. Bafut's tribal peoples were governed with benign despotism by an intelligent, wealthy and eccentric paramount chief, or king, known as the Fon. His palace, Gerald learned, was set amid rolling grassland and forested valleys with a wealth of interesting and valuable creatures: chimpanzees, bush babies, mongooses, lions, leopards, cobras, green mambas. 'What the king says goes,' the DO advised Gerald. 'He's a most delightful old rogue, and the quickest and surest way to his heart is to prove that you can carry your liquor.' That afternoon Gerald sent a messenger to the Fon's capital carrying a bottle of gin and a note requesting permission to visit his kingdom to collect rare animals. Four days later the messenger returned, bearing a letter from the Fon himself:

> Fon's Office Bafut, Bemenda Division
> 5th March 1949
> My good friend,
> Yours of 3rd March, 1949, came in hand with all contents well marked out.
> Yes, I accept your arrival to Bafut in course of two month stay about your animals and too, I shall be overjoyed to let you be in possession of a house in my compound if you will do well in arrangement of rentages.
> Yours cordially
> Fon of Bafut

Gerald made arrangements to leave for Bafut at once.

11 March: We shot out to Bafut and arrived there about half-past three. The guest house is built on the side of the road on a steep bank, and a flight of about fifty steps leads up to the balcony and then into the house. Standing at the top of this flight you look across the road at the fort-like compound of the chief or Fon, with its small brick guard-houses, and then beyond that the chief's own small villa, surrounded by the grass huts of his numerous wives. As I stood there at the top of the stairs I could see the Fon with a crowd of council members approaching across this vast square. I went down and met him at the foot of the stairs, where we shook hands and beamed at one another like long-lost brothers.

The Fon was a tall, slim man with a lively, and humorous face. Even though he was modestly garbed in a plain white robe and simple skullcap, there was no mistaking who he was, for his bearing was regal and his presence palpable. In the Fon Gerald was to meet his match, and in him he recognised a kindred spirit, as he was soon to discover. His diary continued:

After an exchange of flattering remarks about each other's character and great solicitude for each other's health, the Fon retired, saying he would come and see me after I had unpacked. So I went upstairs to unpack the whiskey and gin. When it was getting dark a messenger came over to say that the Fon would like to come and talk with me if I had 'calmed' myself after my journey. So then I got the glasses out alongside the bottle of Irish. The Fon arrived together with an interpreter, which at first I thought was unnecessary. We drank each other's health (he mine in neat Irish, I his discreetly watered) and started to talk about beef. I brought out books and showed him pictures, made noises like the animals I wanted, drew them on bits of paper, and all the time his glass was being replenished with a rather frightening regularity. The bottle was full when we started, and in two hours, when he lurched to his feet to depart, there was about three fingers in the bottom. Towards the end his speech became almost incomprehensible, and I understood the presence of the interpreter. As we reached the top of the steps (down which the Fon nearly took a toss) he turned to the interpreter and told him to drink. He had a full glass of whiskey in his hand. The man went down on one knee, made a funnel of his hands into which the Fon poured half the whiskey, while the man sucked it up greedily. Then it was obviously my turn, and with a certain repulsion at treating a human being like a pet dog, I poured my glass out also. It was rather disgusting. However, after the Fon had wended his unsteady way home I could hear the drums beating, telling Bafut to bring beef.

Life henceforth was to be so action-packed, what with the endless drinking sessions with his friend the Fon and the ceaseless stream of beef coming in from the countryside, that there were times when even Gerald could barely cope. 'Today I have become nearly mental,' he wrote in his diary on 15 March. 'Beef rolling in and nothing to house it in . . . I am dead beat.' The following day the pace had quickened even more, and he scribbled desperately: 'Today I *have* become mental . . . Hell let loose.' Besides the animals the Fon's subjects were bringing in, Gerald and his hunters were collecting their own, sometimes flushing them out of the mimbo-palm plantations with a posse of boys, sometimes shaking them out of the trees, sometimes burrowing for them, sometimes smoking them out, sometimes trapping them. A large collection of animals and birds of all sorts began to form on the veranda of the enormous guest house, many of which had rarely, if ever, been seen in any zoo. They ranged from brilliantly coloured sun-birds about four inches long to vultures the size of a turkey, from pigmy dormice that would fit into a teaspoon to giant rats the size of cats. On 14 March Gerald encountered a form of hunting that was entirely new in his African experience – a sort of beagling for beef.

What I love about Africa is that you set off into the bush with the firm resolve to catch some special beef, and almost always come back with something quite different. Today I was going out to capture Allen's Galago [a bush baby] and Hammer-heads [hammer-headed bats]: we caught neither but brought back something quite different . . .

There was Joseph, myself, four hunters, and two dogs that looked as though they had just come out of Belsen. I was assured that they were first-rate hunting dogs. There was a slight altercation with one of the hunters who wanted to bring his dane gun: not wanting to return home with bits of rusty nail and flint in my backside I was firm and said NO. We worked our way through several mimbo plantations, flushed a squirrel and lost him, and then came out into the grassland proper. This is about six foot high and looks like a pigmy bamboo. The leaves have a sharp cutting edge which makes it painful to walk through.

So we continued on our way. Soon the dogs made a great pother, and the hunters assured me that they had found a Cutting-grass i.e. a Great Cane Rat. While some hunters went into the grass with the dogs, the others spread their nets in a haphazard sort of fashion along the edge of the undergrowth where it joined the path. I thought the dogs were probably on the track of a lame Tree frog (they didn't look strong enough to run after anything faster) so I sat myself down with the thermos and started to imbibe tea. I was gently sipping my second cup when great yodelling screeches went up from the hunters, there was a great crashing in the undergrowth and something that looked the size of a well-developed beaver dashed past, crashed through the grass and leapt headlong into the net. Joseph and another hunter (whose name I am assured is M'erwegie) fell on it, and to show the brute's strength it bucked and kicked so much that they were both lifted off the ground. After much shouting and good advice we got it into the beef bag, and sure enough it was a Cutting-grass, and a very large one at that, about two foot long, with a round fat beaver-like face. *Praomys tullbergi tullbergi* is the correct name for this huge rat.

Shortly after this we flushed another, which ran almost between my legs. We were off after it in full cry and ran after it for about a mile. It reminded me of beagling: first the dogs yapping and snarling, the little bells they wear round their necks clonking like mad; then the hunters and myself, and a trail of small boys scream-ing behind. Through the long grass, getting cut to hell, jumping (generally unsuccessfully) over streams, pushing through mimbo swamps. At last we came to a sweaty and gasping halt to find the dogs had lost it. As I lay on the ground trying to regain my breath a boy appeared from nowhere holding a dirty calabash, the long neck of which was stuffed with leaves. Joseph peered inside and then started, gurgling with delight, for inside was a 'shilling', or Allen's Galago. This makes the pair that London wanted!!

Though the really big 'stuff' continued to elude Gerald, the quantity and variety of smaller creatures was prodigious. On 16 March alone he acquired hyraxes, pouched rats, skinks, mongooses, great cane rats, a Nile monitor, three kinds of squirrel, feral kittens ('wild as hell') and, 'prize of the bunch, the thing that London wants very much, two huge Hairy Frogs!!!!! I was so pleased that I sent a message over to the Fon asking him to come and have a drink with me tomorrow evening.'

The visit was a memorable one, as Gerald noted in his diary entry for 17 March:

This evening the Fon came in about seven and left about eleven having consumed a bottle of gin. Later in the evening he sent for his wives, and they came and sang and beat drums below the house. When he noticed that the gin was finished he decided to go, and arm in arm, preceded by three men with lights, we went down the long flight of steps, at the bottom of which was this mass of stark naked females, all dancing and singing. As both the Fon and I were now well lit up, we nearly fell down the stairs together, but saved ourselves at the last minute, amid cries of horror from the population. Then we crossed the huge compound, the wives dancing in front of us, backwards, and then into a large hut, where the Fon and I sat on wicker chairs and watched the dance.

After I had developed a sore throat shouting compliments about the wives, the dance, the music, we were friends for life. Then he asked me if I could dance. Fearing what was coming, I quickly said no, to my everlasting regret I could not dance. This stopped him for a second, then he beamed all over his face, rose swaying to his feet, grasped my arm and said: 'I go teach you native dance.'

Reluctantly I went to my fate, and clasped in each other's arms we staggered round the room. It was not a great success, owing chiefly to the fact that his very long and highly coloured robes kept getting caught up in my feet, and we would both be jerked to a standstill while six or seven people unwound his clothes from my legs. Presently he was nearly asleep, and so was I, so with deep sorrow at having to break up such a unique party, I said I must be going. He walked to the gates with me, and bade me a fond and slightly maudlin farewell.

What a hangover we will have, but what beef I hope this evening will bring forth.

Two days later the Fon was back. The occasion was a local festival called the cutting of the grass. At four o'clock a court messenger came to fetch Gerald, and with liberal application of a switch he cut a path for him through the crowd to the courtyard outside the Fon's villa. The Bafut council, consisting of some fifty elders, was already assembled, squatting against a wall drinking mimbo ('a milk-like liquid, very fine, light and sweet – and very potent') out of cups made of cows' horn. At the far end of the courtyard sat the Fon, seated on an elaborately decorated chair placed on a raised stone dais beneath a huge mango tree. He was garbed in resplendent ornamental robes and wore a conical felt hat with elephant hairs stitched to it. Gerald was made to sit at his right hand (a great honour), and one of the Fon's wives poured him a glass of mimbo.

Then came the ceremony of the feeding of the masses. In return for bringing grass to thatch his roof, the Fon traditionally provided his subjects with a feast. The Fon rose and with Gerald at his side strode down the double rank of bobbing and clapping council members, his wives 'uttering cries such as the Redskin is supposed to produce'. In the outer courtyard the crowd greeted them with a burst of screams and claps. With Gerald again seated on the Fon's right, more mimbo was poured as lesser chiefs from outlying parts made their obeisance, retreating backwards after a regal nod from the Fon.

In his diary Gerald described a strange modification of the traditional ceremony – a modification for which he was entirely responsible:

By this time I had drunk about five glasses of mimbo, and was feeling very pleased with life. Then to my horror a table was brought and on it were two glasses and a bottle of gin – a brand I have never heard of and never want to again. The Fon poured out about four fingers for me, and I asked for some water. The Fon gave a rapid command in his own tongue, and a man rushed forward with a bottle of bitters. 'Beeters,' said the Fon proudly, 'you like gin wit dis beeters?' Yes, I assured him, it was very fine, and the first sip of the drink nearly burnt out my throat: it was the most filthy raw gin I have ever tasted. Even the Fon blinked a bit. He had another sip, mused a bit, and then leant over and confided to me: 'We go give dis strong one to all dis small small man, den we go for my house, for inside, and we go drink WHITE HORSHE . . .' We both smacked our lips. I wondered how I would feel with White Horshe on top of gin and mimbo.

By this time an endless series of men had been streaming into the compound carrying an amazing variety of food and drink. There were calabashes of palm wine, mimbo and corn beer; huge stems of plantains and bananas; meat in the shape of cane rats, mongooses, bats, hunks of python meat, all smoked and spitted on bamboo. There were dried fish, crabs and dried shrimp; red and green peppers, pawpaw, oranges, mango, cassava, sweet potatoes and so on. This was the feast for the people. While they started on it, the Fon called his counsellors one by one and poured gin into their mimbo. Then we rose and proceeded to his house, where the White Horshe was produced.

While we finished the bottle we discussed many things ranging from various types of guns to the Russian question. Then the Fon, by now well lit up, sent for his wives and made them play and dance in the courtyard outside. They played some special dances, and one of the tunes had a perfect Conga rhythm. Feeling then very bright I suggested to the Fon that I should teach him a special European dance. He was thrilled to bits and we adjourned to the dance hall. Here, with the Fon sitting in state, I stood up and asked him to let me have five council members to teach. Five of them rose and joined me on the floor.

In the deathly silence you could hear their robes swishing as they approached. I made them all join on behind me, holding on to each other's waists, gave the band a nod and off we went: One, two, three, four, five, KICK, one two, three, four, five, KICK. It was a huge success: all the other council members took the floor, and about thirty of the Fon's wives, all joining on behind. Nothing loath, the Fon, supported by a man on each side, tagged on behind.

We must have danced about two miles. I led them all over the Fon's courtyards, up and down steps, in and out of rooms, with the band running behind us beating like mad. I did every step I could think of, leaping, twisting, turning, and the huge tail of followers all repeated them, grinning all over their faces and shouting at the tops of their voices 'ONE TWO THREE FOUR FIVE ... YAARRRRRR ... ONE TWO THREE FOUR FIVE ... YAARRRRRR.' In the end we all collapsed in a sweating and panting heap. The Fon, who had fallen down once or twice during the dance, was escorted to his chair gasping and panting, and beaming with delight. He clapped me on the back, nearly dislocating my spine, and told me that my dance was 'foine, foine, vera foine.' Then we had some more mimbo and started all over again. I did everything I could think of, a dreadful combination of ballroom and jitterbug, with a bit of ballet, Fred Astaire and Victor Sylvester thrown in.

After about two hours of this the Fon quite suddenly called over a girl of about fourteen, one of his daughters, and pushed her into my lap, saying that she was mine and I must marry her. I had to think damn quick. Taking a hasty look round to see how many of the council members had spears, I wiped the sweat from my brow and wondered what to do. If I accepted, there was a chance he would remember in the morning and hold me to it; and yet he was so drunk that I could see my refusal would have to be very tactful not to annoy him. I started by saying that I was deeply grateful for this great honour he was doing me, but that of course, being so well versed in the stupid customs of Europeans, he realised that by the laws of my country I was only allowed one wife. He nodded sagely and agreed that it was a stupid custom. This being the case, I continued, he would realise how very sad I felt at having to refuse his kind honour, as I already a wife in my own country; but I assured him that if this was not the case I would gladly have married the girl and settled in Bemenda for the rest of my life. This was greeted with loud cheers, and the Fon wept a bit that this wonderful thing could never be realised. Then the party broke up, the Fon and everyone accompanying me to the steps of the house doing the Durrell Conga.

What a hangover I will have.

Collecting wild animals, as Gerald and his African hunters knew only too well, was an activity fraught with risk, for the animals as well as the humans, especially if less kindly methods were used to catch them. Gerald's care for the halt and the lame knew no bounds. He recounted in his diary on 21 March:

A man came with a female Patas which had been caught in one of those bloody steel gins. Three toes are missing from one of her hind feet, and the whole foot was swollen and starting to smell revolting. The poor little thing must have been in the trap about two days, as she was so exhausted she just collapsed as soon as I took the rope off her. My first thought was to kill her, an idea I did not relish, but then I thought I would have a shot at getting her well. The first thing to do was to get some food into her. She was too far gone to take any solid food, so I made her some Horlicks and managed to get about half a cup down her. She seemed a little brighter. Then I had to attend to her foot, a job which nearly made me sick. The bones of the three toes were sticking out quite free of flesh, and these I had to amputate. Then I discovered that the whole pad of the foot was filled with pus, and this had to be squeezed out and dettol and water poured into the cavity. Then I bandaged the foot up and wrapped her in a blanket and put her in a box to sleep. About five o'clock she woke up and ate a small bit of banana and drank some more Horlicks; but I don't like the look of her foot. However, she is keeping the bandage on, which is something for a monkey. The poor little thing has decided that I am trying to help her, and will let me handle her, though she gets very frightened if the boys come near. I do hope I can save her.

Gerald himself had so far led a charmed life, wading up snake-infested rivers and rummaging in animals' burrows with his bare hands; but now he was to suffer a series of misadventures. Perhaps because of bad luck, perhaps because of increasing exhaustion or recklessness or over-confidence, he had several near-misses at the hands of a variety of animals, followed by a palpable and very nearly fatal hit, which almost put an end to his life, not to mention his career as an animal collector.

The first close shave occurred when he bungled an attempt to put down an injured cobra with a formalin injection in the head. Then on 22 March a full-grown booming squirrel bit right through his glove and into a vein in his wrist, so that he bled 'like a stuck pig'. Shortly afterwards, dressed only in shorts and sandals, he was attacked by three very agile and very deadly green vipers. 'Boy, did I jump!' he wrote laconically in his diary. 'It gave me quite a fright.'

On 24 March he drove the entire Bafut collection to date back to Mamfe, 'leaving Smith with a tent full of animals all shouting and screaming'. Gerald was now showing distinct signs of over-tiredness and irritability, especially on days of solid rain. In this enervated, lacklustre state he was to encounter nemesis in the form of what he thought was a harmless burrowing snake, brought to the guest house one morning by a tribeswoman clad only in a slender G-string. On 13 April, more than two weeks after his last diary entry, he recounted what then transpired.

> Having ascertained, as I thought, that it was a blind burrowing snake, I tipped it out on to the ground to have a look at it. It certainly looked like a burrowing snake, so I picked it up by the neck. As I looked at its head I saw it had a pair of large, evil black eyes, while a burrowing snake is quite blind. Still, like a bloody fool, I kept hold of it instead of dropping it, only remarking to Pious that it had eyes. As I made this classic discovery the brute turned its head slightly and drove one fang into the ball of my thumb.
>
> I dropped the snake as if it had suddenly become red hot. I squeezed frantically, while rushing into the house. It was fortunate that Pious had been well drilled in what to do, and within three seconds I had a tie round the base of my thumb, and, not without an effort, had slashed the bite with a razor blade and rubbed in P. of Potash. By this time the thumb was quite swollen and beginning to throb slightly. My pulse, as far as I could tell, was normal. This was about five minutes after the bite.

Gerald's predicament was dire. A quick check in a reference book revealed that the snake that had bitten him was a burrowing viper, whose poison causes death within twelve hours through paralysis of the heart and nervous system. Only the appropriate serum could save him, and there was none in Bafut, and very possibly none further afield, for this was a true backwater of bush Africa. There was a British medic in

Bemenda, some forty miles away across rough country – a five-hour drive – and perhaps he had some serum. If not, Gerald Malcolm Durrell, twenty-four, animal collector, would very likely be dead by nightfall. His diary entry continued:

> While I sat in a state of scientific panic, noting my symptoms, a boy had been despatched for the driver of the Fon's kitcar to take me into Bemenda. I was doubtful if they had any serum there, but at least there was a doctor. Within half an hour my thumb and a part of my hand and wrist was very swollen and getting very painful. The skin was red, which may have been due to the tightness of the tie, but the area immediately around the bite was quite white.
>
> The driver arrived and of course the bloody kitcar would not start and had to be pushed up and down the road while I stood on the steps of the house gulping a brandy and shouting curses at the two hundred odd people who were pushing the car. By the time the car was started the glands in *both* my armpits were swollen and painful, and my right arm (I was bitten in my right thumb) was aching.

In fact his right forearm was now as big as his leg, and the glands under his arm as big as walnuts. And his head and neck ached furiously and he felt 'ghastly'.

> We dashed off as fast as the road would permit and first stopped at the Basle Mission. Here there was a nursing sister, who was not sure what to do, but tied two bandages round my arm, one on the forearm and one on the biceps. These were so tight that my hand turned quite blue within a few seconds. Then the Basle man, Angst by name, took me into Bemenda in his car, as it was faster than the kitcar. So, within an hour of being bitten, I was descending a trifle unsteadily at the doctor's house. 'Hallo, Durrell,' the doctor said cheerily, 'what's bitten you?' To my surprise, he had some serum, and I was rushed inside and given five injections, three in my thumb and two in my arm. These were very painful, and I got quite dizzy and stupid with the pain. When the doc had finished he gave me a large whisky, which I made short work of. Then I had a hot bath and was shoved into bed on a light supper. My arm was still very painful, but what with fright, exhaustion and relief I slept like a top. The doctor told me that when I arrived the pupils of my eyes were contracted to pinpoints.
>
> As my arm was swollen and stiff, for several days I could not

type this epic, nor could I do any work. I had to go back to Mamfe at the end of the week and was a bit depressed as no beef worth while had been brought in. Then came the climax, the day before I left. I was lying down before tea, when Pious came in to say that a man had brought a 'bush dog', and I staggered out expecting it would turn out to be a civet or genet. The fellow was clutching a large bag, from inside of which came the most fearsome noises. We proceeded to open the bag carefully. As I peered inside I could have yelped with surprise, for there was a half-grown Golden Cat, hissing and snarling in the bottom of the bag.

London Zoo, Gerald reflected with triumph, had not had a golden cat for fifty years.

Towards the end of April it was apparent to Gerald that the expedition was running into trouble. A collecting expedition, he began to realise, is subject to a kind of inverse mathematical law, and its very success contains the seeds of its impending failure: the more animals you collect, the more time you must devote to looking after them, therefore the less time you have to collect more of them and the fewer you succeed in collecting. Though they had acquired a substantial number of smaller animals, some of them were ailing in captivity, and every day a few more died from sickness, trauma or dietary problems, absorbing Gerald's available time. His detailed inventory of the collection up to 26 April showed that of the 394 animals caught to date, thirty-four had escaped and 108 had died – nearly half of them *Idiurus* – a loss rate of almost 40 per cent.

However, a cold statistic is not a fair way of judging Gerald's skill as a collector. Some animals are easy to take into captivity. Some are very difficult indeed. Some are virtually impossible, as Gerald found to be the case with the *Idiurus*. A collector's ability should be measured by the way he looks after his animals – how much he cares for them, how clean they are, how well sheltered, how well fed and so on – and by this yardstick Gerald measured up to the highest possible standard. But it was a very, very difficult job. On 28 April he noted in his diary the death of the royal antelope and the only surviving hairy frog, along with two of the remaining *Idiurus*. 'Now I have only one young specimen of *Idiurus* left,' he lamented. 'I put in some ordinary potato tonight and to my delight he ate quite a large amount of it. If only I can get them eating that sort of stuff they will be simple to get back alive.'

Feeding such a diversity of creatures was a nightmare. None of the carnivorous animals cared for goat meat, but they would gobble up brains from any source. Some liked their meat bloody, some liked it with fat in it, others liked it chopped into little pieces. All the insectivorous birds adored winged termites, and Gerald would spend hours collecting them round the lamp at night. The fruit bats preferred their bananas with the skin on; the pangolins lapped up egg and milk but refused it if it was sweetened, the golden cat was more partial to it if brains were added; and the young owls had to have bits of cotton wool in their food as roughage. One species of monkey only ate oranges, throwing away the fruit and eating the peel. The precious *Idiurus* remained an almost insuperable problem. 'I have never met such stubborn creatures,' Gerald recorded.

Gerald had so far been unable to secure any spectacular big-game animals – elephant, hippo, leopard – which would have solved the expedition's financial problems at a stroke. Worse, his application to the local authorities for a gorilla permit had been turned down, though he still hoped to acquire a specimen from the French side of the Cameroons border. He now pinned his hopes on trapping a hippo from a colony near the camp on the Mamfe River by laying a grass noose trap along one of the hippos' nocturnal trails on a mid-river sandbank. But this plan depended on the assistance of his unreliable band of hired hippo hunters. 'Still no signs of the bloody hippo hunters,' he scrawled on 24 April. 'If we don't get a hippo we are really in the soup financially, and won't be able to go collecting again.' He fumed with frustration as he listened to the hippos snorting and bellowing barely two hundred yards from the camp. 'Bugger the bloody bastards!' he fumed, referring to the hunters, adding for good measure: 'Blast the bloody complacent sods of zoo officials who think collecting is easy.'

Though Ken Smith assured him that what they had collected already would cover the cost of the trip, they were down to their last £50, and on 28 April Gerald had no alternative but to write to his mother asking her to bail them out. 'A hundred or two would cover us wonderfully,' he wrote. 'There is no danger of it being not paid back because we will *definitely* sell our present stuff for a thousand *minimum*. That is without hippo. If we get hippo we shall be making a profit, and seriously, the chances are about ninety to ten for. If you can't spare it don't worry. We shall raise the wind somehow.' A few days later Ken wrote a follow-up letter to Mrs Durrell and Leslie, even more bullish in tone, in which he assessed the value of the collection at up to £2500 (£50,000 in today's money) 'at minimum market values'.

Still, getting a hippo was critical to the expedition's fortunes. Several attempts at snaring a specimen from the colony near the camp proved abortive, much to the relief of Smith, who was less convinced of his immortality in the proximity of big game than was his younger companion. 'If your mother knew I had let you go down on to that bloody bit of sand surrounded by hippo and with no retreat,' he remonstrated with Gerald after one night-time foray, 'she would never forgive me.'

Before long the villagers were objecting to these escapades, on the grounds that the nearby hippo colony was juju. Gerald was advised to try a more distant herd near Asagem, four hours downriver by canoe, and on 30 April he set off on one last major effort to catch a hippo. 'Gerald left yesterday for Asagem,' Smith wrote in a reassuringly avuncular letter to the long-suffering Mrs Durrell, 'to attempt to bring the hippo hunt to a successful conclusion. I have stressed to him the importance of conducting the task without undue risks, and I think my constant insistence on this point has driven the matter home.'

The wild habitats of the tropical lowlands of the Cameroons consisted of the river and the forest. The forest was opaque and potentially hostile, a treasure house of fauna to be plundered and admired with caution. The river, by contrast, was open and friendly, a dreamland ribbon of wilderness where the cavalcade of nature slid past as if on a rotating stage. In his diary entry for 30 April Gerald recounts his impressions of the day spent drifting down the Mamfe to Asagem, allowing his new-found narrative gift full range in prose that is simple, vivid and measured.

The canoe arrived at some ungodly hour and the loads were carried down the hill and across the white beach and piled into it. We shoved off and raced down stream at a fine pace, and, once we had left the white man's tropical suburbia, the river plunged into the proper jungle.

It was here that I decided that travelling down an African river in a canoe is one of the most enchanting and lovely occupations one can conceive. For perhaps three miles the river runs unbroken by rapids, the waters like a black mirror sliding softly between the grey slopes of rock. The solid tangle of trees and shrubs runs right down to these rocks, two lines of green running down the river as far as the eye can see. The various shades of green are infinite, some rich and shining, some so delicate and ethereal they defy description: jade green, olive green, bottle green, emerald green, chartreuse green, all woven into this incredible filigree of leaves and branches. Even the rocky slopes themselves are covered, sometimes almost obscured, with a blanket of quivering ferns and patches of gleaming moss.

You pass several beaches, white as ivory and dazzling in the sun, with the bleached skeletons of trees lying across them. Everything is drenched in sunlight and silence. The only sounds are the piping cicadas, the soft, husky, plaintive coo of the Emerald Doves, and the pleasant, lazy plop and splash of the paddles in the waters. Then, far away, you hear a murmur, a sound so faint that it merges into the insect and bird calls. Slowly it gets louder, from a murmur to a chuckle to a full-throated, frightening roar. The placid waters seem suddenly to stir themselves to life, and you feel them seize the canoe in a fierce and exultant grip. Long shining black waves appear, moving restlessly along the sides of the canoe. The paddlers stop work – a few strokes to keep an even course and the river does the rest. Then you reach the bend in the river. The great rocks stretch across the river, tangled and jagged as the vertebra of some prehistoric monster. Through the gaps the river squeezes its waters, churning itself into a creamy froth and throwing a thousand glittering rainbows above the rocks. The roar of the waters is now so loud that you have to shout to be heard. The canoe hurtles forward, and for an awful moment it seems as though you are heading straight for solid rock; then suddenly a cleft appears, and you are carried through on a polished stream of water. Suddenly it is all over, and you are drifting through the shallows where the waters hurry along, chuckling and clinking on the smooth brown pebbles.

A river trip of this sort is ideal in so many ways. You go just slow enough to examine things around you. You get a wonderful view of the forest, for it is as if someone had cut a great cleft in it and allowed you to see the various stratas of foliage, from the tiny ground plants to the feathery tops of the hundred foot trees. Above all there is the delicious lazy peace of it, the warm waters, the endless horizon of the trees, and the tameness of everything.

Sometimes, where the river curved into a deep pool with shady banks, a hippo would rise from the depths and regard you with watchful but not unfriendly eyes. Then he would submerge silently, leaving only an ever widening circle of ripples and a few drifting silver bubbles. In the shallows where we bathed even the fish were tame, and little silver and green fellows some three inches long nosed gently around you and nibbled at your toes. We passed a troop of Mona monkeys coming down to drink and they shouted what I think were insulting remarks at us. Then an outcry arose, for there on the bank stood an adult Harnessed Antelope, the first one I have seen. It looked simply magnificent, a gleaming chestnut coat covered with great white stripes and strokes like giant writing. The hunters begged me to shoot, so, feeling that my reputation was at stake, I took careful aim at a spot about fifty yards to the right of her and let fly. Groans of disappointment, and suspicious looks from Pious, who knows I am quite a good shot really. The antelope stood stock still for a moment, then bounded up the bank and into the undergrowth, with my blessing.

We arrived at Asagem about four, and it turned out to be a tiny little village boasting about seventy inhabitants, sixty of whom were senile and rotting and the other ten young and festering. I was met by the Chief, a dirty old man, who was suffering from so many diseases that he looked as though he would fall to pieces if one blew at him, and he conducted me to the juju house where I was to stay. Here I unpacked and my bed was arranged under several skulls, a row of juju drums and other oddments of 'medicine'. Then I went off into the forest, walked about five miles and saw a lot of stuff, including a huge troop of Mona monkeys, moving through the trees. They made a great noise in the trees, and the swish of the leaves when they jump sounds like giant surf on a beach. Then I went home and slept the sleep of the dead, juju house and all.

The events of the following day or two proved to be by far the most distressing of Gerald's brief career. The plan was to snatch a hippo calf, and it was an iron rule of the river that it was impossible to do this without killing the parents first, for an enraged adult hippo is an utterly lethal creature.

At about six on the morning of 1 May Gerald and his little band of African hunters set out from Asagem, paddling upriver till they reached a small herd consisting of a hippo bull, cow and calf of about the right size. 'The idea was to shoot both the parents,' Gerald recorded afterwards, 'and then catching the calf would be easy. Accordingly I landed and worked my way down stream through the bushes until I reached a spot where I got a good view of them. The first shot I fired missed the cow completely, as I had never fired the .450 before and was a bit timid about the kick. She submerged with a splash and I thought she would swim off, but she came up again a few yards to the right and this time I shot her right between the eyes.' In the split-second it took for the bullet to shatter the hippo's brain, Gerald Durrell underwent a sea-change. He watched the consequences of his act with horror: 'She sank at once into the gloomy depths, and I was filled with an awful remorse.'

He still had the bull hippo to deal with. 'I felt that I must try and get rid of him without hurting him,' he wrote in his diary that night, 'as one hippo on my conscience was quite enough. Accordingly we leapt into the canoe and raced down the river towards him, while I fired shot after shot into the water just near him. We chased him about two miles down stream, and he made a great fuss, snorting and roaring and at one moment looking so ugly I thought he would attack the canoe.'

With the mother hippo dead and the father repelled, Gerald judged it was safe to retrieve the calf. But it was nowhere to be seen, having sunk beneath the surface of the river. When it failed to reappear it was assumed a crocodile had eaten it, and eventually a crocodile did indeed rise to the surface near the last spot where the baby hippo had been seen. 'The self-satisfied smirk on the croc's face enraged me,' Gerald wrote after-wards, 'so I shot him neatly between the eyes.' As he had feared, the remains of the baby hippo were found inside the crocodile's stomach – 'blast the bloody thing!'

Later the mother hippo was hauled up from the riverbed and dragged to the village, where the carcass was set upon by the protein-famished population 'like a pack of animals, fighting, tearing, screaming and push-ing'. One old woman got hold of a rib almost as big as herself, and finding herself beset by a hungry mob leapt into the river with it under one arm. 'She was a game old thing,' Gerald recorded, 'and she was a good twenty or thirty feet from the shore when they caught up with her and the rib and its owner disappeared under a forest of waving knives and bobbing black heads. The old lady at last swam back to shore, weeping and moaning, with a nasty cut on her forehead. I got her a large bit of meat and gave it to her, then I escorted her up to her house to see it was not pinched from her, and bathed her wound as well as I could. Now, every time she sees me she starts dancing and clapping her hands.'

Profoundly conscience-stricken by the day's events, Gerald wrote in his diary: 'I don't think I have ever felt so depressed. If I had got the baby I would not feel so bad about shooting the cow: but it seems such a shame to shoot a fat, lazy, funny-looking animal like a hippo for no reason.'

As far as is known, the hippo and the crocodile were the last animals that ever met a gratuitous end at Gerald Durrell's hands. When, four years later, he came to write his best-selling book about his second Cameroons venture, *The Bafut Beagles*, he made no mention of his shooting exploits, for they no longer represented something he wished to remember or be remembered for. In future years, even the distant sound of a pheasant shoot would pitch him into a mood of outrage and impotent despair, knowing all the tiny deaths the gunfire implied. By then the poacher had long become an ardent gamekeeper. 'For me the road to Damascus had been a very slow road with only one lane,' he was to confess years later.

It was on the hippo hunt near Asagem that he met his blinding light.

With two hippo dead and gone, Gerald's permit had been used up. Dejected, he retreated to Bakebe, where he settled himself in some style in the courthouse, a huge place with three-foot-thick walls all round. 'Having ensconced myself,' he recorded on 10 May, 'I then sent for all the local hunters and planned the capture of every beef from the French border to the foot of N'da Ali.'

This ambitious if desperate scheme did not go entirely to plan. Gerald's luck, it seemed, was out. He began to go down with sandfly fever, and though he had set a number of traps, including three for leopard, they yielded little of value. The leopard business was particularly frustrating, for though he could hear them at night and see them by day, none of them was tempted to take the fresh meat with which he baited the snares. The reason, he complained, was that the local tribesmen, many of them leopard worshippers, believed that the animals were inhabited by the spirits of their ancestors, and so placed a ju-ju on Gerald's traps.

What with one thing and another, his diary lapsed, and from 14 to 22 May there were no entries at all. 'Got all behind with this bloody thing again,' he noted on the twenty-third, 'owing to hard work on the traps and sandfly fever. The other day I received a very rude letter from Ken accusing me of not working, and all sorts of things, so I wrote back a carefully controlled snorter and received his apology today.'

In spite of the daily aggravations, Gerald was not yet – nor ever would be – impervious to the spell Africa could cast. He wrote in his diary in late May:

Today, somewhat to my surprise, I awoke at five-thirty, just as it started to get light. Staggering from my bed to attend the pangs of nature I was treated to one of the most lovely sights that I have ever seen.

The mist, white as snow, was starting to drift and disperse, and as it twisted its way into the sky like smoke the forest and mountains came into view. Everything was a deep jade green, and the mist, hanging in great swathes along the base of the mountains, made them look like dark islands in a white sea. The sky above the mist was a pale apple green tinged with gold where the sun was just starting to come up over the forest. As it rose higher and higher, the sky turned from green to gold and from gold to a lovely pink. Down in the village the cocks were crowing lustily and across the pink sky flew three hornbills, honking in the wild and hysterical way that hornbills have.

Gerald stood stock still, staring in awe and humility as if at the dawn of creation, and with his feet rooted firmly in the mud and his eyes fixed firmly on the sublime he responded to the call of nature in more senses than one. Etched in his memory for ever, this scene would recur to him in other places and at other times, a permanent testimony, an article of faith perhaps, to the lost world before man – precious, transcendental, but perishable.

The Cameroons diary ends on 23 May. Apart from a letter to Mother a fortnight later, Gerald left no written records of the remainder of the African adventure. Towards the end of the month Ken Smith wrote to Leslie, thanking him for his part in arranging for money to be sent to keep the collectors alive and functioning. Gerry was still at Bakebe, he reported, but as soon as he returned to the base camp at Mamfe they would start crating up, prior to moving down to the coast and the port of embarkation. Ominously, perhaps, the long rains were starting. 'Most days now, or at nights, we get heavy thunderstorms and torrential rain. Fortunately the jolly old tent stands up to it well, otherwise we should be washed away. It seems strange to think we will be back in England (blast the place!) in 8 weeks time.'

Then came calamity. The two Englishmen had hung on in the Cameroons desperately hoping to take delivery of a young gorilla that had been promised them. They had even cancelled their bookings on a cargo ship sailing from Tiko on 3 June, on the basis that the enormous sale price of a gorilla in Britain would well outweigh the extra cost of staying on in Africa. But the gorilla never turned up, and with the next available boat not due for another two months, they faced a grim wait in the torrential rains that now began to drown the country in earnest. No gorilla, no boat, no money – their circumstances were so straitened that Gerald was forced to sell his precious shotgun and .318 rifle, and anything else that could be spared. On 8 June he wrote to his mother:

> We are now hung up till August the sixth, so won't be home till the 20th. Our position at the moment is that we have enough stock to sell at stupidly low prices and still make enough profit to pay back our debts, but I don't think it will leave enough to go collecting again. This is an awful thought, and we are straining every nerve to try and get something big before we leave. Our collection is zoologically wonderful, but just needs the one or two big items which the zoos will buy for their bloody Public.

Stranded in Mamfe, his thoughts began to turn to home, and particularly to his long-lost girls of home: 'Please ask Margo, if you ever see her, to give my love to Rosemary and Connie at the Barn Club. What's wrong with Diane [Ursula]? She wrote me a very back-up letter . . .'

Gerald and his companion now reversed roles, and it was Ken Smith who set off into the interior, aiming for the Endop Plain, right up in the mountains, for as big a trawl of the local wildlife as he could manage in the time remaining. 'This is his first real trip by himself,' Gerald wrote, 'and he went off as excited as a schoolboy. He certainly deserves it.'

For all its remorseless routine of cleaning the cages and feeding their occupants, being stuck at base camp was almost as much fun as collecting in the wilds, as Gerald wrote home:

> Going to bush, you get the thrill of seeing new places and of catching new animals. Here you can really study the animals day by day, and each day learn some new thing. For example, Mary, the female chimp, is cleaned out in the morning, and by night her straw is all dirty. So, before going to sleep, she turns the whole lot over and sleeps on the nice clean underside. She has a habit of lying on her back and looking at you daringly, then if you blow on her bottom she will cover it up with her hands and scream with laughter. This is now referred to, even by the animal boys, as Blowing Mary's Wicked Parts. Mary has a passion for clothes, and will lure a native up to her cage by patting her tummy or turning somersaults or some other trick, and then, when he is within reach, she will shoot out her hand, and there will be a loud ripping sound mingled with yelps of fright, and the now shirtless native will be left glaring with rage while Mary puts the shirt over her head and looks coy. Both chimps are so fat they can hardly move. The other day I thought I would see how greedy Charles, the young male chimp, really was, so I kept on pushing bananas through the bars and he ended up by having two in his mouth, one in each hand and one in each foot – and still screamed when I wouldn't hand him any more. He is very ticklish on his collar-bones and will start screaming with helpless laughter before you even touch his neck.

Gerald was no longer just a zoological mercenary, a bring-'em-back-alive bounty hunter. Though he had no formal qualifications as a zoologist, his intimate, round-the-clock association with a vast horde of some three hundred creatures from a huge range of species and his minute observation of their physical forms, habits and mannerisms, as well as the environments and micro-habitats from which they came, represented a prolonged and intensive field-study course which would have been the envy of any zoology department in the world. It was to be the foundation of the formidable knowledge of animal behaviour he was to build up over the years. Out of the zoo collector was emerging the zoological polymath.

'No two animals are alike,' he was to say later. 'They are irritating, annoying, frustrating, but never boring. They vary as much as humans do. There are the great characters among them, the natural comedians, the wide boys, the problem children, the greedy ones, the inquisitive ones, the hypocrites, mental defectives, split personalities and so on. Watching them once you have got them is one of the chief charms of the trip. So I gave short shrift to a man who once said he couldn't understand why I liked animals so much, they were all so dull, all the same.'

But it was killing work. 'There is little time for anything, even sleep,' he wrote to Mother, 'as it seems that no sooner have you given the Red River Hogs their midnight feed than it is dawn and you have to start cleaning out all over again.' Only after the nocturnal animals had had their evening feed was it possible to relax a little. 'You then have three lovely hours to yourself, and can do anything you want to: generally there are some specimens to bottle and a few to skin. Then your bath, a few quick ones, and chop. After chop you fill in the diary and the additions book, feed the Bushbaby and the Red River Hogs and give a last bottle to the baby Chevrotain, then crawl into bed.' As for being asked out to dinner, 'you are so near to sleep that your host might as well carry on a conversation with his bookcase'.

So the weeks passed, and the rain continued to pour and the grass to soar and the bugs to swarm and the creatures in their cages to complain. Eventually Ken Smith returned from the hills with a large new batch of animals, and by the end of July the collection had increased to some five hundred specimens, including a number of unspectacular species of largely scientific interest, for Gerald was no longer just a menagerie collector, but a field zoologist anxious to make a contribution to knowledge. Finally, in early August the time came to dismantle the base camp overlooking the Mamfe River and to transport the collection down to Tiko and the boat home. 'It was,' Gerald was to recall, 'one of the worst journeys I can remember.'

Three lorries and a van were needed to shift animals and stores the two hundred miles down to the coast, travelling at night when it was cooler for the animals. Every three hours they had to stop to sprinkle the boxes of frogs with cold water, and twice each night they had to stop again to bottle-feed the younger animals with warm milk kept in thermos flasks. At dawn they would pull off the road and park in the shade of the trees, unloading every cage and cleaning and feeding every animal. On the morning of 7 August they reached the docks and began to load the cages on to the forward deck of the banana boat SS *Tetela* – the very same ship in which Gerald had sailed home the previous year.

One unwelcome task remained. Gerald had been told that at a banana plantation not far from the port a drainage sump had been uncovered that was found to be full of snakes. Even at this stage – in spite of having nearly died of snake-bite recently – Gerald found the prospect of a pit full of snakes irresistible. But the circumstances were not propitious. For one thing, time was short and the collecting would have to be done at night. For another, the snakes turned out to be Gaboon vipers – one of the most deadly species in West Africa. They were not only poisonous, but were equipped with particularly long fangs to enable them to inject their venom deep into the victim's body, to much quicker effect. Moreover, their habit was to hunt for food at night, so they would be very much awake.

With considerable trepidation Gerald was lowered into the viper pit on the end of a rope, equipped with an unreliable lamp, a collecting bag and a Y-shaped stick. As he descended he could hear ominous hisses rising up in protest, and glimpsed thirty or forty snakes writhing and spitting below him. This was the most perilous and nightmarish foray of his collecting career, requiring a very cold courage and a high degree of skill. For half an hour Gerald was in the pit. One of his shoes fell off, the pit wall was crumbly, and the lamp went out, leaving him in darkness till a replacement was lowered down. Then at a signal he was hauled slowly up, his collecting bag packed with a dozen wriggling snakes. 'I sat on the ground,' he was to recall, 'smoking a much needed cigarette and trying to steady my trembling hands. Now that the danger was over I began to realise how extremely stupid I had been and how exceptionally lucky I was to come out alive.'

Next day they set sail. Gerald's main concern was to keep the sole surviving *Idiurus* alive till they got to England. The creature had developed a taste for avocado pears, and though these were out of season in the Cameroons, they were able to keep up the supply by raiding the ship's captain's private hoard. But in spite of all their efforts, having travelled four thousand miles and got within twenty-four hours of Liverpool, the *Idiurus* died. Though most of the other animals survived, including the two chimpanzees and the hairy frogs, Gerald was devastated by the loss of his last precious pigmy flying squirrel. 'I was bitterly disappointed,' he was to recall, 'and black depression settled on me.'

It was not a wildly happy homecoming when the *Tetela* finally nosed into Garston Docks on 25 August 1949, but Gerald and his staunch and able companion Ken Smith had much to be proud of. They had survived disease, hardship, destitution, danger, solitude, a poisonous snake-bite and the wilds of Africa. They had even survived the notorious difficulties of travelling in the Cameroons – the homicidal lorries and the deathtrap bridges. And they had returned with five hundred living creatures, representing seventy species and housed in 139 crates – eighty-one of them containing mammals, forty-two containing reptiles, fourteen containing birds and two containing land crabs. In all the expedition had cost £2500, and would probably make a modest profit of around £400, not counting the equipment, which could be resold for about £900. It was an achievement of substance.

The press evidently thought so too. Reporters from most of the national papers swarmed on board, flashbulbs popping. 'Two Men Sail in with a New Noah's Ark' ran the *Daily Express* headline. 'Jungle Hunters get Bag of 500' splashed the *Star*. Hot on the newsmen's heels came the representatives of the London, Edinburgh, Manchester, Bristol, Paignton, Chester and Dublin zoos, and an animal importer by the name of Robert Jackson, who was 'here for the snakes'. They crowded the well deck, discussing prices and zoological fashions and inspecting clawed toads, moustached monkeys and the hissing golden cat. Their vans and shooting brakes lined the quay, and business was brisk. Eventually over a third of the collection was taken by Chester Zoo, while London took some of the rarities of special scientific interest, many of them never before seen alive in Britain, including the hairy frog and a large number of insects.

Though the expedition had failed to acquire any truly spectacular animals, the lesser creatures paraded before the crowd on board were intriguing enough. 'Dock workers unloading bananas from the steamship *Tetela*,' reported the *Yorkshire Post*, 'stopped work in astonishment when a fair-haired young man on deck put his hand in a wooden crate and dragged out a wriggly, two-foot-long black object with long, hairy legs – the first creature of its kind ever to be brought into this country. The hairy frog appeared to be displeased with its first glimpse of Britain. It uttered weird, low-pitched croaks and thrashed its long, hairy legs.'

The collectors, now attired in jackets and ties, posed for the photographers – a balding Ken Smith clutching a baby broad-fronted crocodile, a tousle-haired Gerald Durrell with a little guenon, or moustached monkey, perched on his shoulder. Though it was Charlie the chimpanzee who won the hearts of the newsmen, it was Gerald who held their attention. 'An unconventional young man,' as one reporter described him, 'with his aesthetically lean face, long-fingered hands and well-cut suit.' Others saw him differently. 'At a glance,' reported the *Illustrated London News*, 'you might imagine Gerald Durrell, aged 24, height five-feet-eight, was a prosperous young farmer, for he has the clear eyes, fresh features and broad shoulders common to men whose working lives are spent in the open air. His conversation, however, gives no hint of crops and cows, for he is concerned with sterner aspects of nature.' Such as snake bites and hippo hunts, juju curses on leopard traps and beagling across the grasslands of Bafut with dogs wearing little bells. It was all good, exotic stuff – and it was Gerald Durrell's first big press call. He was a star, if only for a day or two. It was a step down a road he did not yet realise he was following.

As he prepared to go ashore, Gerald let it be known that he and Ken Smith were planning a third collecting expedition in a few months – this time to South America. But though further encounters with the animal denizens of the tropical wilds seemed Gerald's next goal, it was an altogether different kind of meeting that was to shape his immediate destiny. At the back of his expedition notebook he had listed the British zoos he proposed to visit in connection with his latest collection, and the last name on the list was – 'Manchester'.

TEN

New Worlds to Conquer

Love and Marriage 1949–1951

Gerald Durrell was one of those men who genuinely liked women. Brought up in the warm, womb-like ambience of a female household, he had always seen them as a source of comfort and security, and by his late teens he saw them as something else as well. As his dallyings in the Guinea Pig Palace at Whipsnade indicate, he could be as sexually driven and obsessed as any normal young man of his age. It helped that he was exceptionally good-looking, with his fair hair flopping casually over his forehead, his frank, quizzical blue eyes that always seemed to be laughing, and his square jaw and long, rather aesthetic face. But it was his personality that proved even more alluring to women, for he was endowed not only with charm but with presence and humour as well.

When Gerald returned to England he took every opportunity that came his way to compensate for his six-month deprivation in matters romantic, cutting a swathe through the North Country as he progressed from Chester to Dudley and Wellingborough on zoo matters. Eventually, around mid-September, he reached Manchester, where he had business at the Belle Vue Zoo, and checked in at a small commercial hotel run by a Mr John Thomas Wolfenden. Gerald's arrival at this seemingly unpromising venue was to be a rendezvous with fate.

The hotel was crowded with the female *corps de ballet* of the Sadler's Wells Opera Company, then spending two weeks of its provincial tour in Manchester. The arrival of a dashing young African explorer and animal catcher caused some commotion amongst the horde of dancing girls, as the hotel proprietor's nineteen-year-old daughter – a bright, rather aloof, *gamine* young woman called Jacqueline, familiarly known as Jacquie – tartly noted. The chattering ballerinas, she later recorded, 'could do nothing but talk about some marvellous being who apparently had everything any woman could possibly desire. Then one wet Sunday afternoon the peace was shattered by a mass of female forms cascading through the living-room door and dragging in their wake a rather delicate-looking Rupert-Brookish young man. Judging by their idiotic behaviour, this could only be Wonderboy himself – and it was.'

Jacquie was usually scornful of people she judged to be 'shallow, spoilt and wholly extrovert', and Gerald Durrell appeared to her to fall into this category. He looked remarkably like the American film star Dana Andrews, she thought, and behaved exactly like a cock in a hen run. Then he became aware that she was watching him, and looked in her direction. Their eyes met for the first time, his fixing hers with what she was to describe as a 'basilisk stare', before she looked away in embarrassment. The memory of this first moment of mutual awareness, literally across a crowded room, was permanently engraved on Gerald's memory: 'There, sitting by the fire, surrounded by all these girls, was something that looked like a baby robin, and I can remember it to this moment, absolutely vividly, it went boom, just like that, into my face, and I thought feebly, Gosh, she's stunning.'

Jacquie beat a hasty retreat from the room, disconcerted and not a little aghast at the man, though also 'rather amused by his posturings'. She was less amused when she discovered that he was conducting simultaneous affairs with three of the ballerinas in her father's hotel – Durrell himself in later years could only recall one – and all the more determined to have nothing to do with this objectionable but happily transient young man.

During the remaining two weeks of Gerald's stay Jacquie saw next to nothing of him. But one morning her stepmother asked her if she could escort Mr Durrell to the station, as (unbelievably) he appeared to have no idea where it was. Jacquie agreed, but made it plain she was doing so under protest. She recalled: 'Having finally satisfied himself that I was not overjoyed at having him as a companion, Mr Durrell went out of his way to exert every facet of that very great charm which was so much admired by females in general. When this did not produce any marked results he switched to humour and, much to my annoyance, he did amuse me – so much, in fact, that I was sorry to see him go.'

Never expecting to see Gerald again, Jacquie put him out of her mind and concentrated on her studies for a career as an opera singer. She had a rich contralto voice and a promising future, and went so far as to change her surname from Wolfenden to Rasen on the advice of her teachers, who thought a less cumbersome name would help her career. It was therefore something of a shock when, in the late autumn, with the hotel turned upside down for extensive renovations, the debonair young man returned.

He was planning a new animal collecting expedition to British Guiana, he announced, and was visiting zoos in the area to get orders. Though he was out most days, he was in most evenings, taking his meals with the family, 'exchanging saucy badinage with my stepmother,' Jacquie was to record, 'and engaging my father in long, involved discussions on current events. He quickly became everybody's friend except mine.'

Gerald was well aware how Jacquie felt about him, but that didn't stop him asking her father if he could take her out to dinner one evening. 'When I got used to the idea I was pleased,' Jacquie remembered. 'I was between boyfriends and thought it might be amusing to spend an evening with such a "man of the world". Much to my astonishment, I thoroughly enjoyed myself and we got on extremely well together.' Gerald's adventures as an animal catcher fascinated her, and she was intrigued by his tales of his unusual family and exotic upbringing on Corfu. Jacquie had never had any real family life of her own, as her parents had separated when she was two and for some years she had been passed from one relative to another, so she envied Gerald his secure and happy childhood. She found herself telling him things she had never told anyone before. 'By the time we returned home,' she recalled, 'I had lost any feelings of distrust or animosity I had had, and really felt that I had at last found a friend whom I could talk to and relax with.'

In a day or two Gerald was off again. Preparations for the British Guiana expedition were all-preoccupying, and Jacquie did not hear any more from her new-found friend before his departure.

Early in the New Year of 1950 Gerald found himself clambering on board yet another scruffy little cargo boat at Liverpool Docks. By now he was an established collector for all the major zoos in Britain, a profession which, he reckoned, brought him into contact with around a hundred animals for every human being he encountered. But collecting animals, he knew only too well, was not a way to get rich quickly. It was just that he couldn't think of anything else he would rather do. 'If it comes to that,' he over-modestly informed an acquaintance just before he set sail, 'I can't think of anything else I could do, even if I wanted to. My qualifications are very elementary. I can treat snake bites, paddle a hollow-log canoe, use a rifle, ride a horse, move quietly through undergrowth, and sit still for hours on end. That's about all I can do. Fortunately, that's about all an animal collector has to do.'

On 27 January he disembarked at Demarara, British Guiana, and set foot in the New World for the first time:

Guiana was absolutely ravishing, because it was so different. It looked as though a florist's shop had been emptied over every tree or bush. I heard an odd noise, quite inexplicable, and was drawn to a tree rioting with orchids and giving out this susurration far more subtle than bees, and then with difficulty – for everything so fabulously new is experienced with difficulty – I saw that something like two or three hundred hummingbirds were feeding off the orchids and making that intent perishable sound. And then on another occasion I was skimming in a canoe down the black tributaries and the whole surface was covered with water plants that had minute leaves rather like mustard-and-cress with a satiny haze of pink bloom hanging over it, so that miraculously your canoe was sliding without the faintest sound across a pinkflowered lawn. God, I must get back there, quick, quick, quick, before it's too late. It's getting too late everywhere. Will I ever wake up again as I did one morning in Georgetown? All so very apparently normal, like a suburban house in England, and not knowing where I was, expecting to spring awake and see the ship's cabin around me. But I looked out hazily, all I had to do lying on my pillow was to open my eyes, and there was a huge magnolia tree with big glossy leaves like plates, all pullulating with three different species of tanager, red and black, cobalt, white and green, hovering in and out of the leaves as they fed. Such moments are beyond belief. They make me feel that at least I'm the centre of my own life. Being considered mad by everyone, mad and fanatical, suddenly makes sense. And the pampas was the closest to true peace I had ever known.

With Ken Smith looking after the main collection in Georgetown, the capital, Gerald travelled far and wide up country in pursuit of strange animals, helped by a companionable itinerant artist by the name of Robert Lowes. They had to wade through swamps, struggle through forest and grassland, swim across lakes and rivers, sit for hours on end in narrow canoes, eat and sleep surrounded by a fantastic assortment of birds, beasts and reptiles. Their destinations were many and varied – from the small town of Adventure on the Essequibo River (where they hunted the moonshine uwarie) and the Karanambo ranch of the legendary Tiny McTurk in the Rupununi savannah far to the south (where they galloped after the giant anteater and stalked the arapaima, the largest freshwater fish in the world, and the capybara, the largest living rodent), to the creek lands at the ocean's edge, an intricate system of narrow, tangled, twisting water roads, where they spent at least half their time afloat, hunting the pipa toad and paradoxical frog, the pimpla hog and tree porcupine ('the only real comedian in the animal world').

The creek lands cast a magic spell. 'We paddled back along the silent creeks,' Gerald was to write of their haunting, primordial air, 'the black waters reflecting the star-shimmering sky with such faithfulness that we felt the canoe was floating through space among the planets. Caymans grunted among the reeds, strange fish rose and gulped at the myriads of pale moths that drifted across the water. In the bottom of the canoe, spreadeagled in a tin, lay the amphibians that had made our evening so perfect. Every few minutes we would glance down at them and smirk with satisfaction. The capturing of an incredibly ugly toad: of such simple pleasures is a collector's life made up.'

Gerald had promised to write to Jacquie from British Guiana when he had a chance, but he never did, and with some relief – for she sensed the danger of getting far too involved with someone like him – she turned back to her opera studies and the long Manchester winter, and put him out of her mind.

But Gerald had not forgotten her. Try as hard as he might, he could not. 'Normally on a trip everyone I knew vanished,' he recounted, 'but this wretched face kept recurring when I was cleaning out the cages or floating down the river in a canoe; all the time it kept flashing into my mind, and I thought, Why should the others be so unmemorable while this one keeps intruding on my brain? So I made a mental note that, should I be able to inveigle her into a corner, I would try and get to know her better.'

Not even encounters with a vast range of dramatic species – from a fer de lance snake that could kill in seconds and an anaconda eight feet long and as thick as a male ballet dancer's thigh, to a score or more of delicate little squirrel monkeys which, when clustered along a branch, looked (so Gerald noted) 'like a bed of pansies' – could entirely obliterate the image of the young Manchester girl from his mind. Not even a no less dramatic brown-skinned girl called Rita could do so. Gerald had met Rita at an 'at home' held in a Mrs Clarabelle's Georgetown boarding house. Among the host of beautiful girls of all colours who filled the room, his attention was riveted by one whose beauty made all the others fade into insignificance. 'She had very pale, chestnut-coloured skin,' he was to write in a private memoir, 'the sort of shade you get by mixing half a bar of Cadbury's chocolate with a pint of cream. Her hair was long, black, curly and as magnificent as a lion's mane. She was slender, lithe, warm and tenacious, with superb legs, wonderfully expressive hands and a rich, musical laugh, as fresh and enchanting as a lark's song. I sat down beside her.'

'My name is Gerry,' he said, opting for the near ultimate in chat-up lines, 'and you are the most beautiful girl in the world.'

'And you,' said Rita, opting for the near ultimate in brush-offs, 'are something else, man.'

By April they had run out of money, and it was decided that Gerald should return to England with the main bulk of the collection, leaving Ken Smith behind until Gerald could remit funds to pay the debts incurred by the expedition, as well as the freight charges and the cost of Smith's ticket home. Gerald sailed on the cargo boat *Arakaka* on 27 April 1950. It was not an agreeable voyage. Quite apart from the worry about present debts and future insolvency, he went down with a recurrence of the malaria he had contracted in the Cameroons.

It was a shock to Jacquie when she found Gerald back in the living-room of her father's hotel one May afternoon, 'looking extremely fit and well and (even to my jaundiced eye) attractive'. Gerald was in Manchester because that was where the majority of the animals from British Guiana were being housed. His plan was to sell them off as soon as possible and send the proceeds out to Ken Smith, so that he could catch another batch of animals before returning home. Though Gerald was out for much of the day and night cleaning and feeding his charges, Jacquie was 'appalled at the idea of having this disturbing influence around for so long', and 'even more determined to be off-putting'.

But, to her discomfort, Gerald appeared to be developing a more sharply focused interest in her. She was not his normal type – not one of the 'clumping carthorse blondes' (as he once called them) towards whom he had instinctively veered in the past. 'I always used to go like a bullet for the blondes,' he confided to a friend a long time later, 'but the ones I gave my heart to were the dark ones.'

Jacquie, it seems, had a precursor, her name lost to memory, but her physical form evidently became the prototype to which Gerald's eventual 'true love' would have to conform. 'My first amour,' he recalled of this proto-Jacquie, 'swam into my life when I started dancing lessons in Bournemouth, and there she was, looking extraordinarily like Jacquie. In years I only kissed her once.' When the real thing came along, therefore, Gerald recognised her at once – love not at first but at second sight. With her petite frame, large brown eyes, pert mouth, dark brown hair and youthful manner Jacquie was attractive enough. But she was more than that, as Gerald perceived early on.

For one thing, she was a personality in her own right, intelligent, perceptive, and highly individual. She had a mind of her own and often spoke it, in the frank, forthright manner of the North Country. As a person she was mature beyond her years, self-assured, poised. Crucially, she was possessed of a keen sense of humour, and was quick to appreciate the humour of others, especially when it was as unpredictably original and fantastical as Gerald's. In many ways she was a complement to Gerald, possessing some of the qualities he lacked. Where he was dreamy and romantic, she was practical and down-to-earth. Where he dithered, she was decisive. Where he was incompetent, she was competent. In her company Gerald became twice the man he was, the pipe dream became a blueprint, and the impossible possible. Above all, she never bored him. 'There's only one person I could tolerate for any length of time,' he once told a friend, 'and that's Jacquie ... She's so quick, she stimulates the mind like an extra dose of adrenaline.'

From the outset Gerald refused to be put off by Jacquie's rebuffs. 'She could be very brusque,' he was to relate. 'All her other boyfriends were comparatively inexperienced, whereas I was the first semi-adult she had encountered – she was a bit scared and didn't know how to handle me. She knew that I was a man of the world, whatever that means, that I'd actually had "affairs" with "ladies". So I suppose she found me a bit off-putting, fighting a rearguard action in case what did happen might happen.'

His first move was to try and fire her interest in what impassioned him most – the animal world. He had to draw up a lot of long lists of the animals he had brought back from South America for the zoos, he told her. Was there any chance she could help him type them up on her father's typewriter? Jacquie agreed, calculating that the sooner Gerald completed his business the sooner he would be gone. But the task proved gargantuan. She had never guessed that there were so many different birds and animals in the world, with so many strange and incomprehensible names. She bombarded Gerald with endless questions, enabling him to make his second move. Perhaps, he suggested, she ought to come up to the zoo to see all the creatures she was asking about with her own eyes.

'This did not appeal to me at all,' Jacquie wrote later,

> as I held very strong views on the ethics of keeping any wild creatures in captivity. Strangely enough, Gerry did not try to persuade me or pressure me into going with him the next day, neither did he defend zoos in general, but he did try to explain what the real function of a well-run zoo should be, and how vital it was, in the face of the population explosion and the spread of civilisation, that wildlife should be preserved for future generations.

Zoos, he argued, would eventually be the last sanctuary for wild things as man increased in numbers and slowly encroached on the natural habitat. It was inevitable that when the interests of man conflicted with those of wildlife, the animals would go to the wall. His most cherished ambition in life was to create a special zoo where he could keep and breed some of these creatures in the hope that they would not be completely exterminated, and the one thing he felt passionately about was that all zoos must cease to be mere showplaces and become true scientific institutions where the welfare of the animals was of paramount importance.

They reached Belle Vue Zoo and entered the large wooden building which housed Gerald's loudly squealing and chattering South American collection. Jacquie's previous experiences of zoos had convinced her that they were 'horrible, smelly places where I would not dream of keeping a dead cat'. It was immediately obvious that this was different. The prevailing odour was sweet and pleasant, a mixture of fresh straw, good food and warm animal bodies. Even more impressive was Gerald's relationship with the creatures in his care:

> Suddenly, this seemingly shallow young man became a different person. Gone was the diffident air as he walked solemnly up and down the lines of cages, giving each creature titbits and talking to them. He really cared about them, and they, in a funny way, returned this love and interest with obvious trust. Like small children, they would scream out to attract his attention, or jump up and down eagerly, waiting to be noticed. I followed slowly behind him along the passageways and peered, I admit rather timidly, into each cage, becoming quite absorbed by these lovely creatures. Without doubt all these animals knew that they were being looked at in a special way, and yet they did not appear to resent my being there.
>
> We spent quite a long time there, while Gerry gave every animal a second feed and renewed any wet straw, and I just sat on a box and watched him. He worked quietly and efficiently, obviously enjoying himself, and talking to every animal as he passed. He had certainly forgotten that I was there, and concentrated his entire attention on the animals. The whole thing fascinated me.

Following the zoo visit, the friendship between the two developed fast. Jacquie was working in her father's town office, and the phone never stopped ringing as Gerald bombarded her with invitations to dinner, coffee, tea, theatre, cinema. Noticing the amount of time she was spending out of the office, her father grew worried that she was succumbing to the attentions of a man who was, as she put it, 'totally different from my usual male friends'.

The crisis seemed to have been averted when Gerald announced one morning, much to the relief of Jacquie's father, that the time had come for him to leave Manchester. All the animals he was keeping there had now gone to their various zoos, and it was time he paid a visit to his mother, whom he had not seen since he left England in January.

Jacquie took Gerald to the station, bade her goodbyes, and returned to her office. Soon afterwards, her father rang. Had Gerald caught the train all right? Yes, she said, he had gone. As she put the phone down the door burst open, and there stood Gerald, framed in the doorway, thrusting a large bunch of faded chrysanthemums in her direction.

'These are for you,' he said.

He half turned to leave, then hesitated.

'You wouldn't like to marry me, would you?' he asked.

Receiving no positive response, he shrugged his shoulders and gave a wry grin. 'I didn't think you would.'

Gerald made his second exit of the morning, and this time he didn't come back. But soon, by every post, letters, postcards, parcels and lengthy telegrams began to arrive at the hotel. Jacquie's father was dismayed. What was going on between her and the Durrell chap, he demanded. Obviously the Durrell chap was hoping to take advantage of her, if he hadn't already. The world was full of men who led innocent young women astray. The Durrell chap was obviously one of them. 'After all, who is he?' her father asked. 'On his own admission he comes from a very dubious background, and he certainly has no money, nor is ever likely to have.' If Jacquie was going to marry anyone, it would have to be someone more substantial, 'like a lawyer or a doctor,' she recalled, 'who could support me if my singing voice ever gave out'.

Looking back, Jacquie could see that he did have a point. 'My father had no reason to believe that Gerry would be any different in the future than what he seemed to be then.' Gerry gave every impression of being indolent and unambitious. He was penniless and thriftless, carting about with him a suitcase of unopened bills. He believed that he was washed up, that he would never go on another collecting expedition. And having acquired a taste for whisky in Africa, he frequently resorted to it in England, in the belief that it had the power to dissolve all his problems away. It was this, probably, that alarmed Jacquie's father most of all. 'My father's father died at a relatively early age through alcohol,' Jacquie remembered. 'Father himself, given a couple of drinks, turned into a raving lunatic. So, with this built-in abhorrence of drink, anyone who to his mind was inclined that way had to be left severely alone, especially if this chap wanted to get mixed up with his daughter.'

But Gerald would not give up. When Jacquie angrily rebuked him over the phone for pestering her with letters and gifts, he quietly suggested he come up to Manchester to talk with her father and straighten everything out. Two days later he was back at the hotel, closeted in a room with Jacquie's father. But instead of the raised voices and vituperation Jacquie had expected to hear, there came only the sounds of chat and laughter. Gerald eventually emerged, smiling happily. Her father had no objections to him personally, he told Jacquie, nor to him going out with his daughter. As Jacquie was to comment later: 'Gerald took it as a right to get everything he wanted, and frankly no one could refuse him.'

Jacquie was furious with Gerald for persisting, and with her father for giving ground. To punish her father, she calculatedly encouraged her suitor. If her father really believed she was emotionally involved with Gerry and might run off with him – well, she would be. She persuaded Gerald to stay on a few more days, then spent every available moment with him, staying out until all hours, infuriating the older man while leading the younger one on. 'I had entered into this game as a way of getting back at stupidity,' Jacquie recalled, 'but I suddenly realised that our attitude to each other had changed. Having spent every spare minute together, it soon began to dawn on us that we were getting emotionally involved and that it would not be easy to say goodbye.'

Gerald returned to Bournemouth. By now Mother's house was in the process of being sold, and she had moved into Margaret's house across the road, most of which Margaret had converted into a number of small flats for rent. A warren of rooms on three floors was inhabited by a troupe of eccentric lodgers, from jazz trumpeters and a painter of nudes to a battered wife and a Maltese transsexual. Margaret recalled Gerald's arrival vividly:

> His arrival eclipsed all else for the next twenty-four hours. Mother's face, unlike mine, cheered delightedly at the sight of her youngest son. I groaned aloud as the familiar boyish face, very like my own, grinned at the mob racing to the gate to greet him. He stepped from the car, tall, fair and debonair, holding a sack carefully in one hand as if carrying a rare gift, but I knew better than that. There was an involved gesticulated discussion which seemed to involve the house, the garage and the large wooden cage that was

resting on the boot of the taxi. I knew the meaning of the sack and the wooden box.

'If he puts one foot over my threshold,' I said in a voice of doom, 'I'm done for.'

'Too late, dear,' said Mother in a queer voice, as many hands lifted the crate and it cleared the gate tipped at a crazy angle.

'Just a few monkeys,' Gerald called out airily, seeing Mother and me for the first time and throwing a saucy eye heavenwards towards an upstairs window, where two half-clad female bodies, disturbed from their slumbers, watched him.

'I hope there is nothing dangerous in that sack, dear,' Mother enquired, kissing her youngest tenderly.

'It's a six-foot python,' Gerald replied carelessly, 'but harmless.'

Gerald was now penniless – 'living on ten Woodbines a day and a lot of tea'. He had not made the killing he had hoped for from his expeditions, his assets amounted to no more than £200, and he had no job. Worse, his health began to go steadily downhill, probably the after-effect of the malignant malaria he had contracted in the Cameroons.

What to do? It was a difficult situation. As things stood, marriage was impossible. For one thing, Jacquie was still under age. The best option would be for Gerald to get a job. The only thing he knew anything about was the animal world, but zoo jobs were hard to get, and his hopes were not high. It was a dire handicap that he had fallen foul of George Cansdale, the Superintendent of the London Zoo and a powerful figure in the Federation of Zoological Gardens of Great Britain and Ireland.

'Cansdale hated Gerry's guts,' Jacquie recalled, 'and did everything in his power to thwart him. Cansdale was extremely jealous of Gerry because he regarded himself as "the only" authority on West African fauna and deeply resented anyone who intruded into his private domain. The thing that really sealed Gerry's fate was when he brought back an extremely rare mammal that had eluded Cansdale called an angwantibo. It was the first time a live specimen had been brought back to the UK and naturally caused a zoological stir at that time. Apart from this, Gerry was never slow to criticise zoos, and London Zoo in particular. He regarded them *all* as commercial sideshows, not much better than circuses.'

David Attenborough, a near contemporary of Gerald's whose first *Zoo Quest* series for BBC Television in 1954 told the story of a London Zoo collecting expedition to West Africa, believes that Gerald had every reason to be critical: 'A great proportion of the animals were not bred in the zoo, so specimens had continually to be taken from the wild; and the zoo still had the Victorian idea that a scientific zoo had to exhibit the maximum number of species, like a stamp collection. George Cansdale could be very overbearing and was not really a popular man at the zoo. Eventually he was sacked for alleged irregularities of one kind or another and quite a lot of people were very pleased to see him go. So to have an ex junior trainee from Whipsnade pipe up and say all this was nonsense would not have pleased him at all.' And indeed it did not. Gerald was blackballed by the British zoo establishment – in the form of an *ad hoc* group of directors of non-commercial zoos – to whom Cansdale sent a round-robin letter unfairly accusing him of neglecting his animals and incompetence as a collector.

From the hubbub of Margaret's house, whose collective night noises reminded him of the Amazon rainforest before a storm, Gerald continued the fruitless search for suitable work. Finally, despairing of finding a more senior post, he used his contact with the Belle Vue Zoo to obtain a short-term job looking after its aquarium, sometimes keeping an eye on the reptile house as well, and this kept him busy for much of the second half of 1950. Gerald was never to write a word about this obscure period of his working life, mentioning it only twice, once as an aside to a friend, and once in a letter to his bank. Despite his diffidence about it, this relatively low-key post kept him in funds after the losses he had incurred on his last expedition; and more importantly, it kept him close to Jacquie, at whose hotel home he was to live throughout that time.

Margaret remembered Gerald's eventual departure from Bournemouth almost as clearly as his arrival: 'Disorganising the entire household, Gerald collected up his python with a showy tenderness and, putting me in unwilling protesting charge of the monkeys in the garage, he left me with the unhappy thought that he would be back soon, the only consolation being that so far none of my lodgers had given notice.'

The moment Gerald's back was turned, the monkeys in the garage saw their chance and bolted. The first Margaret knew about it was when a huffy neighbour called Lord Booth telephoned her.

'There is an animal in my bedroom,' he growled, 'that has knocked over the light and is eating my tobacco!'

Shortly afterwards a police car pulled up outside the house.

'Good morning,' one of the officers said. 'Are you missing anything? Some monkeys, perhaps?'

Twelve had gone missing, and only three had been sighted so far. The rest had made their way into town, where the local paper started a daily column with news of sightings and of the escapades they had been involved in. Gerald arrived to take charge, and one by one the prodigals returned.

'They greeted their foster father with recognisable cries of welcome and touching shows of affection,' Margaret recalled. 'Touching, that is, to those who had not suffered the galling indignities of chasing a monkey, or its bites!'

Jacquie, meanwhile, had come of age and no longer needed parental consent to be married, but this only made life with father at home more strained. It was a relief, therefore, when Margaret invited her to visit Bournemouth for a long weekend in the late autumn. Margaret was getting married again, and thought this was a good opportunity for Jacquie to meet the rest of the family, especially as it looked as if she might become a part of it herself in due course.

Gerald brought her down to Bournemouth, and it was quite late by the time they reached the boarding house, the new fulcrum of the Durrells' family life. Any prior knowledge Jacquie had about the family was based on what Gerald had sketched out for her – but that was enough. 'I was quite frankly terrified at the thought of meeting them all,' she admitted. 'It would be unpleasant to live so close to them if I was not completely accepted.'

Her first encounter was with Margaret and her second-husband-to-be, a strapping twenty-one-year-old corporal in the Life Guards by the name of Malcolm Duncan. Margaret was sitting on a divan in a long tartan housecoat, in a room with 'what looked like half an orchard protruding out of the fire'. The walls were covered with brightly coloured oriental rugs and picture postcards of faraway places. To Jacquie's untravelled eye the ambience of Margaret's home in this staid part of the South of England was unexpectedly Bohemian.

Margaret greeted the new arrivals with a cheerful grin. Mother had grown tired of waiting up and had gone to bed, she said. There was food in the larder and their beds had been made up. They sat around the fire, talking and eating. If ever Gerald and Jacquie did get married, she said, she could put them up in one of her flats till they got themselves sorted out. So far so good.

But not everyone was pleased to see Jacquie, as Margaret recalled: 'When Gerald was staying with me he had a bit of a fling with one of my lodgers, an attractive young nurse, a rather Swedish-looking girl with dyed blonde hair, and a lot of fun. She was really very fond of Gerry and she was terribly upset when he brought Jacquie down to stay and realised it was all over between them. I don't think that she knew he had been playing the field around Bournemouth, and had also been going out with a young redhead whose family lived at the bottom of the hill.'

Next morning Gerald introduced Jacquie to Mother. 'I was astonished,' Jacquie recalled of that first encounter with the linchpin of the family. 'She was completely different from how I had imagined her; instead of the tall, rather forbidding woman I had always pictured, here was a tiny, gentle person with merry blue eyes and silver hair.'

'Thank God you're not a blonde, dear,' said Mother, grinning wickedly.

'I gathered later that all her favourite son's past girlfriends had been blonde and blue-eyed – cow-like is how Mrs Durrell described them – and she had an absolute horror of one of them becoming her daughter-in-law.'

It was not just Mother who was surprised by the girl Gerald seemed to have chosen to marry. Petite, pretty, elfin, boyish, Jacquie was almost adolescent to look at, and was so different from anyone Gerald had ever come home with before that Margaret and Mother wondered what had induced him to fall in love with her. Not even Jacquie herself was sure of the answer – but they took to her immediately.

Two down and only the two other brothers to go. Larry was away in Yugoslavia with the Foreign Service, but Leslie's turn came later in the day. 'He came bursting into the living-room, looking for his mother, scowled at me, turned on his heels and went into the kitchen,' Jacquie recounted later. 'Gerry brought him back into the room and introduced us. He was a dark-haired young man with penetrating blue eyes, and like the rest of the family, apart from Gerry, not much taller than me.' Jacquie liked Leslie, indeed she liked them all, and she found it hard to drag herself away from the warm, cheery, supportive family home and return to the oppressive, disapproving atmosphere of her father's hotel up north.

Life with father went from bad to worse. Though Jacquie no longer needed his approval to get married, she hoped at least for his blessing. But he bitterly opposed the idea of her marrying Gerald – indeed, he probably opposed the idea of her marrying anyone. 'Nothing would make my father relent,' she remembered sadly, 'and in the end he even refused to discuss it with me.' A crisis loomed. Gerald was pressing her for a decision. Margaret renewed her offer of accommodation. Mother Durrell said she could help financially till Gerald, who had finished his stint at Belle Vue, was earning again. 'I felt dreadful,' Jacquie wrote later. 'I didn't want to alienate my father or go against his wishes, and yet I felt that this was my one opportunity to break free once and for all and have a life of my own.'

Jacquie lived in a whirl of indecision. There were many things to consider. Gerald had no job and no money, and her father would cut her off without a penny if she married against his wishes. She had a promising career in music which she would have to forgo if she married Gerald.

Gerald needed someone who shared his interest in animals and foreign travel, and she was not sure she could commit herself to all that. True, he was an amusing and charming companion, and she felt she could rely on him utterly. On the other hand, she recorded, 'there was the question of temperament – we had absolutely nothing in common ... Ours was the attraction of opposites. With our totally different natures we complemented each other perfectly.' She was left-wing and he was right-wing. She was fascinated by history and politics, but he wasn't. She was a city-lover, while he hankered for wide-open spaces. She loved cricket, but he couldn't stand the game – or indeed any games at all. She was thrifty and took life seriously, while he was extravagant and lived for the moment. The only points of contact between them were animals and possibly music, but here again, while she loved opera and jazz, he did not.

A resolution to the dilemma came unexpectedly. Towards the end of February 1951, Jacquie's father had to go away for a few days on business. Shortly after he had gone Gerald arrived unexpectedly at the hotel. There was nothing else for it – Jacquie would have to make up her mind once and for all, and in short order. 'If you're going to marry me,' he told her, 'you've got to break your strings with your father, so do it sensibly.' She promised him an answer within forty-eight hours. For the next two days neither of them raised the matter, and at the end of that time they went out to see a film and have supper. It was late when they got back, and everyone in the hotel had gone to bed. The two of them sat in the living-room and talked and talked, though not about marriage. 'Suddenly I felt very tired and was horrified to see that it was five o'clock,' Jacquie recounted afterwards. 'In our mad rush to get out of the door we both somehow jammed in the doorway, and as we were disentangling ourselves Gerry said very quietly, "Well, will you marry me?" As my resistance is always at its lowest ebb at that hour of the morning, I said, "Yes, of course I will," and so the trouble was over.'

Father was due back any time now. There was only one course – to elope. Jacquie and Gerry decided to run off to Bournemouth and get married as soon as they could. They only had £40 in the world between them, but it was enough. To the consternation of Jacquie's stepmother, the pair spent much of the next day feverishly packing up Jacquie's possessions – and not a few of Gerald's – into tea chests, boxes and brown-paper parcels. By six the next morning they were piling into two taxis with all their baggage and heading for the station to catch the first train south. As they piled the stuff in to the carriage, an elderly guard looked mournfully on.

'Are you two getting married?' he asked at length.

Struggling with her pile of bursting parcels, Jacquie answered a frantic 'Yes.'

'Well Gawd 'elp yer,' the guard replied, and waved his flag.

'The guard was right, of course,' said Gerald a long time later, 'but then fortunately He has.'

As the train bore the eloping couple in the direction of London, Jacquie's father returned to find no daughter, a wildly agitated wife, and a brief explanatory note. He never forgave her: 'I never saw my father, or my stepmother, or my two half-brothers, or my two half-sisters, or any of my family ever again.'

Returning to the Durrell *ménage* was like passing from night to day. The whole family had gathered to welcome the pair, bubbling over with enthusiasm for the prospective wedding. Even Larry had written from Belgrade to say how much he approved. All they had to do was fix the day. Gerald thought it ought to be as soon as possible, in case Jacquie's father turned up with a shotgun. So plans were laid and roles delegated, and next morning Jacquie and Gerald set off to besiege the register office, while Margaret took charge of the catering and Mother and Leslie saw to the drinks. The wedding was fixed for three days' time, Monday, 26 February 1951. The cake was ordered, the flowers arranged, the ring – 'modest, slim, octagonal, gold' – chosen, a little flatlet in the attic of the house made ready for the future newlyweds. 'The whole atmosphere was absurd,' recalled Jacquie. 'Everyone else was thrilled and excited, whilst Gerry and I were carrying on like an ancient married couple.' In the middle of all this turmoil Margaret's first husband, Jack Breeze, arrived, and was instantly roped in as best man.

'You poor thing,' said Jack to Jacquie. 'How did you get embroiled with the Durrells? You didn't have to, did you?'

The morning of 26 February was, as Jacquie recalled, 'the dreariest day, grey and muggy'. The couple duly presented themselves at the register office, with Margaret and Jack as witnesses. Jacquie was wearing an old coat, a borrowed blouse and a new pair of nylons. 'Durrell had even cleaned his shoes,' she recorded, 'a really startling phenomenon.' Though the ceremony was short, it was still long enough for Jacquie to have doubts.

'It's too late,' whispered Gerry, squeezing her hand in the car on the way back to the house. 'I've got you now.'

At least, that's what Jacquie thought he said. Gerald remembered it differently. 'Without wishing to be too unkind,' he corrected her later, 'and while prepared, at a pinch, to admit my memory may be at fault, I was under the strong impression that what I actually said was "It's too late. You've got me now." '

The deed was done. Gerald Malcolm Durrell, zoologist, aged twenty-six, and Jacqueline Sonia Rasen, music student, aged twenty-one, were man and wife. Like all newlyweds, they now had to live with the consequences. Most marriages are a journey and an adventure, and most have modest beginnings. Gerald and Jacquie's was no exception. But theirs was to be no ordinary marriage, for it was also a kind of strategic alliance, at least for a while. For Gerald certainly, and for Jacquie to a lesser degree, life would never have been the same if they had not married one another. They were two utterly different people – different in both temperament and outlook – who complemented each other exactly for a period of time. Without Jacquie to prime and blast him into space, so to speak, it is possible that Gerald might never have fulfilled his potential, and no one would ever have heard of him. 'I knew life with Gerry would involve me in an entirely different world,' Jacquie was to say, 'but I cared for him so much that I was certain this wouldn't worry me.'

ELEVEN

Writing Man

1951–1953

The little flatlet in Margaret's boarding house was fun, a tiny attic room overlooking a large back garden, with a view to the rising ground of St Catherine's Head in the distance. There was no money for a honeymoon, but married life was novel enough in itself. 'We had our honeymoon on the carpet,' Gerald recalled happily of those basic beginnings, 'in front of the sitting-room fire.' The room was just big enough to take a double bed, a small desk, a wardrobe, a chest of drawers and one fireside chair. It was simple but cosy, especially when there was a fire burning in the little grate, and it didn't matter much that there were no cooking facilities, as they ate downstairs *en famille*.

Their pleasures were simple, but they were never bored. 'There were masses of books to read,' Jacquie remembered, 'lovely country for us to walk in, and dear Jack Breeze had given us an old radio. So far, Gerry had two main vices – cigarettes and tea drinking – and I was determined that whatever happened he was not going to give these up.' Jacquie was to look back on the days in the flatlet as the happiest period of their marriage. She enjoyed a good relationship with the rest of the family, and there were no outside distractions, nothing (as yet) to knock Gerald off kilter.

'Jacquie was very good for Gerry in the early days,' recalled the Durrell family's Bournemouth GP, Alan Ogden. 'In those days Gerry had a sense of insecurity which he tried to conceal, and he lacked the self-confidence with which he later matured. Jacquie was an uncomplaining support, accepting the tough times and providing the backing of practical optimism.'

Money was the enemy. There was none, and no obvious prospect of getting any. Gerald's three expensive collecting expeditions had burned up his inheritance, and only earned enough to pay for their costs. The couple were too poor to afford a daily newspaper, so every day they trotted down to Bournemouth Central Library to look through the job ads. Gerald's lack of qualifications was a handicap, as was his lack of business training or experience. When all his efforts to find a job in England came to nothing, he decided he would have to look abroad – one of the game departments in the African colonies, perhaps, or even emigration to Australia. They looked up the addresses of all the zoos in Australia, America and Canada, and fired off applications to every one of them, enclosing a CV outlining Gerald's experience in the animal business to date. Few bothered to reply, and those that did had no vacancies. Gerald was so depressed by his situation, Margaret noted, that at times he was reduced to tears.

The feud with George Cansdale at London Zoo did little to help. 'Cansdale behaved in an appalling way,' Jacquie said later, 'and tried to destroy Gerry in the most despicable ways. Fortunately Gerry did have a few friends in the zoo world who warned him of Cansdale's intentions, so he was prepared to a certain extent. However, it was due to this vendetta that we spent the first years of our marriage without money and living in a room measuring twelve feet by nine. The whole business really soured Gerry and reinforced his determination to show the zoo world what he could do as an example of how to run an animal institution properly – where the animals came first at *all* times.'

As a stopgap, Gerald agreed to fill in as temporary relief manager of a little menagerie, part of a seaside funfair at Margate, belonging to a former associate of his. For Gerald the job was really the end of the world. This establishment represented everything he loathed about the zoos of the time, most of which were nothing more than peep-shows, badly-run components of the holiday business. But anything was better than nothing, and though all he would get was free food and lodging in lieu of salary, he jumped at the chance of working with animals again. For Jacquie – 'deeply involved in skinning bananas, peeling oranges, destoning cherries, bottle-feeding babies and generally learning about animal keeping the hard way' – the experience was a revelation.

But before long the couple were back in their tiny Bournemouth room, still penniless and without prospects. It was then that Jacquie began to explore another possibility. In between cutting up fruit and clearing out cages in Margate she had tried to work out what untapped resources they could harness to raise a few pounds. Gerald, she knew very well, was a born raconteur, and could keep a company spellbound or splitting their sides with his tales of his childhood in Corfu and his adventures in the African wilds. Perhaps he could present these stories to a wider audience.

She had no idea whether he could write, but there was already a proven writer in the Durrell family. Larry, so she gathered, had always tried to encourage Gerald to write when he was a boy, and even if Gerald couldn't write for toffee, perhaps Larry could help. Jacquie recalled: 'If one Durrell could write and make money out of it, why should another one not try? So began Operation Nag. Poor Durrell suffered. For days I went on and on about him writing something for somebody.'

'I can't write, at least not like Larry.'

'How do you know you can't write until you try?'

'What can I write about anyway?'

'Well, about those trips you've been on.'

'Who on earth wants to know about all that?'

'I do, so get on with it.'

But Gerald hated writing. And he couldn't spell. None of the Durrells could, apart from Mother. Oblivious of the vividness and fluency of his African diaries, Gerald was convinced he had no literary talent whatsoever. It required something more positively goading than a nagging wife to force him to a desk, and in May 1951 this arrived, in the form of the ebullient and persuasive Larry, hotfoot from Belgrade with his new wife, the raven-haired and exotic Eve.

Larry had taken extended leave from his Foreign Service job so that Eve, now in the late stages of pregnancy, could have her child in England, and called in on the family in Bournemouth before continuing on to Oxford, where Eve was due to check in to the Churchill Hospital for her confinement. Eve was the third new spouse to be presented to the Durrell clan in three months, for a month after Jacquie and Gerald's wedding, Margaret had married her Life Guard, Malcolm Duncan, with Gerald and Jacquie as witnesses.

Jacquie had been somewhat daunted at the prospect of meeting Larry. She had heard a lot about him – about his brilliance, his intellectual energy, his *avant garde* attitudes and Bohemian lifestyle, his ways with women – and his reputation had grown ever more formidable in his absence. She was relieved that the encounter, in the end, proved less fraught than she had feared: 'Although a meeting with the genius of the family was a bit awe-inspiring, I must admit that he was far nicer than I had ever imagined. Larry was small and stocky and instantly recognisable as a Durrell, with all the Durrell charm and humour, though far more sophisticated and suave.'

Larry was greatly concerned to hear that Gerald was down on his uppers, and without a job.

'Why on earth don't you write a book about these dreadful trips you go on, and make some money for a change,' Jacquie remembered him hectoring his recalcitrant young brother. 'After all, the British simply love stories about fluffy animals and jungles, and it's so easy to do.'

Gerald was unconvinced, but reckoned he could just about squeeze a book out of his three expeditions.

'My dear boy,' said Larry, aghast, 'you are not seriously suggesting that you write three trips up as one book, are you? You must be mad. Surely to heaven you can get a book out of each one?'

Gerald was unmoved. He couldn't write. He had nothing to write about. He hadn't even got a typewriter. It was a rotten idea. He wanted nothing to do with it. But Larry persisted. Try it and see, he told him. He'd be happy to read the first few chapters and give an honest opinion and any practical help he could. He was even prepared to give Gerald an introduction to his own publishers, Faber & Faber. 'Take my advice,' he warned, 'don't bother with agents. They cheat you and take your money for nothing. They only put themselves out when you are a success.'

Alan Thomas drove Larry and Eve up to Oxford, and at the end of May Eve duly gave birth to a daughter, Sappho. In Bournemouth, meanwhile, Gerald's malaria lingered on, and Alan Ogden came to check him over. 'Gerry was lying on a mattress on the floor in a sparsely furnished room,' he recalled. 'He would often come back from trips to the tropics and ask me what was wrong with him, and often I'd have to say "G.O.K." – God Only Knows. This time it was the malignant malaria again, a serious condition of the *plasmodium falciparum* variety. I started him on quinine, but when I suggested to Jacquie that she should give him a very light, high-fluid diet, she asked if bread and tea would do, as that was all they had.'

Jacquie realised something had to be done. 'We were holed up in a room measuring twelve foot by nine and costing £2.10.0 a week and we were subsisting on a diet of bread and tea,' she recalled, adding wryly: 'We would still be sitting there living on bread and tea if I hadn't kicked his butt and forced him to get up and do something.' Gerald's resistance to the very idea of writing began to break down before her persistent cajoling. The turning point came a few days after Larry and Eve had left. Gerald had been listening to a BBC radio talk about life in West Africa, and complained how bad it was. Jacquie rounded on him. If he thought he could do better, then why didn't he give it a go? 'Promise me that you'll do it,' she insisted. 'At least it's better than rotting here.'

Several days passed, and nothing more was said. Then one morning Jacquie overheard Gerald asking Margaret if she had any friends who could lend him a typewriter. Jack Breeze had an old one, Margaret told him, but he was away, so Gerald would have to wait till he got back. But by now Gerald had got the bit between his teeth. He couldn't wait. He'd hire a typewriter. Since he couldn't afford the charge, he'd sell some of his precious books to raise the money. The loss of the books seemed to spur him on. He sat down and began to make tentative notes about his African adventures, searching for an episode that might make a fifteen-minute radio script.

'I've got it,' he proudly announced to Jacquie one morning. 'I'm going to write about the Hairy Frog and how I caught it.'

So Gerald Durrell embarked on his first piece of professional writing. Reluctantly seated at the tiny desk in the tiny room at the back of Margaret's house, kept going by endless pots of tea supplied by the ever-attentive Jacquie, the agonised tyro tap-tapped with finger and thumb on his clackety old hired typewriter, and slowly, laboriously, painfully, with much staring into space and many sighs and groans and (to the alarm of Jacquie) occasional total silences, the words went down, the lines filled up, the story unfolded and *The Hunt for the Hairy Frog* began to take shape.

As each page filled up with type it was passed over to Jacquie, who gave her comments and corrected his spelling by a painstaking method that entailed typing each correction on to sticky paper, cutting it out and pasting it over the offending word – 'a tedious business, but it did get the damn thing finished'. Jacquie recalled: 'I became engrossed in the story of the strange amphibian with thick hair-like filaments on its hind legs, that Gerry had found, captured and brought back to the London Zoo, and I simply could not wait for the pages to roll off the typewriter.'

The story began:

Our base camp in the Cameroons was in a clearing on the banks of the Cross River, at the edge of the forest. Here we erected a huge marquee, and in this we lived, together with our specimens. As the news of our arrival spread, hunters from all parts came to our camp clearing, bringing animals to sell to us. Sometimes the capture would be in a basket, sometimes wrapped in leaves or tied on the end of a stick, and occasionally it would arrive wrapped up in its owner's loin cloth, and the hunter would stand there naked and unembarrassed while he bargained fiercely with us over the price . . .

Jacquie anxiously turned the page as the story moved on.

All the hunters that we interviewed knew the animals we wanted. They knew them all, that is, except the one we wanted most . . . the Hairy Frog. They had never even heard of such a thing: frogs, certainly, but frogs with *hairs* . . . ! With the air of someone humouring a child they would suggest that perhaps what I meant was a water rat. No, I did not mean a water rat. A frog with hair on its legs was what I wanted, and nothing less would please me.

Another page emerged from the tiny room where the tethered Gerald sipped his tea and tapped his keys. Jacquie read:

Night after night the hunters and I would wade up and down these icy watercourses, turning over rocks and looking into holes, shouting to make ourselves heard above the roar of the waterfalls. I had just decided that we were going to be unsuccessful once again, when I caught sight of my first Hairy Frog. He was perched on a rock at the side of a deep pool, a great, fat, beautiful, choc-olate-coloured frog, big enough to cover a saucer, and his legs and sides were covered with a thick pelt of hair. I knew that if he jumped into those dark waters there was no chance of catching him, so I flung myself forward and grabbed him by one leg. But I had overlooked this frog's defensive armoury: his claws . . .

Jacquie was beside herself. The man could write after all. And he could write like a dream. Gerald's simple, seemingly artless, deceptively straightforward story, devoid of literary pretensions, embodied everything that he had learnt from his haphazard reading and desultory literary discussions with Larry in years gone by, and went beyond the best of the set-piece descriptive passages in his Africa diaries. Vivid, fluent, direct, accessible, funny and enlightening by turns, Gerald's writing possessed the common touch but also a fully fledged professional expertise.

The script was posted off to the BBC Talks Department, and the couple waited in hope and mounting penury for the reply. But no reply came, and soon Gerald was mooning about the tiny flat just as before. 'You do realise, don't you, that Larry has had many things rejected,' he told Jacquie. 'So don't pin your faith on one little talk.' Later, inexplicably, he said: 'Why don't you have your hair cut? I'm tired of you looking like a central European refugee.' Without more ado Gerald and Margaret took Jacquie to the bathroom and sheared her locks off with a pair of scissors. By the time they had finished she looked more like a boy than ever, but she and Gerald were pleased with effect, which emphasised her elfin good looks. Jacquie was to wear her hair short for ever more.

Finally, in the autumn, they received a letter from a Mr T.B. Radley, a BBC talks producer. He had read the hairy frog script and enjoyed it very much, he wrote. In fact he thought it was quite delightful. Could Mr Durrell give him a ring at Broadcasting House so that they could discuss it further? There was great excitement at 51 St Alban's Avenue – but no phone, so they all rushed down to the off-licence where Leslie lived with Doris. In some trepidation Gerald picked up the handset, dialled the number he had been given and was put through. Yes, Mr Radley confirmed, he wanted to broadcast the hairy frog script. The fee would be fifteen guineas, and he wanted Gerald to read the script himself.

On Friday, 7 December 1951, Gerald travelled up to London for an hour's rehearsal in Studio 3D. On the following Sunday, 9 December, he did the real thing in Studio 3G, and the talk was beamed out live on the Home Service to whoever in the kingdom happened to be sitting near a radio set between 11.15 and 11.30 that wintry morning. Gerald proved to be a natural broadcaster, with a warm, engaging, curiously charismatic baritone voice not unlike that of Dylan Thomas, who was also broadcasting stories and poems around that time.

More radio broadcasts were to follow – *Animal Mysteries*, *How a Zoo Gets its Animals* and others – but more pressing was the question of a book. The success of the *Hairy Frog* had finally persuaded Gerald that it might conceivably be worth having a shot at writing a book. He had a subject – the first Cameroons expedition – and even a title: *The Overloaded Ark* (for if Noah had confined himself to species from the Cameroons alone, the Ark would have been overloaded). A book was a different kind of beast to a fifteen-minute radio talk, though – bigger, more complex, more time-consuming, a test of character as well as talent. Gerald began to write, sustained by an allowance of £3 a week from Mother.

This was the beginning of a strange existence which put not a little strain on the marriage. Gerald found he preferred to work at night, when the world was quiet. But Jacquie was a light sleeper, and the clatter of the ancient typewriter, only a few feet from her head in the tiny room, kept her awake for much of the night. Things improved when Jack Breeze turned up and lent Gerald his quieter portable, but the book was a physical and psychological ordeal for both husband and wife.

Though *The Overloaded Ark* was a first book, it was far from being an absolute beginner's book. Gerald knew what he was striving for, and had a fair idea how to achieve it. Years later he recounted to a friend, the author and critic David Hughes, the techniques he used to tell his tale:

It all started long before, when Leslie used to come home from Dulwich on holiday and tell me Billy Bunter stories. He used to embellish them with his own bits and pieces, add a dash of his own school adventures, imitate a master or two in a very clever and vivid fashion. He had the same gift as Larry, only untutored, not so well developed, and unconsciously I must have been absorbing the fact that this was the way to tell a story. Because when I started writing *The Overloaded Ark* I found it difficult to convey a character until I discovered how to do it by description and a trick of speech – and most people have tricks of speech. My first impulse was to imitate physically what I was trying to get over to the reader, but you can't imitate on paper. So I had to sit down and learn the knack of translating an imitation into words by means of timing and suitable exaggeration and knowing how, in the film sense, to cut. I was learning to edit events so that they offset one another funnily, highlighting an episode that may have happened at the tail-end of an expedition by twisting the whole plot to put it up front.

The older Gerald makes all this sound quite fun. The younger Gerald, however, loathed every second of it – it was not nearly as attractive as cleaning out a monkey's cage. 'As a form of manual labour,' he said at around this time, 'I find it one of the most unexciting and exhausting known to man. I took up writing in desperation, having spent all my capital. If I had been able to obtain an unending stream of finance I would never have written a word. But to suddenly find yourself possessed of a wife, two pelicans, a capuchin monkey and £40 in cash as your total assets is, to say the least, disconcerting.'

Often he wrote while lying on his stomach on the floor, smoking more cigarettes than he should and drinking vast quantities of tea. 'When I show signs of flagging,' he complained, 'my wife, far from soothing my sweating brow, goads me on by showing me a bank statement.'

He had two main concerns as he wrote his book: how to reconstruct what he had experienced in the Cameroons, and how to present it to the reader in the most effective way. He had hoped his expedition diary would solve the first problem, but he was mistaken. 'Diaries, I have discovered, are almost completely useless,' he said. For one thing, they were usually written late at night after a hard day's work. For another, the pages were full of distracting marks and stains (tea, whiskey, medicine, squashed bugs, blood) which took hours of brain-racking detective work to interpret.

There was an even more fundamental drawback. The raw material of travel diaries often reads like an inchoate muddle, a raggle-taggle of random incidents, seemingly without order or purpose. Even at this early stage in his literary career Gerald was canny enough to realise that a non-fiction author could not ignore some of the techniques necessary to a fiction author: reorganising his material by means of selection, compression, inversion and the rest, in order to leach out the inner essence of his story and recreate his experiences on paper to best effect. What he was trying to do as he struggled to complete his first book was to express an imaginative truth rather than to relay a collection of bare facts. 'Truth and fact *may* be related,' wrote another new travel writer, Gavin Maxwell, then also struggling with the mysteries of his craft, 'but they are more often opposed, and a collection of facts, no matter how conscientious, does not constitute truth unless by accident.' Durrell concurred: 'Except to verify a fact or two, diaries are a dead loss.'

Not surprisingly, therefore, much of what is in the Cameroons diaries is not in the book, and much of what is in the book is not in the diaries – including much of their author. The Gerald Durrell who appears in the book is a reconstructed, tidied-up version of the Gerald Durrell in the diaries of four years previously. Gone (with Jacquie's help) are the big white master and mighty African hunter posturings, the raw, brash, opinionated young man with a mercenary streak and a taste for whiskey whose ambition was to get rich by bagging the really big game. In his place emerges another, no less authentic Durrell – charming, humorous, modest, resolute and selfless, with an abiding passion for the smaller, rarer creatures in his charge and a fond respect for the African villagers on whom he depended.

The inadequacy of the diaries as a source of copy did not matter hugely. For Gerald, like his brother Larry, was gifted with almost total recall. 'It's almost vulgar, the way I remember photographically in the colours of a glossy magazine,' he was to say. 'My memory is so exact that I have to go through it mentally with a pair of scissors to make sure I don't overwrite the bloody thing.'

As for the second problem in his writing, that of presentation and interpretation, Gerald was clear from the outset that he did not want to follow in the footsteps of a preceding generation of writers about travel and animals: 'I have tried, firstly, not to be boring, and to try and create some sort of word picture of the lands through which I travelled. Secondly, I have tried very hard to show that even the most ugly – by human standards – mammals, birds or reptiles have some interesting or charming characteristic about them, if you will only take the trouble to watch them with an unprejudiced eye.' So – evocation of place, uncluttered with place names, dates, facts or figures; and wild animals alive on the page in an utterly new way, not the old-style stereotypes of alien, ravening beasts, but individual characters of fascination, idiosyncrasy and delight, the intrinsically precious co-denizens of our planet.

There was one other crucial ingredient in the mix. 'I read a book in my childhood called something like *Ninety Years in Tibet*,' Gerald was to tell a colleague, 'and there wasn't a glimpse of humour in it. I was aghast at the dullness of it and I determined that if I wrote travel books I'd put plenty of humour into them.'

The work was intense and absorbing. 'Durrell himself worked on this book as I had never known him work,' Jacquie was to remember, 'and every morning there was a pile of pages for me to read and correct, and slowly the book began to take shape. We were both consumed with excitement, and again I found myself completely engrossed in the story, which was surprising as I had always loathed animal-travel books, but this was different from anything I had ever read before.'

Here again was George, the drum-playing baboon, and Chumley (short for Cholmondeley), the beer-swigging, cigarette-puffing, gentleman chimp; the rare angwantibo, black-legged mongoose, and giant water shrew; the water-snake rivers and python caves; the spectral beauty of the forest at night and the thrill of the chase in the dark; the trusty hunters Elias ('short, stocky, with ape-like forehead and protruding teeth') and Andraia ('very tall and extremely thin, drooping artistically, drawing patterns in the dust with his long toes'); a carnival of strange animals, a plethora of wild places, a whale of an adventure.

There were, too, passages of hypnotic magic that had Jacquie utterly beguiled:

> As you enter the forest, your eyes used to the glare of the sun, it seems dark and shadowy, and as cool as a butter dish. The light is filtered through a million leaves, and so has a curious aquarium-like quality which makes everything seem unreal. The centuries of dead leaves that have fluttered to the ground have provided a rich layer of mould, soft as any carpet, and giving off a pleasant earthy smell. On every side are the huge trees with their great curling buttress roots, their thick, smooth trunks towering hundreds of feet above, their head foliage and branches merging indistinguishably into the endless green roof of the forest ... There is no life to be seen in the forest except by chance. The only sounds are the incessant rasping zither of the cicadas, and a small bird who follows you as you walk along, hiding shyly in the undergrowth ...

Jacquie began to have a sneaking feeling that the book might make them 'quite a lot of money'. But it seemed to go on and on: 'It began to look as if Gerry was trying to write *Gone With the Wind*.'

In fact, when she counted the words in the finished typescript it came to sixty-five thousand, which was on the short side of average for that kind of book. But it was enough, and soon it was stitched between two pieces of stiff cardboard, given a typed sticker on the front with the title, the author's name and address, and the number of words. Then Jacquie wrapped it up into a neat parcel and posted if off to Faber, with a note saying that it came from Lawrence Durrell's brother.

Gerald and Jacquie settled down to another long wait in penury, and to catch up on their sleep. There was a flurry when two overseas job opportunities cropped up, one in the Uganda Game Department and the other in the Khartoum Museum in the Sudan. Gerald went to interviews for both. He rejected the Sudan job straight off, because it would not allow him to bring Jacquie out for two years, but he was confident he stood a good chance for the one in Uganda. But a new cost-cutting Conservative government had recently been elected, and in a wave of economies the Uganda post disappeared overnight.

Six weeks after he had sent off the typescript, Gerald received a letter from Faber. They had now read *The Overloaded Ark*. They thought it was wonderful. Could he come up to London to talk about it? Gerald couldn't. He didn't have enough money for the train fare. If they wanted to haggle, it would have to be by post. Faber were used to indigent authors, and felt no pressing need to improve Gerald Durrell's status in this regard. The best offer they could come up with for an exciting new book by an unproven writer was £25, followed by another £25 on publication. Gerald accepted, reluctantly. He was broke, and he needed the money. Above all, he wanted the book to be published.

Increasingly Gerald began to have doubts about Larry's strictures regarding literary agents. In his dealings with Faber he realised it would have been helpful to have had someone in the business to argue his corner. So worried was he about the vulnerability of his position that eventually, in the autumn of 1952, he decided to write to Larry's own agent, Spencer Curtis Brown, son of the founder of the firm that bore his name, the Fortnum & Mason of London literary agencies, whose clients included names like Noël Coward, Somerset Maugham and A.A. Milne. Curtis Brown replied immediately, asking for a copy of the manuscript, and Faber were asked to supply a galley proof. A few days later another letter arrived from Curtis Brown. Could Gerald come up to London to see him? Once again Gerald and Jacquie trooped down the road to borrow Leslie's phone. The whole Durrell clan waited in the living-room in a state of hushed anxiety while Gerald explained that he couldn't come up to town because he couldn't afford the fare. They heard him put the phone down, and the next they knew he had burst through the door.

'What do you think?' he yelled with excitement. 'He's so anxious to see me that he's sending me some money to travel with.'

The money came by return of post – and to the value of rather more than the fare, for inside the envelope Gerald found a cheque for £120. 'This was fantastic,' Jacquie was to write of that benchmark day. 'It really was the first time that anyone had given us any concrete evidence of their faith in Gerry's abilities.'

Gerald insisted that Jacquie come to London with him. After eighteen months cooped up in the flatlet it was like being let out on remand. They found Curtis Brown in his office in a quaint old building – 'like something out of Dickens' – near the Covent Garden fruit and vegetable market. Curtis Brown was in his forties then, and had gingery hair and a military moustache. He had a reputation for being impulsive – he had once thrown Dylan Thomas out for being sick all over his office – but Gerald and Jacquie found him affable and encouraging. He told them how much he liked the book, and that if it was handled properly it might prove a very valuable property.

'If Fabers haven't done anything about the American rights,' he said before they left, 'can I have your permission to show your manuscript to an American friend of mine I'm having dinner with this evening?'

Back in the little room in Bournemouth, Jacquie went down with a bad bout of flu. She was feeling wretched and unusually sorry for herself when she heard someone running up the stairs. The door was flung open. It was Gerald, looking very excited and pleased with himself.

'Here's some medicine that should make you feel better,' he whooped, thrusting a telegram at his prostrate wife.

Jacquie read the words 'HAVE SOLD AMERICAN RIGHTS FOR £500 CONGRATULATIONS SPENCER' (£500 then would be worth about £7500 now).

'We were on our way,' she recalled.

One sad event unexpectedly blighted the general euphoria. Gerald had last seen his favourite chimp, Chumley, some six months after he had been delivered to London Zoo by Cecil Webb in 1948. Chumley, wildly delighted to see his old friend again, had rushed into Gerald's arms, held his hand and contentedly smoked a cigarette. Gerald was unaware that anything was amiss until he saw an article in the *Daily Express*:

CHUMLEY THE CHIMP
- Boards a 53 bus
- Bites a woman
- Wrestles with man
- Acts as King Kong

Chumley had become a highly popular animal at London Zoo, and had been seen by millions on television drinking tea and smoking cigarettes. His problems started when he developed toothache early in 1952, and was taken to see the dentist in the zoo sanatorium. Chumley took a dislike to the dentist and made a break for it. Pushing aside his keeper, he swung open the door of his cage, got out through a skylight and legged it across Regent's Park, stepping into the middle of the road and holding up a number 53A bus. He got on board, and put his arms round a woman passenger's waist. When she screamed, Chumley bit her, got off the bus and made his way towards a queue of people at a bus stop, all but one of whom, a blind woman, fled. Chumley then felled a passing ex-sergeant-major-*cum*-nightclub bouncer before climbing on to the balcony of a house where, according to an eyewitness, 'he beat his chest and cried out like King Kong'. Terrified in a frightening and alien world, Chumley climbed gratefully into his keeper's arms when he at last caught up with him.

'Chumley is a darling,' a member of the zoo curator's family told the press later that day. 'He would wring any mother's heart – the funny little soul. If he bit anyone it was out of sheer fright.'

That seemed to be the end of the matter. But on Christmas Eve Chumley escaped again, loping across Regent's Park once more and banging on the doors of a few cars at Gloucester Gate in the hope of a lift. This time there was to be no second chance. 'He was a moody animal,' George Cansdale, the Superintendent of London Zoo, told the *Daily Express*, 'gentle as possible at times, a positive terror at others. And on Christmas Eve he was in a mood to be a terror. Regretfully I decided the only thing to do was to shoot him.'

Gerald, jolted out of the jollity of a family Christmas in Bournemouth, was aghast at the news, and took the opportunity to insert into the proofs of *The Overloaded Ark* a valedictory epilogue to his chimpanzee friend.

Chumley decided that if he had a walk round London on Christmas Eve, he might run across someone who would offer him a beer. But the foolish humans misconstrued his actions. Before he had time to explain his mission, a panting posse of keepers arrived, and he was bundled back to the zoo. From being a fine, intelligent animal, he had suddenly become (by reason of his escapades) a fierce and untrustworthy monster, he might escape yet again and bite some worthy citizen, so rather than risk this Chumley was sentenced to death and shot.

'The Chumley affair really soured Gerry,' Jacquie recalled, 'and he blamed London Zoo and George Cansdale in particular for incompetence and total lack of appreciation of what this particular primate needed to survive happily in that confined environment. Again Gerry was rather vocal and left no one in any doubt how he viewed London Zoo's competence and capability.' In years to come Gerald was to wage a ceaseless passage of arms with London Zoo, the top establishment organisation of the British zoological world. It is hard to believe that the fate of Chumley did not have something to do with the implacable contempt he felt for much of what London Zoo then stood for.

By now Gerald was well into his second book, *Three Singles to Adventure*, a light-hearted account of his third collecting expedition, to British Guiana. Even though *The Overloaded Ark* had not yet been published, Spencer Curtis Brown had suggested that Gerald keep writing while he still had a head of steam, so that he could fulfil the expected public demand for a sequel. *Three Singles to Adventure* took him only six weeks to write, and since Faber were not prepared to offer him any more for it than they had for the first book, Curtis Brown offered it to Rupert Hart-Davis, who ran an up-and-coming publishing house and was prepared to offer this up-and-coming author a substantially bigger advance. After a brief respite Gerald embarked on a third book, *The Bafut Beagles*, about his second Cameroons expedition. In the midst of this punishing literary endeavour *The Overloaded Ark*, beautifully illustrated with line drawings by Sabine Baur, was finally published in Britain on 31 July 1953.

By a remarkable coincidence, Gerald Durrell's first book came out at exactly the same time as his brother Lawrence's new one, a discursive literary essay on the Greek island of Rhodes entitled *Reflections on a Marine Venus*. Faber promoted the two books in tandem in an advertisement which read: 'Quests animal . . . and human – a dual demonstration of the enviable art of Durrelling.'

Both books had appeared at exactly the right moment. A new golden age of British travel writing had dawned. Memories of the war years were receding, and post-war austerity was at an end. There was a feeling of standing at the beginning of a new era. Young men woke up to find that the world was once again their oyster, and not just a place you went to on a troopship. At almost exactly the time the Durrell brothers' two books were published, a galaxy of talented travel writers, including Laurens van der Post, Gavin Maxwell, Patrick Leigh Fermor and Norman Lewis, were also bringing out new books, while one-off accounts of new worlds conquered or explored, such as Jacques Cousteau's *The Silent World*, Heinrich Harrer's *Seven Years in Tibet* and John Hunt's *The Conquest of Everest* – all published in this same *annus mirabilis* of 1953 – were in huge demand.

The Durrells' books basked in this sun. 'Glorious Press for the Brothers Durrell!' ran the publishers' ads. While Larry's book was received with almost reverent acclaim by the literati, Gerry's was singled out as a Book Society Choice, *Daily Mail* Book of the Month for August, and BBC Book of the Week in December, and greeted with rave reviews in the press and hot-cake sales in the bookshops. 'Congratulations,' Lawrence told Gerald. 'We are now a circus act. Clad in sequinned tights, three hundred feet above the ring, you will fling yourself into space, while I, hanging by my knees, will attempt to focus my bleary eyes sufficiently quickly to catch you by the ankles as you sweep past.'

All the quality national newspapers devoted space to *The Overloaded Ark*, and several of the most eminent reviewers of the day turned their critical attention to it. Most commended the book for its charm, its freshness, its humour, its totally new approach to wild animals and wild places, and the vivid quality of its writing. Most praised the author's courage, sensitivity, humanity and devotion to the animals in his charge ('what he did for them,' wrote one, 'would equal the services of the most devoted mother'). All adored the animals he wrote about – 'like so many guests at a Mad Hatter's cocktail party'. Some tried to compare the book to putative literary antecedents – Victorian adventure books for boys, for example, or (more persuasively) recent best-selling books which shared Gerald's view of animals as creatures of interest and individuality, such as Colonel Bill Williams' *Elephant Bill* and Konrad Lorenz's popular study of animal behaviour, *King Solomon's Ring*.

'As a person Gerald Durrell has a warmth of sympathy and a good humour you would expect to find in an elderly keeper of a baboon house,' wrote Nigel Nicolson in the *Daily Dispatch*. 'As a zoologist he is a modestly disguised expert. As a writer he has almost everything – clarity, great humour, a vivid style and an exact knowledge of how not to be dull without being flippant . . . It is a splendid book.'

Laurens van der Post, writing in the *Countryman*, also found a host of reasons to be impressed by the book: 'His chase after live fauna reveals something of the abiding Africa in its more tender, intimate, mysterious and darkly domestic moods. What a relief to read a book about Africa without drums and lion and elephant stories!'

Peter Quennell in the *Daily Mail* judged the book 'fascinating . . . he shows an enviable gift of discovering the apt phrase'. Raymond Mortimer in the *Sunday Times* found it 'exhilarating' and had no doubt it would appeal to all ages and tastes. John Hillaby in the *Spectator* saw it as one of a new breed of books about wild animals 'characterised by a new and refreshing level of realism'. Gavin Maxwell in the *New Statesman* wrote that Gerald 'communicates every detail of his experience with just the right degree of zest'. Within a few months *The Overloaded Ark* had sold twenty-seven thousand copies, putting it near the top of the best-seller list. It has rarely been out of print since.

But the acclaim was not universal. One or two of the stuffier old hands in the British animal-catching business looked askance at Gerald as a novice and an upstart, and poured sour grapes on his book, calling it 'lightweight' and comparing it unfavourably to the recently published autobiography of his Cameroons rival Cecil Webb. And while most critics commended his affectionate treatment of his African helpers, some wondered whether the use of pidgin English for most of the dialogue – for all the accuracy of its transcription – might not be seen as colonial and demeaning. (Conversely, one critic regarded the book's pidgin English conversations as 'amongst the best and kindliest things I have ever read about Africa'.)

More seriously, a few reviewers queried the ethics of what Durrell was actually doing in Africa. The *Irish Times*, for example, questioned the morality both of zoos and of collecting wild animals to put in them. 'We are tempted to ask: "What of the birds and the mammals and the reptiles, or do they not remember at all?"' Remember, that is, the days of their freedom in their native land. But as another reviewer pointed out, 'even those who disapprove of caging the wild will not be able to help following Mr Durrell on his journey with rapture and enchantment'.

Nobody could have predicted the potential impact of the book on public thinking, its value as propaganda for wildlife, especially among the young, in the dawning age of environmental consciousness to come. In fact there is not a glimmer to be found in the book – or, for that matter, in its immediate sequels, *Three Singles to Adventure* and *The Bafut Beagles* – of Gerald's views on the proper role of zoos, on animal conservation in general and on the captive breeding of endangered species in particular.

His silence on these issues in his early books is puzzling. It is clear that Gerald was thinking about them as far back as the war years, when he was in his teens. In later books he records how his ideas in these matters were virtually fully fledged while he was still a student keeper at

Whipsnade in 1945 and 1946. Yet before the mid-fifties there is no written evidence at all of any particular interest in animal conservation or in environmental matters as a whole. Why this lack of any reference in his early books to the concepts he claimed to have developed in his youth, and on account of which he was to become world famous in his maturer years?

Was it because his ideas about these matters were not yet evolved and solid enough to be expressed in public? Or because the relatively novice author judged those early books were not appropriate vehicles for advanced zoological dialectic? Or because he felt that the cultural climate was not yet ready for what he had to say? Or because he was not yet confident and secure enough to go out on a limb and risk the ridicule of the zoo establishment on which he believed he still depended for a livelihood?

One reviewer above all came near to divining the man and the message – or lack of it – in *The Overloaded Ark*. Writing for *Country Life*, the influential critic Geoffrey Grigson saw Gerald Durrell as a latter-day literary equivalent of a primitive painter or *naïf* like Henri Rousseau, who also depicted jungles of a sort. The vision, Grigson perceived, was child-like, and so was the author – a child of nature. The book as a whole was like a dream of childhood in a childlike world of wonders. The big questions went unanswered, though not necessarily (buried deep in the sub-text) unasked, wrote Grigson:

> Mr Durrell does not consider too much the dangers, the difficulties, the drudgery. He does not consider his own destiny, he does not involve himself in the problems of life or its duties, he does not weight the pros and cons of collecting. Animals from under a stone, from inside a cave, from water, from the high branches of the forest – these are like birds' eggs to the small boy in the April holidays. Some live, some die. Some things go well, some go badly, but the happy collector is unruffled. He likes the world. He likes his tall, thin hunter and his short, stocky hunter. He likes pidgin English. He likes the forest . . . This writer accepts, he enjoys, and he hands on his enjoyment.

In September 1953 *The Overloaded Ark* was published by Viking in the United States (and in due course in many countries in Europe), and met with the same rapturous reception it had received in Britain. All the major papers heaped praise upon it, and unlike their British counterparts the old Africa hands and collecting professionals of America generously commended the author – described as 'Britain's youngest wild animal collector' – for his 'absolute fidelity to the truth' and his 'mastery of the fundamental law of jungle conduct'.

Virtually overnight Gerald's present life, and probably his future career, had been transformed. His brother Lawrence, who had been writing for years but had as yet attained neither fame nor fortune, greeted his instant success with generosity. 'Don't you think the little devil writes well?' he commented. 'His style's like fresh, crisp lettuce.' To his friend Henry Miller he reported: 'My younger brother has scored a tremendous success with his first book, and he is making a deal of money. How marvellous to have one's career fixed at 25 or so and to be able to pay one's way.' And to Richard Aldington he wrote: 'My brother Gerry? He is delightful, Irish gift of the gab on paper . . . do you know these blasted books about animals sell thousands of copies. My agent says that it is the only sure-fire steady *eternal* market. I wish I liked animals enough.' Lawrence did not experience – or at any rate betray – a shred of envy, not even when Alan Thomas, who was now running Commin's bookshop in Bournemouth, reported that a woman who had read a good review of *Reflections on a Marine Venus* telephoned the shop and told him: 'I want to order a book by a Mr Durrell. Not THE Mr Durrell, it's not about animals at all.'

Rather to his surprise, Gerald was now passably well off. He was also becoming a celebrity. When he appeared on the popular BBC TV magazine programme *In Town Tonight* to promote the book and chat about his unusual career, he was followed by the dazzling London-based Swedish film star Mai Zetterling, who had just returned from Hollywood. As it happened, she was to become one of Gerald's greatest friends, and to marry one of his greatest friends. It is a measure of the dramatic change in his social and professional status that from living on bread and tea in a seaside garret he was soon to move effortlessly within the aura of Hollywood's stars.

TWELVE

Of Beasts and Books

1953–1955

Gerald was now better off than he had ever been. Rather than invest his new-found money in property or shares, he decided to embark on another collecting expedition, his fourth. Jacquie had hardly travelled at all, and never outside Europe, so to her fell the choice of destination. Perhaps because of the romantic resonance of the name, perhaps because of the evocativeness of the images she associated with it – tango, gaucho, pampas, Evita Perón – Argentina had always cast a siren spell for her. 'Durrell, of course, was carried away by the thought of South America,' she recalled, 'and had visions of embracing Chile and perhaps Paraguay in our itinerary.'

The preparations began. Gerald was still in the middle of writing his third book, *The Bafut Beagles*, and though it helped that Jacquie was on hand to shoulder much of the burden of organising the Argentine expedition, it was soon obvious that too much was happening for the two of them to cope alone. What they needed was a secretary. A suitable person was soon found. This was Sophie Cook, whose mother had been a refugee from Hitler's Germany, a quiet, rather shy, totally dedicated woman of around forty – the first of a band of secretaries who were to underpin a crucial part of Gerald's future life and work. Sophie typed up the manuscript of *The Bafut Beagles*, corrected Gerald's spelling and took over most of the secretarial burden of the Argentine expedition. It was a memorable but uncomfortable time. With three people crammed into the small flatlet in Margaret's boarding house there was barely room to move – especially when the room began to fill up with expedition paraphernalia, from lambs' teats and hummingbird feeding-pots to film cameras and hot-weather clothing. 'Our small flat really did look like a junk shop,' Jacquie was to write, 'and poor Sophie could hardly get in in the mornings, never mind reach her desk. But she never grumbled or fussed, and stoically went on with her typing and tea-making.'

With a third person on board, everything proceeded smoothly. On the advice of Larry, who had had plenty of experience of Argentinean red-tape, Gerald dealt with the diplomatic side of things at the highest level in the Argentine Embassy and Foreign Office in London, with the result that the expedition acquired the status of an 'official mission'. But never had an official mission set off in more incongruous style. Their travel agent had booked them on a ship bound for Buenos Aires, promising them quality accommodation at a knockdown fare. Towards the end of November 1953, in great expectation – for Gerald and Jacquie intended to enjoy the voyage out as the honeymoon they had never had – they bade farewell to the family assembled to see them off at Bournemouth Central, joined the boat train at King's Cross and disembarked at Tilbury Docks, where their ship was waiting.

The honeymoon boat turned out to be an immigrant ship, a former wartime troopship that now ferried Spanish and Portuguese immigrants out to Latin America. The Durrells' tourist-class ticket entitled them to accommodation a notch above the near slave-trade conditions of the other passengers – but only just. Their cabin – 'like an overgrown coffin', Jacquie recalled – had no portholes, no fresh air, no daylight. Their beds consisted of two bunks one on top of the other, and there was barely room to stand, let alone store baggage. Gerald was beside himself with fury, but things were to get worse. The ship was infested with cockroaches, the communal bath was filthy, the gloomy, rudimentary saloon served only beer, and the food was execrable. Perversely perhaps, Jacquie enjoyed the trip. 'I loved every minute of it,' she was to write, remembering the tropic nights on deck, the immigrant passengers singing and dancing to their guitars, and the exotic ports of call. 'But poor Durrell could not get over his acute disappointment.'

The ship made its first landfall in the New World at Recife, in northern Brazil, then made its coasting south, first to Rio and then to Santos, before shuffling up the muddy Rio de la Plata to where the beautiful skyline of Buenos Aires loomed through the morning mist. Gerald's spirits lifted. Nothing could compare with arriving in a new land on board an old ship. On 19 December 1953 the delayed honeymoon couple set foot on Argentine soil for the first time.

Since they were on what was ostensibly an official mission, the press were there to greet them. The journalists of Buenos Aires were bemused that the couple should have come all this way to scrabble around in the backlands looking for dumb beasts. 'When you're interested in animals,'

Gerald was to recall, 'people are generally kind wherever you are because they think you must be feeble-minded.' The Argentinean press duly hailed Gerald and Jacquie – stylishly dressed as a smart couple about town – as 'scientific adventurers in an heroic world', the latest in a valiant line of conquistadors that stretched from Cortes and Pizarro to Bougainville, La Condamine and Darwin.

'Gerald Durrell is no old-style big game hunter,' reported the weekly news magazine *Vea y Lea*. 'He works for science. He looks for unknown animals which he takes back to England alive *to study their behaviour and breed them in captivity.*' 'And Jacqueline's job?' one reporter enquired. 'I'm going to use her as live bait to catch jaguars,' Gerald replied, without a hint of a smile.

'They are a perfect young couple,' reported *El Hogar*. 'She is small and slender with a charming fringe that looks like the last memento of childhood. In fact, she looks like a little girl at her husband's side. He is a youthful looking man, a bit dishevelled and on the lean side, with auburn hair and the bright clear eyes of a boy. At every step in his quest for strange beasts in the wilds of Africa and British Guiana he has risked sudden death.'

Anyone arriving in a strange country to look for wild and possibly dangerous creatures needs a fixer. Shortly before Gerald sailed for Argentina, Larry had sent him a note suggesting he contact Bebita Ferreyra, a friend who lived in Buenos Aires. 'She was the nearest approach to a Greek goddess I have ever seen,' Gerald was to write. 'We fell under Bebita's unique spell during our first meeting, and from then on we practically lived at her flat, eating tremendous and beautifully constructed meals, listening to music, talking nonsense. Very soon we came to rely on her for nearly everything. The most fantastic requests never ruffled her, and she always managed to accomplish something.' But not even a fixer of Bebita's abilities could arrange everything, and the expedition was to be blighted by events beyond even her control.

It had always been part of Gerald's plan to venture into the bleak southern wilderness of Tierra del Fuego to collect ducks and geese for Peter Scott's Severn Wildfowl Trust, so he was mortified to learn that his chances of getting a flight down to that part of the world in the immediate future were practically nil. As a fall-back, he and Jacquie decided to make a short journey to the pampas beyond Buenos Aires, staying with Anglo-Argentinean friends at their *estancia* 'Los Ingleses'.

'Argentina is one of the few countries in the world where you can go on a journey, and when halfway there you see both your starting point and your destination,' Gerald recalled. 'Flat as a billiard table, the pampa stretches around you, continuing, apparently, to the very edge of the earth.' It was in the pampas around 'Los Ingleses' that Gerald began collecting, his first captures including eight burrowing owls and a pair of Guira cuckoos. The most common of the birds around 'Los Ingleses' were also the most endangered. These were the chajás, or 'great screamers', goose-like birds that earned the wrath of the local farmers for devastating their fields of alfalfa. Few birds Gerald ever collected in his entire life proved as memorable as Eggbert, a baby chajá he acquired in those few days at the *estancia*:

> He was quite the most pathetic, the most ridiculous-looking and the most charming baby bird I had ever seen. He could not have been much more than a week old. His body was about the size of a coconut, and completely circular. At the end of a long neck was a huge, domed head, with a tiny beak and a pair of friendly brown eyes. His legs and feet, which were greyish-pink, appeared to be four times too big for him, and not completely under his control. He was clad entirely in what appeared to be a badly knitted bright yellow suit of cotton wool. He rolled out of the sack, fell on his back, struggled manfully on to his enormous flat feet, and stood there, his ridiculous wings slightly raised, surveying us with interest. Then he opened his beak and shyly said 'Wheep'. As we were too enchanted to respond to this greeting, he very slowly and carefully picked up one huge foot, swayed forward, put it down and then brought the other one up alongside. He stood and beamed at us with evident delight at having accomplished such a complicated manoeuvre. He had a short rest, said 'wheep' again, and then proceeded to take another step . . . Now I have met a lot of amusing birds at one time or another. But I have never met a bird like Eggbert, who not only *looked* funny but also acted in a riotously comical manner whenever he moved. I have never met a bird, before or since, that could make me literally laugh until I cried.

The Durrells' next destination was Paraguay, and the small settlement of Puerto Casado on the Paraguay River, where they planned to explore the swampy cactus plains of the hinterland, the Chaco. From Casado there were three ways of entering the Chaco – on horseback, by ox-cart, or by *autovia*, a beaten-up Ford 8 motor car mounted on a narrow-gauge railway that ran for two hundred kilometres. With the help of the *autovia* they began collecting, though sometimes, to reach areas where the *autovia* could not go, they took to horseback, discovering at every turn the unexpected delights of a strange land – like the river of flowers they encountered one day as they crossed a prairie of golden grass.

Halfway across the grass field we found it was divided in two by a wide, meandering strip of wonderful misty blue flowers which stretched away in either direction like a stream; as we got close to it I discovered that it really was a stream, so thickly overgrown with these blue water-plants that the water was invisible. There was the haze of blue flowers and, underneath, the glint of glossy green leaves growing interlocked. The blue was so clear and delicate that it looked as though a tattered piece of the sky had floated down and settled between the ranks of brown palm-trunks. We took our horses across the river, and their hooves crushed the plants and flowers and left a narrow lane of glittering water. When we reached the other side and entered the shade of the palm-forest again, I turned in the saddle and looked back at the magnificent lane of blue flowers, across which was marked our path in a stripe of flickering water, like a lightning flash across a summer sky.

So the days passed in the wide wastes of the Chaco, under the big sky, in the orbit of soaring wings and galloping claws and plopping amphibian bodies, never knowing what the day would bring. Their own efforts, combined with the help of the area's male population, soon produced a flood of fauna, from Budgett frog to yarará (or fer de lance), crab-eating racoon to bare-faced ibis. After two months the collection was vast. Since the Chaco was such a paradise for birds, they outnumbered all the other creatures in the collection by two to one.

'In any collection of animals there are bound to be two or three which endear themselves to you,' Gerald noted, citing Cai the douracouli monkey, Pooh the baby crab-eating racoon and Foxey the grey pampas fox. But none could compare with Sarah Huggersack, a baby giant ant-eater. Sarah was only a week or so old, measured just two and a half feet from the tip of her curved snout to the end of her tail, and made a noise 'like a foghorn suffering from laryngitis'.

When Sarah was taken from the sack in which she had arrived, she staggered round in vague circles, bellowing wildly till she discovered Jacquie's leg and shinned up it. When Gerald unhooked the animal, she attached herself to his arm like a leech and then clambered up and arranged herself across his shoulders like a fox fur. 'So Sarah Huggersack entered our lives,' wrote Gerald, 'and a more charming and loveable personality I have rarely encountered. To begin with, she was tremendously vocal. Keep her waiting for her food, or refuse to cuddle her when she demanded affection, and Sarah battered you into submission by sheer lung-power. Sarah's one delight in life was to be hugged, and to hug in return.'

Sarah had been with the Durrells for some weeks when the first rains of the Chaco winter started. Now was the time when they would have to start thinking about travelling back the thousand-odd miles to Buenos Aires to catch their ship; but at this point revolution broke out in Asunción, the capital of Paraguay. Gerald's luck had run out. He was advised to get out of the country at the first available opportunity. The only way out was by light aircraft – and that meant leaving the animals behind. On receiving the dire news Gerald was plunged into one of the blackest moods of depression he could ever remember. There was no alternative but to open the doors of the cages and let the main part of the collection go. This was easier said than done, for many of the animals showed no desire for freedom at all. To encourage them Gerald arranged them in a circle round the camp, their noses pointing out towards the wide open spaces, but they just sat there, moping, waiting for their next feed. Gerald chose a handful of animals, the maximum that could fit into a small plane, to keep and take back with him to Buenos Aires – among them Sarah Huggersack.

During a lull in the fighting the plane arrived to take them back to Asunción on the first stage of their journey home. They were safe – but they were sorry. The expedition had cost Gerald virtually all the £3000 he had earned from *The Overloaded Ark*, and the acquisition of a few more animals in the final days in Argentina could not recompense him for the loss of most of those he had collected in Paraguay.

Soon it was time to leave South America. The animals were securely stowed on the forward deck of the *Paraguay Star*, with tarpaulins tied over them against the wilder Atlantic weather to come. In the smoking-room friends had gathered to bid their farewells over a parting drink. As the day faded, they filed down the gangway back to the shore. 'We waved and nodded,' Gerald was to write, 'and then, as our friends started to disappear into the fast-gathering dusk, the air was full of the deep, lugubrious roar of the siren, the sound of a ship saying goodbye.' For Jacquie especially the occasion was a sad one, for she adored Argentina, and resolved that one day she would return.

The all-demanding routine of animal care soon banished melancholy. At first light a cup of tea, then clearing out cages and washing feeding pots up on deck – an agreeable chore in tropical waters, when the birds could be sprayed without risk of a chill and Sarah was allowed the run of the deck three times a day, but a lot less so as the ship entered more northerly latitudes.

It was not all slog. Unlike the boat that had brought them to the Americas, the *Paraguay Star* was a pukka liner, and the accommodation was sumptuous, the food good, the booze ample and the service punctilious. There were good friends to make and parties to throw and hangovers to spend hung over the rails in the grey morning light. At the ship's fancy dress ball Gerald and Jacquie, disguised as Paraguayans in traditional costume, ran off with the first prize. Only the ship's master looked on askance at the creatures and their mess and the ceaseless distractions they caused to his junior officers.

In July the *Paraguay Star* tied up at London's Victoria Docks. The animal collection was tiny, so was quickly disposed of. Paignton Zoo took most of the birds and animals, including Sarah, the star of the ship. 'It was heart-breaking in many ways,' Jacquie reflected, 'to part with all these lovely creatures.' She added, significantly: 'I began to realise how Durrell must have felt on his previous trips and why he had this burning ambition to have a zoo of his own, so he would not be forced to part with the animals he brought back.'

From the far horizons of the pampas and the broad sweep of the Atlantic the couple returned to Bournemouth and the tiny room in Margaret's house. Gerald attempted as best he could to focus on his literary chores and to contemplate the options in his long-term strategy of somehow, some day, starting a zoo of his own. His second book, *Three Singles to Adventure*, had come out in the spring, and Gerald riffled through the reviews. On the whole they were good, commending once again the charm, modesty and good humour of the author, his story-telling skills and the delight his encounters with strange animals provided.

But one review in particular rankled. It was in the *Daily Telegraph*, and was by George Cansdale, the London Zoo Superintendent who had shot Chumley two Christmases ago. Cansdale had little time for Gerald, and had been riled by the bitter account of Chumley's death in *The Overloaded Ark*. Now he took the opportunity to get his own back, and he pulled no punches in a peevish attempt to put Gerald down as a feckless amateur. He conceded that Gerald wrote 'infectiously', but he and his party seemed very much like 'innocents abroad'. 'If they did live as he describes it,' wrote Cansdale, 'it is surprising that they brought themselves back alive.' The book was prepared in haste, he declared, and more work would have improved it. The grammar was flawed, the treatment superficial, it contained too little information and too much 'backchat', and not enough about 'trapping and collecting and natural history'.

This was bad enough to come home to, but worse was to follow. In Gerald's absence his publishers, Hart-Davis, had decided to publish *The Bafut Beagles* in the coming autumn, rather than waiting till the following spring. This meant that instead of having a book in hand, Gerald would now have two books coming out in 1954, and nothing on the stocks for 1955. With extreme reluctance he began to face up to writing a fourth book, *The Drunken Forest*, an account of the Argentina-Paraguay foray. Sometimes Gerald found it difficult even to sit at his desk unless he was cajoled and bullied by Jacquie and Sophie Cook.

The situation grew even more intolerable when, to offset the financial losses of the Argentina expedition, Gerald undertook to begin a fifth book hard on the heels of the fourth – a collection of true stories for children based on his collecting trips to the Cameroons, Guiana and Paraguay which he called *The New Noah* – a not insignificant title. 'For some unknown reason Durrell just did not want to finish this book,' Jacquie was to write, 'and in sheer desperation Sophie and I set about writing the final chapter. This was naturally tossed aside with scorn by the genius when we had completed it, but it did inspire him to rewrite it and get the thing out of the way.' 'Why can't you two hags realise I am not a machine?' Gerald complained. 'I can't just turn on a tap when I want to. I have to wait for inspiration.'

When Jacquie suggested that he adopt a system like brother Larry, who got up at half past four in the morning to write for a set number of hours, then used the rest of a day to earn a living and get on with anything else he felt like doing, Gerald retorted: 'The subtle difference between us is that he loves writing and I don't. To me it's simply a way to make money which enables me to do my animal work, nothing more. I'm not a serious writer in that sense, merely a hack journalist who has the good fortune to be able to sell what he writes.'

He was buoyed up, though, by the sales figures for *Three Singles to Adventure* and by the way the launch for *The Bafut Beagles*, due out on 15 October, was shaping up. A Scottish newspaper had bought the rights to a twelve-part serialisation, and later the BBC ran a fourteen-part radio adaptation of the book on *Book at Bedtime* and a dramatised version called *The King and the Conga* on New Year's Eve. The mass-circulation book club World Books made it their Book of the Month, and on the strength of the sales guaranteed from this alone Hart-Davis held a lavish dinner in Gerald's honour at the Savoy.

Gerald was outwardly pleased but secretly embarrassed by his success as an author. He had little esteem for himself as a literary figure compared to the likes of his elder brother, whom he deemed a 'true' writer, even though he couldn't (as yet) make a living out of it, and felt the only good thing that could be said about his own literary career was that it funded his zoological one. In this he seriously demeaned himself. It was patently clear from his first three, relatively youthful, books that Gerald had a highly original talent and an innate grasp of the essentials of narrative: a facility with language that was fluent, lucid and sensitive; a naturalist's precise powers of observation combined with the aesthetic sensibility of a poet; the story-telling gift of a born raconteur, with an ear for dialogue and an eye for the eccentric and the absurd; and a highly individual comic sense, based *au fond* on an intense reverence and affection for life of all kinds, human and otherwise. His talent put him in the forefront of the nature writers of his age and among the best comic authors in the language, and at its very best his writing could sing with the true voice of poetry. Even the *Poetry Review* was to commend his works for 'their innate poetry shown in the masterly use of imagery which brings the creatures and landscapes most vividly to life and can compare successfully with the diction of Gerald's poet brother, Lawrence'.

Gerald himself remained unconvinced about the merits of what he wrote. 'The only thing that worries me,' he was to write to Larry, 'is how long is the great British public going to continue to read this sort of slush without getting bored by it. Hart-Davis seemed to think it might be a good idea if I interspersed it with something of a different type.' To this end he wrote a book of short fiction stories for children, only to have Hart-Davis turn it down on the grounds that it was too 'precious'.

On 13 November 1954 Gerald gave an illustrated lecture at the Royal Festival Hall in London. The idea appalled him, as he loathed any form of public speaking. Often he was literally sick with worry at the prospect of such an occasion, and it was only when Rupert Hart-Davis persuaded him of the enormous publicity value of a lecture in the Festival Hall that he agreed to go ahead.

The lecture was widely advertised. 'A Feast of Flying Mice', chattered the posters. 'Dancing Monkeys ... Hairy Frogs ... GERALD DURRELL!' The seats were soon sold out. 'The whole family bore the strain and worry of the venture,' recalled Jacquie. Gerald was cajoled into donning a freshly pressed dark suit, crisp white shirt and respectable tie, and was driven to the Festival Hall feeling as if he was being taken to his execution. But the moment he stepped on to the stage in the huge auditorium, he metamorphosed from a neurotic almost incapacitated by terror into a brilliant natural speaker, funny and captivating, commanding rapt attention by the warm, compelling timbre of his voice and the charisma of his stage presence.

'Most people,' he began, 'think that collecting animals consists of six months of tropical paradise, sitting in a deck chair with a glass of whisky while the natives do all the work. To try to correct this sort of idea, I would like to give you some sort of picture of an average collecting trip.' He talked about his unusual experiences as an animal collector, the travails, the surprises, the comedies (though not the tragedies). He was a gifted cartoonist, and introduced every animal with a lightning crayon sketch on a large sheet of paper mounted on an easel beside him. By way of variation he showed a sequence (the capture of a giant anaconda) from his abortive South American film – its first and virtually only screening. Because of the Paraguayan revolution, he explained, he was forced to do two months' filming in four days, but he hoped the audience would overlook its deficiencies – 'especially as the National Film Theatre is so close'.

Then he came to the *coup de théâtre*. 'Now I would like to introduce you to two members of the opposite sex,' he announced. 'I collected them in various ways. One I caught in the Chaco and the other I married. Ladies and gentlemen – my WIFE ... and ... SARAH HUGGERSACK!' Jacquie came on to great applause, but when it was Sarah's turn it was no artist's impression the audience were introduced to, but the real thing – furry, sinewy, eager and honking wildly as she lolloped across the stage. 'The lecture was a tremendous success,' Jacquie recalled of that memorable occasion. 'But it was Sarah Huggersack who stole the show. She accepted completely the adulation that was showered upon her from all sides and became so excited that she did not want to get into her box.'

The Bafut Beagles was published in Britain and America in the autumn of 1954, and later in most European languages and in South America. The reviews were terrific, and so were the sales. In Britain it was one of the top twenty Christmas books, with Gerald rubbing shoulders with long-established best-selling authors like Agatha Christie, Paul Gallico and Colette. The first impression of ten thousand copies sold out almost overnight, and a second was rushed through to meet the demand, with a third soon afterwards. The book never stopped selling, and has remained in print ever since, being translated into more than twenty-five languages. Even the eminent Swiss psychologist Carl Jung was a fan, it seemed, and kept a copy of *The Bafut Beagles* with him wherever he went. Gerald's fan mail became truly global, many of the letters coming from the younger end of his vast readership, and particularly from those who lived within the Communist Bloc. They ranged from the moving to the incomprehensible, but all were impassioned by a love for the natural world, and often by a poignant sense of deprivation and longing.

'Expensive Gerald Durrell. How-do-you-do?' wrote one. 'My name Alosha. I live in the Rossia. I read many yours book. I very love your book "The Bafut Beagles". I very, very want have toad dry-leaf. I very, very requests send me toad dry-leaf. And if shall send, then write what feed. And expensive Gerald write me letter. Plise. Good-buy. Alosha.'

More coherent was a letter from Elena, a fifteen-year-old girl who lived in Sofia, Bulgaria. 'You are popular in the midst of young people here,' she wrote. 'I like most "Three Tickets for Adventure" and "The Drink Wood". I love animals very much and I am terribly sorry that in our house there is no room to turn, let alone for domestic animals. But I have sponge. His name is Klavdy. He live in one jar and eat only sea salt. He has four/five children. Sponge, pitiful sponge . . .'

Critics in Britain and America responded with similar enthusiasm. *The Bafut Beagles*, most agreed, was Gerald's best book yet. It was the best thing they had read about Africa for a long time, the best about animals, the best about travel, the best about anything. 'I have seldom enjoyed a book so much,' wrote novelist James Hanley. The zest, the fun, the humour, the acute observation were there as before, and so was the author – 'a faunlike, almost furry personality of exceptional charm'. And there was the Fon.

This bibulous African giant – a source of great embarrassment to politically correct African nationalists of future years – strides through the book like an empowered black Falstaff. 'The gin-loving King of Bafut is a creation of pure joy,' wrote *Time and Tide*, while another reviewer declared: 'I am glad that he should have joined Agamemnon and Sir Tickeji Rao III and found a poet to make him immortal.' The *Saturday Review of Literature* in New York enlarged on this theme: 'Mr Durrell, who appears to have as formidable a head for liquor as any private eye in print, joined the Fon in guzzlings that earned the potentate's profound respect. In the course of these alcoholic shindigs Mr Durrell conducted some of the most peculiar conversations on record, but achieved in serious-ness an intimate understanding of the native chief. The depth and dignity under the 100-proof exterior came through to Durrell, and he catches this in a portrait that is tender, absurd and penetrating.'

But the praise was not unstinted. In a world increasingly critical of the old relationships between animals and zoos and between natives and colonies – the one a metaphor for the other – some critics were surprised by the absence of any sign of a moral standpoint towards these matters. 'He attempts no explanations;' wrote the *Spectator*, 'he passes no moral judgements; he is absorbed wholly in particulars.' Moreover, he had 'no recipes for the future of the dark continent', and seemed convinced that 'smaller animals are, and feel, better off in zoos.' David Attenborough noted that there was next to nothing of 'the anxieties and tragedies and horror of a collecting expedition' in the book. From America came another cautionary word: this book was unsuitable for any 'fond Aunt Emma'. For one thing, Gerald was not without a fancy for lavatorial references, and for another, he had a cheery, chortling way of discussing such matters as the sexual antics of monkeys. 'And, of course, there is the drinking. It goes on by the case.'

By now Gerald had realised that he was becoming public property. He therefore decided the time had come to straighten out the meandering course of his earlier life somewhat, and to re-present himself to the world at large in a more acceptable form. Abashed to find himself described in the papers as a 'scientist', he beefed up his credentials for the benefit of book jackets and press releases. He now emerged newly (though not truly) authenticated with an education in France, Switzerland, Italy, Greece and England before the war (two-fifths correct), and involvement in agricultural research and the study of animal ecology during it (some way wide of the mark).

With three best-sellers to his name in the space of two years, and two more in the pipeline – *The Drunken Forest* and *The New Noah* – Gerald was beginning to be reasonably affluent and seriously well-known; so much so that his brother Lawrence was to write to Henry Miller that Gerald was 'a more famous writer than all of us put together', though he remained 'completely unspoiled by his fame and just the same as ever'. For the first time Gerald's lifelong dream of having a zoo of his own began to look like more than a fantastical dream – though a proper full-blown zoo was far beyond even his much-improved current means. The more determined he became, the more alarmed grew his family and friends. 'But why take on a zoo?' they asked, 'and not a biscuit factory, or a market garden, or a farm, or something safe and respectable?'

'The first answer,' Gerald was to write later, 'was that I never wanted to be safe and respectable. Second, I did not think that the ambition to own one's own zoo was so outrageously eccentric. To me the thing was perfectly straightforward. I was deeply interested in all creatures that lived with me on the planet and wanted them at close quarters so that I could watch them and learn about and from them. What simpler way of accomplishing this than to found my own zoo?'

Rationalise it how he might, Gerald's dream went deeper than mere logic. It was more an obsession, seemingly almost as predetermined as genetic programming. Certainly he was driven by an unbroken sense of mission that ran from his childhood to his death, an instinctive perception of his own destiny. It mattered little whether his ambition was eccentric or not, and even less that it would involve Herculean labours. 'In those palmy days,' he recalled, 'I had no conception of the amount of money and hard work that would have to be put into such a project before the dream could become a reality.'

But where, and when, and how? By now his thinking about his projected zoo had made considerable advances, and he felt confident enough about both his ideas and his status to seek the advice of three of the most eminent naturalists and conservationists in the land – the biologist Julian Huxley, who as Director General of UNESCO had helped to found the first truly global nature protection body, the International Union for the Protection of Nature, in 1948; Peter Scott, who had founded the Wildfowl Trust at Slimbridge in 1946 and was later to become Chairman of the World Wildlife Fund; and James Fisher, one of Britain's leading ornithologists and natural history broadcasters. He also visited Jean Delacour – 'the most incredible aviculturist and ornithologist' – who had a famous bird collection at Clères, in France. 'Jean gave me a lot of advice about my scheme,' Gerald was to write, 'and coming from a man with his vast experience his advice was invaluable.' At the end Gerald asked the great man if he thought there was any hope for the world. Delacour thought for a moment. 'Yes,' he declared. 'There is hope – if we take up cannibalism.'

On 24 October 1954, a few days after the publication of *The Bafut Beagles*, Gerald had written to Lawrence, outlining an ambitious scheme that had long been on his mind:

> I wish to propound an idea to you on which I should like your help and co-operation. I am now, I think, sufficiently well known to attempt something which I have had in mind for a number of years. To you, no doubt, it will sound completely mad and a lot of rubbish. I want to start a Trust or organisation, with land in somewhere like the West Indies, for the breeding of those forms of animal life which are on the borders of extinction, and which without help of this sort cannot survive. I had always privately thought that such a scheme would be too hairbrained to have much chance of success, but when I met Julian Huxley (who wrote me a very nice crit on the *Ark*) I put my idea to him and he agreed that it was very necessary and an excellent idea all round, but, as he pointed out, while I could get nearly every known zoologist on my side in such a scheme, very few of them have sufficient funds

to help financially. What I would like to know from you is, who do you know that is stinking rich? . . . I can get a glittering array of scientific names on the prospectus, and also probably one or two rather faded nobility. Unfortunately, nowadays, it is neither the nobility nor the scientific world that has the cash.

If he could find three or four people who could put up £10,000 between them, Gerald reckoned he could get the whole thing started. He also wondered if Lawrence could help with big names as well as moneyed ones – the author and Arabian traveller Freya Stark, for example, and Osbert Lancaster, Igor Stravinsky and others known to Lawrence personally. Gerald's accountants were already working out how the Trust could be organised. The next step would be the big money and the big names.

In a later letter to Lawrence, dated 14 December, Gerald gave news of brother Leslie. Back in March 1952 he had finally married Doris Hall, his divorcee lady friend – 'big-hearted, big-voiced, laughing Doris', who at nearly forty-six was some eleven years older than he was – and now the couple had emigrated to Kenya, where Leslie was to manage a farm (on their marriage certificate he was described as an 'agricultural implements mechanic'). Gerald had high hopes that he would at last settle down to doing something worthwhile with his life. The first signs looked promising. 'An absolute cataract of letters tell us that he is thoroughly enjoying himself,' Gerald told Lawrence, 'and likes his work and the life, which I thought he would.'

Lawrence's own life had been peripatetic and tumultuous in the last two years. At the beginning of 1953, faced with a new posting to either Russia or Turkey, he had resigned from his position as information officer at the British Embassy in Belgrade and retreated to Cyprus to rediscover his Greek and Mediterranean roots and rekindle his creative fire. He was working hard to finish his novel *Justine*, the first volume of what eventually became the *Alexandria Quartet*, which was to make his fame and fortune. In a little village called Bellapaix a few miles from Kyrenia, he bought a small house near a medieval abbey on a hill overlooking a landscape of orange and lemon trees. His dark-eyed baby daughter Sappho was with him, and so for a while was Mother, standing in as housekeeper and nanny for his wife Eve, who had suffered a serious nervous breakdown.

Cyprus itself was also entering a period of breakdown, and before long, as Greek Cypriot complaints over British rule turned from protests and strikes to open resistance and the outright armed war of the struggle for *enosis* (union) with Greece, Lawrence's peace was shattered. Before long, against his instincts, he once again found himself in government harness, this time (because of his knowledge of the Greek language and Greek mind) as director of information services for the British colonial authority in Nicosia, a post some Cypriots thought made him tantamount to being a British spy.

In the midst of all this it was clear that Lawrence and Eve's ailing marriage was beyond all repair, and was descending into a deeper circle of recrimination and pain. A stream of visitors alleviated the tedium and duplicity of Lawrence's job and the nastiness of the private hell, and early in 1955 Gerald and Jacquie came to stay for two months. 'Knowing Gerry's fascination with films and film-making,' Jacquie recalled, 'Larry suggested that he might get to know the island by making a film about it. Gerry needed no excuse for leaving "Pudding Island" and soon we were once again surrounded by odd bits of equipment.'

There may have been another reason for visiting Cyprus. Like his brother, Gerald was not a committedly English Englishman, and had no problem with the idea of pitching camp elsewhere. He was still haunted by the magic of his childhood on one Mediterranean Greek island, and entertained a faint hope – though Cyprus was no Corfu – of gaining a foothold on another in his maturity. More, he fancied that perhaps some-where in Cyprus might be found an ideal location for an ideal zoo – a dream zoo on a dream island, warm, Greek and indulgent. At the end of 1954, at his brother's request, he had written an article for the *Cyprus Review*, a quasi-governmental periodical which Lawrence was editing, on the subject of the potential for a zoo on the island: 'It strikes me as surprising that no one has yet started a zoo in a place like Cyprus ... The advantages are considerable, the main one being the climate. It is amazing how a good climate can cut down the costs of such a project, and most creatures, including some of the more rare or delicate beasts, could be bred there with success.'

Gerald and Jacquie arrived in Cyprus on 31 March 1955. It was Gerald's first glimpse of the Mediterranean since he left Corfu as a boy before the war. 'My young and very successful brother arrived this morn-ing,' Lawrence wrote to Freya Stark, 'for a two month stay to finish a book and make a couple of television films in colour. He is bursting with energy and enthusiasm.' Among a stream of guests who passed through Lawrence's house were the writer and philhellene Patrick Leigh Fermor and his wife, who overlapped with Gerald for a couple of days. 'We were delighted and very amused to see how very alike the two brothers were,' Leigh Fermor recalled, 'in looks, voice, laughter, outlook, humour and zest for life.'

But Gerald's high expectations of Cyprus as a possible location for his zoo were almost instantly scuppered. Lawrence had arranged a small cocktail party to introduce his brother and sister-in-law to Cypriot society in Nicosia. Later that night, the two brothers were having a drink when a series of bomb blasts went off all over the city, followed by an enormous explosion from the direction of the radio station. It was the beginning of the Cypriot terrorist war of resistance against the British. Lawrence rushed out of the house, shouting: 'My classical records!' Gerald rushed after him. 'Wait!' he shouted. 'If you're going to be such a damn fool as to get yourself blown up, I can't let you go alone. Wherever I go,' he complained, remembering Paraguay, 'there's a bloody revolution.'

The plan of travelling around in a government van to make a film of the island was hurriedly abandoned. Instead, Gerald and Jacquie stayed on at Bellapaix to make a film about the importance of a water supply to a Cypriot village – an oddly earnest subject for a man of Gerald's disposition. He remembered enough Greek to get on good terms with the local Cypriots, and was treated with friendly hospitality even in hostile areas of the island, but an island at war was no place for a zoo, and a family at war no place for a brother. When a television project cropped up in London, Gerald and Jacquie were happy to leave Cyprus to its troubles and Larry and Eve to theirs.

THIRTEEN

The Book of the Idyll

1955

On 12 June 1955 Gerald and Jacquie returned to England and settled into another rented flat, this time at 70A Holden Road, Woodside Park, on the northern edge of London. Here Gerald went down with a bout of jaundice and was put on an austere diet of steamed fish, dry bread and no alcohol – 'something no sane person will put up with', he was to complain.

Never had he been so fortuitously laid low. Agueish and ailing, confined to his room, removed from the obligations and routines of daily life, waited on hand and foot by Jacquie, Gerald had a rare opportunity to roam mentally at will, turn over stones, re-form the scattered fragments of the past into new patterns and meanings that had not been perceived before – indeed, there was nothing much else for his mind to do.

As he entered the fourth decade of his life, Gerald began to rediscover the terrain of the early part of his second – the paradise years on Corfu before the war. The island had never been far below the threshold of his consciousness. He had never stopped talking about it. A childhood experience of such intense and transcendent joy, a happiness so powerful it was like an ache, is always with you. In many ways Corfu had made Gerald what he was now, had firmed and channelled his interests in natural history, taught him a way of life and fashioned a point of view, an insight into the nature of existence, human as well as animal, that hidebound, sclerotic old England could never have done. In his illness Gerald allowed himself the luxury of reliving those halcyon years in a wallowing of nostalgia that was both exquisite and sad, like the remembrance of a perfect love that is for ever past and gone. 'Corfu,' he told his friend David Hughes years later, 'was like Christmas every day.'

On Corfu, he realised, 'what I really learned was pleasure . . . Sun and sea. Music. Colours. And textures: rocks, tree barks, the feel of things.

Then bathes, swimming, water on the body ... The island was perfect for it, like a film set, the cypresses stagily against the sky, the olive groves painted on the starry backcloth of the night, the big moon hanging over the water – a Hollywood of the senses.'

Gerald had first exhumed his childhood memories in a systematic way some three years previously for a radio talk entitled *My Island Tutors*, broadcast on the BBC Home Service in December 1952. The talk confined itself to the four eccentric expatriate tutors – to whom he gave the names Thomas Johnson (i.e. George Wilkinson), Michel (Pat Evans), the Belgian Consul and the Polish humpback (Krajewsky) – who had been hired to instil some learning into the obdurate flint of his juvenile head. The characters of this bizarre foursome were brilliantly and hilariously drawn, and occasionally Gerald allowed a brief peep of the broader backcloth of the island and the boy's true interests there – dusty goat tracks through olive groves down to beaches white as snow and seas as clear as crystal and warm as blood; the cobbled streets and bright stalls of the Jewish quarter of Corfu town, overrun by an army of cats; the intricate, intimate nether world of the trapdoor spider; a matchbox full of scorpions; an attic full of singing birds ...

Gerald had barely skimmed the surface of his memory for this broadcast, and notably missing was his true island tutor, Theo Stephanides, who counted as a friend and mentor rather than a hired hand, along with the rest of his family. But it was a beginning, and now, laid up in bed in the flat in the very different environment of an outer London suburb, he began to forage wider and delve deeper, till a whole vanished world lay bare before him. Here, he realised, set out like an array of riches in some exotic bazaar, was the raw material of the one book he really wanted and needed to write – the story of his enchanted childhood in the never-never land of Corfu. 'It was,' said Jacquie, 'the one book he had been talking about for years.'

Gerald was artist enough to know that here was the stuff of true literature, and hard-headed enough to know that if he did it right, he had a winner. Two opposing but complementary forces began to work on the idea. On the one hand, whole scenes, whole chapters even, began to gush out like a verbal oil-strike – crude oil, perhaps, but the genuine stuff nonetheless – complete and fully formed, apparently without the intervention of any human agency between memory and pen. On the other hand, the way Gerald set about fashioning the raw material of his story entailed a great deal of calculated, professional cunning.

In conversation with David Hughes years later, Gerald intimated that he had 'sat down consciously to manufacture a best-seller'. Hughes recorded: 'To mix the magic, Durrell maintained he had started off like a good cook with three ingredients which, delicious alone, were even better in combination: namely, the spellbinding landscape of a Greek island; his discovery of its wild denizens, both animal and Greek; and the eccentric conduct of all the members of his family. The first offered escape, sunshine, paradise, peace; the second adventure in the natural world; the third, fun, light relief, situation comedy.' The trick, Gerald reckoned, was to ring the changes on the three ingredients, so that the reader never had a chance to grow tired of one before being hit with another.

'I made a grave mistake by introducing my family in the first few pages,' Gerald was to write towards the end of this intensive exercise in total (but reconstituted) recall. Once they appeared, he complained, 'the family took the book over, as characters often do, developing a life of their own on the printed page'. Only with difficulty, he said, did he manage to squeeze his animals in at all.

There is no doubting the meticulous care with which he originally planned the book. 'I plan my chapters with great care,' he explained later, 'and also the order in which they appear. It's a bit like a layer cake.' He would put a bit of descriptive writing here, and a bit of humour there, followed by some natural history just so, so that there was a constant variety in the flow.

The first question to be settled was the title, for a book without the right title is like a battle without an objective; a good title not only evokes but defines, and without one there often lurks a text without a concept. Gerald listed the possibilities as they occurred to him. First 'A Young Man's Fancy', 'Childhood with Scorpions', 'World in a Nautilus'. Then, as the Family began to creep in, 'Quinqueniad'. Later, as the true theme of the story became clearer, 'The Map of Paradise', 'The Chart of Childhood'. Finally he decided to go with 'The Rose Beetle Man'. Unlike the other titles, which were mostly trite or obscure, this one at least evoked a hard, visual image, though one too focused to serve as a metaphor for the whole book.

Next came the structure. There were to be three parts, one for each of the family villas – the Strawberry-Pink Villa at Pérama, the Daffodil-Yellow Villa at Kondokali, the Snow-White Villa at Criseda. Each part would consist of four chapters (later increased to six), and would be twenty thousand words in length. Some complicated sums scribbled on a page of chapter titles produced the astonishingly precise figure of 105,076 words for the total length of the book. Possibly an addendum in the form of a preface, described as 'small description of me', accounted for the additional 45,076 words.

Then came a list of the book's characters – many of them provided with cartoon portraits drawn by Gerald in ink outline – and their principal characteristics. For example: 'Larry – unctuous, posey, humorous'; 'Mother – vague and harassed'; 'Spiro – typically Greek, volatile, explosive, coarse, kind'.

Next in Gerald's meticulous plan came a schedule of the characters' speech and mannerisms. The cast of human characters was followed by a cast of animal ones – Roger, Widdle, Puke, Aleca, Ulysses, Dodo, and a horde of extras that included magenpies, geckos, sea slugs, ant lions, spider crabs, mason wasps, giant toads and many more.

There followed a cue-sheet with the order of appearance of every character, human and animal, in all their permutations and combinations, at the end of which, suddenly realising that some of the human ones might still be alive and potentially litigious, Gerald made exhaustive attempts to rename them. His Polish tutor, Krajewsky, for example, went through more than twenty variations, from Quarenski and Petrogubski to Vedzardopski and Mulumnivitski, before Gerald settled on an anglicised approximation of his real name, Kralefsky.

Finally, Gerald composed a two-page overview, entitled 'Explanation', of what he thought constituted the premise of the new book (which he now retitled 'Beasts in my Belfry'). It was, he wrote, 'the tale of a rather curious apprenticeship', of how, having become by the age of six 'a confirmed zoophilist', he went to live in a rambling villa on a remote Greek island in the Aegean (sic) Sea, which he proceeded to fill with the largest assortment of animals he could find.

Woodside Park was not the place to write the book. Gerald's landlord objected to the two monkeys he was keeping in the flat, and after a few weeks of ailing creativity, with Gerald's yellow complexion now fading to a healthier pasty-white, Margaret drove up to London to convey him back to the bosom of the family in Bournemouth. Here he began to write: 'The book was written sitting in bed in my sister's house, with an endless procession of family and friends coming into the room to gossip, drink tea or wine, fight or just simply to tell me how the book should be written. That I managed to write anything at all is a constant source of astonishment to me.'

Gerald had found most of his books a chore to write. This one was different. Writing it became a joy, a passion, for he was now engaged in reliving, reshaping the paradise years of his life. Looking back, he came to the conclusion that he didn't actually write it at all: 'In some curious way, a gremlin seems to have done it for me.' Jacquie remembered: 'Never had I known Gerry work as he did then. It seemed to pour out of him and it was all that poor Sophie could do to keep up with the output. Six weeks and 120,000 words later, Durrell collapsed gracefully. It was finished – and so, nearly, was he.'

What he had written was a wonderful utopian tale of an island idyll, a classic of childhood seen through the eyes of a grown man who was still that same child at heart.

Halfway through he had second thoughts about the title, and this time changed it (not very felicitously) to 'Merrily we Lived', a phrase adapted from a couplet in Shakespeare's *The Tempest*.

But as soon as the book was finished, in a final, exhausted *frisson* of inspiration – 'a fit of pique,' he called it, 'because the family had taken up so much space' – he crossed out the latest title and in its place scribbled a new one, dreamed up by his literary agent's son-in-law:

MY FAMILY AND OTHER ANIMALS

Gerald's first thought was to send a copy of the typescript for checking by his old mentor Theo Stephanides. Theo put it under the microscope of his exhaustive scholarship, correcting the spelling of Greek names and recondite details of Corfiot history and biology. 'Oranges do not start to turn red till about November,' he pointed out, 'they are a *winter* fruit . . . Are you *quite* sure that land tortoises eat tiny snails – they are supposed to be vegetarians . . . I have never seen luminous fire-flies in Corfu after the month of May, only on Mt Olympus did I see them in July . . . "Turkish" should be "Persian" – correct this for goodness sake or you'll have the critics trying to be clever about the Turks at the Battle of Thermopylae!'*

With the typescript safely through this preliminary test, copies were packed off to Curtis Brown and Rupert Hart-Davis. They reacted swiftly. It was a brilliant book, they enthused, the best he had ever done, and would beyond doubt sell in enormous numbers. Hart-Davis would put their whole weight behind its launch, but since it was such an obvious Christmas book they proposed holding back publication until the autumn of 1956, even though that was a year away. They were sorry to hear the book had half-killed him, but the good news was that it was perfect as it stood, and would require absolutely no editorial changes.

By now Gerald was suffering from total exhaustion. Alan Ogden recommended that he remove himself totally from the cares of the world and give his mind a complete break. The Scilly Isles was suggested as a good place for this sort of mental anaesthesia, and Gerald and Jacquie

---

* Unusually, Theo was wrong about this: it should have been 'Marathon' and not 'Thermopylae', as the book's Greek publishers eventually pointed out.

spent two weeks under the wind and sky, walking, birdwatching, drinking home-made parsnip wine and working hard at thinking of nothing at all. Corfu, for the moment, was out of his system.

In the meantime, the Family was reading the book. Their reactions were more bemused than amused. Apart from Larry, none of them had been put in the public eye before, and they had some difficulty recognising themselves in the form that the boy Gerald had evidently once seen them. Mother, to whom the book was dedicated – 'We can be proud of the way we brought her up,' Larry remarked of her; 'she is a credit to us' – was heard to remark: 'The awful thing about Gerald's book is that I'm beginning to believe it is all true, when it isn't.'

Larry, by contrast, came to the opposite conclusion: 'Gerry has turned his watchful animal-lover's eye upon his own family with a dreadful biological fidelity. He has successfully recreated his family with the devastatingly faithful eye of a thirteen-year-old. This is a very wicked, very funny, and I'm afraid rather truthful book – the best argument I know for keeping thirteen-year-olds at boarding-schools and not letting them hang about the house listening in to conversations of their elders and betters.' There were two first-rate portraits in the book, Larry added: that of his mother, which was executed with feeling and perfect fidelity; and that of Corfu, whose beauty and peace had been captured 'with tenderness and poetic skill'. As for Gerry's portrait of Larry himself – 'the grouch with the heart of gold', as one critic described it – it was, he wrote to his friend Richard Aldington, a 'wicked pen portrait of the genius at the age of twenty-one'.

Margaret, it seems was rather put out at being portrayed as empty-headed and boy-mad, but was big-hearted enough to let it pass. There is no record of Leslie's reaction. As for Jacquie, who was not in the book, she laughed uproariously when she was reading the manuscript, only to inform Gerald that it was his spelling that amused her, for not only was it a book about childhood seen through the eyes of a child, but it was even written in the spelling of a child.

Was it all true? Or was it, as some critics believed, more fictive than fact, spun like a spectacular candyfloss out of a spoonful or so of real sugar? Had Gerald adopted the method of his mythomaniac Corfu tutor Kralefsky, of one of whose tales he had written: 'It was a wonderful story and might well be true. Even if it wasn't true, it was the sort of thing that *should* happen, I felt.'

In his preface to the book, Gerald wrote: 'I have been forced to telescope, prune, and graft, so that there is little left of the original continuity of events.' For the sake of the unity of his concept of the Family, for example, he had cut Larry's wife Nancy out of the script, and moved Larry, who in reality had lived a mostly separate existence, back to the family villas in the vicinity of Corfu town. At times he had appropriated Leslie's actions to himself, so that in the book it is he who has the bizarre conversation with the man who turns out to be a murderer on leave from prison.

As Huck Finn remarked of Mark Twain's book about his pal Tom Sawyer: 'There was things which he stretched, but mainly he told the truth.' This was, of course, not unusual in non-fiction, and the same principle of selection and synthesis underpins all great autobiographies, particularly autobiographies of childhood – Laurie Lee's *Cider with Rosie*, for example, and Gavin Maxwell's *House of Elrig*. Even so, some asked, how could Gerald possibly remember with such precision and detail, across a gap of some twenty years, so much about so many creatures, and all those places and landscapes, and their inhabitants, and everything they said and did?

'Gerald's extraordinarily popular story may well be true,' declared Jane Lagoudis Pinchin, a Professor of English in New York. 'But truth is, after all, not an important concern. Gerald Durrell is after fiction. Moreover he is after a particular kind of fiction. Actual names and known places are the real illusion, for they allow us to willingly enter an island idyll.'

Gerald himself denied this: 'I would like to make a point of stressing that all the anecdotes about the island and the islanders are absolutely true,' he wrote in his preface. Later he was to claim that he could recall the events of any single day during his five childhood years on Corfu, stored like a collection of photographs in his head. 'I have a memory like everyone else. I think mine is colour, with 3-D built-in smells and sounds.' Of Corfu he could remember an infinity of sights, smells and sounds, significant or trivial, with blinding clarity and precision:

I can remember the curve of a wrist, the glint of a smile, a wart, a blackhead, an old hand as twisted and misshapen with arthritis as an iris corm patting my shaggy blonde head while toothless gums beamed glisteningly and the yellow rimmed eye peered down and the voice said, '*Na pas sto kako, phili mou, na pas sto kalo*' – a traditional benediction. I can remember the smell of musty clothes, like the wrappings of a mummy, stale sweat, bread, oil, olives and garlic, stockings washing. In her armpits where the hair grew rampant as her head hair, her brassiere grey with water. Peasants drying tea when we had finished with it, popcorn in Maria's house, warm rain . . .

The accuracy of Gerald's descriptions of animal behaviour, and the precision with which he conjures up those long-lost landscapes of Corfu – as anyone who retraces his footsteps today can verify – lend credence to his claims that his memory was uncannily infallible. The guts of the book were true – anthropomorphised here and there, caricatured now and then, souped up a bit when it suited, and humourised in the Durrell family tradition – to the spirit, and often to the letter, of a small boy's first reactions to the wonders of life on a Mediterranean island in those unspoiled halcyon years. And there could be no greater authentication of the book than that by Theodore Stephanides, who vouched for its accuracy, strict chronology apart.

My Family and Other Animals presented a very different view of the island to that of Gerald's brother Lawrence in his Corfu book, *Prospero's Cell*. Both brothers tried to recreate heaven, but they were very different heavens. Lawrence's was the knowing world of his early manhood. Gerald's was a boy's heaven, an innocent, prepubertal heaven, ignorant of evil, a domestic heaven in which Mother is always there, with a ladle and a steaming tureen and a table from which no one is turned away, in a home to which he can return at the end of every momentous day, bringing friends and strays, be they two-legged, four-legged, six-legged, hundred-legged, or entirely legless. The passage of time ensured that such a heaven, once left, could never be revisited – except, perhaps, through the medium of pen and paper, and the exercise of memory and a vivid reconstructive imagination.

FOURTEEN

Man and Nature

1955–1956

By late 1955 Gerald Durrell had written six books in three years, and had carried out five expeditions and foreign assignments in eight. Though in later life he sometimes described himself as 'lazy and timid', this was ramming speed by any standards, representing a huge expenditure of energy, both physical and mental. But he now began to make a significant change of course. Fed up, for the moment, with the confined, sedentary life of an author, he longed again for the relative freedom and adventure of the wilds, and his mind turned to the possibility of another major collecting expedition. Jokingly, he said that as his family were about to file a libel writ against him for what he had written about them in *My Family and Other Animals* he needed 'to go and hide in some tropical forest'.

In fact he had great ambitions for his next expedition. At first, it was to be the mixture as before: he would once again collect rare or interesting animals for zoos and dealers in Britain and (hopefully) America and Europe. He now knew only too well that collecting animals in the wilds, viewed simply as a commercial venture, was an arduous way of going slowly broke; but these trips provided terrific material for his books, and it was his books that kept him in funds. He also wanted to break into making natural history and travel films for television, in spite of the failure of his filming ventures in Argentina and Cyprus, and the adventures of an animal collector in the wilds was a rich subject for any number of films.

He gave the new expedition's destination a lot of thought before deciding it should once again be the Cameroons, in particular the upland kingdom of his old friend the Fon of Bafut. It would help the filming, he reckoned, if he knew the country already, and it would help the collecting if he knew the people and the animals they would help him collect. At first his main aim was to go for the really big, sensational beasts, even though he liked his readers to believe he specialised in the smaller, scientifically interesting, seldom collected creatures. From its early stages the expedition was riddled with inconsistencies and contradictions as Gerald evolved from old ways of thinking towards new ideals.

His first act was to get in touch with the legendary American 'bring-'em-back-alive' zoo collector Ivan Sanderson, whose accounts of a long safari in search of great beasts in pre-war Cameroons had first fired his imagination as a boy on Corfu. Gerald wanted to pick the great man's brains about certain rare, valuable and mythic animals, in particular gorilla and a mysterious giant bat that Sanderson had reported seeing along a jungle river at dusk on one of his expeditions. It was not a propitious time to approach Sanderson. The winter quarters of his famous jungle zoo in New Jersey had just burned down, with all the animals in it. But Sanderson's reply was warm and informative:

> I know all about your past work, and for some time have been a keen admirer of your activities.
>
> Now as to the 'giant bat': I must assert that the darned thing, whatever it was, did not attack me – it was just passing by and dipped down to have a look at us. I gained the impression that it was fishing for frogs that sat in the stream in quantities. Whatever the thing was, it was enormous, had teeth and at least a six foot wingspan, flew slowly, and was apparently known to the locals and regarded with awe by them – and they are NOT easily awe-struck folk but just about as matter-of-fact and logical as any people I have ever met, much more so than most Europeans and certainly Americans! ... The accompanying map shows exactly, almost to the half-mile, where we saw it.*... As to Gorilla, there used to be swarms of them all along the ridge from the huge bare rock mountain to the North which we called the 'Rustic Teat' to way over Bamenda way. The Assumbo knew all the family groups and it was all we could do to stop them catching all the youngsters by killing the mothers and then running very fast. You ought not to have any trouble getting babies but I do not envy you getting them down to the coast.
>
> ... Are you going to take some Potamogale back alive? If so,

---

* Sanderson's sketch map shows that the giant bat was seen a little north of Tinta, along a river that flows through a valley dividing the Mountains of Ogoja and the Mountains of Bemenda. There is an account of the incident in his book *Animal Treasure* (London, 1937, pp. 300–1).

try and ship me a pair – I'll pay a lot of good American dollars for them!

Sanderson ended with an afterthought concerning an odd coincidence. 'Do look up my mother,' he wrote, 'who is living at the Berry Court Hotel, Bournemouth. She is a perfectly fabulous woman, and if you like good food you'll get it with her.'

Gerald replied five days later. The information about the giant bat was fascinating, and made him all the more determined to investigate it. He also wanted to look for a creature resembling a pterodactyl that had reportedly been sighted in the swamps on the Congo–Rhodesian border and might have worked its way across to the Cameroons. 'If we see it and by some fluke I can obtain it,' he told Sanderson, 'I will certainly let you know.'

Regarding the list of stuff that you would like, I love the way you say: 'Are you going to take some Potamogale back alive?' It sent my blood pressure up several degrees when I read it. I have obtained these water shrews, but I found, as you did, that they refuse to eat anything. I shall most certainly make an attempt to get some, and, if I succeed, I am afraid you will have to pay a *lot* of good American Dollars for them, if only to compensate me in some small degree for the mental anguish these beasts have caused me!

The timing of Gerald's second letter to Ivan Sanderson was even less propitious than the first, as the luckless Sanderson's reply makes plain:

This answer to yours of the 28th July has been delayed by considerable disturbances around here, among which some 53 feet of water travelling at about 20 knots roared over my zoo for 36 hours. One of my men got all the animals out singlehanded but we lost everything else. This is the third time we've been cut down to the ankles in twelve months. First a hurricane that blew us into the river, loss $7000. Then a fire that killed all my animals and eliminated all my scientific equipment, lab, dispensary, etc, loss $29,000. Now this, at a mere $10,000. Unfortunately I am not Standard Oil of New Jersey, and even here no man can earn an honest living and $45,000 in one year, so we are having to sell the animals and discharge the staff and go out of business. Hence the delay in writing . . .

If you catch a Pterodactyl you won't only 'let me know', you'll damned well name it after me!

What with one thing and another, notably the writing of *My Family and Other Animals*, it was some months before Gerald returned to his plans for what he was now calling the Durrell Third Cameroons Expedition. In early 1956 the planning began in earnest. Jacquie, with Sophie's secretarial back-up, shouldered much of the organisational load, writing off to manufacturers around the country asking for aid in kind in return for future publicity. Soon Margaret's boarding house was piled high with crates and boxes containing all the arcane paraphernalia required to keep a collecting expedition up and running in the wilds of tropical Africa for half a year or more. 'We had enough stuff to equip an army,' Jacquie recalled, and when the time came to leave, two large trucks were needed to shift the expedition's stores down to the docks.

Gerald, meanwhile, was sounding out the zoos of Britain and America and making formal approaches to government departments. From the Director of the Natural History Museum in London he obtained a *laissez-passer* and a note that 'a gorilla skull will always find a customer', while from London Zoo he received a request for Red River hog, from Dudley Zoo a *carte blanche* for reptiles of all kinds, and from Belle Vue Zoo an expression of interest in gorillas and chimps. In May he travelled to Holland, the world centre for international trade in wild animals, seeking advice from dealers as to what species were in demand, and from the colonial British authorities he received a provisional permit for guns and ammunition 'to hunt, kill or capture animals and birds mentioned in the Schedule to the Wild Animals Preservation Ordnance'.

As the workload entailed on an expedition of this scope became apparent, Gerald added two extra pairs of hands – first Sophie Cook, who jumped at the opportunity, and later an aspiring eighteen-year-old naturalist from Bristol by the name of Robert Golding, one of many people who had written asking for a place on the team, who was finally chosen because of his specialist interest in reptiles.

To John Yealland, his companion on his first expedition to the Cameroons, now Keeper of Birds at London Zoo, Gerald wrote asking for a list of desirable birds and the feeding requirements of the more difficult species. In reply he received an irreverent letter that revealed a sense of humour not very different from his own.

> Dear old Dealer,
> Thanks for your insulting letter. You know perfectly well that if I give you a list of birds (desirable) you will lose it before you leave Bournemouth. Cast your mind back to when you even lost our tickets, not to mention the many lists I have previously supplied.

No wonder you feel that a Cameroon expedition is not the same without me ... Look forward to seeing you when you come up. The fee for all this valuable advice can be settled later. When are we finally relieved of the White Woman's Burden? In other words when do you sail?

In the midst of all these preparations, Gerald was still actively pursuing his greater dream of starting a zoo of his own. In a clear statement of what became his credo, he was to write later:

Like many other people, I have been seriously concerned by the fact that year after year, all over the world, various species of animals are slowly but surely being exterminated in the wild state, thanks directly or indirectly to the interference of mankind ... To me the extirpation of an animal species is a criminal offence, in the same way as the destruction of anything we cannot recreate or replace, such as a Rembrandt or the Acropolis. In my opinion zoological gardens all over the world should have as one of their main objects the establishment of breeding colonies of these rare and threatened species. Then, if it is inevitable that the animal should become extinct in the wild state, at least we have not lost it completely. For many years I had wanted to start a zoo with just such an object in view, and now seemed the ideal moment to begin.

It had become obvious that a zoo nearer to home made more sense than one in Cyprus or the West Indies or any other exotic spot, and he had decided that Bournemouth was as good a place as any – indeed, better in many respects. In the early summer of 1956, as a first practical step towards the realisation of his dream, he drafted a memo on a proposed Bournemouth Zoo-Park which included many of his notions about running a proper zoo:

Bournemouth, as the premier south coast resort, is an ideal situation for the formation of a zoological park, run on the lines of the world-famous Continental Zoo-Parks. Apart from the town's climate and setting, its enormous popularity with summer visitors would make a Zoo-Park an immediate success.

The accent would be on well laid-out park-like surroundings, combined with the most up-to-date methods of caging the animals, wherever possible in natural surroundings. This system ensures that the visitors have excellent facilities for seeing the animals and the animals have ideal surroundings in which to live and breed. The birth of young animals, is of course, one of the main attractions of any zoo; by adopting this method of layout and caging the Continental zoos have had far greater success in the keeping and breeding of wild animals than any zoo in this country.

The entire running of the zoo-park would be under his personal control. His qualifications for the job, he argued, were more than adequate:

During the past nine years I have financed, organised and led a number of major animal collecting expeditions to Africa and the South American continent, bringing back very large collections of mammals, birds, reptiles, fish and, on occasions, even insects for the leading zoos and such institutions as the Severn Wildfowl Trust. Many of these creatures had never been collected before. I have also made a special study of zoo design and management and the problems involved in keeping and breeding wild animals in captivity.

As a well-known author, journalist, lecturer, broadcaster and television film-maker, he wrote, he was exceptionally well placed to generate immense publicity for the zoo-park:

My publishers are extremely keen that I should do a book dealing with the 'birth of a zoo', to be followed by subsequent books on its growth and activities, quite apart from any books I might write dealing with collecting expeditions undertaken for such a Zoo-Park. A Zoo-Park of this kind could make a great contribution to both education and science, and with the growing popularity of television the making of animal films of all types should be a major part of a zoo's programme. As my wife and I are professional still and cine photographers we could therefore undertake this work.

Gerald's first port of call was the local MP for Bournemouth East, Nigel Nicolson, son of Sir Harold Nicolson and Vita Sackville-West, an independent-minded publisher and politician. When Gerald sent him a copy of the zoo-park memo he received an almost immediate reply. 'I think that it is first-rate,' Nicolson wrote, 'and exactly what is required to convince a stuffy Alderman.' As a first step he would send it to the town clerk of Bournemouth – 'a man of great sense and imagination' – and take it from there.

But neither Durrell nor Nicolson had counted on the infinite potential for procrastination of Bournemouth Council and its labyrinthine committees. It was late October before they responded. They liked the idea, they said, and were prepared to cast around for a suitable site. But as they had no intention of coming up with the money for it, perhaps it would be better if the proposed zoo-park was scaled down somewhat and turned into a pets' corner.

By now the Cameroons expedition had gathered an irresistible momentum, and Gerald had no time to wrestle with the apparatchiks at the town hall. He was disappointed by their response, but remained as determined as ever to start his own zoo for the captive breeding of endangered species.

Gerald's grasp of the nature and origins of the environmental and conservation problems facing planet earth had grown broader and deeper over the years. Even in the middle of the twentieth century such matters were the concern of an extreme minority, and were below the threshold of awareness of the general public in most of the world. Gerald was now in the vanguard of this minority. On 29 August 1956, in a talk entitled *Man and Nature* broadcast through the fairly obscure medium of the BBC German Service, he uttered his first public protest at the role of man in the destruction of nature.

Let us consider man, the strange biped that has taken over the earth. Let us consider him scientifically . . .

A genus of catarrhine primate, *Homo sapiens* is to be distinguished anatomically from living catarrhines by a large brain of about 1500cc, and distinguished in behaviour by walking upright, by using tools with his hands, and by speech . . .

Or let us consider him as the poet sees him:

'What a piece of work is man! How noble in reason! how infinite in faculties! in form and moving how express and admirable! in action, how like an angel! in apprehension, how like a god! the beauty of the world! the paragon of animals!'

In fact man is not unlike the Brown Rat. By his adaptability and cunning he has succeeded in establishing himself all over the world, from the coldest and most windswept highlands to the thick, steamy tropical forests. And, like the Brown Rat, wherever man has gone he has created havoc with the balance of nature.

Gerald went on to relate, in a few brief and haunting minutes, a horror story that was global in its range and centuries old, a story fuelled and driven by the need, greed and stupidity of man. He told of the destruction of much of the world's temperate forests, of the overgrazing and destruction of the grasslands that took their place, culminating in dust-storms and deserts. He told of the destruction of animal life wrought by man's familiars – the dog, the cat, the pig, the house mouse and the brown rat: 'While man was busy plundering the land, they were at work hunting and killing the animal life, exterminating creatures that could never be recreated.'

Extermination, he explained, meant the driving out or killing of a species. Carried to extremes it led to the extinction of a species. The most notorious case of this kind was that of the dodo, which would eventually be closely associated with Gerald Durrell and his works for ever more:

> The Dodo was a great ponderous waddling pigeon the size of a fat goose. Secure in its island home it had lost the power of flight and, like the ostrich, lived and nested on the ground. It seems that it must also have lost the power of recognising an enemy, for it appears to have been a tame and almost confiding creature. Mauritius was discovered by the Portuguese about 1507. The settlers brought with them the usual collection of goats, dogs, cats and pigs and released them on the island. These at once set about the task of exterminating the unfortunate bird. The goats ate the undergrowth which provided the Dodo with cover, dogs and cats harried and killed the old birds, while the pigs grunted their way round the island devouring the eggs and young. By 1681 this huge, harmless pigeon was extinct . . . as dead as the Dodo.

But the story was not wholly negative. Man was learning to control the balance of nature:

> All over the world there is springing up a new awareness of nature and a desire to preserve rather than destroy, for by helping nature preserve her capital man can be rewarded by the interest. Laws have been passed to check the pollution of rivers and lakes. Reforestation programmes are under way to try and check erosion and recreate the great forests that were destroyed. The protection and reintroduction of game and fur-bearing animals is meeting with great success. Other species of animal are also being protected, for man has at last realised that it is important to protect all forms of life whether directly beneficial to him or not. Large areas of the world are being set aside, untouched, as Reserves and National Parks, where the flora and fauna can exist untouched, a living museum for future generations.

In 1956 Gerald Durrell might well have had grounds for feeling optimistic about the future of the embryonic conservation movement, and believed that he would himself be one of the standard bearers in a new moral crusade, even if little of this way of thinking could be found in his books.

Shortly afterwards, his account of the childhood in which his part in that crusade had its genesis finally appeared. *My Family and Other Animals* was a runaway success from the moment it was published on 11 October 1956. Each of Gerald's previous books had sold more than a hundred thousand copies in Britain, and almost as many in other countries. *My Family* outsold them all. The first two impressions were sold out before publication, and within a month it was the number two non-fiction best-seller, behind only Winston Churchill's *History of the English Speaking Peoples*. In the Soviet Union the book sold two hundred thousand copies in six days. It was to continue to outsell all Gerald's other books, and in forty years it has never been out of print.

My Family and Other Animals was an archetypal story that appealed to something fundamental in the human psyche, and it was to make its author a household name throughout the world. Its British paperback sales alone are now in the region of one and a half million, and its appeal to other media forms has been constant. Three separate attempts were made to produce a movie version (one of the scripts, the best, being co-written by Gerald himself) before eventually the BBC produced a lavish ten-part drama series shot entirely on location on Corfu in 1987. There was also talk of the book being staged as a Broadway musical to be directed by Stanley Donen, who had directed the hit films *Singin' in the Rain* and *Seven Brides for Seven Brothers*, and of an operatic version to be composed by David Fanshawe.

The reviewers articulated the enthusiasm of the fans. *My Family*, they concurred, was 'a bewitching book', 'the *happiest* of books', 'a joyous narrative', 'a glorious story', 'an uproarious comedy' and 'even more of a spellbinder than any of his previous records of zoological adventure'. All praised his vivid and meticulous observation of the natural world of Corfu. 'The life of every natural thing was to him a perpetual feast,' effused the *Sunday Times*, 'and his fellow human beings aroused in him a loving if irreverent response . . . Across the pages troop and gobble the bent, the bearded and the zany; talk and laughter, dismay and love, fill the villas; chameleon spiders, cicadas, fireflies shimmer and twitter; toads bloat and curunculate, gaze out reproachfully from heavy eyes laced with golden filigree; scorpions dance, claw clasping claw in angular saraband.'

But it was the family – 'marvellously and most attractively crazy' – who stole the show. 'One of the most enchanting collection of pleasantly dotty mortals I've ever come across,' proclaimed a BBC books programme. 'They are ridiculous, illogical, at times infuriating but almost always adorable, and above all they are *real*.' All the critics were doubled up by the sheer comedy. 'As the antidote to a Northern winter this book is invaluable,' wrote Kenneth Young in the *Daily Telegraph*. 'I read the Widdle and Puke incidents and the affair of the good ship *Bootle-Bumtrinket* in a train, but I was obliged to close the book for fear my lowering fellow-Goths should think me unbalanced.' Fellow-author Peter Green summed it up: 'This is an enchanting and utterly unique book, by turns comic, lyrical, mocking, tender and absurd. Mr Durrell is a kind of cross between Fabre the naturalist and a nearly grown-up Kenneth Grahame, with the compulsive fascination of both.' The appeal of the book, suggested the Durrells' family friend Alan Thomas, was that it enabled those who had compromised with life, and become middle-aged straphangers, to withdraw into Arcadia. It was largely on account of *My Family and Other Animals* that Gerald now received the first formal honour of his life, being made a Fellow of the International Institute of Arts and Letters. And his books were to become, in their way, a part of the British popular culture of the late 1950s and the sixties.

Just as three years previously, when Gerald's first book, *The Overloaded Ark*, and Lawrence's *Prospero's Cell* were published virtually simultaneously to ecstatic reviews, the brothers were once again being fêted by the literary world. Lawrence's *Selected Poems* had recently been published in Britain, his novel *Justine*, the first volume of the celebrated *Alexandria Quartet*, was already at the printers, and his third and arguably best island book, *Bitter Lemons*, a portrait of Cyprus during the troubles, was finished in six weeks flat and would sell twenty thousand copies in three months.

Though he was almost completely broke, Lawrence's luck was changing, just as Gerald's had changed. Within a few months his American publishers, Dutton, were to buy the whole of the unfinished *Alexandria Quartet*, plus *Bitter Lemons*. He had recently resigned from his post in Cyprus, where he had been a marked man in daily danger of his life, and had returned to England with his new love, a married woman called Claude Forde, a writer like himself, born in Alexandria (of all places), the daughter of a French banker and a Jewish mother. The couple were temporarily holed up in a borrowed cottage in the depths of the country at Donhead St Andrew, near Shaftesbury, in Dorset, looking after Lawrence's young daughter Sappho while his wife Eve, who was petitioning for divorce, searched for a job in London.

The Durrell family saw little of Lawrence and Claude during their sojourn in 'Pudding Island', and after Gerald's departure for Africa they took off for France, where they were to become permanent residents, eking out an existence (till the money rolled in) in a primitive rented cottage in Sommières in Provence, then later moving to a small farmhouse, or *mazet*, near Nîmes. Lawrence's move to France was one day to prove of the greatest significance in the life of his younger brother.

By Christmas Gerald, Jacquie and the rest of the party were at sea, three days out of Southampton and heading south across Biscay on board the SS *Tortugeiro*, a banana boat with no other passengers. 'It was,' Jacquie reported, 'rather like having one's own private yacht.' The fact that Gerald had converted £2000 of bank securities into cash to pay for the trip helped sustain the illusion. Ahead lay good old Africa and sweaty old Mamfe and the proud old Fon and the whole of a world Gerald hadn't set eyes on for eight years or so. He popped another cork and led the ship's company in another hearty carol as the boat ploughed on. It was going to be a good trip. He felt it in his bones. But he was wrong.

Gerald's intended destination was a new area that had been recommended to him by Ivan Sanderson – the wild and forested Tinta Valley in the Assumbo in the north-west part of the Mamfe Division. This was one of the few places in the British part of the Cameroons where, it was believed, lowland gorilla were to be found in any quantity. The main objects of the expedition were to make a colour film of the gorillas and other animals in the area; to bring back as complete a collection as possible of live specimens of these animals, along with skin and spirit specimens of mammals and reptiles for the British Museum of Natural History; to make a report for the Fauna Preservation Society in London on the status of the gorillas in the area and the problems connected with their protection; and to investigate Sanderson's 1935 report of a giant bat in the region. In addition, the expedition would make sorties to the highlands, the flooded N'Dop Plain, the Oku crater lakes and the border country of the French Cameroons, where they hoped to find an incredible amphibian called the giant frog (*Rana goliath*). 'All these places,' Gerald noted in his initial statement of intent, 'generally yield a tremendous variety of creatures, ranging from mice to porcupines and from pythons to toads.' Last but far from least, Gerald would write a book about his adventures, which would be the main means of recouping his costs.

That was the plan – and it had excited the press. 'Wife off to Film Love Life of the Gorilla,' proclaimed a headline in the *Sunday Express*. 'We hope to find out if a gorilla beats his wife on a Saturday night,' Jacquie was reported as saying, 'but we shall be lucky if we see anything of their courting.'

On 7 January 1957 the ship sailed slowly into Victoria Bay. Though the view was still breathtakingly the same, time had moved on since Gerald Durrell was last there. The Cameroons were undergoing environmental change and approaching independence. As for Gerald, he was no longer the young tiger in the depths of the forest, but was travelling in a rather grander style more befitting a best-selling author, with a wife, a secretary, a teenage assistant and (later) a photographer from *Life* magazine. They ran into trouble the moment they set foot in Africa, as Jacquie vividly recalled.

> We arrived in the Cameroons during the run-up to independence, and shortly after we had landed we were summoned to Government House in Buea and hauled in front of the British Administration. They were not at all pleased to have Gerry back in the country. They wagged a finger at him and tore him off a strip for writing about the Fon the way he had done in *The Bafut Beagles*, presenting a paramount chief as a carousing black clown who spoke comic pidgin English, which is how they saw it. Today they would have called it politically incorrect. Then they just called it embarrassing and unhelpful in view of the changing political situation in Africa. They said that if Gerry was planning to go back to Bafut he should keep his mouth shut – and of course that didn't endear them to Gerry or augur well for the trip as a whole. To make matters worse the Head of Customs, a Brit with the appropriate name of Pine Coffin, wanted to confiscate the special equipment which had been donated to us by British industry, and then tried to have Gerry arrested because he didn't have a licence for his firearms, or so he claimed.

Even the Conservator of Forests, who was in charge of fauna and flora in the Southern Cameroons, was hostile. Grudgingly granting Gerald a permit to film and capture gorilla in the forest reserve provided humane means were used, he poured sarcastic scorn on both the man and his proposed method of capture: 'The prospect of Mr Durrell wresting a baby gorilla from the arms of its irate mother is a pleasing one and in my opinion he should be given every opportunity to try it.'

'Officialdom had progressed considerably in the eight years since I last visited the Cameroons,' Gerald noted wryly. 'Greater patience and agility are needed to cope with this than one needs with the animals. After two rather fruitless weeks we decided to move our base up to Mamfe and establish a camp and wait patiently for our permits.' By the time he got there the authorities had begun to dig their toes in, and an official appeal against granting Gerald permission to enter any forest reserve for the purpose of capturing any protected animal (including gorilla) had been lodged with the highest authority in Nigeria, which had ultimate responsibility for affairs in the British Cameroons at that time. Eventually it was explained to Gerald by the Commissioner of the Cameroons himself, who called on him in Mamfe, that since there were reckoned to be no more than thirty gorilla left in the Southern Cameroons it would require a matter of the first scientific importance for him to issue a licence to capture one. This persuaded Gerald that catching gorilla would not only be difficult, but wrong. At the very outset of the expedition, therefore, he was forced to abandon one of his main objectives.

He now planned to return again to the territory of his old friend the Fon in the grassy highlands to the north. Shortly after reaching Mamfe he wrote to the Fon announcing his intention, and two days later, on 25 January, received a reply from the Fon's palace.

> My good friend,
> Yours dated 23rd. received with great pleasure. I was more than pleased when I read the letter sent to me by you, in the Cameroons again.
>
> I will be looking for you at any time you come here. How long you think to remain with me here, no objection. My Rest-House is ever ready for you at any time you arrive here.
>
> Please pass my sincere greetings to your wife and tell her that I shall have a good chat with her when she comes here.
> Yours truly
> Achirimbi II
> Fon of Bafut

This bucked Gerry up a bit, for clearly, whatever the British might think, the Fon still seemed to be on his side. But the rot had already begun to set in. 'Those first few weeks had all left a very nasty taste,' Jacquie recalled, 'and what with one thing or another Gerry got a mental block about proceeding up to Bafut and hung on interminably at Mamfe, which of course was home from home to him but hell on earth for Sophie and me. I mean, the climate was intolerable. One got up in the morning and had a shower and I don't know why one bothered, because one's clothes just stuck to you all the time, so that Sophie and I ended up covered in sweat rash and there was nothing we could do about it. And we couldn't get Gerry to *move*! We were begging him to go up-country to Bafut, where at least the nights were cool. But Gerry didn't mind it. He'd camped here before.' Besides, they were comfortably housed, and this was good collecting country. Word had gone out that the 'beef master' was back, and almost immediately a large number of creatures of all sizes began pouring in.

Gerald's reluctance to move from Mamfe may have had more deep-seated reasons than disappointment at the reception he had received from the colonial authorities or problems about proceeding inland to the gorilla country in the Assumbo. Indeed, the British were later to give every sign of respect for his zoological status by inviting him to act as the government's advisor in planning a zoological garden in the capital Victoria. Rather, there appeared to be some deep angst troubling him, a spiritual or emotional affliction that snapped his springs of action. Bob Golding had not been privy to Gerald's dealings with the authorities, but during the seven months he spent in Gerald and Jacquie's company it became obvious to him that their relationship was under great strain. 'I had just turned nineteen,' he was to remember later. 'I found the whole trip amazing, exciting and quite frightening. I was just out of school and really wet behind the ears. I had never been out of Europe before, never been in a place like this before, lived a lifestyle like this before, been in the company of people like Gerry and Jacquie before. But it was obvious even to me that Gerry and Jacquie were getting on very badly. There was no rapport between them, no shred of affection or compassion, no physical, emotional, even personal connection – not to each other or for that matter to me.'

At Mamfe Gerald began to crack up. He started drinking heavily, and became depressed, morose and quarrelsome. One evening he had a tremendous row with Pious, his devoted 'boy', for whom he had always shown respect and affection. In a mad after-dinner bet with the District Officer at Mamfe, the two men had run a race round and round the house, during which Gerald, dashing like a madman in his bare feet on sharp gravel, had torn his feet so badly that he had to be hospitalised for the best part of two weeks.

By the time the permits allowing the party to film (but not catch) gorilla in the Assumbo had arrived, Gerald's condition had deteriorated catastrophically. 'I suddenly collapsed and actually lost my sight for a brief spell,' he recorded at the time. 'Rather frightened by this, we sent for the local African doctor, who told me to rest and not to worry. This left me in a quandary – was it fair to either my companions or myself to attempt the three day trek to the Assumbo. After a discussion with both them and the District Officer I decided against it.' For a time it seemed the expedition would have to be abandoned, and to one animal collector in his employ Gerald dropped a note which read: 'I do not want the

Horned Puff-Adder, and as I am returning to England sooner than I planned, please do not bother to obtain more animals for me. I regret to have to tell you that I have been very ill, and for this reason I am leaving your country much earlier.'

It was at this low point, with the entire expedition on the point of foundering, that Jacquie asked a basic question that was to change everything: Why collect a lot of animals for other people's zoos if he was aiming to start up one of his own? 'When we had been considering what we would do with our animal collection when we eventually reached England,' she was to record, 'in a fit of demented enthusiasm I had suggested to Durrell that we keep this collection and use it to blackmail the Bournemouth Council into giving us a suitable zoo site in the town.' From that point forward he would not be collecting animals for other zoos – he would be collecting them for his own.

A new plan was hatched. They would divide their forces. Bob Golding would go on alone to N'Dop to collect reptiles, Gerald and Jacquie would carry on up to Bafut, and Sophie would remain behind to look after the collection at base camp in Mamfe until Bob's return in mid-April, when they would move up to Bafut to join the others.

So the party split up. For Bob Golding his lonely foray to the wilds of N'Dop was an experience of absolute isolation – physical, mental, emotional, social – such as he had never known before and would never know again. Left behind in sweaty Mamfe, meanwhile, Sophie was bombarded with letters, demands and wild beasts by that legendary hunter from Eshobi, Elias Eyong, who had been a star turn in *The Overloaded Ark* and was now a man of status and an up-and-coming local politician. On 1 April he wrote:

> Dear Ma,
> Receive from bearer one animal of the same nature with the first two. I asked you to send me a bar of soap but you sent me a block of 'Sunlight'. Also I want some matches plus two empty cases for animals. If you are still anxious to get this particular type of animal, please inform me. I will like to know the time Mr Durrell will be returning from Bamenda.
> Best and sincere greetings. Yours truly. Elias.
> N.B. Do not put this animals in the same box/case because they fight and kill each other.

By now Gerald and Jacquie had reached the cooler, more open grassland country of Bafut. The Fon had not been in the best of health when they arrived, and was unable to attend a welcoming drink with them on the first evening. 'Good morning to you all,' he wrote to them cheerfully next day:

> I was sorry for I failed coming to drink with you, due to the sickness. I was grateful for the bottle of whiskey and the medicine which you sent me. The thing which is giving me trouble is cough. If you can get some medicine for it, kindly send it to me through bearer. I think the whiskey will also help, but I do not know yet. Please send me some gin if any. I am lying on my bed.
>
> Your good friend, Fon of Bafut.

In a short time the Fon was back on his feet. 'He greeted us very warmly,' Jacquie recalled. 'When Gerry told him about the palaver at Government House he was furious and told Gerry how much he had enjoyed his books, including the one which included himself. "Dis book you done write," he said, "I like um foine. You done make my name go for all the world. Every kind of peoples 'e know my name, na foine ting you do." The Fon really was larger than life – a fantastic looking man with enormous energy, and a wonderful dancer.' Jacquie should know, for one night she and the Fon danced the samba in the Fon's dancing hall, whirling about to the music of the royal band, he standing six foot three inches, she five foot one, and almost completely hidden by his swirling robes. 'People think Gerry had exaggerated him in his written account, but he hadn't – if anything he had underplayed him. The Fon didn't have much time for Europeans in general, but he adored Gerry.'

But Gerald was seriously out of sorts, and generally depressed. He hated anything changing, and had had fond expectations that the Cameroons would be the same magical place it had been when he first arrived there all those years ago. He became more gloomy and disappointed with each day that passed, and according to Jacquie he stopped eating and drank a bottle of whisky a day instead. Then, because he smoked in bed and burned holes in his mosquito net, he went down with malaria again, followed by piles. Finally both he and Jacquie picked up a bug that chewed up their red blood corpuscles, and they began to look like death. Jacquie recalled:

> In spite of all the setbacks, Gerry loved this sort of life. He got on terribly well with the native people. One of the greatest compliments he was paid was that he didn't behave like the English. In the Cameroons he'd sit up at night with the boys on upturned kerosene cans, smoking with them and discussing politics, saying

for God's sake don't get rid of the white man overnight, stick with him and learn what you can from him, and in a lot of ways the Africans appreciated that he was concerned about them, because he saw that it would be the poor little bush man who would suffer – the fat cats, the ones with some education, could look after themselves.

By the middle of May the animal collection was so large that it spread right round the veranda on all four sides of the Fon's rest house. Hundreds of cages contained anything from chimpanzees to mice, eagles to sunbirds the size of a thimble, coal-black cobras and multi-coloured Gaboon vipers. And though they had no gorilla, either on film or in the flesh, they did have a small, wizened baby chimp called Cholmondeley, in honour of his ill-fated predecessor, who grew in mischief as he grew in size, and another called Minnie, who had been wished on them by a local coffee planter and who screamed like a banshee when she wanted attention.

By early June it was time to leave Bafut before the rains made the road to the coast impassable. On their last night the Fon threw a farewell party, and presented Gerald with the robes of a Deputy Fon of Bafut. At dawn they were off on the three-hundred-mile drive to the waiting ship, a banana boat called the SS *Nicoya*. Staring at all the cages and baggage strewn about the deck before they sailed, one of the ship's stewards remarked: 'I've seen some queer things in my time, mate, but I've never seen anyone with a zoo in his luggage.'

FIFTEEN

'A Wonderful Place for a Zoo'

1957–1959

The *Nicoya* docked at Liverpool on 7 July 1957. Gerald Durrell was now a veteran of five collecting expeditions. All told, he had brought back some two thousand creatures from the wilds of Africa and South America, including forty-three species that were completely new to the zoological collections of the world. But this homecoming was different. This time his animals were destined for his own zoo. The gangway had barely touched the jetty before the first reporters were on board. Gerald was anxious to use the press to prime Bournemouth Council about his plans for founding his zoo in their town.

'Zoo Plan for Bournemouth' ran an obliging headline in the *Daily Telegraph*:

> Mr Gerald Durrell, 32, the writer-zoologist, hopes to start a zoo at Bournemouth. 'We trust that the council will be sympathetic to the extent of letting us have some land,' Mr Durrell said. 'If they agree I shall start preparing it this winter and would like to open it next spring.' Mr Durrell and his wife, Jacqueline, 27, have just returned from a seven-month expedition to the British Cameroons. They brought back 200 reptiles, 50 birds, 18 monkeys, 47 bush babies, a nine-month-old Chevrotain deer, thought to be the only one in the country, and a nine-month-old chimpanzee which has been named Cholmondeley St John Durrell.

This collection was to form the basis of the Durrells' zoo. An entire railway goods van had been hired to transport the animals to Bournemouth, but the journey was an agonising one. There was only one seat for the three human beings, and the goods van was continually shunted off and on to trains and in and out of sidings. Of all the hundreds of creatures confined in it, only Cholmondeley seemed to enjoy himself, replete with bread and milk and nursed and fussed over by whoever was sitting in the seat.

After fourteen hours the Cameroons expedition finally reached Bournemouth. A fleet of furniture vans were waiting for them, and the collection from the kingdom of the Fon and beyond was quickly unloaded and transported to the sanctuary of Margaret's house in St Alban's Avenue. Further to the west Bob Golding, an older and wiser young man after his great adventure, reached the haven of his parental home in Bristol, where a few days later he received a meticulously typed bill for £1.10.6, the cost of the orange squash and sandwiches Jacquie had subbed him for in Liverpool.

Gerald and Jacquie were hungry, thirsty and exhausted, but they knew they could not rest until the animals were properly housed. Cholmondeley was handed over to Mother while the grand marquee was hauled into position on the back lawn to house the hardier animals like the civets, mongooses and larger monkeys. The more delicate creatures – the squirrels, bush babies, some of the birds and all of the reptiles – were put in the garage, which had been specially insulated before their arrival.

'The animals seemed no worse for their ordeal,' Jacquie was to write of this unusual homecoming, 'and only wanted to be fed and left alone, while all we wanted was a hot bath and a drink and a good meal. But it was many hours before Gerry or I got it. Cholmondeley was finally put to bed in a large laundry hamper, after being thoroughly spoilt by Gerry's mother and sister, and it was only then that we were free to crawl up to our flat and collapse.'

Within a few days the suburban menagerie was up and running. It presented an odd sight, as Gerald was to recall:

Anyone looking out at my sister's back garden would have been forced to admit that it was, to say the least, unconventional. In one corner stood a huge marquee, from inside which came a curious chorus of squeaks, whistles, grunts and growls. Alongside it stretched a line of cages from which glowered eagles, vultures, owls and hawks. Next to them was a large cage containing Minnie the Chimp. On the remains of what had once been a lawn, fourteen monkeys rolled and played on long leashes, while in the garage frogs croaked, touracos called throatily, and squirrels gnawed loudly on hazel-nut shells. At all hours of the day the fascinated, horrified neighbours stood trembling behind their lace curtains and watched as my sister, my mother, Sophie, Jacquie and I trotted to and fro through the shambles of the garden, carrying little pots of bread and milk, plates of chopped fruit or, what was worse, great hunks of gory meat or dead rats ... It was some time before they managed to rally their forces and start to complain.

The first and most urgent cause of complaint was Minnie, who screamed continuously all day, and was soon removed to Paignton Zoo, where Ken Smith was Superintendent. Before long Minnie was followed by most of the more delicate animals, including all the reptiles, for Paignton could provide the heated accommodation that Margaret's premises could not. Cholmondeley stayed on in the house, not so much a pet as an honoured guest – or perhaps something more than that, as the man from the *Woman's Sunday Mirror*, one of the numerous press reporters irresistibly drawn to this unusual *ménage*, recorded.

At first I thought I had misheard her, but then she said it again. '... I'm mother to a chimp,' she said. 'Come and see.' And that's how I met Cholmondeley, dressed in a pink cardigan and playing on the dining-room carpet of an ordinary-looking house in St Alban's Avenue, Bournemouth, just like a child. Which is the way Mrs Jacquie Durrell, 27, wants it to be. For she plans to bring up Cholmondeley exactly as if he were a human baby – her own baby. Then she explained: 'I have decided I would never have children – the life of an ordinary housewife did not seem right for me. Now I am mother to Cholmondeley – he just steals your affection.'

Jacquie and Gerald were engaged in a serious experiment, the reporter claimed (recording more fantasy than fact). They wanted to see if it was possible to educate a baby chimp in human ways so that he could remain a member of the family when fully grown.

'His day was a simple one,' Jacquie recorded; 'he was awakened in the morning with a large cup of milky tea and then dressed in the exotic sweaters that my mother-in-law had knitted for him "to keep the cold out, dear". Then the rest of the day was spent in plaguing the inhabitants of the house until he was finally put to bed in the evening with the aid of a large mug of Ovaltine, leaving everyone else exhausted and irritated beyond recovery.'

At first the chimp slept in Mother's room, but when it was discovered that she never put the light on for fear of waking him, he was removed to Gerald and Jacquie's small bedsit upstairs, where he soon learnt to put up with light, noise, cigarette smoke and all the pressures of his human friends' hectic life. 'His favourite game,' Jacquie recalled, 'was to swing on the curtains in the front living-room, where he held audience every day for all the children in the neighbourhood.' His preferred haunt was the golf links at the end of the road, where he would climb trees, turn somersaults, chase dogs, distract golfers and pelt people with pine cones. When he grew tired he was trundled home slumped in a pushchair.

'At mealtimes,' Gerald wrote, 'Chumley was exceptionally well behaved. He would sit on my lap and wait patiently until I put some tit-bit on my side-plate for him. Then he would feed himself very delicately, pulling the food to the edge of the plate with his forefinger, and then picking it up with his long, almost prehensile lips. If it was something like peas, he would spit out the skins very daintily, generally managing to get fifty per cent on to the plate, and the other fifty into my lap.'

After lunch Cholmondeley liked a spot of exercise – a game of hide and seek, or pick-pocket, or swinging on the curtains, or rocking to and fro in the rocking chair with ever-increasing speed till the chair tipped over and he rolled on to the floor. Like a human child he was extremely inquisitive, and liked to touch any new object he discovered. He had a few animal friends, including two budgerigars, one green and one yellow, though he seemed to be under the impression that the yellow one was a new kind of banana.

After games came tea. 'Chumley would greet the arrival of the tea tray with shrill hoots of joy,' Gerald observed, 'and then squat as close to it as possible and watch with absorbed interest while you poured him a cup of tea. When you handed it to him he would taste it very carefully by sticking the edge of his lip into it. He was very particular about his tea: it had to be the right temperature and the right colour, not too strong or too weak, and without the slightest trace of sugar. If he felt it was too hot, or perhaps too cold, or that it had too much milk in it, he would put his cup down carefully, and then, catching hold of your hand would place it on the tea pot or the milk jug as a gentle hint that he wanted something done to his tea to make it acceptable.'

At night he slept in a huge laundry basket with a paper bag containing a dormitory feast – a couple of tomatoes, an apple, a handful of grapes, a slice of brown bread, four cream cracker biscuits and a packet of potato crisps. 'This fragment of food,' noted Gerald, 'kept him going during the dark hours and prevented night starvation.' Then it would be morning, and tea again, or better still, four large mugs of cocoa and raw egg.

Cholmondeley became a well-known local character, dressed in football shorts and a sweater. Sometimes he would venture forth around town with Gerry on his motorbike. Once he took part in a BBC radio programme involving an intelligence test, in which he performed extremely well, emerging with the mental age of a human child of seven, though he was a good bit younger than that. If he was sick Gerald would ring up Alan Ogden, who would arrive complaining that this was vet's work, but would stay to inject penicillin for whatever Cholmondeley's ailment turned out to be. On one occasion the long-suffering Ogden was obliged to administer a suppository to an ailing pigmy mongoose which had eaten some of its coir bedding.

Gerald, meanwhile, had begun his search for a place in which to house his animals permanently. His aim had been to persuade Bournemouth Council to rent or sell him a suitable site in the area, using the *fait accompli* of the menagerie in Margaret's garden as both a stick and a carrot. The town should be glad, he felt, to have a new amenity that would cost it nothing. The council was amenable at first, and even came up with two sites, both of which proved to be totally unsuitable. But gradually they went off the idea. The animals were likely to be dangerous and smelly, they claimed, and even if they weren't, they had no land anyway.

Gerald's next move was to launch a press campaign, and soon a stream of reporters from the local and national press were coming to Margaret's house, where they were first softened up by Cholmondeley and then charmed by Gerald and Jacquie. 'Have You a Site for a Zoo? Mr Durrell's Problem', read the headline in the *Bournemouth Echo*. 'If you know of such accommodation,' ran the story, 'Mr Durrell will be pleased to hear from you.'

Gerald received only one letter – from the borough council in neighbouring Poole. They had a place that might be suitable for a zoo, they said – a large but neglected Georgian mansion called Upton House, the former residence of the Llewellin family, situated in fifty-four acres of ground at a beautiful site on the shores of Poole Harbour.

Gerald was greatly excited by this development. An initial inspection confirmed that the house and its grounds were perfect for a zoo, and on 6 August 1957 he sent Poole Council a lengthy letter outlining his preliminary plans for a zoological garden, and an estimate of the likely income and expenditure involved during the first two years of operation:

> I have estimated that the property would cost £10,000 to develop and £6000 to stock. I myself can stock it, and would like you to put up the £10,000 for development. I should like to stress that my motives for wanting this zoo are not entirely mercenary. It has always been my ambition to have a place of my own, to run on my own lines and incorporating many new ideas that I have. Therefore, you can rest assured that I would put my maximum

effort into making the project not just a financial success but something of scientific value recognised throughout the world. In nine years I could make it the foremost zoo in England.

By early October Gerald had finalised a working proposal. Only the land immediately surrounding the house and its walled garden would be developed to start with. The entrance fee would be two shillings, extra for special exhibits. There would be a minimum of seventy-eight aviaries, some with ponds; eleven paddocks, including one each for lions and bears; four pits with ponds for small mammals; a small mammal house with forty cages; a monkey house with six cages; a reptile house; an aquarium and a pets' corner. Money could be saved by converting the squash court into the aquarium, the tennis courts into the pets' corner, the coach house into the store room and animal feed centre, and Upton House itself into a cafeteria, offices and keepers' quarters. Additionally – a nice touch – the shoreline along Poole Harbour could be developed into a complex of channels and islands where various species could be kept and viewed from boats. Some 875 mammals, birds, reptiles and fish would have to be purchased, at a cost of over £2600, but Gerald could provide nearly two hundred animals of his own – 'all young animals in magnificent condition'. A bear enclosure could be got for £400, a station for the model railway for £100, and a shorthand typist for £312.

Though it was obvious that Upton House was currently in no fit condition to house a zoo, it would not have made much difference if it was. With winter approaching, and Margaret's back garden looking, as Gerald put it, 'like a scene out of one of the more flamboyant Tarzan pictures', he was dismayed to learn that the council's decision about Upton House would not be forthcoming until the New Year. The animals could not be expected to last out the winter in an unheated marquee. What to do?

At this critical juncture, Jacquie had a brilliant idea. 'Why not let's offer them to one of the big stores in town,' she suggested, 'as a Christmas show?'

Only one store in town, the huge emporium J.J. Allen, had room for such an improbable Christmas attraction. So 'Durrell's Menagerie' was born. A basement was set aside, roomy cages were constructed to Gerald's design, murals depicting a tropical paradise were painted on the walls, and the ceremonial robes with which Gerald had been presented in his capacity as deputy Fon of Bafut were put on public display. Those animals that were suitable for housing in a shop basement were moved in during the run-up to Christmas, the others being offered winter quarters at Paignton Zoo. 'Durrell's Menagerie' proved such a success that it was kept open for several weeks more after Christmas, but there was always potential for trouble with monkeys in a department store, and one peaceful Sunday morning trouble came. It began with a phone call.

'This is the police 'ere, sir,' came a lugubrious voice. 'One of them monkeys of yours 'as got out, and I thought I'd better let you know.'

The escapee proved to be Georgina the baboon. Gerald grabbed a taxi and rushed down to the store. A large crowd had gathered outside one of the big display windows, which had been carefully arranged to exhibit a wide variety of bedroom furniture. 'It looked as if a tornado had hit it,' Gerald was to recount. 'The bedclothes had been stripped off the bed and the pillows and sheets were covered with a tasteful pattern of paw marks. On the bed itself sat Georgina, bouncing up and down happily, and making ferocious faces at a crowd of scandalised church-goers. I went into the store and found two enormous constables lying in ambush behind a barricade of turkish towelling.'

With Margaret, Jacquie and the two constables guarding the main exits and the approaches to the china department, Gerald approached the errant baboon.

'Georgina,' he said in a quiet, reassuring voice, 'come along then, come to Dad.'

The hullabaloo of the ensuing chase lasted half an hour. Georgina rushed hither and thither, swinging from the Christmas decorations, rampaging through the stationery department, chewing lace doilies and hiding in linoleum rolls before grabbing one of the policemen round the legs in a tackle worthy of a rugby forward. It was then that Gerald leapt out, seized her by her hairy legs and dragged her away.

'Cor!' said the policeman. 'I thought I'd 'ad me chips that time. It makes a change from teenagers, I must say.'

The demands made by the animals – especially the primates – were endless. On 9 December 1957 Lawrence Durrell received the Duff Cooper Memorial Prize for his book *Bitter Lemons* from the Queen Mother in London. He invited Mother to come along, but she declined – she hadn't anything decent to wear, she explained, and besides, she had to look after the chimp.

Christmas was spent *en famille* in St Alban's Avenue. It was not a peaceful time, for Cholmondeley had ideas of his own about how the festivities should be celebrated, and spent much of his time demolishing the Christmas tree, eating the candles, swinging from the paper chains, stuffing a cracker into the gravy boat, burning his fingers on the flaming brandy, running off with the Christmas cake and throwing the duck into the fire.

Gerald was too preoccupied with his efforts to start up his zoo to be able to settle to anything, least of all to writing his book about the latest expedition. His thinking had evolved considerably in recent months, and he had received valuable advice from Peter Scott on ways and means to establish a conservation Trust, based on Scott's experience when starting up his Severn Wildfowl Trust in 1946. Though Gerald was never entirely at ease in Scott's company he came to admire him enormously as a founding father of the conservation movement, and was always to be grateful to him for the encouragement and advice he had given him. 'In those days,' he recalled, 'captive breeding was considered anathema to most conservationists. But Peter was one of that small band of conservationists who realised that captive breeding could be a useful and powerful tool in the preservation of endangered species. Therefore he thought my idea was a splendid one.'

Reflecting what he now saw as the main thrust of the project, Gerald proposed setting up a Trust – a non-profit-making charitable organisation, to be known as the Wild Animal Preservation Trust – to run the zoo, which he now called a sanctuary, where he aimed to do for wild animals what Peter Scott had done for birds at his Wildfowl Trust.

'The objects of the Trust,' Gerald wrote in a preliminary report which in effect spelled out his life's mission, 'are to save animals in danger of extinction, to conduct collecting expeditions to obtain these rare creatures, and to promote the preservation of wild life all over the world.' The establishment of such a sanctuary had never before been attempted, he pointed out, and it would therefore be unique.

The negotiations with Poole Council dragged on endlessly, and Gerald began to complain of the 'constipated mentality of local government' and the 'apparently endless rules and regulations under which every free man in Great Britain has to suffer'. The country, he fumed later, was 'enmeshed in such a Kafka-like miasma of bureaucracy that the average citizen was bound immobile by red tape and it was impossible to get quite simple things agreed to, let alone something as bizarre as a zoo'.

Eventually the basis for a forty-nine-year lease on the Upton House property was agreed. This required that Gerald put up £10,000 towards the costs – the equivalent of about £125,000 in today's money. At this delicate moment his publisher, Rupert Hart-Davis, came forward with an extraordinary offer. His firm was prepared to act as guarantor for a £10,000 loan, he told Gerald, on the understanding that the zoo would provide material for a virtually endless series of books, for which they would have exclusive rights.

On the strength of this bold and generous offer – a huge vote of confidence in Gerald's present and future status as a best-selling author

– Gerald wrote to his bank asking for £10,000 to finance the Wild Animal Preservation Trust. He had a guarantor in place, he said, and expected enough profits from the zoo to pay the money back within six years. 'I regret that I cannot personally deposit any security,' he added, 'but I would mention that my estimated income for the next financial year will be not less than £10,000.' In case his bank manager was still dangling on the ropes, Gerald decided to knock him out of the ring once and for all. 'My activities have put me in touch with a variety of well known people in different walks of life,' he wrote, 'all of whom could be useful, including Julian Huxley, Peter Scott, James Fisher, Somerset Maugham, Freya Stark and Lord Kinross.'

However, when the terms of the lease from the Poole Council were finally made known, they proved quite impossible. Most of Gerald's £10,000 would be swallowed up by specified repairs to the house and outbuildings, which were in a shocking state of repair, leaving next to nothing for the construction of the enclosures, lighting, heating and other necessary services. 'Durrell was bitterly disappointed,' Jacquie recalled, 'and we reluctantly came to the conclusion that we would have to abandon the whole idea of starting a zoo in Poole.'

Gerald was in a bind. Most of his animals were in Paignton Zoo, and would remain there for ever if he failed to reclaim them by a certain date. He had an agreement with his publishers to write a book a year, but he still hadn't written last year's book, and now he had to write another one, for which he would have to make another foray overseas while he was trying to found a zoo back home. Now his immediate zoo plans had collapsed. His instinct was to forget England altogether, since all the local authorities in the land would be bound by the same red tape and tunnel vision. But if not England, where on earth . . . ?

Gerald turned his back on Poole and set his sights on another expedition to Argentina, departing in the autumn of 1958 and returning in the summer of the following year. This time it was not to be simply a collecting expedition, for he was keen to establish himself in wildlife television, as Peter Scott, David Attenborough and the ornithologist James Fisher had already done, and hoped to come back with material for a series rather like Attenborough's *Zoo Quest*, which had been attracting large audiences on BBC.

By now Gerald was quite an experienced broadcaster, mainly on radio, a medium he felt relatively (though never entirely) relaxed in. He was a natural on radio, as Tom Salmon, then a young reporter for BBC West Region, found when he went to St Alban's Avenue to interview him shortly after his return from the Cameroons.

Gerry and I did a little four- or five-minute piece in a modest little house in the suburbs, sitting on a sofa and scampered over by a chimp called Cholmondeley, who was dressed in a sort of 1890 bathing costume and plastic pants and seemed to have the run of the house and absolutely terrified me. When I got back to Bristol I sent a copy of the tape to the Natural History Unit together with a note saying I had just interviewed one of the best off-the-cuff broadcasters I had ever come across and I thought he could well help them in their programme-making. Thereafter Gerry reckoned I had marked his path into broadcasting and we became the firmest of friends. The relaxed skill of his broadcasting never failed him, and never once, though he was such a 'name' by then, did he think regional broadcasting was beneath him.

The previous spring, while he was in Africa, the BBC had broadcast Gerald's brilliantly written six-part radio series *Encounters with Animals*, an engaging account of a miscellany of creatures who had impinged on his life in one way or another. It had been produced by Eileen Moloney, Gerald's mentor in the world of radio broadcasting, to whose encouragement and professionalism he owed much. *Encounters with Animals* was repeated three times, and was such a hit that Eileen Molony commissioned Gerald to write a sequel, to be broadcast early in 1958. This was another six-part series, called *Animal Attitudes*, a behavioural study of animals which treated the animal kingdom as an organisational and technological world comparable to the human one, encompassing animal inventors, animal architects, animal warriors, animal lovers, animal parents and animal minorities, the species in danger of going under, or already gone.

It was Jacquie who came up with the idea of amassing all twelve talks from the two series in the form of a book, to be entitled *Encounters with Animals*. This was a relatively easy task, and at a stroke solved the problem of delivering a new book to his publishers for 1958, as required by Gerald's contract. The typescript duly landed on the desk of a copy editor at Rupert Hart-Davis by the name of David Hughes, five years younger than Gerald and an aspiring author in his own right.

One morning Hughes was informed that the famous author of *My Family and Other Animals* was coming into the office at noon to discuss editorial matters concerning his new book. Durrell was one of the money-making stars of the firm, and though Rupert Hart-Davis normally chose not to sully his hands with authors of a popular kind, and was often impatient with people who were likely to make money, he had a rapport with Gerald Durrell which he didn't have with other best-selling non-fiction writers like 'Elephant Bill' Williams and Heinrich Harrer. Durrell, the secretaries in the office decided, was also a ladykiller. He was also, so the office mythology had it, a rewrite job. According to Hughes' predecessor, Gerald was one of those illiterate adventurers whose ungrammatical scribbles required maximum input from his editor in order to turn them into a publishable book. Eventually, went the story, Durrell would be sent the proofs of the book, but not a copy of the original text. 'Thus, legend had it,' recalled Hughes, 'he would never guess that an anonymous wage-slave had guaranteed him yet another best-seller.'

The reality, Hughes found, was rather different. The typescript of *Encounters with Animals* was immaculate – totally literate, perfectly grammatical, punctiliously spelt. 'There wasn't a howler in sight,' David Hughes remembered. 'A flip through the script told me that Durrell seemed to enjoy places, animals, landscapes, jokes, wine, weather and people, in roughly any order. I thought that Durrell might be the kind of wild-eyed enthusiast who would at once intimidate me by his brilliance.' But when Gerald entered David Hughes' office, unannounced, he did no such thing. Hughes' account of his first encounter with a Gerald Durrell still only in his early thirties, and at the very beginning of big things, is illuminating.

> He looked young, blond, handsome, excited and nice, all to excess. After a few words, minding his every comma, he gave me a hard blue stare of amusement and said: 'We're all going to Bertorelli's, if you'd care to join us . . .' All? That 'all' was crucial. I had learned in two seconds that this man was uniquely inclusive. I had discovered Durrell's gift of drawing others irresistibly into his private orbit. His prompt intimacy had found me a friend for life.

> Over plates of pasta he assumed me too to be an adventurer, if not a ladykiller, as well as a very literary fellow well above the sort of tripe he wrote. He had only just had success with *My Family* and was regarding it as a fluke. Meanwhile, as he wolfed his veal, Gerry was working me up with visions of Greece, regretting that by some oversight I had missed that country and therefore most of civilisation, but convinced I would very soon be ordering pints of ouzo with my arm round a willing nymph. Every word was infectious. He had the gift of being as interested in my life as in his own, and as keen to enrich it. As of this lunch I began to see that life of mine in a jollier perspective, riddled with possibilities, ambushed by the unpredictable. It was clear that Durrell had no vanity (and certainly no conceit), only exuberance, a pleasure in

the feel of this piece of bread or that plate, the taste of the second bottle of wine, the look of the decorations in this old favourite among dining rooms, the sound of the waitresses making a fuss of him, the mood of the moment. The last thing he wanted or needed to talk about, or impose on anyone, was himself, because he so distinctly was himself without trying. That defined charisma.

Gerald's ambition to break into television was to prove difficult. He had no innate talent as a cameraman or director, and was ill at ease in front of the camera, at least in the cramped and inhibiting studio conditions of those days. The footage he had shot with Jacquie on his third Cameroons expedition was not wildly promising, but skilfully structured and drastically cut by BBC producer Tony Soper, it stretched to a three-part series called *To Bafut for Beef*, which included studio excerpts featuring Gerald, Jacquie and Cholmondeley.

By now Cholmondeley was well used to making public appearances. He had done several photo-calls for the press to show off his skills with washing-up brush, sponge, mop, kitchen scales, telephone and camera. He had appeared several times on television, and had been a guest at the production launch of a Twentieth Century-Fox movie. 'Brother Gerry has become a television star,' Lawrence wrote to Henry Miller from Sommières, 'owing to a clever little chimp he has brought back from the Congo which does everything but vote apparently.' At a trade book fair at Olympia Cholmondeley had been guest of honour at the W.H. Smith stand, and comported himself impeccably at the hotel lunch afterwards. 'Lunch was served by an ancient and aristocratic waiter,' recalled Gerald, 'who did not bat an eyelid at the sight of a chimpanzee in a Fair Isle pullover, sitting on my lap and eating food from my side plate . . . During the course of the meal he suddenly leant over and enquired softly and deferentially: "Would the . . . er . . . er . . . young gentleman like some more peas, sir?"' Cholmondeley grew quite accustomed to the train journey up to London, which he enjoyed hugely, except for the cows in the fields, which frightened him, but as word of his presence spread great crowds would gather, blocking the corridors and infuriating the guards, so that eventually he had to be taken up to town by car, which was just as much fun, especially the pub stops and the beer and crisps that went with them.

'My beastly brother has started a zoo in Bournemouth and travels everywhere with a giant ape called Chumley,' Lawrence reported to Richard Aldington. 'Dreadful scenes in the dining car of the Bournemouth Belle; but I must admit it is a good way to call on one's publishers when asking for money. Our techniques are widely different. I find that Fabers get awfully scared when I put imaginary titles to books. For a long time I convinced them that *Justine* was to be called "Sex and the Secret Service" or "Not Now Your Husband's Looking". Gerry, who is cruder (with Hart-Davis one must be tougher I suppose), always threatens to write a life of Jesus. I expect they'll come down here and make my life a cicada-ridden mystery before long . . .'

Gerald's television series *To Bafut for Beef* had a mixed reception. Cholmondeley had grown a little cocky with adulation, and behaved unpredictably, while Gerald was so uncomfortable under the lights that he sweated continuously and profusely, an embarrassing phenomenon which the cameras picked up with pitiless precision. 'If Gerry was going to pursue any career in this particular medium,' Jacquie concluded, 'he would have to be filmed on location and not asked to perform in a studio.'

'Durrell is still a tiny bit nervous,' wrote the *Observer*'s reviewer after the second programme, 'but he communicates a good deal of his own charm and all his animals'.' One review in particular, by Jessie Forsyth Andrews in *Christian World*, gave Gerald special gratification, not just because it was favourable but because it was imbued with a way of thinking that was not very far from his own:

What is the right relationship between man and the lower creation? Some humans have almost a passion for animals, tame or wild, familiar or strange; and I cannot believe it is anything but a God-given instinct. I am thinking of the whole range of sentient creatures in earth and sky and sea. Are we their owners – or their trustees?

One of the greatest recent achievements of science has been the long-range photographic lens. We explore space and locate sput-niks with it. But at the opposite end of the scale it brings us acquain-tance with the life-histories of the wild creatures of the jungle and the desert. Some of the best programmes on television have given us the same insight – especially recently the short series of films from West Africa by Gerald Durrell, the genial young explorer who collects what his native friends call 'beef' in the Cameroons and brings them home. He almost made me love the egg-hunting snake – and snakes paralyse me even in pictures.

But in a generation or so will man's knowledge of the wild creatures be gathered only from films and books, and from Whipsnades, small or vast, here and there in the world? Is it to be Man versus Beast henceforth?

There remains for me this question: aeons ago God created and evolved marvellous creatures in the vast spaces of earth where no man was – surely therefore for His own delight in them. For untold millions of years His eye alone has beheld them. By His gift now we partly share His joy in them. Is it His will that they should cease from the earth?

Argentina now began to occupy more and more of Gerald's time and attention. The BBC were keen for him to film the expedition, and though they felt unable to send a cameraman out with the party, they were confident enough to offer Gerald a contract.

'Gerry was obsessed with Charles Darwin's book *The Voyage of the "Beagle"*,' Jacquie recalled, 'and had a secret ambition to go to Patagonia to see for himself the penguins, fur seals and elephant seals that live along its coast.' In Gerald's rough shooting script for a series of eight half-hour films, Tierra del Fuego was to be the subject of the first two (*Land of Fire* and *The Edge of the World*), followed by programmes on the pampa, the Lower Andes and Formosa.

There was a moment of crisis when Gerald discovered that David Attenborough was also heading for South America to shoot another *Zoo Quest* series, this time in Paraguay, but when he phoned Attenborough he found to his relief that they were not really in competition, for their aims were very different. 'Whereas David is really going on another zoo quest for only two or three special creatures,' Gerald reassured the Head of Programmes at BBC Television in Bristol, 'what I am trying to do is to present a complete picture of the pattern of animal life in a vast area ranging from almost polar conditions down south to tropical conditions up north.' Conceived in this way, the proposed series revealed a breadth of vision and a grandeur of scale that was ahead of its time in documentary programme-making. Built in to the series, too, was a conservation dimension that was still rare, for Gerald had drawn up an exhaustive list of animals on the verge of extinction in South America that he wanted to film.

Shortly before Gerald set off for Argentina he approached his colleague and mentor Peter Scott to see if there were any species he particularly wanted for his Wildfowl Trust at Slimbridge. Scott told him that one of his great ambitions was to secure a pair of the rare torrent ducks thought to inhabit the high Andes of Bolivia. 'He was, as always, wildly enthusiastic,' Gerald recalled, 'and he begged me to obtain some Torrent ducks for him. He talked so enthusiastically about the Torrent ducks that at one point I was under the impression that I had already got them for him. His enthusiasm for everything to do with conservation or the animal world would warm you like a fire. Half an hour's talk with Peter and you felt you could succeed in realising your wildest dreams.' Sadly, Gerald was not to secure any Torrent ducks in South America, and Scott never succeeded in keeping the species at Slimbridge.

In the middle of his preparations for the expedition, Gerald's mind returned to the problem of the zoo. What happened next has become part of the mythology of zoo history. There were three stages. The first involved (once again) Jacquie. She wrote:

> I thought that the matter of the zoo had been shelved entirely, but I had overlooked Durrell's stubborn nature.
>
> 'Surely there must be somewhere left that has sensible people in charge who are not hidebound or tied up with red tape and the dear old Town and Country Planners,' Durrell moaned bitterly one day. Before I realised what I was saying, I found myself suggesting the Channel Islands.
>
> 'They've got a better climate than ours and their own government, so I think they're worth trying.'

Gerald agreed. But they didn't know anyone in the islands who could help fix things for them. The conversation petered out, and the flicker of hope faded.

The second stage involved (again) Rupert Hart-Davis. Gerald recalled:

> Reluctantly (for the idea of starting my zoo on an island had a very strong appeal for me) we forgot about the Channel Islands. It was not until a few weeks later that I happened to be in London and was discussing my zoo project with Rupert Hart-Davis that a gleam of daylight started to appear. I confessed to Rupert that my chances of having my own zoo now seemed so slight that I was on the verge of giving up the idea altogether. I said we had thought of the Channel Islands, but that we had no contact there to help us. Rupert sat up, and with the air of a conjurer performing a minor miracle, said he had a perfectly good contact in the Channel Islands (if only he was asked) and a man moreover who had spent his whole life in the islands and would be only too willing to help us in any way. His name was Major Fraser, and that evening I telephoned him. He did not seem to find it at all unusual that a complete stranger should ring him up and ask his advice about starting a zoo, which made me warm to him for a start. He suggested that Jacquie and I should fly to Jersey and he would show

us round the island, and give us any information he could. And this accordingly we arranged to do.

Major Hugh Fraser was waiting for them at the airport. He was a tall, slim man, and wore his trilby hat so far forward that the brim almost rested on his aquiline nose. They drove out of the airport and through St Helier, the island's minuscule capital, into the countryside. The roads were narrow and ran between steep banks and overhanging trees as if through a green tunnel. The landscape reminded Gerald of Devon on a miniature scale, but the farmhouses were built of the beautiful Jersey granite, which contained, Gerald observed, 'a million autumn tints in its surface where the sun touches it'. Within a remarkably short time they had viewed two substantial properties with what could be called zoo development potential; but neither seemed quite right, and spirits began to sink. Then they headed for the district called Trinity, where Major Fraser himself lived. They turned down a drive, and there before them was Fraser's family home, Les Augrès Manor (The House of Ghosts), one of the most beautiful houses on the island.

'The Manor was built like an E without the centre bar,' Gerald was to write of that fateful encounter; 'the main building was in the upright of the E, while the two cross pieces were the wings of the house, ending in two massive stone arches which allowed access to the courtyard. These beautiful arches were built in about 1660* and, like the rest of the building, were of the lovely local granite. Hugh showed us round his home with obvious pride, the old granite cider-press and cow-sheds, the huge walled garden, the small lake with its tattered fringe of bulrushes, the sunken water-meadows with the tiny streams trickling through them.'

The party walked back into the sunlit courtyard. It was, Gerald agreed, a wonderful place. He turned to Jacquie, and by way of a polite, idle aside he said: 'Wouldn't it make a wonderful place for a zoo?'

As far as Gerald knew, there was no question of the manor being available. It was therefore fortunate beyond belief that he happened to say what he did just then. In future years this sort of thing came to be known as 'Durrell's luck'.

'Are you serious?' said Major Fraser. 'Come inside, dear boy, and we'll discuss it.'

They discussed it over aperitifs. They discussed it over lunch. They discussed it over brandies after lunch. Major Fraser, it seemed, was finding the upkeep of the property a bit beyond his means, and was thinking of

* In fact the oldest parts of the building date back to the fifteenth century.

moving to a smaller place on the mainland. Perhaps, he suggested, Gerald might be interested in renting the manor for the purpose of establishing his zoo?

'So, after a frustrating year of struggling with councils and other local authorities,' Gerald was to write, 'I had gone to Jersey, and within an hour of landing at the airport I had found my zoo.'

The Durrells returned to the mainland in a turmoil of emotions – elation, anticipation and relief mixed with anxiety, and doubts as the daunting demands of the enterprise began to sink in. When Gerald announced the good news on his return to Bournemouth, it was greeted, he recalled, 'with alarm and despondency by all who knew me'. Only Margaret seemed pleased, for though she thought the scheme 'hare-brained', she was relieved that she might soon be able to reclaim her garden from the various denizens of the jungle who still inhabited it.

James Fisher, Britain's foremost ornithologist, who had earlier approved of Gerald's plans for captive breeding, poured scorn on the idea of trying to set about it on an offshore pimple of a place. 'You're mad, dear boy,' he exclaimed. 'Quite mad. Too far away. End of the world. Who the hell d'you think is going to come to some remote bloody island in the English Channel to see your set-up? The whole thing's lunatic. I wouldn't come that far to drink your gin. That's a measure of how silly I think your scheme is. Ruination staring you in the face. You might just as well set up on Easter Island.'

Gerald tried Sir Julian Huxley, the doyen of the biological scene. 'He had always been kind and helpful in the past,' Gerald reported, 'but this was a somewhat grandiose idea and I was fearful he would treat it in some damning way. I need not have worried, for he greeted it with the infectious enthusiasm he showed for every new idea, great or small.' Gerald and Sir Julian sat down to tea and talked of monkey-puzzle trees and giant sloths and many other things. Then Sir Julian glanced at his watch.

'Have you seen that film young Attenborough brought back from Africa on that lioness . . . you know, Elsa? It was reared by that Adamson woman. They're repeating it this afternoon.'

'So the greatest living English biologist and I,' Gerald wrote, 'perched on upright chairs and in silence we watched Joy Adamson chasing Elsa, Elsa chasing Joy Adamson, Joy Adamson lying on top of Elsa, Elsa lying on top of Joy Adamson, Elsa in bed with Joy Adamson, Joy Adamson in bed with Elsa, and so on, interminably . . .' By the end they felt they had watched the world's first natural history blue movie.

Gerald listened to the advice he was given, then made up his own mind. With less than a month to go before he was due to sail to Argentina, there was no time for prevarication or fine tuning. He could proceed with the zoo on Jersey forthwith, or abort the idea immediately and for good. He had no difficulty deciding. Within a few days the Durrells were back on Jersey to discuss the practical problems of founding a zoo with the island's authorities. The head of tourism, Senator Krichefski, responded enthusiastically to the idea and promised his total support. Other officials were equally helpful, and appreciated the need for speed. All this was a far cry from the red tape of the local bureaucracies on the mainland. Meanwhile Hugh Fraser's advocate was drawing up a lease to grant the tenancy of Les Augrès Manor to the Durrells. The dream was on the verge of becoming reality. All that was left was the matter of the zoo itself.

It helped that Gerald had already had a dry-run in Poole, so the basic aims and principles had already been thoroughly worked out, and many of the detailed specifications could simply be transferred to Jersey, with modifications here and there to suit the lay-out of the manor and its grounds and buildings. Gerald's plan was for the zoo to open to the public in the spring of 1959, while he was still in South America. He would ship the Cameroons animals over from Paignton once their cages had been set up, then add his South American collection when he returned. To manage the zoo and supervise its establishment in his absence, he persuaded his old friend Ken Smith to take over as Superintendent. 'Smith was always eager for change and advancement,' Jacquie recalled, 'so it was very easy to persuade him to come to Jersey. Smith collected all the Jersey staff. He insisted on *carte blanche* in everything as the price of his leaving Paignton. I strenuously opposed this for various reasons and was, alas, proved to be only too right.'

In the middle of this hectic time, *Encounters with Animals* was published. To Gerald's surprise – for the book was essentially no more than a rehash of his two radio series – it was well received, and sold moderately well. 'If animals, birds and insects could speak,' wrote one reviewer, 'they would possibly award Mr Gerald Durrell one of their first Nobel prizes ... His creatures are as alive as his style.'

Finally, on 18 October 1958, the day after he signed the lease for the zoo site in Jersey, thereby becoming the 'Lord' of the Manor of Les Augrès in the Parish of Trinity, Gerald set sail from Plymouth on board the *English Star*, a cargo boat of the Blue Star line, bound for Buenos Aires in the company of his wife, his mother (who was going out for a two-week holiday) and his secretary. He had mortgaged his future to start his zoo, but he did not regret it: it was not his own future that was now his major concern, but that of the wildlife of the world.

Gerald liked Argentina and its inhabitants almost as much as Jacquie did. He found a warmth, charm and eccentricity in their character which matched his own, and before long the couple were surrounded by a band of helpers and friends – Bebita, Josefina, Rafael and his sister Mercedes and his cousin Marie Renee Rodrigue and many others – whose cheery devotion and hospitality was unflagging. Without them the venture could hardly have succeeded; with them even its hardships became a joy. Only the Customs were a pain, keeping the party waiting a whole month before finally releasing their equipment.

The broad plan of the expedition was simple – first, to collect animals for the new zoo, and second, to shoot a number of television wildlife programmes. The itinerary was no less straightforward. First, head south out of Buenos Aires by Land-Rover, crossing the pampas to the wastes of Patagonia and the huge penguin colony beyond Puerto Deseado and the fur seal and elephant seal colonies of Peninsula Valdes, where Gerald hoped to shoot at least two programmes of his proposed television series. Second, return to Buenos Aires, regroup, then charge off in the opposite direction to the fauna-rich far north-west of the country, where the land rises towards the snow-white heights of the Andes.

Patagonia was bleak, strange, disorientating, a monotonous desert of scrub and black sand dunes haunted by the ghosts and relics of long-exterminated Indian tribes. The penguin colonies, numbering some two million birds and reeking of stale fish, stretched for miles along a shore pockmarked with nesting hollows like tiny moon craters. 'Strange, plodding, sturdy little birds,' Gerald scribbled in his unpublished notes, 'walking with a shuffling flat-footedness, like elderly waiters whose arches have long ago collapsed under the strain of a lifetime of carrying overloaded trays.' The fur seals dwelt in a bedlam of their own making – 'exactly like a volcano about to erupt', Jacquie was to recall. 'Roar. belch, gurgle, bleat and chough,' Gerald jotted, 'a constant undulation of sound like the boiling of an enormous cauldron of porridge. Gleaming gold in the sun like a restless swarm of bees.' 'Durrell was busy shooting roll after roll of film,' Jacquie recorded. 'He was drunk with pleasure and so madly in love with the seals that it was with the greatest difficulty we prised him away.'

The delay seemed to have been disastrous, for the small beach where the elephant seals should have been found contained nothing but a scattering of curiously shaped boulders, and it was assumed that the creatures had headed off to Tierra del Fuego. Sitting among the boulders, the party rued the length of time they had spent with the fur seals. Then something very odd happened. 'Marie, with the air of someone who is used to disaster,' Gerald was to write, 'seized a bottle of wine, and as the cork popped out of the bottle a large, slightly elongated and egg-shaped boulder some ten feet away gave a deep and lugubrious sigh, and opened a pair of huge, gentle, liquid-looking eyes of the deepest black, and gazed at us placidly.' Miraculously, another eleven lumps of rock turned into living flesh – giant creatures, some of them more than twenty feet long. Gerald shot his film and the party returned to Buenos Aires in good cheer. But not for long.

Before setting off for Patagonia, Jacquie had been injured in a traffic accident in Buenos Aires. Josefina was at the wheel, and failed to notice that the traffic lights – the only ones in the city – had changed. 'Lights!' Jacquie had shouted a split-second before the Land-Rover ploughed into the car in front. 'The next thing I knew I was being thrown forward into the windscreen,' she remembered, 'then grabbed by Durrell, who pulled me towards him. Streams of blood flowed over the pair of us. People appeared from everywhere, all shouting and offering help. I still felt perfectly fine, except for the blood which was slowly covering us both.' At the city hospital Jacquie had five stitches in her forehead, a white-faced Gerald, far more upset than she was, holding her hand. That had seemed the end of the matter, but during the last half of the Patagonia foray Jacquie had begun to feel very ill, with constant backache and blinding headaches exacerbated by the jolting over the terrible Patagonian roads, and it seemed possible that she was actually suffering from a fractured skull. Once back in the heat and humidity of the capital she realised she could not continue, and that the only sensible course was to return to Britain for treatment as soon as possible. Reluctantly Gerald agreed, and in the middle of February 1959 she sailed away on the only boat which happened to have a single berth free.

Sophie was delegated to stay behind in Buenos Aires to look after the growing animal collection while Gerald embarked on the second stage of the expedition. His destination was the north-western province of Jujuy, a lush, tropical area, bordered by the mountains of Bolivia on one side and the arid region of Salta on the other. His plan was to base himself on a sugar estate in the valley of Calilegua, where he had friends, and from there to begin collecting animals with the help of a tiny, black-eyed, black-haired Argentinean called Luna and a big, blue-eyed, blond-haired Argentinean called Helmuth. With Jacquie gone the expedition had lost its organisational genius; from now on the television film took second place, and Gerald was not destined to fulfil his dream of becoming a leading director-cameraman of wildlife programmes.

This was the first time Gerald had been separated from his wife for a substantial period of time. Although their relationship had occasionally been strained, particularly during the Cameroons expedition, he missed Jacquie desperately, and felt lost and insecure without her. When he was in Buenos Aires he phoned her frequently. When he was up-country on his collecting and filming trips, he would write her long letters that not only conveyed news and gossip about the expedition's progress but expressed a deep yearning to be one with her again, and a terrible gnawing doubt that perhaps, for some reason not explained or even understood, he never would be. From Calilegua he wrote her an account of a foray up a five-thousand-foot mountain range with Helmuth and Luna:

> We went up on horseback, and it was a wonderful experience. At the top was a tiny wooden shack in which we lived, surrounded by the most lovely forest full of tapirs, toucans and parakeets. The floor of the forest was covered with the most extraordinary fungi and toadstools I have ever seen, hundreds of different types and shapes, so the leaf mould looked like a coral reef. We had brought up a group of five hunters and twelve dogs, but in spite of dashing about wildly they caught nothing. However, our horses and the pack mules were attacked by vampire bats, and this was interesting. Just like a dracula film they looked in the morning in the clotted blood in huge stripes down their necks, poor brutes. Greatly interested I decided to see if I could get a vampire to bite me. I was sleeping outside the hut, as inside was full of seven people and I preferred fresh air and less garlic. So that night I shifted my bed nearer the horse and popped my foot out of the blankets, for vampires like the big toe to feed on. Needless to say nothing happened, though I lay there for hours, but the horses were attacked again. Charles said it was because vampires preferred blood to gin that they didn't attack me. Since then I have remembered that the damn things carry rabies, so it was just as well.
>
> . . . In the time I did not do too badly. This is the list. One half grown Puma, one Ocelot, one Geffroys cat, two young Coatis, four blue fronted Amazon parrots, one red fronted Amazon (Blanco), six little parakeets, two yellow necked Macaws (rare, I think, and may be first timers), two Agoutis, six Brazilian rabbits, two Seriamas (one of each species), two very nice Guans, two lovely collared Peccaries, the baby female of which is an absolute sweetie.

The collection was so large that the only way to bring it back to Buenos Aires was by train – an agonising journey of two nights and two days. Gerald wrote to Jacquie:

The train trip was really quite fun, but exhausting. The poor beasts suffered from the heat, but I could not do anything about that. As could only happen on an Argentine train everyone soon knew that I had animals in the van, and they would all lean out of the windows at each stop and ask after the puma, or tell me where the nearest water tap was . . .

In my absence Soph had added a very nice half grown Capybara to the collection and a most lovely pair of young, but adult, Douracoulis. You will love them, darling. Claudius the tapir is fine and is now about the size of a cow, eating like hell and wanting his own way as usual. (Blanco has just come in from the kitchen, climbed on to my shoulder and inquired how I am.)

Darling, you don't have to keep telling me you love me . . . if you didn't you would never have put up with me. All I am or ever will be is due to you. You are a part of me, and now I am without my right arm. In a little over two months I will be able to kiss you and tell you what I mean . . . but remember until I come back that I have always been and will always be yours . . . without you I am nothing.

Gerald had a great many things on his mind in Buenos Aires. For one thing, unbelievably, he was still trying to write his Africa book. 'I'm struggling to finish *Zoo in my Luggage*,' he told Jacquie, 'and hope to be able to do so and send it off before I leave Argentina, so there will be some money in the kitty. It's a bit difficult because I can only write at night, and I feel so bloody tired but nevertheless am keeping at it. It will be very bad but never mind. Don't, darling, *please* don't worry about cash: I can earn enough for anything when I get back, and I promise you I will, so please don't get worried or depressed about that: you know what I can earn if I try.'

He was thinking of going off to Mendoza, in the foothills of the Andes in the far west of the country, for a week, in pursuit of the rare little fairy armadillo. David Jones, an agreeable young Anglo-Argentinean who had become a kind of younger brother and general factotum to Gerald, and an invaluable replacement for Jacquie in all the practical matters of day-to-day living, would accompany him. There was a paved road all the way to Mendoza, and hopefully the incessant rain would stop. 'If it doesn't,' Gerald wrote in desperation, 'I really don't see how I can produce more than three or possibly four programmes. I did so hope that the Elephant seal, fur seal and penguins would make two programmes, but if you remember I was doubtful at the time.'

The growing collection of animals now temporarily housed at the museum in Buenos Aires left little time for other things, but nothing so preoccupied Gerald as his uncertainty about the strength and durability of his marriage.

'Did I mention that I love you?' he wrote to Jacquie. 'That I miss you? That I wish we were leaving tomorrow so I could be with you? Well, I do. Darling I am yours and only yours: not a very good bargain for you but there it is. And now I must stop playing the middle aged lover and go and have a shower as we are going to Blondie's for dinner, and David has just laid out my clothes for me ... if you ever divorce me I shall marry him. I will write again soon, darling. Keep well and safe for me.'

'Darling,' he wrote again soon, 'this is a horribly short note but David and I are off to Mendoza at midnight, and we are in the middle of our packing. I will write you when we arrive there I promise. But I just wanted to let you know that I love you, and I want you so much. It won't be long now darling. Goodnight. G.'

They left for Mendoza at three o'clock in the morning. The trip was uneventful. Gerald slept until dawn and then took over the wheel while David had a rest. 'Suddenly my ears started to pop,' he wrote to Jacquie:

> ... we came to the top of a rise and there before us were the outriders of the Andes, a wonderful chain of weirdly shaped mountains, all wearing a sort of fragile shawl of snow over their heads. It was so lovely and exciting that I woke David up to share it, and all he did was to grunt and then tell me the engine was pinking. This so affected me that I sat down at dinner that night and wrote the enclosed poem that might amuse you.

First sight of the Andes with technical companion

> Pause here, what vistas now unfold
> Bannered with sunset flags of pink and gold
> The Andean vertebrae all striped with snow
> That here and there takes on a ruby glow,
> ('I think the fan belt is about to go') ...
> Here in the sky, like crosses pinned,
> The Condors hang, suspended in the wind.
> Weaving, swooping, bigger circles winding,
> Seeking, ever seeking, rarely finding,
> ('I think the intake valves need grinding')
> Now in the moonlight, watch the snow caps glisten,
> To hear the crackling stars, you only have to listen.

> Silence, silence, hear the flowers dew drinking,
> Wrapt in their shadows, every peak is thinking.
> ('Shut up! I think the engine's pinking') . . .
> Hear now the silence and the bat's wing beating,
> ('I think the engine's overheating!')
> Here then a product of God's imagination,
> ('Thank God, at last, a Service Station!')

When I read this to David he said that the engine was more important to him than the Andes, as he had to maintain the engine but not the mountains, which I suppose is fair enough.

Darling, I love you. Since you left I have lost all real enthusiasm for the trip: I have no one to yell at or blame or be nasty to, no one who knows what a bastard I am and still puts up with me, no one to tell me how good I am when I know I'm not, no one to just be there when I need them, no one to love. I really want to come back to England (and I never thought I would) and I wish we were leaving earlier than May. Whatever you decide eventually to do I shall still love you, and I hope you will love me. All I ask is that you don't make up your mind firmly before I get back. I can't promise to reform and be a good boy and always do what you want me to because you would know that this was a lie and impossible, because you know me. So all I can say is that if you stay with me I shall be the same bastard I have always been, with luck a little better but I can't promise: all I know is that I have discovered just how much I love you since you left.

While Gerald was in Argentina, David Attenborough had been filming and collecting armadillos and other small animals in the Gran Chaco of Paraguay. When he returned to Buenos Aires with his animals at the end of his expedition, he heard that another collector was in town, waiting for a ship to take his collection to England. It was Gerald Durrell. They had met before, when Attenborough was still a relatively junior BBC producer. Now, in Buenos Aires, Gerald was to describe his zoo idea to him. Attenborough remembered:

He was in his early thirties, but he looked ten years younger, with long hair flopping down over his eyes. We were to some extent rivals, but my most enduring memory of him at that time was his huge engaging grin and his rich line in repartee. We had a lot of common interest to talk about: how you could cure an armadillo's diarrhoea by mixing soil with its meals of minced meat and condensed milk; how astonishing it was that the favoured food of that most extraordinary of the dog tribe, the maned wolf, was not meat but bananas. As the evening wore on and we moved from beer to cheap South American brandy, Gerry talked more and more about his plans. He told me he was starting his zoo and I just thought he was mad. How could anyone, except a millionaire, start his own zoo? Gerry was undaunted. He had already proved he could write a best-seller. He would write a few more and use the royalties to finance the zoo of his dreams.

Such a zoo, Gerald informed Attenborough, would be very different from the average zoo, of which he was bitterly critical. Most cages and enclosures, he complained, were designed more for the convenience of the public than the comfort and needs of the animals. And most zoos kept the wrong kinds of animals – big, dramatic creatures such as lions and tigers, rhinos and hippos, which cost a lot of money to keep and took up a lot of space. Smaller creatures like marmosets, armadillos, scorpions, butterflies and even ants could interest the public just as much if they were properly looked after and displayed. 'Most of all,' Attenborough recalled, 'he was critical of zoos which made no attempt to breed their inmates. Sometimes they did not even bother to keep them together in pairs. When one died, the zoo simply sent somebody to catch another . . . He was going to change all that.'

Years later, looking back on the task that faced him as he prepared to leave Argentina, Gerald was amazed at his temerity, his hubris – and grateful for the naïve optimism that blinded him to the immensity of the undertaking on which he was now embarked.

PART THREE

The Price of Endeavour

SIXTEEN

A Zoo is Born

1959–1960

In the makeshift menagerie in Margaret's back garden in Bournemouth, the hardier animals were bracing themselves for their third winter in Britain. Across the water in Jersey, the manor house lay empty and shuttered, huddled in the hush of its tree-enshrouded valley grounds, poised – after five hundred years of unbroken rural domesticity and calm – on the brink of a more dramatic and clamorous history.

During the winter the first wave of animals took possession of the manor farm that was to be their home. With the help of Ken Smith and Gerry Breeze, Margaret's eighteen-year-old son, the cages were loaded up and driven to Weymouth docks to catch the ferry to Jersey. At Les Augrès Manor they were stowed in outbuildings and barns while the serious business of building more permanent enclosures and cages began. Gerald was not there, but he was kept informed. 'Les Augrès Manor was a scene of frenzied activity,' he was to record. 'Carpenters and masons rushing about laying cement, making cages out of everything they could lay their hands on. Cages on legs we called them, made out of untreated wood, chain link and chicken wire. Packing crates were wonderfully converted into shelters and every available piece of iron piping or wrought iron from the junk yard was grist to our mill. We transformed the things people discarded as being of no further use into animal havens and shelters: cages ungainly and ugly but serviceable sprouted everywhere.'

The generally young, unfailingly willing assistants Ken Smith recruited locally or brought over from Paignton to help lay the foundations of what would become one of the world's foremost zoological establishments included his wife Trudy (who was Head of Mammal Section), Timothy Carr (Bird Section), Nigel Hanlan (Reptile Section), Roderick Dobson (an ornithologist) as carpenter-in-chief, Nick Blampied as vet-on-call, Les Gulliver (maintenance), Michael Armstrong, Kay Page, Gerry Breeze,

Nigel Albright and Annette Bell. Jeremy Mallinson joined for a summer job five weeks after the zoo opened, followed by Yolande Wilson, Lee Thomas, Peter Glover, Bill Timmis, Lesley Norton, John Hartley, John (Shep) Mallett, Betty Boizard, Stefan Ormrod and Quentin Bloxam. Of these Betty Boizard (later Renouf), Hartley, Bloxam and Mallinson are still at the zoo nearly forty years later, and the latter was later to become its Director and an OBE.

Ken Smith recruited Michael Armstrong, who had an interest in birds and a talent for poetry, as a junior assistant to help look after the birds in January 1959, when there was not much to see in the way of a zoo. 'Smith showed me round the place,' Armstrong recalled. 'He said, "Well, we hope to have things here and we hope to have things there," but all I could see was one cage with two Indian parrots in it. It was a particularly nasty day, it was raining, and the poor creatures looked very miserable. And that was that.' But the work proceeded quickly under Smith's punctilious direction.

The opening day, scheduled for 26 March 1959, in time for the beginning of the Easter holidays, drew near. The hammering and sawing continued at a feverish pace as cage after cage was run up and the animals moved in. A rudimentary car park was bulldozed, a smart little café knocked up, toilets installed and a pay-box erected at the zoo entrance. Ken Smith wrote the first edition of the Jersey Zoo Park guide. Swallowing his proprietorial pride, he splashed a fetching photo of a youthful Gerald Durrell with a Scops owl on his shoulder on the front of the little booklet, with a blurb that left no one in any doubt that Mr Durrell was as big an attraction as Leo the lion cub. The zoo was still in its infancy, Smith explained – not that any visitor could be in any doubt of that – and both the collection and the gardens would be extended substantially. He was careful to include a mention of Gerald's credos. 'The zoo's special aim is the breeding of rare creatures,' he wrote, 'especially those threatened with extinction in the wild state.' However, there was as yet little evidence of this, for in Gerald's absence Smith was creating what he knew best, a conventional zoo whose main aim was to attract the public.

Jacquie's voyage home, *sans* husband and *sans* animals, provided a much-needed rest. She had been beset by a nagging sense of guilt at leaving the rest of the expedition behind in Argentina, but the osteopath she saw in London on her return assured her she had done right thing. Relieved, she set off for Bournemouth, once again taking possession of Margaret's small attic room, and steeling herself for the great change that lay ahead – the move to the manor house in Jersey and the grand opening of the long-dreamed-of zoo.

As soon as she could, Jacquie flew to Jersey to see how the zoo was progressing, and to begin the process of altering and decorating the flat in the manor house where she and Gerald planned to live. Everyone at the zoo was working feverishly to have it ready by opening day, but she was surprised to find that in various respects it was developing in ways that were different from what she had expected. 'I was a little perturbed to notice that Gerry's blueprint for the development had not been followed,' she was to record, 'but this was not my concern and I decided to leave it until Gerry could deal with it himself.'

The flat occupied the two upper floors of the central section of Les Augrès Manor, the grand reception room and other rooms on the ground floor being reserved for zoo offices. It was substantial, but not immense, accommodation, with a light, spacious sitting-room whose high windows looked out over the large gravel forecourt beyond the main entrance, providing fine views over the wooded, undulating grounds beyond. Soon Jacquie was as busy in the flat as the zoo workers were outside. A kitchen had to be installed, fresh paint applied to the dun-coloured walls, carpets laid, furniture ordered, curtains hung, and a room got ready for Mother Durrell, who would be sharing their new quarters.

Meanwhile, to drum up public interest Ken Smith took to going to St Helier and patrolling up and down with a billboard luridly decorated with lions and tigers to advertise the zoo. Later he would picket the airport, waylaying newly arrived tourists with news about the zoo, or calling through the windows of their cars: 'Are you looking for the way to the zoo? It's straight on, first right, keep going . . .' The local paper, the *Jersey Evening Post*, took up the cause, and by the time opening day came, no one on the island could have been unaware of the zoo's existence. Mike Armstrong's diary logged the events of 26 March 1959 – a day that would one day be looked back on as a historic one in conservation history – from his own point of view:

> Fine but fresh S.W. wind. 58°. Up early for opening day of zoo by 7.15 a.m. A rush to open by 10 a.m. First visitor buys in shop 10 a.m. 900 visitors during day and packed out in afternoon . . . All labels up on cages and quite a good show. Reptile House quite a good show. There is also a large cage of multi-coloured fishes in the Animal House. The monkeys of course are a great attraction. The mandrill succeeded in acquiring a gentleman's pair of glasses. One or two complaints re the mandrill grabbing at children. However it seemed a good start on the whole and I heard a lot of people who were impressed.

Next day the gate increased almost fourfold, to three thousand, and on the fourth day the attendance reached six thousand. The zoo was up and running. Milling hordes crowded round the makeshift cages and enclosures, peering intently, even excitedly, at the blue-tongued skink and Cameroon clawed frog, the splendid sunbird and Chinese mocking bird, the dingo and quokka, the cunning cat squirrel, slow loris and needle-clawed lemur – 'brought back from the Cameroons by Gerald Durrell in 1957,' proclaimed the placard on the cage, 'and believed to be the only specimen in Europe.' Apart from Gerald's Cameroons collection, many of the early denizens of Jersey Zoo were exotic little creatures from all over the world which had been picked and purchased by Ken Smith from dealers' catalogues for their crowd-pulling qualities – 'singers and dancers', in zoo parlance. There were no large animals, no elephants or rhinos; not only were they expensive to buy and look after, but they did not conform to Gerald's vision of his zoo as a home and sanctuary for smaller creatures of greater interest.

Mike Armstrong summed up the zoo's first week under Ken Smith's suzerainty in his diary:

> I feel it is a very good little zoo and they have done wonders with it . . . Mr Smith is a very pleasant man when not worried by the job. He is a good organiser and administrator but allows little personal love towards his animals. I feel it is just a business to him and if the animals are uncomfortable or in temporarily inadequate cages, he is in no hurry to put things right for them, so long as the zoo is presentable as a paying concern.

Jacquie, meanwhile, was dashing frantically back and forth between Jersey and Bournemouth, clearing out the flat in Margaret's house where so many plans had been made, dreams dreamed and books written, packing up the goods and chattels of one phase of married life for shipment to Jersey and the beginning of another. She was at the quayside to meet Gerald's ship, the *St John*, as it nudged into Tilbury Docks, and they greeted each other warmly. During their separation Gerald had undergone a dramatic metamorphosis. He now sported a ginger beard, and looked a bit like Ernest Hemingway in his big-game-hunter mode. He had grown the beard for her, he told her. 'I did not have the heart to say a word,' noted Jacquie – for after all, it was she who had first suggested it. 'Gerry hated shaving, because he had a very sensitive skin and was always cutting himself. In the Argentine he went around with a sort of stubble and I got fed up with it and told him, "Either grow a beard or shave." So he grew a beard and kept it for ever after.'

Gerald's South American animals were offloaded and entrained for the Southampton steamer that would take them to Jersey. Gerald sailed with them, while Jacquie flew over that evening, so as to be at the zoo when he and the animals arrived on 16 June. 'Durrell was so excited by everything,' recalled Jacquie, 'that he did not know what to do first: look round the grounds or supervise the release of his collection into their various cages.' The manor house and its grounds had undergone considerable modification since Gerald had last seen them. The fifteenth-century hay barn was now the Tropical Bird House; the cowshed was the Monkey House, with the Quarantine Station on the floor above; the cider press now housed the large and small mammals; the garage had become the Reptile House; and the pig pens sheltered more exotic beasts such as racoons, pumas and dingoes. The little orchard on the bank behind the manor now had a range of paddocks and aviaries, and the apples fell on the plump backs of peccaries, tapir and wallabies. The stream in the sunken meadow had been dammed up to produce a shallow lake dignified with the name the Waterfowl Gardens (but known in-house as the Peter Scottery), where black-necked swans, mandarin duck and other graceful waterfowl drifted slowly by.

'As I had suspected,' Jacquie wrote, 'Durrell was slightly put out that his blueprints for the zoo's development had not been followed, but this was softened by his delight at having all his African and South American animals safely back with him again.' The zoo at this point did not match his prior vision of it. 'Gerry had always had definite ideas for his zoo layout,' Jacquie recalled, 'but naturally this had to be modified according to the site, terrain and buildings available. He definitely gave Smith a full and detailed blueprint for Jersey but Smith largely ignored it.' Smith claimed that all Gerry had left him by way of a blueprint was a few doodles on the back of an envelope, and that lack of time and money had dictated the result. The fact remained that Ken Smith and his team had created a zoo at Les Augrès Manor where none had existed before – a zoo where at least the animals were fed, sheltered and cared for to the best of everyone's ability.

Gerald, Jacquie and Mother settled into their new quarters in the manor. Though these were expansive by comparison with Margaret's flatlet they soon filled up with animal guests, most of them ailing and most of them requiring a room temperature of eighty-five degrees. Cholmondeley the chimpanzee was brought back from his human foster mother after Gerald's return, with a slipped disc that needed nursing. He was followed by his girlfriend Lulu, who had a nasty abscess behind one ear, a big Aldabra tortoise with a mouth infection, a sick peccary, a ten-foot python with mouth canker, four baby squirrels making loud and irritable trilling noises as they waited for their next bottle-feed, and various birds, including a parrot with a chill which wheezed and bubbled by the fire in a melancholy manner, Dingle the chough and several oiled gulls. Mother, meanwhile, kept a marmoset called Whiskers in her bedroom, along with a huge avocado pear tree, raised from a stone, which had grown up one wall and down another. Of Mother and Whiskers Gerald wrote:

At the moment she is acting as foster mother to an extremely rare little creature, an Emperor tamarin, one of the marmoset family, which are the smallest of the monkey tribe. This diminutive chap was in a very forlorn condition when we got him, and it was obvious that he would not thrive unless he was given a great deal of love and attention. So, inevitably, my mother was chosen to take on the task of nursing the tiny creature back to health and strength.

When he arrived he could fit comfortably into a tea cup, and his skinny little body, combined with the enormous white curling moustache which these tamarins have on their upper lip, suggested not a monkey but an elderly leprechaun. Within a fortnight my mother's careful treatment of him had worked wonders. He had put on weight, his coat was glossy, and his snow-white moustache so luxuriant and curly that it would have been the envy of any brigadier.

Moreover, from being a timid and retiring creature he had become very self-confident, even cocksure. He rules my mother with a rod of iron, and as soon as he is led out of his cage he takes over her room like a dictator. If she lies on the bed to rest he must either lie with her under the covers or, if he does not feel like a siesta, then Mother has to provide him with amusement by wiggling her toes beneath the bed-clothes, so that he can stalk them and leap on them from what must seem to him a great height.

He talks to her the whole time in a high-pitched, twittering call that is extraordinarily birdlike, and, as my mother has pointed out, it is difficult to get forty winks when you have what appears to be twenty operatic canaries singing volubly into your ear.

Every evening he crawls under Mother's pillow and settles himself for the night, in the hope that we will not notice his absence from his cage and will leave him there. When he is hauled out and put to bed properly in his own cage his screams and twitters of indignation can be heard all over the house, and it is only when the front of his cage is covered that he reluctantly stops shouting and makes his way into his own bed, which consists of an old blanket and an apron belonging to my mother.

One of the advantages of a small zoo was that all the animals could receive individual attention and be treated more as pets than merely exhibits. One of the earliest beneficiaries of such intensive care was Topsy, a young female Humboldt's woolly monkey from South America. Gerald had found her lying half-dead at the bottom of a cage in a dealer's shop in England. She had acute malnutrition, bad enteritis and a severe chill bordering on pneumonia. 'She was huddled up in the sawdust,' he recorded, 'her arms over her head, breathing stertorously, and when I tapped on the wire she turned to me a small black face with such a lost and tragic expression on it that I knew I had to rescue her, whatever the price . . . At first, being so young, she wanted something to cling to, but she was too scared to transfer her affections to a human being. A teddy bear was therefore introduced and for three months this was treated as the "mother".'

Gerald started the little monkey on the road to recovery with regular doses of Chloromycetin and injections of vitamin B12. Within a week she was looking worlds better: her fur was starting to shine, she was eating well, putting on weight and throwing off her various infections. Soon she was too big for the teddy bear and was transferred to an amiable guinea pig with a vacuous expression. 'At night she slept on top of the unfortunate animal,' Gerald wrote, 'looking like an outsize jockey perched on a Shetland pony. Their marriage has been – and still is – a very happy one, but the guinea pig is not getting any younger, and so we are training a young ginger-and-white one to act as a substitute in case of accidents.'

Another endearing waif who arrived very early on was Piccolo, a black-nosed capuchin from Brazil. He was the pet of a sailor who sold him to a restaurateur in Jersey, who in turn gave him to the zoo in 1960. When he arrived he was permanently crippled, for he had been confined in a cage that was too small and fed on a diet that was hopelessly inadequate, and though he received expert veterinary care, his condition was never to improve. But Piccolo was a survivor *par excellence*, and while he had to be kept on his own because he could not get on with other monkeys, he did like people and had many human friends who visited him regularly. Eventually he became the longest-surviving resident in the zoo, dying only in 1997, rickety, balding and nearly toothless, at the ripe old age (in monkey terms) of around forty-five.

When Gerald first told David Attenborough about his plans to open a zoo of his own, Attenborough had thought he was mad. But he soon changed his mind, and was to write: 'He laboured tirelessly and practically. He had to an amazing degree the zoological equivalent of green fingers. You could see it in the way he handled animals and in the way they responded to him. You could sense it when you watched him watching them and deducing just what was necessary to make them happy. And he was a wonderful persuader. He gathered around him a team of companions and inspired them with his own enthusiasm.'

Many of the animals emerged as highly individual characters. One such was Peter the Cheetah, who had been presented to Gerald by the film director Harry Watt when he was working in Kenya, where the animal had been hand-reared and kept around the house like a dog. Peter loved to take Jeremy Mallinson out for a run round the zoo, or to put the young man through his paces in a one-a-side football match which he invariably won by means of a variety of devious fouls.

Another animal who displayed a uniquely outsize personality was Trumpy, a grey-winged trumpeter, a South American bird with a bugle-like voice. Trumpy was the zoo's village idiot, and had the run of the premises and for that matter the road outside. In cold weather he took to dossing down in the Mammal House, one of the warmest places in the zoo. Come the spring, he emerged to strut around the grounds, occasionally opening his wings wide, trumpeting wildly and rushing up to some astonished visitor as though he was a lifelong friend he had not seen for years. Sometimes Trumpy would accompany the last visitor out of the zoo and down the road to the bus stop, where he had to be physically restrained from boarding the bus into town. Trumpy's most endearing quality was the way he treated new boys. He was the zoo's chief 'settler-in'. Whenever there was a new arrival Trumpy would dutifully waddle down and spend twenty-four hours outside, or preferably inside, its cage, till he was satisfied that it had settled in. He did this with the swans, for example, down at their flooded water-meadow, standing up to his ankles in water for twenty-four hours, oblivious to all entreaties to come out.

Not all the animals were so endearing, however, and a few had distinctly unsociable habits, as Gerald noted in an early animal log at the zoo, an inventory of meticulous behavioural observation:

Cherry-crowned Mangaby: Obtained Mamfe, Brit. Cameroons, January 1957. Behaviour: Has typical baby Mangaby habit of sucking penis. This becomes almost obsessional.

Palm Civet: Obtained Mamfe, approx. two weeks old. Behaviour: was always, even when quite young, savage and untrustworthy.

Potto: 1 male, 2 females: Obtained Eshobi. Behaviour: It is possible to sex adult Pottos by smell, for when frightened the testicles of the male give off a quite strong odour like pear drops.

Collared Peccary. Obtained: Jujuy, Argentina, March 1959. True pair. Behaviour: Both of them frequently rub their faces on their mate's scent gland. When excited they indulge in a 'waltz'-like action: the male seizes the female's hind leg in his mouth, and she seizes his hind leg, and then, grunting and squealing, they revolve round and round for a few minutes.

The most spectacular (and expensive) beast in residence was N'pongo, a young lowland gorilla born in the Congo, who had been purchased from a dealer in Birmingham and at the beginning spent most of her time on Mother's lap. Later she was to become the favourite playmate of Caroline, Ken and Trudy Smith's two-year-old daughter, whose nickname was Moonbeam. Gerald noted:

Although the young ape is bigger than Moonbeam, and tremen-dously powerful (it takes three adults to get her back into her cage if she doesn't want to go back), when playing with Moonbeam she is astonishingly gentle and tolerant. To watch them sharing a bag of candies is a sight worth seeing. Both sit there, looks of extreme concentration on their faces, while Moonbeam carefully opens the bag and rations out the candies into N'pongo's immense black paw. When the candies have been equally divided they will sometimes sit back to back, like a couple of bookends, while they eat, both of them occasionally spitting the semi-masticated sweets out into their hands to have a close look at them.

N'pongo loved nothing better than a game of tag. If she played with Gerald she usually managed to bring the zoo's Honorary Director to the ground with a determined rugby tackle. If it was Moonbeam, however, she would content herself with plucking at the little girl's clothes in a teasing, gentle way. 'Both love to be tickled,' Gerald observed, 'and they will roll about in the grass hysterically when you do it. Moonbeam's shrill giggles contrasted strangely with N'pongo's gruff laughter.'

Since there were no funds to finance the purchase of N'pongo, Gerald had rung all the wealthiest people on the island, inviting them to buy a share in the first gorilla at the zoo – Gerald's first foray into begging-bowl fund-raising, an activity that would preoccupy him for much of the rest of his life. Among those he approached was the Earl of Jersey, who recalled their first encounter vividly.

When we met, Gerry asked for a subscription to a fund to raise £1000 to buy the gorilla N'Pongo. I was sure he would never do that in subs of £25. On the other hand I felt that if the island was to have a zoo it had better be a good zoo – and a good zoo must have a gorilla. In the event I guaranteed him an overdraft for £1000 so he could get N'Pongo at once. As a baby N'Pongo was great fun and gurgled like a human if you tickled her tummy. I need hardly say that when the bank wanted to close the account I had guaranteed, I was presented with a bill for £900 – and a few pence. Gerry had no sense of money. He had an almost pathological antipathy to people he thought of as Bankers. He seemed to picture them sitting at large mahogany desks wearing bowler hats and saying 'No.' (Incidentally I myself was also a Banker.) Discussing some new venture I would tell him: 'We will have to wait till we can save enough money.' He would scoff at this. 'Oh! Nonsense,' he would say. 'Pennies from Heaven. We'll start at once.' Maddeningly, of course, pennies did always seem to come from heaven.

The zoo occupied every minute of Gerald's waking thought. He was absorbed by it, lost in it, utterly enthralled. It was a world of its own, always engaging, idiosyncratic, full of incongruities, as he was to record in an account of an average day written during the first year:

If you lie with half-closed eyes in the first light of dawn, you sometimes wonder exactly where you are in the world, for robins and blackbirds are endeavouring – not very successfully – to out-shout seriemas and crested screamers from South America, glossy starlings from Africa, and the jay thrush from Asia ... It is very wearing to the nerves of even the most ardent ornithologist to be awakened at half-past five every morning by a chorus of peacocks under his bedroom window, all yelling 'Help ... help ... hel ... l ... l ... p!' in harsh and despairing tones ...

One of the chief difficulties of living in your own zoo is that there is so much going on the whole time that you are constantly being lured away from the stern duty of writing articles or books. A message is sent up to you that one of the rare lizards is indulging in a courtship display, and so you have to rush down to watch it. Someone tells you that the bushbaby is giving birth, and so, casting the typewriter aside, you dash to gloat over the smug mother and a baby the size of a walnut – and apparently composed entirely of eyes – that muzzles into her soft fur.

In many ways, evening is the best time in the zoo. The public has gone, the sun has sunk, and all the night animals are on the prowl. The slender, elongated genet, in its handsome gold coat spotted with black, performs miracles of acrobatics among the branches in its cage; the bush-babies are awake, staring at you with enormous eyes, taking prodigious leaps about their cage, landing with as much sound as a piece of thistledown.

Now is the time when you can take a tinful of succulent snails and go down to the Reptile House. There the Guiana dragon awaits you, his mouth curved in a perpetual and benign smile. His great, dark eyes watch you anxiously as you tip the snails out into his pond, and then he slides into the water and mumbles one of them into his great jaws. He throws back his head, half closes his eyes in ecstasy, and scrunches the unfortunate snail to bits, with a noise like someone walking very slowly over a gravel path.

Then you make your way back to the manor house and as you pass beneath the arches you hear the lion quietly trying out his new trick: roaring. Then, from the cage by the archway, comes a soft, sweet voice saying 'Goodnight, darling,' and you wish the cockatoos 'Goodnight.'

No, it's not much like being a country squire, but it's a lot more fun.

Though funds were low and Gerald had a publisher's contract to fulfil, he found it hard to lock himself away in a room to finish his infinitely neglected book about his Cameroons expedition of over two years before, *A Zoo in My Luggage*, let alone to embark on a new book about his recent expedition through the Argentine. It required ceaseless nagging on Jacquie's part to extract even a minimum of words from the recalcitrant author. It didn't help that Sophie Cook had had to resign in order to go and look after her gravely ill mother.

Lesley Norton, who as a teenager fresh from school had come to the zoo in its first months, took over as Gerald's secretary (her mother, Betty, was a great friend of Gerald's mother). 'He'd make every excuse, every excuse,' Lesley recalled, 'not to write a word or go near his typewriter to type a word. I mean, days on end would go by and you'd be trying to shuffle the pages under his nose, but he obviously found writing very, very difficult at that time.' Working for Gerald, Lesley found, was like being an intern in a hospital. 'It was like working twenty-four hours a day, seven days a week.'

It says much for Gerald's professionalism that *A Zoo in My Luggage* was to prove one of the most popular and enduring of all his books, and was received with enthusiasm by the critics when it was published in England in 1960. The *Daily Telegraph*'s reviewer spoke for most of them: 'He describes the individual personality traits of his captive creatures with a hilarious fondness, and though an ape is an ape, one such as Cholmondeley St John (otherwise referred to as "you bloody ape") soon becomes a very deep anthropoid friend of ours ... He has a novelist's ear for dialogue and a poet's sensitivity to the mood of the African landscape. He has, too, a genuine humorist's awareness of the incongruous and tells many very funny stories.'

It puzzled the zoo's staff that they saw less of the establishment's founder than they had expected. At first this was put down to Ken Smith's proprietorial pride. As Superintendent his job was to keep the place running with military precision, and he achieved this using the factory-style working practices typical of many zoos at that time. It was Smith who rang the zoo bell for work to start and work to stop. It was Smith who made it a habit once or twice a day to tick someone off or dress someone down *pour encourager les autres*. During the first few months after Gerald took up residence at the manor, Smith discouraged him from involving himself in the day-to-day running of the zoo or having much close contact with its staff. Gerald Durrell was a famous author who wanted to be left alone to get on with his own work, Smith explained to his workers, which was writing, not zoo-keeping, and under no circumstances was he to be disturbed. So the affable Gerald, to whom the zoo owed its entire existence, was seen at first as a remote founder figure who remained mostly holed up inside the manor house and was very rarely spotted outside in the zoo of his creation.

Meanwhile, 'the zoo of his dreams', built on a shoestring, left much to be desired. The cages were for the most part makeshift and rudimentary, cobbled together out of any material that came to hand. Inevitably, from time to time animals fells sick, and a few died. Though holiday-makers continued to pass through the turnstiles in a steady stream at two shillings a head, money was desperately short.

The staff lived on a pittance. Even some years later, when Quentin Bloxam joined the zoo as a live-in helper on £5 a week, he found himself having to work seven days a week, with two afternoons off, in extremely primitive and labour-intensive conditions. 'There were no hoses to wash down the yards, for instance,' he recalled, 'and we had to carry the water around in old metal milk churns instead. Even shovels and wheelbarrows were unobtainable, as all the money went on food and veterinary services for the animals. Staff turnover was high, and this wasn't helped by the fact that we had to live three to a room in very damp conditions. But a small nucleus of people stayed on, out of loyalty to Gerry and a kind of missionary zeal arising from a belief in what we were doing.'

To run a zoo properly – that is to say for the benefit of the animals to the utmost possible degree – is a colossal undertaking, requiring tremendous expertise, ceaseless care and vigilance, and not inconsiderable sums of money. Gerald Durrell wanted to have the best small zoo in the world, a zoo moreover that was dedicated to the welfare and salvation of animals and the enlightenment and understanding of man. In the early days it was a steeply uphill struggle, partly because he was finding his way, and partly because there was never enough money.

The shadow of bankruptcy was always just around the corner. One day, a year or so after the zoo had opened, all the staff were summoned to a meeting. The ship was almost on the rocks, they were told. Maybe it would sink, maybe it would not, but anybody who wished to leave should do so now. Nobody volunteered. Instead they rallied to keep the zoo going by all possible means. Peanuts dropped near the monkey cages by one lot of visitors were gathered up, rebagged and resold to the next lot. The island's rubbish dump was rummaged over for discarded park railings, wire netting and old packing cases that could be recycled as cages. A local cabaret duo called Tony and Dot (stage name 'Katinga the Queen of the Snakes') devoted all their spare time to scouring St Helier's market for junked fruit and vegetables for the animals. With meat for the carnivores in short supply, John Hartley and Shep Mallet would rush out with knives and food bins whenever they heard news of the death of a carthorse on a farm, cutting up the carcase and sawing off the legs and head, half asphyxiated by the stomach gases. Even Gerald's elderly mother joined the battle. 'Mother was frail but very anxious to help,' Alan Ogden recalled. 'Gerry suggested to her that if she really wished to assist, she could look after the ladies' loo and take the money, as that part of the complex generated a better cash-flow than any other.'

The survival of the zoo that had been founded to save animals from extinction was itself under threat, and for the first few years it was a far cry from its founder's revolutionary vision. 'There was a big credibility gap,' Jeremy Mallinson recalled of that time. 'We thought about the things Gerry was saying, we even talked about them, but he'd have had a hard job matching his vision with any signs of it at the zoo.'

The gruelling zoo routine was broken now and then. Sometimes a keeper got bitten. Old Etonian Tony Lort-Phillips was bitten three times by the monkeys ('They all wanted to bite his bottom,' a colleague recalled), but it was Mike Armstrong who was the most accident-prone. Early on he put his back out for three weeks when he jumped off a high wall while in pursuit of an escaping goliath heron. Later he was bitten on the behind by N'pongo ('She wasn't being nasty,' he recalled, 'it was just play, really') and half squeezed to death when Bali the female orang utan got him in a love hug while she was on heat. Finally he suffered a straight left to the nose when he tried to give a temperamental chimp called Beebee her milk. 'It was a terrific punch,' he remembers. 'It nearly floored me. I staggered out of the cage with the milk bottle and Beebee ran off some-where, and do you know my nose has never been the same since. I've got what boxers get. My nose is much narrower on one side than the other and gets all stuffed up at night.'

More often some creature escaped. Birds were the most frequent absconders, usually just vanishing out to sea, but Chumley the chimp was the most accomplished. He had little difficulty with locks and cages, and he and his girlfriend Lulu soon found a way of unravelling wire mesh like knitting. Before long Chumley was often to be seen making his way across to the manor, where he would lollop up the stairs for a cuddle with the ever-patient Mother. One evening she heard a loud bang at the door and found both Chumley and Lulu on the stairs, looking cheerful and expectant. Nothing daunted, she invited them in, sat them down on the sofa and opened a large box of chocolates and a tin of biscuits. When Gerald remonstrated with her for letting them in, she protested: 'But dear, they came to *tea* – and they had jolly sight better manners than some of the *people* you've had up here.'

One Christmas Chumley led all the other chimps in a mass breakout, totally wrecking the staff's Christmas Day lunch. The first anyone knew about it was when an American student peered in and asked: 'Do the chimps always go out for a walk every day?' Chumley was finally caught in a bedroom over-excitedly rummaging through the drawers, and was eventually pacified by John Hartley in a rather novel way. 'I discovered,' he recalled, 'that if you put your hand behind his back legs and held his balls in the palm of your hand, it had a calming effect.'

But it wasn't just the chimps. One day the crashing of glass alerted the keepers to the fact that a spectacled bear had got out and was smashing its way through the cold frames in the zoo grounds. The first member of staff to encounter the bear took one look at the charging beast and locked himself in the zoo's pay-box. Claudius the tapir got out one night and romped around a field of gladioli in a thunderstorm – 'chomping all the flowers up and eating them like anything'. The New Guinea bush dogs were out for three days, and when Major Newgate, a wallaby, escaped, people were ringing the zoo to say: 'Something strange has just hopped past – we think it must come from your zoo.'

On occasion the urge to escape was almost as strong in the humans as it was in the animals. In the early days the zoo owned a huge reticulated python by the name of Pythagoras, twelve feet long and as thick, as Gerald put it, 'as a rugger blue's thigh'. Normally it took three keepers to clean out Pythagoras' cage in the Reptile House – two to restrain him and another to do the cleaning out – and the golden rule was that on no account should any member of the staff attempt the job on his own. One evening at dusk after the zoo had closed Gerald happened to walk by the Reptile House when he heard a muffled cry for help coming from inside. When he investigated he found John Hartley, then a new recruit straight from school, and built (as Gerald put it) 'on the lines of a giraffe', bound but not quite gagged in the coils of the giant python. 'John had done the unforgivable,' Gerald was to record. 'The great snake had thrown its coils around him and bound him as immobile as if in a straitjacket. Fortunately, John still had hold of his head, and Pythagoras was hissing like a giant kettle.' Wasting no time, Gerald seized the creature's tail, but no sooner had he unwound a few coils from Hartley than the snake rewound the coils around Gerald. 'Soon we were both as inextricably linked as Siamese twins,' Gerald wrote, 'and we both started to yell for help. It was after hours and I feared that the staff would have gone home. The idea of standing there all night till someone found us in the morning was not a happy one.' So Gerald, John and Pythagoras remained entwined together coil by jowl in the hushed island dark. It was pure good fortune that eventually a member of the mammal staff heard their cries and came to the rescue. The experience of being jointly throttled by a giant snake evidently created a kind of bond, and eventually Hartley was to become a key member of Gerald's team.

Gerald had never run anything in his life before, and it did not come naturally to him to administer anything. He had little grasp of money or business affairs, and his approach to his subordinates was to become comradely and sociable rather than managerial. It was Jacquie who provided the modicum of steel, and she did not shirk tough action when it was required. Gerald's nephew Gerry Breeze, who was at the zoo for the first eighteen months of its existence, recalled: 'Uncle Gerry had a heart of gold, but Jacquie was the captain. Handing out orders was not his way of doing things. He was only concerned with the animals, not with administering anything. But if he was going to do something he would do it, and nothing could change his mind. Not even Jacquie.'

Despite the zoo's financial problems, Gerald was boyishly bullish. 'We've got some nice new stuff,' he wrote to his Cameroons companion Bob Golding in July 1960: 'Pigmy Marmosets and Olingo, Emperor

Tamarin and so on. Among the reptiles the Bafut Skinks are still doing wonderfully well and the babies have grown like mad. Our lovely trek Boa (the New Guinea one) is doing well, thank the Lord, and also our Madagascan Green Gecko. Perhaps the best new arrival we have had are four baby Aldabra Tortoises. I am very pleased with these as normally they won't let you have more than a pair, but I spun the old bull about preservation, and they let me have the four.'

But four years of struggle were to follow, as Gerald and Jacquie battled desperately against the odds to establish the zoo on a firm footing. Every new problem – veterinary, cash flow, personnel, personal – was an exercise in crisis management. Through all this time, failure and the dissolution of Gerald's lifelong dream was but a breath away.

Gerald's first and most urgent task was the overriding question of funds. Though he always had difficulty with detailed accountancy, he had a visionary's grasp of strategic finance. It was clear to him that the zoo had to raise more capital. It was still a new venture, and it would take a little time for it to become an established attraction for the island's holiday-makers, who represented its only significant source of income at that time. Gerald therefore decided to approach the bank again for another £10,000 loan, and once again Rupert Hart-Davis agreed to guarantee that sum.

Jacquie was horrified. Their total indebtedness now amounted to £20,000 – almost a quarter of a million pounds at today's values. Night after night she would lie awake wondering how the money was ever going to be repaid. This burden was compounded by the fact that from the outset Gerald had insisted that his position as Director of the zoo should be entirely honorary, and that the zoo should not be encumbered by having to pay him and his wife a salary. All they would receive would be the flat to live in and free electricity to run it, while Gerald supported them entirely by his writing, which would also serve to publicise the work of the zoo and to spread the word of Gerald's long-term, worldwide mission. All he asked was that the zoo in its turn should be solvent and self-supporting.

Confronted with this financial imperative, Gerald began to write in earnest. During 1960 and 1961 he followed his Cameroons book with two children's books – *Island Zoo* (in collaboration with the celebrated photographer Wolf Suschitsky), a Disneyish, highly anthropomorphised collection of stories about some of his favourite animals in the zoo, and *Look at Zoos*, a young person's guide to zoo-going – and an account of his Argentine venture, *The Whispering Land*. To these he added various radio talks and television appearances on television, a series of articles for the *Observer* and an anecdotal portrait of a favourite animal for a children's magazine called *June* every week for a year – a task so interminable that Jacquie took over the writing of the last few.

It was not all toil, though it mostly was. And there was respite ahead, for Gerald was planning to return at last to the idyll of his youth.

SEVENTEEN

'We're All Going to be Devoured'

Alarms and Excursions 1960–1962

In May 1960 Gerald wrote to his brother Lawrence to tell him that he and Jacquie were taking Mother to Corfu for six weeks – their first view of the island since their enforced departure twenty-one years previously: 'I expect to find Corfu hideously changed, but they can't possibly change the colour of the sea or its transparency, which is what I am really going for.' In a reference to Larry's cohabitation with Claude, Gerald added: 'I think it's disgusting my own brother should be living in sin.'

Gerald looked forward to his return to the land of his childhood idyll with tremendous anticipation – but also trepidation. 'There is always an element of risk,' he wrote, 'in returning to a place in which you were happy, and the risk is greatly increased if it is a place in which you spent a part of your childhood.' Twenty-one years was a long time, and anything could have happened. Endlessly on the journey he eulogised the island to Jacquie – the giant moon, the million fireflies, skies blue as jade, sea transparent as soap bubbles. On 26 May the party took a small plane for the last hop from the toe of Italy, and suddenly there it was, lying like a misshapen scimitar in the sea – his beloved island.

It was colder and greyer than he remembered it, and the hailstones were the biggest he had seen in his life. The worst summer in history, his island friends told him. But he need not have feared. The unseasonable weather passed – and nothing had changed at all. The lobsters were still as sweet as he remembered, the moon as large and burnished, the view from Pérama across to Mouse Island as enchanted. Only his knowledge of Greek had changed, sunk to a deeper layer inside his skull, with only the zoological bits at easy beck and call.

They took a short lease on a tiny, secluded cottage called 'The Annexe' near the beach below the sea-cliff at Pérama, on the other side of the road from the hill where his two childhood homes – the Strawberry-Pink

Villa and the Snow-White Villa – were situated. In the evening they would repair to a tiny café down the road. 'Here at a table under the mimosa trees,' Gerald was to recall, 'we would watch the sunset on the sea, turning it from blue to silver, and then, suddenly, lighting it up with a blurred peacock iridescence that was unbelievable. Presently, drifting casually through the gloom, our friends would arrive to join us. Wine would be drunk in silence until the last faint colours had been smudged from the sea, and then the singing would begin . . .' No, he was not disappointed, the magic was as it had always been. One day, he reckoned, he would be back to find a new home here and revive the island idyll so long interrupted. Or so he hoped, little guessing that Corfu might have other plans.

At the end of the year Lawrence and Claude and the young Sappho, along with Margaret and her two boys, planned to come to Jersey to celebrate Christmas at the manor. Gerald was looking forward immensely to this family reunion – as was *Life* magazine, which was sending one of its crack photographers, Loomis Deane, over from America to shoot a photo-feature about the celebrated author of the *Alexandrian Quartet* at a family gathering with his no less celebrated brother at the latter's zoo.

Christmas was a zoo event as well as a family get-together. Since many of the staff were necessarily on duty that day, Gerald cooked a huge turkey for their Christmas dinner downstairs in the manor house, and was unstinting with the drinks at the pre-prandial warm-up. Then he went back up to the flat to rejoin his other family. Everyone lent a hand. When Claude found Mother in the kitchen stirring a big pot with one hand while holding a totally swaddled baby in the crook of her free arm, she asked if she could help. 'Well,' said Mother, 'I suppose you could take *him*.' Claude took the small bundle, which after a few minutes began to stir, and a long hairy arm reached out and casually wrapped itself round her neck. The baby turned out to be a young chimpanzee which had been brought into the flat for special care. Christmas passed amid the familiar family jocularity of old. But it was not an entirely peaceful occasion. From time to time there would be a tremendous rumpus from the chimps or lemurs in the zoo outside. 'You see!' cried Lawrence, who was never entirely at home in the company of wild beasts. 'They've broken loose and we're all going to be devoured!'

For many of the animals, especially the primates, Christmas was the most boring day of the year. There were no human visitors to stare at, no human antics and eccentricities to keep them amused, no titbits pushed through the wire netting. But the season was not without its little bonuses. Special treats had been prepared for them – crackly pieces of turkey skin for Claudius the tapir, a handful of liqueur chocolates for Pedro the spectacled bear, crystallised fruits for the marmosets, mince pies for the smaller monkeys, turkey bones for the smaller cats, grapes for the birds. The *pièce de résistance* was the apes' Christmas tea party – a sumptuous spread of sugar-covered biscuits, chocolate bars, grapes, apples and pears, a large iced cake and their favourite tipple of well-watered red wine, all laid out on a table in the courtyard in front of the manor house, complete with a Christmas tree hung with stockings stuffed with sugared almonds and marshmallows. N'pongo, Chumley and Lulu made short shrift of this seasonal set-piece. The tree disintegrated as Chumley tried to grab the fairy at the top, both chimps brawled over each other's wine, and N'Pongo systematically stuffed herself with everything in sight. 'We carried them, full of wine and sweets, back to their cages,' Gerald wrote, 'where they crawled exhaustedly into their straw beds and lay there belching gently. If they were exhausted, we were doubly so, and crawled back to the flat to revive ourselves.'

The following spring Gerald and Jacquie took Mother by car for a holiday in Spain, stopping off on the way south to visit Lawrence and Claude at the Mazet, near Nîmes. This was Gerald's first glimpse of the out-of-the-way farmhouse in Languedoc that was to play such an important role in his future existence, and he warmed at once to its rural simplicity and the spare, herb-scented hills all around. The party carried on to Spain as planned, but Gerald was not inclined to linger there, for the pull of the little *mazet* was too strong. From Cadaqués on the Costa Brava Jacquie wrote to Alan Thomas and his wife Ella: 'Larry's house is charming and the area very Greek-like. We go back there next week as Gerry does not feel like sight-seeing in Spain and wants to investigate the Camargue fauna.'

Though Gerald was close to his immediate family, he did not seem to have any great yearning to have a family of his own – not, at any rate, at this time. The reasons for this cannot be known, but they may have been reinforced by his awareness that the conservation battle he was helping to fight was against the consequences of a human population explosion that was out of control. 'How lost in admiration and envy the fleas and rats and rabbits of this world must be,' he used to say, 'when they regard the fantastic reproductive record of the human race.' 'Gerry didn't want any children,' Jacquie was to state. 'We both felt the state of the world was such that we didn't want to bring anyone into it.' On the two occasions when she did become pregnant – she miscarried both times – he was quite upset. 'On the first occasion,' she recalled, 'he even refused to speak to me for something like three weeks, addressing me, when he had to, through a third person.' The matter became academic when Jacquie underwent a partial hysterectomy on medical grounds in the autumn of 1961, at the age of thirty-one. Gerald was consumed with worry while she was in the nursing home, and when she came home after ten days he fussed over her like a nursemaid. 'I had a wonderful time,' she recalled, 'being waited on hand and foot with nothing to do all day but read or play records while my ever-loving husband attended to everything.'

The news was more procreative, so to speak, on the zoo front. Gerald noted that 'we have so far, in our first year of existence, bred eleven species successfully.' The excitement attendant upon these births was considerable. Juan and Juanita, a pair of collared peccaries, were a case in point. Juan was two feet long and had been bought by Gerald in northern Argentina from an Indian who was fattening him up for Christmas. Juanita was a baby measuring only six inches in length when Gerald acquired her. Despite the discrepancies in age and Juanita's ill health, the pair soon produced their first baby in Jersey Zoo, to Gerald's intense gratification. 'To look out of the kitchen window,' he wrote, 'and see Juanita, her husband and baby playing a new game they have invented, fills me with pride.'

But to obtain pairs of the larger endangered species was an expensive business. Gerald took to hanging a collection box on the outside of N'pongo's cage so that visitors to the zoo could contribute some of their small change towards the £1500 needed to buy her a mate. Not long afterwards a new gorilla did arrive, but it was another female, called Nandi. She was followed by a female tapir called Claudette (a mate for Claudius), and in 1962 by a female cheetah called Paula (a mate for Peter).

During 1961 Gerald made another foray into television. Of the hoped-for six-part series he had shot in Argentina, only one programme could be salvaged for transmission in a BBC nature series called *Look*. Now the BBC Natural History Unit in Bristol asked him to do a short series of programmes, to be called *Zoo Packet*, for broadcasting that summer. The idea came from Eileen Moloney, Gerald's early radio talks producer and friend, who had recently crossed over to television. She felt that for all his palpable anxiety in front of the camera there was still a place for Gerald in television, given his charm, humour and passion for animals. *Zoo Packet* was intended to provide a relaxed format in which he could relate his animal stories and introduce his favourite animals from the zoo.

The logistical problems were considerable. Special display cases with glass fronts had to be constructed and the animals flown to the BBC studios in Bristol in a chartered plane. The largest dressing-room was set aside entirely for the animals, while the unflappable N'pongo was given a smaller dressing-room to herself. Far from being relaxed, Gerald was beside himself with anxiety over the well-being of his animals, their behaviour under the blinding studio lights, and his own performance. 'It was surprising,' said the programmes' director Chris Parsons, 'that he did not collapse with nervous exhaustion at the end of each show.' Many of the animals were nocturnal or forest creatures, and retreated from view the moment the lights were switched on. Others were going to be a handful whatever the circumstances. 'Never before have eleven representatives of the primate family been shown live together in a television studio,' Jacquie was to write, 'and judging by what happened, never again will they be allowed to be.'

Chris Parsons had first met Gerald when he had gone to Bournemouth to film some of the animals he was keeping in Margaret's back garden. Now, off the set, he began to perceive in Gerald some of the qualities Eileen had so wanted to show on screen – his powers as a raconteur, his humour, his enthusiasm, his gift for friendship. 'If Gerry started making rude remarks about you,' Chris decided, 'you knew that these came out of a feeling of affection rather than hostility ... If Gerry had something to offer television it was most likely to be on location, where he would be relaxed amongst the animals and the wild places which he loved.' This notion was to bear fruit before long.

Towards the end of 1961 Gerald wrote to Lawrence in Languedoc, giving him a progress report, a round-up of the year. The news, by and large, was good. Stanley Donen, the Hollywood director, had approached him about making a Broadway stage musical based on *My Family and Other Animals*, and if it was successful he would go on to make a movie version of it. He was serious, Gerald reported, and Curtis Brown was having talks with him about it: 'I've got to get each member of the family to sign a chit to say they won't sue him providing that the character on the stage is like that in the book ... Mother is very thrilled and I am giving her singing lessons in case they can't get anyone to play her part.' That was not the last of the good news. Gerald continued: 'The zoo has done very well this year; we are up a third on last year. This is still not good enough, and we are in for another hard winter, but I reckon that within another two years we shall be reasonably happy. The lion, you will be glad to know, is having a mate, arriving tomorrow, a gift from a fan in Uganda. The books do help sometimes.'

Now in his mid-thirties, Gerald was approaching the height of his powers. A best-selling author around the world, marathon globetrotter, budding television personality and founder of his own zoo, he was also a man of extraordinary charisma. Harold Macmillan had had him round to 10 Downing Street for an official reception during the state visit by the President of Peru, while the Queen had invited him and Jacquie to Buckingham Palace for a state banquet to mark the official visit of the President of the Cameroons. Even authentic stars were drawn into Gerald's orbit. 'One day,' Gerald recalled, 'I received a long, handwritten letter from Jamaica signed Noël Coward. Suspecting a hoax, I wrote a guarded reply. Then I got another letter, from Switzerland, and I was forced to believe that I could number the master among my fans, and I was very flattered.' Coward, it seemed, was a devoted animal-lover and convinced conservationist, and adored Gerald's books. They carried on corresponding for several years, and when Coward came to London to act in three of his plays, he suggested that he, Gerald and Jacquie meet up. Gerald was diffident about making contact, but Jacquie nagged him into telephoning. Coward was delighted, and asked them round to supper at the Savoy the next evening. When Gerald, still bashful, asked what he should wear, Coward thought for a second, then suggested: 'How about leopardskin tights?'

Unlike Gerald, Jacquie was not a great fan of Coward's, and thought it might be better if Gerald went without her. 'Don't be silly,' Gerald told her. 'This is like having dinner with Oscar Wilde.' He repeated the story over supper. 'Oh, dear,' responded Coward. 'I hope it doesn't have the same repercussions – but then, Wilde didn't go in for beards, did he?' Later Coward had Gerald and Jacquie to stay at his house in Switzerland.

Friends, colleagues, reporters, visitors of all kinds fell in thrall to Gerald's magic aura. His powers of persuasion were prodigious, and his success in life was largely thanks to his ability to have an idea, a radical or even revolutionary vision, and then to persuade others to turn it into reality. He didn't just have charm; he had (when he chose to raise his game) mega-charm. In part it was due to his physical impact: the astonishingly bright, piercing blue eyes above the raffish beard; the frank, intelligent gaze of a child; the engaging, ever-ready laugh. 'He laughs with that infectious staccato peculiar to the Durrells,' David Hughes wrote. 'Joking irresistibly, he can get you hysterical in two minutes flat, setting off jokes like fireworks.'

Partly also it was the range and style of his conversation, its sideways looks, its darting insights, its unorthodox trajectories, the underlying anarchy of his approach to people and ideas, the stories conjured out of thin air, preposterous and hilarious by turns, but harbouring a kernel of truth. 'Glass in hand,' noted Hughes, 'he conveys a sense of his preoccupation with worlds that are closed books to us: "boyish" is the word that fits.

He comes to us adults only to share our pleasures – drink, talk, laughing – and then he pushes off. He cuts straight through our system of pretences. Class doesn't count, prestige is drivel, the social pattern is good for a laugh. In every company he is vulgar and detached.' Gerald's charisma also owed much to his larger-than-lifeness, his deeply engaging eccentricity. For those who played the game and observed the rules he was an unnerving proposition, for he undermined polite conventions, promising something different – risqué perhaps, fun certainly, unpredictable always. Only when it came to animals, and their care and conservation, did the man of laughter turn to the man of steel. Animals, about which he wrote with such affectionate comedy, were in reality no laughing matter to him. Over things about which he cared deeply, Gerald Durrell was a profoundly serious man.

'I'm tired of human beings,' he told David Hughes when they met in Jersey towards the end of 1961. 'They've made such a mess of it. It's odd how human beings in a crowd become the most stupid of animals. It's usually the other way round. A herd of buffaloes is more intelligent than a single buffalo.' It was unbelievable how some of the public behaved when they came to the zoo, Gerald told a couple of French reporters. One oaf had slipped a packet of aspirins into the chinchilla cage, and one of the animals had died. Other morons had given razor blades, lipstick, even lighted cigarettes, to the monkeys. 'If only people had the intelligence of gorillas,' he sighed.

'It's a complex business, how to treat an animal,' he said. 'Any human being who has a rapport with an animal will gain something. It makes you aware of other spheres. Just watch a dog sniffing like a connoisseur and imagine the whole field of art that lies unexplored in that.' His attitude to animals, he went on, was not anthropomorphic, as some people believed. He didn't look on animals as little furry humans, and he would have no compunction in shooting one and eating it, if need be.

Gerald was well aware of the emotive views of those who held that it was cruel to keep wild animals penned up in zoos. Zoos went down in the public's estimation in the 1960s, when the young were proclaiming freedom and love and conservationists were revealing the extent of the biological catastrophe that was overwhelming much of the planet. Some maintained that there was no such thing as a good zoo. Gerald understood that view, and where the zoos were bad, he sympathised with it. 'The average zoo is pretty bloody,' he declared. 'It might pose under the wonderful banner of a scientific society, but it's nothing more or less than a three-ring circus, run either by businessmen or illiterate showmen.' However, he shared the position of Florence Nightingale, of whose

Gerald at around the time he met Jacquie Rasen in Manchester. With his film-star looks he was, she reckoned at first, 'shallow, spoilt and wholly extrovert'.

Gerald (twenty-six) and Jacquie (twenty-one), zoologist and trainee opera singer respectively, shortly after their marriage on 26 February 1951. They had only £40 between them, and Gerald had no job and no prospects.

The attic room in Margaret's boarding house in Bournemouth where Gerald wrote his first best-selling books, including *My Family and Other Animals*. Secretary Sophie Cook is at Gerald's typewriter, and Chumley the chimp is at his ankles.

A best-selling author is born. Book signing on publication day of *My Family and Other Animals*, Gerald's most successful and enduring book, with sales running into millions.

The tall, regal, gin-slinging Fon of the Kingdom of Bafut in the Cameroons, wearing his ceremonial elephant-hair headdress.

Jacquie dances the samba with the Fon while Gerald happily revolves by himself, Bafut, 1957.

One way of catching animals in the bush – doing it yourself. Gerald with African companions nets a giant monitor lizard in the wilds of Bafut.

Another way of catching animals – getting others to catch them for you. At the Fon's rest house Gerald surveys a crowd of children who have brought anything from bugs to snakes inside their hollow calabashes.

Gerald and Jacquie attend to their collection of Cameroons creatures in the back garden of Margaret's boarding house, 1957. In Gerald's arms is Chumley. In the background is the wedding marquee used to house animals on previous expeditions.

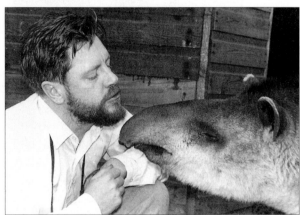

Above: Les Augrès Manor, the sixteenth-century Jersey manor house that became the Durrell home and zoo headquarters in 1959. The dodo in the centre of the gate is the Trust's symbol.

Left: An early resident of Gerald's embryonic zoological garden – Claudius the tapir from Argentina.

Paula the cheetah taking zoological director Jeremy Mallinson for his morning run.

A young orang utan quizzically pondering his human chum. The rapport between man and animals at Jersey Zoo was always a hallmark of its success.

Chumley, Gerald and Lulu enjoying choir practice, 1959.

Gerald with Swedish film star Mai Zetterling and her husband, writer David Hughes. Mai is holding the young female gorilla N'pongo.

Gerald and his brother Lawrence with a rhesus monkey at the manor house, 1960.

Durrell family reunion, Les Augrès Manor, Christmas 1960. Only Leslie, then in Africa, is missing. The dog is Keeper the boxer.

Left: Mother and son, Jersey, early 1960s.

Right: Gerald and Jacquie, Jersey, 1969.

With albino emu,
Australia, 1962.

Above: Gerald and John Hartley
(crouching) during shooting of *Catch me a
Colobus* in Sierra Leone, 1965. Behind
Hartley is director Christopher Parsons.

A split-second of the formidable Durrell
charm – Gerald photographed during a
newspaper interview on Corfu, 1966.

achievements he was a great admirer. The fact that she criticised bad hospitals did not mean that she was opposed to all hospitals. For while even a good zoo – like Jersey Zoo – did indeed keep animals in confinement, it also gave them significant freedoms that greatly enhanced their quality of life: freedom from fear (especially of predators); freedom from hunger and disease; freedom to live and bring up their offspring in shelter and security and even (with luck) freedom from extinction. The majority of human beings would be happy to live out their lives on such terms. In any case, animals in their wild state defined their own limits, which amounted to cages of their own making. A mouse throughout its entire life might seldom move out of an area of twelve square feet. A lion needed a much bigger territory, but even he marked out his own natural cage. In Gerald's view no zoo could be considered good if it did not breed the animals it housed. Not only did this reduce the need to draw stock from the wild, but it raised the possibility of returning species to it. And where this was not feasible, at least a good zoo provided a sanctuary in which species on the brink of extinction might continue to draw breath.

'I have the same interest in politics as a gamekeeper has in stoats,' Gerald once said. 'The only view I hold strongly, which I suppose is political in a far-flung way, is that human beings should stop reproducing themselves. The pronouncements of Kennedy and Macmillan are just not important. Our problems are biological: overpopulation.' In 1961 – prior to such seminal dates in the history of the modern environmental movement as the publication of Rachel Carson's *Silent Spring* (1962) and the politicisation of green protest with the foundation of Friends of the Earth (1971) – such views put Gerald Durrell well ahead of his time.

So far as his own role was concerned in practising what he preached, Gerald was disarmingly selfless and frankly self-willed by turns. 'I am a charlatan,' he told David Hughes. 'I am lazy and stupid, vain and greedy and selfish. But I'm terribly broad-minded when it comes to me. I've got, you see, all the normal human virtues.' On the other hand, he was pursuing a cause, to which he was prepared to sacrifice even himself. 'If you're an intelligent mammal, apart from giving your body to the earth and thus creating new life, I think you should leave something behind. If you go through life taking and not giving, then it's detrimental to you.'

Early in February 1962 Gerald and Jacquie set sail from wintry Rotterdam bound for the southern hemisphere, at the start of another grand adventure. First dreamed up by Jacquie, then taken up by their friend Chris Parsons at the BBC Natural History Unit, the plan was to make a series of television documentaries about the conservation work being done in

New Zealand, Australia and Malaya – new ground for both the Durrells. On 4 April they stepped ashore in Auckland. Chris Parsons, who would direct the series, and Jim Saunders, the cameraman, were making their own way there, and would meet up with them shortly.

Gerald wrote a long letter to his mother (the last he was ever to write her, though he never quite finished it or even posted it) giving an account of the New Zealand section of the expedition:

> In Auckland, to our astonishment, we found ourselves greeted like royalty. The red carpet was unrolled in no uncertain fashion. We were interviewed, photographed from seventy different angles, recorded, televised, and generally exhausted. We found the Wildlife Department had – to use a New Zealand expression – jacked up our whole tour for us, and had detailed one Brian Bell from the Department to be our guide throughout our stay.

From Auckland they proceeded, via the black swans of Lake Fongapay and the mud geysers of Rotorua, to another red-carpet welcome in Wellington, followed by lunch with the entire New Zealand Cabinet. 'Can you picture me sitting there surrounded by the Minister for this and the Minister for that?' Gerald wrote to his mother. The lunch was not without its moments. Gerald expressed concern at the environmental damage inflicted by sheep grazing. Some members of the Cabinet were themselves guilty of this, and when they protested that a little bit of erosion did nobody any harm, he replied: 'It's a bit like having a Rembrandt. Once it's destroyed, you can't replace it. If you had a Rembrandt, would *you* destroy it?' 'Really,' he said to Jacquie when he emerged from the encounter, 'they're just a bunch of hick farmers like the rest.'

A mile off the coast lay the island bird sanctuary of Kapiti.

> Though the birds are wild they are incredibly tame. The first we saw were the Wekas, dumpy brown birds the size of a chicken with very worried expressions. They prowled around our feet, examining us and the equipment with great care, and consulting each other with a most curious noise, like someone beating softly on a tom-tom. Then George Fox, who looks after the island, said he would call the Kakas; these are large parrots clad in rather sombre shot silk feathering, and with very large, strongly hooked beaks. Fox shouted out for a bit and then, suddenly the birds appeared out of the forest, screeching excitedly. They flew down and perched all over us to eat the dates Fox had provided. One of

them decided that my head was the ideal perch, and as their claws are long and sharp I was nearly scalped.

Their next venture was to a pair of rocks called The Brothers, where they had to be hauled ashore by crane. The Brothers were home to the rare Tuatara lizard, and much else beside.

There were Giant Geckos all over the rocks, and I collected a number of these which I sent off by air and which I hope are now settled in happily at Jersey. All five of us had to sleep in a tiny hut that night, and our slumbers were not of the sweetest as two pairs of Fairy Penguins had their nest burrows under the floor, and spent the whole night braying at each other like four donkeys; even banging on the floor with a boot did not have the slightest effect on their singing . . .

After this came the highlight of our trip: we had been granted permits to go into Notornis Valley. The Notornis [commonly known as the takahe] is that bird that they thought was extinct until they rediscovered it in this remote valley in the mountains. They think there might be about four hundred pairs. The valley is, of course, strictly protected, and no one is allowed to go in without permission.

But the visit to the remote valley where the strange, flightless takahe had been rediscovered was a disappointment. 'We made our way down the whole length of the lake without seeing anything,' Gerald wrote in his film commentary. 'It was one of the most unpleasant bits of country I had ever been in.' A few days later he did succeed in setting his eyes on a number of takahe in captivity at Mount Cook, where the New Zealand Wild Life Service was attempting to breed them. 'But it was another rarity being kept there that raised Gerry into almost a quivering state of excitement,' Chris Parsons was to recall. 'This was the one and only kakapo [nocturnal owl parrot] in captivity. Since then more kakapos have been discovered in the wild and translocated to safety, but the possibility of breeding such endangered species in captivity and reintroducing them to the wild was already prominent in Gerry's mind.'

Unlike the Durrells' previous expeditions in Africa and South America, the one in New Zealand had all the characteristics of a tightly organised, official guided tour. By contrast, in Australia the itinerary was less structured. This was perhaps one of the reasons Gerald and Jacquie adored Australia from the moment they landed there. 'We all fell in love with Australia, completely and instantly,' Gerald was to write. 'If ever I was compelled to settle down in one spot – which God forbid – Australia is one of the few countries I have visited that I would choose.'

The animals and birds they went in quest of – wombat, bandicoot, platypus, cassowary, lyre bird, kookaburra and many more – were primordial and extraordinary. But none gave Gerald so much pause for reflection as Leadbeater's opossum, which, like the takahe, had once been considered extinct. The film crew visited the animal's secret location at night, and the narration Gerald wrote for this sequence is of particular significance:

> As far as has been discovered, they're only found in a piece of forest about a mile square. Such a small area could only support very few pairs of these little creatures. Should a bushfire ever break out and sweep through this area, the Leadbeater's Opossum would be doomed for ever. Probably the only safeguard for their survival would be to establish some in captivity, to breed them and then introduce them into other suitable areas so that at least if this forest was burned, they would still survive elsewhere.

The travellers were growing weary by now, but they still had Malaya to go. 'Dreadful voyage on Italian liner,' Jacquie wrote to Mother in early July. 'Got to Singapore July 1st, two days there, then Kuala Lumpur by road. Fascinating country and people but dreadful climate – sticky heat all the time. How long I'll be able to put up with it – being sopping wet all the time – I don't know. Filming situation difficult – not laid on as in Australia and New Zealand.' Their itinerary in Malaya took them first to the Terman Negara, the country's largest national park, a gigantic slab of untouched forest which was home to the Sumatra rhino, tiger, leopard, gibbon and king cobra; and then to Dungun, on the east coast, an area rich in reptiles.

At last they came to the end of a journey which had taken them some forty-five thousand miles through three countries, during which they had encountered dozens of fascinating species. Gerald later summed up what he had learned from this conservational grand tour:

> The picture of conservation that I found in New Zealand, Australia and Malaya was distressingly familiar. Small bands of dedicated, underpaid and overworked individuals are fighting a battle against public apathy and political and big business chicanery. By and large people are apathetic because they do not realise what is going on, but the most dangerous part of the problem is political apathy, because it is only at top level that you can get things done. Most

politicians would not risk their careers for the sake of conservation, because firstly they do not think it is important, and secondly they treat conservationists with the disregard they would display towards an elderly spinster's ravings over her pet peke. But unlike us, animals have no control over their future. They cannot ask for home rule, they cannot worry their MPs with their grievances, they cannot even get their unions to agree to a strike for better conditions. Their future and their very existence depends on us.

Gerald and Jacquie had planned to carry on to East Africa when they finished shooting in Malaya, but the news from home was not good. The state of things at the zoo had deteriorated to a point of crisis. So had Mother's morale. Her loneliness had become acute over the months that Gerald and Jacquie had been away, and her friend Betty Norton and Eileen Moloney, who was staying in the manor in the Durrells' absence, urged Gerald to forgo the last stage of the expedition and to come home as speedily as possible. The travellers changed plans and ships. By the last week of August they were in Aden on board the Glen Line cargo boat *Glenorchy*, and in the second week of September they docked in London.

Gerald and Jacquie were given a warm welcome when they finally returned to Jersey in the late summer of 1962, but they were dismayed by the lacklustre look of the zoo. Although it had enjoyed a record season at the turnstiles, it presented, Jacquie recalled, a 'shabby' and 'uncared-for' appearance. Underfunded, understaffed, dilapidated and down-at-heel, the zoo was evidently near to financial ruin. Jacquie blamed Ken Smith, who had been given *carte blanche* in Gerald's absence, and she was outspoken in her criticism. 'He not only ignored Gerry's plans for the zoo,' she was to claim, 'but imposed his own ideas.' He was really a zoo man of the old school, she felt: 'He didn't have a clue what Gerry was about. I tried to persuade Gerry to get rid of him and put somebody else in charge. But this revealed the weakness in Gerry's character. He couldn't bring himself to do it.' Instead, Gerald staunchly defended his old friend and colleague. Jacquie was furious: 'Things got to a point when, after I'd had a couple of barneys with a member of the staff who was incompetent, Smith came storming into our flat and told Gerry that if he didn't keep his wife's bloody nose out of it, he'd leave. And Gerry supported him and not me!'

Smith's wife Trudy saw things differently. 'Ken and I had got on pretty well with both Gerry and Jacquie,' she recalled. 'But in the winter of 1962 ill-feeling began to develop – I don't know why. We all felt it was a parting of the ways. Probably Gerry wanted to take over the reins, change things, bring the Trust into being. Probably he thought Ken had run his course and done his bit.'

The writing was on the wall, and the senior staff of the zoo were under immense pressure. By the time Gerald got back from the Far East he had run up debts of £17,000. Drastic action was required to halt the three-year-old zoo's slide into insolvency. Gerald's accountant Eddie Ray, from the London firm of Spicer & Pegler, was invited to Jersey to audit the books and produce a financial survey of the administration and its day-to-day running costs. His report confirmed their worst fears. The books were in a mess, money had leaked away, and the establishment was getting nowhere. The zoo was on the verge of folding.

EIGHTEEN

Durrell's Ark

1962–1965

The crisis was total. Gerald's dream was on the brink of dissolution, and instant action was required. Neither he nor Jacquie was in a position to run the financial side of the zoo. There was nothing for it – they would have to bring in a professional, an administrator and troubleshooter who could sort out the mess. They advertised in the local paper, and the response was overwhelming. Among those who applied was Catha Weller, who had previously worked in advertising in London, and had recently come to Jersey when her husband Sam was posted there. She was summoned to an interview at the manor on a Sunday morning in December 1962.

'Only Gerry could interview somebody on a Sunday morning,' Catha recalled. 'I walked into the room and I could hardly speak. I am a clairvoyant, and years before I had described to Sam in detail a room I had seen as a sort of vision in my head. And when I walked into the room in the manor I realised straight away that this was the room I had seen, precise in every detail. It was uncanny. So I said to myself: "Well, of course, this is where I am destined to work."'

Gerald and Jacquie had already interviewed some twenty no-hopers that morning, and were beginning to despair. But Catha was clearly something special. 'She waltzed into my office for her interview,' Gerald recalled, 'diminutive, round, with sparkling green eyes and a comforting smile. Yes, she knew how to do book-keeping, shorthand and typing – the lot. I looked at Jacquie and Jacquie looked at me. We both knew instinctively that a miracle had happened.'

Three days later, on 12 December 1962, Catha started her life-saving job at the zoo, though when she turned up for her first day's work she formed the impression that she had been brought in simply to wind the place up: 'I thought the job would last about six months. They were in dire straits: there was no money, nothing at all, and I had never done any fund-raising in my life. I thought, well, in six months I can get this all sorted out for the Receiver.'

Catha ruled the zoo's finances with a heart of gold and a hand of iron. Not even the smallest transaction could be entered into without her approval. If a zoo worker asked her for a new broom with which to sweep out the cages, he was required to bring the old one for inspection, and if it retained a single bristle his request was denied. If a keeper indented for twenty bananas, his order was cut to eighteen. If a member of staff was caught eating an apple, he or she was reproached with the words: 'You are taking food from an animal's mouth.' If the month's budget was spent in three weeks, it would be short commons all round for the remaining week. Payments of bills were deferred with a polite note. Though such penny-pinching alone would not save the zoo, it was symptomatic of a state of mind that might. 'What we would have done without this ally who sorted out our administration,' Jacquie was to record, 'leaving us free to deal with animals, I cannot bear to think; we shall for ever be in her debt. Slowly but surely she introduced routine and order, and with the help of our many friends, things began to settle down.'

But it was hard going. By now the zoo had 650 animals and a staff of forty to look after them. The work was hard and dirty, and the hours could be unsociable. The pay was poor – nevertheless it was an expense that had to be met, week in, week out. The feeding statistics were even more daunting: 180,000 apples a year, eighty thousand pears, fifty thousand oranges, countless tons of onions, tomatoes, carrots, potatoes, tens of thousands of eggs, an untold quantity of milk, all that meat. 'Money ... this obsession ... money,' Gerald complained to a visiting journalist, sighing deeply. 'There's never enough in a zoo.'

Gerald had always seen the development of his zoo as taking place in two phases. The first was the establishment of the basic structure, with a stock of animals sufficient to attract a paying public in numbers large enough to guarantee the continuance of the embryonic institution. The second phase would be the zoo's evolution into a public body and serious scientific establishment whose primary function was the captive breeding of species threatened with extinction. At the request of Julian Huxley he had delayed pushing this through in order to give priority to the foundation of the World Wildlife Fund, which came into being in 1961. But now, with Jersey Zoo on a stable, albeit still impoverished footing, Gerald decided the time had come to move to the second phase of the organisation's development and transform his small local zoo into a world-class charitable scientific Trust.

With the help of a friend, James Platt, a director of Shell International and the main architect of the zoo's recovery, the metamorphosis began. 'Without Jimmy Platt,' Jacquie was to recall, 'we could never have done it. The first thing he did was to take me on one side and ask me point blank: "Do you want the zoo to carry on?" He liked Gerry very much, he said, but Gerry was a dreamer and I was a practical person. So before things went any further he needed to know if my heart was still in it or if what I really wanted was to call it a day. And the temptation was very great, from a personal point of view, for the sake of my marriage, even at this early stage, to say, no, close the place down. But I didn't, because obviously it would have been a dreadful thing to have done. I mean, we had the animals, we had the huge debts, we had the young staff living on a pittance of £3 a week and pledging their support to bring the place round, we had all those years of struggle to get to this point. So I said, yes, I wanted to carry on.'

Gerald's long-cherished dream of a Wildlife Preservation Trust was a bold and ambitious proposal, but it was readily accepted by the influential people Jimmy Platt persuaded to take an interest in the zoo's affairs. 'He convinced them that Gerry was not getting a penny out of it,' Jacquie was to relate, 'and gave the whole thing an aura of respectability. Because of this, our creditors were willing to let us carry on.'

Matters now took a decisive turn. In January 1963, in a sad parting of the ways, Ken Smith left the island, along with his wife Trudy and a number of animals of his own which had been kept at the zoo. They had contracted to work at Jersey Zoo for three years, and had stayed for four. It was time to move on. Gerald's sister Margaret greeted Ken and Trudy on their return to England. 'I felt a traitor about him,' she recalled. 'Suddenly Jacquie and Gerry would go off people. Like Ken. It was me that picked up all his animals in a van and brought them to St Alban's Avenue. It was me that kept all the heaters going to keep the little things alive and then drove them down to Paignton Zoo for safe-keeping.' Smith, she felt, had not been given sufficient credit for his part in the establishment of the Jersey Zoo. But within a short while he had bounced back and established his own small zoo in Exmouth.

Steps were now taken to wipe out the zoo's outstanding debts. An appeal was launched, and the *Jersey Evening Post* published a letter signed by twelve prominent people concerned with the zoo, asking islanders to contribute to a public subscription in support of the zoo, which was not only a jewel in the island's crown but potentially a leading light in the cause of animal conservation around the world. Gerald had kept all his fan letters, and with the help of Catha Weller and the new zoo secretary,

Betty Boizard, he wrote to every fan at home and abroad asking for help.

The money poured in. Donations ranged from £1000 from the island's well-heeled to a small boy's pocket money. The zoo staff, despite their meagre incomes, clubbed together to contribute a donation which touched Gerald and Jacquie deeply. A hundred and fifty residents of Jersey banded together with others interested in wildlife and raised a total of £13,500. Jersey was well-known as a haven for the wealthy, although the source of their wealth was sometimes obscure. One day, following a tip-off from his bank manager, Gerald approached a certain 'Mr X' for a donation. The man – tall, charming, urbane – received Gerald in his palatial home, listened politely to his embarrassed, half-choked request, then calmly wrote out a cheque for £2000. Gerald gratefully resolved to name one of his orang-utan babies after this kind and munificent fellow, but three months later, Mr X suddenly hit the headlines. 'It seemed that he had, allegedly, swindled a large number of sober Jersey citizens out of their wealth and was, in consequence, forced to spend a short period of time in one of Her Majesty's less salubrious prisons. I wished I had known him a lot sooner. He could have taught me a lot.'

Gerald's own financial contribution was by far the biggest. Against the advice of many who were close to him, he agreed to shoulder the whole burden of the £20,000 bank loan, waiving any right he might have had to reclaim the money – thus, in effect, donating it to the zoo. Since his only income was from writing and television – unreliable livelihoods both – he had condemned himself to unremitting toil for years to come. But he was adamant.

In May 1963 Gerald made another critical decision, and appointed Jeremy Mallinson, then only twenty-seven, as his deputy. The two had first met in June 1959, shortly after Gerald had arrived in Jersey from Argentina, when Jeremy had a summer job as a casual hand in the bird section. Fervently interested in animals and the natural world, he had left his first job as a trainee in his father's wine and spirit business in Jersey to join the Rhodesia and Nyasaland Staff Corps as a regular soldier, his main motive being to explore as much of Africa and see as much of the continent's wildlife as he could. When he returned to Britain he turned down the prospects of a career in the Hong Kong Police or tea-planting in Assam in favour of working with animals, first on a dairy farm in Devon and then in dog kennels in Surrey. When he returned to Jersey his plans to establish kennels of his own were thwarted by financial and planning restrictions, and in desperation he applied for a summer job at the newly opened Jersey Zoo, not because he was interested in zoos but because he had just read and been captivated by *My Family and Other Animals.*

The temporary job stretched into the winter, and as he moved from the tropical birds section to the mammals Jeremy became increasingly intrigued by the work: not simply the problems of daily care, but the bigger picture, the threats to the survival of animals in the wild, and Gerald's plans to rescue endangered species from extinction. 'With his Duke of Wellington nose, his buttercup-coloured hair and his bright blue eyes,' Gerald was to record, 'Jeremy was as devoted to our animals as if he had given birth to each of them personally. His habit of referring to human male and female acquaintances as "fine specimens" was an indication that his job tended to creep into his everyday life.' As Jeremy's knowledge of the maintenance and breeding of exotic species began to grow, he began to feel he should extend his education to include a collecting expedition of his own, and in October 1961 he set off for southern Africa in search of wild creatures.

When he returned to Jersey Ken Smith had gone, and Gerald and Jacquie needed someone to take over the day-to-day reins. 'Gerry asked me up into his office,' Jeremy recalled, 'right at the top of the manor house. "Jeremy," he said to me, "would you be very honoured to become my deputy – the Deputy Director of Jersey Zoo?" He gave me two days to think about it. Well, I had been his disciple right from the start. He was the master. He couldn't have been more supportive to me. I was a total sort of backwoodsman, really, but he always encouraged me and gave me a tremendous amount of confidence. He was a very charismatic man, and like all great men he couldn't care less who you were or what your background or qualifications were. If he saw some quality in you which he liked he would support you. He could never work with someone he didn't like in some way, no matter what their qualifications were. He had this tremendous insight into people, you see, though he never bothered to quantify or qualify it. So after two days I went back to him and said: "I'd be proud."'

But Jeremy Mallinson was soon aware that he had not one superior but two, for Jacquie was even more active than Gerald in practical matters to do with the running of the zoo. (When Tony Lort-Philips found himself on the receiving end of Jacquie's orders, he answered back: 'If this was a ship, I would expect to take my orders from the ship's captain, not his wife.') 'Jacquie was very direct,' Mallinson says. 'She shot from the hip. She was an intelligent woman and if she saw something she didn't like she'd say so. Right at the start I had an altercation with Jacquie over something, and I said to her: "Look, either you do it or I do it, but I can't do part of something." When Gerry got to hear of this he was very annoyed. "I don't employ a dog and have to bark myself," he said [to Jacquie]. "I expect him or her to have the authority and I don't expect that to be undermined by you, even if you are my wife, or anyone else." To give Jacquie her full due, I never had any problems after that. She would say what she thought but would never sulk about something or harbour grudges. And I can understand the enormous pressures she was under, as Gerry was too.'

But Jacquie was not amused. She had always tried to maintain a rapport with both the animals and the staff, as part of the 'open-door' policy she and Gerald pursued at the zoo. 'The staff felt they could speak freely to me about anything,' she was to say, 'so that I was a sort of conduit to Gerry. This he happily accepted until one day – for no discernible reason – he objected strongly to all this "hob-nobbing" and proceeded to give me a pompous lecture about how to comport myself both in the Zoo and in the island generally. Being even more Irish than Gerry I exploded and told him what he could do with his precious Zoo and committees.'

By now Gerald's eleventh book in nine years, *The Whispering Land* – an account of the expedition to Argentina back in 1959 – had been published. Gerald was among the best-selling authors in English. His adventurous spirit, his spontaneous gift for narrative and anecdote, his talent for divining the characters of the rare creatures of the wild with the same clear, humorous and unsentimental eyes with which he regarded the people he met in remote places – all served to make him a master of animal and travel writing. To have maintained such unfailing standards of entertainment for more than fifteen years could only be described as a triumph.

Gerald started work on a new book, *Menagerie Manor*, a description of the first four years of the Jersey Zoo. At the same time he was heavily engaged in writing the scripts for Chris Parsons' seven-part documentary series *Two in the Bush*, an account of the journey through New Zealand, Australia and Malaya. But the manifold problems besetting the new book's subject itself were causing him angst-full days and sleepless nights. He made a number of attempts to write the book, and but for Jacquie's intervention would have torn up the lot. 'Never have I wished so fervently that I could write the book for him,' she said.

Gerald's distaste – revulsion, even – for putting pen to paper had become almost pathological. In part, the problem was an acute case of literary burn-out. But also, the whole process of scribbling simply seemed trivial to Gerald compared to the real work in hand: the survival of the zoo and the formation of the Trust. Yet there were times when Gerald did dimly perceive that it was actually his writing that empowered him. It was his writing that provided him with fame, money, popular status and the attention of the media. Without his books he could never have set up his zoo in the first place.

The distractions caused by the establishment of the Trust were formidable, but at long last they were overcome. It was announced that the first Trustees were to be Lady Coutanche, wife of the ex-Bailiff of Jersey, the Earl of Jersey and Jimmy Platt. There was also to be a council consisting of a number of interested local people, ranging from the editor of the *Jersey Evening Post* to the local bank manager, who was Honorary Treasurer.

The bank manager was soon to be replaced by a much more heavy-weight figure – a corporate chief and ardent conservationist by the name of Sir Giles Guthrie, Bt, OBE, DSC, a senior merchant banker who was shortly to move into the airline business. Peter Scott came to Jersey to help launch the Trust, and in due course became one of its first scientific advisors.

On 6 July 1963, the second act in the drama was finally concluded. 'It was a great day,' Gerald recorded, 'when we assembled in the dark depths of the impressive Royal Court in St Helier to hear ourselves incorporated and thus made legal. Lawyers, like black crows in their gowns, flitted through the gloom; they all chatted together in hushed voices. So finally we emerged blinking into the sunlight and went to the nearest hostelry to celebrate the fact that the Jersey Wildlife Preservation Trust was no longer a dream but a reality.'

Gerald had handed the ownership and management of his zoo to the Trust, with himself as its Director (honorary, unpaid), Lord Jersey as its Chairman, the dodo as its logo, 'the stationary ark' as its concept and the bleak cautionary message 'Extinction Is For Ever' as its shibboleth. Soon the Trustees and Council were meeting monthly, two Council members had been co-opted on to the zoo management side, and the scientific advisory committee was up and running. 'The Jersey Wildlife Preservation Trust has been formed to protect all animals in danger of extinction,' Gerald announced, 'but with a particular emphasis on the smaller, more neglected and perhaps less publicly glamorous ones. Our aim is to track down animals in danger and breed them here in captivity. We can then build up a colony of them and restock the areas where they were in danger.'

With the Trust now in proper working order, Gerald, Jacquie and Chris Parsons set off to Nîmes in July for a fortnight to recce locations for a proposed Camargue film, to be called *A Bull Called Marius*. Afterwards Gerald and Jacquie joined Lawrence and Claude at the Mazet in Languedoc, where Mother was enjoying a short holiday, for a crash convalescence that involved large doses of sun, food and wine. 'Not looking forward to our return at all,' Jacquie wrote to Alan and Ella Thomas on 24 July.

The problem was not just the workload but the lifestyle, in so far as the two were distinguishable. Gerald's legendary Jersey way of life was established at the outset of his occupancy at the manor as an adaptation of the open-house family life of Corfu and Bournemouth. He and Jacquie lived over the shop. Beneath them lay the council room and offices, and all around them stretched the zoo. Gerald wrote his books and scripts on the kitchen table (he never liked to be out of sight, even in the throes of composition), handled any impromptu zoo business discussions in the living-room, and conversed and caroused with his intimates into the early hours around the dining table. The front door was open to all comers at all times, and the tramp of feet up the stairs to the flat on some zoo mission or other became the *leitmotif* of the Durrells' days. There was rarely much privacy and precious little peace. Such access and transparency in the conduct of Gerald's affairs was both a matter of personal instinct and professional policy. It did not suit everybody, least of all Jacquie and Mother: 'Visitors daily in and out till one feels like screaming,' Mother complained in a letter to Larry and Claude on 12 October 1963.

For Jacquie, life in the flat – life on the island, for that matter – became increasingly claustrophobic and oppressive with each day that passed. 'Gerry ate, lived and slept zoo,' she recorded. 'He never had any time for any private life. He disliked going out to social events, especially cocktail parties, which he thought were inane, and eventually he hardly even went out into his own zoo. It began to get to the point when really I saw the zoo as a sort of Frankenstein monster.'

In a sense, Gerald had become a captive in his own zoo. John Hartley recalled:

He never spent a lot of time out in the zoo when he was here. This was an aspect of the man I never quite understood. It was said he couldn't stand the pressure from the public, being mobbed by his fans. But it couldn't have been just that, because there were slack times of the year when there was hardly any public here, and when later he took to getting up at five in the morning the zoo was closed anyway. And yet when I went off to Africa with him on one of his trips, he was really into his animals, looking at them all the time, playing with them, talking about them morning, noon and night. But when he was here he never did that. I don't remember him ever once coming for a walk with me round the zoo. I tried to talk to him about it. It wasn't exactly a no-go area, but I never got a proper explanation ... The driving ambition of his life was to have his own zoo, but once he'd got it he couldn't even bring himself to play with it. When we got to see a lot more of him, after Ken Smith left, he would talk to us as individuals for hours about what was going on and what we were doing and what we thought and so on, and he'd get tremendous pride and pleasure from that, but it was sort of second-hand.

Jacquie had noticed this curious reclusive trait too, but could never coax an explanation from her husband. Was it shyness? Or disappointment that the reality did not measure up to the dream? Or a sense that in the struggle to survive his place as general was not down in the trenches with the chaps, but in the command post, masterminding the battle? Or something altogether more elusive and deeply buried in the psyche, an inner feeling of solidarity with the creatures he had brought here, perhaps, a sense that if it was he that kept them cooped up in their cages in the grounds, the least he could do was to keep himself cooped up in the flat? 'I think Gerry was taken aback at what having a place like that entailed,' Jacquie believed. 'Although he had a really dedicated staff – something he genuinely appreciated – he still had to face many unpleasant things, and I think he found it hard.'

Gerald and Jacquie had been planning to have another get-together at Christmas 1963, with Lawrence and Claude coming up from Languedoc and Alan and Ella Thomas over from London, and a number of other friends besides; but it was not to be. The year had taken its toll of all the members of the Durrell family in the Les Augrès Manor flat. Writing to the Thomases on 14 December to apologise for cancelling the festivities, Jacquie explained: 'We really are both nearly demented with the awful pressures of this last gruelling year and felt we could not cope with being even basically sociable.'

There was, besides, an added complication. Mother was getting on for eighty now. She was growing frail and had begun to develop cataracts in both eyes. There were indications, too, that she was growing weary of life, and was feeling lonely and abandoned. Jacquie arranged for her to go on a short cruise with Sophie Cook, and while she was staying with Sophie in Bournemouth before their departure, she fell seriously ill. According to one account, she reverted to a favourite old remedy for moments of crisis, and drank a bottle of gin. If she did, it didn't work – or worked only too well. She became irrational and disorientated. Alan Ogden was summoned, and recommended that the old lady be moved to a small nursing home nearby. There she was successfully treated for heart trouble and pneumonia, but she began to go downhill fast. 'She was not her normal self,' her daughter Margaret recalled. 'She was very subdued, hardly spoke, just lay on the bed staring blankly out of the window in a strange, abstract sort of way. I think she just wanted to die.' Margaret began to get a room ready for her in St Alban's Avenue, but Mother's condition continued to decline, and it was clear that there was something seriously wrong. Renal failure was diagnosed, and the prognosis was grave.

It was Sophie Cook who sat with the old lady as she lay dying, for none of her children could bear the prospect. On 24 January 1964 Louisa Durrell passed away. Her last words were: 'Is that brandy on the sideboard for medicinal purposes, dear?' Margaret recalled: 'When Mother died, all she had were a few belongings you could wrap in a handkerchief like a Buddhist priest – a prayer book, a St Anthony, one or two things like that.' Her one significant asset was the rights to *My Family and Other Animals*, which Gerald had given her some years before. In her will those rights were bequeathed to her daughter-in-law, Jacquie.

Mother's death was a colossal blow to Gerald. She had always been there in his life, the body beside him in the bed when he was a boy, the shoulder to cry on, the guardian angel and protecting spirit. And now she was gone. He was beside himself. The funeral at the crematorium in Queen's Park was an oddly muted affair. Jacquie didn't go. Larry came over from France, and seemed numbed by the wintry bleakness of the occasion – the low-key, suburban setting and the Protestant rites. Gerald could hardly bear it. With Alan Thomas's support he was half-carried in to the back of the church, but when his mother's coffin was borne into the chapel he rushed outside, choked with anguish.

Back at Nîmes, Lawrence wrote to Henry Miller: 'I've just got back from the decent burying of my mother. She had an obsession about "being a trouble to people" and this time she performed her ploy to such purpose that she almost slipped away before anyone knew where they were.' 'Everyone missed her,' Jacquie was to write, 'for she was one of those rare people whom everyone loved, even if they had only met her quite casually. The house was a very sad place without her.'

Gerald was never to be quite the same man again. He now felt himself alone in a strange, awesome sense. 'I have always thought his mother's death was a major catastrophe for him,' Jacquie was to reflect. 'He never came to terms with it, he was utterly unable to accept it, he couldn't even grieve for her, in fact he refused to grieve for her, so the hurt was never assuaged.' In Jacquie's view, his response to Mother's death was typical of him: 'As a child his life was so idyllic, especially in Corfu, that he came to believe that life would always be like that, and when it wasn't, when something untoward occurred, he just couldn't cope. He would run away from problems, and just drink, or take drugs such as tranquillisers, or combinations of both.'

Though Gerald was to sparkle with charm and fun and infectious humour until the end, his underlying mood was to grow darker from this time forth. The severance from his roots that his mother's death had brought about; the growing sterility of his marriage; the frustration caused by the ceaseless difficulties with the zoo; the mounting anger he felt at the ways of man, hell-bent on mayhem in the world of nature – all these things began to affect him, and to bow him down, inch by bitter inch.

The change in the nature of the inner man was reflected in the physical appearance of the outer one. As if to acknowledge his growing status in the world at large, Gerald's latest passport gave his height as five feet eleven inches, miraculously a full four inches taller than in the one issued when he was twenty-two and fully grown. But his passport photo revealed a different story. When David Attenborough had met him in Buenos Aires less than five years previously, he described Gerald as looking ten years younger than his age. Now he was beginning to look ten years older, his bearded face presenting a wearier, fuller, rather battered image to the unforgiving lens.

If nothing else, the face revealed the cost of Gerald's journey. Until recently he had been lean of visage and slender of frame. No matter how much he ate and drank he had remained as slender as a beanpole. But in the last few years he had been steadily filling out, and was now emerging as the stout, round-faced man most of his fans were to remember. According to Jacquie, this metamorphosis had begun soon after his return from his third expedition to the Cameroons. The bug he had picked up in Africa had left him anaemic, and to remedy this in the most agreeable kind of way, Alan Ogden had suggested he take a daily drop or so of Guinness, which was rich in iron as well as alcohol. Gerald took to this medication with alacrity, and was soon knocking back not a bottle a day, but a crate. 'That's when he started ballooning out,' Jacquie recalled. 'When I complained to Dr Ogden, he said he hadn't expected Gerry to take him so literally – or the Guinness so copiously.' As the expense of the elixir began to soar, Jacquie wrote to their accountant enquiring whether Guinness consumed for medicinal purposes was tax deductible (it wasn't).

For Gerald, Jersey had meant not only a change of location but a change of life. He became not just an individual, but an institution. He no longer worked on his own behalf, but on behalf of the animal life of the world. There was a price to pay for a career of dedication such as this. Gerald's ark and all it stood for had already cost him his privacy, his peace of mind, and to a degree his happiness and well-being; in time would cost him his marriage, his health, and perhaps even his life as well.

Gerald Durrell was a square peg, a rebel. 'He was looked on by the zoo establishment as a meddling upstart, a dangerous lunatic,' a friend and colleague was to recall. 'Here's this chap, they said, no degree, no qualifications, goes around giving interviews saying we're making a mess of things and tapping funds that could be better spent. My God, we can't have amateurs wandering round the world causing trouble. Dammit, his chimps are *bonking*! What's more, he seems to think it's a *good idea*! Gerry always used to think he was under siege, an outsider, didn't have the respectability, the backing. He had to start with a blank piece of paper and create his own structure – so you could hardly blame him for feeling paranoid. His sense of isolation – I'm a man against the universe – came out a lot in conversation. Never bitterly, but he felt rejected because ideas he thought central were regarded as bone-headed and eccentric.'

When a symposium on zoos and conservation was held at the Zoological Society of London in the summer of 1964, Gerald was not invited to contribute. Instead he sent a memo to the organisers drawing attention to the mission of the new-look Jersey Zoo and Trust, particularly building up colonies of threatened species, including smaller creatures that were normally neglected because they were not spectacular enough, and therefore not commercial enough, to be of interest to the general public. 'I believe we will be the first zoo in the world to attempt to devote all our resources and energy towards conservation in this manner,' he proclaimed. 'I believe that eventually the zoo here will be unique, as everything that the public sees will be underlining the importance of conservation.'

It was around this time, when the Trust stood on the brink of a challenging but uncertain future, that Jacquie began to undergo a profound change. When she had arrived back from the Far East she had told a magazine journalist: 'Despite the unusual situations that stimulate our lives I am enormously happy as Gerry's wife. I have become as interested as he is in his collection of wild creatures, in which he sometimes even includes me.' But now she began to think differently. Despite the establishment of the Trust, Gerald seemed to be even more taken up with the zoo and Trust matters than before: 'I seldom saw him alone or had a conversation that was not interspersed with zoo problems,' she remembered. 'I began to loathe the zoo or anything to do with it. The flat was becoming a second office, with a constant procession of people trailing up. I finally put my foot down and made Durrell promise to discuss zoo and Trust matters in his office downstairs, and leave us one small haven where we could relax and be on our own. But it was an uphill struggle and I often felt that I had married a zoo and not a human being.'

On the face of it, Gerald need not have chosen the difficult path he did. At his best he was one of the great nature writers in the English language – perhaps in any language. He was up there with the classic nature writers of the past – Thoreau, Richard Jefferies, W.H. Hudson, John Burroughs, William Beebe – and the best of his own time – Henry Williamson, Jim Corbett, Konrad Lorenz, Gavin Maxwell, Joy Adamson, George Schaller, and was also a masterly practitioner of comic writing. His books sold by the millions. He could well have afforded to retreat to a life of comfort and tranquillity in the South of France like his brother, writing a book a year. But he eschewed the easy way, the life of the self. He did not choose to do what suited him best, but was driven to do what he considered right.

In the spring of 1964 Gerald and Jacquie joined Lawrence and Claude for a short holiday on Corfu. On their return to Jersey, it was mayhem as usual. 'Since our return,' Gerald wrote to Alan and Ella Thomas on 2 May, 'we have had a right basin-full. We have been fighting to save our lioness and she is still very ill, but we have great hopes of pulling her round. On top of this, there has been a thousand and one things to do for the Trust, so I am afraid that we have lost all sense of time and everything else.'

In an effort to keep part of their lives private and free, Jacquie withdrew her active support for the Trust and the zoo. The immediate cause was her reaction to what she perceived as her exclusion by Gerald from the daily affairs of the zoo, but the overriding motive was her disillusionment with the life she was living. Though Jacquie continued to run his personal and business affairs, she and Gerald were no longer a duo with a shared aim. Up to now he had relied enormously on her dynamism and support. It was she who had started him off on his career as a best-selling author, encouraged his ambition to establish his own zoo, suggested Jersey as its site and kept a practical and disciplined eye on its development during its critical early years. From this point forward, however, the work and achievements of the Trust, and the programme it had set itself to save animals from extinction, would be down to Gerald alone. At this point his life went into contrary motion, his professional career advancing, his personal life retreating. For while Jersey Zoo began to take off at last and the Jersey Wildlife Preservation Trust to go ahead full-blast, Gerald's marriage began to fall apart piece by piece – and with it much else besides.

The extent of the schism soon became apparent. Jacquie was anxious for them both to get away from Jersey, and at this critical moment Chris Parsons intervened, suggesting they undertake another filmed expedition 'before the glow of *Two in the Bush* has gone off'. Gerald responded favourably to the idea, but was unclear where they could go that others hadn't been to before. Argentina, Guiana and India were rejected. An island-hopping journey through the West Indies, ending up on Little Swan Island, home of a unique hutia, a type of Caribbean rodent that would one day become extinct, was rejected as too expensive. 'So that,' Gerald informed Parsons, in a curiously myopic view of the world's wild places, 'only leaves West Africa really, and I've already written three books about that area.'

'Well, you once mentioned Sierra Leone as a possibility,' Parsons replied.

So the die was cast. They would make a series of six programmes telling the story of an animal collecting expedition in the wilds of Africa, from departure to return. There were a number of advantages in such a project, Gerald reckoned. It would provide substantial publicity for himself, the zoo and the book about the expedition, and would enable him to collect more animals, with the BBC funding part of the cost. But Jacquie responded bleakly to the glad tidings. If it was to be Sierra Leone, she announced, then she was not going. 'I don't like West Africa,' she informed Gerald, 'either the sticky heat or the tropical forests, and as you know I get exasperated with the Africans. So if you don't mind, I think I'll miss this one.'

Gerald had half expected this, but he was still hurt to the core. 'Sierra Leone was a serious crisis in our marriage,' Jacquie was to recall. 'Gerry really didn't think I'd ever come back to him. I hadn't made up my mind either way then, but I began to think Gerry didn't need me at all any more. He was so wrapped up in his zoo. I was just someone extraneous who managed his affairs, the hostess, and that was that. I wasn't very important to him any more.'

They were going their own ways: and not just metaphorically. Jacquie proposed that while Gerald headed south for Africa with the BBC, she strike west to Argentina with two long-term friends and supporters of the Durrells, Hope Platt and Ann Peters, to reconnoitre a possible future collecting trip. For some months they would be continents – as well as hearts and minds – apart.

In the middle of January 1965 Gerald and his young assistant John Hartley set sail for Sierra Leone. John was aware that all was not well between Gerald and Jacquie. On their last night in London before joining the ship they had gone out to dinner, accompanied by John's mother, and afterwards Gerald sat up very late talking to her. Next morning she took her son to one side and told him he would have to look after Gerald in Africa, as he was having a difficult time and was rather distressed. 'I thought this a bit rich,' John recalled. 'I mean, here I was, twenty-two and never set foot in Africa before – I thought I was supposed to be looking to *him* for support.'

By an extraordinary coincidence Gerald's boat and Jacquie's coincided at Las Palmas in the Canaries. From his deck Gerald could see his wife standing on hers with Ann Peters and Hope Platt, and he shouted and hollered excitedly before grabbing a bottle of champagne and rushing down the gangway. When he was stopped by immigration officials he went berserk, and an unseemly altercation ensued before he was allowed to board Jacquie's ship. For a brief, frantic and rather embarrassed quarter of an hour husband and wife were reunited before they went their different ways to opposite corners of the South Atlantic.

Agonised by fears that his marriage was breaking up, Gerald began writing letters to Jacquie almost as soon as he set foot in Africa, expressing the depth of his love for her, the extent of his need for her. But he was addressing thin air, for few of the letters ever reached her, and those that did took an eternity. The first was written in Sierra Leone's capital Freetown shortly after his arrival.

> Darling,
> Well, we've got this far. We arrived at the crack of dawn (both with hangovers). Freetown is quite extraordinary: it's just like a sort of multicoloured Georgetown. A charming mess of bad new buildings and lovely clinker built houses on stilts. The first thing that hits you is the difference between these Africans and the Cameroon lot. Ninety per cent of them are really beautiful, particularly the women . . . a wonderful sort of refinement. Imagine a market or a street filled with male and female Harry Belafontes. They are a very lovely shade of pale bronze, and watching the women has given me as much pleasure almost as watching the Fur Seals. With lovely faces and long slender necks they drift down the streets like flocks of elegant deer.

Almost as soon as they landed, offers of help poured in. In the vanguard was the wealthy Diamond Corporation of Sierra Leone, who laid on a chauffeur-driven limousine and luxury quarters in the company's Hollywood-style apartments ('the Dicorp flats') on the edge of town. 'They drove us through the enchanting, multicoloured streets filled with beautiful women,' Gerald wrote to Jacquie, 'out of Freetown and up on to a hill. Here we found the very primitive accommodation from which I am writing. A flat with two double bedrooms, bathroom, bog, sitting-cum-dining room approximately seventy feet by forty, air conditioning in the bedrooms, a steward and, most important, a fridge filled with beer. To cap it all the view from our balcony is straight down over rolling hills to Lumley Beach.'

There was a frustrating wait for the expedition Land-Rovers to arrive on a ship which had been delayed by storms at sea, and then they were ready. 'At last we are off,' Gerald wrote in his letter,

> having in the meantime engaged two charming ruffians called Sadu and Lamin as cook steward and small boy. We set off in great style on the hour we said we would. We had planned to make Kenema that day (it can be done) but on reaching Bo John was so exhausted that we crept into the U.A.C. [United Africa Company] rest house and spent the night. The next day we set off and just outside Bo we hit the laterite, with attendant corrugations and dust. At one point we were so covered with red laterite that we decided to stand in the next local elections.

At Kenema they were informed they could put up at a deserted chrome mine up in the foothills about fourteen miles out of town – a convenient spot, they were assured, to make a base.

> Having told Hartley what terrible privations we would suffer once we got up-country, I was slightly taken aback. The mines themselves were at the base of the escarpment, which is about 800 foot high. Then there is a twisty road leading upwards with something like ten or fifteen perfectly good houses absolutely empty since the mine closed down. Our house is about the size of John Henderson's [in Mamfe]. Big living-dining room, large bedroom, bath and loo, larder place and kitchen attached by covered-in way. Running water and electricity. Bedroom with mosquito proofed windows. From the back veranda we look down over a vast plain with a series of smoothly rounded hills in the distance. We get up before sun up and the whole of the plain is covered with thick white mist, just the tops of the hills showing through. Then the sun comes up directly opposite us looking like a frosted blood orange. We were having tea the other morning and in a tree about fifty yards down the hill a troop of five Red Colobus were feeding: as the sun came up it hit the tree and floodlit it. You can imagine: a vivid green

tree with pink fruit full of monkeys that are jet black on the back with rich fox red on the tummy, throat and insides of arms and legs, all making purring noises like gigantic bees. Behind them was the backdrop, ever changing, of the mist and the mountains . . . It is quite weird living here, like a ghost town, or being the last people left in the world . . .

Darling, I wish you had come on this trip. I wish it for a great variety of personal reasons, but particularly because I know you would have enjoyed it: it has been really Waldorf Astoria all the way, what with air conditioned flats, bathing on Lumley beach, chauffeur driven cars and now this wonderful house cut off from everything. The climate here is not a bit like Cameroons, but more like Corfu, and perched up here in this house it's cool enough in the early morning and evening to wear a sweater. Also the forest is not as high nor so impersonal as the Cameroons: it seems to welcome you. I have never seen so many flowers of so many different colours; everywhere you look there is pink, purple, scarlet, white or yellows in great masses. It's an enchanting country and would give you a completely new idea of West Africa . . .

If the trip is not a success it will not be due to lack of help from both Africans and Europeans. Oh, yes, I have got the Prime Minister to agree to appear in one of the films. I quite frighten myself with my own powers sometimes.

After seeing you briefly in Las Palmas I expected you to write and say you wanted to leave me. I wouldn't have blamed you as I'm far from the perfect husband, but the thought did not make me feel happy.

Darling, life's so bloody short, let's try not to be parted again, either mentally or physically. I know I'm difficult to live with and very demanding, but I will try and reform. The trouble is that when I feel you drifting away from me I get so hurt and angry that I get bloody minded and this makes you drift still further. Let us both love in our own silly ways and try and shove that love on to a sort of no-man's-land where we can both meet.

I miss you terribly. I must end now. I love you. Keep safe and return. Have a wonderful time and return refreshed to me. Send for me should you need me and don't take risks. By God's Power we have a lot more loving to do yet.

I love you now and always.

Gerald's plan was to make a start with the animal collection, so that by the time the BBC crew arrived a fortnight or so later the collecting would be in full swing and they could start shooting without any delay. By the time Gerald wrote to Jacquie again, on 25 February, he had renamed the chrome mine, for some obscure reason, 'The Treacle Mine'. He was later to change the name again, more appropriately, to 'The Beef Mine'.

> Darling,
> ... All goes well with us as I hope it goes with you. We have at long last managed to assemble something like a collection. So far it consists of: two baby male chimps called Fluffy Frogsbottom and Amos Tuttlepenny. Apart from these two thugs we have two Hinge-back tortoise (to John's delight), a Kingfisher, a young Woodford's owl (mental), a mongoose, and the most wonderful baby Genet which measures about five inches in length and is full of personality: I think you will love it, and we can keep it in the flat if you want to. We have called it Pickin. So at least the veranda of our house here looks now as though we are collecting. A woman near Freetown is giving us a tame pair of Timothys (God Help Us All), a forest squirrel of some sort and a python . . .
> John Hartley is shaping very well indeed. He finds driving on these roads in this heat a bit trying (the laterite gets in his eyes) but he never complains. He is first class with the animals, who all take to him, and is very good in his dealings with the Africans . . . He is a very good companion, he does not get flurried and has learnt that in this sort of country a sense of humour and limitless patience are necessary unless you want to go quietly round the bend. In fact I think he'll do.
> Darling, this trip must be doing you good: *two* love letters from you in such a short space of time. Your first one was an injection to my soul, as was the second. I mooned over your first letter like a love-sick schoolboy, and carried it about with me and re-read it at frequent intervals. Unfortunately, they have a mania for washing clothes here, and I had the letter in the pocket of my pyjamas (so I could re-read it last thing at night) and the idiot washboy seized them the following morning and washed them, letter and all. By the time I had discovered this all the ink had run. I was furious. Luckily I had read it so many times I knew it by heart.
> Darling, I miss you like Hell. What I miss most is that I can't talk to you . . . I am hoping that when Chris and all arrive there

will be so much work to do that I won't have time to miss you, but I doubt it. I want your physical presence. It is now ten to ten: blue sky, sun, cool wind and I am writing this and drinking beer. Outside I can hear the staff giggling over some joke, the carpenter banging away, and the chimps 'oooooing' over some tit bit they have found. I can see the great bush of scarlet and mauve bougainvillaea at the end of the veranda alive with purple and green sunbirds. This is all fun, but you are not here and so every sound and every colour is slightly off key: like looking at a sunset through dark glasses . . .

I love you so much, and I can't wait to hold you and kiss you again. Please keep safe and don't do anything silly; remember that a woman alone anywhere in the world is lawful prey. Come back to me safe and happy and love me a little. You say that you need me: double that feeling and you will know what my views are on my need for you – you are my life.

Day by day the animal collection increased and the filming proceeded. Two major animal requirements were still lacking, however – leopard and colobus monkey. The only way to catch colobus, it was clear, was to organise a monkey drive through the forest with the help of the local Africans, who were well versed in this method of hunting. But dreaming up a monkey drive was one thing: pushing it through was another, as Gerald recounted to Jacquie.

Darling,
All goes well with us but it is, as I feared, a fight against time and African procrastination. We are working among the Mendes, and for sheer inertia they knock the Mamfe-ites into a cocked hat. Example: go to village. Flock of forty odd black and red Colobus in trees *not one hundred yards from village*. Film them. Good. In village elders all swinging in hammocks: say what about monkey drive. My dear chap, they say, we get monkeys time no dere. But, should you wish to have monkey by the score we can jack it up for Tuesday. Now, are you quite sure about this, says you. Yes, says they, monkey we get time no dere; no be palaver for catch um. Good says you, we go come back Tuesday, early morning time. Ah arrrrrrrrrrrrrr! says everyone. So you go back on Tuesday morning early early and you still find the elders swinging on their hammocks. Which side monkey drive, you ask in a spirit of inquiry (I'm starting to write pidgin now)? Ah arrrrrrrrrrrrrrrrrrrrrrr they all say, dis village na small village; we do no get SURFISHNT

young men for monkey drive. Ef you go bring some men from Kenema we go catch you monkey time no dere ... whole day wasted by the time you have driven there, done your nut and driven back. I told the BBC that I needed time to organise this sort of thing. This is the last BBC trip I do, except on my own terms. To be paid fuck all money and be expected to produce a Hollywood epic is a bit much, and I am getting too old for it.

Pause while we go on monkey drive.

Later. Well, after all the unkind things I writ above we have at last met with success. We organised a big drive in a village and it really came to something. We had fifty-three Africans (so you can imagine the noise) and they tracked down some red and black Colobus, drove them into a suitable tree, and then proceeded to hack down all undergrowth around the tree. Then a fire was lighted at the base of the tree and the monkeys all dashed down and into the nets. It was terribly noisy (perfect for sound on film) and exciting. The monkeys behaved wonderfully, all getting themselves caught within a few feet of the camera. Every time they caught a monkey all fifty-three Africans would break into a sort of triumphant chant ... wonderful stuff that makes the stuff in *Zulu* look tame. It will make a wonderful climax if we don't get pigmy hippo (and I don't think we will) and so Chris is like a dog with two tails. But it really is tremendously spectacular stuff ... knocks David [Attenborough] into a cocked hat ... and the sound on film makes the whole thing so real. We jacked up a sequence the other day of John and I catching a huge monitor lizard in a pool. As I rushed after it I got my foot caught between two rocks under the water: 'Oh, bugger it,' says I, 'I've got my bloody foot caught.' Chris is going to leave this in, so we are really trying to get naturalness into the programmes ...

Just recently we have all had a mild go of sandfly fever. Hartleypools first, then Chris, and now me. So I am writing this in bed where they have insisted I go. But this is a much more healthy place than the Cameroons, and we have all been very well. I must say our staff (an irritating, shiftless, ham handed, mentally defective and utterly charming bunch) have thrown themselves into the work with wild delight. Every new arrival is crooned over, they listen to the recording we make with great attention, and take part in the film shots acting and delivering their line with consummate acting ability.

Now to more important matters. Darling, I love you so much.

Nothing I do or see or eat or feel is the same, because you are not here. And then, after all I have written to you, I find that you haven't got the bloody letters. I think of you all the time, and I have never wanted to get back from a trip so much. I want to lie in a warm bed with you and kiss you and feel your silky body under my hands; I want to see you in a rage when you go all white and lose your breath; I want to see you in the bath with your hair all covered with soap, looking about five years old. I want you more than hunger or thirst affects one . . .

I love you G.

PS . . . I am dirty, love-sick and full of faults. But I love you and, if ever one human being can possess another, you have me. I wish you were here.

To say that I miss you is stupid, it's rather like saying: 'Isn't it curious, the sun fell out of the sky yesterday . . . do you find it dark?' It's rather like being deprived of both arms and a pair of eyes. If you are willing, I never intend it to happen again – not of my making. You said I have changed, and everyone does, but the one thing that has changed in the right direction (probably the only thing I have done that *has*) is that my love for you has increased to the extent where it is not just a feeling but a physical pain, rather like walking round with a few red-hot coals under your ribs. We do not live forever and while I am alive I want nobody else but you. If you left me tomorrow, and this was best for you, then OK . . . With you – and without anything else – I have the whole world. Without you I am nothing.

Goodnight and I wish to fucking hell you were here.

I love you. G.

Then came the setbacks. Though the black and white Colobus monkeys that had been caught in the monkey drive gradually settled down, the red and black ones grew sullen and morose and seemed to withdraw into themselves, eating next to nothing. Eventually it became obvious that there was no alternative but to let them go, and this, with great regret, Gerald did. At around the same time Gerald suffered an accident that threatened his further participation in the venture. He had been sitting on the tailgate of the BBC Land-Rover when the vehicle hit an enormous bump at speed and he was thrown upwards and sideways, badly bruising (perhaps cracking) the base of his spine and breaking two ribs. Henceforth he was in pain every time he sat down, or bent down, or even breathed. Doing the filming and the work that the collection required was difficult, and as the pain increased Gerald realised he would need help on the voyage home. He sent a cable asking Jacquie, who had recently arrived back in Britain, if she could possibly come out to join him, which she did.

Gerald was not there to greet her when she disembarked at Freetown, and arrived to find her standing in the docks and 'looking mutinous'. The reunion was unusually tense, as he recorded later.

'Where have you been?' she said, as a nice, wifely greeting.

'Trying to get on to the bloody docks,' I said.

She came forward to kiss me and I said, 'Don't squeeze me too hard because I've got a broken rib.'

'What the hell have you been doing?' she asked belligerently. 'Have you been to see a doctor? Are you strapped up?'

So, after this demonstrative greeting of a husband and wife who had been parted for some four months, we made our way to the Land-Rover and drove back to the flat.

A fleet of army lorries took the animals down to the docks, and the cages were slung on board, followed by Gerald, Jacquie, John Hartley and Ann Peters (a 'brisk and efficient blonde' who had flown out to help), along with Chris Parsons and his cameraman and sound recordist. The voyage home was uneventful, but the onward flight from Liverpool to Jersey was a nightmare. 'How Durrell stood the strain of coping with his rib, his tiredness and the worry of the animals, I shall honestly never know,' Jacquie was to recall, 'but I felt he was pretty near to collapse.' By comparison, most of the animals were completely unaffected by the stress and strain, and happily settled into their new quarters in the zoo.

'Durrell was happy, as indeed we all were,' wrote Jacquie, 'and he could now collapse – at least for another twenty-four hours.'

NINETEEN

Volcano Rabbits and the King of Corfu

1965–1968

Though the expedition had not been entirely fun, it had been broadly successful. 'Just back from Sierra Leone,' Gerald wrote to a friend in New Zealand on 2 June 1965. 'We got a very nice collection of 90-odd animals, the rarest and most important of which are 7 black and white colobus monkeys and a pair of nice young leopards.' The homecoming had been gratifyingly upbeat as well. 'One of the best bits of news on my return,' Gerald continued, 'was that our pair of Tuataras had hibernated, so we are keeping our fingers crossed that we will go down to their house one day and find lots of baby Tuataras galloping about the place . . .'

Gerald now began to write up his account of the expedition to the Antipodes and Far East of four years before, to which he gave the same title as the television series based on it, *Two in the Bush*. While he was thus occupied, Jacquie decided to try her hand at writing her own account of her life with Gerald, his family and other animals – to be called *Beasts in my Bed* – and advertised in the local paper for a secretary with shorthand to take it down and type it up. One of the applicants was an attractive young blonde by the name of Doreen Evans, whose parents had recently moved to Jersey. When she turned up at the manor for her interview, she was confronted not just by Jacquie, but by Gerald and Catha Weller as well. Halfway through, Gerald leaned across and put a question to her.

'Would you,' he asked, 'be prepared, if need be, to breastfeed a baby hedgehog?'

His voice was deadpan, but Doreen could tell from his eyes that it was a joke. 'That's when I realised we had a lot in common,' she recalled '– that and a common love of nature and the countryside.'

During the early part of 1966 Doreen typed Jacquie's book in a small office at the top of the manor, with two lovebirds in a cage for company.

When she had finished she was asked if she would like to stay on as Gerald's secretary and take down *his* next book as well.

This book was to mark a departure for Gerald. He now found himself confronting the dilemma which eventually faces all non-fiction authors whose books are based on their own adventures: the adventures begin to dry up – or at any rate, the zest and sense of novelty that the author once felt in undertaking them. Travelling round Sierra Leone with a film crew at the age of forty was not the same as plunging into the Cameroon rainforest for the first time at the age of twenty-two. One way out of the dilemma was to change genre, to move from non-fiction to fiction and write about what was inside one's head rather than in front of one's eye. Gerald was not sure whether he had the talent to do this, but he could try. His next book, he decided, would be a fictional story for children, to be called *The Donkey Rustlers* and set in Greece. This was not too daunting a challenge. He was half-child himself, and a born raconteur, and he loved Greece. He chose to compose this new work in a new way – by telling the story out loud to his new secretary.

'We started at about ten in his office,' Doreen Evans recalled. 'He planned the whole book first. Then he planned the chapters in his mind. He set himself a target of a chapter a day. He didn't have any notes and he didn't make a lot of corrections, he just walked up and down telling the story to me, and if any of it made me laugh then he'd laugh too, with that bubbly giggle of his. After lunch I'd type it up and he'd read it at the end of the afternoon in his sitting room, walking up and down smoking his Gauloises cigarettes. Most of his writing seemed to involve walking up and down when I knew him.'

Doreen also handled Gerald's fan mail. Though he couldn't answer every letter himself, he always made a point of signing every reply personally, and he was particularly attentive to letters from children and young people. *My Family and Other Animals* had recently been chosen as a set book for GCE examinations in England, so a lot of letters from schoolchildren coming in – 'How do I become a zoo keeper?' or 'There's something wrong with my budgie and what can I do to make him better?' 'He treated the kids' letters with as much attention as if it was a scientist writing about a rare species,' Doreen remembered. 'They were the next generation and they needed to be encouraged in their love of animals. That's how he had been when he was a little boy and he knew how important it was to help a child.'

In February 1966 the BBC began transmitting *Catch me a Colobus*, the series of six television programmes shot on the Sierra Leone expedition. It was well received. 'There is no better practitioner in this field of interest than Gerald Durrell,' wrote the *Times Educational Supplement*. 'The Colobus is an elusive little African monkey with a fantastic capacity for leaping from tree to tree and outsmarting his pursuers. Gerald Durrell's documentary of his efforts to capture these agile creatures has been a weekly delight, for it has involved not only the excitement of the chase but also a sympathetic and amusing depiction of the Africans whom he recruited to assist him. Gerald Durrell never cheats, he never sacrifices veracity to satisfy the whims of a cameraman. He is also a most expressive and perceptive narrator, and his running commentary has been as brilliant as the photography. He has produced one more television classic in natural history.'

The programmes roused enough interest for the *Daily Mail* to send a reporter to Jersey to find out what sort of fellow Gerald Durrell was. What he was, the reporter discovered, was someone disturbingly different from the comic writer and cuddly animal-lover of his popular image. Instead, here was a man whose capacity for concern had brought him near to the end of his tether, a man close to buckling under the weight of humanity's guilt. You could get people to watch a series like *Colobus*, Gerald told the reporter, but they didn't want to know about the larger issues. They didn't think it concerned them when forests were pulped for paper napkins, when topsoil was destroyed by the quick crops of greed, when species were made extinct. It was so difficult to get these ideas across, he said, it was like mumbling in his beard. Even other naturalists asked: 'What are you getting aerated about, Durrell? This is an inevitable process.' But it had to be stopped. Half the animals he had on display at the zoo were rare, threatened, or liable to be threatened.

He handed the reporter a horned toad, handling it as if it were an Etruscan vase. 'Get some of that mud off and it's lovely,' he said. 'People ask what use it is. They never stop to wonder what use *they* are. Why should anything go for a burton because of greed? It's got a right to live.' Sometimes he felt he was doing something useful, he went on. Then a letter would come in from a television viewer who hadn't quite got the message. 'One of my correspondents said that I was the most evil man he knew. It was against God's law to shut up little creatures in cages. If he had his way he'd have me locked in a cage for life. There's a snag in that argument somewhere, don't you think?'

On 16 May 1966 Gerald, Jacquie and Doreen Evans left Jersey to drive in slow and easy stages through France and Italy – 'eating every mile of the way' – to Venice and the leisurely sea-ferry voyage down the unspoiled Dalmatian coast to Corfu. Gerald had four aims – to take time off on his beloved island, to dictate another book, to look at locations for a proposed BBC film about his childhood on Corfu, and to find an old villa to live in or land to build on. They stayed in a flat belonging to Philippa Sanson, Theo Stephanides' sister – a huge apartment occupying three sides of the top floor of an old Venetian building at 35 Arseniou Street on Corfu town's waterfront overlooking the harbour. The flat was sparsely furnished, so they were obliged almost to camp in it.

Gerald's routine was invariable, Doreen recalled.

He'd get up at crack of dawn, around five-ish, and make me a cup of tea with condensed milk in a big thick green cup. Then I'd get dressed and he'd start dictating, walking up and down the huge sitting room with its wonderful view over the sea and the little islands. He'd do this till about mid-morning and then that would be it for the day, and I'd type it all up while Jacquie was out buying things for lunch – chicken and tomatoes and fresh bread and yoghurt and so on – and then we'd all set off for an olive grove by the sea somewhere. Barbati was a favourite place, a long unspoiled beach some way out to the north of the town. There'd be no one else there in those days, just the keeper of the olives, and we'd swim and have a picnic under the olives and the almond trees, and then Gerry would read what I'd typed and perhaps make a few corrections and have a siesta. Then when the sun started going down we'd potter slowly back. Sometimes we'd stop at a little place called Luciola's at Ipsos, which hadn't been built up like it is now. There was a little restaurant there which sold the most wonderful chicken pies and had green tree frogs in the trees, and we'd sit there having our evening meal, which in Corfu could take a long time, and drinking our wine. Occasionally we'd go for a picnic to the south of the island, which was further away, and then when we got back we'd eat in Gerry's favourite restaurant in town, called Themis, near the Platia, which was run by a friend of his called Vassili. Quite rarely we ate in and Gerry would do the cooking. His fish pies were very good, but his prawn Provençale, with prawns fresh out of the sea and herbs fresh out of the ground, was absolutely brilliant. We'd sit in camp chairs round the huge dining table and have a few drinks while Jacquie played her favourite classical music on the gramophone, and the air outside would be warm and the sea starlit.

One day they went to a cricket match between Corfu and the British Fleet – a match the Fleet had strict instructions to lose – and one evening they went night fishing, the phosphorus shining like fire on the water and their hands, trailed in the sea, coming up 'dripping with diamonds'. So the summer passed.

In early September they were back in Jersey. Lawrence and Claude moved into a big house they had bought in Sommières at the end of that month, and Gerald and Jacquie took over the Mazet near Nîmes on a two-year lease, the beginning of an association that was to last the rest of Gerald's life.

By now *Two in the Bush*, Gerald's account of his six-month filming expedition through New Zealand, Australia and Malaya in search of rare animals with the BBC Natural History Unit, had been published in Britain. By this time Gerald had changed publishers. Amid some bitterness and recrimination he had (at Jacquie's suggestion) moved from Hart-Davis, who had subbed him at the start of his careers as an author and zoo-owner, to the richer pastures of William Collins, who ran a large and successful natural history list. The reviews of Gerald's first Collins book were mostly favourable. The *Daily Mail* thought it 'delightfully readable and often very funny', while the *Evening Standard* proclaimed that it would 'delight fans and armchair naturalists everywhere'. Maurice Wiggin in the *Sunday Times* found it 'Easy to read, difficult to put down, with many sidelights on the human side of the expedition. This absorbing narrative reveals the ardours, ironies and disappointments, the organisational miracles and the hilarious human mishaps, which lie beneath the bland, sure surface of Mr Durrell's nature films.'

Towards the end of 1966 the Trust held its annual grand fund-raising ball for members, well-wishers and the island's high society. The event was a great success, the highlight being the arrival of a regal-looking, dark-skinned, clean-shaven gentleman, splendidly garbed not in the statutory dinner jacket but the robes of the deputy chief of the kingdom of Bafut. He was greeted as the celebrated Fon himself, but closer examination revealed a pair of twinkling blue European eyes and a voice that spoke pidgin English in an unexpectedly cultured accent. So the ruse was laid bare – Gerry had arrived at the Black and White Ball disguised as the all-black Fon, having shaved off his beard for the first and only time in his life in order to perfect the disguise.

By this time much of the fund-raising on the island was in the hands of Lady Saranne Calthorpe, a young woman who had become a close friend of Gerald and Jacquie. She had first come into their life a year or so before, when Gerald had met her by chance at Jersey airport selling flags for a local charity, and was bowled over by her beauty, intelligence and Irish charm. Born in Eire, she had been an Aer Lingus air hostess before marrying one of its pilots, a hereditary Irish peer by the name of

Peter Somerset, Lord Calthorpe. At Gerald and Jacquie's invitation, Saranne Calthorpe teamed up with Lady Jersey to organise many of the Trust's fund-raising events on the island – balls, recitals and the like – and to approach Jersey's richer residents for donations.

But funds raised in this way could provide only a drop in the ocean of what was now desperately needed. During the winter of 1966–67 the zoo faced its worst crisis yet. There was no money to pay the staff's wages or the bills for the animals' feed. With the National Provincial Bank in St Helier on the verge of foreclosing, Gerald sought out its manager, Ray Le Cornu, to make a last-ditch plea for a stay of execution. He was in bed at home with 'flu, but Gerald knocked on his door one evening clutching a bottle of champagne – his panacea for all ills. For an hour he sat on the edge of the bank manager's bed, desperately pleading his case and using all his formidable powers of persuasion to change the sick man's mind. At last Le Cornu agreed to give the zoo one more chance, then turned over, exhausted, and fell into a fitful slumber as a grateful Gerald tiptoed out of the house. From that moment everything changed. Upon receipt of the news, Lord Jersey stepped in, offering to pay the staff's wages and to help keep the place afloat till the spring.

At this time most of the animals were still housed in the makeshift cages the zoo had started with, and the main thrust of the enterprise, captive breeding, was not yet properly under way. If the zoo was to develop, it was clear that substantial funds would have to be raised.

'We have formulated a ten-year plan,' Gerald announced, 'which will require £200,000 to complete [£2 million in today's money]. Of this £100,000 will be spent on property expansion and new buildings and £100,000 for the wider objects of the Trust.' The public could help by becoming members of the Trust, or by making donations or sponsoring particular projects.

Even while he was writing this report, Gerald reckoned, four animal species had been irretrievably lost to the world for ever, and the fate of four more – the orang utan, the okapi, the whooping crane and Leadbeater's opossum – hung in the balance. The situation was dire, the need overwhelming.

In the meantime he remained preoccupied with Corfu. Earlier in the year he had approached his BBC friend Chris Parsons about a possible television adaptation of *My Family and Other Animals*. For a few days that summer he had taken Parsons around some of the key locations on Corfu. Beguiled by both the story and the locations, Parsons had proposed devoting an entire evening to Corfu on BBC 2, which was about to start Britain's first colour television service under its new controller, David

Attenborough. Parsons' idea was for the Corfu evening to be structured around an adaptation of *My Family*, with travel and natural history programming thrown in.

When David Attenborough pointed out that the Natural History Unit had no experience of drama production, Gerald came up with the idea of a more straightforward documentary, to be called *The Garden of the Gods*, in which he would revisit the haunts of his island childhood. Gerald dreamed up the device of travelling round the island with his town-bred 'godson', played by Andreas Damaskinos (son of Corfu's Director of Tourism), a kind of junior *doppelgänger* invented for the film, who would look at the wonders of Corfu through the eyes of just such a boy as Gerald had been, but with Gerald as his mentor; at the same time Gerald would be accompanied by his own real-life mentor from boyhood days, the now-venerable Theo Stephanides.

Gerald looked forward with great anticipation to the making of the film on Corfu during the coming summer. But his spirits were quickly dashed by dire news from France. On New Year's Day 1967 Claude – the one real love of Lawrence's life – died in a Geneva clinic, succumbing quite suddenly to pulmonary cancer, leaving Lawrence bereft and Gerald 'very upset and worried' about his brother.

Some distraction from the pervading family grief was provided by the new book Gerald was writing, a comic novel (his first work of adult fiction) entitled *Rosy is my Relative*, and by the arrival of Chris Parsons and his television crew to shoot a programme for a new series called *Animal People*, one of the first to be made in colour by the BBC. Each programme was to be about a well-known figure who was involved in some way with animals – Peter Scott was another of the subjects. Shot over a period of nearly two weeks, the Jersey film attempted to portray a typical day at the Trust headquarters from dawn to dusk, ending with an evening sequence in Gerald and Jacquie's living-room in the flat in the manor house. Chris Parsons recalled:

> I knew from personal experience that this was an extremely enjoy-
> able part of the day. I had always looked forward to the moment
> when the animals had the floor – literally. Firstly, there was Keeper,
> an amiable boxer who loafed around the Durrells' flat most of the
> day. Then there were the African squirrels which lived in cages in
> the corner of the sitting room. Undoubtedly the squirrel with the
> most attractive personality of all was Timothy, an African ground
> squirrel. In the evening, when the traffic in and out of the Durrells'
> flat had died down, Timothy's cage was opened. This usually sig-

nalled the start of an hour's entertainment which was better than any night-club cabaret I had seen. For it seems that African ground squirrels are nature's comics – at least Timothy was – and his routine and thorough inspection of the room and its occupants was conducted with such mischievous showmanship and perfect timing that every little action brought ripples of applause.

What with the camera and the lights and a room full of technicians, it took several evenings of filming before Timothy could be said to be 'in the can'. This provoked Gerald to indulge in a little good-humoured mischief of his own. When the filming was finished, he wrote a lengthy letter to the Programme Executive at BBC Bristol, Frank Sherratt, whose facility fee for shooting at the zoo he considered none too generous, announcing that he had been appointed agent for the two animals which had performed in the film, and that he wished to negotiate terms on behalf of his clients:

Timothy Testicle was required to have his own private room infested by a vast series of lights, combined with an array of ham-handed and apparently inebriated technicians and was then expected to go through a routine that would have made even Bertram Mills' wife think. He was expected to do a Bolshoi ballet across the carpet; to lie supine upon a large and potentially savage carnivore, to wit a dog; to stand on his hind legs with his nose wiffling (looking not unlike a young BBC producer) and then undergo the ignominious experience of lying upside down in my wife's hands, displaying an astonishing proportion of his more intimate anatomy, while giggling hysterically.

I think you will agree, my dear Mr Sherratt, that as he so willingly took part in something for which he had not signed a contract, it is up to the Corporation to show a certain amount of generosity. I am therefore empowered on his behalf to request the Corporation for the following fee:

    1 cwt bag of hazel nuts
    300 copies of the Radio Times (for bed-making)
    2 bottles of Chanel No 5
    A year's supply of Smith's potato crisps
    1 female ground squirrel, approximately 3 years old and of
        an uninhibited disposition.

For Keeper the dog Gerald requested a similar 'fee', including a boxer bitch, four tons of chocolate drops and 'a yearly visit from the lady at Tring whom I believe has made a life work of collecting fleas'.

On 23 May 1967 Gerald, Jacquie and Doreen Evans arrived back on Corfu, where they again stayed in the flat in Arseniou Street. Gerald had sent Spencer Curtis Brown the typescript of *Rosy is my Relative* shortly before leaving Jersey, and he found a rather negative response from Collins waiting for him in Corfu: the editor wanted to change the title, it seemed, and much of the story as well. Gerald dug his toes in. 'You know I have not got a very high opinion of myself as an author,' he protested to Curtis Brown, 'and am perfectly prepared to have things changed at the editor's discretion, but I am terribly sorry I am absolutely firm on the point of the title. It is to be called *Rosy is my Relative* or else it is not going to be published at all and you can send the MS back to me. I am here for a rest which I desperately need, so I am not prepared to do a lot of re-writing at this juncture for what I consider to be silly reasons.'

In July the Durrells were joined by Theo Stephanides, now a white-bearded old gentleman with the bearing of a soldier and the air of a Victorian naturalist. When Chris Parsons and an unusually large BBC production crew flew in for the start of shooting on *The Garden of the Gods* they checked in to the Aegli Hotel, owned by Menelaos Condos, a childhood friend of Gerald's, on the road below the Snow-White Villa and Strawberry-Pink Villa, and conveniently close to many of the locations in the film: the chessboard fields, the Venetian salt-pans, the olive woods, the small hills, and the bay and Mouse Island just across the water. The filming was scheduled to last a month, and was timed to coincide with the festival commemorating St Spiridyon, the patron saint of Corfu, whose embalmed body is carried in grand procession through the streets in a special casket.

'*The Garden of the Gods* was a particularly enjoyable film to make,' Chris Parsons recalled, 'because it involved such a delightful mixture of topics. There was a little of the history of Corfu, something of its music and dance, beautiful scenery, and running through it all, a series of incidents concerning wildlife – usually linked to memories of Gerry's childhood experiences or lessons with Theodore.'

But there were jarring undertones. 'For me,' Parsons confessed, 'the experience was spoilt a bit by a running battle with Jacquie going on in the background.' This was due in large part to Jacquie's determination to keep Gerald's workload to a minimum following a mild heart disturbance he had suffered in Jersey earlier in the year. For Gerry things were spoiled by the sheer impossibility of revisiting paradise, let alone recreating it, in the irreverent, knockabout ambience of a film crew on location. He grew morose, feeling the emotional burden of his past was being compromised by the human mêlée of the present, and he complained loudly to camera about the plastic bottles, ice-cream cartons and other debris left by the tourist trade along the island's once-pristine shores. 'In such a vein,' Parsons recalled, 'Gerry wouldn't listen to reason and he could become maddeningly opinionated and bigoted and extraordinarily irritating. But he was so endearing and charming in other respects you just put up with it.' On screen Gerald, still only forty-two, looked fit and well, swam and rowed boats with gusto, presenting a charismatic, powerful, unusually serious presence – so serious, indeed, that he gave little impression of having much sense of humour at all.

This was to be the last film Chris Parsons would make with Gerald, whose personality, he believed, never quite came across on camera. 'He would be terribly polite and self-effacing in front of camera,' Parsons recalled. 'He was at his best when he was relaxed and informal, and then the Durrell charm would come out and he'd become a different person – a terrific raconteur, totally indiscreet, very rude, utterly bawdy – the sort of stuff you couldn't put on air except on some obscure cable channel in the middle of the night.'

King Constantine of Greece was staying on Corfu that summer with his wife Queen Anne-Marie and his mother Frederika, an ardent conservationist and animal lover. When he heard that Gerald was making a film on the island he invited him and Jacquie to lunch at his palace. The other guests included the King's uncle Prince George of Hanover and his wife Sophia and the future Queen of Spain. 'I am not a royalist and approached them with some doubts and misgivings,' Jacquie recalled, 'but I was won over by their "normalcy". We found them all a charming, amusing bunch and thoroughly enjoyed the whole thing. I remember the King and his sister exchanging bread rolls over the heads of the others; the wine flowed and the food was excellent (not Greek!) The King was genuinely interested in Gerry's views on everything and Gerry didn't tone down his remarks at all, save for not swearing, as was his wont when talking about contentious subjects and human folly. Both appeared to be in agreement about most things. Queen Frederika naturally took part, and the King offered to fly Gerry around the mainland and the islands to see the environmental situation for himself. But it was not to be. Greece was now under the rule of the Colonels and before long the Monarchy was abolished and the Royal Family sent into exile.'

Gerald and Jacquie returned to Jersey in the middle of September 1967. Not long afterwards, Gerald's attention was drawn to the plight of a strange little rabbit called the volcano rabbit, or teporingo, which was found only on the slopes of the volcanoes round Mexico City and was in imminent danger of extinction, through encroachment by cattle and crops. On paper the volcano rabbit was a protected species, but the Mexican authorities found it almost impossible to patrol the area in which it lived, and though its flesh was not good to eat and its fur was useless for commercial purposes, local hunters liked to use it for target practice and for training their hunting dogs. 'This, I thought, was a job for the Trust,' Gerald was to record. 'It was an animal we could easily cope with because of its small size, and I felt certain that, with a certain amount of patience and perseverance, we would be able to do it.' There were some technical problems – the rabbit fed exclusively on zacaton grass (alfalfa), which was unobtainable in Jersey, and lived at altitude, while Jersey was at almost sea level – but Gerald reckoned it was worth a shot. So the Mexican expedition was born, a kind of conservation lightning strike, the plan being to secure enough rabbits to form a viable breeding colony at Jersey Zoo and thus save the species from extinction.

On 15 January 1968 Gerald and Jacquie, Doreen Evans and Peggy Peel, a BBC friend, sailed from Antwerp on board the German cargo boat the SS *Remschied*. Three weeks later they arrived in Vera Cruz, Mexico, and shortly afterwards were joined by Shep Mallet, Curator of Birds at the zoo, and an Anglo-American student by the name of Dix Branch, resident in Mexico, who acted as interpreter, driver and general factotum.

During the first week the party travelled south to the Guatemalan border looking for various species of rare birds, particularly the thick-billed parrot, another creature in danger of extinction. Then they set up their headquarters in a flat in Mexico City, within easy reach of the volcanoes where the rabbits eked out their perilous existence. The prospects were not wildly promising. No visitors from abroad had ever shown any interest in the rabbits before, the local zoo had no specimens and the Mexican Fauna Department could offer little assistance. Most people who heard about Gerald's plans shook their heads sombrely and declared the project would be *muy difícil*.

One difficulty was the very scarcity of the animals on the ground. Another was the terrain where they lived – the vast, rough and (at ten to sixteen thousand feet) exceedingly high slopes of the great snow-capped volcanoes of Popocatepetl and Ixtaccihuatl. Another difficulty was that the guards of the Popocatepetl National Park, who were supposed to protect the rabbits, often caught and ate them instead.

The first foray after the rabbits was to prove typical. Gerald wanted to be on the spot before dawn, hoping to find the rabbits as they came out of their burrows, so the party had to leave their flat at four-thirty in the morning. By the time the sun was rising they were high on the slopes of

Popocatepetl, bouncing about in their Land-Rover across Alpine terrain, everything still and no sign of life anywhere. All day they searched and toiled, breathless in the thin, high air. At one point a volcano rabbit scuttled across their path and vanished into the thick grass. In a clearing in a wood they found some rabbit droppings, and first one burrow, and then another. But the first was found to be empty, and the second contained nothing but a tuft of fluff. All day they dug in the black lava soil – volcano rabbit burrows can be forty feet long – but not another rabbit did they see.

The disappointment was acute, and Gerald lapsed into a state of gloom. Back in the flat in Mexico City he sat slumped in silence in a chair. He barely moved, his face was dark and haggard-looking, and Peggy Peel began to wonder whether he might not be suffering from something more substantial than mere disappointment – the beginnings of some sort of clinical depression, perhaps.

On their second sortie the party drove to a different part of the volcanoes, climbing up to fifteen thousand feet from the little town of Amecameca. They had the help of a number of local Indians this time, and after working hard all morning they achieved their first success, digging out a female teporingo. The excitement was palpable. They were on their way – or so they thought. The teporingo was an appealing little creature, chocolate brown in colour and very small. 'Gerry pointed out how she differed from the rabbits we know,' noted Peggy Peel. 'Apart from a difference in skull formation, her ears were much smaller and her tail almost invisible, hidden in her fur. Apparently teporingos don't hop in a rabbit-like way, but run everywhere. And they have a "voice" – they communicate through little, muffled squeaks. But one of the most interesting things about them are their fleas. It's a kind of prehistoric flea, only previously found in fossils, before it was discovered alive and kicking on the teporingo.'

The rabbit was borne off in triumph to Mexico City, where she readily adapted to a diet of apples, carrots and alfalfa, and soon became very tame. But what good was a single rabbit if your plan was to establish a breeding colony? Gerald abandoned the idea of catching the rabbits himself – the altitude was too exhausting, the rabbits too elusive. Instead he resorted to a method he had first refined in his early days as an animal collector in the Cameroons – pay the locals to catch the animals for you. For three weeks the search continued as the local Indians dug away in the hot, dusty ground high on the volcanoes. But time was running out, and Gerald grew increasingly despondent, for he faced the prospect of returning to Jersey with only a single rabbit to show for an expensive three-month expedition – an absolute failure by any standards. Then, in the middle of March, four more volcano rabbits were brought in – but all of them were female. And that, it seemed, was that. No male – so no breeding colony in Jersey.

A few days later Shep Mallet flew home, taking with him the five female teporingos and some rare birds (most notably three pairs of thick-billed parrots, along with breeding groups of Mexican black-bellied tree ducks and Emerald toucanets). Five days later the rest of the party sailed from Mexico on board the cargo boat *Sonderburg*, bound for Antwerp on a five-week voyage via the southern United States. Dix Branch remained behind, charged with the task of finding a male teporingo by fair means or foul, somewhere, sometime, somehow . . .

On the voyage out to Mexico Gerald had dictated the first half of his new book, a long-awaited sequel to *My Family*. On the long voyage home he managed to dictate the second half, but his thoughts remained with the volcano rabbits, and after arriving back in Jersey in early May he waited anxiously for word from Dix Branch. Eventually Branch was able to procure six more rabbits, two of them male, and had them flown to London at once. Held up by red tape at London Airport while awaiting onward freighting to Jersey, one of the males died. In Jersey the remaining male and two of the females died of a disease called coccidiosis, and though four baby volcano rabbits were born at the zoo, all of them were female and three of them died in infancy. This left a non-viable colony of eight female rabbits – all there was to show for months of endeavour. Today the volcano rabbit is still threatened with extinction.

This failure was counterbalanced by success with the white eared pheasant – Jersey Zoo's first really significant breakthrough in the captive breeding of endangered species. The white eared pheasant was a graceful and beautiful bird which once inhabited the highlands of China and Tibet, but due to hunting and habitat destruction was on the verge of extinction. Only eighteen birds existed in captivity, none of them capable of breeding. Jersey Zoo was fortunate to obtain two pairs of white eared pheasant from a dealer in Holland, and, against the odds, succeeded in breeding them. Gerald wrote: 'It was a red-letter day for us when Shep Mallet and I stood gazing fondly at no less than thirteen delicate and fluffy babies clad in fawn down marked with chocolate blotches, who peeped and trotted around their bantam foster-mother like so many wind-up clockwork toys.' If these birds were indeed extinct in the wild state, as was feared, Jersey Zoo had made a major contribution to their conservation.

By the time Gerald had settled back into the manor house he had completed his new book and given it the title *Birds, Beasts and Relatives*. Spencer Curtis Brown seemed to like it, Gerald told Alan Thomas, 'but whether any of the family will still be speaking to me after it is published I really don't know'.

As an antidote to the desecration of modern Corfu, Gerald found it therapeutic to try and recreate yet again the unspoiled wonderland of his childhood. Corfu never lacked the power to reawaken in him the yearning for the sensuous languor, the freedom and wonder of his island childhood, as his latest book again made clear.

Birds, Beasts and Relatives was published the following year to unanimous family approval and highly favourable reviews. 'A delightful book, full of simple, long-known things,' wrote Gavin Maxwell in the *New York Times Book Review*, 'but above all, childhood moulded by these things and recalled intimately in middle age.' The *Sunday Times* went further: 'He effortlessly immerses us in the glittering bays and sun-shivered olive groves, teeming with weird astonishments – the private life of the rotifer, the mating of snails in impassive hermaphrodite bliss, the use of a female cuttlefish on heat to catch ardent, undistractable males. The expert's scrutiny is blended with the boy's wondering gaze in a way Hudson himself never excelled. The crystal-clear dreamworld he has made of it, that gives delight and hurts not, expands the spirit and demands our gratitude.'

In June there was another tremor in the ranks of the Durrell family when brother Leslie and his wife Doris precipitately decamped from Kenya, arriving back in England with only the clothes they stood up in and £75 between them. They were put up in the attic flatlet of Margaret's house in St Alban's Avenue while they tried to sort themselves out.

Leslie, it seemed, had got himself into a bit of a mess in Africa, and Gerald had first heard of the developing scandal the previous autumn. On 6 October 1967 a Mr Wailes had written to Gerald from South Devon to inform him that 'your brother Leslie has got himself into considerable financial trouble and this unfortunately involved my mother, at Diani Beach, Mombasa. Leslie informs my mother that he has written to you in this connection.' Leslie, it seems, had conned the woman out of a substantial sum while he was working as bursar at a school near Mombasa on the Kenyan coast. Gerald immediately fired off an angry letter to his brother: 'It seems you have implied that I would be willing to get you out of whatever mess you have got yourself into,' he fumed. 'I am not in any position to help you financially and I do strongly object to receiving letters from complete strangers implying that my only function in life is to rescue you and save their mothers.' Not only would Gerald not help;

he wanted nothing to do with a criminal sibling whose antics might taint the reputation of the Trust if ever the press got hold of the story. With nowhere else to turn, the helpless Leslie lost his job and the house that went with it. With Africanisation in full swing in Kenya following independence, his prospects of finding another job were virtually zero, so he and Doris had no option but to take the first plane out, leaving all their possessions behind.

Eventually the press got hold of the story. Lee Langley of the *Guardian* tracked Leslie down to a bare flat in a basement at Marble Arch, where he and Doris were working as a caretaker couple looking after an apartment block. 'He looks very like his brother Larry,' Langley noted; 'short, stocky, with a pouchy, leathery face and bright blue eyes; a quiet polite man of 53 in a stiff white collar and the sort of tweedy suit an empire builder would have put on when he was home on leave. He stirs a cup of Bovril carefully and agrees that of course he's inhibited about having such successful brothers. "It was terrible in Africa sometimes," he said, "when people found out I was Gerry and Larry's brother. I felt like something out of a zoo. They'd come and stare at me . . ."' The caretaker job wasn't much, but at least it provided a home and some stability. Leslie had written a children's book, he said, and had given up shooting: 'I used to shoot a bit in Africa – a duck or so for dinner. But there seemed such a lot of shooting going on. I felt I could not add to it. Lost the taste for it somehow.'

Though Margaret continued to see Leslie and Doris from time to time, neither Gerald nor Larry would have anything further to do with their wayward brother. There were those, however, who saw a different Leslie, and who held him in high regard. Among them was Peter Scott (no relation to Sir Peter Scott), who had been his friend and employer in Kenya for three years and was to testify to his reliability and kindness, and to the happiness of his marriage to Doris. Leslie was also, Scott said, a brilliant raconteur, who should have been a writer. But 'he was one of life's losers – a middle brother with no obviously marketable talents, scarred by a bizarre childhood. His contact with Lawrence must have been minimal. He once tried to visit Lawrence at his home in Paris, but Lawrence's wife refused to admit him. He probably wanted to borrow money.'

TWENTY

Crack-Up

1968–1970

In the last week of July 1968 Gerald, Jacquie and Doreen Evans set off once again for Corfu, this time in a small convoy consisting of a Rover saloon car and a four-wheel drive Land-Rover intended for the ruggeder parts of the island. They were to spend two months there, during which time Gerald was to pass from a kind of heaven to something more closely resembling a private hell.

The sojourn had started well enough. The film rights to *My Family and Other Animals* had been bought by a London-based production company called Memorial Enterprises, run by the British actor Albert Finney and the producer Michael Medwin. Gerald was anxious to write a draft screenplay for the film on Corfu, in collaboration with his friend the actor Peter Bull, who was due out soon for a flying forty-eight-hour visit. Large and round, funny and kindly, a lover of all things Greek and an obsessive collector of old teddy bears, Peter had appeared intermittently in the Durrell family's lives ever since he first met Larry in London before the war and his brother had tried to marry Margaret. Gerald and Jacquie had re-met him on Corfu a few years earlier. A favoured member of their inner circle, it was Peter who had been instrumental in persuading Albert Finney and Michael Medwin to buy the film rights in *My Family*.

At the end of the first week in August Finney flew to Corfu to meet Gerald and discuss what form the film should take. By dint of concentrated application, waking Doreen Evans at six most mornings for a four-hour session on the screenplay, Gerald completed a first draft by the last week of August, and early in September Doreen retyped the whole script with three carbons – 'an enormous task' – in time for Finney's return. Unfortunately Gerald and Finney were unable to form much personal rapport, for Finney regarded Gerald as an overprivileged product of the Raj – or so it seemed to Gerald – while Gerald grew weary of Finney's exegesis of his own underprivileged working-class childhood. Of all the screenplays written around *My Family*, Gerald and Peter Bull's was the best by far, but eventually Finney became disenchanted with the project and sold it on to EMI. Time and again international funding proved illusory, and sadly the film of the book was never to make the big screen.

Corfu that summer turned into a caravanserai of the Durrell clan and their friends. Margaret came out for most of the time, followed by the formidable Aunt Prue and then brother Larry, still bowed down by the death of Claude, unusually subdued, sticking close to the crowd but saying little. ('So many friends have died,' he wrote in a letter, 'that I feel ringed with graves ... Damn everything.') Dix Branch came out from Mexico, and Alan and Shirley Thomas, Mai Zetterling and David Hughes, and Xan and Daphne Fielding, the former a war hero who had fought behind the German lines in Greece, the latter (so Gerald enthused) 'a really fabulous creature'. Peter Bull brought an American boyfriend called Don, a quiet, good-looking dancer. For Doreen Evans the casual coming and going of film stars, celebrities and royalty was heady stuff.

'Last night was *the* big night,' she wrote home excitedly on 21 August. 'The Corfu film we made last year, *Garden of the Gods*, was shown at the Casino to all those who helped in any way or are important. Everyone was there from the fisherman who arranged the night fishing to the Archbishop with his long beard and the military Colonel in charge of the island under the new regime. Also Prince Philip's sister and her family and many German princesses!! It was a big success and everyone was impressed by the film.' On 12 September Doreen wrote again, with as much *sangfroid* as she could muster, to report how they had all taken Prince Michael of Kent – 'a nice, unaffected, very lonely boy' – on an excursion to Sidari in the north of the island.

The weather was unseasonably cold and wet that summer, but that did not deter the party on their excursions to other parts of the island and across to Paxos and Antipaxos in the *benzina* (the local motor-boat). One day they all drove off to Afra, the grand but decaying old Venetian country mansion belonging to the aristocratic Curcumelli family. 'We drove up to a high village in the south,' Doreen reported. 'The streets were so narrow we had to leave the cars outside and walk. Immediately we appeared we were surrounded by a group of boys who proudly took us on a tour of their village. It is the richest in the island – but the dirtiest. Everyone lined the streets, standing in their doorways. They had to touch my face and hair and Margo took great pains to explain that not only was I "beautiful" but "good"! This was greeted with approval and applause, but she rather spoiled the effect by explaining that the only word of Greek I understood was "bed"! Typical of Marg, who never thinks before she speaks.'

Afra was the most famous and romantic of all the grand old estates on Corfu, built on the ruins of a thirteenth-century monastery by an eighteenth-century ancestor of the Curcumelli family. With its weathered roof of Roman tiles and its rusty pink Venetian façade, its luxuriant garden of magnolias and olive trees, its ancient, richly furnished interiors, Afra was both grand and lovely. Its current owner was Marie Curcumelli, a gallant old lady who had become another of Gerald's Corfiot friends. 'She is an enchanting woman,' he wrote to Alan Thomas, 'and lives all alone in this vast crumbling mansion which she is trying desperately to keep up, but it is a losing battle as she is so poverty stricken.' Gerald hoped Alan could come out and cast an eye over her antique book collection, with a view to selling it to raise funds for the mansion's embattled denizen: 'She has got a damned great cellarful rotting away. Some dating as far back as her grandfather and even her great great grandfather.'

Gerald's trips around the island made him increasingly despondent. If Mexico had been an exercise in futility, Corfu was an essay in destruction. A case in point was Palaeokrastitsa, one of the most beautiful spots on the island, with a lovely scalloped little bay and an ancient monastery perched on a high hill above. Throughout the whole of the twentieth century until now Palaeokrastitsa had remained unchanged – two houses, a tiny hotel, peace and silence on land and sea. But not any more. 'They have turned it into a Greek Margate,' Gerald was to lament to a friend. Soon, he reckoned, the rumble of the cement mixers would be drowning the birdsong in the secretive little Eden he called Nightingale Valley. Palaeokrastitsa was a metaphor for change on Corfu, and Corfu was a metaphor for change in the world. 'We are like a set of idiot children,' he was to protest, 'let loose in a complex and beautiful garden that we are turning into a barren and infertile desert.'

But could one deny the aspirations of a poor people to a better life, some asked, simply because a privileged few, mostly foreigners, wished to keep the island preserved in aspic as it had been for the last hundred years? Was it possible to decree that an inhabited part of the planet remain frozen in time? It all depended, Gerald argued, on why it was changing, and how. Corfu wasn't just being changed, it was being ruined, he reckoned. 'When a Greek peasant designs a hotel, he makes the bad taste of a provincial Frenchman look like a stroke of genius. Total lack of control, total rapacity, total insensitivity. In the old days we used to have – think! – as many as fifty tourists coming ashore every two weeks, producing indescribable chaos and panic on the island. Nowadays . . .'

So upset was Gerald about what he saw as the rape of Corfu that he wrote a memorandum on the subject to the Greek Prime Minister, concluding: 'I do hope that the necessary authorities in Athens will see their way to giving more power to the people on the spot, who are as worried as I am at the all too rapid and tasteless development of the island.' Underlying Gerald's disquiet was a sense of guilt that he had himself played a not insignificant part in the destruction of the thing he loved, by popularising the island in *My Family and Other Animals*. He was no less concerned that his recent film *Garden of the Gods* might have the same effect: 'I am afraid that in spite of all my efforts it will promote rather than reduce tourism to Corfu,' he wrote to his friend Marie Aspioti.

At that time the development on the island was more an intimation of things to come than an intolerable reality. The roads were still few and for the most part unsurfaced. Many parts of Corfu, especially the Durrell family's old haunts along the north-east coast, remained unspoiled. Gerald was negotiating interminably to buy – from an eccentric old owner who wouldn't sell – an ancient and beautiful olive press with a garden at the head of the little bay at Kouloura, not far from Lawrence's old haunt at Kalami.

When Sir Giles Guthrie and his wife announced their intention of visiting Corfu, Gerald gave them some typically irreverent advice about who and what to see. 'In order that you should not create unwanted disturbances and offend any friend of mine,' he wrote, 'I am issuing you with the following instructions which I hope you will abide by.' Everybody in Corfu was mad, he advised. If they wanted anything fixed they should see Spiro's son. If they wanted anything cooked – especially octopus – they should see a man called Vassili ('face like a camel and the fastest, wittiest and most vulgar repartee in the whole of Corfu') who ran his favourite restaurant, the Themis. 'For your cultural activities you must approach Miss Marie Aspioti,' Gerald advised. 'She is the nearest approach to the White Queen outside the book. She is absolutely enchanting and her knowledge and love of Corfu is incredible.' A rather well-preserved bandit called Christos was worth knowing, he went on – they couldn't mistake him 'because he has got a voice like a toad with laryngitis and a brand of English which makes Shakespeare turn in his grave'. The Manisses were three extraordinary brothers and were worth a visit. They were the uncrowned kings of the island, lived in one of the most gorgeous villas on Corfu and could do anything from providing you with a basket of new potatoes to getting you off a murder rap. 'When you have finished insulting all my friends,' he continued, 'you may get Lady Guthrie to row you round the island. I am enclosing an Admiralty chart which was done in the 1800s and I have marked on it the places which I think would enchant you. If they don't, then I think you have what I always suspected – incredibly bad taste!'

It was during their sojourn on Corfu that Jacquie noticed Gerald was beginning to behave rather strangely. His drinking had increased to the point where he was downing a bottle of ouzo before lunch, and he was becoming so difficult to live with that she started to wonder whether it was possible to live with him at all. The exact nature of his deteriorating condition was hard to pin down. One symptom took the form of compulsive-obsessive syndrome. He would play the same music – usually Vivaldi or Scott Joplin – over and over again on the record player. On one occasion he turned his camera on his favourite view at Pérama – across the water to Mouse Island – and proceeded to take twenty identical shots of the same view, almost as if he were trying to will the scene to transform itself into the enchanted world of his lost boyhood of long ago, when he was happy, carefree – and loved.

Part of the problem, clearly, was Corfu itself. 'He becomes quite intolerable from the moment he sets foot on the quay,' Jacquie was to tell a friend, 'and realises it will never be what it was. That's why I loathe Corfu – for what it does to him now.' On Corfu in the summer of 1968 Gerald seemed to be turning into a tortured soul, shrouded in gloom and fear, bad-tempered, intransigent, contradictory, subject to long silences and furious outbursts of temper. One day he told Jacquie, 'I keep having these deep depressive doubts. I feel I want to commit suicide.'

Margaret, too, was aware that something was seriously amiss. 'I remember Gerry weeping in the car,' she was to relate, 'weeping, weeping, weeping, and I said, "What is the matter?" He wouldn't say. Something was very wrong and I knew it was to do with Jacquie.' Margaret reckoned that Ann Peters – an on-off long-term secretary-cum-friend whom Gerald had first met on Corfu in the early sixties – was in love with her brother. 'He'd have done better to have married her,' she felt. 'I could fall in and out of love like a yoyo, but Gerry couldn't – this was the problem. Gerry remained fond of Jacquie long after she had ceased to be fond of him. He had bouts of weeping and drinking himself to death. I don't know how he managed to do the things he did with all those pressures that were on him.'

The best course seemed to be to return to Jersey and seek medical help, but the return journey involved a detour to Basle Zoo to consult with its director Ernst Lang on zoo business, and it was almost the middle of October before Gerald and Jacquie returned home. Dr Hunter, their local GP, examined Gerald and decided he needed specialist care and recuperation. Jacquie felt his breakdown was the result of gross overwork, after years of unremitting pressure at the zoo. This was undoubtedly a major contributory cause, but Dr Hunter thought it was also alcohol-related. He was all for leaving it till Gerald raised the subject himself, but Jacquie told him, 'If you wait that long, he'll probably hang himself.' So arrangements were made for Gerald to be admitted to The Priory, in Roehampton, south-west London, an expensive private clinic in a splendid Gothic building for people with depressive conditions, especially alcohol- and drug-related ones, and early in 1969 Gerald was quietly slipped off for a three-week 'cure'.

The big question was: why had Gerald Durrell cracked up? He was drinking anything by this time, Jacquie was to recall. He drank for all the usual reasons – to cope with stress, to cover his shyness, for Dutch courage, for *joie de vivre*, to drown his sorrows, to escape. The conventional attitude to alcohol addiction was to blame it on weakness of character, but in Gerald's case it was much more likely to be due to something beyond his control – an alcohol gene which he and his brothers had inherited, most likely from their mother. Sometimes it seemed that Gerald was addicted to the simple physiological mechanism of drinking, for whenever he couldn't get booze he would drink tea, and even water, in vast quantities.

The only absolute cure for such a genetically driven compulsion was total abstinence, and though occasionally Gerald had attempted this, the inordinate stresses in his life made it difficult to persevere with, for alcohol was more an enabler than a disabler for him. He got to a point where, like his brother Larry, he couldn't function without it – or at least, where he functioned better with it. Life was hard. So much to do. So little time. He worked constantly, mind pelting, and when he stopped he drank. You had to get through the day.

The medic in charge at The Priory was a Dr Flood.

'He's just an alcoholic,' Dr Flood told Jacquie at their first meeting.

'Are you trying to tell me something I don't know?' she retorted.

'Well, he's been having affairs, I suppose?' Dr Flood went on.

'No,' Jacquie replied. 'He hasn't, actually.'

'Well, then *you've* been having an affair.'

'No,' Jacquie told him. 'I have not.'

Dr Flood, having run through the usual options, paused for a moment.

'So,' he went on. 'What do *you* think is the cause?'

Jacquie told him she thought it was his mother's death, and his inability to come to terms with it. But the doctor only spoke to Gerry twice while he was there, and never got to the bottom of it. Possibly Gerald's breakdown was a combination of many things – stress, overwork, alcohol, Corfu, the zoo, the death of Mother, mid-life crisis, the fate of the animal kingdom, the after-effects of malaria, hepatitis and all the other tropical bugs, the frustrations and inner contradictions of body and soul – the whole package, the intolerable burden of being.

It could not have helped that in the previous year Jacquie's book, *Beasts in my Bed*, had been published by Collins. In it she proclaimed to friends and public alike: 'I began to loathe the zoo or anything to do with it ... I often felt that I had married a zoo and not a human being.' Reading his wife's message of disillusionment and renunciation, Gerald may well have felt that if his mother's death had triggered his troubles, his wife's withdrawal of total support had exacerbated them, for he was now doubly deprived, orphaned twice over.

Whatever the cause, Gerald was put on the clinic's standard regimen for such cases, a heavy cocktail of tranquillisers, to which was added (since there seemed no enforced restriction) crates of booze brought to his room by his many well-wishers. On Dr Flood's advice Jacquie's visits were restricted, though Saranne Calthorpe called regularly on her behalf.

The publication of his two non-fiction books did little to alleviate Gerald's problems, though he was proud of the fact that with his picaresque comic novel *Rosy is my Relative* he had finally succeeded in writing something straight out of his head, just like Lawrence. The story of Adrian Rookwhistle's adventures travelling around Edwardian England with Rosy, an amazing elephant with an unfortunate penchant for alcohol, was described by the *Washington Post* as 'a descendant of the traditional, rambling, good-natured British novel which goes back at least to Smollett'. Gerald's fiction works tended to be curiously old-fashioned, almost as Edwardian as Adrian Rookwhistle in tone and outlook, and never found a readership comparable to his non-fiction. He wrote only one other novel for adult readers, most of his fiction being aimed at a juvenile audience. Published almost simultaneously with *Rosy* was *The Donkey Rustlers*, a charming and ingenious tale of two English children who hold a Greek village to ransom by rustling their entire stock of donkeys in Wild West style and keeping them hidden away on a tiny island. Both books soon attracted the attention of the film industry, and it was *Rosy* that brought home the bacon when Ken Harper, an independent British producer, paid £25,000 for it. The film was never made, but the deal solved all the Durrells' financial problemss at a stroke, including the original loan they took out to found Jersey Zoo.

After three weeks Gerald was released from The Priory and went to stay in Jimmy and Hope Platt's London flat in order to acclimatise himself to being back in the normal world. Dr Flood advised Jacquie to leave him be for a time, and it was not until his return to Jersey in February that they were reunited. This proved to be a mixed blessing. 'Though I did all I possibly could to support him throughout this bleak period in his life,' Jacquie recalled, 'all this naturally put a tremendous strain on our already creaking relationship.' Drugged up to the eyeballs with medication, Gerald was 'almost like a zombie', and for Jacquie it was painful to watch him trying to get back into a normal routine.

On 6 February Gerald scribbled a note to Alan Thomas: 'I am feeling much better but still under these bloody drugs so one cannot really tell whether one is making any progress or not, as one is wandering around in a state of euphoria. I sometimes wake at night to find myself standing in the middle of the bedroom and wonder what the hell I am there for.' Try as he might, Gerald found it virtually impossible to focus on his work, and was forced to admit to the Trust's Scientific Advisory Committee that owing to illness he would be away from the island for part of the coming summer and all of the following winter. On 18 March Jacquie told Lawrence that Gerry was getting much better, but needed complete rest. In the following month Gerald left Jersey again for a recuperative sojourn on Corfu with Jacquie and Saranne Calthorpe.

They were to be away for more than three months, returning to Jersey in late July 1969 after a short diversion to the Greek mainland. They did not stay at home for long. Since their visit to Australia Gerald and Jacquie had felt an affinity for the country and its people, and now Gerald dreamed up a reason for going back there – not a collecting expedition this time, nothing too heavy or demanding, more a look-see, a conservation fact-finding mission, with the possibility of a book on the Great Barrier Reef thrown in if he felt up to it. In reality the trip was a kind of purposeful stretch of R & R designed to put Gerald and his shattered psyche in order again. With a long sea voyage out and a long sea voyage back he would be out of contact with the world of the zoo and the Trust for a full nine months.

For company he was taking two other women in addition to Jacquie – his assistant Ann Peters, and Saranne Calthorpe, whom he invited along when it became clear her marriage was foundering. Gerald enjoyed flirting with women, and while strangers who noticed this often jumped to the conclusion that he was a compulsive womaniser, in fact he was not. 'I'm not interested in sleeping with anyone else,' he declared. 'It only even occurs to me to be unfaithful when Jacquie gets on my wick (which she frequently does). I see lots of girls whom I think it would be nice to take to bed, but it's just a harmless fancy.' One such fancy was the beautiful

Saranne, with whom he gave every impression of being infatuated. But he never stepped over the line, never spoke a word or laid a finger out of place.

On 22 August 1969 Gerald and Jacquie travelled to London and checked in to the Buckingham Hotel for a week. On the twenty-sixth they threw a farewell dinner at Bertorelli's. On the thirtieth they were in the Swedish port of Göteborg to catch an Australia-bound cargo ship. Next day they sailed.

A little under six weeks later they made landfall in Australia. There they were met by the press. 'What is it like being married to a world-famous zoologist and author?' one newspaperman asked Jacquie. '"*Bloody*," she says . . . but with a glint in her eye that makes you doubt her meaning. But there's no doubting one thing – that marriage to Mr Durrell is a case of "love me, love my animals". Luckily Mrs Durrell is fond of animals. "I've been married to them for nineteen years – but I don't eat, sleep or drink them." Mrs Durrell described her marriage as a successful partnership. "I do all the jobs Gerald loathes doing."'

When the party arrived in Melbourne they were met by Peter Grose, the Curtis Brown agency's representative in Australia. 'Gerry struck me on that first meeting as a great big honey bear of a chap,' Grose recalled, 'a bearded, boomingly extrovert, hugely overweight bon viveur who was knocking it back with great gusto. Sometimes he would go into a serious mode but basically he was jokey, fun, good company. The only odd thing was the bizarre *ménage à quatre* with which he was proposing to make his way around Australia. It seemed pretty clear to me that he was a bit besotted with Lady Saranne.'

There was no evidence of Gerald's recent breakdown – as far as Grose could see he was firing on all cylinders. The problem was his entourage. Saranne and Ann Peters did not get on at all, the latter loathing the very sight of the former, perhaps out of jealousy, for Ann Peters was infatuated with Gerald, while Gerald was infatuated with Saranne – a potentially disastrous triangle, even without counting in Jacquie. When the party set off into the outback, heading for Queensland via Canberra and the Blue Mountains, it was in an atmosphere of mounting emotional stand-off that boded ill for the harmony of the trip.

From the rainforests of north Queensland Gerald sent a postcard to Alan and Shirley Thomas depicting 'the famous and wondrous Curtain Fig Tree' near Cairns – an amazing tangle of close-thicketed aerial roots. 'Have just had my females cut through this tree,' he joked. 'It was hard work and two of them died – but the show must go on. Have discovered several new places and called them Sidney, Melbourne and Dicky-Pricky

Creek. Found a thing with a bill like a duck but found it was Lady Calthorpe.'

Christmas Day found Gerald and his female entourage heading out across the Great Barrier Reef aboard a small launch laden with provisions to instil some Christmas cheer into a most un-Christmas-like, scorching, tropic day – iced champagne, cold turkey and ice cream. In his time Gerald had spent a number of unusual Christmases abroad – in a waterlogged tent in West Africa nursing a sick chimpanzee; lying roasting on a cliff in Patagonia filming a vast conglomeration of fur seals below him; dining on manioc cakes and cold alligator tail while floating through the creek-lands of Guiana in a canoe. But no Christmas in his experience compared with that on the Great Barrier Reef. This one day was like a metaphor for the entire, six-month, twenty-thousand-mile expedition through Aus-tralia – a dazzling and incomparable interlude in a teeming, near-pristine Antipodean Eden – a Christmas with corals.

Gerald had a special interest in the Great Barrier Reef. A great bastion of coral guarding Australia's north-eastern shore against the gnawing blue rollers of the Pacific, the reef sheltered a string of coral islands within its protecting wall and an underwater world that contained one of the most breathtakingly beautiful, complex and extraordinary animal communities on earth. It was a place of a very special order, a world of nature quite unlike any he had ever experienced – 'more colourful than a Matisse,' he was to record, 'more intricate than the Bayeux tapestries, structurally much more beautiful than the Acropolis'. Though he never wrote his intended book about the reef, he did leave behind a rhapsodic account of a day beyond compare spent exploring this as yet unravaged paradise.

Their first stop, as they throbbed their way across the milk-smooth sea, was a group of small islands that formed part of the breeding area of a bird he had long wanted to meet, the Torres Strait pigeon. Dropping anchor in water as transparent as gin, they scrambled ashore over a graveyard of coral that scrunched and disintegrated under their feet – 'like walking over the whitened bones of a million dinosaurs'. The pigeons, large and milk-white, with huge jet-black liquid eyes, showed little fear of man, and this was costing them dear, for though they were a protected species they were mercilessly poached, and their numbers had dropped alarmingly.

They sailed on across a placid sea towards the outer rim of the reef, then put on flippers and masks and submerged in the lukewarm water. Gerald had known roughly what to expect, but what he saw so stunned him that he cried out in astonishment and swallowed a lungful of water for his pains:

The coral gardens lay spread in a million different shapes and colours and textures. It was like floating over the multicoloured roofs of a medieval city, here a church spire picked out in russet red, gold, and magenta, there a row of lesser houses with steeply canted roofs, white and brittle as sugar, studded with gold and blue cowries. Moving busily through all this were red and white spotted crabs, yellow and black eels, and above all, fish – large fish and fish so small they were like little glinting embers, fish green-gold as a tiger's eye, working their way assiduously over the craniums of brain coral, each the size of a dining-room table. There were beds of anemones, pink and white and as frilly as a Victorian bonnet. And everywhere, it seemed, prowled that great enemy of the Barrier Reef, the crown of thorns starfish, each the size of a soup plate or bigger. The variety of living things was bewildering. It was an enormous biological firework display.

It wasn't just the colours – it was also the shapes. There were fish encrusted with spines like hedgehogs, others with horns like cows, others shaped like a box or elongated like a tape-measure, some shaped like harps or hatchets, some like boomerangs and some like kites. 'We were like children in a toyshop, clinging to coral, pointing out to each other the fish that nosed gently around us, and everywhere the great rainbow-coloured sculptures of coral.' 'You realise,' Gerald added happily, 'that nature can still do things better than Hollywood.'

They climbed out of this underwater Arcadia to have Christmas dinner, then, replete with turkey and champagne, sank gratefully back into that primordial maelstrom of colours. It was late in the day before they could tear themselves away. The evening sky was pale leaf-green. Their bodies were burnt scarlet by the sun, their skin rough with dried salt, their heads spinning. Then, across the water, they saw something strange. 'We looked to where the sky seemed to have developed a hundred twinkling stars,' Gerald wrote, 'which shot nearer to us until we realised they were the wing beats of the Torres Straits Pigeons flying back to their nests, cool white against the green sky, gleaming like shooting stars.'

Gerald vowed to spend another Christmas on the Barrier Reef before he died, and though he never did, this incomparable marine wonderland remained for ever dear to his heart. Not surprisingly, he took up the cudgels during the controversy that ensued when it was proposed that drilling for oil should be permitted on the reef. Though conservation had made great strides in Australia since his first visit eight years before, the local politicians (like politicians all over the world) seemed oblivious of the issues at stake. 'The average Australian,' he protested in a public letter to a Melbourne newspaper, 'now realises he lives in one of the most fascinating and biologically unique continents in the world and he is aware of the necessity of trying to preserve what is left of it before it is too late. Unfortunately, he appears to be badly served by his politicians, who display an astonishing ignorance on any subject that is not immediately connected with sheep, opals, minerals or anything else that can make them a quick buck ... The problem the conservationist has is a difficult one: it is how to educate the politicians, for by and large they are like retarded children.'

From Queensland the party headed up across the northern half of Australia, and in March 1970, shortly before setting sail for home, Gerald filed a progress report for the Trust's newsletter back in distant Jersey:

I'm writing this from Alice Springs in the Northern Territory, and the temperature is 104 in the shade if you can find any. Travelling by road, as we have done, gives you a much better impression of the country and its vastness, and we are unanimous in our conviction that this is one of the most fascinating continents in the world. We have been lucky enough to see a great cross-section of Australian wildlife, from the Pigmy Flying Possums the size of a walnut to Red Kangaroos as tall as a man, from the bizarre duck-billed platypus to the almost equally strange green mountain possum, from the spectacular Wedge-tailed Eagles and huge and brilliant Cockatoos down to the tiny Spinifex bird and weeny multi-coloured Parrakeets.

But it wasn't just the wildlife that delighted them. The Australian people they met, including many members of the Trust, impressed them greatly – 'all dedicated in one way or another to the conservation not only of Australia's unique fauna but also the magnificent landscape it lives in'.

Early in May 1970 Gerald, Jacquie, Saranne Calthorpe and Ann Peters returned at last to Jersey. A little later Gerald had lunch with his publisher in London. He might do a book on Australia, he said. He had even thought of a title for it: 'Bonking Round Oz with Three Sheilas'.

TWENTY-ONE

Pulling Through

1970–1971

During the course of 1970 Gerald's life seemed to return to a more even keel. He had got over the worst of his nervous breakdown, though he was not yet back to work. He had managed to kick whisky and nicotine (he now smoked cigarettes without inhaling), and as an antidote to stress he eventually turned to yoga. Rising early, he would drink his first cup of tea of the day, then gently lower his corpulent frame on to the floor, where he would not only look like Buddha but act like Buddha, sitting practically immobile as he began to ease himself into a slow-motion half-hour routine of cobra, lotus, headstand and bow. If it hadn't been for yoga, he reckoned, he didn't know how he would have coped after his crack-up – it virtually saved his life. The exercises were relaxing, but it was what they did to his mind that was so important. Yoga, he once told a friend, was like a perfect wife – 'It only asks what you want to give it.' If he had had his way he would have made it compulsory in schools, instead of football.

By now Gerald was taking little other exercise. He was not a physically active man. When the world traveller and bushwhacker was at home he would remain strictly within his own confined orbit, and might move no further than fifty feet from his chair or desk or kitchen table in a day. Though he was a nomad at heart, he was sedentary by inclination, and his pleasures were mostly domestic ones. 'I adore cooking,' he was to reiterate time and again. 'It's very soothing. My idea of bliss is to have eight people round to dinner and cook a gorgeous repast for them.' He was a passionate and highly accomplished cook, with no moral reservations about cooking and eating animals, be they fish, flesh or fowl. 'Of course I will eat a salmon,' he once declared defiantly, 'provided it's not the *last* salmon.' 'You can't be sentimental and run a zoo,' he would say. 'You have to feed animals to the animals. Can you imagine feeding a lion on dog biscuits?'

In his time Gerald had eaten all sorts of creatures: iguana ('revolting'), crocodile ('unpleasant'), hippopotamus ('even more unpleasant'), python ('high grade blotting paper'), cane rat and pouched rat ('both delicate and delicious'), bear's paw ('wonderful'), beaver ('a test for all your organs'), porcupine ('wonderful casseroled or smoked'), guanaco ('pleasant but you don't yearn for a second helping'), paca ('delicious gamey meat'), horse ('delicious if cooked carefully'), seagull ('never again'), peacock ('heavy and rich'), penguin ('ugh'), black swan ('very good') and rook ('nice'), along with anaconda, emu eggs, conger eel, termites, locusts and much else besides.

When he was in the flat at the zoo it was generally curries that were the order of the day. Down at the Mazet, however, where life was more leisurely, he gave his repertoire full rein. He delighted most in the richer, naughtier end of classic French cooking – all calvados and cream, brandy and blood, calories and cholesterol: *bisque de homard*, hare with olives in wine, quails stuffed with raisins and pine nuts, marinated venison. This was the kind of fare he defined as 'sexy' – 'The way to a girl's bedroom,' he once remarked, 'is through her stomach.'

Entertaining was part of the same pleasure, but it had to be strictly on his own terms. He was generally uncomfortable at other people's parties, and always happiest at his own. In London the venue could be Bertorelli's restaurant, where the company as often as not included Theodore Stephanides, Peggy Peel, Peter Bull and Alan Thomas and his wife. In France it was the Mazet and his brother Larry and his present companion, David Hughes and Mai Zetterling, the sculptor Elizabeth Frink and her husband, and his artist neighbour Tony Daniells. In Jersey (eschewing island society for the most part) it was the flat and his closest and most trusted friends and colleagues at the zoo, including Sam and Catha Weller, Jeremy Mallinson, John Hartley, and later Simon Hicks and Tony Allchurch – the last four comprising a group Gerald knew affectionately (to their embarrassment) as 'the boys'. 'In Jersey,' noted Peter Grose, who was now at the London office of Curtis Brown, and had taken over Gerald's literary affairs from Richard Scott Simon, 'Gerry never ran a salon for interesting new faces but often held a court of familiar old faces. If you went to stay at the manor the same people would come to dinner every time – huge meals in which Gerald himself would play a huge part, serving up enormous plates of dead animals galore. He always kept a coterie of close and trusted friends, but when he travelled the faces would change and he would set off with an entourage, usually of women, because he was at home in the company of women and liked to flirt with them all.'

Gerald loved giving, and his generosity knew no bounds. He would take his friends out to lunches and dinners at the very best restaurants for the very best food and wine, all paid for out of his own pocket. His generosity was not the flamboyant, self-serving kind, but an expression of genuine love and friendship. When his film and television agent Dick Odgers had to go to hospital, Gerald went to some pains to have two bottles of champagne delivered to his bedside 'to cheer the old bugger up'. When his former secretary Doreen Evans, who had become an air hostess, was badly injured after falling out of an aeroplane, Gerald sent her an unusual get-well present – a huge scarab beetle of the kind sacred to the ancient Egyptians, which had been blown across to Corfu by the *khamsin* wind early one hot summer, and which he had found and had mounted and framed especially for her. Birthday and Christmas celebrations were fulsome and unstinted. Anniversary or invitation cards were usually designed by Gerald himself with pen-and-ink artwork, often depicting cartoon animals or himself and Jacquie.

Reading was a lifetime's passion. 'Apart from my own books, which I always read at bed time as a soporific,' he once declared, 'I am omnivorous in my tastes and, to most people's horror, I read five or six books at once, leaving them in different parts of the house and devouring a few pages as I pass. It might be anything from the latest Dick Francis (a splendid writer – I'm very jealous), to a book of poetry, an erudite tome on the sex life of the Patagonian weasel or the *Dictionary of Phrase and Fable*. To me, a house without books is an empty shell. To have well-stocked bookshelves cuddling you is like having a thousand sights, sounds, smells and sparkling ideas. Books are things to be cherished in the same way people cherish jewels, great paintings or great architecture. It is an honour to turn the pages of a book.' When he was in the right mood and in congenial company he would recite his favourite verse or prose passages, usually comic ones, from memory. He could reduce an audience to tears with his rendition of Lewis Carroll's 'The Walrus and the Carpenter'. If his memory failed him he would invent his own limericks, most of them rude.

Often he would switch on the television in the sitting-room at the flat as a way of marking the end of the working day – the more mindless the programme the more definitive the demarcation. He was an avid film-watcher – almost always on television, for he virtually never went out to a cinema, or for that matter anywhere else in the evening if he could help it, unless it was to a close friend's for dinner. He had an interest in the paranormal, and particularly enjoyed horror movies with really good monsters in them. If he had not sought a career in the zoo world, he reckoned, he might have made a passable film director, for he adored the medium, and the business of story structure and visual interpretation and cutting and splicing, and felt comfortable in the company of actors and stars.

Music was important to Gerald, and his tastes were catholic and far-flung, though he played no instrument and only rarely sang. His preferences in classical music were different from Jacquie's: while she loved the soaring sounds of romantic grand opera, he preferred what she called 'piddle music' – Mozart and Vivaldi. And while she was a great jazz fan, Gerald's tastes in popular music veered towards cabaret and musicals, though he was also an early aficionado of what is now called world music, the popular music of other lands and cultures. When he appeared on the marathon-running BBC radio programme *Desert Island Discs* on 7 August 1961, his eight chosen records included parts of Beethoven's 8th Symphony and Mozart's *The Magic Flute*, 'A Hymn to Him' from *My Fair Lady*, Eartha Kitt singing 'An Old-Fashioned Millionaire' and Flanders and Swann performing 'The Gnu Song', as well as Zulu music, an Andean tune and a Greek folk song he had first heard on Corfu when he was a boy. As his luxury item he chose writing materials (much as he claimed to loathe writing), and for his book he cheated a little and asked for the *Encyclopaedia Britannica*.

Drawing, especially cartoons, was another favourite pastime, and when combined with his charisma and his talents as a raconteur, his lightning sketches could keep an audience spellbound. 'He was able to hold a capacity audience at a Cambridge University meeting of the Fauna and Flora Preservation Society for two hours,' John Burton, then the society's secretary, was to recall, 'with nothing more than a few sheets of paper and a felt pen – and he raised several hundred pounds at the end of the evening by auctioning off his vivid cartoons . . . He could be even more hilarious when describing certain members of the zoological and conservation establishment. It was humour without malice, but he was a doer and had little time for conservationists who spent most of their time going from conference to conference.'

Little of Gerald's occasional writing ever saw the light of day, though its range, variety and ingenuity was considerable. He was for ever bubbling with ideas, and at one time or another he sketched out a stage play called 'Uncle Amos', set on a Greek island; an animation film idea for children called 'AESOP' (Animal Emergency Survival Operation); an unpublished collection of short stories; a cookery book called 'Cholesterol Cooking'; a spy novel and a thriller called 'Mengele'; an autobiographical television series; and a musical set in Dracula's castle in Transylvania entitled 'I

Want a Stake in Your Heart' (with songs that included 'It's a Lovely Day for Doing a Bit of Evil' and 'You have Something to Hide, Dr Jekyll').

His favourite form of literary doodle was the limerick. These could pop into his head at any time of day or night, especially with a drink inside him, and would be scribbled down on whatever was to hand – beer mat, menu card, nightclub notepad – wherever he happened to be. In the spring of 1970, by way of a little creative psychotherapy to speed his recovery along, he turned to a form of his own devising, the bawdy limerick with animals, and before long he had elaborated this into a grander scheme – an illustrated bestiary of creatures, twenty-one in number, each the subject of its own limerick. To this concoction Gerald gave the name 'The Lady Saranne's Bestiary'. The least ribald of the limericks convey the work's broad flavour.

The Llama

There was once a newly wed Llama
Who was given a copy of 'Kama'
He tried ninety-six ways
In forty-one days
Which did more to alarm her than calm her.

The Song of Saranne

A voluptuous young mink called Saranne
Said 'I've thought of an excellent plan
If we have a reversal
Of what's universal
Then I could be wearing a man.'

With the help of these diverting little five-finger exercises Gerald perked up sufficiently to face the world again. For much of the summer he pottered around the South of France, eating, drinking and making merry with friends on a strict convalescent regime of wine, women and uproar. Towards the end of June he pitched up at the Hôtel le Select in Arles with a large 'harem' in tow (including Jacquie, Saranne Calthorpe, Peggy Peel and an American assistant by the name of Anne Valentine) to meet up with Chris Parsons for discussions about a possible BBC television programme on his favourite naturalist, Henri Fabre, and a recce of key locations. But Gerald did not linger long, confessing to Parsons: 'I was faintly at the end of my tether, so you were well shot of me.' He and his entourage moved on to visit Lawrence at Sommières. 'My brother turned up with an entourage of females,' Lawrence reported to Henry Miller. 'He travels with a permanent seraglio like a Turkish potentate. Or do I mean imbroglio? It often amounts to the same thing.' By 7 July the party had headed off to the family flat of Odette Mallinson, Jeremy's wife, at Cros de Cagnes on the Côte d'Azur, where they parted from Saranne and hoped to meet up with 'the Zets', Mai Zetterling and David Hughes.

The days passed happily in a blur of excursions, shopping, swimming, lunches, siestas and dinners. Gerald often stayed behind when the rest of the party sallied out for the day in order to get on with a new book of short stories, *Fillets of Plaice*, and on 22 July he finished it. Not long afterwards, on 4 August, he suffered a serious relapse in the middle of dinner. 'He had his first seizure,' Jacquie recalled, 'an attack of grand mal, the first and only attack that I know of in the time I was with him. The local French doctor and later a consultant neurologist in Nice told me that his attack was solely due to the horrendous drug treatment he had been prescribed in England plus the booze, and if he stayed with the regimen given by the French doctor things would stabilise themselves.' This regimen prescribed half a bottle of red wine as the limit of his daily alcohol intake – a fraction of what he had grown used to. But he stuck to it, and as a result began to lose all the weight he had gained through his previous illness, and to look better and younger than he had for years.

At the end of August Gerald and Jacquie finally returned to Jersey. They had been away, a few short visits apart, for the best part of a year and a half. For Gerald the recuperation from his near total collapse in 1968–69 had been a long one. In October Jacquie wrote to Lawrence: 'You will be pleased to hear that Gerry is still looking absolutely marvellous and he is actually keeping to his regime. Whatever it was that affected him in France certainly was miraculous because all the tensions and general woes have gone and he is now like his old self.'

This was all too evidently true. In November Chris Parsons visited Gerald in Jersey to talk further about the proposed programme on Henri Fabre. Gerald had ambitious ideas for an elaborate dramatic treatment of the French naturalist's life, but Parsons felt that this might prove too costly for the BBC. After Parsons left, Gerald wrote him a characteristically mischievous letter, enclosing a revised treatment of the subject.

> Dear Wellington,
> It was, as usual, a horrible experience having you here but one from which we are recovering. I know that you spend ninety percent of your time in bed with a blonde, so I felt that I ought to write and jog your memory. I watched the Modigliani programme as you

suggested and it has given me lots of ideas on how to do the Fabre film. I enclose a rough draft of the opening sequence which I am sure will win your approval.

Yours

Napoleon

The rough draft was brief but original.

This film opens simply but, I think, effectively with an enormous close-up of Fabre's external genitalia. Across the screen crawls a small dung beetle dragging behind it a banner on which we have the title, 'Furry Fabre, the Prick of Provence'. As the beetle reaches the edge of the screen, it is hit with a bottle and the screen goes black and remains that way for approximately three and a half minutes, during which a rather soulful Provençal tune is played on a comb and paper ... That is as far as I have got so far, but I think you will agree that the meat of the Fabre story is coming over.

Parsons suggested a less Rabelaisian approach, but Gerald lost interest in the project, and ceased to be involved in it.

When Parsons came out to Provence with his wife and a BBC crew to shoot the film in the summer of 1972, he had barely checked into his hotel before the manager brought along a bottle of champagne which had been left, he explained, by a Mr Gerald Durrell in the hope that it 'might help Mr Parsons overcome his shyness'. Asked what this was supposed to mean, the manager replied that Mr Durrell had told him (falsely, of course) that the couple were on their honeymoon, and needed all the help they could get. The incident was to generate hoax and counter-hoax. When Parsons arranged for a telegram to be delivered to the Mazet with the message 'FILM DEAL NOW IMMINENT STOP IMPERA- TIVE YOU FLY NEW YORK IMMEDIATELY', Gerald plotted an elaborate riposte. Parsons recalled:

The next day we were all due to drive north to a party at the lovely old Provençal farmhouse of Elizabeth Frink, the sculptress. After the meal, when everyone was in jovial mood, Elizabeth's husband, Ted, brought out a curious package addressed to me which he said had been left by an eminent zoologist who had heard I was in the area. I opened it suspiciously, finding inside six objects resembling the cocoons of emperor moths – one of the subjects we had been filming. Curious to see how the cocoons had been made I started unpicking one of them, for I could hear something rattling inside.

I discovered a small piece of paper, tightly rolled. Unravelling it I saw it bore a message – it was something extremely rude about the BBC. Once more Durrell had somehow managed to have the last word.

Meanwhile the work of the Trust was making dramatic progress. Its ethos had been honed down to a simple agenda – simple, that is, to express, though far from simple to achieve. Gerald was to declare:

We are not a zoo in the accepted sense of the word, we are a reservoir of threatened wildlife from all over the world. A sanctuary where they can live and breed in peace.

   Our objectives are firstly to provide a safe sanctuary for a species and then to build up a colony of them. You see, unlike a zoo, we have to deal in colonies. Once you have created your colony surplus, animals can be sent to other organisations all over the world, until the creatures are safely established under controlled conditions. Then, when it is safe, you can start on the final problem: taking your surplus animals and returning them to the wild, reintroducing the species to areas where it has become extinct.

By now Jersey Zoo, the first collection of its kind in the world to turn its activities entirely towards conservation, had begun to earn international recognition for its work. It had established a number of breeding colonies of rare animals, many of which had never been bred under controlled conditions before. Despite the limited means at its disposal, thirty species of mammals, forty-nine species of birds and four species of reptiles had been bred there.

   All this represented a remarkable achievement for a man whose only formal education amounted to half a term at prep school. However, it was difficult to see how the organisation could ever be totally secure when it did not own the buildings and grounds on which it stood. The Trust's lease was due to run out in fifteen years' time, when the owner, Major Fraser, might choose to move back in or sell the estate off for development. It was clear that unless a substantial sum could be raised to secure outright ownership of the property the zoo and Trust might lose their home and to all intents and purposes cease to exist, for unless they owned their place of work no charitable foundation would be willing to give them grants.

   Sir Giles Guthrie, the financial adviser to the Trust, led the charge. Major Fraser said he would be prepared to sell the estate for £120,000, and a public appeal launched in the autumn of 1970 raised £25,000. Sir

Giles was anxious to scotch rumours amongst the wealthier residents of the island that Gerald was lining his own pockets from the proceeds of the zoo and the money donated to the Trust. It was the Trust that received all moneys, he told the local press: 'Mr Durrell gives his time freely and without payment and has in fact given over £20,000 in cash to the Trust. His expeditions are paid for out of his own pocket with the income from his books.' Satisfied on this point, in March 1971 the States of Jersey agreed a minimal-interest loan of £60,000 to help secure the property. On 18 March Gerald wrote excitedly to a friend: 'Life here is hectic in the extreme but there is one very big piece of news. We have at last managed to raise £120,000 to buy this property which will become ours on April 2nd. I cannot tell you what a relief this is to us. It means that we can now go to various foundations and get grants and we are also embarking on a large-scale fund-raising operation directed mainly at North America.'

Gerald's agent Peter Grose was always to regard Gerald as one of the three great people he had been privileged to know in his professional life, the other two being Christopher Isherwood and the Australian Nobel Prize-winner Patrick White. But it was not on account of his literary achievements that he so admired him. 'When I took him on,' Grose remembered, 'his best books were well and truly behind him and he was beginning to scrape the barrel.' Gerald had become a rather slack writer by now, Grose reckoned, and though Sir Billy Collins, the Chairman of Collins, remained a staunch champion, his editors, Adrian House and Philip Ziegler, were having to do a lot more work on his manuscripts to bring them up to scratch. The downturn in the quality of Gerald's literary output was evident in *Fillets of Place*, and even more so in his long-delayed and still unfinished account of the Sierra Leone expedition, *Catch me a Colobus*. Not that his books did not still sell well, particularly back titles like *My Family and Other Animals* and *The Bafut Beagles*, and they were widely translated, being especially popular with the pet-starved inhabitants of the Soviet Union and Communist Eastern Europe, who loved Gerald's slightly mutinous view of the world. Rights in three of his books were optioned for the big screen – *The Donkey Rustlers*, *Rosy is my Relative* and *My Family* – though none was ever made into a film.

Peter Grose recalled:

Gerald never had a high regard for his writing. He saw it as a means to three ends. First, as a source of money. Second, as a platform for his ideas. Third, as a route to stardom (for he did have real star quality and a genuine affinity with showbiz and the stars) – and stardom he could use to further his real life's mission. I used to go to that zoo and I was awe-struck – here were animals that might have ceased to be had it not been for the intervention of this man. That does seem to be a monument beyond the imagination. To have that vision and the drive to achieve it was just astounding in those days. I admired him hugely as a human being. You lose sight now of how far ahead of his time he was, and how what he was expounding in the fifties and sixties is now the current orthodoxy. In those days he was still looked upon as an upstart amateur expounding mad ideas. The pressures on him, the anxieties and doubts, were enormous. The zoo and the Trust were phenomenally expensive things to run, they chewed up money at such a rate, so fund-raising was his biggest single preoccupation – all that PR glad-handing, speeches at dinners, touting for money and so forth – he was under the same pressure as a comedian who's got to be funny every single night. So under those circumstances he tended to drink as an anaesthetic to take the pain away. The drinking escalated as the pressure escalated, till in the end he was drinking quite ferociously. I remember staying at the manor and getting up at eight o'clock one morning and finding Gerry with an *enormous* brandy balloon into which he poured a huge quadruple slosh of brandy and a pint of milk on top – and that was breakfast. For elevenses he would open the first bottle of rather fine claret of the day. Drinking like that damages you – not that I *ever* saw him drunk or incapable when he was in working mode or at functions and engagements where he had to make speeches and be on parade.

In April 1971 Gerald and Jacquie again repaired to France with Peggy Peel and Anne Valentine, staying at the Mazet for the summer for Gerald to get on with the writing of *Catch me a Colobus*. He was having immense difficulty with the book, for he had not altogether enjoyed the Sierra Leone expedition, and his antipathy towards the highly unionised BBC camera crew deprived him of a lot of the source material that a book of this kind needed, with its reliance on eccentric human and animal characters.

On the sixteenth Gerald took time off to drop a note to Lord Jersey, brimming with enthusiasm over his immediate plans for the zoo – a new gorilla cage, better accommodation for the Congo peacocks, and completion of the water meadows ('a lovely focal point for the whole zoo'). 'I have finished two chapters of a new book,' he added, 'and eaten a lot of delicious French food and drunk a lot of delicious French wine, so I am feeling, if not a giant refreshed, at least like a coherent pygmy.' With Lawrence's house at Sommières only a relatively short drive from the Mazet, Gerald saw a lot of his brother, meeting up for an informal meal or a binge, or a wide-ranging, deep-diving *tête-à-tête* in which they would put the world to rights or pick it to bits. The two had always been close, and now they were to grow closer still. Disappointingly, however, it proved impossible for Gerald to buy the Mazet from his brother as he had hoped. He could not afford the asking price, he told Lawrence on 11 June, 'even if all three films suddenly materialised', so he would like to rent it for five years instead.

A few days later Sir Giles Guthrie wrote from Jersey outlining the latest Trust plans: Lady Saranne Calthorpe to raise £20,000 'to keep the wolf from the door'; the scientific committee to recommend a conservation programme 'which will bring joy to all working at the zoo'; and 'you, dear boy, to make an exploratory trip to the States in the autumn', to be followed by a full-blown assault in the spring of 1972, when Gerald would 'set out like a knight in shining armour to conquer the Americans and replenish the coffers at Les Augrès Manor – essential to the successful expansion of your life-work'. Later in the month Lord Jersey wrote to reinforce the importance of Gerald's activities in America. 'Fund raising in the States depends entirely on you,' he wrote, and quoted a remark made by an American friend of Sir Giles: 'If Durrell wants any money he better come and get it himself. It's no good him sending his stooges.'

But these plans came badly unstuck. The first casualty was the lovely but luckless Saranne Calthorpe, with whom Gerald and Jacquie had enjoyed a long and intense friendship. Indeed, some who were close to the three of them considered the friendship to be obsessive, and even unhealthy. Without a trace of a grin, Gerald had proposed the appointment of Lady Calthorpe as the Trust's special fund-raiser on Jersey at a solemn committee meeting because, he said, 'as everybody knows she's the sexiest bitch on the island'.

Saranne's post was conditional on her remaining single, Gerald informed her, since he did not consider it a suitable job for a married woman. A married woman would have too many other distracting commitments, he claimed – not admitting even to himself the jealousy and possessiveness he felt on Saranne's account. He was therefore greatly dismayed to learn that following her divorce from Lord Calthorpe she proposed to marry again, this time to Tony Lort-Philips, who had worked at the zoo in the early days. Gerald's reaction was demonic. From the Mazet he wrote to Saranne in terms that suggested he regarded her decision as a personal betrayal.

'From the very outset of this affair,' he raged, 'you have behaved with a crass stupidity which I had hoped was only a temporary manifestation due to your private life. This latest effort, however, leaves me no alternative but to believe you imagine this job to be a sort of plaything, a hobby . . . As you say, happiness tends to make one incoherent – so does imbecility. I would be glad if you send your letter of resignation direct to Lord Jersey.'

Gerald never saw Saranne again. Her second marriage broke up like her first, she drifted about the island, helpless and forlorn, then took to the bottle in a systematic, suicidal way, and after crashing her car a few times in Jersey's narrow, stone-walled lanes, died prematurely of drink in a Jersey nursing home.

In Saranne's place Gerald proposed John Hartley, a highly diplomatic but determined young man. 'He is genuinely devoted to the Trust,' Gerald advised Lord Jersey, 'loves being loved by people, and is really quite ruthless.'

The second casualty was Gerald himself. He was back in Jersey in the autumn, but his doctor doubted if he was yet well enough for such a strenuous undertaking as a fund-raising tour of the United States. On 19 November Gerald wrote to Lawrence that the doctors had vetoed the proposed visit next year as well, 'because they think the pressure of a whistle-stop tour would unravel my psyche again'. He wrote again later: 'I have broken the drug cycle [medication] but still get enormously tired very easily, with occasional great dollops of depression which only last for about five or six minutes but are rather terrifying in their intensity.'

In a way Gerald was relieved not to have tackle the States so soon. 'I do not share some Council Members' opinion,' he told Sir Giles Guthrie, 'that all I have to do is walk down the gangplank in New York to be immediately handed a cheque for a million pounds.' In any case, he was fed up with having to wrestle with money matters year in year out. 'It has, among other things, affected my health, so that I really feel now is the time to make an all-out effort to get ourselves into a financial position where I can concentrate on intelligent conservation work and not be constantly harried by the world of accountants and bank managers, about which I know nothing and care less.'

TWENTY-TWO

The Palace Revolution

1971–1973

For some time a move had been afoot among the senior members of the Trust Council to push through a radical review of the organisation and direction of the Trust and zoo. This was to mark the second great crisis in the organisation's history. The first had been the battle for survival. The second would be the battle for power.

In September 1971 Lord Jersey had drafted a preliminary memorandum, the main thrust of which was that the organisation had to adapt to keep up with change. There was the faintest hint that the biggest obstacle to that adaptation was Gerald Durrell himself:

> A complete review of the organisation is urgent. Les Augrès Manor is fast becoming a very important specialist zoo, and is no longer merely a collection of animals. The animals are, and must continue to be, pets; that is the charm of the zoo. But the collection now has a wider, vastly more important function, and we must be ready for it. We must not forget that the zoo centres on Gerald Durrell, the author, and his books, and the TV personality and his films and appearances, and the zoo is linked to him in the public eye and in the minds of the Trust members . . . As the Trust and Zoo grow bigger and increase in scope, one might think it more efficient to decentralise, but this would only be possible up to a certain limit. We must do nothing to break the impression that this is Gerry Durrell's private zoo, and that the animals are all his pets.

Gerald's value to the zoo, in other words, was as the star turn in an elaborate fiction. But the days had long passed when he knew most of the animals in the zoo by sight, if not by name, and when some of them, companions from the earliest weeks of their lives, had been an integral part of his own past. It was impossible for a scientific institution run on the most rigorous lines, with new animals constantly coming in from all over the world as part of a systematic conservation programme, to continue to be run as a personal fiefdom of private pets, and had Gerald never intended that it should, though most of the public still believed it was.

Gerald did not at first pick up any scent of danger in the radical rethink now afoot. He did object to certain things in Lord Jersey's memo, however – the idea that the Trust was in danger of becoming moribund, for example, or that a way of improving the organisation's efficiency was to increase the number of committees, to the point where, as he put it, it was 'all balls and no brain'. But he did not yet perceive that his own role was under threat.

Christmas 1971, therefore, was to pass in relative peace and contentment, after a rather good year for the Trust and not a bad one for Gerald. His newly published collection of stories, *Fillets of Plaice*, was 'going a bomb,' he told brother Lawrence, and the reviews were good. The book was a miscellaneous collection of short pieces based on fact – a bizarre dinner party in Africa, an ocean picnic in Corfu, a nose-bleed in a London taxi, a sojourn in an eccentric nursing home in the Home Counties – with a title that was an affectionate spoof on his brother's recent literary paean to the *deus loci*, *Spirit of Place*. 'Dotty, painful and amusing,' declared the *Evening Standard*. 'An element of what can only be called "niceness" invades everything which Gerald Durrell writes,' Ronald Blythe wrote in the *Listener*. 'His books accept life in a generous, unshadowy way and are a testament to getting on with it. They remind human beings that the earth is not exclusively theirs to rape and ruin but also belongs to a vast population of other creatures which looks at it with observant eyes, breathes its air and listens to its sounds.'

There was a *frisson* of excitement when a film option on *My Family and Other Animals* was taken up, and it looked as if it might go into production the following year, with Christopher Miles as director, Gerald as 'technical adviser' and Ingrid Bergman as Mother. This choice did not please everybody. 'She might be a beautiful and very talented actress,' complained Jacquie, 'but she doesn't possess an atom of comedy in her bones.' Alternative names put forward for the part included Maggie Smith, Glynis Johns, Joan Greenwood and Audrey Hepburn. But though Christopher Miles visited Corfu to check locations, the production came to nothing when the British unions slapped a ban on filming in Greece because it was still under military rule.

As for the rest of the family, Lawrence was stuck fast in Provence, and Margaret was working as a hostess aboard a Greek cruise ship. 'No word, fortunately, from the Bovril-drinking brother,' Gerald wrote to Lawrence about Leslie, 'but I still scan the *Police Gazette* nervously over my morning coffee.'

As the New Year of 1972 dawned, Gerald was preoccupied with the publication of his book *Catch me a Colobus*, a potpourri of animal encounters and travel adventures, including a belated account of his expedition to Sierra Leone seven years previously and his foray to Mexico to catch volcano rabbits four years ago, with a colourful résumé of the last ten years or so at Jersey Zoo thrown in. The book received mixed reviews: some found it a lacklustre and pedestrian effort compared to the dazzling and infectious virtuosity of his earlier works. But it sold well enough, and raised more public interest in the work of the Trust than any other of Gerald's books. Shortly afterwards the Royal Society of Literature invited Gerald to become a Fellow, in recognition of his contribution to the world of books. 'FRLS' became the second set of letters he could put after his name, and many more were to follow, including (not long afterwards), FIB, or Fellow of the Institute of Biology. Gerald was at the Mazet when he heard the news, working hard on a new book, an account of his year at Whipsnade more than a quarter of a century ago, to be called *Beasts in my Belfry*.

At the zoo the future of the two half-grown female gorillas, N'pongo and Nandi, was giving some concern, first because they were growing out of their accommodation, and second because, without a mate, they had begun to lavish their affections on each other. The first problem was solved when Brian Park, a Jersey resident (and a future Chairman of the Trust Council), happened to see Gerald on local television bemoaning the lack of funds for development at the zoo, and donated £10,000 towards the new Brian Park Gorilla Breeding Complex. The second was solved when Ernst Lang of Basle Zoo, the first man to breed a gorilla in captivity and then persuade the mother to rear the baby herself, presented Jersey Zoo with a young adult male gorilla called Jambo, the first mother-reared gorilla in captivity and a proven breeder.

On 30 April 1972 the new Gorilla Breeding Complex was officially opened by the film star David Niven. The Durrells' connection with Niven had come in a roundabout way. Gerald had bought his first volume of autobiography, *The Moon's a Balloon*, as a present for Jacquie. She had loved it and thought Gerald would get on well with Niven, so when they were searching for a celebrity to open the complex and act as best man at a gorilla wedding she suggested they ask him. Fortunately Dick Odgers, their television agent at Curtis Brown, knew Niven's son Jamie, and so it came about that Niven agreed to come to Jersey.

'He did it wonderfully,' Jacquie recalled. 'He and Gerry took to each other like soul mates and in fact Niven said it was like meeting his twin. Throughout his association with the Trust he was marvellous and did all we asked of him.' The opening ceremony was not without its moments. Niven – armed with an appropriate bouquet of celery, leeks, cabbage, cauliflower and curly kale, and dressed in an extremely elegant dove-grey tailcoat – had no sooner declared the complex open, and 'married' its two newly introduced occupants in a speech of immense charm and humour, than the newly-wed Nandi and Jambo began to copulate in full view of the assembled dignitaries and the deeply gratified zoo staff. Niven turned to Gerald and declared in a loud stage-whisper: 'Wherever I go this sort of thing happens. I have this effect on primates.'

On 1 May 1972, the day following the opening of the Gorilla Breeding Complex, more than three hundred conservationists, zoo keepers and field scientists from around the world gathered in Jersey for the First World Conference on Breeding Endangered Species in Captivity, organised jointly by the Jersey Wildlife Preservation Trust and the Fauna Preservation Society of Great Britain. The theme of the three-day conference, the first of its kind, was the captive breeding of endangered species.

An outline of the scope and aims of the conference was given by Gerald as Director of the Trust and Sir Peter Scott as Chairman of the Fauna Preservation Society. Later Gerald was to give a clear and trenchant account of where captive breeding came from and where it was heading. Saving endangered species was a matter of the most urgent concern, he declared. Over a thousand species were under threat at that very moment. The only practical way of saving them was by protecting their habitats and, as a safeguard, creating 'zoo banks' in which viable breeding groups could find sanctuary in which to live and breed in security until their numbers were sufficient for them to be reintroduced, if possible, back into the areas from which they had vanished.

The concept was not new, he said, but it had been an uphill struggle to persuade some conservationists that it was a respectable, let alone a viable, one. 'Even now,' he told the conference, 'if you mention it at some august body of conservationists they tend to regard you as if you had advocated war as an ideal form of population control.' There were even those who thought it was better a species became extinct in the freedom of the wilds than 'languish' within the confines of a zoo. Many (and Gerald was one of them) acknowledged that most zoos were thoroughly bad places, with high mortality rates and near-zero breeding records, that did more to deplete animal populations than conserve them. But a few world-class institutions were doing a first-rate job, including Jersey (where they had successfully bred the West African colobus monkey and the Chinese white eared pheasant), Basle (lowland gorilla and Indian rhino), Antwerp (the extremely rare Congo peacock), Phoenix (Arabian oryx), and Prague (Przewalski's wild horse). Gerald went on:

> First, and perhaps the most important thing to stress, is that this Trust has never claimed – nor would it be foolish enough to claim – that captive breeding of an endangered species should take the place of conservation of that species in its natural habitat. We have always maintained that controlled breeding should be used *as well as*, not *instead of*, conservation in the wild.
>
> Second, we have never claimed to be able to help *all* species currently in danger of extinction. Out of this long and melancholy list we can only aid a few – generally the smaller and more obscure ones which tend to be ignored by zoological gardens and conservation schemes generally – but we feel that even this is a worthwhile undertaking.

The Jersey Trust, a model of its kind, did not run a zoo in the usual sense: it was a dedicated breeding centre, not merely a showplace. As such, it had many advantages over the conventional zoo. For example, it could concentrate all its energies and funding on conservation. It could design its cages and enclosures for the needs of the animals, and not the public. 'With luck,' Gerald declared, 'we may be groping our way towards a goal all zoos in the future should aspire to.'

'I am afraid that we must face up to the fact,' Gerald continued, 'that a vast number of species in our lifetime are going to become extinct in the wild state and will – with luck – exist only under controlled conditions, provided we set up programmes now. Let us strive wherever possible to save habitat, and the creatures that live in it, but as a precautionary measure let us also set up breeding centres *now*.'

There were, he acknowledged, possible problems inherent in prolonged breeding programmes, about which they were still largely ignorant. For example, would animals bred for many years in controlled conditions undergo genetic change? Gerald contended that a certain amount of hope was to be gained from the fact that the golden hamster, lost to science for a hundred years, now had a world population probably numbering millions, all originating from one gravid female found in Syria in 1930. Or again, what sort of reproduction programme would have to be evolved to train creatures of say, the seventh or eighth generation born under controlled conditions, so that they could be reintroduced into a wild that they had never known, full of dangers from which they had no protection?

'The future of controlled breeding bristles with questions of this sort,' Gerald warned the conference, 'but it is precisely these challenges which make the task worthwhile.' Already a few species had been released back into the wild, among them the white rhino, the Hawaiian goose and the eagle owl.

Gerald ended with a rallying cry. 'We realise,' he said, talking of the Jersey Trust, 'that at the moment our work is only a small part of the whole complex machinery of conservation, but we feel it is important for three reasons. Firstly, no one is doing it on the scale that we are; secondly, it is practical; thirdly, judged as a rescue operation, it is something that can – funds permitting – be done *today*, and with luck bears fruit almost immediately.' As the Trust grew, he explained, he hoped that one day it could function as a training base where staff from around the world could be trained to establish similar breeding centres in the places where they ought to be set up – in the natural habitats of the creatures concerned. There were many who were to think that inherent in this thought was the germ of Gerald's greatest achievement.

The conference was a huge success, and was widely reported in the press and broadcast extensively around the world. It established the validity of captive breeding as an important conservation tool and finally confirmed the stature of both the Trust and its founder in the eyes of the world's scientific community. Three of the world's most influential conservation organisations – the International Union for the Conservation of Nature and Natural Resources (IUCN), the World Wildlife Fund and the Fauna Preservation Society – had thrown their weight behind the work of the Trust, and some of the world's leading scientists had commended the superlative quality of its ground-breaking endeavours. The Director of the Smithsonian Institution's National Zoological Park in Washington, D.C. wrote to Gerald: 'Having visited Les Augrès I can personally attest that you possess personnel so completely imbued with your own dedication to the cause of wildlife conservation that any venture you undertake will most assuredly have the very best chances of success. For many of our lesser known species, your facility and goals represent their only hope of survival. You can already look back on an enviable record.'

One of the contributors to the conference was Dr Robert D. Martin, a young and highly able primatologist, who also edited the proceedings for publication. Not long afterwards he became Senior Research Fellow at the Wellcome Laboratories of the Zoological Society of London, and this appointment led on to a number of projects on endangered species which required samples from numerous zoos. It soon became apparent to him that the Jersey Trust was rather special. Not only was it the best and most reliable source of samples, he reckoned, but it showed the greatest interest in the projects' results and potential applications:

> I was particularly impressed by the personal interest that Gerald Durrell took in such projects. I found him to be very open and receptive to the opinions of others. I was impressed by his approachability, his naturalness, despite his fame, and by his physical presence and sense of humour. He was a person at ease with himself, and unfazed by the antipathy he had attracted from the London Zoo, which in those days (but not later) was anti-Durrell and anti-Jersey Zoo and totally dismissive of the viability of captive breeding as a way of saving endangered animals.

When he was eventually invited to join the JWPT Council, Bob Martin became more impressed still. The Trust, he felt, never stood still, never drifted into complacency. Jersey Zoo was always one jump ahead in the field of captive breeding. It was far more productive per working unit than anywhere comparable in the world. However much it achieved, it was always firmly concentrated on the next stage in the process. Not only did it invite assessments from outsiders, for example in the fields of scientific research and education, but it actually put the advice it received from such sources into practice. This continuous readiness for change and openness to inputs from others was a hallmark of Gerald Durrell's deep concern for endangered species, and was consistently reflected by all members of the JWPT team.

It was Gerald's personality that drew the whole thing together. 'I owe a personal debt to Gerald Durrell for his inspiration and friendship,' Bob Martin was to recall. 'It is no exaggeration to say that his example and philosophy exerted a major and comprehensive influence on my own interests, teaching and research activities. He was never a theorist. Rather he was a communicator; and the idea he articulated throughout his life was of mankind's communion with all animals. He was ultimately trying to save life, in all of its forms, and to export the message. You could say he was the Florence Nightingale of the animal world. He gave a broad brush-stroke to the movement, and his life, his books, his zoo have had a universal and unique impact on both animal and man.'

The growing stature of the organisation was further enhanced later in May when Princess Anne paid a visit to the zoo. This had not been easy to arrange. The zoo had not been on the itinerary for the Princess's official tour of Jersey, and when Gerald rang up the powers-that-be who organise these things they were very dismissive. Show the Princess a zoo? Never! She had more important things to do, like visiting the island's new sewerage works. Gerald was down at the Mazet when the phone rang. There had been a change of plan, he was told: the Princess had asked to see the zoo. She was a fan of his books, it seems – the first one she had read had caused her acute embarrassment, she was to confess later, because she was on a train and couldn't help guffawing out loud.

Gerald had never been involved in a visit of this kind before, and he was unprepared for the swarm of detectives who fanned out over the premises in a hunt for bombs and undesirables, the men with stopwatches who calculated ways of squeezing a tour of seven hundred animals spread over twenty-odd acres into twenty-five minutes, the posse of pressmen 'clicking like a field of mentally defective crickets'.

'The imminent approach of royalty has an odd effect on one,' he noted. 'What was I going to say to her? All of a sudden our achievements and our aspirations seemed as interesting as a vicar's sermon. The whole thing seemed a great mistake. I wished I was back in France.' But the moment the royal car drew up and the Princess stepped out all his fears vanished. 'I was taking round a beautiful, elegant, highly intelligent woman,' he was to recall, 'who asked unexpected questions, who was interested.' The only way Gerald and Jacquie could escort the Princess round the zoo in the allotted time was to show her only the more spectacular or interesting animals – and none was more spectacular than Frisky, the male mandrill. At that moment, as it happened, Frisky was at the multicoloured climax of his sexual display. Gerald was to record the encounter:

> He was in full bloom. The bridge of his nose, the nose itself and the lips were scarlet as any anointment by lipstick. On either side of his nose were bright, cornflower blue welts. His face, framed in gingery-green fur and a white beard, looked like some fierce *juju* mask from an ancient tribe, whose culinary activities included gently turning their neighbours into pot roasts. However, if Frisky's front was impressive, when he swung round he displayed a posterior which almost defied description. Thinly haired in greenish and white hair, he looked as though he had sat down on a newly painted and violently patriotic lavatory seat. The outer rim of his posterior was cornflower blue (as were his genitals) and the inner rim was a virulent sunset scarlet. As we approached the cage, Frisky grunted and then swung round to display his sunset rear.
>
> 'Wonderful animal, ma'am,' I said to the Princess. 'Wouldn't you like to have a behind like that?'

Gerald heard a deep insuck of breath from the entourage behind him and realised – 'with deep gloom' – that he had said the wrong thing.

The Princess examined Frisky's anatomy closely. 'No,' she said, decisively. 'I don't think I would.'

They walked on.

After Princess Anne had left, Gerald had several large drinks to steady his nerves. He had made a sow's ear out of a silk purse, he reckoned. He had meant to ask her if she would become the Patron of the Trust. It was too late now, he thought. But some weeks later, after relentless prodding by Jacquie, he wrote to her and put the question. 'To my incredulity and delight,' he recalled, 'she replied that she would. I am not sure how much he had to do with it, but I took Frisky a packet of Smarties – whose virulent colours so closely resembled his own – as a thank-you gift.' Since August 1972 Princess Anne has carried out her duties as Patron of the Jersey Wildlife Preservation Trust seriously, supportively and with great enthusiasm.

At this high point in the zoo and the Trust's history, some of the leading trustees decided the time had come to take a fresh look at where the organisation stood and how it might capitalise most effectively on its opportunities, rather along the lines of Lord Jersey's preliminary memo a year previously. On 1 September 1972, while Gerald was away in the South of France, the Zoo Management Committee recommended that a special committee of the council should look into the organisation, administration and running of the Trust and the zoo.

This was eminently sensible. No organisation can stand still, and it was obvious that improvements could be made across a whole range of matters. There was no question that the main mission of the organisation was sacrosanct, but it was felt that the time had come for it to be administered more like a well-run commercial company than the vaguely *ad hoc* creation of a philanthropic enthusiast, and that the overall direction of the zoo and Trust should be placed in more professional and experienced hands.

Implicit in the committee's proposals was the understanding that those hands did not belong to Gerald. He was the founding father, creator, visionary; but he had no head for sums, or time for committees, or reverence for reputations, or room for corporate mind-sets and the rule of accountants, or any bent for administering anything or anybody in the sense the trustees implied. He was a dreamer of extraordinary dreams, and his job was to try to make those dreams come true. When rumours of what was afoot reached him in distant Languedoc, Gerald grew restless and resentful. He returned to Jersey post-haste, and when he read the minutes of the management committee's meeting he grew more restless and resentful still. 'I think that both Lord Jersey and Sir Giles Guthrie were genuinely concerned that Gerry was being overwhelmed by the affairs of the Trust,' Jacquie was to reflect a long time later, 'and were seeking ways to alleviate the problem. It was just unfortunate that neither of them approached either Jeremy Mallinson or myself before springing it on Gerry.'

In a memorandum in early September, Lord Jersey recommended a recourse to that typically English organisational stratagem, the committee system, as a cure for all ills. Gerald bridled. 'The apparent cure for lack of funds and its attendant difficulties,' he noted with scorn in a memo to the management committee, 'is to proliferate committees and sub-committees like mushrooms. I cannot stress too strongly that I myself would not be prepared to work for any more committees than we have at the moment.' Then he came to the real nub of his resentment. 'Arising out of this,' he stormed, 'comes the criticism that everything "comes to a standstill" when I am away. This is a criticism, not only to myself, but to my staff, which I do not feel to be justified and which I would like to take this opportunity of refuting.'

But the trustees did not let up. They appointed an investigation com-mittee which swiftly focused on the same main bones of contention. Gerald was not in a position to continue as supremo at the Trust, they reiterated, because he was so seldom there. What the Trust needed, they implied, was a full-time administrator-in-chief. Thus the axe was aimed at the tallest tree. Gerald could now be in no doubt that the main thrust of the Trust's agenda was to remove its founder from his position. In a memo to the investigation committee on 3 October he again defended his absences. When he was away, he said, nothing was left undone that should have been done at the zoo and the Trust. When he was away he was *working* – both on his own behalf and that of the Trust. It was then that he wrote his books. 'I would like to point out,' he continued, 'that the writing of these books fulfils two functions of great importance to the Trust: (1) It provides me with a livelihood, thus obviating the necessity of the Trust paying me a salary commensurate with my worth – a sum the organisation could not possibly afford; (2) It increases Trust member-ship, one of our most important sources of money. It is true to say that without the books there would be no Trust membership and therefore no Trust.' To write his books he had to get away: 'If Trustees and Council lived *with* their staff, were on the job 24 hours a day, and with a café practically in their drawing room, they too would find their powers of concentration impaired.'

If the present structure of management was changed, Gerald con-tended, and all Trust matters were vested in one person, as was proposed, such a person could not possibly cope with all the multifarious complexities of the organisation. The only structure by which the Trust could function, he argued with desperate illogic, was with himself in overall control, Jeremy Mallinson in charge of the scientific and animal side and Catha Weller in charge of finance and Trust business. 'To try and do it in any other way is to treat the Trust as if it were a bank or some similar inhuman organisation. If this is attempted this place will fail: if this is what the Trustees want then I want *no* part in it.'

The trustees were not to be deflected. Again Sir Giles Guthrie led the charge. He believed that what was being proposed was sensible, rational, necessary, above all helpful. As the saviour of BOAC and creator of British Airways he was used to getting his own way. The Jersey Wildlife Preservation Trust was on a much smaller scale, but as an intricate piece of problem-solving the challenge appealed to him. It is also probable that he greatly misunderstood and underestimated Gerald Durrell, who now emerged as not only the main problem, but as his main opponent. Like many people in Jersey and on the Trust, Sir Giles saw Gerald as an amiable, eccentric, bearded best-selling author with a passion for animals, a taste for champagne and a creative bent – but not as a practical administrator. He did not imagine that such a charming chap could re-emerge in a totally different guise, swinging a mailed fist, breathing brimstone and uttering oaths.

At a series of informal meetings mostly held at Lord Jersey's home, Radier Manor, the council members eventually agreed to go ahead as planned, in spite of Gerald's objections, and at a meeting of the Trust Council at Les Augrès Manor on 23 September 1972 it was resolved that a subcommittee of the council should examine the organisation and running of the zoo and the Trust. There was to be a long-term plan for the expansion of the zoo; finance would be under tight control; the structure of management would be changed; and responsibility for the administration of the organisation would be put 'where it rightly should be', on the shoulders of those in day-to-day control. Then came the *coup de grâce*, as Gerald was to see it, delivered with exquisite sleight of hand: 'We feel these recommendations, if adopted, would give G.M.D. his rightful place in the hierarchy of the Trust as its Founder and as originator of the Zoo. They also recognise that it is wrong to tie him down in the routine of the Zoo Administration and Finance.' The council would always be happy to receive the benefit of Gerald's ideas and advice, they said, but in the meantime he would be free to get on with his writing.

Gerald saw the council's recommendations for what they were – or so he thought. The territorial imperative took over. They wanted to dispossess him of the edifice he had created, disengage him from running his own show. They wanted to sideline him as a celebrity fund-raiser who could extract rich pickings from American audiences. Though much of what the council recommended was sensible and constructive, to Gerald it looked like a *coup d'état*, a palace revolution. He tossed all the documents in a paper file and scrawled across it the words 'Judas File'. 'I felt deeply hurt, bewildered and angry,' he told Sir William Haley, the former Director-General of the BBC and editor of *The Times*, who lived on Jersey, not long afterwards. 'The rules governing my actions in the future I found totally unacceptable.'

'When Sir Giles Guthrie suggested that Gerald should become a kind of figurehead Director-General of the Zoo Trust,' Jacquie recalled years later, 'and withdraw himself from the daily hands-on running of the zoo, that's what I wanted as well. Let Jeremy take over, so we could have some life of our own. But they set about it the wrong way – more like a takeover or palace revolution. Giles went at it like a bull at a gate and caught Gerry on the raw. Gerry, of course, just hit the ceiling – there was no possibility of his leaving now. He was all for doing a bulldozer job and all we could do was lock him up in the flat and tell him not to answer the phone while Brian Le Feuvre, a local journalist and friend of the Trust, handled the press. It was a pity Rhona Guthrie was away at the time because she and I could have sorted it out between us.'

To Lord Jersey, the Trust's President, Gerald fired off an intemperate riposte on 13 November 1972: 'As a piece of insulting, mischievous fatuity,' he exploded, 'I have never seen it equalled. It is really a waste of my time to even comment on it, but since you apparently want my views I will.' And he did. Some of the report he found 'exceedingly offensive', some 'laughable', some 'distasteful', some even 'immoral'. He went on: 'Curious though it may sound to the limited minds of the committee the day to day running of the zoo interests me enormously. They may be surprised to learn that I created the place because it *does* interest me enormously. I am tempted to say that I know more about the day to day running of the zoo than the Trustees and Council and I have never at any time suggested that I want relief from the day to day running of the zoo in order to get on with my writing and television appearances. What does *not* interest me is having to waste my time constantly as a fund-raiser owing to the complete inertia of the Trustees and Council.' If they thought he was going to relinquish control – 'after nine years of steady growth from tiny beginnings into an organisation known throughout the world' – they had another think coming. 'If the committee seriously imagines that I intend to have my authority undermined in this way,' he finished off, 'their collective intelligence is less than I had always supposed it to be. I am stating here and now – and for the last time – that I would not dream of accepting any of these proposals. I do not intend to implement any of them. Should the Trustees and Council wish to implement anything like this then I am afraid they will have to ask for my resignation.'

Gerald's reaction caused some confusion in the enemy ranks, but they quickly regrouped and returned to the fray. Lord Jersey asked for an apology. A meeting was convened for 8 December at Les Augrès Manor. Gerald was fired up, fighting mad, taking no prisoners. He was battling for his dream, for his baby, for the cause. He spared no one. He did not hide his contempt. He did not mind his language. He spat fire and four-letter words in an attack such as the staid and distinguished gathering round the council table had never heard – or at any rate had never heard directed at themselves.

The council's ultimate weapon, as they thought, was mass resignation, which would leave Gerald without a remit, without a mandate to continue. At a meeting at Lord Jersey's home, letters of resignation were circulated among the trustees, and all but one – Brian Park – signed.

To Gerald the crisis looked terminal. He instinctively took evading action, telephoning his literary agent, Peter Grose, in London. Grose recalled:

He rang me up in a pretty agitated state and said, 'The whole Trust has quit on me.' I said, 'I'm on the plane,' and I went straight over to Jersey. When I got there Gerry was in a great state of fury and mouthing many expressions of disgust in pretty fruity language. 'This is appalling. I've written a letter to the local paper.' He gave me the letter to read. It was a defence against what he called 'charges'. 'Barmy!' I said. 'You can tear that one up straight away.' The public didn't give a damn about the directors, I told him, what they wanted to know was what was happening to the animals. What we had to do was take the initiative, issue a press statement, get the TV people up here, tell the world – a bit like Harold Macmillan at the time of the Profumo scandal – that there had been 'a little local difficulty' but that now it was 'business as usual at the zoo'. So I drafted the press statement and got the TV cameras in, and that night, when Jeremy Mallinson and his wife, and John Hartley and Sam and Catha Weller came up to the flat to have a rallying dinner with Gerry and Jacquie and me, we watched it all on the TV news, all the animals as happy as lambs and the public pouring in as if nothing had happened. So we had won the day –

so far. But the idea you could run the Trust without Gerry was preposterous and grotesque. You had to have Gerry, warts and all.

Next day Gerald wrote to Lord Jersey, apologising (as requested) for any offence caused by his letter of 13 November, but reaffirming that he could not accept the substance of the report. Two days later Lord Jersey, a very kind, gentle man and a staunch supporter from the beginning, wrote to confirm the resignations of the trustees. 'May I say we all still firmly believe in your ideals of conservation,' he wrote, 'and sincerely wish the Trust and the Zoo every success in the future. After so many years it is only with regret and sadness that we have come to this decision.'

But they had not read the small print. The Jersey lawyer who had drawn up the laws of the council had included a loophole that provided for a quorum to take over. It turned out that Jeremy Mallinson (Zoological Director), John Hartley (Trust Secretary) and Catha Weller (member of the Board of Management) were legitimate council members with a vote. A quorum was formed when some of the council members who had resigned crept back. Gerald was happy to accept the resignations of the rest. He could now replace them. He had won the day.

Looking back soon afterwards, Gerald blamed Sir Giles Guthrie for the whole affair. 'This has been a power struggle, pure and simple,' he wrote to a colleague in America on 14 December. 'For several years now, one of the Trustees has felt that I was a thorn in his side, for the simple reason that as I am unpaid he cannot boss me about. This whole sorry business was because he hoped that he could back me into a corner and force me out of the way. As you can imagine, I was distressed beyond all measure at the despicable way the Council was forced into a position of resigning as a body. This whole distasteful business has at least shown me where my friends lie.'

But it was a sad business from the viewpoint of either side. Like Lord Jersey, Sir Giles Guthrie had been one of those rare creatures, a tycoon who was also a dedicated conservationist. And he had not just paid lip service to the cause. He had periodically donated £5000 to the Trust over a lengthy period, as well as his pet alligator, while his wife had contributed £1000 per annum on her own account, and a lump sum of £10,000 towards the orang utan enclosure.

The Times had picked up the story, and the Curator of Mammals at London Zoo, Dr Michael Brambell, was moved to write a letter of commiseration to Jeremy Mallinson which included a testimony to the current stature of the Jersey Zoo and Trust: 'I think Jersey Zoo is the most exciting new venture in the field in this country, and one of the four worthwhile zoological efforts at present going in the animal collection business in the British Isles, two others being Peter Scott's set-up and on a smaller scale Philip Wayre's [Pheasant/Otter Trust in Norfolk].'

Looking back with the gift of hindsight, it is clear that the Trustees were probably right to propose improving the efficiency of the organisation. But they set about it in the wrong way, provoking a defensive and hostile reaction from Gerald, who went right over the top. Nearly twenty years later Lord Jersey wrote to Sir Giles Guthrie's widow, Rhona, wondering what all the fuss had been about. 'Looking through our Report with today's eyes,' he reflected, 'it seems so very mild and to the point. I am amazed it resulted in all the kerfuffle, and amazed that practically all our recommendations have, bit by bit, been adopted.'

Gerry and Jacquie had not emerged unscathed. Jacquie was condemned to life as before, but in the process had lost a number of her Jersey friends. Gerry had emerged with his position enhanced, but there were mutterings behind closed doors that he had now kissed goodbye to any prospect of a knighthood.

Gerry wasted no time in dusting himself down. He had ambitious plans for 1973, when the tenth anniversary of the Trust would be celebrated, and he had a new council to form as soon as he could. In February he announced a new 'all-star' line-up. Sir William Collins, chairman of Gerald's publishers, had agreed to join the council, along with Gerald's celebrity chums Noël Coward and David Niven. Other new members included Lord Craigton, Vice-Chairman of the Fauna Preservation Society and Chairman of the British Council for Environmental Conservation, and Robin Rumboll, a prominent Jersey accountant and politician, who replaced Sir Giles Guthrie as financial adviser.

Gerald's New Year *tour d'horizon* was bullish. The zoo collection now comprised nearly eight hundred animals. The breeding programme was forging ahead and the scientific excellence of the establishment was now almost without peer. The animal records were among the most comprehensive of any zoo in the world, and the annual report was one of the most impressive zoological publications of its kind. The education programme, so dear to Gerald's heart, was expanding. In the last few years over eleven thousand British and nearly a thousand French school-chidren had visited the collection, and a classroom and a full-time teacher were to be added to the Trust's facilities. Great importance had always been attached to the landscaping and planting of the zoo grounds, and with the tireless devotion of Vi Lort-Philips (a local resident and staunch supporter of the zoo) and Lady Rhona Guthrie and the Gardening Committee the greening of Jersey Zoo had proceeded apace, with the impressive botanical collection – matching where possible the natural habitat of the animals – a worthy and sometimes even a rival complement to the zoological one. In the first month of the year alone, Gerald reported, Trust membership had gone up by over two hundred, and nine mammals and thirteen birds had been bred. A new reptile and amphibian breeding unit – the most sophisticated of its kind in the world – was going ahead with money from a Canadian Trust member, and a marmoset and tamarin breeding unit was being built with the help of a £5000 donation from a British member.

'We hope to make this tenth anniversary year the best in the history of the Trust,' Gerald told the press. And he was now ready to take the campaign to the world's richest country.

TWENTY-THREE

Gerald in America

1973–1974

Though Gerald Durrell, now approaching fifty, could still be a very funny man and could still write very funny books, he had become a deadly serious player in a deadly serious game. The image he presented to the world was no longer just the product of his genes and upbringing. The fifteen often brutally tough years since he had arrived in Jersey and taken on the zoo and the Trust had moulded him into something more complex and frequently more contradictory and paradoxical than his earlier persona. From being a purely private person he had become a political animal, with all that entailed – subtler, more volatile, more desperate, not always as jovial and cuddly as his physical appearance, resembling a kind of bacchanalian Father Christmas, led his fans to expect him to be.

There was though, still a strong sense of sheer mischief in the man, and this mischievousness could be ludic or demonic, depending on his mood. David Hughes saw something of this schism in his personality:

> I think he had enormous difficulty in controlling himself in a Jekyll and Hyde-ish sort of way. He could often be wickedly teasing, trying to find a person's soft spot and put thumb pressure on it. You had to be fairly tough to stand up to it really. He did it with me. He never let me off the hook at all, so there were occasions when I came quite close to being hurt, though he wouldn't have wanted that to happen. It was more than a game, it was more a way of controlling people. Probably he couldn't have run the zoo and the Trust without it. It was his way of being the big male boss gorilla, the super silverback. If you're anarchic, not in a conventional power structure, you've got to have something over and above normal charisma to get people to follow you, and getting behind people's defences was one way of keeping control. That's

how his devoted staff not only remained faithful to the idea but to the man who had set that idea in their minds. In a way, too, it was his way of expressing his shyness. Because he *was* shy. This wasn't observable in terms of normal shyness – he didn't stutter or go inside himself, but he did have to compensate.

Peter Olney, Curator of Birds at London Zoo and an old friend, had watched Gerald grow in status and in stature over the years, turning into the portly, prophet-like figure he now presented to the world. But in spite of his fame and authority, Olney felt Gerald was still *au fond* the same rather diffident and modest man he had always been:

He admitted he didn't like meeting strangers greatly, and he had to force himself to come forward. When he was talking about something that he was passionately interested in he was able to overcome this, but he hated having to go to formal things like banquets and cocktail parties, and hated giving public speeches, though once he had got to his feet he could be brilliant. He was not only shy and modest but he laboured under a sense of inadequacy as well, certainly in the early days, and especially surrounded by academic zoologists – he didn't speak the same language, didn't know the genetics and so on. He never really understood why he was so famous, though he quite enjoyed it, or why people took him so seriously, though he enjoyed what fame gave him. When I got to know him I regarded him not so much as a father figure but as the older brother I would like to have had, someone whose ideas I was very much in sympathy with.

In May 1973, with his forthcoming visit to the United States in mind, Gerald contracted an independent documentary film-maker by the name of David Cobham to make a short promotional film about the work and achievements of the Jersey Zoo and Trust which he could show to American audiences. The film was scripted and narrated by Gerald. On his home patch, away from the bright lights and artificial atmosphere of a television studio, he blossomed as a performer in front of the camera. 'He was very impressive,' Cobham recalled. 'He did long takes to camera absolutely convincingly and without a single fluff.'

The film opened with Gerald sitting at a desk lit only by a single candle. On the desk were two fluffy baby representatives of an endangered species of African owl. 'All over the world,' Gerald said to camera, 'animal life is in danger of extinction by the direct or indirect intervention of man. Over a thousand species and sub-species of animals are in danger of vanishing for ever. Here on the island of Jersey the Wildlife Preservation Trust has created a rescue operation that is quite unique. We're a reservoir of threatened wildlife from all over the world – a sanctuary where they can live and breed in peace.'

In two and a half days flat the film was in the can. It ended as it had begun, with Gerald seated at his candle-lit desk. 'Every year,' he said, 'we spend millions of pounds on man-made things, on beautiful buildings, monuments, libraries and art galleries to house books and works of art. But in a way, isn't the animal world God's art gallery, aren't the animals God's works of art? You can recreate an art gallery, but you can't recreate an animal species once it has been destroyed, and to exterminate an animal species is as easy as snuffing out a candle.' Gerald's finger poised over the candle flame. As he snuffed it out, the baby owls disappeared into darkness.

Gerald's newfound ease and fluency with the film medium was not lost on David Cobham, or on Gerald himself – or on others in the business. 'He was rather like Peter Ustinov in some ways,' Jacquie was to remark. 'He had a wonderful facility for involving you when he was relating an incident, a tremendous gift for telling a story and captivating you.'

David Cobham was very struck by Jacquie's role during his short sojourn at the zoo. 'Gerry was enormously dependent on her,' he recalled. 'She drove the whole circus. She could be very forceful with people, very tough when it came to looking after Gerry's interests. If Gerry was like the exalted subaltern at the head of the platoon, Jacquie was like the platoon sergeant, the one who really kept the troops on the march and the show on the road. I never saw any hostility between them then. In fact quite the reverse. One evening I had to double back to the flat because I'd forgotten something and I just went straight into the flat without knocking and found Gerry and Jacquie curled up in each other's arms, cuddling on the floor with their backs against the sofa. It was a lovely image and it moved me greatly.'

Gerald spent the early part of the summer of 1973 at the Mazet. By now *Beasts in my Belfry*, his humorously written but seriously intentioned account of his year as a student keeper at Whipsnade, had been published, to a favourable reception from reviewers and readers alike. Dominating his thoughts, however, was his forthcoming visit to Canada and the United States. A crucial step in the furtherance of the Trust's activities worldwide, the tour had two objectives: first, to publicise the work of the Trust and to raise funds from wealthy American supporters; and second, to develop the American arm of the Trust, known as SAFE (Save Animals from Extinction), which could continue to generate funds *in situ*.

Gerald viewed the visit with excitement, awe, and absolute dread. 'Off at crack of dawn tomorrow,' he wrote uneasily to Lawrence on 26 August, 'and not looking forward to this bloody American trip one bit, but I hope it will be a success. I'll be back in Jersey in mid-December so come over and be introduced to the baby gorilla.' The baby was Assumbo, four pounds nine ounces, son of Nandi and Jambo, Jersey's first-born gorilla, the pride of the zoo, currently being kept in an incubator and hand-fed every three hours by his human father-substitute, Jeremy Usher-Smith.

Gerald was never altogether comfortable in America. He was a confirmed Old Worlder, perfectly at ease in an oriental bazaar, an Arab kasbah, a Greek country taverna, an African hut. But while the Americans spoke more or less the same language as he did, collectively they seemed to him to come from another planet. The pace, the drive, the pressure, the glitz, the noise, the way of life and way of thinking of American big cities terrified him, but also mesmerised him. America was the big time. America had money – lots of it. And Americans could fix things – lots of things. He had no alternative. Everyone at the Trust was counting on him. Besides, the Americans had the best and longest animal conservation record in the West. It was the Americans who had first taken up the challenge of a beleaguered environment and who had first set aside great swathes of their country as national parks. Above all it was the Americans who decades ago had pioneered the breeding of an endangered species, in the form of the American buffalo.

On 27 August 1973 Gerald set off in trepidation. He did not like flying, preferring to see the world at ground or sea level, so he crossed the Atlantic on the SS *France*. Jacquie did not accompany him, though she planned to join him in New York at the end of the trip. Instead he sailed with a couple of old friends he had first met on a trip to Corfu – Peter Waller, who for some years had been Assistant Administrator at the Royal Opera House, Covent Garden, and Steve Eckard, a Princeton man and a teacher, who with Waller had founded the American School in London. These two were to be the key and linchpin of the tour, Gerald's fixers and minders, booking hotels and buying train tickets, leaving Gerald free to concentrate on the task in hand – lecturing about the Jersey Trust and persuading rich Americans to part with their money.

Waller and Eckard's countless friends included many of the rich and famous, and they selflessly used these contacts to help Gerald in his ceaseless quest for support and funds. Eckard was a long-time friend of Margot Rockefeller, wife of a scion of the great American family, having taught her to ride when she was young, and by great good fortune – a classic example of 'Durrell's luck' – she happened to be on board the SS *France*, along with her husband Godfrey and their two children. Within a few hours they had all met up, and were soon working their way through Godfrey's inexhaustible supply of whisky in the Rockefeller suite. By the time the ship was nosing past the Statue of Liberty the Rockefellers were among Gerald's best and closest American friends. They were poor Rocke-fellers, Gerald was told – relatively speaking, that is. Nevertheless they were to play a crucial part in his life and work in future years, and to be a critical connection in the evolution of American involvement in the Trust.

On 5 September, after a convivial but sometimes storm-tossed crossing, Gerald and his companions disembarked in a smoggy, heatwave New York. During his first few days in the Big Apple he fortuitously encoun-tered someone else who was to prove a critical figure in his American plans. He had been shopping in Macy's in Fifth Avenue and had just emerged when his young female companion Martha Reeves, who had set up the tour and helped set up SAFE, uttered a piercing squeak. 'Look,' she cried. 'It's Tom Lovejoy.'

Dr Thomas E. Lovejoy was a Yale-educated environmentalist and tropical biologist in his early thirties. At this time he was based at the Academy of Natural Sciences of Philadelphia. Like many zoologists and conservationists of his generation, his commitment to conservation had been nurtured in part by his reading of Gerald Durrell's early books when he was a schoolboy. Gerald later recounted their first meeting: 'I saw a slight young man dancing down the sidewalk towards us, tousled dark hair, dark eyes with a humorous glint in them, a handsome face with an endearing grin. I liked him at once and felt that he liked me.' Tom Lovejoy, too, vividly recalled that chance near-collision: 'I was steaming full tilt like a New Yorker up Fifth Avenue, and almost ran up on the back of Gerry's heels. "You must be Gerald Durrell," I said (careful to avoid the American mispronunciation Doo-rell), and he turned, fixed me with those blue eyes, and we both knew in an instant, in a form of love at first sight, that the other was a true believer, in that conservation and zoos represent callings to which there are none more noble.' It was a partnership and bond, Lovejoy was to say, which endured to the very end.

Though this first encounter happened by chance, the two men were not unacquainted, for Gerald had been in touch with Lovejoy by letter about his American plans. 'We dragged him off to a nearby hostelry,' Gerald recorded, 'and filled him with beer while I told him what I was trying to do in America. He listened quietly and gave me some excellent advice, and promised to see me when I returned from my trip so that we could discuss how best to set up the Trust in America.'

Gerald normally did not care for cities, but he fell in love with New York. It helped that just as he was about to begin his first lecture, at the Explorers Club, he was handed a telegram with the news that N'pongo, Jersey's other female gorilla, had given birth to a male baby, whom Gerald immediately named Mamfe. 'My audience must have thought I was a little bit distraught,' he recalled of this big moment in the Trust's breeding history. 'But it's not every day you hear that your gorillas have successfully given birth to two babies within weeks of one another. This marvellous news on its own would have been enough to fortify me throughout the whole tour.'

Spirits lifted, Gerald set off on his coast-to-coast tour. Philadelphia was fine, but he did not like Chicago, where he lectured to a packed, expectant and daunting audience of two thousand, and though he adored San Francisco he hated Los Angeles. The lectures were a great test of his nerves, although his practice of drawing lightning sketches of the animals he was talking about helped. 'If you mention an animal like a capybara,' he was to explain, 'you can't expect everyone to know what you're talking about, but if you can draw it, even if it's only a caricature, they've got a much better visual impression. They love the drawings and fight for them afterwards.' It also helped to focus the attention of American audiences on his theme of endangered species if he could connect conservation with patriotism. That emblem of the American nation, the bald eagle, he pointed out, could be gone in ten years' time – how would they feel if they let the funny-looking bird on their dollar bills become extinct?

His last speaking engagement on his three-month marathon was at an exclusive country club. The place was full of *nouveau riche* Americans, many of them women on the wrong side of middle age. 'They were bejewelled like Christmas trees,' Gerald recalled, 'and tinkled like musical boxes as they walked. I felt that if I could lure one of them behind a bush and strip her of her baubles, it would probably keep the Trust solvent for several years.'

Even Gerald was dismayed by their capacity for alcohol: 'Dinner was preceded by two hours of solid and lavish drinking on a scale I have seldom seen equalled. A request for Scotch resulted in something the size of a small vase being thrust into your hand, containing half a pint of spirits, four ice cubes, each capable of sinking the *Titanic*, and a teaspoon of soda in which three or four errant bubbles were enmeshed.' By the time dinner was served the audience was half sloshed. By the time dinner had been consumed it was half blind.

'I launched into my heart-rending plea on behalf of the animals of the world,' Gerald was to relate, 'to an audience of quite the most unprepossessing mammals I had ever encountered.' Against a rising babble of conversation – for none of the audience could fathom what he was talking about – he realised he was competing for attention with the woman seated next to him. Weighed down by a passable imitation of the Crown Jewels, she had passed out during his address and her head had fallen into a plate containing the remains of a large strawberry soufflé. 'As she breathed stertorously, the strawberry soufflé bubbled merrily with a loud gurgling and popping noise, reminiscent of somebody trying to suck a complex fruit sundae through a straw.' At the end of this terrifying ordeal Gerald received donations from his audience of pie-eyed super-rich that totalled just $100.

Gerald returned gratefully to New York for a series of radio, TV and press engagements. He was a happy to tell a few whoppers if they helped the cause. When American families came to the British Isles on vacation, he told America, there were only two things their children wanted to see – Buckingham Palace and Durrell's zoo. It was in New York that Gerald and Tom Lovejoy worked out the formula which allowed SAFE (later renamed Wildlife Preservation Trust International – WPTI) to proceed. 'To be more accurate,' Gerald noted, 'I said what it was the Jersey Trust needed and Tom hammered out the master plan of how to obtain it.' Though its mandate was to change later, it was originally conceived to assist Americans in making donations to the work of the Trust in Jersey and overseas. The Zoological Society of Philadelphia donated office space to house the organisation's headquarters, with Tom Lovejoy as chairman of the board and Jody Longnecker as the administrator in charge.

So Gerald's first great American tour ended with both of its objectives successfully achieved. Jacquie flew out to join him in New York in time to celebrate Thanksgiving with the Rockefellers and her birthday at the Waldorf. Then the couple sailed away, heading for France on a voyage that was to give Gerald, as Jacquie put it, 'a complete rest after all the steam of that intensive time'.

'There are times when the trail of the begging bowl is a hard one,' Gerald was to reflect, 'but in this case it was more than made up for by the wonderful and generous people I met in America. Over the years we have had reason to be more than grateful to our American friends, for most of our big gifts and grants have come from across the Atlantic, and without this magnificent help our progress would have been slow indeed.'

At this point WPTI consisted of not much more than a few hundred card-index records in a shoebox, but gradually it began to grow following regular meetings round Margot Rockefeller's dining-room table with Sophie Danforth, Emerson Duncan and other dedicated American supporters of the cause. Tom Lovejoy soon realised that to really make an impact in the States they needed a patron who was a household name. Jacquie suggested Princess Grace of Monaco, formerly Grace Kelly, one of Hollywood's greats. 'It seemed obvious,' Lovejoy recalled, 'that Her Serene Highness Princess Grace was perfect; a princess but an American. She could do enormous good. Besides, Prince Rainier had a zoo and loved gorillas.'

An approach to Princess Grace was made through David Niven, who was a close friend of the Rainier family, and it was suggested that Gerald and Tom Lovejoy should come to see the Princess in Monaco. So in the spring of 1974 Gerald, Jacquie, Ann Peters and Peggy Peel drove down to Monaco.

'As it is not every day that you are invited to the palace at Monaco,' Gerald was to recount, 'I felt we ought to do the thing in style. Therefore I and my female entourage were ensconced in an extremely lush hotel within note-rustling distance of the casino. The delicious cucumber soup had been delicately sipped and the waiters had, in solemn silence, placed in front of us the fresh salmon poached in champagne and cream, when Thomas Lovejoy made his appearance.'

Lovejoy, Gerald observed, looked like the survivor of an earthquake. His suit appeared to have been slept in by seventeen tramps. His shirt was fish-belly grey. His shoes were 'carunculated and furrowed as any chestnut, the toes standing up like flagpoles, they were shoes in which you felt might lurk any number of communicable diseases'.

'Well, hi there,' said Tom, packing his unsavoury body into a chair. 'Sorry I'm late.'

'My female entourage regarded him as if he were a toad found lurking in their soup,' recalled Gerald. '"We hope you're not going to meet Princess Grace at the palace looking like *that*," they said ominously and simultaneously.'

In due course Gerald and Tom set off up the hill to the fairytale pink palace. They were ushered into the Princess's private office. 'Dazzlingly beautiful and elegant,' Gerald was to recall, 'Princess Grace rose from behind her desk and came forward, smiling, to greet us. It was then to my horror I saw Tom wave a friendly hand at her.

'Well, hi there, Grace,' he said.

'Your Serene Highness is most kind to spare us the time,' Gerald croaked, trying to undo whatever damage had been done. 'This is Dr Thomas Lovejoy, chairman of our American board, and my name is Durrell.'

They sat down on a large sofa with the Princess between them and carefully explained what they were trying to do. It looked at first as though Princess Grace would turn them down. She had so many commitments, she said, so much on her plate.

At this point Gerald played his trump card: 'I slid on to her lap a large photograph of our newly-born baby gorilla, lying on its tummy on a white terry towel.' The baby gorilla was his firstborn, Assumbo, the pride of the zoo and totally adorable.

'Your Serene Highness,' said Gerald, 'these are the sorts of animals we are trying to help.'

The Princess studied the baby gorilla portrait rhapsodically. 'Oh, it's so cute,' she cooed, her eyes misted with emotion, 'I've never seen anything so cute ... Now tell me, how can I help?' She was prepared to think about it, she said. They should stay in touch.

'I knew that gorilla picture would get her,' Gerald told Tom as they jubilantly climbed into their taxi. 'Every woman I've shown it to has gone nuts about it. It brings out the mummy in them.'

But Tom didn't agree. It wasn't the picture, he told Gerald. It was the little piece of egg yoke on his tie.

Later in the summer there was a second meeting in Monaco. This time Gerald and Tom Lovejoy were joined by Jacquie and Jeremy Mallinson at a small informal lunch by the pool in the palace garden. Prince Rainier was swimming in the pool when they arrived. The Princess was wearing dark glasses and moved her head carefully. Last night, she said, there had been the big Red Cross Ball, and she had a hangover. She asked them what they would like to drink. Jeremy Mallinson said he'd rather like a lager, and watched in fascination as the Princess plunged her arm into the heart of the sub-tropical shrubbery and brought out an ice-cold bottle from a fridge concealed in a bush.

'Princess Grace was still frankly rather reluctant to take on animal charity,' Jacquie recalled, 'as her main interest lay in human problems. However, after Gerry had given her a basic outline, with additions from Lovejoy and Jeremy, Rainier threw his support behind our request, for he was a very keen animal man, and had his own zoo. Princess Grace felt that it should be Rainier and not her who should head the US end, but we all – Rainier included – pointed out that it was *her* name that Americans would respond to.'

Later word came through, via the palace private office, that Her Serene

Highness Princess Grace of Monaco had graciously agreed to serve as the American Trust's patron. So now both Trusts, on both sides of the Atlantic, had princesses as their champions.

TWENTY-FOUR

'Two Very Lost People'

1975–1976

The new year of 1975 began as it was to end for Gerald – in catastrophe. In the run-up to Christmas he had cheerfully fired off a clutch of invitation cards illustrated with his own pen-and-ink cartoons to his closest friends:

> This is to invite you to my half-a-hundred party. On 7th January 1975 I will have achieved my half century. As this rarely happens twice in a lifetime I am celebrating the occasion with a select band of favourite friends. If you will grace this orgy by appearing, please let me know so that the chef may be cosseted, oysters ordered, champagne chilled, and the red carpet renovated. Make landfall on the 6th (in case of fog) and plan to leave on the 8th. I look forward to you.

But it was not to be. Five days before his birthday Gerald's health crashed again and Jacquie had to send out telegrams telling the guests that the celebrations had been cancelled. Pneumonia was diagnosed, and it was March before Gerald was truly on the mend. 'For seven weeks I have been bedridden,' he complained, 'coughing forlornly, like a heroine in a Victorian novel – only slightly more hairy and with a better prose style.'

Two events brightened the early part of the year. The first was the publication of his second story book for children, *The Talking Parcel*. The second was the arrival of another film star at the zoo, this time in the shape of James Stewart, an actor whom Gerald greatly admired. Stewart came to Jersey in May to open the Nocturnal House, the safe breeding area for some of the lemurs and the zoo's collection of hutias, which had been funded by the American end of the organisation. He had a great interest in conservation and was keen to meet Gerald, and as he was in London, starring in the stage version of *Harvey*, Fleur Cowles, a wealthy American patron of the arts who had rallied to Gerald's cause at the time of the palace revolution, had little difficulty in persuading him to come over to perform the opening ceremony.

'Stewart was unassumingly himself,' Gerald recorded, 'tall, gangling, a gentle smile on his face, walking with a slight cowboy slouch, drawling sentences in his lovely husky voice.' After lunch Stewart opened the hutia complex with characteristic charm, explaining that had loved hoot ears ever since he had first set eyes on them, which was five minutes ago. Ordeal over, Gerald and Jacquie led the party off for a tour of the zoo. Stewart and his wife and daughter (who worked with Diane Fossey and the gorillas in Rwanda) were enchanted to be introduced to the baby gorillas, who in the warm summery weather were let out on the lawn in front of the manor, where they picked the flowers and played with a wooden rocking horse, their favourite toy. Later the group moved on to the house of a friend and neighbour of Gerald and Jacquie, where they all repaired to the drawing-room after dinner. There was a piano in the room, as Stewart, who seemed to be suffering from something resembling jetlag (though the flight over had taken less than an hour), slowly perceived.

'Gee, it's a piana,' he said.

'Jimmy, no,' said his wife Gloria, warningly.

'Yes, sir, a piana, a kinda little baby piana.'

'Jimmy, you're not to,' said Gloria.

'A little toon . . .' said Stewart musingly, a fanatical gleam in his eye. 'A toon – what's that toon I like?'

'Please, Jimmy, don't play the piano,' said Gloria desperately.

'Oh, I know . . . "Ragtime Cowboy Joe" . . . Yes, siree.'

'Jimmy seated himself at the piano,' Gerald was to write:

He lifted the lid and the baby grand grinned at him like a crocodile. We were immediately apprised of two facts. The first was that James Stewart was tone deaf and the other was that he could not play the piano. In addition, he had forgotten all the lyrics except the basic one of the title. He played all the wrong notes and sang out of tune. In his husky, croaking voice he sang the title of the song over and over again, going back to the beginning when he thought he had left something out. It was excruciatingly funny, but you did not dare laugh as he was taking such pride in his performance. In the end, he exterminated 'Ragtime Cowboy Joe' to his satisfaction, and turned to us, happy in his achievement.

'Would anyone like to hear some other toons,' he enquired.

'Jimmy, we must go,' said Gloria.
And go they did.

Another great name of the movies who passed through around this time was Katharine Hepburn, who was staying with the Durrells' near neighbour Bill Rose, a film writer with hits like *Genevieve* to his credit. Hepburn often went for walks around the zoo grounds, during the course of which she struck up an acquaintance with Shep Mallet, the Curator of Birds. When Mallet mentioned this to Gerald, who was an ardent admirer of Hepburn, he asked Mallet to let him know when she came again. 'A few days later,' Jacquie recalled, 'John brought her up to the Manor together with her secretary. Gerry was over the moon to meet her. She was charming and totally relaxed and Gerry thoroughly enjoyed her visit. Before she left she agreed to sign our visitors' book, and when her secretary hesitated to do this as well, Hepburn said: "Go ahead, but *sign real small*." '

Gerald still hankered to get back into the film or television medium. It seemed his ambition was doomed to be frustrated when David Cobham's planned BBC Television version of *The Donkey Rustlers*, starring David Niven and Peter Bull, was abandoned when Greek co-production funding fell apart a week before shooting was due to start on Corfu. Another of Cobham's projects was more promising, however. In the previous year he had commissioned Henry Williamson to write a screen adaptation of his classic novel *Tarka the Otter*. When the ageing Williamson became too ill to complete the job, he recommended that Gerald Durrell take over. When Gerald heard of this he said to Cobham: 'If you don't let me write it, I'll kill you.' So in 1975 Cobham came to Jersey with Bill Travers, who with his wife Virginia McKenna had produced and starred in such box-office hits as *Born Free* and *Ring of Bright Water*, to discuss the possibility of Gerald adapting *Tarka* for the big screen.

'Although we didn't take to Travers at all,' Jacquie recalled, 'because for a start he was a dedicated anti-zoo man, Gerry agreed to try and tackle this filmically difficult book. It wasn't an easy time for him – he had a lot on his mind – and it took him a while to work out an angle, but eventually he came up with an idea and the script was written.' In fact what Gerald wrote was a hundred-page treatment on which David Cobham based the finished screenplay. Eventually the film was made to great acclaim, with Gerald and Cobham sharing the screenwriting credit and Peter Ustinov speaking the part of the narrator.

Even more promising was Gerald's burgeoning association with a dynamic young Canadian television executive by the name of W. Paterson

Ferns, a director of a production company called Nielsen Ferns Productions, whose wife, a Durrell fan from childhood, was to become the first unpaid Executive Director of Wildlife Preservation Trust Canada. In April 1973 Ferns' business partner Richard Nielsen had visited the Mazet to ask Gerald if he would be interested in doing a television documentary for their new company. 'Gerry's response was that he was not interested in doing a documentary,' Ferns was to relate, 'as he had done many documentaries for the BBC. What he was interested in doing was a television *series*.' When Nielsen returned from France, therefore, he gave Ferns the responsibility of putting together a series with Gerald. 'The idea we presented to Gerry,' Pat Ferns recalled, 'was to use his forthcoming book *The Stationary Ark* – which he described as his first "serious" book – as a basis for a series that could be shot in his zoo on Jersey. Gerry's strengths as a presenter were obvious. He was a great storyteller, and his capacity to relate the telling anecdote made him compelling TV fare.'

In October 1974 Pat Ferns flew to Jersey to negotiate a deal with Gerald's television agent, Dick Odgers of Curtis Brown – 'The best agent I ever encountered,' Ferns remembers. 'He was a gentleman, he was fair, and he represented Gerry brilliantly.' The series got under way with the filming of a gorilla birth shortly afterwards, and principal photography began on 8 May 1975. 'It was obviously a difficult period in Gerry and Jacquie's relationship,' Ferns recalled. 'During filming Jacquie would walk straight on to the set if the mood took her and start berating Gerry for something or other with the cameras rolling!'

That summer Gerald, Jacquie, Peggy Peel and Penny Roche, a local Jersey girl, set off in two cars for the South of France, where they were to stay at the Mazet for much of the summer. Much of his time there Gerald spent working on the commentary script for *The Stationary Ark*, for which David Cobham's short promo film of the same title now turned out to be a kind of pilot. The series presented a detailed look at the workings of the Jersey Zoo and Trust, above all the captive breeding agenda.

During the year Gerald's friend David Hughes paid a series of visits to the Durrell *ménages* in Jersey and the South of France to gather material for a proposed biographical memoir about Gerald, which had been contracted by Collins. Hughes found Gerald and Jacquie strangely semi-detached, occupying the same living space without making any but the most routine and perfunctory contact. They had gone far beyond the staleness or even boredom of a long marriage, and had reached a stand-off in which there was no sharing of interests or meeting of minds. 'Sadly Gerry's and my relationship had deteriorated over the years,' Jacquie was to record, 'something we both did our best to hide from outsiders, for we hated displaying our woes in public and always presented a "happy face" for the benefit of the Trust.' But by the mid-seventies it was becoming apparent to some people at the zoo that the marriage was in serious trouble.

To Hughes it seemed Jacquie was the background figure who addressed her husband as often as not by means of a shouted question or instruction from a distant room – 'What are our plans?' 'Where are we lunching?' 'How can I do lunch for ten people single-handed?' – to which Gerald would respond with a nod, or a grunt, or by raising his eyes to heaven, no more. Jacquie was the practical major domo of the household who kept things in running order. In France it was she who masterminded the daily shopping, did the packing, drove the car, planned the route, checked the petrol, oil and water, booked the restaurant, paid the bills, kept an eye on the booze, brought Gerald round when he ate and drank too much. On Jersey she acted as his business manager, controlling the secretariat, supervising the cash flow, handling the schedules and appointments. When Jacquie spoke, Hughes noted, she was clear and cool in tone, with a touch of a Mancunian accent. 'The round face ended in a firm chin,' he recorded, 'that suggested both determination and the humour to use it wisely. I felt at ease with her acerbic attitude to Gerry and his excesses, the way he pushed his luck, his tendency to domineer given half a chance, the boyish need to be king of the castle. She was both Durrell's match and more than a match for Durrell. She detested cant. She loved wit. She shared his humour.'

But they didn't share much else. She had gone on record as saying that from the day they first met in grey old Manchester more than a quarter of a century ago they had never had a thing in common except animals and travel. Although that was quite a lot, the things that divided them were more – especially when it came to human beings, for while Jacquie was a socialist who supported the aspirations of the working man, Gerald viewed the human race as a failed, stupid and infinitely destructive species, and in response adopted a stance that some (Jacquie for one) would say was right-wing and misanthropic. Once, in half-hippie Avignon with Jacquie and David Hughes, Gerald surveyed with distaste the throng of jeans-clad, guitar-toting teenagers wandering through the main square, and remarked: 'Man is an unattractive mammal. These are the very people for whom I am slaving out my guts.'

Gerald liked to travel in the grand manner of an Edwardian satrap, and to live on a gargantuan scale which often pained his more prudent and thrifty wife. Money meant little to him, and when he ran out he would sit down and scribble away to make some more. Though Gerald had earned a fortune in the last twenty years, he had little to show for it in terms of property or capital, for the flat on Jersey was a grace-and-favour dwelling, while the Mazet was rented from his brother. Most of the money had gone on the good life, on travel, expansive dinners for his friends, expensive presents – and, of course, the zoo.

The tedious details of daily life were beneath Gerald. He seldom carried either cash or a chequebook, for both bored and irritated him, and on the very rare occasion when he had to pay for a taxi himself, he would pull a wad of notes out of a pocket and tell the driver to take what he needed, as he had no knowledge of the denominations. He was an inveterate traveller but rarely if ever drove a car. The necessary arrangements to support his highly peripatetic and eccentric life plan he left to others. He adored the more creative side of cooking, but the routine preparation and clearing up he delegated to minions.

Gerald loved to throw large parties, and took pleasure in giving pleasure and entertaining in every sense of the word. But often he would pass through one mood after another, and the flow of wine was a matter of ceaseless vigilance and altercation on Jacquie's part. 'What we all need is a drink,' Hughes records Gerald brightly piping up at the end of a long, vinous lunch party at the Mazet, to which Jacquie crisply riposted: 'Oh, do shut up, Gerry! Everyone's had quite enough, including you.' His favourite *leitmotif*, uttered at virtually any time of day, ran along the lines of: 'The moment has arrived to press a tiny glass of red wine to the left kidney.' If this got short shrift, he would try a more plaintive version, such as: 'Can we stop somewhere and press to our lips, like a little nosegay, a pungent little pastis?' While Jacquie – slim, trim and brimming with energy – toiled unglamorously in the house or garden, Gerald – 'a Herculean chunk of hero with a beard', as Larry described him – would sit in the shade in Olympian fashion and declaim his lofty thoughts on man, nature, creation and the inner workings of the universe and his own sometimes troubled mind.

Gerald's intense, abiding, undeflectable passion, Hughes noted, was 'a single vast issue'. It was Archilochus, one of the lesser-known poets of ancient Greece, who divided people, or at any rate writers and thinkers, into those who resemble the fox and those who resemble the hedgehog. The hedgehog relates everything to a single central vision, a universal organising principle, while the fox pursues many unrelated and contradictory ends, without any single overriding moral principle. Gerald was a hedgehog (like, say, Dante), whereas his brother Larry was a fox (like, for example, Shakespeare). As Hughes observed at first hand, the brothers were both serious men of similar temperament, always mischievous, for ever laughing, but where Larry was ultimately a dazzlingly clever man without faith of any kind, Gerry was a simple man of unshakeable conviction. In short, one was an intellectual and the other a believer. Lawrence not only believed in nothing, but believed that nothing could be done, while Gerald not only believed in something but believed that something should be done, even though he might well lose the battle in the end.

But the price was high. 'His vision of the world's future,' David Hughes was to write, 'was entirely at his own expense, inconveniencing him at every turn, wrecking his bank balance, disturbing his peace of mind.' Being a celebrity is itself a kind of penance, for the more the adulation is piled on, the more worthless the recipient may feel himself to be. 'I am a charlatan,' Gerald was to repeat like a litany, wrongly. 'I suppose self-deprecation helps to keep me sane, if you can call me sane, which you can't. I have to be constantly on my guard against adulation. For a cause like mine it's quite in order to boast a certain amount, but not to believe what you boast yourself. In the end you're taken in by whatever you're shouting, by which time, like all propaganda, it has become quite untrue. What I'm after is truth. No, that's pretentious. Validity. That's what I'm after.' He had accomplished very little in his life, he claimed: 'My achievement has been like chipping away at the base of Mount Everest with a teaspoon.' The sheer size and gravity of the problem inevitably put him in his place. And if he compared his achievements at fifty with those of Darwin or Fabre, they shrank to nothing. 'Where the hell did they find the bloody time?' he complained, with some reason. 'In Jersey I go mad trying to locate half an hour to do anything in.'

Much of Gerald's dark side – his despair, his sporadic rage, his misanthropy, his recourse to food, drink, travel, sun in larger and larger doses as means of escape – was a direct result of his gnawing fear that it was possible his life had been in vain, and that nothing he had done, or could ever do, would stem the tide of destruction at the hand of man. Every hour of every day at the zoo, reports came in from all round the world chronicling the remorseless erosion of wilderness, wildlife and resources – myriad cases of eco-vandalism in every shape and form, initiated at international, governmental, corporate, private or individual level, all spelling out the same accelerating and catastrophic trend. 'If I live to be seventy,' Gerald blazed away at David Hughes, 'the whole deteriorating mess will just about see me out.' And then, changing tack somewhat, he gave utterance to a holistic credo that left a tiny chink for faith and hope: 'As far as I'm concerned there's only one world, and I'm in it and it's inside me, like the duck we had for lunch, and those louts in the square, and Jacquie, and the handful of mountain gorillas getting fewer every day, and wine, and my horrible cousins, and Larry writing his incomprehensible masterpieces, and breeding white eared pheasants and anything human, animal and alive.'

Even now – overweight, disillusioned, off whisky but with his marriage creaking – Gerald Durrell retained his intense, boundless reverence for life, his gentle, humble love of the creatures of the world. The alertness and appreciativeness with which he beheld an ant or a wasp or a flight of birds across the rising sun was something solid and permanent in his life, where all else might seem to be shifting sand. 'His gravity of manner,' David Hughes wrote of Gerald's concentrated fascination with the micro-wildlife that crawled and buzzed around his chair on the patio at the Mazet, 'often suggested a child trying to be grown-up. His enthusiasm for the swiftly identified butterfly, the ants dragging overweight seeds, was infectiously boyish. All his life he had kept this freshness; his interest in nature, in animals, was obsessive from birth.'

But all was not well. Since March Judy Mackrell, who had first met the Durrells on Corfu a few years previously, had been the Trust secretary. When she went down to the Mazet that summer she found Gerald and Jacquie behaving 'like two very lost people'. 'They weren't even friends,' she recalled. 'There was not a single spark of affection.' Jacquie was very lonely, Judy reckoned. 'As for Gerry, I think he was probably never a really emotionally mature person, and romantically I suspect he was a rather inexperienced, frightened kind of man, for all his harmless flirting. He was a wonderful person and he did amazing things but he was undoubtedly difficult to live with, what with his impatience and his distress at what was happening to the world. One day Jacquie told me she had thought of a sequel to her book *Beasts in my Bed*. She was going to call it "My Life with an Animal". But she did share Gerry's conservation vision and his love of animals, no matter how lowly. Before she had a shower, for example, she would pick up all the spiders very carefully and take them out of the bathroom. And when she'd finished they'd all trundle back in.'

As the summer went by, Lawrence was forced for tax reasons to decide against selling the Mazet to his brother, and asked him to move out. Jacquie and Peggy Peel set off to find another suitable rental in the Alpes Maritimes region of the South of France, and after a great deal of searching they found a house, 'La Chèvre Blanche', at Le Tignet in the vicinity of Grasse, a country of scented limestone plateaux and splendid olive-covered hills. In late November 1975, just before Jacquie's forty-sixth birthday, she, Gerald and their new secretary Sue Bateman, along with

Peggy Peel and David Hughes, drove down to the Mazet to pack up all the Durrells' belongings there. Then they set about getting the new house – 'perched up like an eagle's nest over a big valley', Gerald told Larry – organised.

The atmosphere was tense. Gerald was drinking and moody and irritable, and David Hughes was feeling lost and footloose after the break-up of his marriage to Mai Zetterling the year before. 'The house was almost a metaphor for the emotional state of the people inside it,' Hughes recalled. 'It was stark, blank-walled, almost empty, terribly modern and totally topsy-turvy – the bedrooms were where you went in and downstairs was where you went to sit or eat. Gerry and Jacquie were getting on appallingly badly. There was a lot of verbal violence hurtling about, most of it from Gerry. Jacquie seemed to be at her wits' end. "I'm wedded to someone who's wedded to something else," she said. It was all a bit like something out of Scott Fitzgerald – a terribly fraught emotional atmosphere taking place in terribly expensive restaurants, everyone eating and drinking enormously well but dying deep down inside. I think by the end of this Jacquie was going right off the male sex, which of course stoked Gerry up even more.'

It didn't help much when Hughes began a tentative flirtation with Sue Bateman, which annoyed Gerald, though he left it to Jacquie to remonstrate with them. 'I was virtually sent back home on the next flight,' Hughes recalled. 'And at my own expense, I need hardly add. £80 one way.' That was the last time David Hughes ever set eyes on Jacquie.

Back on Jersey, Gerald was preparing to go to Assam in north-east India on a conservation fact-finding tour, with special regard to the desperate plight of the endangered pygmy hog. Built into the Assam expedition was a second objective – a television documentary for the BBC *World About Us* series entitled *Animals are my Life*, to be produced by David Cobham. The programme was to be as much about Gerald Durrell, his way of life and his never-ending self-imposed task of saving endangered animals from extinction as it was about Assam.

By now Jacquie was finally resolved as to her future course of action. 'I told Gerry I could no longer tolerate his behaviour,' she said, 'and proposed to go away on my own.' This was the bombshell that Gerald had probably been long waiting for. It blew away what was left of his marriage, which by now was precious little, and shattered his entire existence. When Judy Mackrell told him she wanted to leave her job at the Trust – she loved the zoo, she said, but not life on Jersey – Gerald was so distraught that he banished her from his sight and cut her off from everything. The walls were falling in.

Jacquie recalled of the traumatic countdown to break-up:

He had become very difficult to live with. It wasn't just the drink, though that was reason enough. He had become very touchy. As he got older his humour became less spontaneous and more studied. He got more cynical, took less delight in things. He became very morose and desperate about the way the world was going, the colossal destruction of nature and wildlife, the global stupidity of mankind. On his fiftieth birthday he formally announced he wouldn't suffer fools at all, let alone gladly. That just about summed up his attitude. At the same time he became more and more bad-tempered and he would explode all over the place for no apparent reason. Mostly it was just a lot of sound and fury but it was very wearing. It's very hard to live with someone who is so wrapped up in a project that they can't see anything or anybody else. I began to think, what on earth am I doing here? Here I am at forty-six – there must be more to life than this. I began bitterly to regret giving up my own career as a singer.

Living with Gerry got very difficult. You never knew what state of mind he'd be in when he got up. Little things would irritate him and he tended to bring his irritations with everybody else to me, and I just got tired of it. When I protested, he said: 'Well, you're my wife, that's what you're here for.' I began to think, what the hell! In spite of all the humour – because he could still be very funny when he chose – the day could be depressive or oppressive. He had become seriously depressive by now – ever since his break-down in 1968, when he was depressive and suicidal as well. Gerry was *never* the same after the breakdown.

It was a truly wretched period for both of us, and that is why I was determined to leave, for by this time it was getting to me and I really felt I had to escape if I was to save my own sanity. I had hung on year after year for the sake of the Trust, for the sake of the animals, really. But once the Trust was on a firm footing, which by the mid-seventies it was, I felt it was now or never. I had been married to Gerry for more than a quarter of a century – a life sentence!

But the flak was not all one-way – it rarely is in marital cataclysms on this scale. To some close observers of the warring couple Gerald occasionally seemed to be getting almost more than he was giving. None was closer to the combatants than the Zoological Director in Jersey, Jeremy Mallinson, an old friend of both of them: 'I was very close to the agonies of it all. It would be a wrong picture to view Gerry as the only guilty party. It was really six of one and half a dozen of the other. For her part, Jacquie appeared to be highly jealous of the zoo and Gerry's devotion to it and his preoccupation with making it a success. There were times when she became quite vindictive towards Gerry, and by the mid-1970s things had got a lot worse. Jacquie almost caused his demise in the process. I mean, she almost destroyed him.'

By Christmas Gerald was not his normal self. He had loved Jacquie profoundly – why, she never knew – but for a long time the marriage had been a sham. Now Jacquie had ripped the mask away. He was deeply distressed, as was all too evident at the annual Christmas party in the manor, though few were aware of the source of the problem. 'Gerry was very peculiar,' Sam and Catha Weller recalled. 'There was an atmosphere. It was very strange. Gerry was really uptight and odd. Things were clearly not right between Gerry and Jacquie, there was no rapport, there was something emotional in the air.' Michael Armstrong detected it too: 'Gerald began to get so drunk that Jacquie actually had to manhandle him, push him away, and I heard her rebuke him with the words: "Without me you would have been nothing."'

With the Assam expedition far from ready to proceed, and his marriage in ruins, Gerald found himself in an unendurable limbo in Jersey, still cohabiting with Jacquie, though he was no longer meaningfully married to her. It was then that Jacquie came up with an idea: Gerry was not well, she told his personal assistant John Hartley. Why didn't John take him off somewhere sunny and warm? As it happened, for the last two or three years the Trust had had a growing interest in conservation problems on Mauritius, the island that was, appropriately, the graveyard of the long-extinct dodo, the emblem of the Jersey Zoo and Trust. Compared to Assam, Mauritius was easy to travel around, and local contacts were already well-established. A six-week fact-finding mission to Mauritius and offshore Round Island was quickly organised, with the departure date set for the end of March.

For her part, Jacquie was keen to go to Australia to gather material for a book on the conservation work of Australian women – a trip which would also give her a perfect opportunity to reassess her life and the future of her relationship with her husband. Reluctantly Gerald accepted this proposition, but insisted she take someone with her, and suggested Sue Bateman, who had resigned as his secretary just before Christmas.

Gerald meanwhile had gone to hole up in the Palace Court Hotel in Bournemouth, promising to contact both Alan Ogden, the family GP, and his sister Margaret. But the solitude and bleakness of his situation soon threatened to unhinge him. Drinking heavily while he passed his time morosely thumbing through the whole nine volumes of Havelock Ellis's *Studies in the Psychology of Sex*, which he had bought at Commin's Bookshop ('Anyone who breeds rare animals knows how important sex is,' he was to claim in justification of his obsession with the subject at that time), he began to slide towards the abyss of another acute depression. Concerned about her husband's state of mind, Jacquie rang Alan Ogden, who found Gerald drinking heavily and in a dreadful state, and had him transferred to a private nursing home. He rang Jacquie and warned her that it might be advisable to postpone her Australian trip. It could unravel Gerald's psyche still further – and she might be needed. Reluctantly she agreed and set off for the house near Grasse instead. There she stayed for the whole of the separation period from January to March. It had not taken her long to realise that there was indeed no mileage left in the marriage, and she found that she rather liked being able to do what she wanted to do, and to have space and time to think of other things. 'I remember saying to myself: "It's now or never!"' she recalled. 'I only wish I'd done it before.'

There was one other casualty in all this. David Hughes went to see Gerald in his Bournemouth hotel, to be told that, with Jacquie's decamping from the scene, his biographical memoir of Gerald Durrell and his world, on which he had laboured for most of the previous year, was now unpublishable. The implosion of the marriage was not the sole reason. Gerald considered there was too much conversation and not enough conservation in the book – 'Not you at your best, dear boy,' he later told Hughes. Collins cancelled the contract without paying the last instalment of the advance, and Hughes departed for the stiller but more profitable waters of American academic life.

Gerald returned to Jersey in a distraught state. John Hartley picked him up at the airport, and realised at once that he was in no condition to be left on his own. 'He was tearful, sullen and very distressed,' Hartley recalled. 'I saw a person I was fond of at the end of his tether. The zoo was a lonely place at night and there wouldn't be many friends passing by. I felt the best thing would be to move into the manor house myself during the next few critical days.' John went home, told his wife what he was doing, picked up a few basic things and returned to the manor to camp there for as long as he thought was necessary. 'We talked a lot,' he remembered, 'played music, had a few drinks and generally decided the world was a miserable place.'

For Gerald this was the inner circle of hell, the dark night of the soul. Shortly afterwards his sister Margaret arrived to lend a hand, followed in due course by Tom Lovejoy from America. 'Gerry was very broken up,' Margaret recalled. 'He couldn't bear one millimetre of loneliness. He'd always had to have a woman around, even if she was only banging around in the kitchen, and he felt unnerved when there wasn't one. But in spite of his state of mind, he said to me one day: "If ever Jacquie is in a bad way and knocks at your door, I hope you will let her in."' From time to time friends came to keep him company. 'He was very, very down,' recalled David Cobham. 'In fact he had reached rock bottom. It was very sad. I know he drank too much and I'm sure he was difficult to live with, but he was a wonderful man doing tremendous things, and it was a shame he had come to this.'

Hell on earth though it may have been, in the long run the break-up was probably as good for Gerald as it was for Jacquie. By any definition of the term 'marriage', this one had fallen apart long ago. The pain Gerald felt was partly because he had lost a loved one and partly because Jacquie's departure had left him alone – a state he found intolerable. 'Had I not been the first to make the move towards our separation when I did,' Jacquie later observed, 'we would eventually have come to the conclusion that it would be the best course for either of us to take. Remember the old adage – once respect goes, love follows? Gerry, of course, was very angry and told me he would do all he could to erase my memory and all my connections with the zoo. And he certainly kept that promise. I think he was upset because my departure left such a large gap in his life. Although Gerry fervently and continually protested that he did *not* want me to go, I sincerely feel that it was not only because of his professed great love for me but because it was also a great inconvenience to him. He had become totally dependent on me and my judgement. I did every-thing for him. Even though I was no longer involved with the zoo, I had continued to be his business manager, his bank manager, his filing systems manager and so on. So now he was bereft. Not emotionally, especially, but practically. It wasn't till I left that Gerry realised how much I did for him. It was rather telling that he protested to his own lawyer that he had been forced to employ three people to do what I had done single-handedly throughout our married life.'

As a cure for heartache and nervous collapse Gerry distracted himself by writing animal verse, just as he had done after his crack-up in the late sixties. On 27 February 1976 he wrote to Shirley Thomas from the zoo: 'I am, in my spare time, trying to outdo my elder brother by writing poetry. I am doing a series of animal poems called "Anthropomorphia", and I am hoping that they will allow me to illustrate them myself. Natur-ally, my poetry has a much more mystical, philosophic quality to it than

Larry's has, as you will see from the enclosed piece. I feel that there is nothing quite like a good dramatic piece of poetry to make one feel better when one is suffering.'

Given the circumstances, the 'enclosed piece', the subject of which was one of the endangered species in the zoo, was remarkable.

> Up in the snow covered Andes,
> There's only one beast you will see,
> Who is clever enough to learn all the stuff
> That one needs to obtain a degree.
>
> The Spectacled Bear is a wonder,
> The Spectacled Bear is no fool,
> The Spectacled Bear, with a wisdom that's rare,
> Paid attention when he went to school.
>
> The Spectacled Bear learnt Spanish,
> The Spectacled Bear learnt to draw,
> The Spectacled Bear with time and with care,
> Could multiply twenty by four.

The Spectacled Bear was a paragon, Gerald went on. He learned to write, paint, knit, weave and sing. He learned history and how to add up his sums without using his thumbs. But one thing made him 'awfully depressed' – he couldn't spell, and had to sign his name with a cross.

> But one day someone gave him a parrot,
> (A bird that was badly behaved),
> But one thing it did well, and that was to spell,
> So the Spectacled Bear was saved.
>
> With this bird as his constant companion
> He writes letters to friends now with glee,
> And always you'll find they are carefully signed:
> 'Spectickled Bere, B.Sc.'
>
> So if ever your teacher should ask you
> To spell words like 'Zephyr' or 'Claret',
> The thing I'd suggest that would be the best
> Is to go out and purchase a parrot.

On 25 March 1976, shortly before his departure for Mauritius, Peggy Peel met Gerald in London and noted in her diary: 'Jacquie was not there.

I asked no questions but suspected she had left Gerry. He was very low. Ann Peters was with him and I gathered she was going with him to Mauritius too.' As his girlfriend, it should be said – 'the first girl on Gerry's rebound', as John Hartley put it.

In April, following Gerald's departure, Jacquie returned to the flat in the manor house at the zoo for the last time, to do Gerald's accounts and collect a few personal items. It was at this point of terminal flux that a new appointee, Simon Hicks, arrived to take up the senior post of Zoological Co-Ordinator at the Trust (later Trust Secretary). 'There was a sort of subtle chaos afoot,' he recalled of his first few days, 'and I just walked straight into it. Goodness, I said to myself, what have I let myself in for? Gerald Durrell had gone abroad, and his wife was clearly packing up and walking out. There was a TV crew there. "Mr Durrell here?" they asked. "No," I said. "He's miles away. I'm new here and I can't keep up with these two. I'm totally confused." No one let me into the secret, they just let me clump around all over it. I couldn't work out what was happening, except that the situation was grave.' When Jacquie left she directed a parting word to Jeremy Mallinson: 'Well, goodbye, and I hope I never see this bloody place again.'

By this time Gerald was far away in body and mind. He had first become involved with Mauritius, second largest of the Mascarene Islands to the east of Madagascar, in a rather casual and roundabout way, little dreaming that one day it would become the scene of the Trust's longest-running and most defining conservation project.

In March 1976, stressed and ailing, his marriage in ruins, Gerald flew to Mauritius with John Hartley and Ann Peters for a six-week foray which was originally intended to be no more than – as John put it – 'a bit of R&R in the sun'. Mauritius was still a relatively remote and little-known island then, and Gerald's first glimpse from the air – 'green and smouldering, mountains smudged blue and purple, ringed with the white foamed reef on the dark blue of the Indian Ocean' – was voluptuous and reassuring. Ecologically, though, the island was in many ways a wreck, and it seemed fitting that the plane should land on a runway from which the skeletal remains of the long-dead dodo had been recovered in past years. Most of the island's unique fauna had been exterminated by early human interlopers or the no less lethal animals they had introduced – dogs, cats, pigs, rats, monkeys, mongoose and the rest. Within a remarkably short time the island's giant parrot, giant tortoise and dugong had followed the dodo into extinction. 'All that was left of a unique and harmless fauna,' Gerald wrote, 'was a handful of birds and lizards. These, together with what is left of the native forest, face enormous pressures.' None more so than the Mauritius kestrel, pink pigeon and echo parakeet, which qualified as the world's rarest kestrel, pigeon and parakeet – victims of marauding troops of Javanese macaque monkeys that wreaked havoc on their eggs and chicks.

Inevitably, as Gerald learned more about the plight of the island's wildlife, what had originally been planned as a holiday with a conservation agenda attached became a conservation agenda with a holiday attached. His first port of call, therefore, was the headquarters of the Conservator of Forests, Wahab Owadally, with whom he and John Hartley formed an immediate friendship. He was helpful and enthusiastic, and insisted that as well as the haunts of the pink pigeon and the Mauritian kestrel and parakeet, the party should visit nearby Round Island, which in his opinion was 'Mauritius' answer to the Galapagos', but was in grave ecological danger.

To find pink pigeons in the wild would be difficult, given the bird's puny numbers, and as the only viable method was by torchlight at night when the bird was roosting. But for Gerald the foray into the cryptomeria groves of Pink Pigeon Valley in pursuit of the elusive birds was a timely adventure, for it took him far from the pain of his broken marriage and the cares of Trust business in Jersey, and he found himself once again in a close-contact world of animals, resembling his long-ago boyhood in Corfu. Just how close-contact astonished – and delighted – even Gerald. At sundown, perched high in a tree waiting for the pigeons to come flighting in to roost, he found himself an object of intense curiosity to a flock of passing birds. He was to write later:

The sun was now very low and the sky turned from a metallic kingfisher-blue to a paler, more powdery colour. A group of zos-terops, minute, fragile, green birds, with pale, cream-coloured mon-ocles round each eye, appeared suddenly in the branches above me, zinging and twittering to each other in high-pitched excitement as they performed strange acrobatics among the pine needles in search of minute insects. I pursed up my lips and made a high-pitched noise at them. The effect was ludicrous. They all stopped squeaking and searching for their supper, to congregate on a branch near me and regard me with wide eyes from behind their monocles. I made another noise. After a moment's stunned silence, they twit-tered agitatedly to each other and flipped inch by inch nearer to me until they were within touching distance. As long as I continued to make noises, they grew more and more alarmed and, with their heads on one side, drew closer and closer until they were hanging upside down a foot from my face, peering at me anxiously and discussing this strange phenomenon in their shrill little voices.

Only when two pink pigeons flew in and Gerald raised his binoculars to watch did his Lilliputian audience take flight. Eventually the first pigeon was caught, dazed with sleep, and Gerald plucked it from the special catching net:

I received it reverently into my cupped hands. It lay quietly, without struggling, merely blinking its eyes in what appeared to be mild curiosity at this strange experience. It was a remarkably handsome bird. Gazing at it, feeling its silken feathering against my fingers and sensing the steady tremor of its heart-beat and its breathing, I was filled with a great sadness. This was one of the thirty-three individuals that survived; the shipwrecked remnants of their species, eking out a precarious existence on their cryptomeria raft. So, at one time, must a tiny group of Dodos, the last of their harmless, waddling kind, have faced the final onslaught of pigs, dogs, cats, monkeys and man, and disappeared for ever, since there was no one to care and no one to offer them a breeding sanctuary, safe from their enemies. At least with our help the pink pigeons stood a better chance of survival.

Not that the pink pigeon exactly did a lot on its own behalf, he noted: its notion of reproducing seemed to involve perching on the end of a branch and releasing its egg into the void below.

The next stop was Round Island, which lay fourteen miles north-east of Mauritius. In area it was no more than 375 acres, yet it contained a remarkable range of unique or endangered plant and animal life, including eight species of native reptile, six of them endangered (two geckos, two skinks, two snakes); at least ten species of threatened native plants (six of them endemic); and the only known breeding ground of the rare Round Island petrel. 'This volcanic island,' Gerald was to report, 'probably has more unique and threatened species per acre than any other piece of land in the world.' Introduced goats and domestic rabbits had ravaged the landscape, browsing down the vegetation, including the dense forests of rare palms and hardwood trees such as ebony, till the island looked like a moonscape. In the process the cover and insect food supply of the island's rare lizards and snakes had been destroyed. The Mauritian government was aware of the dangers, and was contemplating steps to reduce the goat population, eliminate the rabbit and re-afforest the island, though little as yet had been done.

But Gerald was bullish. 'When this is an accomplished fact (in perhaps thirty or forty years' time),' he wrote, 'Round Island will have been pulled back from the brink of total obliteration and serve as one of the most exciting examples of conservation as it should be practised.' Meanwhile the party had a chance to save some of the island's threatened creatures. Gerald had been given permission to bring back some of the rare endemic lizards, and after four days he departed with a breeding nucleus of Round Island geckos and skinks.

The visit to Rodrigues was a more far-flung venture. Some 350 miles east of Mauritius, and only forty square miles in area, this dry and dusty island had once been the haunt of the giant tortoise and the strange solitaire bird – both exterminated by ruthless hunting and habitat destruction by French venturers in the eighteenth century. Gerald and John's aims were to carry out the first proper survey of the fruit bat population for a number of years – they arrived at a figure of between 120 and 130 – and to catch enough of them to form captive breeding colonies in Jersey and Mauritius, using mist nets and a bait consisting of nearly rotting fruit, including the sweetly-sick stinking jak fruit.

The Rodrigues woods at night were not a place for the faint-hearted. The mosquitoes half-devoured Gerald and his friends, and the torrential rain half-drowned them. The locals built crude banana-leaf huts for them, but these were half-chewed-up by an army of noisily browsing giant land snails. Eventually, however, they were successful in their quest, returning to Mauritius after four days with eighteen bats.

Gerald's hotel in Mauritius was at the head of a casuarina-fringed beach of frost-white sand leading to a lagoon and the coral reef beyond. The waters of the reef were a revelation to him, a hallucinatory other world. 'You suddenly become a hawk,' he wrote, 'floating and soaring over the forests, mountains and sandy deserts of this marine universe. You become like Icarus.' This, he felt, was the ultimate paradise, and he hoped that one day soon the Mauritian government would have the sense to declare its reefs marine national parks, as Tanzania and the Seychelles had already done. On his last day he found himself swimming among a huge concourse of some two thousand leaf fish around a reef he called the 'flower garden':

> I swam with them for half an hour, and it was unforgettable: one
> moment it was like being in a forest of green leaves greeting the
> spring, the next like floating through bits of Mediterranean blue

sky that had miraculously fallen into the sea in the shape of fish. At length, drugged and dazzled, I found a smooth coral head free from urchins and scorpion fish and sat on it in two feet of water. I took off my mask and there, in the distance, were the mountains of Mauritius humped and shouldering their way to the horizon, like uneasy limbs under a bed covering of green forest and a patchwork quilt of sugar cane. Across this were looped no less than five rainbows. I decided I liked Mauritius very much indeed.

When Gerald returned to Jersey in May he found Jacquie packed up and gone, having taken her personal belongings and (by mutual consent) their Mercedes car. Later that month they had a final meeting.

'We met again in Bournemouth,' Jacquie recalled, 'which was semi-neutral territory. By and large our meeting struck me as a calm and well-considered affair and Gerry struck me as being extremely well balanced within himself. I told Gerry that I didn't want to come back to him, but he refused to accept this. He said he was sorry for the way he had behaved, and he said that if I came back he'd take me to Russia or anywhere else I wanted to go. He also insisted that I have another forty-eight hours to think about it, which I did. In the meantime I consulted a solicitor, because although Gerald had said he would divide everything equally between us, there was nothing in writing to this effect, and when Gerry realised I really wasn't coming back he might not be so well disposed. It was from my solicitor's office that I finally rang him and confirmed I wasn't coming back. Gerry absolutely exploded on the phone and promised that in view of all this he was going to be as bloody and obstructive as he could.'

Nearly four years of dispute and bitterness lay ahead. The separation was total. Jacquie never saw Gerald again, and both sides were deeply embittered by the schism. Though Gerald remained at the heart of his zoo, his life was shattered, and he was in a parlous state. As for Jacquie, she felt an exile, and carried about with her her own large burden of pain. 'I will never forget the trauma of that time,' she remembered with reluctance. 'I was subjected to so much stress and vindictiveness that I was only saved from a total breakdown after I left Jersey by the loving support of close friends.'

On 19 July 1976 Gerald wrote to Lawrence to confirm the worst: 'Jackie [sic] has departed. It is nice of you to ask me to come and join you but I prefer to lick my wounds in private. I am going down to Grasse. If we manage to see you on the way back, we will try and arrange that there is a bull fight in Sommières, as I think I would like to see somebody else getting beaten.'

This plan was changed, however, and shortly afterwards Gerald, John Hartley and Denise Liddelow, a lissom young Afro-Caribbean woman who was then a secretary at the zoo, and whom he called Rainbow, set off for the South of France to stay in the white-walled, bougainvillaea-clad villa of a well-to-do couple in Cannes by the name of François and Sheila Brutsch – Sheila being a member of the wealthy American Johnson & Johnson pharmaceuticals family and a generous contributor to the Trust. 'Gerald was toying at writing a book about Mauritius at the time,' John Hartley recalled, 'but spent most of the time eating and drinking in the restaurants and then coming back to the house to drink some more and talk about everything under the sun, sitting up on the rooftop terrace with the lights of Cannes twinkling all around, sometimes till four or five in the morning. It was really a sort of boozy R and R – but it helped.' It gave Gerald great satisfaction, and his *amour-propre* a much-needed boost, to be able to saunter into the bar of the Negresco, one of the world's most exclusive hotels, with a tall and beautiful young black woman on his arm. He was finding his way back.

Meanwhile the solicitors' letters went back and forth 'He was making a lot of silly accusations,' Jacquie was to relate. 'A lot of it was pique really. It was only when I threatened to go into court and talk about his nervous breakdown and various other things that he began to be more reasonable.' Gerald didn't quite see it that way, and wrote to Lawrence on his return from Cannes in August: 'I fear Jackie will not return to the fold as she is suing me for divorce on the grounds of cruelty. Apparently I beat her up with monotonous regularity. I was unconscious of this but she seems convinced of it.'

Gerry resisted Jacquie's lawyers tooth and nail. 'Jacquie was about to subpoena a number of us for a full divorce battle,' Jeremy Mallinson remembered. 'It was Gerry, against his personal financial interest, who in order to protect the Trust as much as possible, came to the final divorce settlement.' The grounds for divorce that were finally agreed in a British divorce court in the spring of 1979 were 'irreconcilable breakdown'.

Because Gerald was not a UK resident the court did not award Jacquie half of his estate, which she felt she was entitled to, arguing that it was she as much as Gerald who had created it. Instead she was granted an index-linked maintenance award, worth £7000 per annum at the time, which Gerald could claim as tax deductible. 'He didn't want to give me anything,' Jacquie recalled, 'and eventually he had to be ordered by the court. But in order to get a single penny I had to sign away *all* my rights to what we had in Jersey. However, I must say in all fairness to Gerry that though it took quite a long time to get any money out of him, and though I didn't get anything like I should have done, he never once defaulted on my maintenance by one halfpenny, no matter what his circumstances were.'

But the taste was bitter. Both Gerald and Jacquie in their different ways felt angry, hostile and betrayed. Gerald had for long loved Jacquie more than anyone or anything in the world. He was aghast that it had come to this, and laid the blame entirely on his former wife, on the grounds that it was she who had ended the marriage by walking out on it. For this he now found he had to pay alimony that in his view was munificent by any standards. He remained outraged. 'I have decided to give up the house near Grasse,' he wrote to Lawrence, 'as it is really rather expensive and I have to watch the cash at the moment, since I am being stung a hideous amount of alimony. It is wonderful, the law being what it is, that I have to pay alimony when the break-up of the marriage was nothing to do with me.'

Jacquie, of course, saw it differently. She had walked out because Gerald had made it impossible for her to stay. 'That I managed to hang on for all those years never ceases to amaze me now,' she was to reflect years later. 'I willingly sacrificed all I ever held dear – family, career and health – for twenty-eight of the cream years of my life, in return for which I got hurtful abuse and financial neglect. I was deprived of my rightful place in the annals of the zoo and Trust and treated as if I had never existed.'

Mutual recrimination is a characteristic of every bitter divorce, but through the gunsmoke Jacquie saw one thing plain: 'Gerald Durrell was a flawed human being, like most human beings tend to be. But as a champion of the animal world and a pioneer of animal conservation he was one of the great men of our age, and his immense contribution to the cause is only now beginning to sink in.'

Gerald was now approaching ground-zero. The twin components of his life were flying apart. While the zoo and Trust he had created grew ever more monumental and famous (with fifteen thousand members worldwide, two hundred thousand visitors per annum, scientists of international eminence on the scientific committee, five awards for distinction from the Zoo Federation, one of the best animal record systems and annual zoological reports in the world, and the world's first captive breeding of more than a dozen species to its credit), his personal life had collapsed and his professional life as an author seemed to be in eclipse. His books no longer received the attention or achieved the sales they had once done, and by 1975–76 his income had plummeted to little more than a third of its previous level. Gerald Durrell's fortunes had sunk to a desperate level, and it was unclear in what way they might ever be revived.

TWENTY-FIVE

Love Story: Prelude

1977–1978

Gerald Durrell always considered he had been born lucky and lived lucky. There were abysses and chasms, of course, and in recent years he had plummeted down a number of these. But he had always bounced back, and not all of these fortunate rebounds could be attributed entirely to his own unaided endeavours. His friends and colleagues often attributed his miraculous changes of fortune to 'Durrell's luck', and never had this struck so unexpectedly and to such wondrous effect as it did during his fund-raising visit to North America in the spring of 1977, when it was to set in motion a chain of events that was to transform his life.

For the first few weeks of late April and early May Gerald was in the United States treading what he called the trail of the begging bowl. He did not enjoy it, but it was the most effective thing he could do for the cause, and it gave him an opportunity to spread the word. 'Species Extinction is Like Killing Ourselves: Durrell', ran a typical headline in a newspaper in Aiken, South Carolina, which reported his apocalyptic message on its front page: 'As a cumulative effect, the extinction of species is going to be our own death. We're committing suicide, it's as simple as that . . . Man is a thinking pest who is pretending to play God, a dangerous thing to do. Man has made such a muck of the world that pretty soon nothing will tick.'

From Aiken it was but a step to Duke University at Durham in the neighbouring state of North Carolina, which was famous for having the largest collection of lemurs outside Madagascar, and for its breeding successes and the studies it was carrying out. Before leaving Jersey, Gerald had heard that Duke's lemur collection was to be disbanded for lack of funds, and he was anxious to offer a home to one or possibly two species at Jersey Zoo before the animals were dispersed beyond recall. He flew to Durham, where he was met by Margot Rockefeller, whose daughter

Caroline was an undergraduate at the university, then taken round the lemur collection by a gaggle of professors on a red-carpet tour. 'For the next three hours I was in my element,' Gerald recalled, 'peering at cage after cage of beautiful animals.' At lunch the conversation was confined entirely to lemurs. So was the rest of the afternoon. By the time they staggered back to their motel Gerald and Margot were exhausted. Their respite was brief, however. Back at Duke the professors had laid on a dinner party for them. More lemur talk. More polysyllabic words. Gerald was to write:

> With the aid of a bottle of Scotch, we tried to get into the party spirit. Fortunately, everyone was on their third drink. All the professors had brought their wives and they talked polysyllabically as well. I was gazing round the room desperately, searching for a nook or a cranny to secrete myself in, when my glance fell upon a young woman who was sitting on what used to be called a pouf, nursing her drink and looking remarkably attractive. I glanced at her hands which were ringless. I glanced around to see whether any muscular young man was exuding a proprietary air and there was none. One of the delightful things about America is that you can introduce yourself to complete strangers without having them faint with horror. So I drifted across to the girl.
>
> 'Hullo,' I said, 'I'm Gerald Durrell.'
>
> 'I know,' she said. 'I'm Lee McGeorge.'

Lee McGeorge was a beautiful, twenty-seven-year-old zoology graduate from Memphis, Tennessee, who had recently spent two years in Madagascar studying the ecology and social behaviour of lemurs and the vocal communication of Malagasy mammals and birds in the wild. Back at Duke she was working as an instructor in the zoology department, and in her spare time working on her Madagascar results and starting her Ph.D dissertation. While in Madagascar she had holed up for a time in a mission station at Fort Dauphin in the south, and in the library there she had first come across several books by Gerald Durrell, including *My Family and Other Animals*. Lying on her pallet at night in her attic room she read these books by the light of a paraffin lamp, while her pet baby fruit bat, which could not yet fly, fluttered around in circles, wings and elbows clunking on the bare wooden floor. She had enjoyed the books, but never thought she was likely to meet their author, so she was greatly surprised when her professor at Duke had rung her and asked if she'd like to go to dinner with Gerald Durrell.

Lee McGeorge had never met a famous person before. 'He lived up to his star billing,' she recalled. 'He was quite dapperly dressed. He wasn't wearing a sober dark suit like the rest of the men. He was much more flamboyant and with his flowing white hair and beard he looked quite dramatic. But he had total and absolute charisma, an aura of energy, which set him apart as someone special. The room was full of silverback professors, but he was a silverback who was different: he wasn't an academic, there was a freshness about him, he was doing something exciting and interesting. His Englishness probably had something to do with it. I'd been to England twice before. London was the first place I'd been to abroad. Then I went to a big conference in Cambridge and I just adored being in Cambridge and going punting and so forth. So I was totally taken aback when a brand new Englishman with this terrific charisma walked through the door in Durham, North Carolina, and came up and started talking to me. I was only there as a token student who happened to have done something exotic that was faintly in the same line of business as his.'

As Lee began to talk, Gerald stared at her in stupefaction. 'If she had told me that her father was a full-blooded Indian chief and her mother a Martian, I could not have been more astonished,' he was to relate. 'Animal communication in all its forms happened to be a subject in which I was deeply interested. I gazed at her. That she was undeniably attractive was one thing, but to be attractive *and* studying animal communication lifted her almost into the realm of being a goddess.'

'The fact that he paid so much interest in me was overwhelming,' Lee recalled. 'It was flattering. No one had flattered me in that way before. It was clear that Gerry was romantically interested and this also was very flattering. I mean, boyfriends in those days didn't flatter you much. But I was too star-struck to respond in that kind of way – and anyway I had a boyfriend I was becoming very involved with.'

For the next two hours the fifty-two-year-old Englishman and twenty-seven-year-old American woman debated animal communication – and practised it themselves. When the whole crowd drove off to a restaurant in town, Gerald and Lee continued their discussion in her car, full of dog hairs and dead leaves. Lee's car was leading the way, 'followed by a sort of funeral cortège of professors and their wives', but she and Gerald talked so much that they got lost and didn't reach the restaurant till ten, the rest of the party still following, 'going round and round in circles like Japanese waltzing mice'. They talked unendingly over dinner till two in the morning, when Lee drove Gerald back to his motel.

'Next morning,' Gerald recalled, with a little difficulty, 'I awoke and discovered that the slightest movement of my head spelt agony. Lying quite still I thought about Lee. Had it, I wondered, been an alcoholic haze that made me think her so intelligent? Beautiful, yes, but intelligent? I put in a call to Dr Alison Jolly, the doyenne of Madagascar studies and the winsome ways of lemurs.

'"Tell me, Alison, do you know a girl called Lee McGeorge?"

'"Why, yes," she said, "Duke University."

'"Well, what do you think of her?" I asked, and waited with bated breath.

'"Well, she's quite one of the brightest students in the animal behaviour field that I've come across for many a year."'

Without more ado he picked up the phone and rang Lee. He wanted to say hello again, he said, and tell her how much he'd enjoyed meeting her. He was going to be on the move now, so couldn't meet up – but he'd be back. A few days later he wrote her a letter – the first of many.

> Dear Lee,
> Apologies once again. However when you reach my age you have to move with a certain speed to accomplish anything. You were so ravishing, refreshing and intelligent that you seduced me. So, while apologising, may I still say this: should it ever happen (God forbid) that your love life comes unstuck and you think a trip to Europe to stay with me would not be too repulsive, write or phone me. You are one of the most beautiful and intelligent girls I have met in a long time and the sort of person I need. I don't just mean for obvious reasons, but I have a hell of a lot I want to do and places I want to go to and I need an assistant.

Gerald's aim was to impress. He might no longer be youthful, lissom or handsome, but he led an enviably exotic and romantic life, and enjoyed an exalted status in several spheres. He would be in the States for a few more days, he told Lee, and would be back in the middle of May to receive an honorary doctorate.

> Then I return to my zoo in Jersey, and go down to my house in the South of France until early September when I come back to Jersey for Princess Grace of Monaco to open our new vet complex. After this I go to Mauritius to lie face downwards on a reef for the winter. I wish I was young and beautiful then you might consider doing all these things with me. Never mind. After Mauritius I hope to go to Assam in the Spring and then Peru and Madagascar. So you see I mean it when I say I am busy.

I beg to remain, your very obedient servant, Gerry
PS: To hell with good manners – I *still* think you're ravishing.

Gerald's honorary degree was awarded at Yale on 16 May. When he woke at dawn in his hotel room on the day of the ceremony, his first act was to write a letter to his deputy, Jeremy Mallinson, in distant Jersey:

My very dear Jeremy,
It is 5 a.m. on the day I am to receive my doctorate and I felt I must write to you ... I am fully aware that the honour that is being done me today is for both of us, since I know I could not have achieved anything without your help, hard work and dedication. So when I receive the doctorate, I want you to know that I will be receiving it as much on your behalf as my own, since it was your efforts that put me in this position.

Prior to the conferring of the honorary degrees, the recipients – who included the former President of the United States, Gerald Ford, and the blues musician B.B. King – walked in procession through the campus preceded by the college band and surrounded on all sides by under-graduates and their parents and friends. 'I had watched many processions but up to now had never taken part in one,' Gerald recalled, 'and I'd never realised how hot the whole procedure was, since the temperature was up to 80 deg. and wearing a mortar board and gown was sticky to say the least.' When it was Gerald's turn to receive his award the entire Yale Faculty of Forestry and Ecological Research got to its feet to cheer him. The President of Yale then read out the citation:

A gifted writer whose wit and graceful prose have given us both entertaining and informative excursions into the lives of animals, you have introduced nature to millions. To the established scien-tists, your work has contributed to a public awareness of the needs and aspirations of modern conservation. Through a sophisticated programme of breeding rare and endangered species to prevent their extinction, you have developed concepts both original and successful. For your humour, your remarkable mind, and your talented contributions to our world, Yale is proud to confer upon you the degree of Doctor of Humane Letters.

Gerald did not meet Lee again on this American visit, but he had not forgotten her, or his seemingly intractable dilemma: 'How did one attract a young, pretty girl,' he asked himself, 'when one is portly, grey and old enough to be her father? To one who had collected mammals successfully in all continents, the problem of this capture seemed, to say the least insoluble.'

Clearly, though, the problem was *not* insoluble. There was little Gerald did not know about the science and practice of sexual attraction in mammals. After all, it was his business to know. It was what captive breeding was all about. 'This zoo is sex mad,' he had once told a party of visitors he was showing round it. 'How do I get the animals to breed?' he said to one reporter. 'I go round their cages at night and read them the *Kama Sutra*.' 'Suddenly,' Gerald wrote, 'I remembered the one unique attribute I had: a zoo. I decided that I must get her over to Jersey to see my lonesome asset. But how could I do it without arousing the darkest suspicion in her bosom? I was struck with a brilliant idea. So I phoned her up.'

Over the phone Gerald talked with bubbling, if devious, enthusiasm about his plans for the Jersey Trust, and the part he felt Lee could play in them.

'You will remember,' he told her, 'that I was anxious to set up a behavioural study and sound recording unit?'

That at least was true. What followed was not.

'An old woman, a member of the Trust, has died,' he went on, 'and very generously left us some money in her will. It's only a small amount of money, not enough to build anything, but enough to do the preliminary research on its viability. So I was wondering ... if we should use it ... to bring you over to Jersey to give me advice on setting the thing up. How does that strike you?'

'Well,' said Lee, 'I'd certainly love to do it, but I couldn't come over till the end of the semester.'

From Jersey on 23 May Gerald followed up his phone call with a formal invitation by letter.

> As I told you on the phone, we had a tiny windfall, the spending of which is up to my discretion. I would be most grateful if you would allow us to fund you on a trip to Jersey. I would like you to see our general set-up, but particularly I would like you to suggest areas of research which we could profitably put into operation. I am exceptionally interested in your theory about animal communications. If you decide to come, I hope by that time that I will have some interesting material on the whales and a rather fascinating paper on the frequencies of bird cries.

She could stay for as long as she liked, Gerald told her, but not less than four weeks. He would send her the air ticket and reimburse her expenses.

So the trap was sprung – though the quarry was to take a long time falling into it.

The summer was full of so many major distractions that it was a little while before Gerald found time to write to Lee again. Indeed, for a while it seems she almost slipped below his emotional horizon, for she was still a remote dream in a distant continent, whereas his existing women friends remained firmly in place. His Argentinean friend of many years standing, Marie Renee Rodrigue, came over to keep him company for a while, followed by Wyn Knowles, whom he had met when she was the producer of BBC Radio's *Woman's Hour*. A New Yorker in her late twenties by the name of Trish, who had helped organise the historic rock concert at Woodstock – 'a nice person, rather like Jackie Kennedy, and great fun' – went with him on his return visit to Mauritius, with John Hartley and Margo also in tow. Later he set off for a holiday in the villa near Grasse and an excursion to Venice, with Margo and John Hartley again in the party, along with a friend of Margo's called Virginia.

From La Chèvre Blanche he resumed contact with Lee in a letter dated 20 June, in which he extolled the beauties of France, which he hoped he would one day show her in person: 'I have never seen France looking so lovely as we drove down . . . Every hedgerow was a vast floral arrangement . . . Everywhere butterflies in great droves . . . The rivers like green satin . . . and every village and cottage covered with roses . . . As you can gather, I love France. I wish you could have seen it though.'

Gerald's emotional life continued to drift vaguely and inconsequentially through the summer of 1977. With Lee a bright but faraway figment of his memory and Trish banished for smoking pot and wearing trousers at a dinner with the Governor of Mauritius, Gerald saw a lot of a statuesque Jersey woman in her forties, with whom he enjoyed a relationship that was relatively casual on his part, less so on hers. It was with her that he travelled down to the South of France in July to check out the Mazet prior to taking it over from his brother Larry in October. Into this merry-go-round stepped Alexandra.

Alexandra Mayhew was the daughter of an English father and a Greek mother, who had been born in Bombay. Now a striking, elegant, dark-haired and independent-minded zoology graduate of twenty-three, she had known Gerald since she was twelve, when she and her mother used to see the Durrells now and again during their summer holidays on Corfu, when they were staying at their hereditary grand house at Kavavades. When she applied for a job on a zoology magazine in London in the summer of 1977 she contacted Gerald about using his name as a reference.

'I had been living in Athens for several years,' Alexandra was to relate, 'working for the Greek Animal Welfare Society, but that summer I developed a kidney stone, so I drove back through Europe to see a specialist, and I was staying with my grandmother in Tunbridge Wells when Gerald wrote to me and said come over to Jersey to stay and we'll talk about the job interview. I went with my boyfriend for a couple of days, then fell ill with a terrible tummy bug and ended up staying a week or so. Gerry christened me "Parasite" and used to write letters to me that began "Dear Parasite" and ended "Your loving Host". He didn't like the chap I was with, mainly because he was the chap I was with. He used to bring me up a tray in bed while I was ill, and one day he said: "Oh, you ought to get rid of that awful man. You're wasted on him. You should come back and marry me." He was serious. I was young and attractive and we had Greece and zoology in common. He had only met Lee once at that time and though he was very taken with her it didn't seem that it was going anywhere. Later he told me that there were only three women he had ever really felt tremendous physical attraction to and wanted to marry – me, Lee and Jacquie. But there wasn't a thing between us at all, because much as I liked and respected him – he was fascinating to listen to, wonderful company and terribly generous, a larger than life, bucolic, bacchanalian St Francis figure who went around uttering four-letter words – I just didn't fancy him, frankly. He wasn't in good nick, either, and he was an emotional wreck at the time.'

So Alexandra returned to Athens and Gerald returned to his plans for an expedition to Assam. His aim was to make a fact-finding tour to determine the status of the endangered pygmy hog and the chances of acquiring a few pairs for captive breeding in Jersey. The pygmy hog had recently been 'rediscovered' in the Himalayan foothills, having been feared extinct as a result of the settlement and cultivation of its original habitat, above all the seasonal burning of the thatch-scrub jungle in which it lived.

For the Jersey Trust to intervene in the fate of the surviving pygmy hogs was not easy. There were considerable political hurdles to clear, and negotiations with the Indian government had to be conducted at the highest level. In the previous year the Chairman of the World Wildlife Fund, Sir Peter Scott, had intervened on Gerald's behalf and approached the Prime Minister of India, Indira Gandhi, with a request for two or three pairs of pygmy hogs. She replied: 'This animal had reached the very edge of extinction, but because of our strict protection, it is now making good recovery and we are able to spare some for breeding. I hope they will do well in Jersey.'

So far, so good. Gerald initially planned to travel to Assam in the spring of 1977 with William Oliver, his research assistant at Jersey, but he had picked up a strange amoebic bug in Mauritius which laid him low. 'It makes me feel as though I am 142 years old,' he noted, 'and excrete blood in a way that would be envied by Dracula.' Though William Oliver eventually went to Assam to carry out his own studies into the pygmy hog, Gerald had no alternative but to postpone his visit to the following spring. The question now was, who would accompany him?

In October he returned to America on another fund-raising tour. Following Alexandra's fond but firm rejection of his tentative advances, he was all the more determined to woo Lee to his side. But how? The first thing he had to do was to meet up with her again – preferably at something prestigious somewhere exciting. He was due to give an important lecture in Washington, DC. He would invite her to that. It went without saying that he would pay for her flight and accommodation.

Lee had never heard Gerald speak in public, and the lecture in Washington reinforced his charisma for her. 'It was brilliant,' she recalled. 'He drew cartoons, he told stories about his collecting trips, it all just seemed off the top of his head. But it wasn't. He had a phrase: "You must always practise your ad libs." He always gave a standard lecture, which started with his animal experiences, going all the way back to collecting animals for zoos, then on to founding his own zoo and Trust, culminating in the work of the Jersey Trust and promoting the American Trust. His strongest point was telling stories and doing sketches and making people laugh. It wasn't his forte to deliver something terribly serious and straight up and down. He wasn't very good at facts and figures or programmes and strategies. Oddly enough, he wasn't very good at asking people for money either. He was brought up in the days when it was considered vulgar to talk about money, so he was very embarrassed about begging for it. Usually social events were arranged round these lectures by Jody Longnecker or Tom Lovejoy or people on the board of the American Trust, many of them very wealthy themselves, who had good contacts with other rich people. Gerry would say: "Point me in the right direction and I will be terribly nice and charming and talk about animals and our work and the terrible problems we're having, and you follow up behind me and make the pitch." But though he was the Trust's chief fund-raiser, he rarely made the pitch himself.'

Over dinner in Washington Gerald cast another fly onto the stream. He was due to go to Assam in the New Year. Perhaps, he suggested, Lee might like to come with him – ideally after she had been over to inspect his facilities in Jersey. Idea implanted, Gerald flew off to Jersey and Lee flew back to Durham. A few days later he wrote to her there.

Dear Chipmunk.

It was nice having you in Washington (or *not* having you in Washington) and to find that you are as attractive as I remembered.

Re Assam, I will try and put it off to March/April if possible, in case you can join me. It should, as I say, be a red carpet trip and it is supposed to be a very beautiful part of the world – I am sure the trip would amuse you, even if I do not.

With much love, Yours, G

Though absence might make Gerald's heart grow fonder, distance made Lee's grow shrewder. With the source of all the charisma now marooned on a tiny island 3500 miles away, she began to have, if not second thoughts, then at least more considered ones. On 26 November she wrote a devastatingly frank and intermittently logical letter which should have stopped Gerald dead in his tracks.

Dear Gerry,

I enclose a flyer on the tape recorder I've asked you to buy. Beautiful machine, isn't it? Talking of beautiful machines, I'm not one. You can't just push a few buttons and expect me to come out with 'fuck off' or any other short, catchy phrase. On the other hand, I can't reply with some suitably pompous soliloquy to your push on the state of my mind and the plans for my life. I can't, not because they're inherently unstable but because the people around me and my circumstances are so subject to change. So here are my honest thoughts on you and me.

I do realise what you're offering me. You're a marvellous man, someone I'd like to spend a lot of time with. You're like me in my good ways and not like me in my bad ways – that's why we hit it off so well. And you plan to take me to the most fantastic places in the world, glorious places with all the animals and wild lands I'd ever hoped to study. Believe me, it makes my head swim. But all this has come about at the right time in your life and the wrong time in mine.

Wrong for me in that I've found a person whom I'd marry. I couldn't very well expect him to wait for me while I'm off being your friend and lover for a few years. He – his name is Lincoln – has his faults, and our life together wouldn't be the easiest for several reasons – his obsession for his child and his dear, ever-present ex-wife – but still, I love him and he loves me. I'm not so foolish as to think it will last forever. When we've lived together a bit longer, *then* I'll know whether to commit myself.

What I'm trying to tell you is that I cannot go to Assam with you because of my thesis, but that going other places with you as your lover, friend and intellectual companion is still in my thoughts.

I sense urgency on your part, Gerry, so it wouldn't be very fair of me to expect you to wait while I make up my mind. Don't wait. Do what you've got to do. If another lady comes along who can take my place, so be it. I'd be sorry for myself, but glad for you.

My problem must be in my Episcopalian upbringing. (Did I tell you I became a non-believer when my Sunday school teacher told me that animals don't go to heaven?)

Love, Lee

So the lady was not only intelligent, she had a mind of her own. She not only understood animal communication, but the human variety as well. She declined to be had, but prudently kept her options open. The game was still all to play for, but now there were two players, not one. Gerald seems to have treated this stand-off in the only way that he felt open to him: by ignoring it. At the end of the month he wrote cheerily as if nothing had happened:

Dear Chipmunk,
. . . I am sorry it took you so long to recover from Washington. It may take you even longer to recover from Jersey in January. I assure you that it will be cold although not snow cold, so bring warm clothes, rain coat and a hat. By all means bring your bikini because I can enjoy watching you sunbathe under my sun lamp.

My love to you.

Yours ever, Gerry

The next day he wrote again with an important afterthought.

I have been having second thoughts about you sun bathing under my sun lamp in your bikini. On mature reflection I have decided that I would prefer you to sun bathe under it without your bikini.

With much love, Yours sincerely, Gerry

By the New Year of 1978 it was settled. Lee had got her tape recorder and she would come over to Jersey and put it to use. The weather was bad on both sides of the Atlantic. Kennedy Airport in New York was snowed in, and for two days Lee had to camp there, sleeping in corners, starving because the food had run out. It was snowing on the other side of the Atlantic too, but that did not dampen Gerald's elation. Jersey was surrounded by water on all sides. His flat was inside a manor house inside a zoo. There was nowhere to run to, and Lee couldn't fly.

'Gerry met me at the airport,' Lee remembered.

He had a bottle of champagne in an ice bucket in the back of the car and during the short drive between the airport and the zoo we got through most of it. I must have been there for four weeks or so. For me it was all very heady and dramatic stuff. In the day I would go round the zoo with my tape recorder and in the evening Gerry would cook marvellous dinners, and we'd eat in the dining room by candlelight, and sometimes we'd sit by the fire in the sitting room, drinking wine and talking and talking. Sometimes the 'boys' would come up and talk conservation business and sometimes we'd go to dinner at their homes. I mean, I was being regally entertained. Perhaps they saw me as the next Mrs Durrell. Gerry had got this pretty much fixed in his mind early on. Even before we'd discussed anything he said to the cleaning lady: 'That's the girl I'm going to marry.' Obviously there was a romantic sexual interest right from the start, but I'd been a bit tangled up in my personal involvement back in the States. This other person knew about Gerry lurking in the wings but I don't think he gave much thought to it. I was very involved actually, but with Gerry's flattery, his flamboyance, his humour, everything – I was very easy to reel in. It was becoming evident that Gerry wanted a longer relationship, a physical relationship, and wished for me to share in lots of things with him. Then one evening by the fire he started talking about my being at the zoo more permanently while still doing my research.

'Do you mean a job here?' I asked.

'Oh yes, of course,' he said.

'Do you think my boyfriend could come and apply for a job as well?' I asked.

'I'm afraid not,' he replied gravely.

'Do you mean you want me to live with you?' I asked.

'Well, I had a bit more in mind than that,' he said.

'Like what?' I asked.

'I want to marry you.'

'Oh, right,' I said.

'So what do you think?'

'I'll have to think about it,' I said.

This is generally understood to mean 'no', but in Lee's case it meant what it said. She was still trying to work the man out, and to think through the implications of the offer he had made her. With Gerald's encouragement she flew off to Paris to talk to the world's leading lemur expert, Dr Alison Jolly, about various kinds of primates, including Gerry. She then went to Cambridge to meet a fellow graduate student from Duke University by the name of Dan Rubenstein, a brilliant ecologist who later became head of department at Princeton. She talked to him about Gerry too, and his response was encouraging enough for her to go back to Jersey with her mind made up. She recalled:

> I had to make some decisions. Marrying Gerry would mean not becoming an academic, not pursuing the career I had always envisaged. This wasn't difficult, it really wasn't. I'd messed about with animals all my young life and went into zoology out of a passion I'd formed for conservation. So in marrying Gerry I would be going into the very thing that so impassioned me. Unlike for Jacquie, the zoo and everything that went with it was for me a complete world into which I stepped, a world I really wanted to be in, though not the world I had been heading for. So I had in front of me the prospect of instant fulfilment at the side of a man at the cutting edge. So I went back to Jersey and I went up to Gerry and I said, 'Yes, I think it's probably quite a neat idea,' and he said, 'Oh good, that's settled then.'

'I am a modest man by nature,' Gerald was to relate later, 'but I have achieved one irrefutably unique thing in my life, of which I am extraordinarily proud. I am the only man in history who has been married for his zoo.'

'It was odd, really,' Lee recalled, 'considering the twenty-five years that separated us, let alone the entire Atlantic Ocean, that we had so much in common, so many shared interests. The age gap never bothered us. He didn't have the crusty mind-set of a retired admiral, so to speak. His mind was so wide-ranging, and his interests so broad, he was so stimulating and flexible and fun, so ready to do all sorts of things, that it was as if he never grew any older, had never grown old or grown up at all. Mind you, though he wasn't set in his ways, he did have some set ways, some opinions about things. The culture gap never bothered us either. Gerry often said that, with all his travels and upbringing, he didn't think he belonged to any one culture or nationality at all, so it was easy for me to fit in to such a broad spectrum.'

Gerald was due to fly to Calcutta on 27 February for his journey through Assam in quest of the pygmy hog. When Lee turned the trip down because of the demands of her Ph.D dissertation, Gerald invited Alexandra Mayhew, another qualified (and attractive) zoologist, to take her place. There would be no funny business, Gerald assured Lee. Indeed, shortly before their departure Lee and Gerald met Alexandra and her mother for a farewell curry supper in London, Gerald and Alexandra's mother vying with each other to see who could eat the hottest dish.

Gerald believed passionately that fidelity was an inviolable rule once a commitment had been made, and on the eve of his departure for Assam he composed a declaration in verse, entitled 'Marriage Vow', affirming his love and faithfulness to Lee.

> Dearest, best beloved Lee,
> I send this note from me to thee
> Over forests, mountains, ocean
> To tell you of my deep devotion
> To tell you that my love won't falter
> That I'll bring you to the altar
> After that, as time grows longer
> You will find my love grows stronger
> No-one else I want to keep
> With no-one else I wish to sleep
> With no-one else I want to travel
> With no-one else would I unravel
> Nature's cunning mysteries
> And doing so I hope to please.
> I hope within the long hereafter
> To hear your voice, your flute-like laughter
> To see your lovely flower-like head
> There beside me in the bed
> With eyes of autumn woodsmoke shade
> A face that's from perfection made
> The dusky hair like storm clouds billow . . .

The fear of losing his beloved, Gerald went on, made his heart 'writhe in a knot', for he would be left alone 'in a world that's cold . . . sans perfume, colour, sound'. But he tried to take a sanguine view, trusting that he could 'truly forge' a love with Lee.

> And since she now means everything
> And makes the very stars to ring
> So I say 'God? D'you envy me?

Enjoying thus the fruits of Lee?'
And somewhere dim I hear a voice
'We cannot but approve the choice.'

Accompanying the poem was a large handwritten note in red ink: 'HAVE GONE TO ASSAM BACK SOON'. It was decorated with a heart pierced by an arrow and inscribed with the words 'I love you'.

The Assam expedition did not have a propitious start. After their farewell lunch together in London Gerald and Lee parted and went their separate ways. Soon afterwards, Gerald realised he had left behind in the restaurant his little shoulder bag containing his and Alexandra's plane tickets, his passport, medical certificates, credit cards, and the cash and travellers' cheques for financing the entire expedition. By the time he got back to the restaurant the bag was gone, and he was stranded – as was Alexandra, waiting for him with soaring impatience at Heathrow. Their departure was postponed for a week.

Alexandra was not as yet fully aware of the distracted state of her co-expeditionary's mind. The problem was that Gerald had, to his surprise, fallen head over heels in love with Lee. 'I'd been married before and was on the point of getting divorced,' he explained later. 'After my wife left me, I thought: "Well, OK. Now let's play the field. To hell with it. I don't want anything more to do with women except in bed." I suppose it was rather an arrogant attitude to adopt. But it was the result of being hurt. But then, of course, I met this creature, and made the fatal mistake of falling in love with her. Absolutely fatal. A man of my age, falling in love with a woman who's young enough to be his great great granddaughter.'

Even as he prepared to leave for Assam Gerald's thoughts were still focused on Lee rather than on the expedition, as the letter he wrote that evening from his hotel showed.

Dearest and beloved McGeorge,
I just want you to have it in writing that I love you deeply, that I cannot wait for your return, and that you are the most wonderful thing that has ever happened to me in a life that has been not uncrowded with wonderful things. I still cannot really believe you are going to share my life. I feel like a man who has succeeded in capturing a rainbow – filled with a sense of awe and delight.

I promise I will not give you any cause for regret. I promise I will devote the rest of my life to making sure you always have a light in your lovely eyes and a smile on your ravishing mouth.

Your devoted servant. G.

Gerald returned to Jersey while the chaos was sorted out. Alone in the flat, with Lee halfway to America and himself all dressed up with nowhere to go, he experienced a solitude akin to vertigo. To ease the burden he sat down and wrote a letter to his love, and so long as they were apart he would never stop writing to her – not only letters but poems and illuminated manuscripts, telegrams and extended narratives, paeans to her beauty, love stories and comic sketches, bawdy limericks and intimate reveries, a vast outpouring from heart and mind intended to salve the trauma of separation and cross the barrier of distance. Taken together, the letters must rank as among the most remarkable in the entire history of zoology. While they were at first sporadic and exploratory – though there was no doubting Gerald's barely hidden agenda – from now on they became prolific and uninhibitedly intimate.

> Dear Lady –
> I have just returned from the airport to an empty and silent room and I miss you like hell already. There are reminders of your lovely presence everywhere – cigarettes in the ashtray, beautiful black hair in the bathroom, on the bed, in my diary, the faint, delicate smell of your body (like jonquils) lingering on the pillow, the towels, in the air . . .
> We have such an exciting future in front of us and I can't wait to get started on it. I want nothing but your happiness and contentment. I want each day to be a carnival for you, full of joy and as brightly coloured as a bed of flowers. I want to hear you laugh often, your flute-like bird-like laugh, and I want to warm and protect you with my love. You are now the most important person in my life and the most important single thing in my life. I have been wandering like a blind man and you have restored my sight.
> I love you, G.

Next day he wrote again, trying another tack. This was, he told Lee, 'a very difficult letter to write', but it was best to be honest, even if the truth was brutal. He had met another girl, and they had fallen deeply in love. Her name was Araminta Grubble, a knitting instructress, eighty-four years of age, 'but *slim*'. Once they were married they were going to open a polar bear farm in Baffin Land and make a fortune taking photographs of people's babies on the polar bear skins. 'If at any time you are passing through Baffin Land,' he concluded solemnly, 'please do drop in and have your babies photographed on one of our best bear skins. It would be our pleasure.'

On 3 March 1978 Gerald and Alexandra finally arrived in Calcutta. This was Gerald's first sight of the land of his birth since he left it nearly fifty years ago, when he was three. 'We were totally walloped by the culture shock,' Alexandra recalled, 'the heat, humidity, smells, squalor, indifference to human life, human suffering. Just the road from the airport to the city centre was enough. The central reservation comprised an entire linear community of the deprived, all living in rag tents, not an inch of space between them.' The travellers, by contrast, as guests of a tea company, McNeill & Magor Ltd, were treated like royalty, for the whole trip was personally arranged by Richard Magor, the director of the company, who was to prove very generous to the Trust and its pygmy hog work over many years. The Raj-style guest house in Calcutta was sumptuous beyond belief, with air-conditioning, an English garden, white-turbaned, bare-footed servants everywhere anticipating every wish, yet with squalor lapping at the walls of the compound like a seething tide of flotsam. 'Gerry was very taken aback,' Alexandra remembered, 'though he was a bit too preoccupied to notice. For much of our time in Assam he was rather distraught. He felt he should be staying in touch with Lee and not running around after a tiny pig on the other side of the world.'

Throughout his sojourn in India Gerald's life revolved around finding means of communication with North Carolina. He was desperate to receive word from Lee and to send word back. Above all he needed to know how her announcement of their proposed marriage had gone down in America. In his first letter from Assam on 4 March he wrote:

> My darling McGeorge,
> I will have you know that I am nearly dead with frustration. I have been trying to telephone you for two solid days. First in Calcutta they said your phone was not answering. We tried all day and up to one o'clock last night – no reward. Then we flew up to Assam today and I started all over again. *Now* they have just told me your phone is *out of order*. Suicide seems the only answer – I will go and throw myself under an elephant.
>
> My sweet Lee, I arrived in Calcutta and the first thing I received was your wonderful telegram. Darling, I am delighted about your parents and friends being pleased, but even more delighted that you are pleased – and said so. But then, when you told me to take care and then signed it 'love Lee' my head started to swim and I fell down several times. 'LOVE?' '*LOVE?*' Whatever happened to my cold blooded zoo-digger? Whatever happened to flint hearted, wishy washy McGeorge, the girl who kept saying she didn't love

me, eh? Whatever happened to our cold, calculating McGeorge
who was only going to marry me for what I could give her, eh?
The next thing you know you'll be writing and telling me you miss
me. Get a grip on yourself, McGeorge, for Heavens sake and don't
go around sending telegrams like that.

Unless you mean it . . .

So I will end as you ended and mean it as much as I hope you
did.

Take care, my sweet and lovely creature.

Love Gerry

Gerald and Alexandra travelled round Assam in (or sometimes on)
whatever vehicle was appropriate – jeep, plane, elephant, inflatable
dinghy. Their first stop was at Gauhati, a cleaner, serener place than the
big city. Here they lived in a bungalow perched on a hill above the
Brahmaputra river and visited the local zoo. 'We were shown around in
great style,' Alexandra recorded in her diary, 'closely followed by a whole
army of keepers, directors, vets and this and that – it was like a state
visit! And at last I caught my first glimpse of the famous pig. They are
absolutely enchanting creatures – about the size of a small dog, hairy,
sharp little tusks, move like greased lightning.'

From Gauhati they moved on to the Kaziranga National Park, a refuge
for Indian rhino. From the Kaziranga Forest Lodge, a riverside bungalow
at Arimara, Gerald wrote to Lee on 6 March, describing the difficulty he
had experienced in attempting to send her a telegram from the local post
office:

> They were very charming, and looked in a big book to see how
> much it was to send a love telegram to North Carolina. Here they
> hit a snag of some sort. They all gathered around the book like a
> flock of ants, gesticulating and arguing. Eventually they brought
> the Post Master himself into the fray. He had a large turban,
> chewed betel nut and looked like Orson Welles. Even this magnifi-
> cent specimen could not solve the problem, so they called me
> around the counter and into the inner sanctum. There they showed
> me the magnum opus. In the book was written the baffling phrase
> 'NORTH-SOUTH CAROLINA' and then the rate. Why, they
> enquired, puzzled, had I only put North on the telegraph when it
> clearly stated in the Post Office Bible that North-South was the
> correct way of putting it? I pointed out that there was a North
> *and* a South Carolina and the book merely put them with a hyphen
> to show that the rate was the same. They looked at each other

aghast. How could the Post Office Bible be so obtuse and cunning? Impossible! By this time the entire staff of the post office was gathered around me trying to solve the problem of North and South Carolina, while at the other side of the counter a great wedge of humanity who merely wanted to buy stamps or post letters or send telegrams to ordinary places like Calcutta, got more and more restive. Meanwhile the Post Master General arrived. He looked about a hundred and eight with a beard that fifty macaws could have nested in. Everyone shouted at him at once and I thought the sheer noise would make him faint or have a heart attack. Eventually, when they had all explained it to him several times and he had heard my explanation (out of politeness only, since no one believed me) he took out a very dusty pair of glasses, put them on and peered into the Bible. The silence was such that you could have heard a dandelion clock landing. Then he took off his glasses, cleared his throat and proclaimed in a tremulous and dignified voice, that I was right – there *was* a North *and* a South Carolina and the rates were the same. The outlet of held breath was like a whirlwind. Then everyone beamed at me, the clever white man. They smiled at me, patted me on the back, shook my hand and brought me a cup of pale white and horribly sweet tea to drink while my telegram was handed round so everyone could read it. Thank God they did not read it aloud. Then they made out a receipt and I was free to go, having refused more tea. The little man who started it all apologised for the delay but, as he pointed out proudly, they had to get it right. It was, after all, *the most expensive* telegram that had been sent *in the whole history* of the Post Office.

Five days later Gerald and Alexandra had reached Pertabghur, *en route* to a camp on the Subansiri river, where they aimed to look for a rare Indian freshwater crocodile with a long pointed snout called a gharial. Gerald wrote to Lee from there on 11 March:

Darling McGeorge,
I have just arrived at the above estate and got your telegram. My sweet, you should not send telegrams like that unless you mean it – it makes my heart turn over and my mind spin. 'I love you' forsooth – *do* you mean it or are you simply saying it because you think I want that and are feeling guilty? Dear McGeorge, if it is true I cannot say how delighted and flattered I am. But I must say once again – I *do not expect* it. I asked you to marry me knowing

full well the terms and with my eyes wide open, so please don't feel you have to force yourself to love me against your inclinations. I shall not be OFFENDED.

If, however, by some alchemy, you have really got your feelings involved then my world is made. I will move mountains for you, pluck the moon out of the sky for you to wear behind your ear, plait rainbows into tresses for you and guard you from harm like an elderly tiger. Please write and tell me what is and what is not true . . .

You'll be delighted to know that all the women in Assam are quite beautiful and if I can remain faithful to you here I can do it anywhere. We leave tomorrow to an elephant catching camp, then to a place to see cock fighting, then to the place to see pygmy hogs, then back here. After that we go – for Easter – to a place in the hills called Shillong, and thence back to Calcutta when I hope I can phone you and hear your lovely voice . . .

I cannot contemplate an existence or an experience which does not include you and that will not be enhanced by your presence. I love you, McGeorge, and if you feel about me even remotely as I feel about you then I am the luckiest man on this planet.

As always and forever, G

By now Alexandra had begun to get the measure of her travelling companion. He had a habit of sniffing down his nose when he talked, she noticed, and of snoring extraordinarily loudly when he slept. He was quite jolly in the main, even though he was so churned up about Lee, but he could become angry when he got on to the subject of conservation. 'He could get very vitriolic about it,' she recalled. 'In his career he must have seen phenomenal destruction. Sometimes I think he would have cheerfully wiped out half the human race to get the numbers down. He has a passion for every living thing, especially the lowly, including man on an individual basis, but not man *en masse*, because their record was too damning. He didn't bat an eyelid about eating animal meat and he was fairly sanguine about the natural system where everything eats everything else. It was just the mass destruction he couldn't stand. He talked about all sorts of things. He talked like his books, in flowery language, with lots of similes and metaphors. He was very graphic in his speech and he could be terribly funny. He said he would have liked to have had children but it was never to be. He missed having a dog, too, but it was impossible, given the way he lived, travelling all the time.'

Gerald was not at all fit, she noticed, but he had tremendous energy, and he looked very sweet sometimes, perched on top of a loudly farting elephant or trying to photograph a butterfly on a sandbank with his big round khaki-clad bottom pointing to the heavens. Not that he was exactly travelling rough. All the VIP perks and privileges in the gift of a wealthy tea company in a country where tea was gold were laid on for him, and he was fêted everywhere as a famous and important person. The camp on the Subansiri river was no backpackers' bivouac but a luxurious tented pavilion fit for a prince, with servants in attendance and a tented loo containing (Alexandra noted in her diary) a formidably gigantic spider commensurate with the *de luxe* facilities.

'Gerry was a bon viveur,' Alexandra recalled, 'even out in the sticks. He was totally larger than life and did everything to excess. He had formed a passion for Indian beer. This came in 2-litre bottles, and when we set off up the Subansiri river he took three crates of it in our rubber inflatable, making 72 litres all told, plus a few bottles of brandy. This didn't appear to affect him adversely at all but it affected the boat. There they were, these crates, sitting on the plywood base of the boat and weighing a ton, with Gerry, who was no lightweight, sitting in the lotus position on top of them, high as a kite by now, and we got into a set of rapids. It was really very frightening. The poor little chap who was trying to steer the boat *and* bale it out with an empty baked bean can at the same time began to get quite frantic. Then I noticed that the base of the boat was tearing away from the inflatable sides and it looked as if the whole contraption would disintegrate before very long. "Gerry!" I shouted across to him. "I think we should jettison the beer! Chuck it out!" But he refused point blank. "Chuck it out?" he said. "I absolutely will *not*!" God knows how we made it back to base. We nearly didn't.'

Though Gerald was treated everywhere as a celebrity, this did not stop eyebrows being raised, since he was travelling in the company of a beautiful woman less than half his age whose presence was never fully explained. 'A lot of people thought there was something going on,' Alexandra recalled, 'which was ironic considering Gerry's mind was full of nothing but Lee.'

Throughout his travels in Assam, Gerald was eaten up with frustration, doubt, angst, fear on account of Lee. By now the travellers were receding further and further from the civilised world. On 18 March they made a lightning leap into the restricted mountain kingdom of Bhutan, as Alexandra recorded excitedly in her diary. 'Out in jeep to jungle. Didn't see anything. Then into Bhutan! Fantastic, really weird atmosphere. Most uncanny. And totally illegal!' 'Don't let on,' Alexandra wrote to her mother of the love match she occasionally glimpsed through the wrong end of a telescope, 'but it's a business deal. She's not a gold digger, doesn't pretend to love him, in fact loves a man in the States, but he wants someone to look after the zoo and the Trust when he goes and he's willing to do anything for her.'

On the day of the Bhutan adventure, Gerald wrote again to Lee:

> My dearest, delightful, delectable, delicious, dreamy darling . . .
> I miss you. In fact I miss you so much that I have got to the stage of not believing you exist. I am convinced that you are a figment of my imagination. You appeared in a dream. Nothing outside a dream could be so perfect . . .
> I have just got back from a quick and illegal trip over the border in Bhutan. Wonderful, just like Tibet, the people with lovely copper coloured skins and hair like ravens feathers. Have investigated the Pygmy Hog area both on foot and from the air and think their capture next year may be easier than I anticipated. I hope . . .
> Lovely, languid, loveable, lecherous Lee – magnificent, meritorious, marvellous McGeorge. How I wish you were in my arms. How I wish I could kiss you and gloat over your beautiful hands and feet and other excitement-making bits of your anatomy.
> Darling, I adore you and I can't wait to start sharing your life. *Please* write and tell me where we are to be married and what I can bring your parents as a present when I come over.

On 19 March Gerald and Alexandra had gone back into Bhutan, where they put up in the King of Bhutan's bright green guest-house bungalow in the Manas Wildlife Sanctuary before venturing further up-country by elephant and riverboat. The wildlife was abundant here – golden langurs, buffalo, mongoose, hog deer, birds and butterflies of all kinds and breath-taking flights of greater Indian hornbills gliding across the river at dusk. So far they had seen nothing of the object of their expedition, no pygmy hogs in the wild anywhere – probably because they had arrived at the time of year when the hogs went up into the hills and were even more difficult to find than usual. By 23 March the pair were on their way to Shillong, the Assamese capital, where every minute of Gerald's time was taken up with meetings, visits, talks, interviews and broadcasts.

On 27 March they finally returned to Calcutta. It had been a fantastic trip, in Alexandra's opinion, but the fate of the pygmy hog remained 'unfinished business', just like the volcano rabbit in Mexico. 'Unfinished business' it was to remain for some time, it transpired, for before long a revolt by Naga tribesmen would prevent all hope of going back in the foreseeable future, and nearly twenty years were to pass before a pygmy hog recovery programme, with the Jersey Trust as a key player, could finally be put into effect.

There were no letters from Lee waiting for Gerald in Calcutta. After lunch they paid a visit to the zoo, then went shopping in the New Market. 'GMD had my pearl and garnet clasp copied for Lee's ring,' Alexandra noted in her diary, 'also earrings to match. Back to the flat. Dinner alone, then GMD's call to Lee came through. He felt there was someone in her flat with her.'

Next day, Gerald's suspicions were confirmed when a letter Lee had written on 14 March was finally delivered to him. 'Gerry v. upset,' noted Alexandra.

> My dear Gerry,
> I am still living with Lincoln. The clean surgical cut required to break off the relationship was too painful for both of us at this time. We tried it for a few days, but whenever we saw each other – in the halls at school or in my office – we both started weeping. I know that I cannot live with him in the future (and he knows that I won't), but I cannot live without him at the present. We both have a lot of work to do during the day, and he must do this season's field work at night – but simply being together for a short while – over supper and in bed – quiets the raging emotions that each of us feels and gives us some comfort and peace . . .
> I know what you must be feeling now – to see that the girl you love and will marry is living with someone else. God, how could I do it to you?! But you're doing it *for me*.
> I can hardly wait 'til end May when you come over – the present phase of my life will be done and my new, marvellous life will begin.

Soon afterwards, Gerald received another letter from Lee, written on 21 March.

> My dear Gerry,
> How I wish I were sitting with you on the veranda overlooking the Brahmaputra, or better still, swaying gently on elephant back pushing through the thatch. As it is, I'm sitting madly at monstrous computers, trying to push back the frontiers of knowledge.

Gerald did not reply immediately. He had engagements in Calcutta to fulfil, talks to give to the British Council and local clubs and schools. But he was, Alexandra noted, 'very upset and flustered about Lee'. Finally it all boiled over and he exploded in fluent telegraphese in a vitriolic cable despatched from Calcutta on 30 March.

BOTH LETTERS RECEIVED STOP YOUR AUDACITY IN THINKING I WILL AGREE TO AND CONDONE YOUR PRESENT ACTIVITIES IS UNBELIEVABLE STOP HAVE NO INTENTION OF UNDERWRITING OR AGREEING TO PUERILE UNINTELLIGENT AND ADOLESCENT AFFAIR STOP IN VIEW OUR DISCUSSIONS AND DECISIONS ON JERSEY I CONSIDER YOU HAVE LIED AND BROKEN FAITH AND AM ASTONISHED THAT YOU THINK ME FOOLISH AND WEAK ENOUGH TO ACCEPT THIS WITHOUT PROTEST STOP APPARENTLY I CANNOT TRUST YOU NOW SO SEE NO POINT IN FURTHERING OUR RELATIONSHIP THEREFORE WILL NOT BOTHER CONTACT YOU AGAIN STOP NOTHING YOU CAN SAY WILL ALTER MY VIEWS ON YOUR STUPIDITY BUT WOULD REMIND YOU OF OLD MAXIM ABOUT NOT BEING ABLE TO HAVE YOUR CAKE AND EAT IT STOP SHOULD YOU WISH TO BEHAVE IN AN HONEST ADULT AND INTELLIGENT WAY ABOUT US YOU KNOW WHERE I AM BUT SUGGEST YOU MAKE YOUR MIND UP FAST AS I HAVE NO INTENTION OF WAITING AROUND WHILE YOU INDULGE IN SCHOOLGIRL HISTRIONICS STOP PITY YOU ARE SO SHORT SIGHTED AS TO DESTROY A MAGNIFICENT FUTURE FOR AN EPHEMERAL PRESENT BUT THAT IS YOUR DECISION AND MISTAKE.
    DURRELL

In far-off North Carolina, Lee took the telegram square on the jaw, and lammed straight back in a forthright letter written on 31 March.

Now, let me tell you in general what your telegram indicated to me. Your lack of sympathy means you do not understand me – you know nothing of my motives and fears, of my capacity for love, sorrow and happiness, nor do you want to know. It is now very clear to me that the woman you want to marry must in fact be subservient to you, a puppet to you, for the moment she takes any action that you perceive crosses you, she is out on her ear. You would not have the respect, decency and honor even to ask why she did what she did, because you are incapable of understanding and loving anyone beyond yourself. Life with you on Jersey and out in the world would be magnificent and glorious, full of laughter and whistling and planning and dreaming together, until I realised that I was being kept in a cage like a rare specimen. This is all right for other animals, because they are unable to cross their captors. But human beings can and will cross each other . . .

Don't worry, my dear, puppets and slaves are a dime a dozen and I'm sure you'll find yours soon.

I cried mostly about two things on the afternoon I got your telegram. The first on account of my shutting myself out of participating in the hopes and dreams of the Jersey Trust . . . How could a thing as illusory and short-lived as love (both mine for Lincoln and yours for me) – it usually lasts for less than a human generation – have prevented me from realising my *raison d'être* – which would be felt for many generations to come – in the best possible way? But there it is. The second reason I cried is about something you so cruelly pointed out in the telegram. You can't trust me any more. You could not believe how that hurts me. I have failed. Why, God knows, but there it is.

Back to rare specimens . . . I am rare, and I feel sorry for you that you've lost me. I don't think you realise how much you've lost. But on the other hand you are rare, and I feel sorry for myself. The reason I signed my first two telegrams to India with 'love' was that I must have been coming to love you in a way I didn't think possible back in Jersey – simply because I truly missed you. Lee.

This letter expressed how she felt in the raw heat of the moment, but second thoughts prevailed and she decided finally not to post it, writing instead a more considered and conciliatory note, posted to Jersey on the day Gerald and Alexandra flew out of Calcutta.

Dear Gerry,

I am truly sorry that you perceived my actions as betrayal. Superficially and conventionally considered, my actions were a betrayal. I can only conclude that your response was due to my breaking convention, and that surprises me. You're one of the most unconventional people I've ever known. I spoke to mother on the phone last night – she said she thought I was being very naive, that any man she ever knew who was worth his salt would have responded in much the same way as you did . . .

So let me tell you how I see the situation. We met and you asked me to marry you, and, after much painful consideration over the uncertainty of my future with Lincoln, the man I love, and the certainty of the future with you, the man I adore, but do not love,

I said yes. You knew the details of my deliberations at every step and you still pressed me to marry you. What I do not forgive myself for is having decided to marry you without talking first to Lincoln. I had lived with and loved him for a year, and although we hadn't spoken the words of a marriage commitment, I think he had the right to hear that I was considering marrying you. Anyway, I returned to Durham, you went to India, and you know the rest of the story ... No matter what happens, I want you to know that I love and respect you and dearly wish that you feel the same about me. Lee.

Lonely and forlorn on Jersey, Gerald perked up hugely when Lee's letter arrived. He did not reply at once, but when he did it was with passion tempered with clarity and perspective.

> Empty Bed Avenue, Lonely Flat, Love Lorn, Melancholia
> 11 April 1978
> My lovely and most true McGeorge,

Firstly let me say that I found your letter sweet, touching and (if I may quote your mother) more than a little naive. And, dare I say it, I found it more than a little illogical in places.

In Jersey I pursued you relentlessly and you finally agreed to marry me. You say that we never discussed the fact that you were in love with someone else. We did. Endlessly. You say that you should have told Lincoln that you had agreed to marry me. But may I remind you that it was only because I nagged you that you phoned him up, because I insisted that it was refined cruelty to meet him at the airport with the news. Furthermore I said – and you *must* remember this – that if you went back to Durham and slept with Lincoln I felt you would be unfair to him and to yourself, since it would upset you emotionally all over again.

Now, you had agreed to marry me. That as far as I was concerned was a commitment. It was, if you like to talk conventionally, the same as an old fashioned engagement. So from that moment, for my part, I was going to be faithful to you because I do not believe in commitment like this or in marriage if you are going to behave otherwise. If it wasn't exactly a love match from your point of view it was at least a business arrangement if you like, and so I expected you to behave in the same way. When I found that you had not I was greatly hurt. I don't think you can conceive how bitter I felt or how abandoned. Let me explain.

For twenty-five years I struggled to make my marriage work

because I feel if you get married you should work hard at it. I did work hard at it in the face of constant nagging and total lack of love both mental and physical, so much so that I had a severe nervous breakdown. The marriage limped along for a few years after that but then it burst. I don't know how to explain it but it left me feeling unclean; it left me feeling that I had contracted some fearful disease and that I could no longer be in any way attractive to a woman. It was a very degrading feeling I can assure you and I started to drink again. As a reaction I decided that I could no longer feel deeply for a woman nor did I want to. I also decided that they were not to be trusted and I in no way was going to get myself in the position of being mentally scalded that way again. Then I met you.

At first – in my new role as the suspicious and untrusting male – I just thought it would be nice to sleep with you and nothing more. Then I weakened and I thought how pleasant it would be to have you around for a year or two. And then – bloody Hell – I was deeply in love with you in a way that I never thought I could love somebody. I did not want to have you float through my bed and leave no more trace than all the women I had been having affairs with before I met you. I wanted you with me forever, however long forever is. I could not believe my luck in finding you nor my luck in getting you to agree to marry me. I was in multicoloured Euphorialand. Suddenly after months and months of living a life that seemed dead, grey, pointless and out of focus, everything became crisp and clear like the first coloured day of Spring after a long frozen shroud of Winter. I thought of you first thing in the morning and last thing at night. I spent so much of the day mentally planning what we will do together that I found I was neglecting my work. But underneath all this I was still suspicious (not of you, my sweet, but at my *luck* – I could hardly believe it), I was still suffering from a massive inferiority complex and feeling about as unepigamic as a six month corpse.

Then your letter arrived in Calcutta.

To say that I was shattered means nothing. I felt that you had, both mentally and physically, dipped me into a keg of vitriol and all the worst feeling that I had suffered since Jacquie left me returned with glee and redoubled force.

My sweet, please rid yourself of the thought (which is somewhat of a naive excuse as your mother pointed out) that all this was due to a generation gap. Oh, of course we will have generation gap problems, and it will be your fault for marrying a geriatric case. But my sweet idiot, you can't be so muddled in your thought processes or so sheltered from the harsh facts of life that you don't know that anyone can feel jealous, hurt, abandoned, frustrated love and wounded pride, from the age of five to five hundred. So I must make it clear to you that because I love you *I shall react in exactly the same way as I did should the same circumstances arise.*

One more thing and then I will have done lecturing you. You seem to think that, because I said that your not loving me as I love you was unimportant, that I meant that *love* was unimportant. No way. I love you deeply and I know this will sustain and help our relationship. I hope that by working, living and laughing together that your feelings for me might deepen, not into love as the women's magazines depict it, but as a secure and happy friendship combined with a genuine fondness. This is the real love in my opinion and when you have achieved it you will know it and want no other. You said two things in your last letter which I think are of great importance since they have a bearing on the matter. You said 'the certainty of the future with you, the man I adore'. Darling, if you really feel this you are a long way along the road to the state I have been describing. I hope you mean it. It is of great importance to me. In ending your letter you say: 'No matter what happens, I want you to know that I love and respect you and deeply wish you feel the same about me.' Do you realise that you have never before used the words 'adore' and 'love' to me, either in speech or in writing? They did much to restore my morale and to salve my hurts. So I can say that I adore, respect and love you to distraction and I hope you now have sufficient proof of it.

There! I have finished this peroration of self pity, nearly as long as the Bible but not half so well written. The thing is over as far as I am concerned, but remember my dear that adoration, love, respect and trust are all very fragile bubbles and you came within a hair's breadth of bursting them all. So I leave you with this quote from no less a cynical source than Nietzsche: 'It is not lack of love but lack of friendship that makes unhappy marriages.'

You are my dearest love and my friend. While you are these I shall want nothing in life for I shall have everything. I miss you.

Love Gerry.

At last, after many absences and separations, and not a few serious ups and downs, the two lovers stood transparent and unguarded before one another. Lee, having vigorously laid claim to her right to her personal autonomy, had firmly declared her affection and respect for Gerald. Gerald, having swallowed his ego and battened down his male pride, had loudly proclaimed his adoration, respect and love for Lee. It was the end of an affair and the beginning of a commitment. The prelude was over. The finale was about to begin.

TWENTY-SIX

Love Story: Finale

1978–1979

Gerald found it difficult to settle back into a solitary life at the flat at the zoo. Zoo and Trust matters distracted him during the day, but when his colleagues and staff went home and the spring night drew in over this enclave of animal salvation, in which he was almost the only representative of the human species, his mind turned to the only living thing that really mattered to him at that time – his wife-to-be in the faraway American South. Then the only solace for his state of yearning and incompleteness was to make a phone call or write a letter. From this point Gerald's flow of love letters and other missives to Lee doubled and then redoubled. They did not end till she was by his side on a permanent basis, and then he never wrote to her again, for she was rarely more than a room away from him.

Back in Durham, North Carolina, meanwhile, Lee had been doing her bit. The first casualty was her relationship with her former beloved, Lincoln, which was now decisively terminated.

The previous summer Gerald had finally got Larry to agree to sell him the Mazet, which had been standing empty for the last three years or so, and he had moved his belongings into it and taken possession, though the sale had still to be finalised. In April 1978 Gerald set off for Languedoc with his personal assistant, John Hartley, to finish his latest work in progress – a collection of anecdotes entitled *The Picnic and Suchlike Pandemonium*.

The Mas – proper name Mas Michel, more commonly known by the diminutive form of the word, *mazet* – was a white-plastered, stone- and mud-walled farmhouse, set in garrigue-covered hills in a large wild plot of its own that smelled of sage, thyme and wild lavender. Reached by a rough motorable track, a flight of stone steps led up to a flagstone terrace, with the unpretentious old dwelling on the left. Before Gerald redeveloped it some years later, the Mazet consisted of a tiny, low living-room with an open fireplace, a bedroom to the left and a small dining-room on the right, leading to a commodious kitchen at the other end. At the back were three other small rooms – and that was that. It was here that Larry had written some of the best of his *Alexandrian Quartet*, and Gerald and Jacquie had spent several summers there, with Gerald working on his books and television scripts away from the distractions of life at the zoo.

Gerald loved the place. To him, as to Larry, it was like living in Greece – Larry thought it was more like Attica than Languedoc – except that it was easier to get to and the native cuisine was a good deal better. Jacquie had never cared that much for the place, perhaps because she and Larry had never really got on, but Gerald had high hopes that Lee would not only fall in love with the house but, through it, with him. He wrote to her:

The Mas, poor little thing, had been badly neglected by the people who had it after me. It was like an orphan child that no-one had loved. So John and I and Arlette [the part-time housekeeper who lived nearby] set to work and with the aid of polish, brushes and mops, great blazing fires of pine logs in the living room and kitchen, managed to bring something of a glow to its cheeks and a hopeful sparkle to its eyes. However, as I told you, it needs new clothes, so to speak, so I am having our bathroom and bedroom, the tiny living room, the room I am going to make the larder and the kitchen all repainted. Then I am having the vine support redone so we have a nice place to sit (in summer we live and eat out there) and they are going to repaint and fix up the pool. I say 'pool' very grandly but it's really only a giant's paddling pool, but big enough to dive in, swim a few strokes and cool off from the sun.

This is the first day of my diet, by the way, and it is now twelve o'clock and all I have had is one glass of orange juice and two cups of coffee. Oh, I shall be so slim!

So I leave you. I love you. I want you. I miss you. I need you. The only pleasure in being here is to know that I am preparing everything for you.

Keep safe. G.

In Nîmes, the nearest town of substance, Gerald had been busy ordering furniture and other necessities, including a double bed. He duly reported the news of this crucial acquisition, enclosing a brochure:

Empty Bed Mazet, Route Chilly, Hopeful
Lit D'amour
27 April 1978
Darling McGeorge,

In haste I send you coloured photographs of what we can do in our new bed. Mon Dieu! The mind boggles. Please read the instructions carefully. I don't want you pleading ignorance at the last moment. If the bed breaks within a year (so the shop informed me without a smile) we can claim a new one.

I am lonely and I wish you and the bloody bed were here and I wish you were in it and I wish I was crossing the room and sliding between the sheets and then . . .

I love you, both in and out of bed. G.

With a wedding bed ordered and paid for, Gerald's mind began to turn to a wedding to go with it. He had already been in communication with Lee's parents, Hal and Harriet McGeorge, and had recently received a letter from her mother in which she went so far as to say they were looking forward to receiving him in Memphis in due course. The time was getting near, he began to feel, when Lee's folks ought to be given a chance to meet (and, he hoped, approve) their prospective fifty-three-year-old son-in-law. He could, he told Lee, visit the States around the middle of May. She welcomed the idea, writing from Duke University at the end of April:

I hope the weather is nice when you come to Durham, so that we can sit on the porch and have drinks while the sun sets and the birds warble their evensong. It's such a restful place. And we'll need rest at that point because I am *seriously* thinking of organising a small party for later that night.

Love, Lee.

Gerald wrote back on 2 May:

Here, Wish I were there, With you, Always.
Beloved McGeorge,

Today, after two days pissing with rain, the sun came out, the sky was blue and all was right with the world except that you were not here. Went down early to the market. I am most impatient to show you this: it is really splendid, and I really believe it is so beautiful and so filled with exotic food stuff and you can put on a couple of pounds just by walking through it. Did you know that France had five hundred cheeses? And to think I have only tasted about thirty five. Oh, McGeorge, I am going to stuff you like a Strasbourg Goose, except I won't nail your feet to the floor. Maybe I'll just nail you to the bed. Or nail us both to the bed. Or just fill the bed with you and me and a couple of cheeses for strength and then nail up the bedroom door. I hope by now you have had the instructions about the bed. IMPORTANT NOTE: DO NOT PRACTISE THEM WITH ANYONE ELSE BUT ME. I don't mind if you're a bit rusty.

Enclosed with the letter was a small envelope full of dried herbs inscribed: 'This is what our hillside behind the house smells like in the sun'. Under separate cover he sent a ten-page illustrated letter about life and nature at the Mazet, decorated with multi-coloured drawings in the manner of an illuminated manuscript concocted by a medieval Walt Disney. In this lovingly and painstakingly composed letter he beguiled Lee with cameos about the nature of the place, starting with the suicide bees:

The patio – on which we live and eat in summer – is shaded by a vine which lies upon a sort of bamboo raft. These hollow bamboos are a great attraction to one of the more stupid but attractive insects in the area: the carpenter bees. They are now buzzing around, testing the bamboos for size, mating in mid-air (which is quite disgusting) and generally getting themselves ready for the great moment when they start building their nests in the bamboo. Song:

> The carpenter bee is buzzing and blue
> As a piece of the Mediterranean sea,
> But I fear that his eyesight is not very true
> For he's swimming around in my tea
> And then, I assure you, just yesterday eve,
> I was watching the sunset at nine,
> And without as much as a quick 'by your leave'
> He was floating around in my wine.
> He fell in my soup, he fell in my beer,
> He fell – with a splash – in my café au lait:
> But his awful myopia just fills me with fear,
> So I'm buying him a life-belt today.

The first hoopoes have arrived and inspected the wall on the hill at the back of the Mazet where they nest. The cuckoos have arrived too, and they are cucking all over the valley in the most seductive fashion. It's funny how all the other birds fall silent when they hear the cuckoo. She even gives the nightingale pause for thought, and if you knew the nightingales here you would realise that all they seem bent on doing is to spend all day and night singing like a bloody pop group. However, I must admit that the other night was very romantic. We had such a fierce full moon that you could read a book anywhere in the valley. And there were no less than four nightingales in full song around the house . . .

Darling McGeorge I must end this, for it is almost as long as the Book of Kells. You have found it silly? Infantile? Stupid? Then I am all of these things. Soon I will be in America and you will no longer be just a voice on the end of the phone. So, until I arrive, dying of jet lag and love, I leave you with this thought: if you don't think up a good answer to my protestations of love, I shall go nuts.

In the second week of May Gerald returned to Jersey. A telegram was waiting for him: 'HELLO WELCOME HOME BY JOVE I WILL SAY IT FOR REAL IN TEN DAYS YOUR CHIPMUNK'. A week or two later he flew to the States, met up with Lee in Durham and travelled to Memphis with her to meet her parents. Mr and Mrs McGeorge had been fully briefed by their daughter about her unusual choice of fiancé. They had studied his photo; they had even read his books. Apart from that, all they knew was that he was closer to their age than hers.

When Gerald arrived, he was at his most charming and charismatic – shy, deferential, polite, attentive, cuddly. With his English accent, Irish charm, Greek manners and cosmopolitan ways, he was not only likeable, he was irresistible. The age gap didn't worry him, he reassured them, though the culture gap might. But he loved their daughter dearly, and to prove it (rummaging in his pocket) he wanted to present her with this garnet-and-pearl engagement ring, which he had had specially made in India. Lee put the ring on her finger. Now she was engaged. It was time to talk about the wedding. Were they thinking about a large wedding and a small reception, Lee's mother wondered, or a large reception and a small wedding? The first would be cheaper, as they could have the reception at home. The second would be more expensive, but easier for all. The ball was rolling. They parted in an atmosphere of great mutual affection and regard.

Lee and Gerald planned to spend a few weeks of the summer at the Mazet, and early in June she arrived in Jersey on the first stage of the journey. She was just in time to play her first official role as the Honorary Director's right-hand lady, at the formal opening of the Trust's veterinary centre by the American Ambassador to Britain, Kingman Brewster. Gerald gave her parents a glowing report of how she coped with this daunting initiating ceremonial.

Dear Both,
Your daughter is a delight and I am even thinking seriously about keeping her. The opening of the new vet complex in Jersey went off with a flourish. As lady of the manor she looked beautiful and elegant in her yellow dress with a silly white hat we got her, and everyone thought – quite rightly – that she was wonderful. She took over when we got to our lemur collection and gave poor Ambassador Brewster a long discourse on these creatures, telling him, I fear, more than he ever wanted to know about them. He fell asleep several times and had to be woken up by careful pinches from his wife. But the whole day was splendid and was enhanced by your daughter being the hostess. The day ended with a massive dinner, a lot of silly speeches (of which mine was the only one worth listening to) and then – after Amb. Brew. and wife had left – McGeorge and I danced. You did not know that your future son-in-law had such talent, did you? True, I fell down several times, but I *did* dance.

In mid-June Gerald and Lee left for the South of France. 'My brother Gerry is buying the Mazet and is busy knocking it about,' Larry reported to Henry Miller. 'He plans to marry a nice American girl and spend the summers there. He is rich and famous as a zoo man now and has very happily shed his last wife.'
The leisurely journey with Lee through the summer landscape of southern France was a revelation for them both, though in different ways, as Gerald reported in a letter to his sister Margaret.

Dear Marg,
We drove down very slowly and the weather was perfect all the way. We stayed at all the really posh old chateaux that are now hotels and I spared no expense regarding food and wine. I wish you could have seen Lee enjoying it, for she has never seen France, nor has she had that sort of treatment from any of her boyfriends before. She is such a treat to be with as she enjoys everything so much, from just looking at flowers and insects in the hedges to savouring new foods and wines (she is a glutton like me) and she makes an adventure of everything. When we got to the Mazet and walked up on to the patio her whole face lit up and she flung her

arms round my neck and kissed me. As we walked from room to room, all freshly decorated and beautifully organised with fresh flowers by Arlette, Lee got more and more excited. If anything she now loves the place more than we do, which is wonderful, and keeps saying, 'now when it is *ours* let's do thus and thus, but we must be careful not to spoil the atmosphere,' and so on. Although it was warm enough to sunbathe on most days it was still cool enough to have fires: she adored this and insisted on lighting them herself. Then we'd drink wine and she'd get the guitar out and she'd play and sing (she has a very true and clear voice) and then we'd drink more wine and fit bawdy words to the songs that she knew and laugh a lot and then go to bed and make love for hours. I wish to Hell I'd met her years ago, but at least I have her now. As we told you she is not in love with me and has never made any bones about it, but is very fond of me and is most gentle, sweet and considerate. Of late, to my secret joy, she has shown unmistakable signs of developing a crush on me, so I have high hopes of the future. But I am happier than I have been in years and she has given me a new lease of life: I feel eighteen again. We like all the same things, we can sing and laugh together, talk serious scientific talk, we can talk about the future of the Trust and the Zoo – both of which she is mad about (unlike Jacquie who spent all her time nagging me to give it up) – or we can talk nonsense. All the things that for years I have taken for granted have now taken on new colours and charms for me, for I am showing them to her for the first time and her delight and enjoyment doubles my own. Anyway, all this crap is really to tell you that I am as happy as hell: don't tell a soul but we are even seriously thinking about a child, but we have so much that we want to enjoy with each other first and are agreed that a child is not like a pet that you can leave behind to be fed and watered by the zoo staff like a cat or dog. Anyway, we'll see, and we may decide against it.

Though Gerald and Lee were sharing a house all on their own, this did not stop Gerald, an inveterate scribbler, leaving handwritten notes for her around the Mazet, scrawled on any scrap of paper to hand, including kitchen rolls. And everywhere, like giant confetti, in kitchen, bathroom and bedroom, the ubiquitous and sempiternal message 'I LOVE YOU'.

The couple stayed at the Mazet for a little over four weeks, and on 12 July Lee flew back to the States. A few days later Gerald reverted to his old habits and wrote another love letter.

From the Desk of: Dr Genius Durrell P.H.D. V.D. C.I.A.
Founder Member and President
The Foundation of Research into the Sexual habits of the Sciuridae [squirrels and chipmunks]

My darling,

I have been home two days and I am sad as Hell. Oh, it was nice enough to get back and see all the new births. But darling it was so *empty* . . . I have never realised until then how much I had come to rely not only on you but your beautiful voice. If I was on speaking terms with Dante I would get him to add the best torment of all to his Inferno: to be without McGeorge. It is like being deprived of all your senses except that of pain. To wake in the morning and not see your flower-like face next to me, to not be able to press your body to me strikes me like a physical blow and depression sets in to start the day blackly . . . I can't tell you what exquisite pleasure it gave me to be with you in France, to watch you day by day, to watch your pleasure, to *pretend* to myself that we were really married . . .

You are my whole life now and will be until the end of my life; if I lost you now – for whatever reason – my life would have no meaning for me without you. I only tell you all this so that when I behave stupidly you will – because you are so gentle and intelligent – attempt to understand, if not condone. I know I am not an easy man to live with and can be just as big a shit as the next man, so you will have plenty to complain of; however, I hope that my deep love of you combined with other, slightly more material advantages, will outweigh my bad points. I must also warn you that I intend to leave no stone unturned in my efforts to achieve the impossible task of making you love me. So there! . . .

Let me tell you about this place. It looks wonderful. The new Pink Pigeon place is very posh and the birds look really lovely in it: they are really beautiful birds when you see them in the sun, but so stupid they don't deserve to survive. It was super, also to go into the Reptile House and see all the baby Gunthers (and more eggs to hatch yet) and all the baby Telfair skinks . . . Then we went to look at the bats and that House has *really* worked, my honey, they look wonderful in it. It was another feeling of triumph to see all the babies – including the newest one – flying round and round, bickering and grooming, just as I saw them in the wild. We now have enough Gunther geckos and Telfair skinks to found colonies elsewhere (hopefully the Bronx) and soon we should have enough bats to do the same, as well as Pink Pigeons. Who said Captive Breeding Won't Work???? Who Said Durrell Is A Fool????? Who Said He Will Surely Fail?????? Well, to be quite frank with you, they all did. He He He.

Now for the *best* news: we are going to embark on our first re-introductions into the wild!!!!!!!!!!! As you know, the Waldrapp [bald ibis] was widely spread in Europe in the Middle Ages and it would be a wonderful thing to put them back into the wild. People always ask us what we have re-introduced into the wild and up until now we have been forced, blushingly, to say 'nothing'. Now, however, I hope we will be able to point to a triumphant success of the re-introduction of the Waldrapp after some five hundred years.

Though Gerald's divorce from Jacquie still seemed no nearer, he was keen to press on with his wedding plans, as he informed Margaret in mid-July.

The wedding in Memphis is going to be very funny, I think. Jeremy is going to be my best man (he had a little emotional weep when I asked him, dear man) and both John, Simon and Sam and Catha are coming. Mum McGeorge (who is a sweetie with a great intelligence and sense of humour) has purchased a tome on How To Do A Wedding Properly and I am duly being sent a copy. It's going to cost poor Daddy McGeorge a bomb and it's not going to be cheap for me, but as I said to McGeorge (which is what I call Lee in moments of sternness) as this is the only time she is going to be allowed to marry in my lifetime I think no expense should be spared. I am, of course, taking the whole thing very seriously because they *do* take these things seriously in the Deep South and after all Lee is their eldest daughter and so they want to put on a splash. But inside me I shall be one vast grin. You'd think that at my time of life I would know better, but it is such fun and poor McGeorge is torn between trying to take it seriously because she thinks one ought to (this is her strict Episcopalian upbringing) and laughing at a somewhat bawdy and unconventional approach to the whole thing. After the wedding we go to Mauritius and stay at Le Morne (in the old part) and there I want to spend most of the time in the sea, for Lee has never seen a tropical reef and I am looking forward to her wonder and enjoyment of it. Oh, yes, another funny thing: to get married in Tennessee I have to have a certificate to say that I am not suffering from V.D.! How's that?

Gerald was now beginning to think more strategically about his marriage. Lee would not just be his life's partner but his Trust's co-regent, a role for which, he realised, she was unusually well suited. He aired his thoughts along these lines in a letter to her dated 21 July.

Darling, I want you to be a real part of this building. Eventually, I want you to know all about its past history, its present progress and I want you to help me to plan the future. I do not want you to think that I am marrying you only to exclude you, see? I want you to be an important part of *every* part of my life, and I want you to feel that at all times this place and what it does in the future is just as much your place as mine.

Once they were married, he told her a few days later, he intended to pay her a substantial yearly personal allowance which she was free to spend how she chose. 'This helps remove one of the awful constraints of wedded bliss,' he explained, 'where the poor bloody woman has to ask her husband for every penny, which is not marriage as I see it but a form of ankle chain as used in slavery.' A lot depended on his income, of course, and this varied from year to year.

Don't worry, we are far from broke, but last year I spent my *entire* (£56,000) income like water, a lot of it stupidly because I was lonely and silly. Also we have to think we may want a child or two, and also consider the chances of my dropping dead suddenly. Now, enough of this sordid commerce. Let me turn to other things.

You don't know how much I miss you. The bed has now grown to the size of the Sahara and as cold as the Arctic wastes: I need a telescope to see from one side to the other, but I know there is no sense in looking because you are not there – I would not see your beautiful face, the smoky blue of your eyes, the curve of your ravishing mouth, your wonderful neck, your cloud-like hair, your ears like pink edible mushrooms. That's above the sheets. Going beneath I would not see your beautiful body, your elegant legs and feet, your super fine-boned hands ... So as there is no point in looking for you I roll over in bed and look at your ravishing face in your photographs on the bedside table.

I love you so much and I am so lonely without your presence. It is not too bad during the day (pretty bad but not *too* bad) because there are things happening and I really have a lot to do. But when evening comes and I am faced with futile T.V. shows which only make me remember more vividly our times in the Mazet by the fire, watching your sweet face as you played and sang, then it really hurts. Then I switch off the bloody T.V. and play The Only Two records [Pachelbel's *Canon* and a soulful Greek air by Hadjidakis] very, very loud (I think the staff think I am mad) and then, when they are over I go to bed. Then I can't sleep. I get up and take a pill and the bloody thing doesn't work. I turn on the light and, hell damn it, there you are, looking up at me from the bedside table. So I take another pill and read some idiotic book until it takes. Sometimes, late at night when I can't sleep, I have black moments (they only last a moment) when I wish I had never met you or, if I had, that I had never fallen in love with you, or if I had, why could I not have only fallen a *little* in love with you, a tiny crush? Why does it have to be this great multicoloured wave of pleasure and pain that engulfs me. I love you beyond belief.

Enough of this.

On 31 July Gerald sent Lee an extraordinary letter. Beginning with a tormented, ruthlessly self-revelatory and self-flagellatory exegesis, it ended with a moving and deeply felt paean to the beauties of the world he loved and the woman he adored.

My darling McGeorge,
You said that things seemed clearer when they were written down. Well, herewith a very boring letter in which I will try and put everything down so that you may read and re-read it in horror at your folly in getting involved with me. Deep breath.

To begin with I love you with a depth and passion that I have felt for no one else in this life and if it astonishes you it astonishes me as well. Not, I hasten to say, because you are not worth loving. Far from it. It's just that, first of all, I swore I would not get involved with another woman. Secondly, I have never had such a feeling before and it is almost frightening. Thirdly, I would never have thought it possible that another human being could occupy my waking (and sleeping) thoughts to the exclusion of almost every-thing else. Fourthly, I never thought that – even if one was in love – one could get so completely besotted with another person, so that a minute away from them felt like a thousand years. Fifthly, I never hoped, aspired, dreamed that one could find everything one wanted in one person. I was not such an idiot as to believe this was possible. Yet in you I have found everything I want: you are beautiful, gay, giving, gentle, idiotically and deliciously feminine,

sexy, wonderfully intelligent and wonderfully silly as well. I want
nothing else in this life than to be with you, to listen and watch
you (your beautiful voice, your beauty), to argue with you, to
laugh with you, to show you things and share things with you, to
explore your magnificent mind, to explore your wonderful body,
to help you, protect you, serve you, and bash you on the head
when I think you are wrong . . . Not to put too fine a point on it
I consider that I am the only man outside mythology to have found
the crock of gold at the rainbow's end.

But – having said all that – let us consider things in detail. Don't
let this become public but . . . well, I have one or two faults. Minor
ones, I hasten to say. For example, I am inclined to be overbearing.
I do it for the best possible motives (all tyrants say that) but I do
tend (without thinking) to tread people underfoot. You must tell
me when I am doing it to you, my sweet, because it can be a very
bad thing in a marriage.

Right. Second blemish. This, actually, is not so much a blemish
of character as a blemish of circumstance. Darling I want you to
be *you* in your own right and I will do everything I can to help
you in this. But you must take into consideration that I am also
me in my own right and that I have a headstart on you . . . What
I am trying to say is that you must not feel offended if you are
sometimes treated simply as my wife. Always remember that what
you lose on the swings you gain on the roundabouts. But I am an
established 'creature' in the world, and so – on occasions – you
will have to live in my shadow. Nothing gives me less pleasure
than this but it is a fact of life that has to be faced.

Third (and very important and nasty) blemish: jealousy. I don't
think you know what jealousy is (thank God) in the real sense of
the word. I know that you have felt jealousy over Lincoln's wife
and child, but this is what I call normal jealousy, and this – to my
regret – is not what *I've* got. What I have got is a black monster
that can pervert my good sense, my good humour and any goodness
that I have in my make-up. It is really a Jekyll and Hyde situation
. . . my Hyde is stronger than my good sense and defeats me, hard
though I try. As I told you, I have always known that this lurks
within me, but I could control it, and my monster slumbered and
nothing happened to awake it. Then I met you and I felt my monster
stir and become half awake when you told me of Lincoln and
others you have known, and with your letter my monster came
out of its lair, black, irrational, bigoted, stupid, evil, malevolent.

You will never know how terribly *corrosive* jealousy is; it is a physical pain as though you had swallowed acid or red hot coals. It is the most terrible of feelings. But you can't help it – at least I can't, and God knows I've tried. I don't want *any* ex-boyfriends sitting in church when I marry you. On our wedding day I want nothing but happiness, both for you and me, and I know I won't be happy if there is a church full of your ex-conquests. When I marry you I will have no past, only a future: I don't want to drag my past into our future and I don't want you to do it, either. Remember I am jealous of you because I love you. You are never jealous of something you don't care about. O.K. enough about jealousy.

Now let me tell you something . . .

There followed a remarkable prose-poem, an aching, wondrous, soaring distillation of the world Gerald had known through all his senses.

I have seen a thousand sunsets and sunrises, on land where it floods forest and mountains with honey coloured light, at sea where it rises and sets like a blood orange in a multicoloured nest of cloud, slipping in and out of the vast ocean. I have seen a thousand moons: harvest moons like gold coins, winter moons as white as ice chips, new moons like baby swans' feathers.

I have seen seas as smooth as if painted, coloured like shot silk or blue as a kingfisher or transparent as glass or black and crumpled with foam, moving ponderously and murderously.

I have felt winds straight from the South Pole, bleak and wailing like a lost child; winds as tender and warm as a lover's breath; winds that carried the astringent smell of salt and the death of seaweeds; winds that carried the moist rich smell of a forest floor, the smell of a million flowers. Fierce winds that churned and moved the sea like yeast, or winds that made the waters lap at the shore like a kitten.

I have known silence: the cold, earthy silence at the bottom of a newly dug well; the implacable stony silence of a deep cave; the hot, drugged midday silence when everything is hypnotised and stilled into silence by the eye of the sun; the silence when great music ends.

I have heard summer cicadas cry so that the sound seems stitched into your bones. I have heard tree frogs in an orchestration as complicated as Bach singing in a forest lit by a million emerald fireflies. I have heard the Keas calling over grey glaciers that groaned to themselves like old people as they inched their way to the sea. I have heard the hoarse street vendor cries of the mating Fur seals as they sang to their sleek golden wives, the crisp staccato admonishment of the Rattlesnake, the cobweb squeak of the Bat and the belling roar of the Red deer knee-deep in purple heather. I have heard Wolves baying at a winter's moon, Red howlers making the forest vibrate with their roaring cries. I have heard the squeak, purr and grunt of a hundred multi-coloured reef fishes.

I have seen hummingbirds flashing like opals round a tree of scarlet blooms, humming like a top. I have seen flying fish, skittering like quicksilver across the blue waves, drawing silver lines on the surface with their tails. I have seen Spoonbills flying home to roost like a scarlet banner across the sky. I have seen Whales, black as tar, cushioned on a cornflower blue sea, creating a Versailles of fountain with their breath. I have watched butterflies emerge and sit, trembling, while the sun irons their wings smooth. I have watched Tigers, like flames, mating in the long grass. I have been dive-bombed by an angry Raven, black and glossy as the Devil's hoof. I have lain in water warm as milk, soft as silk, while around me played a host of Dolphins. I have met a thousand animals and seen a thousand wonderful things . . . but –

All this I did without you. This was my loss.

All this I want to do with you. This will be my gain.

All this I would gladly have forgone for the sake of one minute of your company, for your laugh, your voice, your eyes, hair, lips, body, and above all for your sweet, ever surprising mind which is an enchanting quarry in which it is my privilege to delve.

At about this time Gerald suddenly became tormented by a terrible thought which agonised him over a period of several days. He loved Lee dearly now, but how would he feel if over time she metamorphosed, like something out of Ovid, into someone totally different? She loved food almost as much as he did – and look what it had done to him. Though Lee remained as lissom as the day he met her, inside every thin girl, he feared, was a fat girl trying to get out. That would never do. Gerald busied about, examining the available diets. One of the most rigorous was the Mayo Clinic Diet – all grapefruit and carrots, boiled lettuce and water, tea without milk, fluid without alcohol. This he sent post-haste to Lee in a bid to head off the dreaded catastrophe of obesity. With it he sent a cautionary verse of his own devising called the 'Food Song'.

Lee Wilson McGeorge
Said: 'I do like to gorge.
I'm as round as a ball
And I've no waist at all
As for my tits
They've both gone to bits:
The thought of them harrows –
They both look like marrows;
While as for my legs
They look like wine kegs
And each of my chins
Proclaims all my sins.
Well, I may be obese
As twelve Strasbourg geese –
But I'll tell you, as well
I'm as sexy as Hell.
This is a grave matter
For as I get fatter
There's one thing I dread:
There's no room in the bed.

Gerald now turned to a more intransigent problem – himself. How should he present himself at the coming nuptials? What should his image be? What should he wear? On a previous visit to the States he had had himself photographed in a studio that promised 'Your Historic Portrait While You Wait'. The resulting picture showed him in the guise of a Mississippi paddle-boat gambler who'd made good, with bowler hat and cane, tailcoat, fancy waistcoat, wing collar and boating tie. This, he thought, might be a suitable costume in which to parade arm in arm with his wife in Episcopalian Memphis. With a twinkle in his eye, he sent off the photo to Lee's courteous and patient parents.

Dear Both,
So that you don't feel fearful of the fact that I may let you down in public, I am enclosing here a picture of the outfit I have had made for the wedding. I *know* it's the sort of thing that you wear in America because I have seen the films. I am sending you this picture so that you will not be uneasy about my appearance in church. My tailor says that he has never seen me look so stunning; do let me know what you think.

However, Gerald began to have second thoughts about his attire. Perhaps, after all, it was a little over the top. On 25 August he wrote again to Lee's father:

> I am glad, Hal, that you appreciated the fact that I am going to be so sartorially elegant at the coming nuptials. You might, however be relieved to know that I am having a suit made up exactly to your specifications, with one tiny addition, and that is that I am having a large heart with 'I Love Lee' picked out on the back in sequins – I do hope you think this is a good idea.

There was still no news about his damn divorce, he continued:

> My wife signed the necessary papers in France but failed to get one of them witnessed by a Notary Public, so the whole lot had to be sent back to be re-done. Once they arrive, however, the wheels can be got into motion, but I still, I am afraid, cannot give you a firm date. Believe me, I am chattering with rage and I do sympathise with you both as I realise the sort of organisation that goes into a task like this. Rest assured that I will cable you the moment I have any news.

Lee was due to come to Jersey at the end of August en route to a lemur conference in Madagascar, at which she would be presenting a paper. Gerald would accompany her. He felt it was time to concoct another illuminated poem, the last of the current series, for they would soon be together again.

> Darling, best beloved Lee,
> I send this screed from me to thee:
> The last I fear with drawings in it
> For now I will not have a minute...
>
> And so, my love, as you well know,
> To Madagascar's shores we'll go.
> We shall hear the Indri call,
> Bouncing through the forests tall;
> We shall see the Aye-Aye linger
> Probing food with slender finger;
> See the Ringtails walking by,
> Tails like banners in the sky...
> Snakes as green as any jade,
> Birds of every size and shade,

Moths as big as birds are found,
And birds as small as moths abound ...

I think I shall never see
A flower as lovely as a Lee;
Nor storm cloud dark that can compare
With the colour of your hair.
No sapphire sea can I descry
To match the colour of your eye.
But why d'you hold me in this thrall
So I cannot get free at all?
Why weren't you born with purple hair?
Why weren't you short and very fat,
With stick-out ears like any bat?
Why don't you waddle like a goose
As though your inside bits were loose?
Why not fingers like Havanas?
Legs as bowed as two bananas?
If you had these ... well ...

Gerald had never before been to Madagascar, with which he and the
Trust would be closely associated for years to come. He and Lee were
there for ten days, then returned to Jersey for another short stay before
setting off for the States, Gerry for another fund-raising tour, Lee to
concentrate on her thesis for her Ph.D, which had to be completed by
November.

Gerald's lectures in America were, as always, a resounding success,
and most sold out well in advance. The press gave him lengthy and serious
coverage, though he always had the power to surprise, as the girl from
the *Chicago Sun-Times* quickly discovered:

The sun was nowhere near over the yardarm but Gerald Durrell
was having a bottle of beer anyway. 'Care for one?' he inquired,
beaming cordially. 'My mouth is like the bottom of a parrot's cage
this morning.'

Durrell, author, conservationist, appears to be the picture of a
sedate, somewhat portly British gentleman. His graying hair and
full beard are meticulously trimmed. He wears a faultlessly tailored
suit. His manners are urbane and amiable. Only the mischief in
his startlingly bright baby blue eyes, surrounded by the kind of
lines that laughter makes, hint that there is a free-thinker who will

jolly well order, drink and enjoy beer at 9.45 a.m. if he feels like it.

Gerald gave the reporter the lowdown on his plans – the captive breeding programmes, the Mauritius rescue project, the mini-university training centre, the plight of the world. Then he confessed what was mainly on his mind that morning. 'As soon as his divorce is final,' she duly noted, 'Durrell will marry Lee McGeorge, "a delicious American girl who's finishing her thesis in animal communication at Duke University. It's a line of investigation we're interested in and now that we've got an expert, we don't have to pay a salary."'

A few days later Gerald was in Philadelphia, sitting in forlorn solitude in a restaurant called The Garden. After the modernity of Chicago, the historic ambience of America's cultured old capital turned his mind to a more classical literary form, and he dashed off a quick verse in praise of Lee, a parody of the popular Victorian doggerel-writer T.E. Brown:

The Garden
> They say the garden is a lovesome thing, God Wot.
> Wine, drink, gin, sin, beer in a pot
> But *my* Garden is a *lonesome* thing, God Wot.
> For here I know just what I've not got.
> How can you in the Garden have a spree
> When I am sitting here and lacking Lee?

By now there was considerable alarm at the tortuous progress of Gerald's divorce. This was ironic, because in the first year or two after Jacquie had walked out it had been Gerald who had proved the obstructive and dilatory one of the two, ignoring all advice to settle round a table, and even failing to turn up to court hearings. Now he was desperately anxious to get the divorce out of the way and to fix a date for the wedding as soon as possible. On 1 October Lee wrote to Catha Weller in Jersey about the stand-off:

> Gerry is very depressed about it all, and seems to think that in some way it will harm his and my relationship – that I'll be bored waiting around a year or so as his mistress. Well . . . I couldn't get bored in a thousand years of his company, and why would I want to leave when we've got so much to do together that it will take three or more lifetimes! I've told him all this, but he is still depressed and afraid. If you have the opportunity, would you reassure him about me? . . . reassure him *wholeheartedly* . . .

This whole new Jacquie thing has upset me considerably, Catha – but not about the delay in the marriage – rather about how it's affecting Gerry. I wish there was something I or you or somebody could do or say to make him feel better about it.

By 3 October Gerald was in the Pennsylvanian town of Intercourse, a name which he found irresistible, and which caused him to pen a few more jealousy-provoking stanzas to keep Lee on her toes.

> As I have not *yet* got my divorce
> (A thing that I am desperate for, of course)
> And as you are not here with all your charms,
> I've had to find my fun in other arms . . .
> This action may annoy you dear, of course,
> This intercourse I've had in Intercourse,
> But can't you, darling, thank the Heavens above
> For giving me one Mennonite of Love?

Before returning to Jersey, Gerald took Lee with him on a short visit to Canada, where she ceremonially fed the killer whale in the Vancouver Aquarium – her second official duty as the lady at Gerald's side. Then by way of a break the couple set off on a train ride through the Rockies from Vancouver to Calgary, Lee working away at her thesis as the train rattled along.

Back in Jersey Gerald occupied himself with the ever-pressing burden of Trust and zoo business and his own career as a writer. When the pressure of Lee's Ph.D thesis began to grind her down and bow her spirit, he wrote her a long letter on several rolls of paper illuminated like an ancient papyrus, intended to raise her confidence and cheer her on with words of encouragement and visions of good times ahead.

He was longing to show her Mauritius, he said – the surreally-shaped mountains, the green chequerboard sugarcane fields, the cool mountain forests and the gorges and the waterfalls falling thousands of feet like fine ropes of silk. And then the reefs – the Crockery Shop, where the coral looked like stacked dishes of brandy snaps, and the Stags' Graveyard and The Garden, shallow, sunlit and brilliant.

As well as affirming his love and devotion, Gerald had various exciting bits of news to impart. An American wanted to make a TV series based on his life ('leaving out all the sexy bits'). The plans for the new training complex at the zoo were splendid, and with a bit of luck it should be up and running by next August, so he'd have to start thinking about who would open it. 'Perhaps the President of the United States?' he suggested to Lee. 'He will, as you know, be so proud of your thesis.' He left the really impressive news till last:

> We are really getting some wonderful breeding results now, exceeding my wildest dreams. I have just been down to the reptile house: we now have a further sixteen Gunther's Gecko eggs to hatch and another eight Telfair's Skink eggs as well. We are now in the happy position of almost being knee deep in both species. In fact, with *eighty five* babies of the Jamaican Boas all flourishing we are knee deep in that particular species. We have now (with the help of Bob Martin's new method) sexed all but one of the Round Island Boas: we have two males and one adult female. So next year we will mix the biggest male with her and hope for the best. You see, so little is known about the damn things; it's not even recorded if they give birth to live young or lay eggs. Also nobody knows how many they have at a time. If they carry on like the Jamaicans we will be able to re-populate Round Island in a year or two. Talking of the Jamaican Boas, we now have so many Boas and Hutias we could do a re-population job if we could find the right place, so I must see if there is a rich American or European who owns an off-shore island where they could let us do a con-trolled try-out at re-introduction. If we could do this together with the Bare-faced Ibis release in Switzerland we would have something solid to start boasting about. The mind boggles when one begins to think about our potential in this field, for in a couple of years we should have enough of both the Fruit Bats and the Pink Pigeons to be able to start thinking in terms of an attempt to put some back in the wild . . .
>
> It is such a comfort to see a dream come true, sweetie, you have simply no idea how satisfying it is. Wait until we have been on a trip together, caught stuff and brought it back and settled it in well and *then* bred it and you will see what I mean. It's such a wonderful feeling of achievement. It more than makes up for all the frustration and hard work that are part of the whole thing. But it requires a hell of a lot of patience . . .

In November 1978 Lee finally finished her Ph.D dissertation on animal communication – 'Circumvention of Noise in the Communication Chan-nel by the Structure and Timing of the Calls of Forest Animals' – and submitted it to the examiners for their judgement. On the twenty-second of the month, the day it was confirmed she had been awarded her doctor-ate, after a three-hour grilling by eight professors (with Gerald waiting nervously in an outside office), she and Gerald flew to Jersey, where she spent her first Christmas away from home with Gerald and his brother Lawrence, now living alone at Sommières. 'I spent Christmas in Jersey at my brother's zoo,' Lawrence, no zoologist, reported to Henry Miller; 'lots of snow of course, but the sound track was pure tropical, which was surrealist. Lions roaring in the night and the sudden screech of wild birds at dawn or the *hugh hugh hugh* of chimps. It is a strange island really, claustrophobic in some ways.'

Gerald and Lee had planned to spend the New Year in Fleur Cowles' castle in Spain. Fleur Cowles was a talented, personable and extremely wealthy American woman of many parts – author, painter, publisher, editor, philanthropist, society hostess and friend of the great and the famous. She and her husband Tom had become great friends of Gerald when she lent a hand and became a Trustee after the palace revolution in 1973. Before their visit Fleur had rung Gerald and told him: 'Now, as you're getting married I'm going to put you in separate rooms, otherwise the servants will talk.' To which Gerald replied: 'Well, in that case we're not coming.'

Fleur Cowles gave way, and on 27 December the couple flew out to Madrid on their way to the beautiful castle near Trujillo on the freezing *meseta* – built by the Romans, restored by the Moors, last occupied by Napoleon's army, then restored again by Fleur and Tom, who had built a wonderful Moorish garden and a beautiful cloister connecting the two surviving Moorish towers. Castles in Spain, a manor house in Jersey, train rides through the Rockies – Lee's life had begun to take off as Gerald had promised it would. But there was a lot more to come, as she was to recall:

That spring we were travelling in Central America and the Caribbean – Costa Rica, Panama, Antigua, Montserrat, and then Gerry's divorce came through and we got back to Memphis ten days before the wedding having done the usual thing and left my mother to handle absolutely everything. Gerry invited everyone over – sister Margaret, and Jeremy Mallinson and his wife, John Hartley and his wife, Sam and Catha Weller, David Hughes, Peter Grose and his wife, and all the WPTI people in America. Everyone was around for all of three or four days and there were a lot of parties. Margot Rockefeller's local Rockefeller relatives threw a big barbecue round their swimming pool, I had a couple of parties, my friends had parties, my mother's friends had parties, even Gerry had a party. In America it's the custom for the bridegroom to give what they call the 'rehearsal dinner'. If you're married in a church the rehearsal dinner follows the wedding rehearsal the day before the actual wedding. But it didn't work out exactly that way because the Church I was brought up in, which was the Episcopalian Church, the American equivalent of the Church of England, wouldn't allow us to get married in it. The minister I'd grown up with said, 'Mr Durrell has been divorced, so we can't marry you.' I didn't particularly mind, even though I'd been to chapel virtually every day there for most of my early life, but Mother was very angry. Anyway, we decided to get married in our back garden, and for his rehearsal dinner Gerry decided to hire a Mississippi paddle steamer and throw a party for all the wedding guests as we steamed down the Mississippi river. I wore my pre-Civil War-style Southern Belle dress – hooped skirts and crinolines and stuff – and Gerry had a stripy blazer, a straw boater, a big bow tie and what he called 'co-respondent's shoes' he'd borrowed from my father. There was a band on board and champagne galore all the way down the river and Jeremy Mallinson as best man gave the rehearsal dinner speech, except that what with the noise of the engines and Jeremy's funny English accent no one could understand a word he said. It didn't matter though, we all gave him a big hand, and the champagne corks popped and the band continued to play ... There was a beautiful sunset over the Mississippi that evening. It was wonderful ...

Gerry was up very early the next morning, wedding day, Thursday, 24 May 1979. It was raining at first but it cleared up later. It was late spring in Memphis now and the dogwoods were out in our garden, and the azaleas were out, and a lot of flowers were showing through. It was such a beautiful wedding. Gerry as the groom was banished upstairs before the final moment, which was the usual custom, so my brother went up with a six-pack of beer to keep him company. At five-thirty that afternoon, as we came out of the house into the garden to get married, a flautist and a harpist were playing Pachelbel's *Canon*, and after a bit the music was taken over by an old black man called Mose who played a whole lot of things on the piano. We were married on the lawn in front of a small grove of dogwood trees under the open sky by a judge who was my mother's and father's close friend, and then there was a big cake to cut and telegrams to read out and dancing on the grass. Then I went and changed into my going-away dress and we had rice thrown over us and then we drove away to a hotel near the airport because we had an early flight to England next morning. We had promised Peter Bull we'd be along to his Teddy Bears' Picnic, a charity do at Longleat, so we went straight there from the airport and snuck into the marquee and Peter was standing up front with the Marquess of Bath and when he caught sight of us he said, 'Oh, oh ... I'm going to blub ... oh, oh ...' And so Gerry and I were man and wife at last. And we were going to live happily for as long as ever after turned out to be.

The wedding stayed long in the memory of all who had been present. After Gerry and Lee had gone there was a feeling of sadness and emptiness in Memphis. 'Y'all was the toast of the town,' Lee's sister Harriet, fondly known as Hat, wrote to the newlyweds. 'Mother got a little teary-eyed when y'all left. Daddy even relit the candles for your good luck. I sho' gonna miss you Miss Scarlett, but I know Mr Rhett will take fine care of you.'

For Lee, the marriage marked the beginning of a great adventure at the side of a remarkable man doing remarkable things. For Gerald it was to prove a kind of miraculous resurrection, with many implications for his life and work and the future of the Jersey Trust – all of them, without exception, wholly good.

PART FOUR

Back on the Road

TWENTY-SEVEN

A Zoo with a View

1979–1980

For both Gerald and Lee, life had been transformed, though in different ways. For Gerald, marriage to Lee meant that his life had not simply undergone a metamorphosis, it had experienced a salvation. His close friend and colleague Jeremy Mallinson was in no doubt: 'Lee was undoubtedly Gerry's saviour. I think he probably would have died long before his time if it hadn't been for the inspiration Lee gave him. He had been in hell, and if that had gone on I think he would have died of a kind of slow suicide. But now his whole dream was life with Lee.' As Peter Olney put it: 'Lee was Gerry's resurrection – just as Gerry was Lee's apotheosis.' In Olney's view, Gerald was very lucky to have found Lee: 'She had a wonderful influence on the last part of his life, and prolonged it by at least ten years.'

The adjustment to married life was greater for Lee than for Gerald. Gerald had been married before, and knew what to expect and what not. But Lee had exchanged the Mississippi for the Channel Islands, a zoology department for a zoo, a career for a cause, obscurity for celebrity and a settled lifestyle for a nomadic one, with a third of the year spent globetrotting to raise money, lecture and collect animals, a third at the Mazet in the South of France, and a third in Jersey at the zoo. Gerald had worked out a way of life that suited him, and he was used to having his own way. He began the day with beer and ended it with brandy, and brooked no protest. 'My doctor says I don't deserve to have such a magnificent heart, liver and constitution,' he would say. You fitted in with this or perished. Lee fitted in. That she did so readily and successfully was a tribute to them both.

Gerald was enormously proud of his young wife and amazed at his luck in having married her. 'He was inseparable from her,' a close friend was to recall, 'and she from him. In spite of the age gap and the culture divide they were a marriage made in heaven.' Though Gerald had always had misgivings about people with letters after their names, Lee was an exception. He valued her Ph.D as highly as if it were his own, and was always anxious to promote her and encourage her in all her undertakings. His sister Margaret sometimes felt he clucked and fussed over his new wife too much. 'Don't put her on a pedestal,' she recalled telling him. 'Don't try and make her something it's impossible to be. She's not a rare and tender plant. Just treat like a really nice, normal, beautiful wife. Just leave it at that.' At first friends like Fleur Cowles wondered how this young and attractive girl and this portly middle-aged man had ever got together. 'In fact Lee was a serious girl with a serious mission,' Fleur recalled, 'and she probably met the right man at the right time – and vice versa.'

In one respect special credit must go to Lee. In marrying a much younger woman, Gerald was often tortured with feelings of insecurity about how long he could hold on to her, especially as they were often in the company of younger men. On a few rare occasions this insecurity erupted in Vesuvian explosions of unfounded and short-lived jealousy. Usually Gerald contented himself with assurances of his own devotion and love, as in the poem he wrote to her for her thirtieth birthday on 7 September 1979:

> Now you're half sixty
> And I'm half a hundred
> In our liaison
> My dear, we've not blundered . . .
> But O! I assure you
> (it's one thing I can)
> Whatever your age
> I'm your faithful old man.

Lee's new home, the flat in Les Augrès Manor, had changed a lot since Jacquie's time. In order to achieve a greater sense of space, Gerald had knocked down a dividing wall between two smaller rooms to create a very large and spacious main reception room, then had it painted white, with a white carpet and yellow and orange Casa Pupo rugs. Gerald's personal contribution to the furnishings consisted mostly of his books, which lined two walls in the sitting-room (general reading there – his wide-ranging zoological library was in his office on the ground floor), his remarkable collection of animal sculptures (some realistic, most fantastical, culled from many countries around the world and fashioned out of almost every material known to man, from clay and wood to glass and old iron), and a multitude of naughty Victorian picture postcards of discreetly naked and heavily rotund ladies which had been mounted in a big gilt frame. The overall effect was light, airy and rather disorientating to the uninitiated. 'I remember walking into that room the first time,' Simon Hicks, the Trust Secretary, was to recall, 'and I'd never been in a room like it – you didn't know where the hell you were, people didn't know how to perform in there, Gerry had them entirely at his mercy.'

It was here he held court, entertaining, haranguing and beguiling a stream of visitors that included zoo directors, biologists, conservationists, architects, publishers and a steady flow of reporters from around the world. He never let an opportunity slip to spread the word about the zoo and the Trust's mission. It was at the kitchen table that he wrote when he was in Jersey (though his books were mostly written down at the Mazet) and met up with his staff over a drink at the end of the working day.

'Gerald Durrell is a passionate man,' noted a reporter from the Canadian magazine *Maclean's*. 'The enormous living room of his home in Jersey is packed with assorted bric-à-brac, yet Durrell, casually dressed and sunk in a red plush chair, overflows the room with a larger-than-life presence. He can talk with fluency and vehemence about anything from poetry to cooking, politics to music. But underneath the fluency lies the bitterness of a man who has devoted his working life to the ever-more-precarious survival of animals; the anger of a portly Cassandra.' Jocular, outrageous, totally without reticence, Gerald was a journalist's dream, the reporter reckoned. But it was a mistake to suppose his ebullient wit and trencherman's paunch summed up the whole man. He was a sensitive, unpredictable soul whose love of the world went far beyond biological curiosity.

Gerald laughed easily, but his mood could change mercurially. He was weary of people questioning his concern about endangered animals by asking 'But what *use* are they to us?' 'What an arrogant attitude,' he exploded. 'Is it not possible for animals to have a right to exist in the world without being of *use* to us? Ever since the Bible was published we have got it into our heads that everything exists for *us*. God tells Adam and Eve to subdue the earth and have dominion over all living things – it is one of His few instructions that human beings have obeyed with enthusiasm.'

It was not only the views *in* the flat, but also the views *from* the flat that riveted the visitor. For Gerald and Lee lived over the shop, so to speak, in the middle of a working zoo. In the living-room, for example, Gerald might be suddenly transfixed in the middle of pouring a gin for a guest by the sight of the Przewalski horses in full gallop, while in the dining-room his carving might come to a halt in mid-joint at a glimpse of the crowned cranes doing their courtship dance. 'Modesty prevents me from relating what can be seen from the bathroom window,' he wrote, 'when the serval cats are loudly and apparently agonisingly in season, moaning their hearts out, screaming with love and lust. However, worse – far worse – befalls you in the kitchen should you lift your eyes from the stove and let them wander. You are confronted by a cage full of Celebes apes, black and shiny as jet, with rubicund pink behinds shaped exactly like hearts on valentine cards, and all of them indulging in an orgy which even the most avant-garde Roman would have considered both flamboyant and too near the knuckle. Close contemplation of such a spectacle can lead to disaster, such as irretrievably burning lunch for eight people.'

Quite apart from adapting to daily life in such an unusual domestic environment, a major task for Lee was to undertake a systematic exploration of the mind and nature of her husband. A flamboyant, robust but occasionally temperamental genius, he did not so much defy analysis as stimulate it. He was sometimes prone to confessionals over a bottle round a table late at night with close friends, though in general he was infinitely more interested in other people than in himself – an essential humility characteristic of human beings bent on great and selfless missions of salvation.

A list of his favourite things he was asked to provide for a magazine gave a clue not only to his preferences but to the subterranean pressures that caused them to break through to the surface. His favourite sexy animal, for example, was the female giraffe: 'For gracefulness of movement, size and lustre of eyes, length and thickness of eyelashes, the female giraffe is incomparable. If there is such a thing as reincarnation, no one should have any complaint if they came back as a male giraffe.' His favourite reptile was the flying snake of the Far East, his favourite poisonous animal the poison arrow frog of the Amazon. No animal was more curious than the narwhal, he reckoned, none more surprising than the mudskipper, none better to eat than reindeer, preferably smoked – 'but it is best not to serve it at Christmas time to children of a sensitive nature'.

One of the odder ways of divining the real Gerald Durrell was carried out on a Channel TV series called *Zodiac and Co.* The idea was for a panel consisting of an astrologer, a graphologist and a palmist to produce a profile of a star guest (whose identity was not revealed till the end of the programme) based simply on his or her gender, date of birth, handwriting and palm prints. Given his interest in unorthodox methodology and the paranormal, Gerald did not require much persuasion to take part in the show, but the uncanny accuracy of the panel's profiles astonished even him.

Observing that the subject had been born with the sun in Capricorn and the moon in Gemini, the astrologer concluded that he was highly ambitious, prepared to take risks, prone to strain and tension, and liable to breakdown. He was very funny man, and also versatile, astute, cunning and stubborn. There was a hint of the poetic and romantic about him, and he was a good talker with high intellectual ability. If he was born in the early evening he could be a painter, poet or architect. If he was born later at night he might be a journalist or broadcaster. He might very well enjoy danger in his profession, and he could probably sell deep-freezes to Eskimos – 'if necessary standing on his head'.

The graphologist described the subject in no less percipient terms: 'The writer has a strong sense of self, but an uncertain sense of identity, resulting in alternation of inferiority and superiority feelings. He is sensitive and becomes uptight through the hustle and bustle of occupational living. He has a need to withdraw from people to recuperate and to experience being himself. He has both vision and practicality. With his vision there goes culture; with his practicality there goes the will to dominate, in order to escape being dominated by others. He is endowed with inspiration and intuition, good observational powers and constructional ability.'

As for the palmist, her report was as unerringly on target as the others had been. The subject was an outdoor type, with a love of nature, love of life, qualities of leadership and a deep sense of justice. He was ambitious, well-adjusted and self-sufficient, inspirational and emotional rather than logical and pragmatic, with a sense of fatalism. He had a touch of humour, sometimes lapsing into facetiousness, and he was gifted with an understanding of animals and a devotion to nature in general. 'At the moment this gentleman is beginning to feel restless in his career,' she concluded, 'and a break in the fate line implies that he may be changing his job in the next few years.'

Gerald's resurrection as a human being following his marriage to Lee was mirrored by his resurrection as a writer and media man. Felicity Bryan had taken over from Peter Grose as his literary agent at Curtis Brown shortly after his marriage. In the publishing world she was advised that he was a 'has-been' as an author and a bit of a wreck as a man. His first more serious book about animals, *The Stationary Ark*, a spin-off from the television series of the same name which dealt with the practice of modern zoo husbandry at Jersey Zoo, had been a commercial disaster by Gerald Durrell standards, although the reviews were favourable. 'Durrell's army of readers,' wrote the *Yorkshire Post*, 'will be relieved to know that despite a new depth in his approach, Mr Durrell has not allowed the flow of rib-tickling anecdotes to run dry; some of them, indeed, seem funnier than ever.' The *Daily Telegraph* was no less enthusiastic: 'He is simultaneously funny, enthusiastic, unsentimental and compassionate. His latest book further enhances his reputation.'

The trouble was that Gerald had had to write *The Stationary Ark* as his first marriage collapsed around him, and by the time it was published in 1976 Jacquie had left. Perhaps because the book reflected that unhappy period in his life, perhaps because it did not deal with the animal world in a totally light-hearted way, it never found favour with the public, and its sales were poor. 1976 represented Gerald's nadir as an author – so much so that Peter Grose described it as 'the disaster year'– though he retrieved some lost ground with his next two titles, *Golden Bats and Pink Pigeons* (an engaging account of his animal rescue mission to Mauritius) and *Garden of the Gods* (the final volume of his Corfu trilogy).

Possibly because Gerald had decided that his fund-raising trips to America on behalf of the Trust should be undertaken in parallel with publicity tours to promote his books, *Garden of the Gods* was particularly well received in the United States, though he himself had little regard for it ('a third work of fiction about our lives,' he told his brother Larry, 'and definitely the last, as I have run out of your similes.') The *Miami Herald*, for example, found the book 'an absolute delight – witty, wonderfully evocative, sharply observant, a joy all the way', while the *Boston Globe* went overboard: 'The best of the trilogy, maybe the best written of all, the stories unerringly shaped and paced, the sentences full of the sound and scent and touch and being of everything they describe. There are so many good stories here, so much hilarity, so much acute observation of nature and human nature that one marvels . . . and one marvels at the prodigal bounty of Creation itself.' But some reviewers had reservations. How could the author remember so much detail, forty years after the events he described? How could he write three books about five years on Corfu without exhausting the subject? 'For what this statistic is worth,' observed the *Washington Post*, 'this is the first of the Corfu books over which I did not laugh aloud, though I could see I was expected to.'

Gerald's status as a best-selling author remained in jeopardy. When his latest manuscript – a collection of short stories entitled *The Picnic* – was submitted to Collins early in 1979, his editor, Philip Ziegler, was not wildly enthusiastic, reporting to Peter Grose:

It is by Gerry and therefore is funny and lively, but I have far too high an opinion of him and his writing to pretend that I think it is anywhere near his top standards. Of course we want to publish it – but I must admit that it is not going to be very easy to promote. It is very distressing to see a downhill trend in Gerry's sales. I do tremendously hope that in his next book Gerry will be able to give us something on which we can base a major campaign – an expedition book which features some really exceptional prey would certainly provide the goods, though I confess the only animal that springs to mind is the panda.

This letter not only underscored Gerald's crisis as an author, but defined a low point in his relations with his publishers. Stung to a vigorous riposte, he described Ziegler's comments as 'condescending', and reckoned that Ziegler had reached a 'low point in my opinion poll of publishers I have known and loved'. Gerald had been trying to get into China for the last ten years, he complained, and if Collins cared to cough up a huge advance he would be very happy to go off and bring back what Ziegler 'so sweepingly calls "the goods"'. He asked Peter Grose: 'Is it time I started looking for another publisher?'

Given this recent history, it is not surprising that at her first meeting with her new author at the manor house in Jersey, Felicity Bryan was greatly taken aback to find herself confronted with a spry, highly energetic and charming figure, brimming with ideas and the joys of life, back in control of his destiny. On a subsequent visit she took her four-year-old son with her, and was enchanted at how well he and Gerry got on together. 'Desmond Morris's summation of David Attenborough – that he personified the intellectual curiosity of a bright fourteen-year-old,' she was to say, 'equally applied to Gerry. At his best he was wonderfully entertaining, and his writing beautifully descriptive.' More to the point, she brought news of a big idea for a book that might revive Gerald's literary fortunes. It was to be called *The Amateur Naturalist*, and its international market was potentially huge. Moreover, the chances that a TV series could be tied in with it were high. Gerald was on his way again. In the course of time *The Amateur Naturalist* was to outsell everything he had ever written, *My Family and Other Animals* included.

Meanwhile the Trust was going from strength to strength, in spite of opposition to everything it stood for from the zoo establishment. As long ago as 1965 captive breeding as a tool to save endangered species had received endorsement in important quarters. At a conference held that year at the Zoological Society of London – the Zoos and Conservation

Symposium – Dr Ernst Lang of Basle Zoo had told the delegates: 'In order to save threatened species from extinction it is not enough to keep and breed them over generations in zoos; there must exist, in addition, the possibility of readapting them to wild life in reserves and national parks. We believe we have enough evidence to show that the scheme can be carried out successfully. The zoos are ready to help the International Union for the Conservation of Nature in their momentous task, provided they are heard and invited to co-operate.'

But more than ten years later there was still entrenched opposition to the whole idea at the highest level. At the second World Conference on Breeding Endangered Species in Captivity, held at London Zoo in July 1976 and attended by Gerald, the conference's Chairman, Professor Lord Zuckerman, revealed his own reservations about the subject of the conference in no uncertain terms. It was the last stand of the old guard against the new believers.

Lord Zuckerman's closing address was precise, thoughtful and specious. Nothing that had happened in the world of zoos and animal conservation had caused him to change his spots. Nothing that had been said at the conference had led him to budge an inch. He remained at heart an unreconstructed pre-war zoo *apparatchik*. The purpose of zoology, in his view, was the promotion of the interests of the zoological scientist, not the zoological animal. 'Species have always been disappearing,' he said. 'There will always be rare species.' If you wanted to leave the remaining species of the world as they were, you would have to get rid of the human species. As that was not an option, *ergo* saving endangered species from extinction was not an option either.

What was more, Lord Zuckerman went on, some animals in the wild didn't deserve to be saved. Some are *pests*. Especially monkeys. And what about *mosquitoes*? 'Man can affect the process of biological selection,' he agreed, 'but regardless of human influence there will always be selection and evolution.' This was true, as any biologist would acknowledge, but was it really a justification for not raising a voice or lifting a finger in the midst of an animal holocaust? The preservation of endangered animals was theoretically desirable as a social good, Zuckerman went on – meaning good for man – but practically impossible. There was no stopping the growth of human populations and the march of progress. And the cost was formidable. Where was the money going to come from? People might queue up to hear circus seals play Beethoven's Fifth Symphony on car horns, but governments are not going to allocate large sums of money to help endangered species whose owners are making money out of them.

To a speechless and by now partly apoplectic audience Lord Zuckerman laid about him right and left. The World Wildlife Fund was driven by a bandwagon of sentimental conservationists and steered by extremists, he jeered. So what if the rainforests of Sumatra are felled to the ground? Surely it's because the people want to improve their standard of living – and who are we to stop them? 'Let me conclude,' spoke the man who styled himself 'a veteran conservationist', 'what we are trying to do is extremely costly ... These things need to be sorted out. Before they are, we cannot expect funds for the general purpose of breeding rare species in captivity. We need to remember' – here Gerald Durrell might well have believed he had been singled out for a personal sideswipe from the eminent chairman – 'that this country does not yet have any laws to prevent anyone, however ignorant, from starting a zoo ... Conservationists should not play at God, idealism must be tempered with realism.'

To many of the delegates it seemed remarkable that the President of the Fauna Preservation Society should have so little enthusiasm for the preservation of fauna, and that the Secretary of the Zoological Society of London should have so little faith in zoos as an instrument for preserving species. Simon Hicks was sitting next to Gerald as Lord Zuckerman delivered his astonishing address. 'I was very confused at what I heard,' he recalled. 'Here was the head of the national zoo and host of a world conference on the conservation of species saying there was nothing zoos could do for the conservation of species. Gerry had gone very red in the face out of frustration and anger, and I remember him saying: "You see! You see what I've been telling you! Why don't those stupid buggers understand?"' Peter Olney, Curator of Birds at London Zoo, was sitting on the other side of Gerald. 'It was appalling,' he recalled. 'My face went red with embarrassment. Most of the staff were equally embarrassed. Lord Zuckerman was a difficult man with enormous arrogance. His attitude to the future of zoos and their bearing on conservation was utterly wrong. I spoke to him about this a few days later and he said: "Oh, do you think I went too far?" I said: "Yes. At the time, you did. That was not the time to say it." And he said: "Well, I thought it had to be said and that I was the best person to say it." Gerry, of course, was furious.'

Gerry was himself well aware that extinctions were a fact of life, and that perhaps 95 per cent of all the creatures that had existed since life began were now extinct. But previous waves of mass extinctions had been the consequence of astro-physical accidents or evolutionary change over long periods of time. The current wave was different, being almost exclusively biologically driven, with one life form (*Homo sapiens*) destroying the others in a relatively short period of time. 'Extinctions in the wild state are part of evolution and will always happen,' Gerald was to say.

'But mankind is creating false extinctions caused by over-population. All species are being pushed to one side by the damage we are doing to their habitats. Mankind continues to act as if there is another world just around the corner which we can use when we have ruined this one. But there isn't.' Unlike all previous extinctions, however, the current one could be slowed, and theoretically even stopped. Not to even try to limit the damage was, in Gerald's view, simply wicked.

The Luddite Lord Zuckerman was not the only critic of captive breeding of endangered animals. It *was* a formidably expensive business; and it was not entirely clear to what extent captive-bred animals could survive if they were reintroduced into the wild. There were even those who felt it was morally better for a species to become extinct in the wild than to be saved from extinction in captivity. When American conservationists asked the Japanese government for permission to remove the last six Japanese crested ibis left in the world from their stronghold on Sado Island so that their numbers could be increased by captive breeding abroad, the local people protested, stating that they preferred the extinction of the species 'alive and free to the last bird'.

Simon Hicks, still new to the Jersey organisation, was initially puzzled as to the zoo's actual role:

> I began to realise that really Jersey Zoo wasn't a zoo at all, and there came a time when I found I simply had to understand Gerry better, get a categorical statement as to what he was about. So I asked him two questions. One: if there weren't any endangered species, would you think it necessary to have a zoo? Answer – no. Two: if it wasn't absolutely necessary, would you feel any obligation to admit the public to your zoo? Answer – no. Those answers contained something extraordinary in the zoo world at that time: a clear statement to the effect that the zoo was not an end in itself but entirely a means to an end – that of fulfilling its role of pulling animals back from the edge.
>
> Of course, Gerry was not a conventional thinker, still less a conventional organisation man. He never worked to a plan. What he would do would be to cut through all the dross. He'd suddenly say – 'Why the f*** don't we do such-and-such?' It's a sort of genius, this childlike clarity of thought, seeing what should be done, though not necessarily how.

'I feel sympathy for the small and the ugly,' Gerald once told a reporter in Indianapolis. 'Since I'm big and ugly, I try to preserve the little ones.' For Gerald, even snakes – the almost universal bane and horror of the

human race – were as deserving of love and protection as any other
creature. Fleur Cowles shared the widespread antipathy to snakes, and
when Princess Anne arrived to open the new Gaherty Reptile Breeding
Centre at the zoo in the autumn of 1976 she asked to be excused: 'I said
to the Princess, "Forgive me, but I can't come into the snake house." She
replied, "That's what you think," and pushed me in.' The Princess's
interest in the work of the Trust was more than routine. She was dedicated
to what Gerald was doing, and formed a close personal bond with him
over the years. 'When the Princess Royal turned up,' remembered Trust
Council member Colin Jones, 'she would spend the whole time conversing
with Gerry, to the exclusion of other people around – something unusual
with the Royals.'

By now penury and periodic financial crises were a thing of the past.
'The whole thing started to take off from 1975,' recalled Robin Rumboll,
Honorary Trust Treasurer during those dynamic years, 'with effective
fund-raising and the designing of visitor-friendly amenities at the zoo. We
thus got away from the annual problem of boom and bust and started
to build up an endowment fund, and the zoo itself was soon to become
the premier tourist attraction on the island, earning £1 million per year.'

The Trust had been a founder member of the Captive Breeding Specialist Group of the IUCN Survival Services Commission, and in 1980 would
host the second meeting of the group, comprising leading conservation
scientists and zoo directors from around the world. 'We have now won
world recognition for our work,' Gerald was proud to announce. 'The
zoo now leads the field in captive breeding programmes, and many other
conservation groups to look to our zoological team for advice.'

The zoo was the headquarters and showcase of the Trust, as well as
a sanctuary and reservoir for endangered animals. The latest breeding
groups included species that were *in extremis*, such as Edward's pheasant
(probably already extinct in the wild), the Jamaican boa (almost extinct
in the wild), the Rodrigues fruit bat (130 left), the golden lion tamarin
of Brazil (350 left) and many more. As the zoo's breeding successes
increased, it became clear that the time had come to move to stage two
of the process: the establishment of *in situ* breeding colonies in the species'
home countries. It also became clear that since next to no one in those
countries had the expertise to undertake this task, a training centre would
have to be established in Jersey – Gerald was to describe it as a 'mini-
university' – where students from abroad could learn the practice of
conservation zoo husbandry and the techniques of captive breeding.
Gerald had in mind a large, specially designed complex, but though funding for the building and for the students' scholarships was raised from

sources in America and Britain, he had reservations about imposing such an intrusive structure in the zoo grounds.

Once again 'Durrell's luck' came to the rescue. Twice a week a local woman by the name of Mrs Boizard came to clean Gerald's flat, and her daughter Betty, who had worked at the Trust since leaving school and was now in charge of the zoo accounts department, often came to have a brief chat with her. One day Mrs Boizard casually remarked: 'I see Leonard du Feu has put his house on the market.' 'Betty looked incredulous, as well she might,' Gerald was to record. 'Leonard du Feu was a neighbour we prized beyond rubies. His Jersey property had been in his family for ever (something like five hundred years) and his fields, as they say, marched with ours. His house lay two minutes' walk from the manor, and was really three houses in one, with a small worker's cottage, a huge coolroom and massive granite outbuildings. We had never, in our wildest dreams, imagined that Leonard would sell the family house. Breathlessly, Betty descended to the office and gave the news.'

Here was their training centre, ready-made and close at hand – an ancient Jersey granite property by the name of Les Noyers. John Hartley immediately rang Gerald in Memphis, and Gerald instructed him to contact Leonard du Feu at once. On 30 November 1979, after much huffing and puffing on the part of the States of Jersey, who had strict laws about the uses to which properties (particularly agricultural properties) could be put on the island, Les Noyers became the Trust's. 'To say we were delighted would be wholly inadequate,' wrote Gerald. 'Instead of the massive concrete block we were contemplating for our training centre, we had an elegantly beautiful old Jersey farmhouse with massive outbuildings and eight acres of land. So, as soon as the property was ours, we started renovations.'

Before long Les Noyers had been transformed into a spanking new international college of specialist education, complete with student dormitories and living quarters, a lecture theatre, a small museum, a graphics and photography area, a darkroom and video suite, and the elegant Sir William Collins Memorial Library, for before his death in 1976 Gerald's publisher had generously given the Trust a copy of every zoological and natural history book that Collins had ever published, and the promise that it would receive every one published in the future.

The first training officer in charge of the centre was Dr David Waugh, selected from a multitude of applicants not only for his Ph.D in biology but for his ability to deal with people from all over the world with tact and sympathy. His first task was to draw up, with what Gerald called 'rigid flexibility', a programme for a diploma training course that had never been taught before. The first trainee – Yousoof Mungroo, who was later to become the first director of the first national park in Mauritius – arrived before Les Noyers was ready, and had to live in the reptile house. Today nearly a thousand students from a hundred countries have been trained in Jersey. These are the men and women who constitute, as someone neatly put it, 'Gerald Durrell's Army'. 'I had never thought to see this, our mini-university, come into being during my lifetime,' Gerald was to write, 'but it seemed no time at all before I was playing croquet on the back lawn of Les Noyers with students from Brazil, Mexico, Liberia, India and China, and that they kindly allowed me to win was in no way the only reason I felt proud. This mix of people from all nations has worked out very well indeed, I think because our trainees share a common purpose, which is saving endangered species.'

The International Training Centre for Breeding and Conservation of Endangered Species was probably Gerald Durrell's greatest achievement. It is still virtually unique, and has spread the Jersey message and Jersey knowhow around the world. As Desmond Morris was to comment:

> There are scores of conservationists and whatnot who sit around pontificating learnedly about this and that. What Gerry did was train local people to do it for themselves in their own countries. Without this you're lost. In many unstable countries, the moment there's a political upheaval, everything falls apart, animals are hunted down, killed and eaten. So you have to have a bedrock of conservation practice, a new attitude inculcated. Setting about doing this was Gerry's great achievement.

Every year over fifty new trainees arrive for courses lasting three months (three weeks in the case of the short Summer School programme), during which they learn the theory of conservation biology, the role of zoos in biodiversity conservation, the biological principles of the proper care and maintenance of animals kept in captivity, the genetic and demographic management of *ex situ* and *in situ* populations, the strategies for habitat protection and reintroduction of captive-bred animals; undertake practical working experience with endangered animals in the mammals, birds and herpetology departments of Jersey Zoo; and conduct research related to the species they will try to save when they return home. Well trained and highly motivated, the graduates of Les Noyers represent an extraordinary international conservation network. Their fondness for Gerald Durrell and his organisation is palpable.

As a result of the vision of a man who had virtually no formal education whatsoever, Jersey Zoo and Trust had undergone an evolution from menagerie to zoo park to survival centre to international conservation headquarters and training centre of excellence. But Gerald's vision could never have become a reality without his closest colleagues – including both his wives and 'the boys' (as he insisted on calling his senior staff). These totally dedicated disciples remained steadfastly devoted to the place, the cause and above all the man. Gerald, in his turn, trusted them totally, for they had been selected to some degree in their maker's image, as committed, talented, congenial and unconventional aides who, like their mentor, could think laterally and stand problems on their heads. 'I trust them as much for their faults as their virtues,' he explained to David Hughes. 'I place absolute faith in them. If I died tomorrow there would be no fear of collapse through lack of directional impetus. They might regret the loss of a fund-raiser, even of a father figure, but they would know just which way to go.' Gerald ran the show like a benign patriarch, but he always had an ear for whatever his staff had to say. To this end it was the usual practice for 'the boys' to come up to the flat for a beer around five o'clock. 'They run the place marvellously when I'm away,' Gerald was to say. 'But as soon as I get back, they say to themselves: "There's that poor old bugger sitting up there, he'll feel unloved and unwanted if we don't give him something to do." So they tell me about all their problems.'

John Hartley – relaxed, humorous, a born diplomat – had been Trust Secretary for a number of years before becoming Gerald's personal assistant in 1976, and knew the man inside out. 'Gerry was brilliant as an ideas person,' he was to recall. 'You know – absolute vision. But he had a total need of the people who were going to say, "Oh, that's a bloody good idea, I'd better try and make it happen." Gerry wasn't an executive; he never ran this place, whatever that means. He was the thinker and where he led we followed – and he was such a remarkable and enchanting man we'd follow him to the ends of the earth. He was magical. You'd come away from an evening with him with a smile on your face. You knew you had been in the presence of somebody who was different to the rest of us – a presence, larger than life, effervescent, terribly funny, a free spirit, a free mind that could go anywhere – and usually did. He did think a lot. Up in the flat he'd spend long periods of time sitting at the kitchen table with a notepad, mulling things over, thinking things through. What a great adventure it was to be with him. What a saga we'd all got involved in.'

Jeremy Mallinson – tall, fair and slim, briskly energetic and bubbling with enthusiasm – had been at the zoo almost as long as Gerald had, and as Zoological Director he was responsible for the day-to-day running of the zoo. Gerald had always regarded taking Jeremy on as a typical case of 'Durrell's Luck'. Jeremy for his part was conscious of a debt of gratitude to 'Mr D' (as he called his friend and mentor in the early days), who had guided his formative years and fulfilled his life. 'Gerry was a great listener,' he recalled. 'He had these lovely blue eyes; they'd fix you, you knew exactly what he was thinking. He was incredibly supportive of people he trusted, no matter what their background was. Even if you made mistakes he'd see you grew out of them. He was an incredibly good chooser of people. He had a tremendous insight into people. He never bothered to quantify it. Basically he was a rather shy, private man, but with someone he liked, or in company where he felt at ease, he could be a very warm person. He would embrace you and mean it. He would even kiss me on both cheeks – very Continental. He was very critical of inhibitions. "If you love someone," he'd say, "tell them you love them." Although he and I were totally different in every possible way, Gerry so inspired me with his philosophy and his dedication that I learned just about everything from him. He inspired all sorts of people all over the world.'

Because Gerald so often railed against the human race and the destruction it inflicted on the planet and the natural world, some people thought he was a misanthrope. In fact it was the nature of the human species he complained about, not humans as individuals. 'We have this awful insular habit,' he had complained to David Hughes, 'of talking about the animal kingdom patronisingly as though it were an inferior form of life on a very remote planet – but we *are* in the animal kingdom, we're a bloody mammal. And the whole educational system supports this appalling divorce, as do politics, social custom, even science – it's all geared to this frightening idea of man being God, instead of the worldwide Frankenstein he has really become.'

Simon Hicks, the new Trust Secretary, was bright, energetic and devout. He looked on his work as not only a privilege and a joy but a calling – 'serving God by saving his creatures'. When he was young Gerry had been his hero ('Wasn't he everyone's?'), but his 'epiphany' had come when, in Africa after army service, he spent two days and a night with George Adamson and his lions under Mount Kenya. After that experience there was only one course for his career to take. He first found himself at Jersey Zoo as a field officer in charge of a squad from what would later be called the British Trust for Conservation Volunteers, digging a pond, building bridges, felling and planting trees. Gerald had been impressed by 'his enthusiasm, the efficiency with which he which handled his team . . . It seemed that Simon was heaven-sent, if we could get him.' Eventually, by luring him back to Jersey on the pretext of looking at more ponds, Gerald did get him. 'The chance to serve another conservation cause in the making,' Simon conceded, 'was just too much to resist.' He arrived on April Fool's Day 1976 – the beginning of a unique adventure in close association with an extraordinary man.

'To Gerry people were just as much part of the animal kingdom as animals,' Simon believed. 'So he saw people as fascinating specimens of the species. In his books people were animals and animals were people. That's why people loved his books – and hence the title *My Family and Other Animals*. Gerry saw people as a child sees people – as characters in a storybook, larger than life, with extraordinary characteristics, usually very funny ones. And if you were in Gerry's company for any length of time, you'd start seeing people as he saw them. People you wouldn't have looked at twice were suddenly transformed into extraordinary characters.

'He not only liked people, he was terribly interested in them. There were times in Gerry's company when you almost began to feel that you were as interesting as he was. He was an amazing listener, and when he talked it was seldom about himself. He had a wonderful way of putting things, a great gift for simile. Once we were having lunch in France and eating haricot beans and I said, "Oh, I love these beans, the way they squeak in your teeth," and quick as a flash he said, "Yes, just like gumboots in the snow." And that's the only squeak you can compare with beans in the teeth. To him the natural world was magic, and he was a conservationist because he hated the idea of the world losing its magic.'

Tony Allchurch had been doing veterinary work at the zoo since 1972, and was later to become its full-time general administrator as well as veterinarian. Though he was within Gerald's charmed circle of 'the boys' at the zoo, he was never on such easy and intimate terms with him as the others. In part this was due to the reservations Gerald had about vets in zoos – 'The two most dangerous animals to let loose unsupervised in a zoo,' he once declared, 'are an architect and a veterinary surgeon.' But Allchurch was unfazed: 'Over the years I'd begun to realise that what was going on here was something very exciting, very challenging, very purposeful. For a vet this is the best job that anybody could ever have, in the best zoo in the world. I work ridiculously hard for a salary that is far less than what I'd be earning if I was still in general practice. But I'm the envy of all my veterinary colleagues.' At Jersey Zoo a vet could be confronted with patients that ranged in size, shape and temperament from a lowland gorilla to a Pacific island snail, the only things they had in common being the fact that neither could explain their symptoms and both were in danger of extinction.

Most veterinary work was handled in-house at the zoo's own small veterinary hospital. But for really major surgery involving sizeable animals a surgical team would decamp from Jersey Hospital bringing all their equipment and support staff – and in the old days, when things were rough and ready, a policeman would stand guard with a loaded gun in case of trouble. From the very beginning, when Gerald's local GP, Dr Hunter, had sometimes been called in to help an animal through a crisis, the emphasis had been on prevention as much as cure. 'If animals are properly looked after,' Tony Allchurch believed, 'properly fed and cared for under the right conditions by people who have a humane approach to them, then diseases and accidents and injuries are going to be rare intrusions into the progress of conservation.'

But there were disappointments as well as rewards. Unlike domestic animals, who generally recognise that the vet is trying to heal them, captive wild animals view him as a mortal enemy, blowing tranquilliser darts at them, stitching them up, pulling their teeth out, bringing back members of their group smelling of strange ointments and spirits. 'The alienation between the patient and the physician is the thing I have found hardest to come to terms with,' Tony was to say. 'Having to try and care for animals who wanted to bite me or run away from me and had to be restrained or even immobilised before I could even look at them – that was hard. If Gambar, our orang-utan, spots me he will immediately go into a rage, and our gorilla Jambo would charge across his enclosure and thump the window if he saw me. I liked to think I was the angel of mercy, yet I was being treated as the angel of death.'

The zoo and the Trust opened up a whole new world to Tony Allchurch. 'It's like sitting on top of a volcano here – brimming with energy, bursting out in all directions. There's no sense of plateau-ing out, the challenges are continuous, the goal is being refined all the time. All this is the creation of Gerald Durrell – his vision, his drive. There aren't many people I've really loved, but he was a most lovely man. And I don't have many heroes but I would certainly put Gerry among them. There was a sage-like quality about him. And gradually over the years I began to see the wisdom of his words.'

Gerald chose his staff more by intuition than judgement. Usually he was unerringly right in his choice. On the rare occasion he was wrong, and he found he had someone who was not on his wavelength, or who turned out to lack the initiative or independence of mind he had expected, he terminated their employment. Of those who remained, Philip Coffey was typical. He had joined the zoo in 1967, at the age of twenty-one, as its first graduate keeper-scientist, a new concept developed by Gerald and Bob Martin. Later he became the first head of the zoo's education department. Coffey was to stay at the zoo for nearly thirty years. 'The reason I stayed so long,' he was to say, 'was because of Gerald Durrell – the dream, the ethics that he put forward for conservation. One of the reasons why the zoo has gone from strength to strength is that it has never stood still, and this again is down to the driving force of Gerald Durrell. He was always happy to listen if you had any problems or any bright ideas. He was a good listener and happy to talk about virtually any subject and ask how you were and how it was going.'

One aspect of Gerald's life and personality was to prove obdurately intractible. By 1980 he had been drinking a lot, for a very long time. It was as much part of the man as his humour, his generosity, or his sense of wonder at the planet and its creatures. But so disciplined was his self-control during the working day that some occasional associates were not aware that he drank at all. To others, though, he displayed no embarrassment, and made no attempt at concealment. When Philip Coffey went for a job interview at the zoo early one morning, he was amazed to find his future employer unconcernedly sipping his way through a breakfast that consisted of a pint of Guinness. Gerald was easy inside his own skin about his drinking. People would have to accept him as he was – and most people did. Occasionally those closest to him would try to persuade him to change his ways. His sister Margaret recalled him telling her: 'If you can say I ever got up drunk, then you can criticise my drinking. But I never have.'

Gerald's fund-raising tours of America were his greatest ordeal. Sometimes he could not even make it to London Airport, so overwhelming was his terror. 'His whole physiology would go to pieces at the very idea of it,' Simon Hicks recalled. 'In my view it was totally psychosomatic, but the physical reaction was quite apparent – he was *ill*.' When he did make it across the Atlantic – and he usually did – he would often summon up the courage to face his lecture audiences by downing a few doubles backstage. To the amazement of all around him, the moment he stepped on to the podium he would appear calm, assured, commanding, charismatic – and completely sober.

In the first year or two of their marriage Lee tried hard to wean her husband off alcohol, convinced that it was merely a matter of affirmation and willpower. 'He'd go in fits and starts,' she recalled. 'Early in our marriage I managed to get him on the wagon for the best part of six months. The medics often tried to do the same – cut it down, or better still cut it out. But then it would creep right up back again. Alcoholism has been described as a condition that rendered you incapable of functioning socially – and there were very few times when Gerry got like that because of drink. It had always been there in his background. The whole family drank wine in Corfu when he was a boy, and Mother liked her noggin – drink was a way of life. At one level alcohol for Gerry was a matter of *joie de vivre*. Good wine was one of the pleasures of life, along with the good food that went with it. But at another level Gerry drank to help get him through moments of deep despair and depression, and later to bear actual physical pain.'

Gerald and Lee had plunged into the hurly burly of television film-making almost as soon as they were married. *The Edge of Extinction*, shot in 1979, was a BBC documentary which took the form of a passionate plea for mankind to take more care of the world we live in and the animals that share it with us. Gerald showed the work being done to save endangered species by captive breeding at Jersey and at the Wild Animal Park in San Diego, California, and accompanied by Lee set off to Mexico in another attempt to catch a group of volcano rabbits and bring them back to Jersey – a more successful rerun of the ill-fated expedition of 1968, producing better breeding results, though this colony too died out eventually. The programme was broadcast on BBC 1 on 6 July 1980, and was well received. 'He's recently had a miniature heart attack,' revealed Richard North in the *Radio Times*, 'a kind of warning shot across the bows: he's determined to take more exercise. "I've got to get down to twelve stone," he says. In his hand is a gleaming – massive – glass of brandy. His eyes are as blue as the Aegean. He is a man, as they say, in the pink: a fifty-five-year-old with a lot to do. But Durrell, after a lifetime lived at what he calls "a colossal pace" may have to slow down now. "It's a shame: this happened just when I'd decided I was immortal."'

The heart attack had happened in the back of a taxi on his way to Jersey Airport. France, as always, was the chosen balm and panacea, and three days after the television broadcast Gerald and Lee were down at the Mazet for a family gathering, with Lee's sister Hat and her parents Harriet and Hal in attendance, soon to be joined by local friends and neighbours, including the sculptress Elizabeth Frink, the violinist Yehudi Menuhin and his wife, the painter Tony Daniells and writer David Hughes. The sun and air of the French South in high summer, the food and drink of its country markets, the long, leisurely meals with friends and the al fresco life at the Mazet were Gerald's very lifeblood. Not even 'the warning shot across the bows' had diminished his boundless appetite for living (and quaffing and scoffing) dangerously, as an illustrated ode with the *double entendre* title of 'Felicity', written in praise of the bounty of France and sent to his literary agent Felicity Bryan, exuberantly proclaimed:

What to say of La Belle France
Where arteries never have a chance?
Where every menu points with glee
The way to adiposity;
With all that wine and crispy bread . . .
(One more coronary – I'm dead).

Mushrooms, big as white umbrellas –
They're minus *calories* they tell us –
But simmered slow in wine and cream:
Dieter's nightmare! Glutton's dream!
But roasted truffles are the best . . .
(What's that hammering in my chest?) . . .

In verse after verse, Gerald hailed the coronary potential of France's fatally irresistible cuisine – quails and suckling pigs and 'livers from whole flocks of geese', eggplants drowned in oil and butter, turbot, lobster and écrevisse. France, he declared, was both his joy and his undoing.

Ah! Belle France, you promised land,
Come, we'll walk now, hand in hand
With oyster, snail and bread and butter
And vintages to make you stutter;
Creamy cheese that eats so well
(Or others with atrocious smell);
Hams and salmon, sunset pink,
Fiery Armagnac to drink . . .
You fill my glass, you pile my plate,
'Tis you who've got me in this state.
Belle France, I love you, there's no doubt,
But one thing I must just point out –
That here and now I do attest
YOU caused my cardiac arrest!

Felicity, my dearest girl,
Do not cast me as a churl,
But I must end, cast down my quill,
Assuring you I love you still –
So please don't think of me a sinner –
But – seven o'clock –
It's time for dinner.

TWENTY-EIGHT

Ark on the Move

From the Island of the Dodo to the Land of the Lemur 1980–1982

Ever since his first foray to Mauritius in 1976, Gerald had been held in the island's spell, and he had become so intrigued by its conservation problems that his mind had begun to turn to a revolutionary way of tackling them. John Hartley recalled: 'One morning at breakfast Gerry and I were discussing the fact that most of the small amount of conservation work being done in the country was by foreigners. For the long term, we agreed, it was clearly essential for the Mauritian community to take part. And then Gerry said:

'"I have an idea. We are seeing the Minister this morning. What I'm going to do is offer him a scholarship for a Mauritian to come to Jersey for training on our specialist conservation programme."'

Hartley gulped on his coffee. He had never heard of any such programme. There was no such thing.

'*What* training programme?' he asked.

'Hartley,' Gerald replied sternly. 'You know what your trouble is? You always get bogged down in the minor details in life!'

'It became obvious as we talked,' Hartley remembered, 'that as usual Gerald had given a great deal of thought to the idea. But at that time we had no programme, nobody trained to do the training, nowhere to house the trainee, and so on, and so on . . .'

The offer was made, the Minister accepted, and in the spring of 1977 Gerald paid a return visit to Mauritius with John Hartley, his sister Margaret and his New Yorker friend Trish. The selection was made, and a local schoolteacher by the name of Yousoof Mungroo became Jersey Zoo's first trainee student.

Another aim of this second foray to Mauritius was to try to catch rare boas on Round Island – an enterprise that was not without its adventures.

The party were camped under canvas on the island one evening when they were subject to one of the most bizarre manifestations of the natural world Gerald had ever witnessed:

As the green twilight faded and the sky turned velvety black, awash with stars, as if at a given signal there arose the most extraordinary noise from the bowels of the earth. It started softly, almost tunefully, a sound like distant pack of wolves, howling mournfully across some remote, snowbound landscape. Then, as more voices joined the chorus, it became a gigantic, mad mass being celebrated in some Bedlamite cathedral. You could hear the lunatic cries of the priests and the wild responses from the congregation. This lasted for about half an hour, the sounds rising and falling, the ground throbbing with the noise, and then, as suddenly as if the earth had burst open and released all the damned souls from some Gustave Doré subterranean hell, out of the holes concealed by the green meadows, mewing and honking and moaning, the baby Shearwaters burst forth.

They appeared in hundreds, as if newly risen from the grave, and squatted and fluttered around our camp, providing such a cacophony of sound that we could hardly hear each other speak. Not content with this, the babies, being of limited intelligence, decided that our tent was a sort of superior nest burrow, designed for their special benefit. Squawking and moaning, they fought their way through the openings and flapped over and under our camp beds, defecating with great freedom, and if handled without tact, regurgitating a fishy, smelly oil all over us.

All night the bedlam continued. Towards dawn the baby birds discovered a new joy they had never known before – sliding down the tent roof, over and over again, their claws making a noise liking ripping calico on the canvas. 'On mature reflection,' Gerald was to record, I decided that this was the most uncomfortable night I had ever spent in my life.' Just before dawn the travellers rose from their inadequate doze and staggered out of their tent, tripping and stumbling over the hordes of baby shearwaters scuttling back into their holes.

Early one morning the party climbed to one of the highest points on the island. From the summit Gerald could see the full, catastrophic extent of Round Island's degradation. With the vegetation cover gone, what soil was left was being washed down to the sea, followed by rocks and boulders. At the summit even the great sheets of hard tuff had dissolved here and there in the night rain and attained the consistency of sticky chocolate.

Father and son: Jambo (left), the silverback patriarch of the lowland gorillas at Jersey Zoo, and . . .

. . . his son Assumbo (below), born 15 July 1973, the first gorilla to be born at the Jersey Wildlife Preservation Trust.

Jill Pook and Jeremy Usher-Smith with young captive-bred gorillas at Jersey Zoo in the 1970s.

Jambo stands guard over the unconscious body of five-year-old Levan Merritt, who had accidentally fallen into the gorilla enclosure, while Nandi and Motaba look on. Film of the incident was shown on television around the world and helped change the image of the gorilla for ever.

Some of the endangered animals that Jersey Zoo and Trust are helping to save from extinction.

Clockwise from top left: Golden lion tamarin and young from Brazil. Pigmy hog of Assam, the world's smallest pig. Black and white ruffed lemur of Madagascar. Aye-aye of Madagascar. Mauritian kestrel – once the world's rarest bird, but now saved.

The wedding of Gerald Durrell
and Lee McGeorge in
Memphis, Tennessee, on
24 May 1979. On
Gerald's left is the best man,
Jeremy Mallinson.
The pianist is Mose.

Princess Anne, the Trust's Patron,
visits Jersey Zoo for the opening
of the international mini-university
for animal conservation,
5 October 1984.

Much of the 1980s was devoted to big international TV series, including *Ark on the Move* and *Durrell in Russia*.

Above: Gerald, Lee and the *Ark on the Move* film team on Round Island – 'the Galapagos of Mauritius' – home of unique and endangered animals that Gerald vowed to save from extinction. Second from the left is John Hartley, far right is producer Paula Quigley.

Right: Gerald and Lee with students and teacher at a school in Siberia during the shooting of *Durrell in Russia*. Gerald was warmly welcomed in Russia, not only on account of his books but for what he stood for – especially among the young.

Deep in the Siberian backwoods, Gerald, Lee and their Siberian friends take a break. Throughout this immense and challenging journey Gerald bore the pain from his hips without complaint – hence the stick and the bottle.

Gerald and thirteen-year-old Darren Redmayne, the boy actor who played his young self in the BBC TV adaptation of *My Family and Other Animals*, on location on Corfu in August 1987.

Gerald and Lee with endangered friends from Madagascar – *above:* Lee with black and white ruffed lemurs.

Right: Gerald with ring-tailed and red-ruffed lemurs.

Grand Old Man and saviour of animals, with two captive-bred species at Jersey Zoo – Round Island boa . . .

. . . and St Lucia parrot.

Lee and Gerald outside Buckingham Palace after he received the OBE from the Prince of Wales in February 1983.

Gerald and Lee in their flat at Les Augrès Manor in the late eighties.

Sarah Kennedy's 'last supper' – Sir David Attenborough (left), Gerald Durrell and Dr Desmond Morris have dinner together – the last time this trio of great naturalists ever met.

Gerald and lowland gorillas in the zoo he founded to
save endangered animals from extinction.

The island was eroding away. Gerald was aghast: 'Gazing down at these slopes of tuff, you realised forcibly that here was a unique, miniature world that had, by a miracle of evolution, come into being and was now being allowed to bleed to death ... this unique speck of land was diminishing day by day. It seemed to sum up in miniature what we were doing to the whole planet, with millions of species being bled to death for want of a little, so little, medicare.'

There was a frisson of panic on their last day on Round Island when the helicopter failed to turn up on time and for a moment it seemed they might be marooned on this intriguing but inhospitable speck of land. Most alarmed was one of their local companions, a young man from the Forestry Department called Zozo who had never been off Mauritius before. Spotting Zozo sitting moodily under a palm tree nearby, Gerald decided to lighten his gloom.

'Zozo,' he called.

'Yes, Mr Gerry?' said Zozo, peering at him from under the brim of his large solar topee which, Gerald noted, 'made him look ridiculously like a green mushroom'.

'It seems as if the helicopter is not coming to rescue us.'

'Yes, Mr Gerry,' he agreed soulfully.

'Well,' said Gerald, in a kindly, reassuring way, 'I wanted you to know that, by an overwhelming vote, we have decided to eat you first when the food runs out.'

But all was well, the helicopter eventually arrived, Zozo was spared, and Gerald and John and Margaret returned to Mauritius with their precious Round Island geckos and skinks as a first step in saving them too. 'As we rose higher and higher, and the island dwindled against the turquoise sea,' Gerald declared later, 'I became determined that we must do everything we could to save it.' It was the beginning of a great endeavour.

With Gerald about to go to America on another fund-raising tour – during which he would make a rendezvous with destiny in the form of Lee – John Hartley became the *de facto* co-ordinator of the Trust's operations in Mauritius. His first action was to return almost immediately to catch pink pigeons for a captive breeding programme in Jersey, returning after a month with eight birds, three of which were left in Mauritius with the ones they already had there, and five brought back to Jersey. There was a steady escalation after that. On the recommendation of the Jersey Trust the Mauritius government had established the Black River Aviaries (now known as the Gerald Durrell Endemic Wildlife Sanctuary) to carry out their own bird rescue and breeding programme, and when the International Council for Bird Preservation appointed a young Welsh biologist by the name of Carl Jones to run the Black River centre in 1983 it was Jersey who funded his work, eventually taking over the whole programme. 'This project was a defining moment for the Trust,' John Hartley recalled. 'It was the first project we developed overseas in a serious way over the years and basically we've learnt an awful lot of what we now apply elsewhere from the Mauritius model. It is also one of the most successful conservation projects in the world, without doubt.'

Carl Jones had no doubts that Gerald Durrell was the inspiration and driving force. 'He saw things very simply,' he was to recall. 'He knew that captive breeding was just one way of saving animals, but he saw beyond this, and realised we had to develop the interface between captivity and the wild state. I spent a lot of time talking to him about this. He was a great visionary. Recently conservation has moved on into questions of animal consciousness and animal rights and whole ecosystems, and Gerry was interested in all these things. He knew that we had to move with the times. He was a great thinker and to my mind a very great man. He was also his own master. He was outside all the committees and in-fighting that ties up so much of the conservation movement. He wasn't like some of the bigger conservation organisations who deal only in high-profile animals, put a load of money in and then pull out. He put local people in on the ground and stuck with the project hands-on *in situ* through thick and thin.'

For Gerald and Lee, much of the 1980s were to be taken up with a succession of international television series on natural history and conservation themes that would take them to almost every point of the globe. The driving force behind this televisual blitz was Canadian production chief W. Paterson Ferns, with whom Gerald had made the highly successful thirteen-part series *The Stationary Ark* in 1975, and who was now head of a Toronto-based production company, Primedia. By the time Gerald and Pat Ferns' association came to an end they would have made five television series (four of them with Lee) and a television special together, a total of sixty-five programmes, plus six related books. The production costs reflected the rising scale of the programmes' ambitions and the increasingly exotic location shooting. The thirteen-part series *Ark on the Move* was made in 1980 on a shoestring, for a budget equivalent to what Gerald was used to when shooting a single documentary for the BBC. By the time they made their fifth series, each episode was costing the equivalent of the entire first series.

During the early part of 1980 Pat Ferns had been back in contact with Gerald about the possibility of making another thirteen-part documentary television series, entitled *Ark on the Move*. The new British network Channel 4's Chief Executive, Jeremy Isaacs, was attracted by the idea of having a major figure in natural history working on the new channel, and as well as commissioning Gerald's new series, he purchased the previous one, *The Stationary Ark*. *Ark on the Move* was a logical sequel to *The Stationary Ark*, reflecting the shift in Gerald's conservation thinking since the first series, and his plans to extend captive breeding operations from Jersey to sites overseas. The idea was to base part of the series on Gerald's animal rescue missions to Mauritius, as described in his book *Golden Bats and Pink Pigeons*, and to shoot the rest in Madagascar, a species-rich island land-mass in dire ecological straits.

It was Pat Ferns' view that Gerald and Lee would be perfect to front the new series together, since Gerald knew Mauritius and Lee knew Madagascar, and each would be showing the other familiar ground. Lee, Pat Ferns reckoned, was a quiet but intriguing presence on film. As for Gerald, Ferns knew that properly handled he was a natural. 'I worked with some of the best television presenters in the world,' he was to say later, 'and Gerry was certainly in the first rank. He wasn't an easy personality but I think he was a first-rate performer with a genuine vision. He was a true storyteller. He loved to regale an audience with a scotch in his hand over dinner or with a lemur on his shoulder in front of a camera. His writing relied on the brilliant simile or metaphor and he was able to translate this into a form of television presentation that captured the comic qualities of his books, while never detracting from the passion of his cause.'

Until Pat Ferns had come along, Gerald's experience of television had not been particularly happy. The long, hard slog of documentary film-making, with the almost invariable crew acrimony and the front-of-camera pressures, had always put him under great strain, making him self-conscious and constrained, and stifling his natural humour and buoyant charm. But working with Pat Ferns had been different, and in *The Stationary Ark* he had finally blossomed in front of camera – 'so full of life and cuddly-cute,' as one reviewer remarked, 'that you felt like reaching out and squeezing him.' So he looked forward to the *Ark on the Move* shoot, and perhaps others to come, in happy expectation.

'In this new series,' Gerald was to write, 'we were to show not only our breeding successes in Jersey but also our rescue operations in the wild. Also, we wanted to show our new scheme for working with governments all over the world to save their animals and to bring people from these countries to Jersey for training in the complex and difficult art of captive breeding.' The plan was to visit Mauritius, Rodrigues and Round

Island in the Mascarenes, where the Jersey Trust was already working with the government, and then to move on to Madagascar, to see what help they could give there.

In the late autumn of 1980 Gerald and Lee met Pat Ferns and the production team in Toronto as they passed through in the course of a fund-raising tour of North America, and at the end of January 1981 Pat Ferns (executive producer), Michael Maltby (director) and Paula Quigley (producer) arrived in Jersey for three days of pre-production meetings. A week or so later John Hartley and the production team flew to Mauritius to set up the production. *Ark on the Move*, the first of the new big series, was under way.

There were the usual hiccups and tensions that befall long film shoots involving talented but temperamental people in uncontrollable situations on unpredictable locations. The Australian film crew were delayed by an air strike, for example, and Gerald and the director began to fall out. But the shooting schedule was kept to, and all the key locations were tackled in turn – Pink Pigeon Wood, Black River Gorges, the Black River Aviaries, and ten days on Rodrigues.

In the last week of March the party moved on to the infinitely bigger island of Madagascar – a strange and intriguing land beset by its own infinitely bigger problems. Lying off the East African coast, a thousand miles long and two and a half times the size of Britain, Madagascar is an island of continental proportions – the fifth largest in the world and home of some of the world's most remarkable flora and fauna, 90 per cent of it found nowhere else. All of Madagascar's chameleons (representing two-thirds of the world's species) and almost half of its birds are unique to the island. Of the four hundred or so known species of reptiles and amphibians, only twelve exist elsewhere. Four-fifths of the plants are found nowhere else, including a plethora of baobab tree (seven different kinds, where Africa only has one). The two dozen kinds of lemur that live there constitute an entirely separate branch of primate evolution, ranging in size from one as big as a five-year-old child to another small enough to fit into a coffee cup. There are woodlice the size of golf balls and moths the size of Regency fans. In short, the island is a natural treasure house – yet four-fifths of it now stood barren.

'Today's acute environmental problems are turning Madagascar, an irreplaceable storehouse of evolutionary knowledge, into a wasteland of barren soil,' Gerald was to lament. 'Eighty per cent of native forests has already disappeared. The conservation of this Eden's rich tapestry of natural history is seen as one of the world's foremost environmental priorities. Indeed, Madagascar has been described as the place with the greatest number of unique species in the greatest danger of extinction.' It was an island of breathless and eerie beauty, he continued, a complex web of past and present, yet riven with wrenching conflicts between changing cultures and fragile environments.

Shortly after their arrival in Madagascar the party flew to the extraordinary reserve at Berenty, at the southernmost tip of the island. To a naturalist it could be said that Berenty has a significance that verges almost on the mystical. It consists of 450 acres of forest of gigantic old tamarind trees, and is famous above all for its lemurs – ring-tailed lemurs, mouse lemurs, nocturnal lepilemurs and sifakas – primitive primates which, having been displaced elsewhere by monkeys, evolved in Madagascar unbothered by simian competition. At first light on the day following their arrival, Gerald, Lee and the rest of the party went into the forest. At the end of the day Gerald dictated his recollections into his tape-recorder.

The first thing that ran across our path was a sifaka. They are the most beautiful and endearing of all the lemurs; not only are they so graceful, but they are so gentle and they have got such sweet, benign faces. They are the ballerinas of the lemurs. Not only are they graceful in the trees, leaping the most astonishing distances, but when they run on the ground they run on their hind legs, holding up their little black hands as though in horror at some remark that has been made to them, twisting the top half of their body slightly sideways as they run, which gives them a terrifically sort of pansy gallop, which is very amusing to watch. Their movement is so beautiful, as light as thistledown.

The ring-taileds, on the other hand, are more baboon-like. They gallop about like dogs or swagger about with their tails up, and when a troop of perhaps twenty or thirty of them walk down the forest paths here it looks like a sort of medieval pageant with banners up going along.

The animals here are so used to being studied and approached by human beings that they treat you exactly as though you are a part of the scenery. They ignore you and just walk past going about their business, sometimes within a foot of you. We have seen a lot of wonderful things. When I started dictating this, for example, about thirty ring-tailed lemurs just walked across the front of the house and any minute now I expect to get a visit from my little troop of sifakas that come and do their funny waddly walk for me and make me laugh.

From Berenty they drove three hours along a bumpy track in an ancient Land-Rover to visit a government nature reserve near a tiny village called Hazofotsy. The reserve protected a spiny forest unique to southern Madagascar, consisting of _Didiereacae_ trees, which looked like giant cacti covered with formidable spikes. In this prickly and inhospitable terrain lived one of the most beautiful of the Madagascar lemurs, the Verrauxi's sifaka. A lovely creamy-white in colour, with sooty backs, black faces and huge golden eyes, they leapt and pounced through their thorny world in the most amazing fashion, jumping twenty or thirty feet from one spike to another without ever impaling themselves. For Gerald and his party, though, it was rough going, as he explained into his tape-recorder: 'As soon as I saw the Spiny Forest I thought to myself that our chances of filming anything at all were very remote. We drove over some roads that were like nothing I had experienced anywhere in the world. They were like ancient river beds which had been under mortar attack for about twenty years.'

That night they slept under the stars – 'the Southern Cross like a gigantic chandelier in the sky' – and woke drenched in dew. 'I looked over to Lee,' Gerald recorded, 'and there she was lying, looking like a Pre-Raphaelite painting of the better sort, with all her hair covered with little tiny beads of dew, like a spider's web.'

The sound-recording equipment and the camera on its tripod seemed to weigh a ton as they were carried through the Spiny Forest. But there were compensations. The spectacle of a Madagascar dawn was one – 'a very odd shade of greeny-blue'. The seemingly limitless abundance of strange creatures was another – a five-foot-long, yellow-and-black-striped snake 'like an animated school tie'; a spider the size of a saucer that spun webs the size of cartwheels seemingly thick enough to catch small birds in; a wood-louse (or pill-millipede) the size of a billiard ball; a 'hissing' cockroach as big as a lemon and the colour of mahogany that sang with a loud ringing-zinging noise when you picked it up.

After two weeks in Berenty Reserve and the Spiny Forest they travelled north to Ankarafantsika, one of the largest reserves in Madagascar. Sadly, owing to the slash and burn method of agriculture used by the local people, two-thirds of this marvellous reserve had been destroyed. A two-week shoot in the nearby forest reserve at Ampijoroa followed, then an excursion to the lush little tropical island of Nosy Komba, off the north-west coast of Madagascar, where the local lemurs – of a kind called black or Macaco lemur – were held by the local people as sacred, and therefore protected. They were incredibly tame – so tame that they would sometimes sit on top of the camera with their tail hanging down over the lens.

Their final port of call was Perinet, a forestry reserve set aside especially for the largest and most spectacular of the Malagasy lemurs, the indri. The size of a five-year-old child, they are marked panda-fashion in black and white, with huge white tufted ears and big staring golden eyes. 'They are the aristocrats of the lemurs,' Gerald was to record, 'and behave in a way befitting their aristocracy. They rarely get up before ten o'clock and are generally in bed by four in the afternoon. While they are up, however, they delineate their territory by singing.' Gerald, Lee and the crew went into the forest to find these creatures and to hear their song, as Gerald related into his tape-recorder:

Well, we went into the forest, and although we heard indri we didn't see any. I've decided their marvellous yowling cry sounds exactly like those underwater recordings of the whale song. It really is a most plaintive and musical and beautiful cry. Finally we managed to catch up with some indri and get a recording of their voices, and this we played back. As soon as the recording died away, we waited and thought, 'No go', and then suddenly from the trees right next to us there rose up this enormous cry which almost vibrates the forest, it is so marvellously loud and rich – and there was this troop of indri sitting almost in our laps, and we hadn't even noticed them. They are marvellous animals with great, fluffy ears that remind me very much of a koala bear's, and these huge, rather maniacal-looking tangerine-coloured eyes stare down at you very fiercely. In fact, they are the most gentle, sweet creatures imaginable. And it's extraordinary how a bulky animal like that can jump through the forest. They just jump from tree to tree like kangaroos, and yet with so little noise. A whole troop can pass you by and the most you may hear is a slight rustle – it's quite extraordinary, the silence of movement.

Gerald was to reflect later: 'It was a privilege to share the world with such an animal. But for how long could we do so? If the forests vanish – and they *are* vanishing – the indri goes with them. The morning before we left, Lee and I walked up the road towards the forest and stood listening to the indris, as the sky turned from green to blue. Their haunting, wonderful, mourning song came to us, plaintive, beautiful and sad. It could have been the very voice of the forest, the very voice of Madagascar lamenting.'

By the end of the first week in May the Madagascar filming was finished and the British Ambassador threw a farewell party for Gerald and the crew which was attended by a number of Malagasy politicians.

During their time in Madagascar Gerald and Lee had had meetings with several Ministers, and had talked with their friend and guardian angel on the island, Professor Roland Albignac, a zoologist working for a French research organisation, about ways of brokering a deal with the Madagascar authorities to enable Western scientists to carry out research and assist in conservation programmes. It was during these discussions that the strategy for what eventually became the crucial Madagascar Conference and Accord, signed in Jersey in 1983, was developed.

In the second week of May Gerald, Lee and most of the film crew returned to Mauritius to film sequences that had been missed first-time round due to time lost at the beginning of the production. Their original director, Michael Maltby, was no longer with them. At Nosy Komba the tension between him and Gerald had become unbearable, and he had been replaced by Alastair Brown. But, after three and a half months on the move, under often arduous and stressful conditions, Gerald's emotional insecurity finally erupted in a most dramatic and unexpected way.

In the first year or two of his marriage to Lee Gerald was always on tenterhooks, afraid some handsome young man would come along and take her away from him. His anxiety reached its most acute stage during the making of *Ark on the Move*, as the series' producer Paula Quigley recalled: 'The film crew consisted of mostly young, presentable, masculine kind of guys. If we went into the forest there would be two or three good-looking young men along with us.' Gerald's jealousy occasionally burst to the surface in full-blown apoplectic rages, and his problems with the original director, were largely due to his groundless suspicions that he had his eyes on Lee. Things reached an astonishing climax one night in Mauritius, as Paula Quigley was to relate:

> We were shooting a special event – a sega dance – out at a special patch of ground. It was night and we'd brought in lights and food and drink, everything to help the thing along, and as the night wore on Gerry was sitting in the middle of it like a great Buddha with everyone around him paying court. Eventually John Hartley had a bright idea to move things along. In Madagascar he had learned a special native dance called a crocodile dance. Why didn't he and Lee do a crocodile dance to keep everyone amused? The director thought this was a good idea, so John and Lee went into the middle, the music started up and they started doing a crocodile dance, jerking themselves across the grass in the press-up position in a series of little jerks – a crocodile mime. There was nothing suggestive about this, there wasn't even any touching, but suddenly

out of nowhere up storms Gerry, roaring with rage, standing there among all those people bellowing his head off, utterly enraged, a deep, seething, volcanic rage from the pits of his being – primordial jealousy incarnate. Well, the music stopped dead, and there was absolute silence, and John was running one way, into the dark of the forest, and Lee was running another way, and Gerry was being led into the shadows, away from the film lights, and the film crew just stood there, totally shell-shocked.

Next morning the crew turned up at the unit hotel at the appointed time, but Gerald didn't show up. Paula went to his room, and found him terribly contrite that he had been so unprofessional as to miss his start time. He was very kind and sweet to the crew after that, but never said anything about the extraordinary events of the night before. But John Hartley wanted Paula to buy him an air ticket home, and eventually Paula told Gerry that he would have to apologise unreservedly to John, which he did, in a most profuse and heartfelt manner.

At the time of the filming of *Ark on the Move*, Paula wouldn't have given good odds on Gerald and Lee's marriage surviving. But after a year or so things began to get easier, and by the time of the next big series Gerald was feeling much more secure about Lee. Paula was also able to head off recurrences of Gerald's outburst, making sure, for example, that he always came out to locations with Lee, and that Lee wasn't left alone with young men.

Gerald and Lee went home to Jersey, where for three weeks they were busy shooting the zoo sequences which opened each episode of the series. Then they were free to spend the summer as they chose. In Jersey Gerald generally tried to steer clear of the island social round, and he had few intimates outside the world of the zoo. He was a naturally shy man, and though his outsize personality and worldwide fame tended to steer him into the company of the rich and the famous, the great and the good, he preferred to mix with them on informal terms, and could only really cope with formal functions with the help of a generous (though discreet) libation or two. There were times, however, when Gerald – a *bon viveur* at heart – entered into the spirit of the big bash or grand do with gusto. His wedding had been one example, and in the summer of 1981 it seemed he planned to continue in that vein.

It began with a visit to the opera at Glyndebourne, one of the finest small opera houses in the world, set in a beautiful mansion and a lovely old garden in the depths of the Sussex countryside. Gerald was determined that Lee should appear looking like a princess. During his travels in India before his marriage he had bought her a quantity of native saris, and in Jersey he found a dressmaker who was able to transform this material into something completely different. 'With her hair up and in this ensemble,' he wrote to Lee's parents, 'she looked like something straight out of Hollywood. I was the envy of every man at Glyndebourne, and there was not a woman there who could touch Lee for either looks or appearance.'

There was something else about Glyndebourne that excited Gerald particularly. Always a great man for seeing like in unlike, he perceived that this opera house was in its way an ideal model for his zoo. 'I was enchanted with the whole thing,' he explained, 'because I have always said that what I want is for this place in Jersey to be small but perfect like Glyndebourne – I am glad that I was not disappointed in my choice of simile.'

The next engagement on the agenda was a garden party at Buckingham Palace – 'one of those intimate little affairs with only about three thousand other guests' – followed by a night out to see Noël Coward's *Present Laughter* in the West End and to meet up backstage with the play's leading lady, the stage and screen star Dinah Sheridan – an encounter all the more jolly for the fact that she and Durrell were each ardent fans of the other. A few days later Gerald and Lee set off for the Mazet on a leisurely, meandering, five-day drive. They aimed to spend three months in their Languedoc retreat, for both needed to unwind, and both had books to write.

Towards the end of 1981 Gerald's new novel, *The Mockery Bird*, was published in Britain, and it came out in the United States a few months later. In some ways the book was a new departure for him – a story with a message for grown-ups, his 'political book' – but its publishing history had caused him considerable aggravation. At the time of his set-to with Collins the previous summer he had complained to his in-laws in Memphis:

> Let me tell you of the thing that almost gave me fourteen coronaries in rapid succession. About ten days ago, I received the page proofs of my new novel (I had not seen galleys) and discovered to my horror that they had passed it over to some awful illiterate little editor who had the audacity to practically rewrite the thing. Snorting wrath I rushed round to my publishers while I was in London and told them they would have to hold up publication on the book. As a result of that, one of the senior members of the firm is flying over here this evening and has been instructed by me to be at the

Zoo at 6 o'clock tomorrow morning; we are going to go through every page of the manuscript and put it back to what it originally was – a mammoth undertaking which I could well do without at the moment – however I can't let such a travesty go out under my name.

Inevitably the book came out late, but at least in a form that conformed with Gerald's sense of authorial integrity.

A cautionary and moralistic tale on a conservational theme, with a few satirical digs at conservationists of the conference-hopping variety thrown in – some of them allegedly thinly disguised real people – *The Mockery Bird* was an ingeniously spun story of events on the mythical island of Zenkali (a fictional version of Mauritius), home of the extinct but revered Mockery Bird and the no less extinct Ombu tree. The hero is a born-again conservationist by the name of Peter Foxglove, who discovers fifteen pairs of Mockery Birds and four hundred Ombu trees all alive and well in a valley scheduled to be flooded as part of a dastardly British plan to turn Zenkali into a military base, complete with a deep-water harbour and hydro-electric dam. Eventually it becomes clear that the economy of the entire island depends on the Mockery Bird, so in alliance with the island's benevolent monarch, Kingy by name, and the genial eccentrics who comprise his court, Foxglove foils the plan and saves the island paradise.

The Mockery Bird was an ingenious and, by Gerald's standards of fiction, relatively ambitious tale, but though it received some good reviews – the *New Yorker* praised it as 'delightful' – it found relatively little favour compared with many of his other books, a reflection perhaps of its troubled genesis.

Gerald meanwhile stumped round the halls on the mainland, drumming up publicity for the book. On 6 December, for example, he gave an after-dinner speech, billed as 'Meet Best-Seller Gerald Durrell', at the Europa Gallery in Sutton. On 9 December he was guest speaker at the London *Evening Standard* Literary Luncheon at the Barbican Centre. His name still pulled the crowds, and there was never an empty seat at these events, and rarely anything but a rapt and appreciative response.

In the New Year of 1982 Gerald sent his end-of-term report to the McGeorges in Memphis. He had been given another conservation award and made an Officer of the Golden Ark by Prince Bernhard of the Netherlands. The reviews of *Ark on the Move* suggested it had gone down very well – 'principally due to the fact that we had a good sex image in Lee, who out-acted even the animals, and that takes some doing' – and the book of the series was going to come out in the States the following year. It had been a busy year, and they couldn't wait to get away 'and relax with a couple of Bloody Marys – or six'.

TWENTY-NINE

The Amateur Naturalist

1982–1984

Gerald Durrell no longer enjoyed an intimate, hands-on relationship with animals on a day-to-day basis as he used to do. He no longer had any pet animals up in his flat, and the animals out in the zoo were in the exclusive care of the staff. The truth was that he was no longer the simple animal man of his youth, but the corporate executive and chief strategist and fund-raiser of an animal preservation society whose business was global. He was also a leading campaigner and evangelist for a cause that was urgent and all-demanding – a cause whose principal tenet was that all life was sacrosanct, that all living forms were of value, that the sanctity of the gift of life was paramount, irrespective of what human politics or religion decreed.

Yet in middle age Gerald retained much of the sense of wonder and enthusiasm of his boyhood, and down at the Mazet, away from his highly professional, ultra-scientific zoo, he was able to indulge his old-fashioned naturalist enthusiasms all over again. 'He loves *all* animals, even wasps, even mosquitoes,' reported journalist Lynn Barber after a visit to Gerald's summer hideaway. 'And, like the small boy that he really is (though cunningly disguised these days as a silver-haired old man) he is never without his private menagerie.' Almost Gerald's only personal association with wildlife these days was the little collection of tiny creatures Lee gathered on a casual basis during their lengthy stays at the Mazet and housed in a motley assortment of dishes and tanks on the terrace – a slow worm, maybe, a scorpion, a praying mantis, a large green bush cricket, a stick insect, wasps saved from drowning in the swimming pool – all of which were let go when they returned to Jersey.

Though Gerald Durrell was one of the world's leading animal conservationists, he remained in a sense an amateur naturalist. Amateur in the sense that (like Darwin and Fabre) he had no professional qualifications

– the average schoolboy visitor to Jersey Zoo was probably better qualified on paper than he, while the Trust's Scientific Advisory Committee could look like a bunch of Aristotles by comparison. And amateur in the sense that in the modern scientific world a naturalist pure and simple could be nothing else, given that the science of biology had moved into utterly new worlds, such as molecular biochemistry and evolutionary biology. As a newspaper in distant New Zealand elegantly put it: 'Durrell's passion for wild things drives his life. He has made nature into his profession, but as a naturalist he is a true amateur: one who does his work for love.'

All things considered, therefore, it was an inspired idea to involve Gerald, with Lee, in a tailor-made project which was to occupy them both for the best part of two years. *The Amateur Naturalist: The Classic Practical Guide to the Natural World* was the brainchild of a young publisher by the name of Joss Pearson, then working for the London-based book-packaging company Dorling Kindersley. The basic plan, evolved early in 1980, was for a lavishly illustrated handbook that would prove essential for the army of amateur naturalists around the world who wished to learn about the best practical ways to pursue their pastime, be it in their own attic or backyard or in the natural habitats beyond. Inherent in the concept from the start was the notion that not only should the book be the best-ever guide to the subject, but the best-selling book of its sort ever. Obviously it was important that such an ambitious enterprise should have a big name attached, and early on it seems that Joss Pearson had Gerald Durrell in mind as the author. He was in many ways an obvious choice: not only was he a best-selling nature writer, but as a boy had been a notable example of the book's ideal target reader – the dedicated young amateur naturalist.

From the outset it was understood that Gerald and Lee would write the book jointly. Both were enthusiastic about the project. Not only did it fall within their areas of expertise, but it allowed Gerald to pursue one of his most passionate concerns – the education of the young around the world in a knowledge of and a respect for all living things and their survival and preservation. Though the initial advance of £30,000 was not over-generous in Gerald's view, the anticipated minimum print run of 160,000 copies (in the end its sales were to be more than ten times greater) was tempting, and the royalty percentage would be the highest ever paid by Dorling Kindersley. In due course there would also be a major television series based on the book, set up initially by a young English director by the name of Jonathan Harris, who would direct six of the programmes and become a close friend of Gerald and Lee.

Joss Pearson had already worked out the book's basic format and design, providing an overall structure in storyboard form to which the Durrells' input had to conform, though it was Lee who decided the order of battle of each individual chapter. The book was to be divided into twelve major ecosystems, ranging from tropical forests to seas and oceans, from meadows and hedgerows to desert and tundra. Within each habitat there would be an account of the flora and fauna of each micro-habitat comprising the whole, together with a number of mini-essays and spreads on the techniques that could be employed by the amateur naturalist in each location, and the recognition and collection of the various creatures inhabiting it.

It was comprehensive, well-informed, hands-on stuff, fired by an underlying sense of wonder and a reverence for life in all its forms. Gerald wrote in the opening section, 'On Becoming a Naturalist':

> Throughout my life it has always astonished me that people can look at an animal or plant and say 'Isn't it loathsome?' or 'Isn't it horrible?' I think that a true naturalist must view everything objectively. No creature is horrible. You may not want to curl up in bed with a rattlesnake or a stinging nettle, and you may find it irritating (as I once did) when giant land snails invade your tent and eat all your food, but these organisms have just as much right in the world as we have ... A naturalist is lucky in two respects. First, he enjoys every bit of the world about him. Second, he can indulge his hobby in any place at any time ... He can be equally moved by the great herds on the African plains or by the earwigs in his back garden.

The work involved in the project was considerable, and it was an enormous help that the Durrells were able to divide the task between themselves – Lee doing much of the research and draft shaping of chapters, Gerald doing most of the writing. Progress was often held up by their many other commitments, not least the filming of *Ark on the Move*, but by 28 January 1982 Gerald was able to report to Alan Thomas: 'Lee and I are at the moment going quite demented trying to finish off *The Amateur Naturalist* book which I think will be really rather splendid when it is finished.' It was frantic work, as Joan Porter, who had taken over as Gerald's secretary and executive secretary to the Trust a few years back, vividly recalled:

> Gerry's writing was diabolical – very scribbly – but I *could* read it. He ended up dictating most of his stuff. So did Lee. Working on *The Amateur Naturalist*, I would take down their dictation and

type it, then they would cut and paste it and I would retype it, working all hours. His books were all dictated during my time, mainly straight from his head. When he dictated his books he would become quicker and quicker as he became involved and excited. Whether he dictated his books to me directly, or sent me a tape to transcribe, I would often find myself laughing my head off at his humour. His previous secretary told me that she sometimes blushed at what she was asked to take down in shorthand and type. Perhaps because I was more mature I was never fazed at what I had to type, although I sometimes thought, 'Cripes, what's the shorthand for *that*?' He never blew his top with me, and I loved him dearly. He was an adorable man. He appreciated effort and kindness in others. I sometimes had bunches of flowers left on my desk, and once, when he had gone off to France, he left a large note stuck on my typewriter saying 'I love you.' But he idolised Lee and certainly never flirted with other women.

By February 1982 the annual fund-raising trip to America was imminent, at the end of which Gerald and Lee planned to spend some time in Memphis before going down to the Mazet. But these plans went badly awry. By the second week of February the big book – 150,000 words in length – was finished, but the struggle to finish it had evidently taken a lot out of Gerald, and on the thirteenth he was suddenly taken seriously ill at the Churchill Hotel in London, on the eve of their departure for the United States. 'I'd seen him with bouts of short intensive depression,' Lee recalled, 'but this was something completely different. He'd been pretty stressed out in the past few weeks but we'd had a few days in London and he seemed OK and was sitting up in bed relaxed watching TV when all of a sudden he went rigid and had terrible convulsions and collapsed unconscious. I had never seen anything like this in my life. I had absolutely no idea what was happening. I thought maybe he was having a heart attack, so I tried to pump his heart, which turned out to be the worst thing I could have done. I called the hotel manager and he came up and peered at Gerry and he didn't know what it was either, so he called the doctor. Then after about twenty minutes Gerry started coming round and he looked up and he saw me and a complete stranger sitting on the edge of the bed and he said to the manager: "Who the hell are you? What are you doing here? Why are you sitting on the bed with my wife?"' Lee had witnessed her first grand mal seizure. Gerry was taken off to the Middlesex Hospital for tests, the American tour was postponed, and on 25 February he and Lee flew out on medical advice for a complete rest in the British

Virgin Islands, where for two or three weeks they stayed on Guana Island, a short walk from the beach and the warm blue waters of the Caribbean

The fact is that Gerald's fund-raising trips to America were utterly terrifying for him, and he tended to suffer various psychosomatic illnesses during the run-up to his departure. Before a later such tour he went down with 'flu and then collapsed into a depressive mess, so that Lee had no alternative but to leave him behind and fly to the States to do the speech-making by herself. 'It may sound surprising, but he was such an unbelievably insecure person,' Simon Hicks recalled. 'He was very contradictory. On the one hand he could be relaxed, laid back, totally cosmopolitan. On the other hand he could make himself ill with worry at the prospect of a formal visit from the Lieutenant-Governor or our royal patron, for example. He hated being unprepared, hated being taken by surprise. He would never make a speech without rehearsing it first, even giving a talk to a bunch of kids screwed him up dreadfully. And it was obvious to all of us in Jersey that the prospect of going to America just made him ill.'

On 2 April Gerald and Lee returned to Jersey, and Gerald reported to Alan Thomas that he was now 'if not completely healed, at least reasonably with it'. He was well enough, at any rate, to accept an invitation to lunch with the Queen at Windsor Castle in honour of the President of the United Republic of Cameroon on 23 April. Gerald thought it was ironic that he and Lee had been invited to such a grand occasion on the basis of a couple of comic books he had written about his adventures hunting for beef in the Cameroons bush when he was a young man who could barely rub two pennies together. But he enjoyed the fare – Avocats Britannia, Pointe de Boeuf Braisée aux Primeurs, Épinards en Branches, Pommes Purées à la Crème, Salade, Chocolate Perfection Pie – and gratefully quaffed as much Zeltinger Sonnenuhr Kabinett and Chambolle Musigny 1969 as he was allowed.

At the end of April Pat Ferns and Paula Quigley came over from Toronto for a pre-production conference about the television series based on *The Amateur Naturalist*, which had excited the interest of CBC in Canada and Channel 4 in Britain. Channel 4 saw the project as a rival to David Attenborough's enormously popular BBC natural history programmes, with Gerald as a different kind of pundit, exploring a more accessible natural world – a genial, spontaneous, boyish uncle figure, who explored the wilderness on his hands and knees, as it were, in a way that the audience could both understand and emulate.

Pat Ferns's plans for the Durrells did not stop at *The Amateur Naturalist*, and in early June there were discussions about a big follow-up series,

Durrell in Russia. Gerald and Lee were now committed to a heavy schedule from the second half of 1982 to the first half of 1984.

On 12 July 1982, a few days after the *Ark on the Move* series began transmission on BBC TV, Gerald and Lee travelled to Unst in the Shetland Islands for the start of filming for *The Amateur Naturalist*. Jonathan Harris – 'dark and somewhat glowering,' Gerald was to recall, 'handsome in a Heathcliffian sort of way' – was directing.

The opening shots proved to be among the most challenging Gerald had ever done. The six-hundred-foot cliffs of Hermaness are the home of one of the great seabird colonies of northern Europe, and the idea was to spend a day filming all the seabird footage for the cliffs and rocky shore programme. The problem was that Gerald had suffered all his life from serious vertigo – flying in an aeroplane always made him panic – and he viewed the filming at Hermaness with considerable trepidation, especially as the script required that he make his way down the cliff from top to bottom. He was to record later:

> Soon we came to the cliff edge. Some six hundred feet below us, the great smooth blue waves shouldered their way in between the rocks in a riot of spray like beds of white chrysanthemum. The air was full of the surge of surf and the cries of thousands upon thousands of seabirds that drifted like a snowstorm along the cliffs. The mind boggled at the numbers. Hundreds and hundreds of gannets, kittiwakes, fulmars, shags, razorbills, gulls, skuas, and tens of thousands of puffins.
>
> 'Now we go down the cliff,' said Jonathan Harris.
>
> 'Where?' I asked.
>
> 'Here,' he said, pointing to the cliff-edge that, as far as I could see, dropped sheer, six hundred feet to the sea below.
>
> There have been many times, in different parts of the world, when I have been scared, but the descent of that cliff was the most terrifying thing I have ever undertaken. The others had strolled along the barely discernible path as if it had been a broad, flat highway and here I was, crawling on my stomach, clutching desperately at bits of grass and small plants, inching my feet along the six-inch-wide path, trying desperately not to look down the almost sheer drop, my arms and legs trembling violently, my body bathed in sweat. It was a thoroughly despicable performance, and I was ashamed of myself, but I could do nothing about it. The fear of height is impossible to cure. When I reached the bottom, my leg muscles were trembling so violently that I had to sit down for

ten minutes before I could walk. I said some harsh things about Jonathan's ancestry and suggested several – unfortunately impracticable – things that he could do to himself.

'Well, you got down here all right,' he said. 'All you've got to worry about now is getting up.'

Afterwards Gerald was to say that that cliff had taken ten years off his life. 'It wasn't much fun when Gerry lost his rag with you,' Jonathan Harris recalled. 'He lost it on that cliff in Shetland. Later on he lost it again when Lee went white-water rafting through the rapids on the River Wye. I did several takes, during which Gerry got very tense, and then I asked for one more take and he went bananas. He was absolutely Vesuvian when he did that.'

But Jonathan had liked Gerald from the moment they met. 'It was the way he came across to me,' he reckoned. 'He wasn't always nice – he could get into terrible moods and say absolutely horrid things about people. But he had a charisma that could transfix a whole room, and though I had a father I suppose there was an element of the father thing. He was terribly proud of Lee, his pretty young wife. He was not a really big number in television – it wasn't really his scene. Not that he didn't care. The impression given by many that Gerry just did television to fund his other work and lifestyle is quite wrong. As a creative person Gerry needed an audience and wanted to perform. And he was delighted to have a new audience for his message about the world in the form of a multitude of television viewers who would never read his books. But the TV pundits didn't rate him a true star performer when I got to know him. For a start, he was terribly unfit. You could only get four hours of work out of him per day on a shoot. He liked to have a break and a siesta – as did the crew – and then begin again when the light got softer at the end of the day. The crucial thing was to get the good animal shots first and then thread in the human shots later. When I grumbled about how uncontrollable the animals were he used to say: "The animals are not under contract." '

In the last week of July Gerald and Lee were back in Jersey with the film crew to shoot the rocky shore sequences for the programme they had begun in the Shetlands. From 9 August to 2 September they were in Zambia, with a diversion for a day or two in Zimbabwe. In Zambia Gerald once again saw hippopotamus in the wild. 'They've got rosy behinds like a bishop,' he was to relate, 'and they get terribly coy and turn their backs on you with those huge behinds. Then they run off on tiptoe like a fat woman in a tight skirt running for a bus. I'd never realised they were so charming.'

On 13 August, during Gerald's absence abroad, his sad, baffled brother Leslie, who called himself a civil engineer but was still working as a janitor in the block of flats at Marble Arch, died of a heart attack in a pub not far from his home in Notting Hill, at the age of sixty-five. None of the family went to his funeral – Gerald was in any case in Zambia, and Margaret (who had sometimes stayed with Leslie and Doris in London) was recovering from an operation. Only his ever-loyal and long-suffering wife, the loud, laughing Doris, and her son Michael Hall, who still lived in Kenya, truly mourned the wayward and luckless Leslie's passing. As for Maria Condos, who had always loved him and who a long time ago had borne his child, she now lived in a world of her own, struck down by advanced Alzheimer's.

After the Durrells got back from Africa in early September they were almost continuously involved in the filming of *The Amateur Naturalist* until early December. In the middle of September they were based in Arles, shooting material for the wetlands programme, *Salt Water Sanctuary*, in the Camargue. During the last week of October they were shooting scenes for the deciduous woodland programme, *A Monarchy of Trees*, in the New Forest. When Gerald went down with gout in early November the desert shoot for the programme *Territory of the Sun* had to be postponed, and the Durrells retreated to Jersey to allow him to recover. Perhaps it was because of faint intimations of mortality that on 1 November 1982 David Niven wrote Gerald a cautionary letter from his home at the Château d'Oex in Vaud, Switzerland: 'One thing I beg you,' he entreated, '*don't* work too hard. I can tell you on the finest authority that if you overstretch the elastic it's bloody hard to get back! PS. How's my hairy godchild?'

By now the book on which the series was based had been published in Britain by Hamish Hamilton. It could have had no sterner critic than Theo Stephanides, who in a sense was its distant progenitor. When Gerald sent him a signed copy, his old mentor, now living in the house of his ex-wife in Kilburn, surrounded as ever by his books and slides, was enthralled. 'A red-letter day!' he wrote back. 'How I wish that I had had such a book when I first came to Corfu in 1907 at the age of eleven.'

It was indeed a splendid book. Published for an international market, and as appropriate for use in the Caribbean as in the Home Counties, it received correspondingly worldwide reviews. 'The beauty of this book,' wrote one Trinidadian reviewer, 'is you don't have to toil up El Tucuche or wade through the Caroni, Nariva and Oropouche swamps or trudge through our tropical forests to study the wealth of wildlife in Trinidad and Tobago ... The reading is easy, often amusing ... The need for us all – young, middle-aged and old – to know more about nature is never more important than now, when man-made bushfires have wreaked more havoc with cane harvests and protective forest cover on our hills.' On the other side of the world, South African radio singled the book out as 'the year's best buy'. Far to the north the *Irish Times* saw it as a perfect remedy for the shameful neglect of native natural history in Irish schools: 'Durrell is a world traveller. He does it with his eyes and ears open, and the book is something of a distillation of his career as a naturalist and conservationist ... *The Amateur Naturalist* will open a whole new world of wonder and delight which will stay with the child as an adult. To give and encourage the gift of wonderment is the greatest gift of all.' Fifteen years later, with over one and half million copies sold and countless millions borrowed, the book has spread this 'greatest gift' around the world.

On 20 November Gerald and Lee arrived in Panama to shoot the reef and rainforest programme, *Tapestry of the Tropics* – the last shoot of the year. No jetlag could quench their happiness at being back in the tropics again, at seeing glittering hummingbirds and butterflies the size of your fist, above all 'to feel the moist, scented hot air, like the smell of plum cake from a newly opened oven, that told you that you were once more in that richest area of the earth's surface'.

This time the director was Alastair Brown, who had worked with Gerald and Lee on *Ark on the Move*. Gerald thought he had probably turned to film as his chosen medium of communication because of the difficulty he had communicating by any other means, for he spoke like a telegram, in a staccato code of unconnected half-sentences.

'Jetlag over?' he said to Gerald when they met again. 'Good. I thought ... you know ... San Blas first. Reefs like ... or perhaps more like ... forests, fish really, like birds only no wings. Don't you think? So islands ... pretty ... you don't ... see when we get there. Then, we know for, er, Barro Colorado, don't we?'

It was up to Paula Quigley, the series producer, to translate. As she had been with *Ark on the Move*, Paula was the linchpin of the production. Gerald called her 'Quiggers', and described her in a thumbnail sketch as 'slender, petite, mop of dark curly hair, snub nose like a Pekinese, curious eyes that can be both blue and green, long eyelashes that can only be equalled by a giraffe, pleasantly feminine soprano speaking voice, but capable of a bellow that came in extremely useful, as we had not budgeted for a megaphone'.

'What Alastair is saying, honey, is this,' Paula explained. 'If we are going to try to compare the forest with the reef, he thinks the reef is going

to be more difficult because it is underwater filming, so he suggests we
go to the San Blas Islands first. OK?'

If Hermaness had been the end of the world, the tiny San Blas Islands
were paradise on earth. Gerald was to write:

> I can never get over the wonder of that moment when you enter
> the water and find your face beneath the diamond-bright surface
> of a tropical sea. The mask is like a magic door and you slide
> effortlessly through a fairyland of unimaginable beauty ... With
> life under the sea you have to learn a whole new language. You
> are constantly asking yourself, why is that fish lying on its side?
> Or standing on its head? What was that one so busily defending
> and why was that one, like some streetwalker, apparently soliciting
> a fish of a different species?

From the San Blas Islands in the Caribbean to Barro Colorado Island
in the Panama Canal was only a short step – but into an utterly different
world. Once again Gerald was back in the dank, vaulted gloom of the
rainforest. 'That lovely, rich fragrant smell of forest enveloped us,' he
wrote, 'the delicate scent of a million flowers, a thousand thousand mushrooms and fruit, the perfume from a quadrillion gently rotting leaves in
the simmering, ever-changing, ever-dying, ever-growing cauldron of the
forest.' He was back in the world of the forest canopy 'as interwoven as
ancient knitting', of toucans with huge 'banana-yellow' beaks, of
hummingbirds flipping among the tiny blossoms of the trees 'like handfuls
of opals', of a morpho butterfly 'like a piece of animated sky the size of
a swallow', of a column of leaf-cutter ants 'like a Lilliputian regatta', of
the buttress roots of the giant trees 'like the flying buttresses of a medieval
cathedral'.

The shoot was not without its adventures. The black howler monkeys,
stoutly defending their patch, set up an almighty roar as the film crew
pitched up – 'like standing in the deep end of an empty swimming pool
listening to the Red Army choir, each member singing a different song in
Outer Mongolian' – and when that didn't work they dropped excreta and
other rubbish on the film-makers' heads. The leaf-cutter ants reacted with
similar outrage when the director and a local hunter attempted to dig
their way into the mushroom beds of an ants' nest the size of a small
ballroom. The ants swarmed up the intruders' legs as if they were trees
and attempted to nip off their private parts as if they were fruits of the
forest.

Gerald made a special plea to camera on behalf of this species-rich
wonderland. The tropical forests were being destroyed at the rate of

forty-three thousand square miles a year, he said. Plant and animal species were becoming extinct before they could even be identified. In about eighty-five years' time there would be no tropical forest left. A great, self-generating storehouse of inestimable benefit to mankind would be lost for ever, and the climate and soil would undergo cataclysmic change. 'We are behaving in a greedy, malicious and totally selfish way,' he told his worldwide audience, 'and this goes for everyone, regardless of colour, creed or political persuasion, for unless we move and move fast our children will never have the chance to see that most fascinating and important biological region of our planet, the tropical forest, or to benefit from it.'

By now the Durrells had been on the move more or less incessantly for the best part of half a year. On 19 December they left Panama for Philadelphia, where they had business to discuss with the Trust's sister organisation, the WPTI, finally coming rest at Lee's parents' home in Memphis for Christmas, where on the stroke of midnight on New Year's Eve champagne corks popped when Gerald officially became an officer of the Order of the British Empire, the honour being awarded for his services to conservation.

By the second week of January 1983 they were back on location, this time in the frozen white Riding Mountains in Manitoba, shooting the coniferous forest programme, *Fire and Ice*. There was a short break in this driving schedule in February which enabled Gerald and Lee to return to Jersey and attend to two major items of business. The first was the signing of a ground-breaking accord with the government of Madagascar. The second was Gerald's investiture at Buckingham Palace.

On 1 and 2 February the Jersey Wildlife Preservation Trust hosted an important meeting to discuss how to aid nature conservation in Madagascar. It was attended by eminent biologists and conservationists from Austria, England, France, Madagascar, Switzerland and the USA, and was chaired by Lee, with Madame Berthe Rakotosamimanana, the Director of Scientific Research in Madagascar, on her right hand. Gerald was greatly impressed by the way his wife handled this major international conference. 'I had never realised, until then,' he wrote to her mother and father on 7 February, 'that I had married a cross between Adolf Hitler and Boadicea. From the outset, she ruled them with a rod of iron and they were as good as gold, accepting with amused resignation that she should boss them about.'

'The crux of the meeting,' Gerald explained, 'was that Madagascar was getting inundated with requests from foreign scientists to work there and all these were ending up on Madame Berthe's desk and she had no way of knowing which ones were good and which ones were not; so for the last seven years she has just been saying "no" to everybody, which has frustrated the scientific world enormously and also was no help to conservation in Madagascar. The idea of this meeting was to try and find a way round this impasse.' This they did. Gerald related:

> This was really a very great triumph for the Trust and for Lee, because all these scientists, plus the WWF, plus the International Union for Conservation of Nature and Natural Resources, had been trying to achieve this for nearly ten years without success, and to do it within twenty-four hours was really miraculous and it showed the amount of hard work and thought that had gone into it. In addition to this, Madame Berthe brought another agreement, which we signed, between the Madagascar government and the Trust here, which allows us carte blanche to go and collect animals from Madagascar and bring them back here to form breeding colonies. Also part of the agreement was that we should train two Malagasy who will come over to us some time during the course of this year. The whole thing was a tremendous *tour de force* and we are all very excited by it.

On 15 February 1983 Gerald received his OBE at Buckingham Palace. He was enormously proud to be given the honour, though always insisting that the real meaning of the initials was 'Other Buggers' Efforts'. 'The OBE is quite a handsome little cross thing, made out of gold,' he reported to his Memphis in-laws, 'so when Lee and I get hard up, we can always sell it ... I was the only OBE to get press coverage.'

It was Gerald's understanding that the next item on the agenda was lunch with Lord Craigton, an influential Trustee of the Jersey Trust, and his wife. He was therefore surprised to find so many other guests waiting on the pavement outside the restaurant, among them Eamonn Andrews, the compere of the popular television programme *This is Your Life* – on which, as Gerald described it to Lee's parents, 'a steady stream of people that you have not seen for ninety years' pounce on you from behind a screen. Instead of the slap-up meal he had been expecting, he was whisked away to a secret room in the BBC studios, where he was kept in purdah from the other guests and fed on sandwiches and champagne.

Then the show started, before a large audience. The first people to appear from behind the screen were Gerald's secretary Joan Porter, Catha Weller, Jeremy Mallinson, Simon Hicks, Shep Mallett and Betty Boizard. Brian Bell had been flown over from New Zealand, and Wahab Owadally and Yousoof Mungroo from Mauritius. An interview had been shot with

Larry, who could not come as he had a commitment to make another film. Also present were Gerald's kindergarten teacher, Miss Squires ('at the age of eighty-seven looking as though she would outlive us all'), Mai Zetterling, Dinah Sheridan, Sir Peter Scott, Margaret and her son. There was even a film clip of Theodore Stephanides, who was apparently too unwell to attend the show.

Or so it seemed. Gerald was thunderstruck when suddenly the real Theo stepped gingerly on to the set – frail and elderly, but as impeccably turned-out and as sharp-witted as ever, and beaming hugely. This was the reunion to end all reunions. Master and pupil embraced as only two old friends whose friendship went back nearly half a century could, knowing that it might be for the last time – as indeed it was. Then Gerald seized Theo's hand and led him forward towards the camera, raised the old man's hand and lifted it high above his head in a gesture of salutation, triumph and love.

Then it was back to *The Amateur Naturalist*. For the next six months Gerald and Lee were on the road, moving from one continent and habitat to another – in March the Umfolzi reserve in South Africa, for the grass-land shoot; in April the Sonora Desert in Arizona, for the desert shoot; in May New York City ('one of the most squalid, repulsive, dirty, beautiful and exciting of cities') to film the wildlife of city dump, cemetery, vacant lot, backstreet eat-house, slum, golf course and apartment block for the city programme; then in England and Wales for the wettest June ever, location shooting for the pond, river and hedgerow programmes, criss-crossing back and forth to catch a patch of sun; then to Corfu for the garden programme, *Matchbox Menagerie*; followed by Canada for the whole of July and August and into September, working on post-production in Toronto and shooting the mountain and remaining conifer-ous sequences in Banff and the Riding Mountains.

'Shooting *The Amateur Naturalist* was very demanding,' Paula Quigley recalled, 'but I think for Gerry it was in general a very happy eighteen-month period (and I should know because I had to supply the scotch!). We had excellent and easy-to-live-with film crews. Gerry knew that he personally was being made to look good and that the animal footage was first rate. Gerry also knew that, for the first time, Lee was being treated seriously (in *Ark on the Move* she was used as window-dressing) and that we were helping to establish her credibility and own identity as a Durrell. And I think he knew he would get a helluva book out of it.'

Perhaps there was no happier period in the whole year's filming than that spent on Corfu – Gerald's first visit to the island since his catastrophic breakdown in 1968. 'Gerry was quite, quite wonderful in Corfu and did, literally, relive his childhood,' Paula Quigley recalled. Many of the sequences were filmed in and around the Snow-White Villa at Pérama, no longer white, but damp-stained, cracking and decayed, on the terrace of which Gerald, at ease with himself and the camera, did a beautiful piece about the joys of being an amateur naturalist. Further afield he caught terrapins in his favourite pond, caught lizards in his favourite olive grove, sailed in a caïque down his favourite coastline, explained how to start a mealworm farm, studied the denizens of a drop of puddle water through the old brass microscope he had used on Corfu as a boy, and sung the praises of a wild, uncultivated garden like the Snow-White Villa's, rich in hidden life.

Wherever he went on the island he was greeted like the wanderer returned. 'People fell all over him,' Paula recalled. 'People he knew from years and years ago. They were so excited to see him back. It was incredible. I hadn't realised how many people directly related their own prosperity to Gerry's book. They really did believe he had brought them a livelihood they had never had before. One day we all went to a celebratory lunch in an out-of-town restaurant given in Gerry's honour by a Corfiot family he had known for years. Afterwards we went for a stroll among the houses and suddenly a man of around Gerry's age stepped out from behind a house and came forward very reluctantly, obviously concerned that Gerry wouldn't recognise him. But Gerry did – they were old boyhood friends – and they hugged each other and chatted away in Greek, and the man was so thrilled to have been recognised and so thrilled to be with Gerry again – it was really very, very touching.'

Gerald and Lee had covered half the world to make the series, travelling forty-nine thousand miles by every means available to the ingenuity of man. In England alone they had flown a hot-air balloon, paddled a rowing boat (sinking up to its gunnels under the combined weight of talent and crew), pedalled a bicycle made for two, ridden a steam train and walked on water on a snowshoe-like affair devised by 'some imbecile inventor'. ('If successful,' Gerald quipped, 'I intend to change my middle name from Malcolm to Oliver by deed poll, so that my initials will more closely resemble my activities and abilities.') At the end of it all they had made a wonderful series which looked at life on earth through the unusual perspective of the eyes of an amateur naturalist – or a child.

One chance encounter in a New York backstreet with that most dangerous and unpredictable species the New Yorker set them back on their heels. Gerald's description of this encounter, besides being an example of his comic writing at its best, is an unnerving examination of the validity of what they had been about all this time.

To show how quickly nature could claim back even a part of a big city when the chance arose, the crew had chosen to film on a rubble-covered, dogshit-plastered vacant lot on the corner of traffic-bound West 87th Street. They had brought along some live specimens of the tent caterpillar, a major pest in America but, as Gerald put it, 'really quite fascinating, in the same way as human beings are'. As they were lovingly arranging the caterpillars on the branches of a deformed cherry tree that struggled for existence in the middle of this urban wasteland, they noticed that a local inhabitant was watching their activities open-mouthed.

'What are youse all doing?' asked the woman, shifting her bulk uneasily in her tight pants and denim jacket.

'We're making a film about wildlife in a city,' said Paula. 'We want to show how even in the depths of a city like New York nature can still be found.'

'Is that what them bugs is for?'

'Yes,' said Paula kindly. 'They're called tent caterpillars.'

'They don't live here, though,' said the woman. 'You brung 'em.'

'Well, yes. You see, there weren't any here, so we had to bring them for the film,' said Paula, slightly flustered by now.

'If there were none here, why did you brung 'em?'

'For the film,' snapped Alastair Brown, who was trying to concentrate on whether he wanted the caterpillars to walk from right to left or from left to right.

'But that's faking,' said the woman, arousing herself out of her lethargy. 'You brung 'em here, and they don't live here. That's faking. You brung them bugs here deliberate.'

'Of course we brung them here,' said Alastair irritatedly. 'If we had not brung them, there wouldn't be any for us to film.'

'That's faking,' said the woman. 'That's not true.'

'Do you realise, madam,' Gerald intervened in the role of peacemaker, 'that 90 per cent of films you see on wildlife, like Walt Disney, are faked? The whole process of filming is in a sense a fake.'

'Walt Disney doesn't fake,' said the woman belligerently. 'Walt Disney is an American. What youse is doing is faking, and faking on our lot.'

'We have permission from the Mayor's office,' said Paula.

'Have you got permission from *the 87th Street Block Association*?' asked the woman, swelling as a turkey to a gobble.

Other locals from the 87th Street Block Association joined in the general outrage. No more faking nature on their lot, they cried. And no more funny bugs. The light in the meantime began to fade, and the crew were forced to abandon the shoot and lock the caterpillars up in the unit van. 'Frustrating and annoying though this was,' Gerald was to write, 'the incident had a certain charm. It was nice to feel that in that giant, brash, apparently uncaring city there were people willing to take up cudgels about a vacant lot covered with dog droppings.'

In the midst of all this, Theo Stephanides, who had played such a critical part in putting the boy Gerald on the path he was to follow when he became a man, died peacefully in his sleep on 13 April 1983, at the age of eighty-seven. Gerald broke the news to his brother Larry: 'Theodore is dead – another dinosaur extinct. He died peacefully. He left a letter for the matron of the hospital saying he wanted his eyes and any other bits of his body used for scientific research, but with a p.s. to ask if they would make *quite* sure if he was dead before they did. So he ends not on a bang or a whimper but a Victorian joke.'

Alan Thomas spoke for them all when he wrote to Gerald on 19 April:

What an irreplaceable gap this is going to leave in our lives. I knew him for almost fifty years. The breadth of his mind, his interests and experiences was greater than that of any other man I know. If we had guests in the house, learned professors would ask him about esoteric aspects of classical learning, simple workmen would listen spellbound while he talked about the moon. But it wasn't only what he knew, but what he was. He had come to maturity, in Corfu, before 1914. He was the perfect embodiment of a classical culture developed in a sane, leisured and peaceful world, such as we shall never see again, and we are fortunate indeed to have experienced it through Theo. And then there was his gentle kindness, his sense of humour, his humility. He was humble in the way that truly remarkable characters sometimes are. As for you, Gerry, I can hardly comprehend what this loss will mean to you. Comfort yourself that you have immortalised Theo. That people all over the world will know Theo through your books. And people as yet unborn will know him.

In memory of the most important man in his life Gerald opened a special fund in his memory at Jersey. Donations to 'Theo's Fund' would be used to plant a grove of trees in the grounds of the Trust, and to contribute towards the education of children in the identification, character and relationships of wild organisms. Gerald also dedicated his new book, *The Amateur Naturalist*, to the man who had showed him the way: 'my mentor and friend, without whose guidance I would have achieved nothing'. Lee for her part dedicated the book to her grandfather, a similar kind of mentor, who had encouraged her early interest in wildlife, 'especially by building palatial homes for my animals'.

On 9 September there was a pre-transmission screening of *The Amateur Naturalist* in London. The reception was enthusiastic. 'I think you've got an absolutely super series,' television distributor Richard Price wrote to Gerald and Lee. 'Both of you come over very well indeed, and I think it is one of the best examples I have seen of an entertaining but highly educative documentary. I am sure it is going to rate well on both sides of the Atlantic.' It was destined to do even better than that, selling to stations in over forty countries and reaching 150 million viewers.

In Britain *The Amateur Naturalist* started broadcasting on Channel 4 on 23 September 1983. Like the book on which it was based, the series was greeted with almost universally glowing reviews in the world's press. '*The Amateur Naturalist* exudes from every frame that most beguiling of qualities – a childlike sense of wonder,' declared the *Toronto Globe and Mail* in Canada. 'Throughout, this series unobtrusively but firmly sets its face against prejudice: that against snakes, flies, spiders, rats – and women,' wrote the *Times Educational Supplement*. Jonathan Harris was commended for his direction and the 'strong whiff of locality' he had created. 'As performers the Durrells have class,' said the *Sunday Telegraph*. 'Gerald Durrell is now the doyen of television naturalists,' agreed the *Guardian*.

Pat Ferns wanted Gerald and Lee to embark on their third thirteen-part international television series, *Durrell in Russia*, as soon as possible after *The Amateur Naturalist*. The basic concept was simple. Gerald and Lee would fulfil a long-cherished dream of studying at first hand the work being done to protect and breed endangered animals in regions as far apart as the wastes of the Soviet Arctic and the deserts of Soviet Central Asia.

But though the concept was simple, its execution was not. The practical difficulties of filming in the Soviet wilderness meant there would be little opportunity to set out with a thesis and search for the most effective way of presenting this on film. They would have to make the most of what came their way. 'I believe it is an *adventure*,' Pat Ferns told Gerald in January 1984. 'It is an event, and the role of the director is to cover this event: its successes, its failures, its frustrations and its revelations. I see very little on-camera prepared scripting during its shooting. Thus for you as presenter the focus of your efforts will be much more in the post-production phase, particularly in the production of an effective narration script. So essentially, we are not making a natural history program, but the reason for making the program at all *is* natural history, and especially your concerns regarding conservation and the natural world.'

On 15 March John Hartley and the proposed series director Jonathan Harris (who had now married Paula Quigley) set off on a fortnight's pre-production visit to the USSR. They found much enthusiasm from the Russians they met, and it was clear that the name of Durrell could provide access that few others had obtained in the past. But a viewing of Soviet natural history films in Moscow revealed that the country's nature cameramen were much inferior to their British counterparts, both as to technique and to ethics – one sequence, showing a tethered goat being devoured alive by wolves, nauseated the British contingent. So poor was the quality of the Russian material that it was obvious the production would have to bring its own camera crew.

Jonathan Harris, though, would not be with them. He argued with Pat Ferns that interference from Soviet bureaucracy was likely to be so pervasive, and the whole project was so underfunded, that there was no guarantee that the series would be of the standard of *The Amateur Naturalist*. 'Over a somewhat difficult evening of high emotion,' Ferns recalled, 'I eventually asked Harris and Hartley to leave so I could pitch Gerry and Lee alone on the value of the Russia series. Fortunately I won the day, and was back in Moscow in July to negotiate our deal. I think the trip through the Soviet Union was one of the most remarkable expeditions in Gerry's life, and despite his health problems he was able to witness a part of the world he had never hoped to visit.' Another Canadian director, Paul Lang, was assigned in Harris's place.

Underfunding was not likely to be Gerald and Lee's problem, for Ferns had offered them a fee of Canadian $350,000 for the series. The books and big television series that they were making through the first half of the eighties were beginning to make them seriously well-heeled. 'Gerry had been sidelined for a long time in television terms,' Paula Quigley was to relate. 'Till Pat Ferns came along he hadn't been on television since the old black and white days, other than on chat shows to promote his books. But now he had a big series on every year, and this made a sizeable difference to his profile and to the growing reputation of Jersey Zoo and Trust. It also created a real role for Lee, which was very important for her. Lee was very attractive on camera and, to be frank, she worked her butt off to do it well, and so she and Gerald were seen as a team, and that made a big difference to their relationship and to her being taken seriously in her own right. And of course Gerry earned a hell of a lot of money out of these series. This was very important, because he'd been relatively poor quite long enough up to then. The money enabled them to develop the Mazet and it put him on the road non-stop, with someone else footing the bill, so that he was able to come back with a tremendous amount of material for his next book.'

1984 marked a double celebration – the twenty-first birthday of the Jersey Wildlife Preservation Trust and the twenty-fifth anniversary of the founding of the zoo, a combined Coming of Age and Silver Jubilee. There was much to celebrate, for the Trust had made enormous progress in the last few years, and had attained many objectives which Gerald had never thought to see in his lifetime. For a start, it had proved that a zoo can and should be a vital cog in the conservation machine, especially through captive breeding. As well as its work in Jersey, the Trust was now establishing captive breeding units in many countries, training foreign nationals and conducting field studies at every stage. By the end of 1984 they hoped to have released Jersey-bred Mauritian pink pigeons back into the wild – their first reintroduction, and an event of great significance.

To mark these anniversaries and achievements there would have to be a great celebration, beginning with Princess Anne opening the Trust's International Training Centre at Les Noyers, and culminating in a dazzling tribute to the animal kingdom on whose behalf they all laboured – a Festival of Animals. On the great day there would be an official opening in the morning, an anniversary lunch, a reception and supper for the Trust's patron, Princess Anne, and finally, the *pièce de résistance*, the Festival itself. During the preceding days there would be special events at the zoo and across the island. There would be a pets' day at the zoo, a mothers' (and grannies') day, an art exhibition, a special programme on Channel TV and an anniversary thanksgiving. A commemorative postage stamp would be issued, as would a wildlife lager from a local brewery. There would be a fund-raising appeal, and anniversary merchandise would include granite dodos, pink pigeon trays and table mats, and wildlife decanter and tumbler sets.

Nobody at the Trust or the zoo had ever planned anything quite so ambitious before, and the bulk of the complex and intricate planning fell on the shoulders of Simon Hicks, the Trust Secretary. Gerald was deeply involved in working out the original concept and persuading the Princess Royal to take part. All the details had to be planned many months ahead. This caused a few problems, as Gerald reported to Hal and Harriet McGeorge:

When we shipped the bare bones of this plan across to the Palace, we had a slightly worried secretary on the phone immediately, saying that no members of the Royal Family ever planned anything further than six months ahead, and she was not at all sure that Princess Anne would want to stay the night, but she thought that probably the sensible thing to do was for us to come across and discuss it with HRH. So we polished our shoes and washed our hair and trotted along dutifully to Buck House. Her secretary ushered us into a room which was arranged as a drawing room but with a big and – I was glad to see – very untidy desk in one corner. HRH greeted us, whisked us over to the chairs and sofa and sat us down. There was nobody else present. We spent over an hour with her and although, having met her before, I had formed a very good opinion of her, I was doubly enchanted this time because she displayed such a nice sense of humour and also a mind as sharp as a razor. She not only agreed to everything that we proposed but actually made some suggestions of her own. For example, she pointed out that on the great day we would want her bright and early, so she thought she ought to come the evening of the day before.

Of the great day itself, 5 October, Gerald reported:

Princess Anne arrived looking very good and officially opened Les Noyers, our New Training Centre, and then met various members of the staff, various members of the American board (many of whom had put up money for the development of the Training Centre), and a selection of students. The Princess then drove round from Les Noyers to the big main gates of the zoo and down into the courtyard, where there was a whole mass of people clapping like mad things. Lee and I had to rush out of Les Noyers as soon as she had left, leap into Jeremy's car and be whisked down the back way, so that we could be standing at the Manor front door when the Rolls arrived.

The first stop on the patron's tour of the zoo was the gorilla complex. Gerald and the Princess were blissfully unaware of the turmoil that was going on inside this haven of primate well-being as they strode purposefully towards it. Four minutes before the royal visitor was due to arrive, a young gorilla called Motaba chose, with split-second timing, to get his head stuck in the bars at the top of his cage, and commenced to wail and scream. Observing their youngster's plight, his devoted parents Jambo and Nandi began to wail and scream as well. Jambo's first idea was to release the distraught Motaba by pulling downward on his legs; then, realising that this solution would speedily result in a headless young gorilla, he wisely decided to support him by his bottom instead. The gorillas' keeper Richard Johnstone-Scott could see the umbrellas of the royal party bobbing their way towards the complex, the floor of which had now been turned into a manure heap, as the gorillas, in their agitation, voided an immense quantity of excrement and urine on to the floor. When Gerald learned of this dire crisis later, he wondered how he would have explained it to the Princess.

' "Oh, yes," I would have said, "we always keep our gorillas knee-deep in excrement, they seem to prefer it. And that little chap in there dangling from the bars like a hanged man on a gibbet? Well, gorillas frequently do this. It's a sort of . . . sort of *habit* they have. Yes, very curious indeed." '

Suddenly, however, the young gorilla managed to find a point in the cage roof where the bars were wide enough for him to extract his head, and he was thus able to descend just as Gerald and the Princess arrived. But there was nothing that could be done about the manure heap.

'All went well and the tour was a great success,' Gerald was to report. 'We kept it as absolutely informal as possible and it was obvious that Anne appreciated this. She then zoomed off in the Royal car and we had about twenty-five minutes to change clothes, brush our hair, wash our hands and rush down to the anniversary luncheon that was put on at the Hôtel de France in St. Helier. This was a luncheon for over 600 people (Trust members from all over the world, local dignitaries, etc.). Again, cutting formality to the absolute minimum, I got up at the end of the lunch and made a short, incoherent speech. Then our Patron rose to her feet and proceeded, in spite of my blushes, to heap praise upon my head.'

Today was the celebration of a unique man and a unique institution, the Princess said. He had pursued his dream, in Jersey and around the world, with determination, charm and, above all, humour. She wanted to congratulate everyone involved in their efforts to fulfil that dream – 'a dream that can now be said to have been wholly realised and established as a vital part of the preservation of wildlife everywhere.' In particular she wished to congratulate the man who had made the zoo and the Trust admired and respected worldwide. 'As a token of that gratitude,' she concluded, 'I would very much like to present him with a little gift from his zoo staff.'

The Princess handed Gerald a little velvet bag. Inside the bag was a silver matchbox, and inside the matchbox was a gilt mother scorpion and a lot of little gilt baby scorpions – a reminder of a famous incident in *My Family and Other Animals*. 'I was so amazed and touched by this gesture from my illiterate, unworthy and flint-hearted staff,' Gerald reported, 'that when I sat down I leant across Princess Anne and said to our Chair-

man, who was sitting next to her, "What silly bugger thought this up?"
I then realised that she was regarding me slightly wall-eyed and had
assumed that the remark had been addressed to her. "I do apologise,
Your Royal Highness," I said. "That's quite all right," she said, "I don't
understand French." But later on she apparently said to the Governor,
"Do you know what? The bloody man swore at me."'

That evening the Festival of Animals was enacted in the great auditorium of Fort Regent in St Helier. All afternoon the performers – the
famed, the professional, the amateur, the infantile – had been rehearsing
their parts. Now they were ready. Gerald came on stage to open the
proceedings, accompanied by Simon Hicks's twin daughters, aged four
and a half, dressed as dodos. 'Your Royal Highness, ladies and gentlemen,'
he began:

> Welcome to the Festival of Animals. As you will see, I am accom-
> panied by two fledgling dodos; alas, not a breeding pair. But it is
> an interesting thought that when the dodo, the symbol of our
> organisation, was discovered on the island of Mauritius, birds were
> taken to both India and Europe, and had there been an organisation
> like the Jersey Wildlife Preservation Trust in existence in those
> days, we would still have the dodo with us. What we are going to
> do tonight is show you how the other animals that share our planet
> with us have influenced us in an enormous number of different
> ways. We want to celebrate the fact that we are sharing the world
> with such marvellous and fascinating creatures.

The show was meant to last for two hours, but went on for three.
Nobody noticed – they were entranced throughout, spectators and performers alike. Children from the island's primary schools opened the
programme with a jolly rendering of a song dedicated to Jersey Zoo
entitled 'Don't Let them do what they did to the Dodo'. The Royal Ballet
School followed with the 'Chicken Dance', The Jersey Children's Music
Theatre and Jersey Musicians performed a jazz oratorio based on a story
by A.A. Milne, Johnny Morris, Isla St Clair, Michael Hordern, Dinah
Sheridan, wildlife artist David Shepherd, David Bellamy and David Attenborough did their bit by depicting animals in art, music, literature, film,
humour and nature, the Moving Picture Mime Show did a rendering of
'Creatures from the Swamp', and Yehudi Menuhin performed with the
Jersey Youth Orchestra.

The show was brought to a fragile and pensive end with Elizabeth
Perry's rendering of Vaughan Williams' *The Lark Ascending*, the violin
birdsong hovering tremulously on the edge of sight and sound, leaving

only a silence in the hushed auditorium. As the applause faded, the sound of a skylark echoed round the vast concert hall.

Dreamed up by Gerald and set up by Simon Hicks, the Trust had put on a show in their small island town that was worthy of London's West End or South Bank. 'Princess Anne reiterated several times to me that she had enjoyed the whole thing enormously,' Gerald related proudly to his in-laws. Many of the hundreds of guests at these events sent Gerald their heartfelt thanks. 'The warmth and love that came over last night was unforgettable,' wrote David Shepherd. 'Just wonderful, wonderful and *totally* deserved. God help wildlife without people like you, you old bugger. Bless you.' Gerald's old friend Alan Thomas wrote: 'Apart from your brother and sister, I don't think there is anyone who has watched your career so warmly and for so long as I have. I was in a perfect position to watch you and Princess Anne at lunch. I saw you both at perfect ease, she laughing at your jokes. At one moment you caught my eye and half raised your glass in an expression of friendship which I returned. Does it sound ham when I tell you that over these two days I often had a lump in my throat and a tear or two in my eyes, rejoicing in your triumph. What happiness it has been to watch your continued achievement. Long may it continue.'

The great celebration ended on 11 October with a Wildlife Thanksgiving Service given by the Dean of Jersey. This was a more solemn and reflective occasion. In spite of the jollification of the past days, all were aware that the natural kingdom had been celebrated in the midst of an animal holocaust. Gerald read an extract from the powerful and prophetic 1854 address attributed to the native American Chief Seattle, about to lose his people's land to the white man. Dear to Gerald's heart and desperately relevant to his mission, the long-dead chief's words, a last cry of pain and admonition from the desert, almost burned in the air. Now, 130 years later, their truth was even more demonstrable, even more a battle hymn for all those who were fighting in the same cause around the world. Chief Seattle had seen a thousand rotting buffaloes on the prairie, he said, left by the white man who had casually shot them from a passing train:

Perhaps it is because I am a savage that I do not understand.

What is man without the beasts? If all the beasts were gone, men would die from a great loneliness of spirit. For whatever happens to the beasts soon happens to man. All things are connected.

Teach your children what we have taught our children, that

the earth is our mother. Whatever befalls the earth befalls the sons of the earth. If men spit upon the ground, they spit upon themselves.

This we know. The earth does not belong to man; man belongs to the earth. This we know. All things are connected like the blood which unites one family. All things are connected.

Whatever befalls the earth befalls the sons of the earth. Man did not weave the web of life; he is merely a strand in it. Whatever he does to the web he does to himself.

When the last red man has vanished from this earth, and his memory is only the shadow of a cloud moving across the prairie, these shores and forests will still hold the spirits of my people. For they love this earth as the newborn loves its mother's heartbeat.

So if we sell you our land, love it as we've loved it. Care for it as we've cared for it. Hold in your mind the memory of the land as it is when you take it. And with all your strength, with all your mind, with all your heart, preserve it for your children, and love it . . . as God loves us all.

One thing we know. Our God is the same God. This earth is precious to Him. Even the white man cannot be exempt from the common destiny. We may be brothers after all. We shall see.

Gerald's voice, slow, soft, measured, vibrant with emotion, died away. He turned, sombre-faced, and left the podium.

Three days later he was heading east towards a vast land that covered a sixth of the surface of the planet. How precious was the earth to the widely scattered peoples of the USSR? he wondered. And would *they* turn out to be brothers after all?

THIRTY

To Russia with Lee

1984–1985

The Soviet Union was *terra incognita* for Gerald Durrell. Within its plethora of natural regions lived a host of wild creatures that were little known and little seen in the outside world, and the rarer forms of the nation's wildlife were the subject of dedicated and often spectacularly successful conservation programmes, some of them dating from as far back as the Revolution.

Besides its sheer physical scale, the USSR in 1984 presented formidable challenges to travellers from the West, particularly travellers who proposed to nose around the country's remoter and obscurer parts. The Soviet Union was still a rival (and mostly hostile) superpower, a monolithic totalitarian police state. Yet, as Gerald was to find out, behind the country's paper-thin Communist mask there lived a mass of humanity that was warm, welcoming, yearning, curiously innocent and reassuringly perverse – a people who by and large took after Gerald's own heart, and whose instinctive camaraderie was underpinned by an alcohol culture as ancient as Mother Russia herself.

On 22 October 1984 Gerald and Lee set off for Moscow, accompanied by John Hartley and a film crew of six. The plan was a complex one. Though both the television series and the book based upon it would give the impression of a single epic journey during which the party would clock up a total of 150,000 miles, in fact they planned to make three separate expeditions over a period of a little under six months, following a complicated itinerary dictated by the complicated illogic of a shooting schedule that was in turn at the mercy of the seasons and of Soviet bureaucracy. Throughout this long perambulation their purpose remained constant – to observe at first hand the work being done to protect and breed species in danger of extinction.

The first stop was the Soviet capital. 'Moscow was damp, dreary, drizzly and dismal,' Gerald reported to the McGeorges in Memphis, 'and did nothing to raise our spirits. One of the things I discovered in Russia to my astonishment, was that I am a sort of cult figure, and everybody appears to have read my books.' This became more apparent when he went to visit the Kremlin. When the policeman on duty discovered who Gerald was, he danced with delight and insisted on shaking his hand, excitedly declaring what a great fan he was. Improbably, he was also the favourite author of Russia's future military supremo General Lebed.

Gerald and Lee's first task was to take a look at one of the most successful captive breeding programmes ever carried out in the Soviet Union. For Gerald the story of the European bison (or wisent) was a benchmark example of how a species can be rescued from extinction by captive breeding. At one time this magnificent animal could be found throughout the forests of Europe and Russia, but hunting and habitat destruction gradually caused its numbers to dwindle, until by the beginning of the twentieth century the only wild bison left were in the Bialowieza forest in eastern Poland and in the foothills of the Caucasus mountains in Georgia. During the havoc of the First World War and the hunger years that followed the survivors were hunted out, until the only European bison in existence were a few individuals kept in zoos. In the 1920s a Frankfurt-based society was formed for their protection and breeding, and by the 1950s their numbers had been built up sufficiently for a small herd to be released into the Bialowieza forest. By 1984 a breeding centre had been established outside Moscow with the aim of reintroducing the bison into the southern parts of its former range.

Gerald's first port of call in the Soviet Union was this breeding centre, at Priokso-Terrasny – a five-hundred-acre range set aside for the bison inside a twelve-thousand-acre nature reserve. Here seventy bison were kept as breeding stock, and the offspring were transported to the Caucasus or the Carpathians when they were two years old, joining other two-year-olds from other breeding stations in the Soviet Union, and released in small herds in the late summer. As a result of this intensive programme, a model of its kind, there were by this time around a thousand bison living wild in the Soviet mountains. Gerald was fascinated by the breeding station, a specialist counterpart of his own establishment in Jersey, but was even keener to see the reintroduced herds in the Caucasus. So after a few days they flew to the resort town of Sochi on the Black Sea coast, and from there, on 28 October, they were flown to the Kafkaz Reserve in the mountains by helicopter.

It was a magnificent flight at low level, over autumn forests, bare heights streaked with snow and great, glittering snowfields. At first it seemed they were out of luck, with not a bison to be seen in the whole of that autumnal wilderness, but as they juddered noisily across a huge hillside patched with snow, they saw them – thirty or so massive animal shapes at full gallop. The pilot landed the helicopter immediately, and Gerald and the others tumbled out and set off in pursuit. But the snow was knee-deep, and soon they were gasping and panting in the thin air, while the bison swept up the hillside, as Gerald put it, 'like woolly express trains'.

The next morning, after a large, vodka-lubricated dinner in their freezing stone-built base in the mountains they set off again, this time by jeep. It grew very cold as they climbed higher, the leaves edged with ice, the snow falling in hard icy flakes that in the intense silence pattered loudly among the trees. They moved on, ever upwards, through the rhododendron zone to where the snowfield lay surrounded by amphitheatres of craggy rock. This was the kingdom of the tur, the chamois and the snow grouse. The tur were there – they could see them silhouetted against the snow. Then the clouds began to well up and they beat a retreat through the snow flurries and banks of cloud like freezing smoke.

Gerald and Lee spent the next evening at the home of the local forester and his wife at Psluch. The stay made a big impression on Gerald. Doing such a job in such an out-of-the-way place, this attractive couple, ex-actors who had lit out from the big city for a life in the backwoods, seemed to have slipped through the interstices of the all-enveloping Soviet state, living a life that was seemingly free and time-hallowed. 'After usual food by camp fire and toasts (endless),' Gerald scribbled in his diary, 'we were whisked off to Victor's and Natasha's place. MAGNIFICENT. Two tiny rooms crammed with possessions: bundles of herbs, pictures printed by Victor's son, photographs of their animal pets (chamois, bear, etc.) and endless books and manuscripts. We were put to bed in such love and comfort.' Next morning Natasha had a splendid Caucasian breakfast ready for them – fresh milk warm from the cow, two types of soured cream like yoghurt (one sour, one sweet), goat cheese, cakes, freshly baked scones, fresh walnuts and tiny wild pears in syrup, and endless tea made from the great-grandmother's huge and resplendent silver-plated samovar.

'The Caucasus are absolutely fascinating and the Georgian people were marvellous, kind and warm-hearted and generous,' Gerald wrote to his parents-in-law. 'They are very like the Greeks in many ways and go in for endless toasts in vodka and much kissing. I think I must have kissed more male Russians in three weeks than Oscar Wilde did in his whole career. They also, for some reason, kept kissing Lee, which led me to suppose that a Communist regime needs very careful watching.'

He had reservations about the Soviet Union in general, however, as he reported to the McGeorges after he and Lee had returned to Jersey at the end of their first trip in the middle of November: 'All I can say is that we are suffering from a sort of love/hate relationship with the Soviet Union at the moment. We saw much that we loved and were enchanted by. We also saw much that we did not care for. I think on balance probably our feelings are that it is a pity that so many nice people are subjected to a system that I personally would not want to live under, and this is made worse by the fact that one has the shrewd suspicion that they know it but cannot confess it.'

In the spring of 1985 they were back, and on 10 April Gerald reported to the McGeorges from Moscow:

Arrived here in one piece (with ninety two bits of baggage) and spent two days in this city, which is not my favourite place on earth. As we had appeared on national TV three days before, we were recognised by *everybody*. We had several good meals (strange for Moscow) and in general, enjoyed this God-awful city more than we had before. Then we had to take an overnight train to Cheripovets and from thence to the Darvinsky Reserve some 120 kms away. At the station in Moscow we were seen off by Nick Drosdov who is a very handsome, sweet and kindly TV star. He thoughtfully brought six little glasses in filigree holders and a vast quantity of brandy with which to fill them. The result was that our sleeping compartment (strictly non-smoking) was soon filled with smoke and loud singing and the clash of glasses, to the despair of our tea lady. The tea lady, I must explain, is found in every Russian railway compartment, and her job is to make tea for you at all hours of the day and night, switch the lights on and off, likewise the radio (which has the Red Army Choir singing stirring songs about the production of tractors) and tell you not to smoke in the compartment. Most of our tea ladies have had to be taken away in ambulances for a rest cure after travelling with us. Can you imagine – 10 of us (mostly foreign) drunk to the eyeballs, and singing and shouting, drinking and smoking, and, what is far, far worse *Disobeying the Rules*. At last ten people left our compartment and the train left Moscow. We drank a little more (for purely medicinal reasons) and went to bed. Comfy night. Dawn brought the tea lady, hollow eyed, with tea and a nervous smile. We were feeling a bit hollow-cheeked ourselves.

Arrived at a station (twelve below zero) with elegant buildings that looked as though they had been designed by Nash in 1780. All painted in pale green with cream coloured facings. Quite lovely and unexpected. Needless to say, all the rest of the town – post Revolution – was ugly beyond belief. Met at the station by the Director of the Darvinsky Reserve, eight jeeps, lorry and a police car. Were escorted out of town, police car in the lead, blue light flashing, siren shouting, forcing all the vulgar peasants into the ditch so we could pass, roaring through red traffic lights. Drove for seven hours over a road that had to be seen to be believed – the thaw had set in, the snow was melting and the road was like chocolate pudding with bumps.

Arrived at the reserve (a village of about fifty people) in the evening. Greeted by lady carrying red embroidered shawl on which was loaf of home made brown bread (round) and on top of it a small bowl of salt. Custom was you break a bit of bread, dip it into salt, give to Lee to eat and then do same for self. We were then taken to our own cottage, two rooms and a hall, heated by a huge stove built into the dividing wall. The lavatory (a two holer) was about a hundred yards away through the snow. Water was brought to us in a bucket from the well. An example of how cold it was, I took the lid off the bucket, filled the kettle, went into the bedroom to wake Madam and by the time I got back there was a film of ice on the bucket.

Gerald never did finish that letter, nor post it. Darvinsky, deep in the forested heart of Old Russia, was the beginning of a punishing schedule in which the Durrells criss-crossed the length and breadth of the Soviet Union in various directions and by various means (jet plane, river boat, skidoo, dromedary, helicopter, train, swampboat, horse and carriage, jeep and shank's pony), pitchforked from summer to winter and back again on an itinerary that defied time zones and latitudes, and stood the seasons on their heads.

The Darvinsky Reserve had been established on the shores of a huge man-made lake to monitor ecological change and to breed capercaillies to restock forests where the bird had been shot out. It was far enough north for the water in your bucket to freeze, but not far enough to ensure that the hibernating bear you had come all this way to film didn't wake up and stroll off the moment you arrived, leaving only its footprints as evidence of its existence. As Gerald was to write: 'Darvinsky, though a fascinating place, was not one of our more successful shoots.'

On 8 April they departed for the Oka Reserve, some three hundred miles south-west of Moscow, a major breeding centre for cranes – seven of the world's fourteen species were represented here, five of them endangered – and also notable for its bird of prey collection and for the great annual rescue of all the animals that had been marooned in the floods of the spring thaw – hares, badgers, racoon dogs, foxes and the rare and cuddly desman, a sort of large aquatic mole, half-shrew, half-vole – whole boatloads of damp, bedraggled and ungrateful creatures ferried to higher ground and then released. On 19 April they made a giant leap to eastern Siberia and the Barguzin Reserve on the still-frozen shores of Lake Baikal, the biggest and deepest body of fresh water in the world, seventeen hours and five time zones from Moscow, and conservation home of the rare and precious sable (bred back from near extinction) and the extraordinary freshwater Baikal seal (once almost hunted out, now strictly protected and back to some seventy-five thousand in number).*

On 2 May there was another giant bound, west-south-west through more time zones, from icy Baikal into the frying pan of the Repetek Reserve, in the scorching Karakum Desert of Turkmenistan in Soviet Central Asia. The shade temperature was 114° though it was still only late spring, and the best way to travel around the desert dunes was by dromedary, a footsure but stealthy approach that gave the travellers an unusual vantage point from which to spy out the vast variety of wildlife that inhabited this hostile place.

From Repetek it was, by Soviet standards, a mere stone's throw of a few hundred miles or so to the ancient and legendary Uzbek city of Bukhara and the nearby desert breeding centre for the elegantly fashioned but inelegantly named goitred gazelle, whose salvation represented another triumph of captive breeding. When the species became extinct in the wild it was realised that a number of individual animals had been kept as pets, and a press and television campaign was mounted to persuade their owners to donate them to a new breeding centre that had been set aside in the desert. Within a short time some fifty goitred gazelle had been gathered, and at the time of Gerald's visit their numbers had risen to more than six hundred. A number of mature animals had been released into the wild, and others had been sent to other breeding centres, and would be used eventually to restock the rest of their original range. Gerald was enchanted by the young fawns that had thus been rescued from eternal oblivion: 'The youngsters were charming little creatures, with coats the colour of butterscotch, huge brilliant dark eyes, and large ears like fur-covered arum lilies. They were completely fearless and either sat in

* By 1998 the Baikal seal was once again an endangered species.

our laps sucking our fingers or else wobbled around us on their long, lanky legs.'

Almost due east of Bukhara lay Samarkand, known to Alexander the Great and Genghis Khan, final resting place of mighty Tamburlaine, staging post of Marco Polo. Gerald was bowled over by the place, by the blue domes of the mosques, by the cavalcade of national costumes in the streets, and by the great market, the trading entrepôt of the whole region, where the young women looked Tibetan, the old women had 'breasts and buttocks like watermelons', and the old men were as 'lean and brown as biltong and had grey beards like Spanish moss'.

From Samarkand the party travelled into the high Tien Shan Mountains, bordered by India, China and Afghanistan. There, in a small cross-section of high mountain habitats called the Chatkal Reserve, Gerald explored an exquisite Shangri La:

> We struck the foothills of the Tien-Shan Mountains and the scenery was unbelievably beautiful. In every direction the knife-edged hills coiled like snakes, green and yellow, their flanks striped with snow. Gradually we dropped lower and lower, chasing our own shadow as it whisked over the snowfields, until we were flying down valleys with the mountains towering above us, the lower slopes shaggy with pine forests interspersed with wild apple trees heavy with blossom and great sheets of yellow flowers that looked like mustard fields. Finally we landed in a tiny valley that was ablaze with colour. The slopes were covered with the yellow flowers we had seen from the air. Amongst it grew wild rhubarb, with dark green, plate-shaped leaves and rose-pink stems, banks of red and yellow tulips, and throughout the valley groves of apple in a froth of pink and white blossom. The sun was brilliantly warm, the sky as blue as a hedge sparrow's egg and the air cool and fresh. We decided that this was the most beautiful place we had so far visited in the Soviet Union.

Very probably no other Westerners had ever been to this remote and ineffably lovely spot, home to some 1400 species of plants, many of them very rare, and a wide variety of butterflies, as well as spectacular birds like the huge griffon vulture and rare animals like Menzbieri's marmot and the Siberian ibex. A welcoming party consisting of the reserve director and his helpers – 'a cheerful group of unkempt ruffians with dark Mongolian faces and glittering black eyes' – was there to greet the travellers.

> They shouldered our bags and equipment and strode off through the wild apple orchards, with toast-brown fritillaries, black

admirals and bronze dragonflies wheeling about their legs as they threaded their way through the tulips and fennel.

Our accommodation was a tiny house nestling in apple trees on the banks of a small busy river, ice cold, clear as glass, sliding down its bed of amber-coloured rocks in a great series of silver ringlets. Its endless chatter day and night was as soothing as a beehive.

Lee and I went for a walk down the valley, along the banks of the stream. There was nothing but the murmur of water and bird-song and the cool, clear air was full of the scent of apple blossom. The great piles of blossom had attracted hosts of bee flies – russet-red, furry as teddy bears, with glittering wings. The trees were full of birds – woodpeckers tapping away like carpenters, jays flashing blue and pink as they flew, shrikes, tree sparrows and a flock of red-fronted serins, the first I had ever seen.

As evening drew on and the shadows slid into the valley, muting the flower colours, it became very chilly and we piled on all the clothes we possessed and huddled round the fire, glad of the warmth we could extract from the director's stock of Georgian brandy. While he had been sleeping, his band of merry men had been up the valley and returned with their hats full of field mush-rooms, each as big as a doll's parasol, fleshy and fragrant. These were added to the *pilov* they were constructing in an enormous battered frying pan. When it was served it proved to be delicious, and when we were stuffed to capacity we tumbled into our sheep-skin sleeping bags.

On 22 May the Durrells left Moscow for a brief rest in Jersey. On 5 June they returned for the third and final stage of their filming adventures. The plan was to visit some of the major wildlife reserves in the vicinity of the two great inland seas in the south of the country, the Caspian and the Black Sea, and on 7 June they arrived in the city of Astrakhan, their gateway to the great Astrakhan Reserve, occupying a large portion of the Volga delta where it debouches into the Caspian.

The Astrakhan Reserve was founded on the orders of Lenin in 1918 – the first reserve in the Soviet Union and still one of the biggest, with a seaward edge of some 125 miles and more than eight hundred river channels threading their way through the reed beds, wet meadows and willow thickets. The reserve is of immense biological importance, particu-larly as a haven for waterfowl, which flock there to breed or moult or overwinter in prodigious numbers, estimated to exceed ten million, including five to seven million geese and duck alone in spring and autumn. However, the main task of the reserve workers is to study and monitor the delta's ecology.

As Gerald discovered, the relationship between the cormorant, the crow and the catfish neatly illustrates the complex ecosystem of the delta. The cormorant, a highly abundant and intensely enthusiastic fishing bird, might be expected to deplete the delta's stock of fish, but as it flies over the waters its droppings keep them rich in the microscopic plants and animals on which baby fish live. The crow, meanwhile, feeds itself by harassing baby cormorants during their parents' absence from the nest and forcing them to disgorge their food, which the crows then snatch. But a portion of this food habitually falls into the water, and into the waiting jaws of the huge catfish, seven feet long and with heads like mastiffs, which in turn excrete waste that is rich in nitrogen and phosphorous nutrients. Because of the huge numbers of cormorants in the area, nutrients which would ordinarily take eight years to be cycled through the delta only take two to three.

Even on the main river, the Volga, the birds were abundant, but when Gerald's convoy of two huge, luxuriously appointed barges turned down a narrow tributary they became absolutely prolific. 'The air was thick with them.' he wrote. 'After travelling several miles through this bewildering ornithological firework display, we eventually came to the reserve headquarters in a nicely laid out tiny village, where we were given a little house to live in, set in a watery meadow full of frogs calling like petulant small children. We settled in and for the next three days had one of the most wonderful times I have had in my life, for not only was the reserve marvellously beautiful, but it was also so rich in all forms of life, overflowing with such an abundance that we were hard pressed at times to know what to look at.'

To explore the intricate network of waterways around their base, the travellers took to a fleet of small boats, using the motors to reach where they wanted to be, then drifting in silence on the current through a labyrinthine dawn of creation: gulls, terns, swallows, hawks, night herons and glossy ibis, spoonbills and little egrets, cormorant colonies and lotus beds, dragonflies and damselflies, wild boar and frogs and catfish: the air was one big blur, the sounds one big cacophony. This was the world as it had once been, and as Gerald fervently dreamed it would one day be again.

But Astrakhan was not just wildness and wet. Away from the riverine delta, in the neighbouring Kalmyk Republic, stretched a desiccated terrain known as dry steppe, the home of one of the strangest of cloven-hoofed mammals, the saiga – half-antelope, half-goat – which Gerald had long hoped to see. This was not easily arranged. The saiga lived far out in the dry steppe, and to reach them took five hours on the river and seven hours over hot and bumpy dirt roads. 'The sky was purple and green,' Gerald recalled, 'the sun like a fire opal, when we suddenly saw, silhouetted against it, a huge herd of saiga grazing placidly, their hooves kicking up little whirlwinds of dust as they moved. They had curiously heavy heads that looked almost too big for their bodies because of their ridiculous bulbous noses, but their horns were delicate and pale yellow like tallow. They were a magnificent sight as they moved slowly across the steppe with the coloured sky and the sinking sun as a backdrop, the young giving strange, harsh, rattling bleats to be answered in deeper tones by their mothers.'

Gerald may well have marvelled, for the story of the saiga is one of the great conservation miracles of the century. In the early years of this century they had been virtually gunned out of existence, and teetered on the very edge of extinction. Then hunting saiga was banned and they began to recover. By the time Gerald and his party set off across the steppe to see them their numbers had increased to over a million, 170,000 of them in Kalmyk alone.*

They drove on. Ahead they could see a cluster of twinkling lights. A local television company had erected a kind of mini-village for them in the middle of nowhere – a travellers' rest in the dry steppe. There was a well-appointed kitchen, an enormous tent for the crew to sleep in, two gigantic *kabitkas*, or yurts, covered with wool felt and floored with gaily woven blankets and mats – one to serve as a dining room, the other as Gerald and Lee's bedroom-cum-living-room – with separate showers and toilets, electric lighting inside and out, and the expedition's transport, consisting of a bus, three lorries, two jeeps, an ambulance and a large biplane, drawn up in neat line abreast behind the kitchen. That evening there was a lavish meal and entertainment provided by two Kalmyk dancing girls in national costume. No wonder Gerald felt compelled to write, when the time came to say goodbye: 'We were sorry to leave: sorry to leave our romantic and comfortable *kabitka*. How wonderful for the saiga to live in this scented world, to eat and move on a carpet of aromas no chemist could reproduce in any test tube and to lie at night on a sweet-smelling bed of flowers.'

Their journey now led them on a clockwise course which would take them out of the arid far south into the no less arid far north, from the oven to the fridge. Late on 16 June they arrived at Askaniya Nova in the

---

* By 1998 the saiga had again become a threatened species.

Ukraine, among the Soviet Union's best-known reserves, preserving one of the last areas of untouched steppe in the world and operating an internationally renowned centre for the breeding and cross-breeding of endangered animals and a unique acclimatisation programme for exotic animals such as elands, llamas, bantengs and zebras. A week later the travellers were in the sixty-year-old Berezina Reserve in White Russia, famous for its protected beavers (six hundred now in residence, a further thousand having been sent to stock other reserves) and wondrous for its profusion of woodland and meadow flowers.

On 8 July they flew off to the Soviet Arctic, passing through four time zones before reaching the land of the midnight sun. The Taimyr Peninsula, which reached 750 miles north of the Arctic Circle and ended less than a thousand miles from the North Pole, was tundra country, flat to the edge of vision, bleak, uninhabited – 'as remote as the moon', Gerald noted. 'You could not tell whether it was midday or midnight.' There were two specific target areas in this vast stretch of wet sponge, the Bikada River Reserve and the Lake Lagada Reserve. Flying in by helicopter from Khatanga, the nearest town, Gerald looked down in amazement at a landscape quite unlike any he had ever set eyes on before. The flat green-gold land was spattered with thousands of lakes and ponds of every conceivable size and shape, and in some areas the winter ice had pushed up the spongy cover of the tundra to form ridges that looked like ancient fields made by some long-vanished polar race of man. Though it was midsummer there were patches of unmelted snow everywhere.

Eventually they landed at a huddle of huts beside a swiftly flowing river, the Bikada, where they were allocated a small three-roomed house. The everlasting light was as unsettling to sleeping patterns as jetlag, but Lee solved the problem by tying a sock round her head. Outside, everything was on a miniature scale, the flowers so tiny you had to crouch down to see them, the trees only knee- or ankle-high. Through this low-level, high-latitude jungle ran the narrow highways of the lemmings, the larder-on-legs of the tundra's population of predators – the hawks, owls and Arctic foxes. The outstanding exception to the miniature scale of this bare green land was the animal they had come mainly to see – the stocky, shaggy, lumbering musk ox.

The story of the return of the musk ox to the Arctic wilds of the USSR is an unusual one, for the creature's extinction was not brought about by twentieth-century man, though its reintroduction was. The musk ox died out in most of Siberia some ten thousand years ago, and vanished from its last stronghold in the Taimyr around three thousand years ago. In the 1930s the Soviet authorities attempted to bring this long-gone animal back home, so to speak, by importing a few specimens from Greenland, but the scheme was interrupted by the outbreak of the war. In the early 1970s the Canadian and American governments sent sixty musk-ox from their own native stocks to Russia as a gift. Half of these animals were sent to Wrangel Island in the Polar Sea, and half to the two-million-acre reserve in the Taimyr. Here they prospered, and at the time of Gerald's visit numbered over a hundred head, though the target figure for the region was ten thousand. The best way to find them was by helicopter.

'Below us we saw the musk ox herd,' Gerald wrote. 'The oxen galloped before us, shaggy as old hearth rugs, with pale muzzles and curved horns looking like the bleached branches you find washed up on remote shore-lines. As they galloped, their cream-coloured stumpy legs thumped the bare ground between the moss patches and raised a miniature dust storm.' As the helicopter landed, the Siberian husky on board, which was known to have a way with musk ox, leapt out and gave chase, quickly overtaking them and running round and round the herd, barking wildly. 'The musk ox then indulged in the classic musk ox manoeuvre. They formed a circle, babies in the middle, all adults with their fearsome horns pointing outward in a bristling and intimidating barrier.' Whenever the dog got too close the leading bull of the herd would break the circle and charge, head down. 'After much head-tossing and irritated snorting the bull would return to the circle. It was an impressive sight to see these powerful animals standing shoulder to shoulder in a circle ... It would take a very brave predator to try and broach the circle to get at the young ones within.'

All this provided wonderful material for the film crew, which was just as well, for by now morale was sagging badly. It was difficult enough to shoot a thirteen-part television series at the best of times, doubly so in a country as vast and cantankerous as the Soviet Union in its declining days, and doubly doubly so when the subject-matter of the series is the rare and elusive wildlife of some of the earth's remotest and roughest wild places. After such a long and arduous – albeit privileged and wondrous – slog from one end of the USSR to another, everyone was exhausted, and tempers were frayed. The Taimyr weather didn't help. Lee's diary turned into a litany of bad days: 'Still bad weather ... Very windy and cloudy, so no filming ... Morning cold and windy ... Everyone upset ... Bad weather again, so sit around ...' At Lake Lagada the river was so low the boats got stuck, the helicopter was called away on an emergency, the wildlife was grumpy and unco-operative, the weather closed down again, the booze ran out, and Gerald blew up and stormed out of the mess tent. There were, though, a few prize moments at the end – a helicopter flight over a five-hundred-strong herd of reindeer, a forest of moving antlers; a rare sighting of a pair of red breasted geese, the world's most beautiful waterfowl. Lee's last diary entries wrapped it all up:

19 July. Chopper comes and goes on reserve business, then returns with a 2 metre, 60 kilogram mammoth tusk. Banquet put on by reserve people in mess tent – much toasting and flowing vodka – Gerry and I presented with a baby mammoth tusk and tooth. Gerry to bed and I stay up – am given a beautiful mammoth leg bone. I get terribly drunk and Gerry furious at me.

20 July. Sleep till 11 and have terrible hangover. We shoot Yury in his pitfall traps and Gerry does a piece on lemmings. I go back to sleep before packing for 1600 departure. Chopper is late.
This ends this diary!

On the plane back to London, cured for all time of any lingering taste for vodka and reindeer meat, Gerald and Lee reflected on the immense journey they had just completed, during which they had visited twenty reserves scattered across a great swathe of the planet, and shot over thirty miles of film footage. 'The conservation work being done in the Soviet Union had impressed us greatly,' Gerald was to write of the situation as it was a few years before the break-up of the old USSR. 'They give it an importance that few other countries in the world can boast, and though it is not perfect (no conservationist is ever satisfied), it is still of very high standard. The nature reserves are numerous and enormous, and each that we saw seemed to be impeccably run by charming and devoted people with deep interests in their jobs. All in all it was a magnificent and fascinating trip.'

By 13 August, barely three weeks after their return from the Soviet Union, Gerald and Lee had finished the final section of the book about their travels there. Gerald seemed to have undergone a slight change of heart about his enlightening but gruelling Soviet experience. He had half a mind, he told Lee, to write a sequel to *How to Shoot an Amateur Naturalist*. He thought of calling it 'How to Shoot the Russians – A Steppe in the Right Direction'.

THIRTY-ONE

Grand Old Man

1985–1991

Gerald Durrell was now sixty. Half a century had passed since he had first been let loose on Corfu as a boy and explored the wonders of the island's natural world under the thoughtful eye of his friend and mentor Theo Stephanides. He had come a long way since then. Though those who knew him believed that his real age – in terms of his undimmed sense of wonder, youthful enthusiasm and effervescent sense of humour – was more like fourteen going on twenty-one, to the world at large he was now indubitably a Grand Old Man, a genial though sometimes apocalyptic prophet and guru with flowing white hair and beard, and a household name around the world.

His recent sequence of major television series had brought him to the attention of an even bigger international audience than his books, while in Britain his already large readership was increasing by leaps and bounds: before long he would enter the ranks of the ten most-borrowed non-fiction authors from public libraries around the country. Much of this was due to the perennial popularity of *My Family and Other Animals*, a permanent best-seller and now a set book in schools as well, albeit in a primly sanitised edition (to the disgust of some juvenile readers, one of whom wrote to the author to protest at 'the silly man who has cut out all the rude words like breasts, bust, udder, knickers, Widdle, Puke and bloody boy'). As a result, Gerald's material circumstances had undergone a transformation. His *net* annual income was to average around the £100,000 mark for virtually the remainder of his life. The revolution in his personal and professional fortunes was matched by the resurrection in his private life, for with Lee he had achieved a happiness that had long eluded him.

The rise and rise of Gerald Durrell the man was mirrored by his apotheosis in the world of conservation. The zoo he had started, which now had an animal population of more than 1200 and a human staff of over forty, was in the top league. 'If you ask people which is the best zoo in the world,' the Director of Dallas Zoo and former President of the American Association of Zoological Parks was to declare, 'some say San Diego, some say Bronx. But if you ask zoo people themselves, people professionally involved with zoos, including zoo directors, they say Jersey Zoo.'

The Trust Gerald had founded, after years of struggle for recognition and funds, was now world renowned and a powerful force in conservation. Long a pioneer in the technique of captive breeding, it was now a model of its kind. In 1983 more than half of the animals, most of them rare, had produced young, an extraordinary record, while the International Training Centre was unique, spreading the method and the word across countries from China to Brazil, Mexico to Nigeria. Following the 1983 accord with the government of Madagascar, a second was signed with Mauritius in 1985, and similar agreements were to follow with the governments of India, Brazil, various countries of the Caribbean and elsewhere.

At the same time a sister Trust, the Wildlife Preservation Trust Canada, came into being to help finance survival programmes for endangered species. Gerald's gratification at this was balanced by his increasing concern at the course being taken by the equivalent organisation south of the border, the Wildlife Preservation Trust International. American tax laws made it difficult to channel US funds to Jersey, so increasingly the WPTI was initiating and operating projects of its own. Though the Americans were undoubtedly doing tremendous work for the cause in general, as Jersey readily acknowledged, it was not how Gerald had envisaged the progress of the organisation, and the gradual parting of the ways was a source of great sadness to him.

Vision undimmed, plans unlimited, it seemed Gerald Durrell was destined to carry on the fight against the extermination of species into the twenty-first century. But as time went by he began to grow increasingly despondent – though increasingly defiant – at the state of the world. 'The zoo has been enormously successful,' he told a visiting reporter in the mid-1980s, 'but not successful enough in the sense that it is such slow progress. You have to grope around for money and persuade governments and every year you read more horrible reports of what is being done to the world around us. The world is being destroyed at the speed of an Exocet and we are riding about on a bicycle. I feel despair twenty-four hours a day at the way we are treating the world and what we are piling up for ourselves. But you have to keep fighting, or what are we on earth for? I believe so much in what I am doing that I cannot let up.' In

1987, almost as a personal crusade, Gerald joined David Attenborough to spearhead a campaign to reverse the decline in the numbers of barn owls caused by changing methods of agriculture. In 1989 he lent his name in support of the work of a new trust, the Programme for Belize, specifically set up to buy and protect tropical forest. 'With Durrell's name involved,' recalled John Burton, the trust's director, '*Today* newspaper donated £25,000. All over the world there are projects doing things that, if it were not for Durrell's involvement, might still be just an item on the agenda of the next meeting.'

As the head of a biological institution of international esteem, Gerald Durrell was on an equal footing with the directors of heavyweight organisations such as the New York Zoo, the San Diego Zoo, the National Zoo in Washington, DC, and the Zoological Society of London. He was even sought out by kings and queens. In November 1984, shortly after he had got back from his first foray to the Soviet Union, he wrote to the McGeorges: 'King Olav [of Norway] came to visit us the moment we got back from Russia. Ever since I married your daughter, I appear to have got more and more inextricably entangled with royalty. I will remember this King, since he giggled all the time. *You* try spending three and a half hours with a giggling King, and at the end of it you are a shadow of your former self.' And in late March 1985 Fleur Cowles invited him to her flat in London to have dinner with the Queen Mother, whom he delighted with his stories and cartoons of the animals in his life.

Such royal contacts made it all the more puzzling that Gerald's achievements never received the accolade of a knighthood. Several representations were made on his behalf, but nothing came of them. Various theories have been put forward – that Gerald was blackballed in the London establishment by Lord Zuckerman, that he had upset a key player with one of his less temperate diatribes, that knighthoods are strictly rationed for non-UK residents – but nothing certain is known. In any case, the work went on just the same without it.

Anyone who knew Gerald in those days was struck by the impression he gave of ceaseless bustle and endeavour on all fronts – conservational, zoological, televisual, authorial, social, familial, personal – a focus of worldwide response and support at every level, from presidents and royals to children and the lonely and ailing. He was everywhere an inspiration, who over many decades had fired countless individuals to devote their lives to the cause. Among his own group he was always the master, the leader, the visionary, the light.

Though Gerald's concern was overwhelmingly for the plight of animal life, he was also aware of the desperate condition of the deprived mass of humankind. 'One should regard the poor and downtrodden of the earth with humility and compassion,' he jotted in a notebook, 'for if the rest of us, with all our privileges and advantages, find it difficult to cope with life, just think what courage and endurance they must have to survive.' People wrote to him from everywhere – Japan, Eastern Europe, Kazakstan, Cameroon, Somerset, Texas – for many, many reasons: to commune with him, to ask favours, to suggest projects, to query strategies and technicalities, to say thank you, to wish well – young and old alike, the obscure and the famous (among them Yehudi Menuhin, Spike Milligan, Lady Bird Johnson, Sam Peckinpah, Stanley Kubrick, Desmond Morris, John Cleese, Dirk Bogarde, Edward Heath, Margaret Thatcher, Prince Rainier of Monaco, Frederick Forsyth and many more).

Attaining such heights had been far from effortless, of course, and for several years it had been literally painful, for Gerald's arthritic hips made it agonising simply to get about, and he now walked with the help of a stick. He had borne this crippling, sometimes excruciating, condition with fortitude, and his rugged forays into the USSR had tested him to the utmost. In February 1986 he underwent an operation for a replacement hip, and duly regaled his in-laws with the details:

My room was pleasant enough, one window showing a fine view of a church and churchyard and the other a tall, mysterious brick chimney that belched forth oily black smoke at intervals in the most suggestive and macabre way. After the eleventh nurse had asked me which hip I was having done my faith in British medicine struck rock bottom. I protested loud and long until my surgeon was forced to visit me with a huge magic-marker to put a cross on my left hip. Then I was given a scalding hot iodine bath that made me smell like any well-run mortuary and then they wheeled me away to the theatre. I took a surreptitious look under my night-gown to make sure my magic-marker cross had not got washed off. We arrived, and the anaesthetist gave me a massive injection which mercifully obliterated everything. I woke after about five seconds, to instant awareness, no sickness, no pain in the hip and a pretty nurse with dimples exhorting me to breathe in oxygen through a dinky little plastic mask. On enquiring when they were going to stop messing about and get on with the operation, I was informed that I had had it. So, free from pain and euphoric as a firework, I recanted. With tears pouring down my cheeks, I blessed the medical profession. I blessed the nurses. I told them that I would build a new wing to the hospital as soon as my wife's new book is published. I even tried to kiss Matron. After a struggle they sedated me . . .

Well, the great day came when I had my first walk – two steps to the door and two steps back to the bed, where I lay feeling as though I had climbed Everest without oxygen. But pretty soon I got better at it and was soon zooming up and down the corridors like a drunken bat. Then they said I could go home and Lee came to fetch me. All the nurses wept and kissed me. I gave them all copies of my books. The night nurses were not on duty, which enabled me to inscribe their books: 'In memory of the wonderful nights we spent together.'

Gerald's morale was raised even further when he received word that the Association for the Promotion of Humour in International Affairs in Paris had awarded him the Noble Prize, an annual accolade accorded to humorist writers.

Within a few weeks things really began to look up when *Durrell in Russia* began its run on Channel 4 on 13 April to favourable reviews, coinciding with the publication of the handsomely illustrated book of the series, written jointly by Gerald and Lee, which reached the top ten best-selling list of non-fiction hardbacks in Britain. Then on 19 April Gerald's old colleague and mentor Sir Peter Scott opened the latest facility at the zoo, the Nubel Bird Propagation Centre, another stage in the unending modernisation and improvement of Jersey's facilities. By now Lee had begun work on an ambitious book of her own – *State of the Ark: An Atlas of Conservation in Action* – a comprehensive overview of the conservation situation around the world, commissioned and researched by the IUCN. Gerald reported to her parents on 21 April:

> Your daughter, of course, is busy being an authoress up in the attic and gets up at seven in the morning and only appears for meals. I am seriously thinking of suing for divorce, but I understand from my lawyer that a computer cannot be cited as co-respondent. Of course, in addition to having to worry about the extermination of wildlife all over the world, I have to do all the cooking and try and entertain my sister, who is staying with us and shows absolutely no sign of ever leaving. So you can see my lot is not a happy one. However, I can now walk without a stick.

That summer Gerald, Lee, Margaret, Lee's sister Hat, Simon Hicks and his wife and three young daughters all headed off to Corfu. Though Gerald had become disenchanted with what he saw as the reckless spoliation of Corfu by uncontrolled tourist development, and had vowed he would never go back there 'except in a coffin', he still couldn't quite keep away from the place, still yearned for the distilled essence of the old magic of his island childhood. 'The most precious moment in my whole life,' he told Simon Hicks, 'was waking up one morning in Corfu when I was a boy. Everything was perfect – the sun, the insects, the colours, the lot. Just simple things. The most wonderful, beautiful things in life are the simple things which we have all forgotten.' They had rented an old converted olive press on the beach at Barbati, which had been one of Gerald's favourite picnic spots in earlier years, and from there they would sally forth, usually by boat. 'He didn't want to see the vast new hotels that they'd erected on that lovely and once pristine coast,' Simon Hicks recalled. 'So we'd warn him when they were coming up, and he'd sit and look the other way, out across the water towards Albania, and we'd tell him when we'd gone past and he'd turn round and look at Corfu, the lovely olive hills he remembered so well, the bright little horse-shoe bays. One night when the others had gone to bed we sat outside at the olive press and settled into the whisky. There was a most glorious full moon shining on the water and a great breathless silence across the sea, and I asked him: "Is it terribly depressing coming back?" And he looked out at this magical scene and thought a bit and then he said, looking up at the moon: "Well, *that* doesn't change."'

By December 1986 Gerald was confined to a wheelchair, his unoperated-on right hip giving him 'Hell with a capital H'. The weeks that followed were 'fairly horrific', he was to complain. Much of the time was spent in London recording the commentary for yet another thirteen-part television series, *Ourselves and Other Animals*, an exploration of the relationship between man and animals, scheduled for transmission in the coming spring. Like Gerald's previous big documentary series – *The Stationary Ark*, *Ark on the Move*, *The Amateur Naturalist* and *Durrell in Russia* – it was being made by Pat Ferns' Primedia Productions. Unlike its predecessors, however, it was largely based on archive footage, although Gerald and Lee were required to shoot several live-action sequences (including one in the Canaries and one with Lee covered in tarantulas), to top and tail the series to camera and to read the voice-over narration.

The series was not essentially Gerald's – he was just the vehicle for it – but it elicited a warm response from his many fans, including Spike Milligan, who wrote: 'What is very good about it is showing the human race as being the drawback in any environmental progress. Everyone who makes a programme like yours should shout out that there are too many people in the world and they are getting manyer.'

Pat Ferns hoped that Gerald's next series would be set in China, but sadly the plan never came to anything. They did do one more programme together, however, a one-hour special on Gerald's work entitled *Durrell's Ark*, co-produced with the BBC. Incorporating archive footage, some special shooting at Jersey, sequences from the previous series and a filmed interview with Princess Anne, the show was presented at a fund-raising gala at the Calgary Zoo on Valentine's Day 1988 during the Calgary Winter Olympics.

The programme would mark the end of the long, extraordinarily rich working relationship between Pat Ferns and Gerald and Lee. Now, and for some while to come, Gerald's main preoccupation was to be the battle for his own body. In mid-January 1987 he underwent a second operation, this time for the replacement of his right hip. 'The operation was successful,' Gerald reported to his in-laws on 12 February, 'but much more painful than the other one because the joint had been in worse condition. However, I made rapid progress and was soon able to pinch the bottoms of the more attractive nurses.'

Gerald's morale rose higher still when he was handed a telex from the Academy of Natural Sciences of Philadelphia informing him that he had been awarded the prestigious Richard Hooper Day Medal, 'in recognition of your many contributions to natural history research and wildlife conservation'. So in fine fettle Gerald was discharged from hospital, as he reported to his wife's parents: 'Wedged in a wheelchair, I was wheeled out of the King Edward VII Hospital between rows of cheering nurses. I will draw a veil over the scene at Southampton Airport. My wheelchair was backed into a freezing corner and all attention was fixed on Patterson [Lee's pet Mexican red-kneed tarantula]. His passport was examined minutely by a bevy of heavy-breathing customs officers, his finger-prints were taken and his birth certificate examined. Finally we were allowed on board and everyone was so interested in Patterson that they did not even notice that now both my hips sounded like Middle Eastern gunmen as they went through airport security. Patterson did not need a drink during the flight, but I did . . .'

Gerald had always known that his powers, either as an individual or as the head of a single organisation dedicated to saving animals from extinction, were strictly limited. It might be possible to slow the remorseless tide of biological extinctions that afflicted the planet, but to staunch it, let alone stop it, seemed beyond his – or for that matter anybody's – reach. This did not mean that one did not have a duty to try, for even a single species saved was a triumph. And since the current wave of extinctions was largely the work of one species (man), it was always possible that in the longer term it could be brought to an end by changing the mind-set and the behaviour of its principal cause. But the realistic goal of animal conservation was damage limitation, not absolute victory over the forces of extinction. It was therefore a matter of profound sorrow, bordering almost on personal insult, for Gerald when he learned that on 14 July 1987 the dusky seaside sparrow of Florida was officially declared to be extinct – an event sad enough in itself, but as a metaphor for the fate of species at the hand of man a tragic and lamentable case. 'Like the canary who warned miners that oxygen was low,' wrote a local Florida newspaper in memoriam, 'the extinction of the dusky seaside sparrow sends a message to us: We are all in peril.'

At the end of July Gerald and Lee flew out to Corfu in order to be present for the last few days of the BBC shoot of *My Family and Other Animals*, to be screened as a ten-part drama series on BBC 1 starting in October. The £2 million production was a combined effort by the BBC's Drama Department and Natural History Unit. It was intended that there should be at least three minutes of natural history footage for every half-hour episode, and twenty scorpions, ten praying mantises, three giant toads, a number of snakes, tortoises, terrapins, barn owls and pigeons trained to dance had been brought to Corfu, together with six hundred frozen mice, as food for the snakes. Hannah Gordon played Mother, Brian Blessed was Spiro, Evelyn Laye the eccentric Mrs Kralefski, and a fair-haired thirteen-year old boy from a comprehensive school in Kent by the name of Darren Redmayne, who had almost no previous acting experience but looked right for the part, was given the challenging role of Gerald Durrell – a role doubly challenging when the real Gerald Durrell, now nearly five times that age, and legendary, bearded and leaning on a stick, turned up for the shoots at the real locations. Gerald had given invaluable advice to the production team at the scripting stage, demanding the power of veto over only one thing – the casting of his mother. He felt Hannah Gordon fitted the bill perfectly: 'She's absolutely superb. She picks up beautifully my mother's slightly flustered, not-quite-with-it-half-the-time air, and not knowing, if the family were squabbling, whose side to take.'

Gerald's presence on the shoot provided a tremendous fillip to the entire production team, and gave enormous delight to Gerald himself, though he found it a curious sensation to watch his own childhood being re-enacted so faithfully in front of him. None of the family's three villas proved to be suitable locations fifty years on, and substitutes had to be found (for the record, the Villa Fundana near Skripero stood in for the Strawberry-Pink Villa, the Curcumeli Villa at Afra was used for the interiors of the Daffodil-Yellow Villa and the Bogdanos Villa near Pyrghi for the exteriors, while the Snow-White Villa was impersonated by Kyriakis' House at Poulades). But it was not so much the visual changes as the sounds of the 1980s that proved most intrusive – the noise of cars, mopeds, motorboats and jet planes. 'In spite of a few setbacks,' Gerald reported to a friend, 'including snow when they arrived, two technicians down with heart attacks and a bright Greek technician who walked backwards into his wind machine and was turned into halva, they seem to be getting along well and are pleased with the results.'

Gerald's enchanted childhood on his enchanted island was finally, after so many false starts, immortalised on film. To celebrate the achievement Gerald sent out a home-made invitation, decorated with his cartoon animals, for all concerned to come to a party and barbecue at the grand and lovely old Curcumeli mansion at Afra:

> The Real Durrells invite the Other Durrells, Spiro, Theo and all who worked on the production (even the Producer). For the sake of the reputation of the BBC, please endeavour to remain sober for at least fifteen minutes.

In the late summer Gerald and Lee were down at the Mazet, enjoying the now familiar routine of rest and recuperation, reading and writing. Both of them were early risers – 6.30 or so. Gerald would usually bring Lee a cup of tea in bed, then they would make themselves busy – Lee wrestling with her plants, perhaps, Gerald scribbling away in his exercise book. Some mornings they might go to the market in Nîmes and have a coffee in the square, but Gerald didn't like to venture far these days. For some years it had been his habit to take a siesta after lunch on the terrace. He would get up around tea-time and get down to another stint of writing or whatever happened to be on the stocks. Then in the early evening he might start to cook dinner – though he always insisted that he did not cook: he *built* a soup, or *constructed* a curry. Sometimes he played the romantic love songs of Arletta, his favourite Greek *chanteuse*, on the cassette player; but he banned anyone from trying to sing or play 'Danny Boy', with its melancholy intimations of impending death.

A close acquaintance since the days of *The Amateur Naturalist*, Jonathan Harris was a shrewd observer of Gerald's private life. 'He drank anything going,' Jonathan recalled, 'sometimes starting with a cold beer after breakfast and sipping steadily all through the day. He was generally OK but if he was really down for some reason he would turn to the whisky, and that was really bad news. I don't think he had lots of close friends – I mean intimate friends with whom he had long heart to hearts.

I was one of his closest friends and I can't remember any occasion when he and I were in that situation. He had lots of acquaintances, but he was never really ever alone with any one of them – in fact he was never alone at all. He was pretty much at the public disposal most of the time. His society was his wife, his family and the "boys". He did have a proximity with Larry and he was always very anxious that Larry, who began to get a bit reclusive in later years, should come over for Christmas dinner, so Lee would have to ring him for days in advance.' Gerald's rapport with his eldest brother had never faltered. Neither saw the other as an angel: Lawrence thought Gerald drank too much, and Gerald always thought Lawrence should have treated his women better. But each would rally to the other's support in times of crisis.

Meanwhile Gerald's new, splendidly illustrated children's book, *The Fantastic Flying Journey*, inspired by the balloon flight that had so thrilled him during the making of *The Amateur Naturalist* a few years previously, had been published, and by Christmas was third in the children's UK hardback best-seller list. The book (which at the time of writing is being made into an animated television series for children) recounted the events of a 365-day aerial voyage round the world by Great Uncle Lancelot and his niece and twin nephews on board a magic balloon – an extraordinary ecological flying machine powered by tree sap, lit by electric eels and heated by solar panels. The voyagers are given the power to talk to animals, and are introduced to the marvels of animal and plant life from the Amazon to the Arctic – marvels that humans are selfishly threatening with extinction. In promoting the book Gerald lost no opportunity to spread his conservation message: 'It's vital for the future that the young should be made aware of the world,' he told a reporter, 'but instead of wagging my finger I wanted to make the book fun. The conservation movement has made several mistakes. They picked out sexy animals like pandas, and everyone thought that was all they were interested in. They didn't explain that it was the whole ecology, *our* ecology too, and that we too will suffer. With the world as it is, greed is the first of the deadly sins. As a species we are one of the most loathsome on earth, and certainly the most dangerous.'

On 20 November Gerald and Lee embarked on a twelve-day Indian Ocean 'Tropical Adventure Cruise' as celebrity guest-speakers on board a new luxury German cruise liner, the *Astor*, sailing from Mombasa to the Seychelles, Mauritius, Reunion and Madagascar. Competing with other attractions such as fancy dress parades, bingo, dance classes and morning jog, they were billed as wildlife experts who would introduce their own exotic worlds of adventure in five slide and video lectures, including

'Gerald Durrell on Corfu', 'Durrell in Russia', and 'Madagascar – The Great Red Island'. Though Gerald was to complain that 'I am put on the list of *Astor* extras as if I were a commodity like Coca Cola or, even worse, Corn Flakes,' the voyage was agreeable, the company congenial, and Lee a star.

Christmas of 1987 was spent again in Memphis. It was almost like old times. Gerald wrote to Hal and Harriet McGeorge on his return to Jersey, 'Many thanks for what was one of the happiest Christmases I have spent since we used to have old-fashioned Christmases when my family was all together.' Then it was back to England and in to hospital for the third New Year in a row – this time for a minor but exquisitely painful operation for arthritis in a toe. Both he and Lee were on a diet, and he had cut his alcohol intake by half, a singularly drastic measure. Indeed, by May things had come to such a pass that Gerald felt obliged to complain to Lee's parents about 'the nine years of almost intolerable suffering that I have had since you forced me to marry your daughter'. However, Lee herself looked very well on it, he said: 'I cannot understand why, when I look in the mirror, I look so much older and more carunculated and when I look at her face on the pillow she looks more beautiful than ever. I think it has something to do with the fact that I have a cataract in one eye.' Later in the year the cataract – though not his carunculated vision of himself – was fixed by a lens implant, the first of two such operations.

On 8 June Gerald received word that he had been nominated for one of the most outstanding awards for achievement that had come his way. This was the United Nations Environmental Programme 'Global 500' Award, the recipients of which were included on the UN Roll of Honour for Environmental Achievement. 'For the last thirty years,' ran the citation, 'Mr Durrell has been one of the world's leading conservationists. In his books and television films he has promoted the conservation of wildlife globally. The Jersey Wildlife Preservation Trust which he founded is noted for its exemplary work in captive breeding of endangered species.'

On 6 July came the twenty-fifth anniversary of the founding of the Trust. 'We are having a marquee in the grounds,' Gerald wrote to the McGeorges that morning, 'and everybody is going to bring a picnic. I have just finished roasting a turkey and wild rice and we are having the Lieutenant Governor Sir William Pillar and his Lady, also the actress Hannah Gordon, who played the part of my mother in the BBC series *My Family and Other Animals*. She and the Governor are going to read extracts while an orchestra plays bits from Saint-Saens' *Carnival of the Animals*, so we are just hoping to God it doesn't rain. Needless to say the fridge is groaning under the weight of champagne and the only thing to spoil our enjoyment is the fact that you are not here to share it with us.'

Gerald had every reason to look back over those twenty-five years with satisfaction and pride. The long struggle was now coming to fruition. That summer, in his review of the achievements of the previous year, he reported: 'You could say that 1987 was an ordinary year for the Trust: two more accords with governments, eight new capital developments, trainees from 22 countries, an island saved, 500 animals bred, four endangered species in the process of reintroduction to the wild, hours of national and international TV time and visitors to the zoo up again!'

But there was no room for complacency. Though captive breeding was now accepted as a significant conservation tool, and though conservation and environmental concern had moved a lot higher on the agendas of many governments around the world, the global situation remained grave. When the Trust's patron, Princess Anne, visited Jersey in December, she officially 'sank' a time capsule beneath the site of the Trust's first interpretative centre (the Princess Royal Pavilion). Among its contents was a letter from Gerald Durrell addressed to future generations of mankind. The simple, direct letter was both an article of faith and a plea to the planet's custodians in the years to come, a kind of last will and testament:

To Whom it may Concern

Many of us, though not all, recognise the following things:

1. All political and religious differences that at present slow down, entangle and strangle progress in the world will have to be solved in a civilised manner

2. All other life forms have as much right to exist as we have and that indeed without the bulk of them we would perish

3. Overpopulation is a menace that must be addressed by all countries; if allowed to continue it is a Gadarene syndrome which will cause nothing but doom

4. Ecosystems are intricate and vulnerable; once misused, disfigured or greedily exploited they will vanish to our detriment. Used wisely they provide boundless treasure. Used unwisely they create misery, starvation and death to the human race and to a myriad other lifeforms

5. It is stupid to destroy things such as rainforests, especially because in these great webs of life may be embedded secrets of incalculable value to the human race

6. The world is to us what the Garden of Eden was supposed to be to Adam and Eve. Adam and Eve were banished, but we are banishing ourselves from Eden. The difference is that Adam and Eve had somewhere else to go. We have nowhere else to go.

We hope that by the time you read this you will have at least partially curtailed our reckless greed and stupidity. If we have not, at least some of us have tried . . .

We hope that you will be grateful for having been born into such a magical world.

Gerald Durrell

Two days after the interment of the time capsule Gerald was awarded an honorary Doctor of Science degree – his second doctorate to date – from the University of Durham. 'In what he has achieved,' ran the citation, 'and in his plans for what is yet to come, we can see the fruit of knowledge, compassion and sheer toughness and determination. It all gives us a hope.'

A visit to the small Central American country of Belize in January 1989 gave a rare and gratifying glimpse of hope. Miraculously, Belize still possessed three-quarters of its natural vegetation (mostly rich tropical forest) and most of its coral reefs (second only in length to Australia's Great Barrier Reef). Moreover the entire population, of less than 180,000, from government officials to jungle-dwelling villagers, realised that their future lay in the wise and careful use of their natural resources – fish-rich seas, fertile lowlands, dense green jungles. Laws were being enacted to protect the reef and the mangrove-fringed coastline. A huge tract of jungle had been set aside as the world's only jaguar reserve. An ambitious conservation programme, called Programme for Belize, was planning to set aside a quarter of a million acres of tropical forest, part as an undisturbed 'core' area for wildlife, part to be used in agro-forestry, selective timbering and honey and chicle production. But it was the Belize Zoo and Tropical Education Centre (whose Director, Sharon Matola, had been inspired to pursue her career after reading Gerald's books when young) which most impressed the Durrells. The animals were in splendid condition – and were breeding. The staff were brimming with enthusiasm, and were anxious to share their knowledge and love of the animals in their care.

24 May 1989 was Gerald and Lee's tenth wedding anniversary. Gerald arranged the biggest and most generous possible bash in commemoration of the marriage that had saved his life. 'I think it should be a good party,' he wrote to the wildlife artist David Shepherd. 'I have ordered some orangeade and a bottle of champagne with extra-large bubbles so that it will stretch to forty-odd people or so.' The venue was to be the huge

Victorian orangerie cum conservatory and surrounding gardens at Trinity Manor, one of the grand houses of Jersey, just down the road from the zoo. All the guests were to have flowers and champagne in their rooms in the best hotels on the island. There would be crystal chandeliers and silver cutlery borrowed from Government House to add a touch of elegance to the anniversary dinner, a jungle of potted plants and garlands of flowers to add an air of tropical magic in the orangerie, and piano music to add a mood of romance to the occasion.

Gerald went to great lengths and no end of expense to find gifts for Lee that matched the splendour of the occasion, including four live tarantulas, a nineteenth-century necklace of Bohemian garnet, a magnificent Noah's ark complete with nearly a hundred animal figures carved in wood in Bavaria in the early 1800s, and two life-size metal baboons from Zimbabwe. 'Among Lee's gifts to me,' Gerald reported to friends, 'was a lovely painting by her uncle, who is a most talented artist, a marvellous silver and glass honeypot in the shape of a giant bee, and a fabulous chair in which I am going to sit in state in the greenhouse that we are going to construct down in France.'

On 24 November 1989 the Durrell Institute for Conservation and Ecology (DICE) came into being at the University of Kent at Canterbury under the tutelage of its founder-director Dr Ian Swingland. Dedicated to drawing on all known resources and disciplines to prevent species extinction and maintain bio-systems, it was believed to be the world's first full-blown academic institution concerned with the establishment of the science of conservation biology. The next day Gerald received yet another honorary doctorate, this time, appropriately, from the University of Kent.

Though it cost £2 million a year to keep the Trust and zoo going, by the end of the eighties the Trust's finances were so buoyant that the Jersey States Treasury suggested it was perhaps a good time to cancel their original loan. In 1989 the Trust's funds became even healthier when, in an unprecedented act of generosity and support, the sum of £1 million was donated towards the running costs of the International Training Centre by the Whitley Animal Protection Trust at the behest of one of its youngest Trustees, Edward Whitley, whose great-uncle Herbert, the wealthy and eccentric founder of Paignton Zoo, had bankrolled Gerald's second Cameroons expedition back in 1949 by agreeing to buy half the animals he brought home and any others that the London Zoo turned down.

Whitley was a young banker with aspirations to be a writer when he first came to Jersey to interview Gerald for an article, inspired by his great-uncle, about eccentric zoo-owners. He had avidly read all Gerald's books when he was a boy, and his first encounter with the man himself was a shock: 'With his white beard, mane of white hair and brilliant blue eyes, he looked like a cross between a country-and-western singer and an Old Testament prophet. Stouter and shorter than I had expected, he lowered himself with some difficulty into an armchair. "My hips gave out on me," he groaned. "I'm now walking on artificial ones." ' Whitley recalled that he was given 'a rather predictable kind of interview', and he thought little more about it. It was only when he wrote to Gerald to say how much he and his literary agent wife Araminta had enjoyed their meeting that things began to happen.

Gerald, it transpired, was obsessed by the name Araminta, and he replied by return: 'When your beautiful lady walked into the room, I was so taken with her looks that I did not register her name, which, if I read your writing correctly, is Araminta – a lovely old-fashioned name which I am very fond of.' So magical was the name to him that during his filming expedition in Australia in 1962 he had invented an imaginary girlfriend with the name of Araminta Jones, and he had later called his car Araminta. When he was wooing Lee he had created a fantasy rival for his affections, an octogenarian knitting instructress called Araminta Grubble, with whom he planned to elope to Baffin Land.

'From then on our friendship flourished,' Edward Whitley recalled, 'and he took me under his wing . . . Within six months I had left my job and become a writer – with endless phone calls and letters of support from Gerry, who became a valued friend.'

When Whitley returned to Jersey in 1989 Gerald took him on a tour of the zoo and Training Centre. He was greatly impressed by what he saw, but was disturbed to learn that the Training Centre was losing the Trust a good deal of money, and might even have to close. 'Using my experience as a banker,' he was to record, 'I wrote a business plan which successfully raised sufficient funding.' The million pounds was the happy outcome. Gerald, Lee and their colleagues were beside themselves with joy at the news, and Gerald wrote excitedly to the bright young man who had masterminded this unexpected turn of fortune: 'We are really over the moon about this. I never thought that the Training Centre would come about in my lifetime and here I am now seeing it underwritten. You really are a splendid man – not nearly as *attractive* as your wife Araminta, but with a beguiling charm of your own. I cannot thank you enough and I look forward to you *and Araminta* coming over so that I can show my gratitude by poisoning you with one of my specially cooked meals.' Not long afterwards Whitley set off on a round-the-world assignment to see how the graduates of the International Training Centre in ten different countries were faring on their return to the sometimes harsh reality of hands-on conservation work in their native lands, later writing a full-length account of what he found in his book *Gerald Durrell's Army*.

After what had become a regular rendezvous in Memphis for Christmas, the summer was spent at the Mazet, which was undergoing substantial improvements both inside and out, paid for by the funds that had come flooding in from the *Amateur Naturalist* and *Durrell in Russia* projects. A new terrace had been constructed, a new swimming pool, a plant-filled conservatory, and a fabulous new study overlooking the pool and the hills beyond, which Gerald christened Delphi – 'whence oracles issue'. Gerald had brought down some of his favourite furniture, and Lee's sister Hat came to advise on replanting the garden. 'I admit that we lead what by normal standards may be considered a very schizophrenic existence,' Gerald wrote to the McGeorges, 'but how lucky we are. We have your beautiful home to go to, full of love, good food and free Scotch. We have Jersey, where our "family" of boys and girls welcome us with warmth, and then we have the Mas Michel, where we can relax and work and mingle with each other in the sun. Over all, we love what we do, in spite of the fact that we frequently wring our hands and moan with despair.'

While 'mingling in the sun' with Hat and Lee, Gerald took the opportunity to pen his long-promised ode in praise of Araminta Whitley. If nothing else, it showed that at sixty-five he had lost none of his sensual delight in the contemplation of the female sex, a pleasure he was never to abjure: even on his deathbed he was to carry on flirting.

> Of all the places I have bin ta
> I have seen some luscious dames.
> Blonde, beguiling redheads yummy,
> Chocolate skins with jewels in tummy,
> Skins like sexy yellow silk,
> Skins like roses, skins like milk,
> Bosom, buttock, legs a-twinkle,
> Girls who have not got a wrinkle.
> Girls beguiling, smiles so winning,
> Girls who like a bit of sinning.
> But in all the places that I've bin ta
> None compare with Araminta.

In the late autumn of 1990 Gerald and Lee returned to Madagascar in search of the aye-aye and other endangered animals. This was to be

Gerald's last major foray into the wilds, and it was very nearly to prove a jungle too far.

Up-country Madagascar is not a place for the faint of heart or feeble of frame at the best of times. There was no doubting Gerald's heart for this endeavour, but his body was to let him down; eventually the pain in his arthritic hips became so trying that there were times when he had to be left behind in camp while his companions plunged into the forest on the kind of adventures he once led from the front.

The aim of the expedition was to obtain breeding stocks of two lemurs (the aye-aye and the gentle lemur), the giant jumping rat and the flat-tailed tortoise (or kapidolo), all of which were in desperate straits as the destruction of natural habitats in Madagascar continued apace. The aye-aye, a shy, nocturnal creature, was perhaps the most remarkable of these species, and its plight the most acute, for it was unpopular with the local population. Slash-and-burn agriculture had reduced its natural habitat to such an extent that it was forced to forage among agricultural crops such as coconut and sugar cane, and thus threatened the local subsistence economies. As if this wasn't enough, many Malagasy believed that, with its round staring eyes, huge teeth, and long, antenna-like fingers, the aye-aye possessed magical powers and was a harbinger of death, so for this reason also the poor creature was looked upon with disfavour.

The plan was to search three specific areas of the island. For the first few weeks Gerald and Lee, John Hartley and Quentin Bloxam, accompanied by a Channel Television film crew, would search for aye-aye in the Mananara region on the east coast of the island. Hartley and Bloxam would then head west to Morondava to set up a camp and search for the rat and the tortoise, while Gerald and Lee would visit Lake Alaotra, the biggest lake on the island, to search for gentle lemur, later joining up with the others near Morondava.

So the party set off from Antananarivo, the capital, more familiarly known as Tana, following the coast northwards, with the roads becoming progressively worse. Gerald was in considerable pain from his arthritic hips, and by the time they reached Mananara ('a one-horse town without the horse') he was unable to walk. But his spirits were lifted when Quentin Bloxam returned from a night-time reconnaissance one morning bursting with excitement. 'Aye-aye,' he bubbled. 'Aye-aye everywhere. They were all dashing about in the trees. It was the most ... well, I can't begin to describe. It was the most fabulous ... we ... it was just incredible. I mean to say ... Aye-aye all *over* the place.'

Quentin had observed what was probably an aye-aye mating orgy. A camp was set up nearby at Antanambaobe, and before very long the first aye-aye was brought in – an individual dubbed 'Verity' who strictly speaking belonged to Gerald's old friend in Madagascar, Professor (*'Pas de problème'*) Albignac, who had masterminded the Man and Biosphere Reserve around which they were to work.

'In the gloom it came across the branches towards me,' Gerald was to record of his first encounter with an aye-aye,

> its round, hypnotic eyes blazing, its spoon-like ears turning to and fro independently like radar dishes, its white whiskers twitching and moving like sensors; its black hands, with their thin, attenuated fingers, the third seeming prodigiously elongated, tapping delicately on the branches as it moved along, like those of a pianist playing a complicated piece by Chopin. It looked like a Walt Disney witch's black cat with a touch of ET thrown in for good measure. If ever a flying saucer came from Mars, you felt that this is what would emerge from it. It was Lewis Carroll's Jabberwocky come to life, wiffling through its tulgey wood.
>
> It lowered itself on to my shoulder, gazed into my face with its huge, hypnotic eyes and ran slender fingers through my beard and hair as gently as any barber. In its underslung jaw, I could see giant chisel-like teeth, teeth which grow constantly, and I sat quite still. It uttered a small, snorting noise like 'humph' and descended to my lap. Here, it inspected my walking-stick. Its black fingers played along its length as if the stick were a flute. Then it leant forward and, with alarming accuracy, almost bisected my stick with two bites from its enormous teeth. To its obvious chagrin, it found no beetle larvae there and so it returned to my shoulder. Again, it combed my beard and hair, gentle as baby breeze.
>
> Then, to my alarm, it discovered my ear. 'Here,' it seemed to say to itself, 'must lurk a beetle larva of royal proportions and of the utmost succulence.' It fondled my ear as a gourmet fondles a menu and then, with great care, it inserted its thin finger. I resigned myself to deafness: move over Beethoven, I said to myself, here I come. To my astonishment, I could hardly feel the finger as it searched my ear like a radar probe for hidden delicacies. Finding my ear bereft of tasty and fragrant grubs, it uttered another faint 'humph' of annoyance and climbed up into the branches again.
>
> I had had my first encounter with an aye-aye and I decided that this was one of the most incredible creatures I had ever been privileged to meet. Since it needed help, help it we must . . .

A local soothsayer was consulted; he gave them a guarantee of success – 'provided your motives are pure' – and the aye-aye hunts began, day and night. A video of Verity was shown to the local schoolchildren to encourage interest, but after five weeks the television crew had to leave, the sound recordist desperately ill with cerebral malaria, blood poisoning and hepatitis, their budget exhausted, their schedule completed and only Verity to show for their efforts. Ironically, soon after they left, two local farmers brought an aye-aye mother with baby, and helpers caught another baby, then an adult male. By the time the Durrell expedition left the island, a full complement of six aye-aye had been acquired. These were immediately despatched by air to Jersey, where they quickly adapted to their new surroundings and settled down to breed – the only aye-ayes in captivity at that time, apart from those at the Duke University Primate Center in North Carolina.

Back in Tana the Durrells were joined by Edward and Araminta Whitley. Edward was on a reportage mission round the JWPT's overseas project areas, a journey that would result in his book *Gerald Durrell's Army*, and at lunch in Tana he found Gerald in good form, eulogising expansively on Madagascar, which had all the good things of France (including a local wine and a native whisky) without the French, and working his way through a hearty dish of frogs' legs – a duty, he claimed, for the legs belonged to an ecologically undesirable form of frog that had been unwisely introduced from India and had all but wiped out the native Malagasy varieties.

From the moment of his arrival at Lake Alaotra, however, Gerald became unwell. Attacked by a dysenteric bug, he was subject to devastating and painful stomach cramps and diarrhoea – 'as though someone were operating on my nether regions with a chainsaw'. Things became so bad that he began to review his life: 'Why, I asked myself, do you do this to yourself? At your age you should know better and stop acting as if you were still twenty-one. Why don't you retire as other men do and take up golf, bowls or soap-carving? Why do you flagellate yourself in this way? Why did you marry a much younger wife who encourages you in these ridiculous acts? Why don't you just commit suicide?'

Gerald's condition was exacerbated by the dismal conditions at Lake Alaotra. The tree cover in the region had long been chopped down, and as a result the surrounding hills had begun to disintegrate, so that now the soil was sliding into the lake and choking it with silt. The area had once been the ricebowl of Madagascar; now the island had to import its staple food. The place was a metaphor for the fate of the country – a progressive suicide for the human race, a holocaust for the other species, among them the gentle lemur, whose only home was the diminishing fringe of reed bed around the lake, currently being burnt off to create yet more rice paddies. All the indications were that unless emergency action were taken now, the gentle lemur – a creature about the size of a half-grown cat, with bronze-greenish fur, huge golden eyes and enormous hands and feet – would soon follow the fate of two species of lakeside birds which were believed to have become extinct recently.

A little before Christmas the Whitleys joined up with the Durrells at Alaotra. Despite Gerald's state of health, things went well. Gerald's method of hunting for gentle lemur, Edward noted, was to go round the villages asking if anyone had any they were willing to sell. One gentle lemur was obtained by these means on the first day, and within three days the required number of ten had been acquired, including four babies, which were fed milk and banana mash by syringe. The animals were flown out to Tana, where they were looked after by Joseph Randrianavo-ravelona, a Madagascar-born graduate from the Trust's International Training Centre, before being flown to Jersey.

Araminta left at this point to return to England, and Gerald, Lee and Edward met up with John and Sylvia Hartley and Quentin Bloxam at their camp, thirty miles from Morondava, in a parched patch of forest that was being ecologically managed by a Swiss aid agency. Around the camp a series of traps had been set up near the entrances to the burrows of the giant jumping rat, and within days the quotas for these creatures – bulky animals that stood a foot tall and bounded along the ground on their hind legs like kangaroos – had been fulfilled, along with those for the flat-tailed tortoise.

To every silver lining there is always a cloud, however, and the cloud at the Durrell camp took the form of a plague of flies – houseflies, horseflies, sweatbees and many more – that swarmed apocalyptically in the heat (40°C by eight in the morning). 'They committed suicide in your beer ten at a time,' Gerald recorded. The tent poles and camp tables were black with them. They settled in clouds over arms, legs and faces. They stung, Gerald wrote, 'as if some malignant millionaire was extinguishing a large and expensive Havana cigar on the exposed parts.' But nature in even its most tiresome form never failed to enthral him. 'Look at a dismembered housefly and mosquito under a microscope,' he was to note, 'and immediately you become captivated by the architectural beauty of their construction. The compound eye of the housefly, for example, is a miracle of design. Indeed, once you have seen the component parts of some of these creatures magnified, you have a faint, guilty feeling at swatting one and crushing such a structural miracle.' Edward Whitley's abiding memory of this profoundly uncomfortable camp was the bedlam of all the creatures of the night – the frogs, birds and animals – in a 'great croaking, honking, roaring mass', above which he could hear a thunderous noise emanating from Gerald and Lee's tent. 'Gerry,' he noted, 'was triumphantly asleep against all comers.'

The aye-aye expedition provided Gerald and Lee with an opportunity to check the state of the ploughshare tortoise (or Angonoka) breeding project on Madagascar – a project which was Lee's specific concern. The ploughshare (so called because of the projection which grows from the shell beneath its neck) was the largest and most spectacular of the four species of tortoise endemic to the island, sometimes reaching almost two feet in length and weighing up to forty pounds. Found only in the scrub country in the Baly Bay region of the north-west, it had become the rarest tortoise in the world, shrinking in range and numbers as a result of the annual burning of the scrubland in which it lived and, apparently, the depredations of the voracious African bushpig, an introduced animal.

In 1985 the JWPT had been asked by the Tortoise Specialist Group of the Species Survival Commission of the IUCN to undertake a rescue operation for the ploughshare tortoise. A site for the project was found at the Ampijoroa Forestry Station near the town of Mahajanga, and in due course Don Reid – 'a herpetological paragon' – was put in charge of the tortoise captive breeding programme there, later assisted by Germain Rakotobearison, a Malagasy trained at the International Training Centre on Jersey. The tortoises had been breeding ever since, as Lee and Edward Whitley could now see.

Gerald had been too ill with fever to travel to Ampijoroa, and had sensibly elected to stay behind in the comfortable Hotel Colbert in Tana, with its cool shuttered rooms, cold beer, cold showers and hot frogs' legs. But an encounter with the tortoise babies on another occasion provoked in him a rhapsodical response. 'Holding four tiny ploughshare tortoise offspring in his hand,' he was to write, 'was like holding four tiny, sun-warmed cobbles, beautifully fretted and sculpted by wind and waves.' Lee crooned over them, admiring the brightness of their tiny eyes like chips of onyx, their sharp, manicured claws, legs encased in meticulously carved scale like fossilised leaves from a pigmy tree: 'There is nothing like seeing and holding the fruit of your labours. Taking these almost circular, still-soft fragments of wriggling life in our hands made all the struggles and begging for money, all the persuasion of bureaucracy, all the months of toil and planning fade away. Cupped in our hands, these funny little pie-crust babies represented the future of their race. Guarded from harm, we knew that these extraordinary antediluvian creatures could breed and go lumbering on into new centuries to remind us how the world began.'

Gerald and Lee took the opportunity to make a return trip to Mauritius, where for the last fifteen years the JWPT had become increasingly involved in conservation rescue operations. A lot of progress had been made in that time. When Gerald first visited the island the Mauritian kestrel was down to four birds and the pink pigeon to about twenty, while on nearby Rodrigues the beautiful golden fruit bat which was native to the island numbered just 120, and on the small islet of Round Island the unique reptile and plant populations were threatened with ecological disaster by the rabbits and goats thoughtlessly imported in the early nineteenth century.

After previous efforts to rectify these problems had petered out, the JWPT had stepped in to help. With the help of the New Zealand Wildlife Service and the Australian Navy (which lent a helicopter), work on Round Island began, and by the time Gerald returned to Mauritius in 1990 the problems of introduced pests on Round Island had been solved, breeding colonies of Mauritian kestrels, pink pigeons and fruit bats had been established on both Jersey and Mauritius, and the cages in the Reptile House on Jersey were overflowing with geckos, skinks and boas. Thanks to brilliant work by Carl Jones in Mauritius the plight of the island's kestrel, once the world's rarest bird, had been dramatically reversed. 'If anyone can be said to have snatched a species back from the brink of oblivion,' Gerald reported, 'then it can be said of Carl and this diminutive hawk.' By 1990 Carl was breeding fifty kestrels a year and had already returned 112 young birds to the wild – a prodigious feat. In one of the last stretches of indigenous forest left in the island, he and his team were now busy with releases of captive pink pigeons into the wild. Gerald wrote:

As we were sitting around chatting, something delectable happened. There was a sudden rustle of wings and a pink pigeon flew into the tree twenty feet above us. Moreover, to our astonishment it was one of the birds we had bred in Jersey and sent out as part of the re-introduction scheme, as we could tell by its ring. It preened briefly and then sat there, full bosomed, beautiful, wearing the vacuous expression all pink pigeons have, looking exactly like one of the more unfortunate examples of Victorian taxidermy. Of course, we gave it news of its brethren, which it received in a stoical manner, and presently it flew off into the forest. It was heart-warming to see a Jersey-bred bird perching on a tree in its island home: that is what zoos – good zoos – are all about.

Later Gerald witnessed something no less miraculous. With Lee and Carl Jones he went out to see one of the many areas where the Mauritian kestrel had been re-introduced. While Carl started a series of 'cooee' noises in a high soprano voice, Gerald stood like a portly Statue of Liberty holding up a dead mouse as bait:

'Here they come!' Carl shouted suddenly.

There was the faintest angel's wing breath of disturbed air, a flash – like an eye-flick – of a brown body, a gleaming eye, the gentlest touch of talons on my fingers as the mouse was deftly removed and the hawk flew off with it. It was an astonishing experience to have this bird, of which there had been only four specimens in the wild and which was now, with the aid of captive breeding, well on the road to recovery, swoop down and take a mouse from my fingers.

Back on Jersey, Gerald and Lee went the round of the zoo to study the new animals they had brought back to save: the beautiful kapidolo ('their shells agleam'); the marvellous snakes ('smooth and warm as sea-sanded pebbles'); the giant jumping rats; the gentle lemurs ('fur fluffed out and healthy'); and finally the fabulous creatures they had gone so far to collect and protect – 'our little tribe of magic-fingered ones'.

'I have met everything from killer whales to hummingbirds the size of a flake of ash, animals as curious as giraffe to platypus,' Gerald wrote later. 'Now to see aye-aye, at last, in Jersey, exploring their cages, to learn that they had settled down and were feeding well was a tremendous relief. One felt one was on the verge of something.' An aye-aye he called 'the little princeling' was handed to him: 'huge ears, magnificent, calm, but interested eyes of the loveliest colour, his strange hands black and soft, his magic finger crooked like a Victorian button hook'. Gerald reflected: 'I thought of the animals we had saved in Mauritius. If only we could do the same for this strange cargo of creatures we had returned with. If, with our help and the help of others, remnants of the wonderful island of Madagascar can be saved and we can return the princeling's progeny – that, in some way, would be man's apology for the way he has treated nature.'

The princeling looked at Gerald with shining eyes, his ears moving to and fro. The creature sniffed his beard and combed it gently. Then, with infinite care, he inserted his magic finger into Gerald's ear. 'We have come full circle,' Gerald was to conclude of this unending adventure, 'but, as we all know, circles have no end.'

*   *   *

While Gerald was in the thick of the Madagascar wilds, his brother Lawrence died at the age of seventy-eight. Lawrence had been ailing for several years. An inveterate heavy smoker at one time, he had contracted emphysema, and even three years previously (as Gerald had observed) it was an effort for him to so much as cross a room. In his declining days he presented a sad sight – ailing, morose, bored, depressed, drinking too much, house shuttered and bat-infested. 'He was so weary of it all,' a close friend reported to Gerald after visiting Larry near the end.

On the morning of 7 November 1990, Lawrence's last partner Françoise Kestsman was to tell Gerald, she had left the house to take her youngest son to school and go shopping for lunch. When she got back Lawrence was dead, having died instantly from a cerebral haemorrhage while having a pee in the bathroom. A few days later his body was cremated at Orange and his ashes interred in the grounds of the little Romanesque chapel in Sommières where Claude's ashes lay.

'I always considered my elder brother to be a somewhat inconsiderate man,' Gerald was to write with mischievous affection. 'This is borne out by the fact that I was in the middle of a highly important animal-collecting expedition in Madagascar in an area that had neither plane, fax, phones, nor even decent roads, when Larry chose to die. The news came to me several days later, when it was too late for me to comfort his two former wives, his numerous lamenting girlfriends and his numerous lamenting friends around the world.' Larry had been his father-surrogate for most of his life, Gerald reckoned. He had always been there to help and advise. It was Larry who had made him believe in himself and who had first helped him to explore the beauties and intricacies of the English language and encouraged him in his writing. 'So he has departed,' Gerald wrote, 'like a comet, leaving a twinkling tail of people who loved, admired and were amused by him. For a host of people he will leave a gap in their lives and they will miss him. So shall I.'

Lawrence left the house at Sommières to Françoise, together with a sum of money to enable her to turn it into an institute called the Lawrence Durrell Centre. 'What with Larry's Durrell Institute [sic] and my Durrell Institute for Conservation and Ecology at the University of Kent,' Gerald wrote proudly to Alan Thomas, 'we Durrells seem to be leaving some sort of mark.'

Gerald had been greatly downcast when he heard of his brother's death, and he was even more dismayed when, in May 1991, it was alleged in an article in the *Sunday Telegraph* that Lawrence had committed incest with his daughter Sappho when she was eighteen, a year after the death of his wife Claude. The evidence for this charge was based principally on ambiguous diary entries by the self-absorbed and unstable Sappho, who in February 1985, at the age of thirty-three, had hanged herself after a series of unsuccessful suicide attempts. Unproven though they were, the newspaper revelations were damaging, and Gerald, Margaret and Jacquie were united in their outrage at the injustice of them.

By now Gerald could smell the faint whiff of mortality in the air. His old friend Peter Bull was dead, and Alan Thomas fatally stricken with cancer. The formidable Aunt Prue, after a long and litigious life, had dropped dead of a heart attack after hurling a brick at a neighbour's cat, leaving £25,000 to Gerald. Gerald himself was inching towards his seventies. It was time to put certain basic matters in hand, tidy up affairs of crucial concern. Most urgent in his own mind was the question of his own passing, and the matter of the succession. Accordingly, on 22 January 1991 he wrote an informal letter to Lord Craigton, the highly regarded patriarch of the Trust Council: 'The recent demise of my brother brings home forcibly to me that none of us are immortal. Therefore, if you agree, I would deem it wise to now move Lee into a position whereby she automatically becomes Honorary Director of the Trust without any undue wrangling or acrimony, should I die.' Lee's academic credentials were impressive, Gerald reminded Lord Craigton – indeed she was far more highly qualified than her husband or anyone else at the Trust. Moreover, the staff respected and liked her, and had taken to bringing their problems to her, rather than to him, such was their confidence in her judgement and tact. 'Lee is deeply devoted to the Trust and its activities and she has initiated and run the Ploughshare Tortoise captive breeding programme in Madagascar, which both WWF and IUCN consider to be a model of its kind. She will be Chairman of the Durrell Trust for Conservation Biology. She will also, at my demise, continue to carry the Durrell name, which will be helpful. One is, of course, powerless from the grave and I would rest more easily if I felt that my life's work were in Lee's most capable hands.' Since it would not be appropriate for Gerald himself to bring this plan before the Council, he asked Lord Craigton to present it on his behalf. Craigton replied immediately that he would be delighted.

As usual, Gerald and Lee went down to the Mazet for the summer. 'The greenhouse is now so full of undergrowth,' he complained in a letter to the McGeorges, 'that I have to employ three local Arabs to cut my way to my desk with machetes.' Lee had taken up horticulture in a big way, he wrote, and the Mazet was now beset by a large number of highly malignant plants: 'There is a sort of creeper thing, with leaves as round as an elephant's fundament and long pink tendrils. Every time I go and sit in the greenhouse these tendrils (which grow about a yard a minute when you're not watching) change direction and start creeping towards me. It cuts into your drinking time of an evening to have to continuously glance over your shoulder to make sure you are not about to be garrotted. There is another plant that looks like the gangrenous remains of a green pekinese. This thing climbs out of its pot and tries to sit on your feet, with God knows what intent on your manhood . . .'

Though Gerald now had a fabulous new study, he seldom wrote there, for to do so meant incarcerating himself alone, and being alone was one thing he could never abide. His preferred place for writing was a small table at one end of the Mazet's long sitting-room, from which he could look out on to the terrace in one direction and in to the kitchen in another, so that he was rarely out of sight of another human being (preferably his wife) while he practised his lonely craft.

By the early nineties, however, his writing had begun to wind down somewhat. Nearly ten years had gone by since his last significant work, *The Amateur Naturalist*, and that had been written with substantial input from Lee. *How to Shoot an Amateur Naturalist* was an engaging spin-off book, while *Durrell in Russia* was an almost literal transcription of his Soviet travel diaries (with informative input from Lee's). In the five years since then he had written six more books, five of them short fiction works, and only one aimed at adult non-fiction readers. His recent productivity as an author, therefore, had been continuous but thin, largely depending for its content on his imagination rather than on his own real-life adventures – a situation dictated by the deterioration of his hips and eyes in recent years.

Anthea Morton-Saner had taken over as Gerald's fourth literary agent at Curtis Brown in the mid-eighties, though she had met him a number of times in France before then when she had been staying at Sommières with Lawrence, for whom she also worked as agent. 'By then Gerry's best books were in the past,' she was to say, 'though you have to remember that by now he was a very famous person and no longer a free spirit. Having ceased to be a voice in the wilderness, he was no longer free to write the kind of books he used to write. Gerry outshone all his peers, except when Larry was present, when both of them had an equally commanding presence. Gerry's rich voice, his incredible gentleness, his quick wit, all combined to have a calming influence on those around him. Nothing was taken too seriously, except his work, which really, really mattered. His anger came to the fore if he heard people mistreating animals, and as the years went by he became more uncivil and impatient and expected you to accept it as part of his friendship.'

Two of the children's books – *Keeper* (1990), a picture book about a boxer dog who works as a zoo keeper, and *Toby the Tortoise* (1991) –

never sold many copies. But *The Fantastic Dinosaur Adventure* – published in 1989 as a sequel to *The Fantastic Flying Journey*, and similarly splendidly illustrated – did a great deal better. In the new adventure a villain steals a time machine and travels back to the age of the Dinosaurs to hunt down the creatures for personal gain. 'He's probably catching baby dinosaurs at this very moment, and the only way he can do that is to shoot the mothers first,' cries the anguished hero at one point, in an uncanny rerun of Gerald's transforming experience of hippo-hunting in the Cameroons in his youth. The story was not merely an entertainment but an education as well, and children loved it.

A new book for adults, *Marrying off Mother and Other Stories* (1991), was no less ingenious and a good deal more hilarious. The stories ranged in location from Paraguay to the Perigord and featured a wonderfully eccentric cast of characters, including Gerald's own family back in pre-war Corfu (among them the mother they were trying to marry off), a gambling nun in Monte Carlo, a prize truffling sow called Esmeralda, an ageing Memphis belle and an alcoholic small-town hangman on the Parana river. 'All these stories are true,' Gerald was to fib with nerveless aplomb, correcting himself a second later: 'To be strictly accurate, some are true, some have a kernel of truth.'

The Ark's Anniversary, published in Britain in 1990, was also occasionally funny, though its underlying theme and final message were deadly serious. 'If you can make people laugh and at the same time get a message across,' Gerald had once confided to his conservation colleague John Burton, then Secretary of the Fauna Preservation Society, revealing his secret formula for the first time, 'you're three-quarters of the way there.' As an account of the struggles and achievements of the Jersey Wildlife Preservation Trust over the past twenty-five years the book was indubitably true – in many ways (though there were inevitably failures and tragedies) triumphantly so. But it was impossible to lose sight of the importance of what was at stake, and the reviewers picked up the bitter-sweet mixture. 'Mr Durrell presents his case for captive breeding with the sincerity and sensitivity of someone who has watched first hand the terrible rape of wild things, both plant and animal,' wrote the *New York Times*, 'yet he always manages to blend in a healthy dose of humor.' The *San Francisco Chronicle* concurred: 'It is impossible for Gerald Durrell to write anything that is less than exuberant, eccentric and amusing. *The Ark's Anniversary* is as sobering as it is delightful.'

PART FIVE

A Long Goodbye

THIRTY-TWO

'Details of my Hypochondria'

1992–1994

Though Gerald Durrell had swashbuckled around the jungles and mountains of half the wild places on earth in the course of his travels in search of animals, he had never been a physically rugged man. As a child he had tended to be on the delicate side – 'a slightly sick creature,' his brother Lawrence recalled, 'always a little bit ailing, fragile and wandlike.' When he was small he had chronic catarrh and found it difficult to sleep at night, and by the time he was in his teens his sinuses were so bad that he failed his army medical. 'You now see this Herculean chunk of a hero with a beard,' Lawrence had once confided. 'But Gerry was enormously fragile as an adolescent and physically timid. Frail, slender, lanky, psychically nervous, jumpy, shy . . . We've all had stresses and strains, but Gerry has had a much harder time of it than any of us. It's quite a remarkable feat to turn yourself into a toughie while remaining friable and tender inside.'

Even as a fully grown, apparently sturdy young man in Africa, Gerald had suffered a more than average number of physical and medical setbacks, from malaria, sandfly fever and dysentery to blood infections and ulcerous sores. Though he was determined and tenacious, driven by a dream and sense of mission, his inner sensitivity and delicacy made him more than averagely vulnerable to the stresses and strains of the life he had chosen, making him subject to depressions and breakdowns. Age had brought other travails: two arthritic hips, cataracts in both eyes, heart malfunctions, a small bladder cancer and diabetes, residual tertiary malaria – a whole litany of wear and tear.

Although alcohol had helped Gerald get through the day, the year, the life, it had brought its own torments in its wake. In later years his intake returned to a level so high that some kind of pay-off was unavoidable. He had already suffered a number of grand mal seizures which were probably alcohol-related. His brother Lawrence – like Gerald a heavy drinker – had been subject to similar seizures, during which he would fall to the ground, have convulsions, bite his tongue and sometimes lose control of his bladder and bowels. There were times when the two brothers wondered whether their shared affliction might not have an inherited genetic origin quite apart from alcohol.

By the early 1990s Gerald was a far from well man. He was all too aware of the ravages he had suffered, and would regard the steady disintegration reflected back at him by the mirror with increasing dismay. At the end of 1991 he looked so awful that his friend Sarah Kennedy, the well-known radio and television broadcaster, was convinced he did not have long to live. She had first met Gerald and Lee in the late eighties when she came to Jersey with the author and zoologist Desmond Morris to shoot a television programme called *The Animal Country Awards*. In January 1992, convinced that Gerald was dying, Sarah held a dinner at her flat in London to cheer him up, inviting David Attenborough and Desmond Morris as surprise guests.

'Sarah said to me: "Gerry's not long for this world," Desmond Morris recalled. 'This surprised me – I'd thought he was OK. But Sarah was very sensitive; she could see he was ill and going downhill. Personally I loved the old rogue. We had a very friendly relationship and I felt close to him emotionally. I had a similar attitude towards animals but we never talked shop because somehow we never needed to – we had this immediate understanding that we shared the same basis of thinking.'

The dinner was to be a get-together of the country's three greatest living naturalists (Sir Peter Scott – 'the man who laid down the bedrock on which international conservation now stands,' as Gerald once said of him – having died over a year before). 'I had to do it,' Sarah Kennedy recalled, 'because I knew instinctively that it would be the last time these three would all be together. Though they all approached the phenomena of the natural world from different directions, they all respected each other very much.'

The surprise was carefully laid. Gerald and Lee arrived first. Gerald was sat in a chair with a bottle of his favourite J&B malt whisky beside him, and Sarah put a record on. After a while the entry-phone buzzed. Sarah picked it up. She could hear David and Desmond downstairs 'giggling like schoolboys'. Determined to spin out the surprise for as long as she could, she said firmly, 'Well, it's a bit bloody late in the day to be delivering the wine now. But I suppose you'd better bring it up.'

The doorbell rang, and the two surprise guests walked in. 'Gerry's eyes were on stalks,' Sarah recalled. 'His mouth fell open and then he grinned hugely. He could be terribly rude to people he was really fond of. He turned to me and he said: "You *bitch*!" There was not a pause for breath after that. The conversation flowed along like silk. They talked about all their lives – they had so much in common. David talked about the time he and Gerry had met in Buenos Aires, when they were both caring for a collection of animals in a different part of the town. What times they were. It was a memorable evening. And as it turned out it *was* the last time they all met up.'

As the year wore on Gerald's letters to Hal and Harriet McGeorge in Memphis began to be increasingly preoccupied with the state of his health. Though he bravely did his best to turn his succession of encounters with the medical profession into yet another funny story, the fact that he wrote about them at all was indicative of his underlying concern. On 5 February he wrote from Jersey: 'I am having to go into hospital for twenty-four hours because the medical profession want to take a peep into my bladder. They can't believe that it is solid whisky.' On 17 March he reported that the problem was getting worse:

> Over the years I have produced something so pale and blonde that it might easily have passed for one of the more delicate Loire wines. Imagine, then, my consternation when instead of this I produced something that looked like a very non-vintage Châteauneuf du Pape. My wife was in the kitchen. Do you think I got sympathy? I was berated for not looking after myself, eating too much, drinking too much, staying up late. So into hospital I went. The Jersey Hospital is famous for its beautiful nurses and for the fact that if you go in to have your appendix out you wake up to find both legs missing and a beautiful nurse pouring boiling pitch over the stumps. Then I was wheeled into a sort of dungeon place where I was strapped – protesting – to a slab and my veins filled with iodine.

And so he went on for four more pages, regaling his in-laws with lurid tales of the Jack the Ripper surgeon and the Marquis de Sade orderly, the ordeal by catheter, the plasma and saline drip – 'like a sort of spiggot and tap that made me feel like a barrel of ale in a pub' – and the indignity of having his internal organs displayed in 'full frontal nude' on a giant TV screen with three nurses looking on. Then the cliffhanger of the diagnosis ('it's a little non-malignant warty thing') and the doom of the cure: 'I must, if I wanted to become sixty-eight, immediately give up women, wine, smoking, eating and drinking.' He had gone in for twenty hours and stayed nine days.

By May Gerald was more or less back to normal, and deeply involved in hosting a major conference on animal conservation – the Sixth World Conference on Breeding Endangered Species. When the First World Conference was held in Jersey in 1972, some of the zoological world still considered captive breeding unnecessary and misguided. Twenty years later it had been officially recognised by the World Conservation Union (the new name for the IUCN) as a significant weapon in the fight against species extinction.

In opening the conference, Princess Anne urged the three hundred delegates from thirty countries to see their zoos as a means of conservation overseas, not as an end in themselves. The conference would be remembered for raising a new challenge – the effective management of captive and wild populations of endangered species as a single problem with a common solution. The almost extinct California condor, for example, removed from the wild under a cloud of controversy, now numbered more than sixty birds bred in two zoos, and the first pair had recently been reintroduced into the wild. The black-footed ferret (the subject of one of Gerald's earliest conservation concerns when he was an adolescent petshop worker) had been returned to the prairies of western America after research had been carried out with a near relative, the Siberian ferret. The Mallorcan midwife toad, known only as a fossil until it was discovered alive in 1980, had been bred in captivity, then returned to secret sites, and was now breeding a new generation of wild toads. Winding up the conference, Dr George Rabb, Chairman of the Species Survival Commission of the World Conservation Union, charged the international assembly of zoologists and conservationists with transforming the nature of the modern zoo to that of a conservation centre.

Gerald Durrell had every right to feel a smidgen of pride, for from his small acorn (and those of a few other like-minded pioneers) a great tree had grown. His own zoo and Trust was now a world leader. Sixty-one endangered species from all around the globe – from snails and lizards to golden lion tamarins, snow leopards, gorillas and spectacled bears – had found sanctuary in this state-of-the-art establishment and were involved in breeding programmes which could one day conclude with their reintroduction into the wild. The whole complex was constantly being improved and developed. Over nine hundred graduates from the Trust's International Training Centre were working on conservation and captive breeding programmes throughout the world. The Durrell Institute for Conservation and Ecology at the University of Kent continued to promote the science of conservation biology. In a few weeks the world's first Earth Summit would take place in Rio, and among the many urgent environmental topics it would address was that of the conservation of biological diversity.

The wheel of the zoo world appeared to have turned full circle. At this moment the mighty Zoological Society of London, with which Gerald had sometimes skirmished furiously from the dog days of Cansdale to the imperium of Zuckerman, was on its knees – rudderless, out of touch, bitterly divided, and on the verge of closing down. Gerald had already become involved on the sidelines. The demise of London Zoo would be as terrible as the sinking of the *Titanic*, he declared. He had lost faith in the Zoo Council many years ago – but there was life after Zuckerman. He wrote privately to a colleague to say that he felt London Zoo's future ought to lie in the hands of zoo professionals of calibre who could 'invade this fossil to give it life and intelligence'.*

A few years previously the zoo world could not have cared a fig for what Gerald Durrell had to say about their affairs, or anything else. Now they hung on his every word and were grateful for his support. On 13 May, triumphant and brimming over with enthusiasm, Gerald reported to Lee's parents:

We are just letting the dust settle after a huge and very successful Conference. We were so lucky to get Annie Girl (our Patron) to open it. She made a wonderful speech and set the seal of importance on what we and other zoos are doing. She is a very remarkable lady and we are so lucky to have her as our Patron. We were also lucky with the weather. For the three days of the Conference there was not a cloud in the sky. The whole zoo looked magnificent, since it is now so park-like, and the people coming from other zoos, which are mainly cement and plastic trees, were overwhelmed. I have never seen the place looking so beautiful. We had to make a short list of people to invite up to the flat for drinks and food and it ended up by being fifty people. As I was more or less immobilised because my hips were giving me some trouble, I had to sit in a chair and everyone had to come and sit on the floor around me. To have all the most distinguished and illustrious zoo directors and conservationists in the world crouched at my feet was a position which I (an inherently modest man, as you know) did not, of course, relish.

---

* Before long Gerald was to mend his long-standing differences with London Zoo to the extent that when a new Director later took over at London he was a Jersey-trained appointee.

Needless to say, he went on, their daughter was magnificent: 'I would like you to know that in this vitally important world conference your daughter shone like a star. She will be, in the future, one of the most important people in world conservation. The fact that you managed to create her is a miracle, and the fact that she managed to join me is another miracle.'

In June Gerald received the first instalment of a hefty £50,000 advance for an undemanding but remunerative new writing project – a series of four slim volumes called 'The Puppy Books', to be given away as part of a promotion for Andrex toilet tissue. He had already written a draft of the first book, *Puppy's Beach Adventure* (which introduced children to seashore life), and the remaining three were soon to follow: *Puppy's Field Day* (animals in the country), *Puppy's Pet Pals* (domestic animals) and *Puppy's Wild Time* (zoo animals). This was Gerald's first experience of what might be called industrial literature, and the statistics impressed him. A £1 million television advertising budget was allocated to the promotion, and an astonishing ten million puppy books would be produced – one of the biggest print runs in publishing history.

In July Gerald was down at the Mazet with Lee, putting his new-found surplus of funds to good use by embarking on an ambitious programme of outdoor improvements and landscaping. He wrote to the McGeorges: 'My wife is convinced that if we spend another £50,000 on it we can turn it into something that Adam and Eve would envy. However, the sun is shining, the pool is soup temperature and, believe it or not, your daughter has become thoroughly unprincipled. She now bathes in the nude and has siestas in a huge hammock. How decadent can you get?'

In the early autumn there was sad news at the zoo. On 16 September, Jambo, the patriarch of the Jersey gorillas, was found dead, only a few months after Nandi, his portly little thirty-four-year-old mate of some twenty years, and one of the founder members of the Jersey gorilla breeding group, had died, with him beside her to the end. A post-mortem at the Jersey General Hospital revealed that Jambo had died literally of a broken heart – his aorta had split, and he had died instantly and without pain. For Gerald, who had arranged to bring Jambo to Jersey back in 1961, it was like the loss of a friend. Jambo had fathered thirteen young gorillas born at the zoo, and was survived by fifteen grandchildren, making him a major contributor to the world's captive gorilla population. He had long been one of the great characters of the zoo – powerful, dignified, gentle. In the summer of 1986 he had appeared on the world's television screens when he gently stood guard over the unconscious figure of five-year-old Levan Merritt, who had tumbled into the gorilla enclosure – an extraordinary incident which changed people's attitude to the gorilla species overnight and triggered a flood of fan mail and a stream of donations from around the world. Later Jambo's keeper Richard Johnstone-Scott wrote the story of his life, *Jambo: A Gorilla's Story*.

In October 1992 Gerald's thirty-seventh and last book (not counting the puppy books) was published. With *The Aye-Aye and I*, an account of his quest for one of the endangered lemurs of Madagascar, he was at last back in form both as a traveller and a writer. For a time his extraordinary literary career had seemed to falter, the *mot juste* becoming as elusive and endangered as the aye aye itself. But as Donald Dale Jackson was to write in his review in *The Smithsonian*: 'It is a great comfort to open a book and discover in paragraph one of page one that you're in the hands of a writer delighting in writing, and thus delighting you. The first and last fact about Durrell is that he's a writer; he's someone you want to listen to or wander with. Durrell's eye and humor and skills are such that I suspect he could transform an account of two weeks in Oakland into a good read.' The *Sunday Telegraph*'s critic enthused that the book was 'a splendid, ebullient tale'.

By the late autumn of 1992 Gerald had gravitated back to the medical world. While in London to publicise his puppy books he 'collapsed gracefully again with this damn tummy bug'. Blood tests proved inconclusive, and eventually he was able to return to Jersey. By now, however, he had become aware of a new pain which he felt mostly in the abdomen, sometimes reaching round to the back. Though not continuous and never unendurable, it was more obtrusive and obdurate than most, and he was concerned that it would never quite go away. At Lee's insistence he went to London for tests, but an endoscopy examination of the large bowel produced negative results.

By early 1993 Gerald felt well enough to embark on a lecture cruise of the west coast of South America – a voyage he was afterwards to describe as 'the trip to hell'. He and Lee had high expectations that a couple of months at sea would be both recuperative and interesting, but they were to be disappointed, as Gerald reported after they got back to Jersey at the end of April. 'Nobody explained to me the ship was a close approximation to a Roman slave galley,' he wrote to friends. The cabin was tiny, the service non-existent, the food indigestible, the noise of the engine indescribable, and the passengers 'very sweet, very frail and approximately 2,000 years old ... when we got to the Galapagos, they had to hitch a chair between two poles and carry me around as in the days of Empire. Then, when we got back to Jersey, my legs had completely given out on me and so I spent five weeks being pummelled and pushed in a nursing home by a physiotherapist who, I think, got her training under the Spanish Inquisition.' It was not only his legs that had given out. He had been quite ill on his return from South America, and while in the nursing home in Jersey he underwent further drying-out treatment, which included administration of the tranquillising drug Valium. In the early summer he set off for the Mazet to recuperate.

His beloved Mazet had for long been the place where he could take time out, rest up, dress as he wanted, do as he pleased. It was also the retreat where he went to write, which he found almost impossible to do in the flat at the zoo. This time his writing programme was much more ambitious than usual. Though he was now approaching his seventieth year, he vowed he would never retire. 'Who wants to retire?' he asked. 'I'm interested in many things – art, poetry, cookery, philosophy. What you need is a wide-spectrum mind. I still have many things I want to try.' All the same, he reckoned he had reached an age where it was appropriate to consider writing the story of his life. Many episodes, of course, had already been told in his numerous autobiographical books, but a complete, coherent autobiography was another matter, and he did not approach the task without a few misgivings. He aired them in his draft preface, entitled 'How to Give Birth to an Autobiography'.

> When you set out to write your autobiography it has, as I have discovered, a very salutary effect on diminishing one's self-esteem. You have, full of enthusiasm, sharpened up your goose quill, the inkwell is brimming, the capacious sandbox is ready to dry each precious sheet of parchment, but then you are suddenly overcome with terrible doubts, the chief one being that, though you know you are the most interesting person in the world, does everyone else SHARE YOUR VIEW?
>
> The author is a lonely soul, like the albatross. He has the black looming shadow always over his shoulder, the knowledge that he can write 50,000 words and not be certain that anyone will read them or, if they do, understand what he is trying to say. It was George III who, when presented with a complimentary copy of Gibbon's *Decline and Fall of the Roman Empire*, said: 'Another damn, great, thick book! Scribble, scribble, scribble, Mr Gibbon, heh?' I hope that these scribbles will amuse.

Gerald was going to call his new book 'Myself and Other Animals: A Sort of Autobiography'. As the title suggested, he did not have in mind a conventional chronological narrative, but something more impressionistic and idiosyncratic. So it is not surprising that among all his working notes not a single date is to be found, nor that in a memo early on he reminds himself to 'dodge about in time – but don't dodge too much'. Very soon he abandoned the idea of squeezing his life into a single volume, and considered spreading it over three: volume one to be called 'Gilt on the Gingerbread', volume two 'Leaning Against the Sun', volume three 'Last Minute Explorations'.

Gerald reported in July that he was collecting a massive file of notes for this *magnum opus*. His health was better, he said, adding that 'the only infliction I find hard to combat is old age, an ailment which cannot be averted, alas'. By August he was able to tell his agent Anthea Morton-Saner that the autobiography was progressing satisfactorily. But now the pain in his abdomen and back returned, with a new tenacity and intensity. At this point his progress with the book ceased to be either structured or coherent. His mind blunted and distressed by his deteriorating condition, he ceased writing sequential narrative, and took to fitfully jotting down a miscellany of maxims and *pensées*, snapshots and reveries. 'Writing your autobiography,' he noted, 'is as terrifying as sleeping alone in a haunted house and dreaming ... My mind is stuffed like the Chelsea Flower Show or Kew – with sights, scents, sounds and the patter of mammalian feet, the whisper of wings. I am never me, I am a thousand bits of a jigsaw.'

Running through these jottings and doodles like a golden thread is the theme which was his life-blood – the wonder, beauty and magic of the world he had known. He wrote of the crystal-clear little waterfalls of the rainforest, the flowers with petals so thick they were like flakes of candle wax, the jungle creeks where the water shone like the finest sherry, the mistral hooting down his chimney and making the fire leap up like tapestry, the shapes of trees, clouds, fires ... He wrote of 'the magic that lies all about us – a fly's wing as intricate as anything that let the sunlight into Chartres Cathedral, a teacup of water teeming with a myriad of life forms as extraordinary as anything you could find by exploring one of the man-made cities of the world – *that* is magic'. Trees obsessed him: 'Trees are loving, immobile friends unto death, giving you a pageant throughout their lives. Trees are like women, we cannot live without them. Trees are the skivvies of the universe. Nobody appreciates them when they are alive but everybody feasts upon their warmth when they are dead.' But over all of this golden theme lay the black shadow of man: 'It was a dark day for the planet when man crawled out of his cave and picked up a rock. Of course we should be interested in our own beginnings, the ladder from sperm to sperm, ova to ova, bone to bone, until the skull was filled with tumultuous ideas that went beyond the necessity of pursuing other animals to survive. As soon as other animals became food they became inferior.' None of this told the story of his life, of course, but it did convey a vision.

Increasing pain made it difficult for Gerald to concentrate, as did the huffing and puffing of the bulldozers that were levelling and landscaping a new terrace garden outside the Mazet. It was at this moment – a point of no return, had anyone realised it – that Lee had to leave for a long-scheduled assignment in Madagascar, where as director of the Madagascar Tortoise Project she was involved in a captive breeding programme to save the endangered ploughshare tortoise, one of the rarest tortoises in the world.

Lee was worried about leaving Gerald on his own, though he insisted he would be perfectly all right provided the wine cellar was full and the deep freeze well stocked. But Lee was persistent, so Gerald suggested that Alexandra Mayhew, the beautiful young woman with whom he had once travelled in Assam, come to stay. 'Lee looked upon this suggestion with all the deep suspicion of a wife whose husband has told her he has to work late at the office with a new, blonde secretary,' Gerald reported to the McGeorges. 'I pointed out that Alexandra was married, now divorced, and had a two year old child who would act as chaperone. Anyway, after some argument, it was decided and Alexandra was telephoned and said she would love to come to a home in the South of France with a swimming pool and a good cook thrown in.'

So Alexandra arrived, bringing her little daughter Siena. 'The child was frail as a whisp (it was four months premature),' Gerald was to record, 'but hyperactive as a squirrel on amphetamines. She rose before dawn, refused to siesta and only went to bed at eight o'clock at night.' Gerry was very good with the little girl, Alexandra recalled:

> He was very patient, very considerate, he related to her almost intuitively. I think he'd have made a good father – on the one hand strict, on the other totally unstructured. He was in appalling shape physically. He looked a lot older than he was and his legs had swelled up so much with oedema and were so tight inside their skin that they looked as if they could burst at any time. And he was drinking with a vengeance. He'd been to a drying out clinic in Jersey before he came down to the Mazet, but his idea of being on the wagon was beer for breakfast and as much wine as he could drink during the rest of the day, and that seemed to be acceptable – as long as he wasn't on spirits. But the moment Lee left he started hitting the whisky. I spoke to him endlessly about it but he said

he needed it for the pain. It had a pain-killing effect on his hips, he said. I felt very guilty about it, because it was me that had to drive him to the market in Nîmes to buy two bottles of whisky every time, and he would drink one a day while Lee was away, on top of all the other stuff. He changed quite considerably during the three weeks I was there. He became maudlin and morose and verbally aggressive. Though he was supposed to be writing a book he spent many days just staring blankly in front of him, sitting at a little desk by the door from the sitting room to the kitchen, not writing a word. It was very sad. It was as though he had pressed a self-destruct button. I quizzed him about it. I said, 'Look, your brother's already died of it, do you want to go the same way?' But he was a bit fatalistic about it. It was karma, he said.

Margaret, too, had noticed a change in her brother in recent years. His liver was not in good working order, she guessed, but sometimes she wondered whether he was mentally affected as well. 'There is an atmosphere of sullen gloom,' she wrote to a friend from the Mazet on an earlier visit, 'with bouts of vitriolic outbursts when he rumbles on like a Kodiak bear with ulcers.' Gerald once told her he knew what would happen if he went on as he was – he had read it up in the medical books. 'It wasn't that he was exhausted with life's struggle,' Alexandra Mayhew noted. 'He still had this tremendous verve and enthusiasm. He was still a zealot as far as his subject was concerned. I didn't see a great diminution in that side of him at all. He just had a sickness called alcoholism.'

A hospital doctor who knew and admired Gerald was to say: 'It's easy to see how he became hooked on alcohol. Even if he hadn't been genetically prone to it, he was the kind of man who just had to escape, protect himself from the harshness of everyday reality, which he found too scary or terrible or depressing in the raw. In his case alcohol did not by and large have an adverse affect on his ability to do his work and function properly as a human being. Well-compensated alcoholics can do that. Going around with a drink inside them is their normal functioning level. Alcohol is a necessary part of their daily intake; it enables them to do the things they do, things they might otherwise not have the courage or verve or effrontery to do. So alcohol can be an enabler as well as a disabler.'

It was Gerald's friend Tony Daniells who picked Lee up from the airport on her return on 5 September and broke the news to her that Gerald was hitting the hard stuff. Lee found him in desperate pain from his stomach, and he said he had turned to spirits in a vain attempt to cope.

Lee had arrived back two days before her birthday, and her sister Hat had flown over to help her celebrate. 'We had invited twenty people to the party,' Gerald wrote, 'for which I had to cook. Trying to cook for twenty-odd people with a two year old child asking you to read, for the fifteenth time, *Baby Bear Goes Shopping*, is one of the experiences that is etched with acid into my brain.' It did not help that Gerald suffered a massive nosebleed, or that the weather turned foul and it rained in torrents, but in the end the birthday party was a great success.

Gerald managed to hang on, though in a steadily declining condition. With increasing difficulty he pegged away at his autobiography, though his thoughts were tending less towards the events of his life than its end:

> Death is a great inconvenience, simply because there is so much more to do and see on this incredible planet. Of course, when it comes knocking at your door you hope it will be swift and painless. What happens after is an intriguing thing which I await with interest. Are you snuffed out like a Shakespearean candle? Do you find yourself suddenly surrounded by compliant and voluptuous houris? Do you awake in some Elysian pasture to be greeted by – horror of horror – all your relatives? Or do you suddenly find you are a tadpole-like creature again, about to metamorphose into a frog in an extremely vulnerable French pond? The ideal solution, of course, would be a sort of delicate omelette of all the more attractive after-life fantasies, a place where the women were beautiful beyond belief, a place where you could – for a short time – feel like a tree, chained to the soil by its roots, or feel the breathless delight of the dolphin as it leapt from one world to another, or feel the wind under your wings like an albatross or a condor, seeing the world from above, using the wind to pillow your scanning. Nothing except possibly love and death are of importance, and even the importance of death is somewhat ephemeral, as no one has yet faxed us back a reliable report.

In November Gerald and Lee returned to London to take part in a pre-launch publicity campaign for the puppy books, and it was then that Lee realised there was something dreadfully wrong with her husband – an illness that was of an altogether different order to anything that had occurred before. 'Gerry and I sort of knew the game was up,' she recalled. 'He was feeling just absolutely horrible, with intense stomach pains for part of the day, and though they would sometimes go away for a bit they would always come back So we stayed on in London so that he could have tests to find out what was wrong.' Later Gerald wrote cheerily to Lee's parents to tell them of his second endoscopy of the large bowel:

I am sure that you are both agog to know all the details of my hypochondria. Everyone kept telling me that what I was suffering from was a spastic colon, so twice I went over to London and they pushed a thing that looked like a gigantic telescope into me and showed me all my internal organs in cinemascope and technicolor on a television screen. There was a strange, small, white, dagger-like thing hanging down and I said to myself, 'so that is where my penis has gone'. I was rather disappointed to find that it was my appendix. However, everything looked rather rosy in every sense of the word and so they kept saying 'it quite obviously is a spastic colon'.

Reassured to some degree, in spite of the continuing pain, Gerald and Lee drove back down to the Mazet in early December. By now Gerald had set aside his autobiography – he had reached the age of twenty-two in a discursive kind of way – and was concentrating all his energies on getting through each day as best he could. 'Starting around Christmas and into January Gerry was feeling awful,' Lee recalled. 'He'd get these terrible, awful stomach pains; they were so bad he'd cry with pain, and of course he'd drink more to deaden them. This was BIG pain, so intense that every afternoon it made him weep.'

Gerald wrote to his parents-in-law: 'The pain became so intense that I simply could not work, could not think and was driving Lee mad because I am not the most docile of patients. So she phoned up our GP and he said 'Tell your husband to give up smoking instantly'; which lowered my faith in him somewhat since I gave up smoking thirty years ago. Then they popped me into the local hospital and got an expert liver man.'

He was in the hospital in Nîmes for four days. On the third day the senior consultant called Lee into his office. The scans, he said, showed a massive cirrhosis of the liver. They also showed a tumour. 'I have no doubt,' he told Lee, 'that your husband has got cancer of the liver.'

'I made the decision not to tell Gerry that,' Lee recalled. 'I did tell him there was some cirrhosis, because that was no big surprise – it had been spotted in previous investigations – but the tumour was absolutely brand new.'

From the Mazet Lee rang their GPs in Jersey and London, Dr Jeremy Guyer and Dr Guy O'Keeffe, and asked their advice. Both recommended that Gerald should come straight back to London, where at least he could swear in his native language, and Guy O'Keeffe arranged for him to be admitted to the private Cromwell Hospital for further tests. Gerald and Lee flew to London on 18 February 1994. Over nearly a month of tests, the original diagnosis was confirmed.

'It was the doctor who broke the news to Gerry,' Lee was to relate. 'He talked it through with him, tried to come up with something positive for him to cling on to. There were treatments available for this sort of thing, he said, and they could put him on morphine to control the pain. They didn't tell him he wouldn't make it to Christmas, which is what they were saying amongst themselves. In fact one of my doctors told me he didn't think he would last more than two or three months without a liver transplant, which was his only option. There was a lot of discussion as to whether he could be transplanted or not. It was his only hope, but there were a lot of things against it, apparently.'

Gerald was a highly marginal candidate for a transplant. He was over the normal age limit of sixty-five, he had an alcohol problem, and his tumour was large and very advanced. What tipped the balance were the facts that his chances of surviving without a transplant were effectively zero – probably no more than three or four months – and that he was a man who was doing good works in the world at large, and who with luck could go on doing so.

So the decision was taken. Gerald was free to go home to Jersey and wait for a replacement organ of the right blood type to become available. He would then be required to return to London virtually instantly. On 18 March 1994, the day following his return to Jersey, he advised Lee's parents in astonishingly courageous and cheery tones of the fate that awaited him:

> Dearest Both
> I am sorry that I have been so dilatory about writing to you but, as Lee will have told you, I spent the summer being a real old hypochondriac and when I am in pain I can't concentrate on writing. However, they have got me on morphine, which makes my eyes glitter like a Venetian virgin's at a ball, and at last has subdued the pain. At first, it made me feel woozy but now I feel almost as fit as a fiddle, but almost as weak as a kitten.
> So I am now back in Jersey, trying to tidy up my affairs, like, for example, whether I should leave my liver to Lee or not, and various matters of moment such as that.
> I hope this in some way explains and mitigates my neglect of you. Rest assured, we will keep you informed of every step of the Hypochondriac's Gallop into Hell.

It was not certain how much time there would be before the call came from the hospital – assuming it came at all. In this precious interregnum, with Gerald out of pain at last thanks to a heady cocktail of morphine laced with alcohol, he and Lee made the best of their time together. 'We put our ducks in a row,' she recalled, 'and made sure our wills were OK. Then Gerry had a farewell chat with the senior members of the Council and the staff. Geoff Hamon, the Chairman of the Trust Council, was there, and Robin Rumboll, the Treasurer, John Hartley, Gerry's personal assistant, and Simon Hicks, the Trust Secretary.' 'Gerry got very emotional, understandably,' Robin Rumboll recalled. 'He thought he was saying goodbye, and broke down and had to leave the room. He was concerned that Lee should be protected and that he was leaving behind a structure that would endure.'

Meanwhile, Simon Hicks reminded Jeremy Mallinson about the matter of the overall review of the Trust's present and future goals, so that no one would be in the dark if its founder did not survive his looming ordeal. Gerald last worked on this memo while in the Cromwell Hospital on 20 February. Entitled 'Statement of the Founder', it read:

> We are dedicated to saving endangered species for which captive breeding is considered necessary to ensure their survival, and particularly those species for which breeding programmes would be neglected by zoological parks because of their lack of 'public appeal'.
>
> Our first and foremost priority is to operate or support these breeding programmes, both in situ and ex situ.
>
> Our second but equally important task is to engage in activities directly designed to ensure these species' ultimate viability in the wild, including research, training and education, protection or restoration of habitats, and reintroduction into the wild.

Gerald Durrell's ultimate strategic goal, however, was rather more drastic. It was to close the zoo down and wind up the Trust. 'This was another of his metaphors,' Simon Hicks explained, 'and it's very clever and very clear. In fact it's more than a metaphor, it's more like a parable. He meant that if there were no longer any species in danger of extinction, he would close the Trust down, because it had fulfilled its purpose and he had no desire to run a conventional zoo. That was the ultimate goal – the impossible dream. Wouldn't it be marvellous, he used to say, to think that one day that could happen.'

By the time Simon went to see Gerald on Trust business on the morning of 27 March, the odds against his mentor's survival had shortened considerably. Simon was anxious to tidy things up in case the worst came to the worst. 'By the end of the discussion he had got very tired,' he remembered. 'He was not feeling at all well, he was in pain. And he turned to me and he said: "Simon, don't be afraid of talking about death. Either there's nothing there at all – or it's a whole new adventure." And then he put his hand in the air and fluttered it in a way that was very typical of him, and that was the last time I saw this wonderful spark – the last time I saw him whole and in the round as we all remembered him.'

That evening Gerald and Lee were watching television up in the flat when at around seven o'clock the phone rang. It was the Liver Unit at King's College Hospital in London. They had a donor organ of the right blood group, B. A plane would be arriving at Jersey at about nine, so an ambulance would be at the zoo at 8.30. 'I went back into the sitting-room and told Gerry,' Lee recalled. 'I said, "That's the call. It's all OK. When you want I'll pour you another drink. In the meantime I'll go up and pack the bags." Gerry seemed to be OK. He was just sitting in his chair as usual. He'd only had a single drink. "I'll be down in a tick," I said. So I was messing about upstairs for twenty minutes or so when suddenly I heard a great crash.

'I came running down and there was Gerry flat out on the drawing room floor with his head at an angle against the bookcase, just lolling there with blood spouting out of the top of his head where he'd hit his crown on a little wooden tortoise. "Oh my God," I cried, "what have you done?" I got a pillow to put under his head and a kitchen towel to soak up the blood, and he said, "I don't know, I think I tried to turn a record over on the record player." It wasn't drink, he just became disorientated and lost his balance. I immediately rang Jeremy Guyer, our local GP, but he was out of town, so the call was referred to his partner. I didn't know whether to cancel the operation because of Gerry's injury, so I rang the liver people to tell them what had happened, and they said it would probably be all right, let's proceed as planned.'

John Hartley arrived to lend a hand, followed by the doctor, and Lee held Gerry's head while the doctor stitched him up. 'Then suddenly we all started howling with laughter – Gerry, John and me. There was Gerry, bleeding away on the floor, about to be rushed over to London for a ghastly ten-hour operation which might save his life, but on the other hand might not – and we were in hysterics, tears of laughter pouring down our faces. The doctor had never met us before and couldn't understand it, he didn't know that this was what we always did in a crisis, try and make light of it. Anyway, Gerry was patched up OK, the liver people rang up to check, and then we went down to the ambulance. Gerry had bright pink hair and we were all laughing our heads off.'

After the ambulance had set off Jeremy Mallinson wrote to Gerald's first wife, Jacquie, to let her know the gravity of what was happening. She replied by return of post:

Dear Jeremy,

Thank you so very much for telling me about Gerry. What a dreadful business, and I feel for Lee. I would like to see Gerry as and when, for I feel very strongly that it is time to settle our misunderstandings and enter a new phase. If you can explain this to Lee I would be so grateful. Basically I just want to tell Gerry that I remember our time together with affection and gratitude, and at least we both tried to repay the joys we've had from wild places and their inhabitants by the creation of the Zoo/Trust. I'm just sad that we left the meeting for so long. I'm deeply upset by this, Jeremy – one can't share twenty-six years with someone without retaining some warm memories of them and all the things we did together – dreams shared and achieved. Just give him my love and blessings.

Jacquie

THIRTY-THREE

'A Whole New Adventure'

1994–1995

Lee had packed a whisky flask before they left Les Augrès Manor, and Gerry took a swig or two on the twenty-minute drive to the airport. By the time they got there he was feeling as relaxed as a condemned man after his last supper, trying to treat the whole thing as a joke. 'We got to Jersey airport about 10.30,' Lee was to recount. 'It was almost deserted at that time of night, just police at the entrance and officials on duty, but as he was wheeled through to the departure gate Gerry was calling out to all and sundry: "Oh, I'm going to get a new Albanian liver, ha ha, I have an Albanian who's got me a new liver, ha ha!" He had a few more swigs on the flight over, then we were met by an ambulance at Heathrow and driven to King's College Hospital in Camberwell.'

The hospital personnel were a little taken aback when Gerald turned up inebriated for his liver transplant. But there was little they could do about it – the countdown had begun, and he was duly prepared for his ordeal. This was a lengthy process, and it was not completed till around six o'clock in the morning of Monday, 28 March 1994. At 6.30 Gerald was given his pre-op drugs, then wheeled along to the theatre for an operation that would last without a break for the best part of the rest of the day.

'I was allowed to stay behind and have a nap in Gerry's room,' Lee related. 'Then later in the morning our wonderful London GP, Guy O'Keeffe, came along with his two children to lend a bit of moral support.' Periodically someone from the medical staff came to give Lee a progress report. At about 3.30 in the afternoon she was told, 'He's out, he's in the recovery room. It's been a great success, but you can't see him yet.' In a little while the surgeon came along to see her. The operation had gone very well, he told her, but he added rather ominously, almost as an aside, that Gerald's pancreas didn't look in good shape at all, but that he had decided to leave it alone.

Next morning, Gerald was still in intensive care. He was conscious, but breathing with the help of a ventilator, so he couldn't talk, and when he saw Lee walk in he became so agitated that he was immediately sedated and put under. Almost as agitated as Gerald was the Transplant Senior Registrar at King's Liver Unit, a young doctor by the name of Christopher Tibbs. He had been a devoted fan of Gerald Durrell ever since his father read him *My Family and Animals* when he was eight, and Gerald remained his lifetime hero. It was as a result of Gerald's influence that the young Tibbs chose to read for a zoology degree at Oxford, only changing to medicine when he found that modern zoology – all maths, statistics, molecular biology and scraping around for grants – was a far cry from the long and honourable tradition of the field naturalist that Gerald Durrell represented. It was therefore an immense surprise when Dr Tibbs came across a familiar face in the intensive care unit the day after the operation. 'My God!' he cried. '*That's Gerald Durrell!*' 'Yes,' someone replied. 'Didn't you know he was on the list?' For as long as Gerald was at King's, Christopher Tibbs remained the senior registrar involved in his case on a daily basis.

By Wednesday Gerald was off the ventilator and out of intensive care. Everything was going well – the liver functions, the wound itself – 'a bloody great wound called a Mercedes cut,' Lee recalled, 'an incredible thing running from front to back' – and Gerald's condition in general. By the sixth day after the operation Gerald was sitting up in bed in a side room, chatting away and as pleased as punch that he had got through the operation – for he had never believed he would.

Shortly afterwards he was moved down to the private patients' wing, and felt well enough to ask for his book manuscript and tape recorder so that he could get on with his autobiography. Asked if there was anything he would like especially, he ordered a brandy, and when he was told he couldn't have one, because he'd just had a liver transplant, he replied, 'Exactly – and now I've got a new liver!' He had emerged from surgery, as far as anyone could tell, the rumbustious, flamboyant Gerry of old. He was even flirting with the nurses.

On 16 April Gerald was moved back to the more comfortable private Cromwell Hospital in Kensington, whose Liver Unit, like the one at King's, was run by Professor Roger Williams. All the signs were that the transplant had been a complete success and that the new liver was functioning perfectly. But he was not yet well enough to be allowed to travel to Jersey for the grand opening of the zoo's new home-habitat for Sumatran orang-utans by Sir David Attenborough (as he now was) on 15 May, so he wrote David a typically jaunty letter apologising for his absence. As far as can be ascertained, it was the last letter he ever wrote.

> I was so greatly looking forward to showing you around and having a little boast. If you could spare the time to pop in and see me when you get back to let me know what you think of our endeavours, I would be grateful. Quite apart from anything else, it would be nice to talk to somebody about something other than livers. Still, I should not complain, as the op has been a tremendous success, and as they only gave me six to eight months to live without it, I have reason to be devoutly thankful. Anyway, if you come to see me I will be delighted, and if you are very well behaved, I might even let you see my scar.

Attenborough's speech at the zoo was heartfelt:

> A lot has happened since I first met Gerald Durrell thirty-five years ago ... This zoo, this Trust, is what Gerry Durrell started, with help from many others – and what a glorious flowering it has turned into! There are some people who argue that there is no justification for zoos. Let them come here! There are some people who say zoos can never make any difference to the great ecological disaster which everyone is talking about. How could they possibly save animals from extinction? LET THEM COME HERE!

Gerald had been put on chemotherapy to mop up any residual cancer cells which might try and form potential secondaries. It was not an intensive course, but it coincided with a sudden dramatic change in his condition. 'He seemed to be getting better till the chemotherapy,' Lee recalled. 'And then suddenly, around the middle of May, he went down with a very bad bout of fever. They didn't put him in a special unit, but they wouldn't let him out of the hospital. Then he went down with a second intense fever and he was put in the high dependency unit.'

It is unlikely that the chemotherapy was the cause of Gerald's fevers. To prevent the rejection of the donor liver following a transplant, the patient is normally put on a course of drugs that suppress the body's immune system. This makes the patient much more prone to infections – in Gerald's case bugs in the blood that caused one septicaemia episode after another. To try to identify the cause of his infection everything was cultured or tested, but nobody was any the wiser.

'What I think was happening,' Dr Christopher Tibbs was to observe later, 'was related to other, different medical problems. Gerry also had pancreatitis – his pancreas was in a mess and not working properly – and this meant that you were dealing with a different biological entity to the pre-transplant phase; in post-operative terms you had completely moved the goalposts. As a result his digestive system was not working properly and he couldn't absorb his food properly, so in addition to septicaemia he had diarrhoea and nutritional problems. Now, according to this scenario, because of Gerry's digestive problems, he very probably had bacteria growing in the part of the gut that shouldn't grow them – the small intestine – and from time to time these bugs would transfer across the gut wall and get into the blood system, causing septicaemia and all these raging fevers. And that went on and on and on. Probably it was the same bug constantly re-colonising in the small bowel. Once it was in the bloodstream we could combat it with antibiotics and it would eventually go away. What we couldn't do was eradicate it from wherever it was coming from. We could do nothing about the pancreas. And we could only cut the immuno-suppressants down to a minimum. More than that and he'd have lost his liver – and that would have killed him.'

The transplant itself had been a success, but as the weeks went by, with Gerald laid low time after time by an endless series of life-threatening fevers and virtually continuous diarrhoea, he began to weaken, and hospital psychosis set in. As a special treat when he was feeling low he was allowed to share a bottle of champagne with the nursing staff while he took a bath. But one day at the end of June, while trying to get to the bathroom using the drip stand as a support, his feet shot from under him and he fell and broke his collarbone, lying helpless on the floor for half an hour till a nurse came. 'That really shook him,' Lee remembered. 'That was the first clear indication to him how far he'd gone down. That was the beginning of his steep decline.'

It was the long-term prognosis that concerned Dr Guy O'Keeffe. 'I told Lee that I feared Gerry might die,' he was to relate. 'It could happen any time. There could be a burst of infection that would be untreatable and could carry him away. There were a couple of occasions when I thought that might have happened. Lee was very shocked by that.'

At about this time, something magical began to happen. In the days of their courtship Gerald had often referred to Lee, only partly in fun, as a 'zoo-digger', and he often claimed to be the only man in history to have been married for his zoo. 'I so profoundly wanted to be part of Gerry's dream and take it forward,' Lee was to recall later, 'that I married without romantic love. I was not worthy of Gerry's enormous love because I did not return it – not at first – though at least I was honest with him from the beginning. But when Gerry became really ill, I began to feel strongly protective towards him, and then, when I realised what I could lose, I began to realise what I had, and I finally fell in love with my husband. I loved him then, and began to tell him so, and he was astonished, as I had for so long refused to use the "L" word, and he was pleased, in a rather childlike way, so sweet, never castigating me for being so stupid and taking so long. Even before the end my heart was breaking.'

In mid-July Gerald was started on a course of steroids. This only treated the symptoms, not the cause, of his sickness, but it made him feel stronger. By the end of the month he seemed to be getting better enough for Lee to take the opportunity to fly to Memphis to see her mother, who was seriously ill with cancer. On the third day she had a phone call from Paula Harris in London: Gerry was in intensive care with a desperately high fever, and it wasn't certain if he was going to live. Lee returned on the first plane, but by the time she got back to London Gerald had pulled through, though he was still on a ventilator.

So the summer passed, with Gerald growing thinner, weaker and more demoralised by the day. Lee was tireless in her support. At the back of the Cromwell Hospital was a tiny private park. She managed to get hold of a key, and a few times she was able to liberate Gerald from the confines of the hospital and take him out in his wheelchair so that he could see the trees and the sky and feel the breeze in his face and watch the sparrows and pigeons and the occasional cat and dog – humble little urban representatives of the great kingdom of the animals on whose behalf he had pleaded and battled for the greater part of his life.

Neither Gerald nor Lee had any doubt that he was going to pull through, and he remained interested in and in touch with events as far as he was able. Jonathan Harris visited him, and was shocked by his wasted condition, but impressed by his positive attitude and unflagging generosity of spirit. 'When I told him that as a new departure I was writing a thriller,' he recalled, 'Gerry was terribly keen to help and spelled out his three golden rules: always try and solve a problem before you stop writing for the day, don't leave it till the morning. Always aim to write no more than you can really manage in a day. Always finish on a high and stop writing when you feel happy about what you've written. And he repeated his brother Larry's Eleventh Commandment for all writers: "Thou shalt never become a bore". Sometimes Paula Harris went to see Gerald about the fund-raising she was organising for the London end of the Trust. 'He never lost his drive when it came to the main thing in his life,' she recalled, 'even when he was ill. He was as keen as ever about what was going on and getting the best out of everybody involved.' But Gerald tired easily now, and soon all thought of continuing with his autobiography was abandoned, and his papers and tape recorder were put aside.

In August, during Lee's brief absence in America, Jersey Zoo was fire-bombed by a deluded animal rights extremist who claimed it was a 'Noah's Ark for cute or weird species' who were being exploited for money. The attack destroyed the £330,000 visitor centre, although no person or animal was harmed. Added to this, Gerald was also worried about the state of his personal finances, for he had been able to do little paid work for some time. 'I'm overdrawn,' he confided to his sister Margaret when she went to visit him. 'Really, Gerry,' she remonstrated. 'You're getting as bad as Mother.'

Towards the end of September, BUPA, which had been paying for Gerald's prolonged treatment, suddenly terminated his insurance. Cover, they announced, was available for acute cases only, whereas Mr Durrell, a valued customer, was a chronic case. He would be required to leave private patient care within the week. On 25 September an ambulance took him back to King's College Hospital, where he was put in a public ward containing five other liver patients, all of them in a serious condition, and one or two of them occasionally demented, so that they would rave incoherently all night and climb in and out of the wrong beds. For Gerald and Lee the move seemed to herald a descent to another circle of hell. After the luxury of the Cromwell, the food was indifferent, and the nursing staff were so desperately overworked that sometimes Gerald, who was now chronically incontinent, would lie for hours, as Dr O'Keeffe put it, 'up to his ears in poo'. The medical care, however, was of the highest standard, as befitted an NHS teaching hospital with a full research team in support.

There were one or two compensations to be found in the public ward in King's which Gerald had not counted on. At the Cromwell he had had a soundproofed room of his own, in which he sometimes felt as alone and detached from the world as if he were in a one-man space capsule suspended in an uninhabited void. But now there was bustle and commotion all around him. He began, bit by bit, to relate to the other five patients in the ward, for lying flat in a hospital bed all were equal in the eyes of the ward sister, let alone the Almighty. His curiosity and powers of observation had not abandoned him even now. He hadn't set eyes on an animal for some while, but man was an animal, one of the oddest of animals, and Gerald set out to observe his fellow man, preferably the female kind of fellow man, like the nurses. Gerald had always been a flirt and he wasn't going to stop now.

'He was a brave fellow,' Dr O'Keeffe recalled, 'and he seemed better than he was. I don't think he ever lost his self-esteem, which is maybe why he did so well. He was also a naughty fellow and he was always cracking jokes with the nurses and being naughty with them. He could be rather inappropriately flirtatious with the nurses. He'd make them blush a bit. But all the nurses liked him. He was an attractive man and he acted like an attractive man to the end. He knew that he was loved. And in turn he loved his life and he loved women. That's quite a motivating factor – quite a mainspring to survival. It confused the doctors. "Oh, he can't be that bad after all," they'd say.'

Gerald was amazingly sweet-tempered, considering. 'Even when he was in a shocking state,' Dr O'Keeffe observed, 'he didn't behave as if he was in a shocking state. Most people are on a very short fuse when they're as ill as he was. Sure, Gerry could be very depressed. "I just don't seem to be getting better," he'd say. But he was never nasty. Neither, for that matter, was Lee. She was extraordinarily calm and strong throughout this long nightmare. I think she really, really loved that man. She was totally devoted to him. There was nothing she would not do for him, even when she must have been absolutely exhausted and fed up herself.'

When Gerald was moved to King's, Lee moved into Sarah Kennedy's apartment, which was relatively close at hand, and from there she visited Gerald twice a day, once in the morning, staying through lunch, then again in the early evening, staying till ten. It was obvious that Gerry was going steadily downhill now. Dr Tibbs was shocked at the sight of him when he returned to King's: 'I hadn't seen him for a while, and now he presented a very different picture. He had lost four or five stone in weight, he wasn't eating anything and he was very weak. Not surprisingly, life was pretty gloomy.'

The fevers continued unabated, and Gerald would become semi-conscious, delirious, not recognising anybody. The diarrhoea got worse till it became virtually unstoppable, so that he was dehydrating badly and losing most of his daily nutrition. To these two ceaselessly recurring components of his personal hell was now added a third – recurring seizures. For the last four or five years Gerald had been taking medication to head off his bouts of grand mal. He was taken off this medication when he went in for his operation, and now the seizures returned. With each one he would vanish into a world of his own, sometimes for a whole week at a time, and there was nothing much anyone could do about it, nor any way they could reach him.

When television producer Chris Parsons called by to help cheer up his old friend and fellow expeditionary, he was appalled by the deterioration in Gerald's condition. 'He looked like a shrivelled monkey on the sheet,' he told a friend. 'He surely can't last long at this rate.' 'I was shocked when I saw him in that hospital,' remembered Margaret. 'He was in such a mess. In fact, when I turned up he said, "Have you come to say good-bye?" And I said, "No, of course not." But it looked as if he was in a death ward. He looked ghastly; he looked as if he was dying. He said he'd even contemplated suicide, and if they did one more thing to him he'd feel like going off his head.'

Day and night Gerald was on drips and infusions and transfusions and high-protein liquid feeds that delivered nutrition in drips through a feeding tube threaded up his nose and down into his stomach. By mid-November he had been in hospital without a break for eight months, and was becoming severely depressed. 'Gerry would watch this constant flow of other people coming in, getting better, going home,' Dr Tibbs remembered, 'and he'd say, "Why am I still stuck in this bloody bed?" During that year we did 165 transplants at King's and only lost two. But the way he was going, Gerry could be the third. I don't think he ever lost the will to go on. Some people do, and then they turn their face to the wall and die very quickly.'

In the end the staff at King's couldn't think of anything more to do for him. He was suffering from a general systemic illness for which there was no apparent cure. It might be better, they suggested to Lee, if he went home to Jersey. Psychologically it might do him good to see his zoo again, to be on his home patch at Christmas. Jersey had a perfectly good hospital, they said, and if they ran into any problems they could always ring King's. Lee recalled: 'I talked to Gerry about it and he said, yes, yes, let's do it. So we did.' 'Going back to Jersey,' Dr Tibbs concluded, 'was a tacit admission that we were not going to get Gerry back to full health and that it was likely to be a pre-terminal event. Whether Gerry realised that or not I don't know. He must have done.'

On 14 November 1994 Gerald and Lee flew to Jersey on a little ambulance plane paid for by the island's public health services. At the hospital in St Helier Gerald was bedded down in a small public ward, and Lee reported the glad tidings to her sister-in-law Françoise, Lawrence's widow: 'We are back in Jersey – ENFIN!!'

A couple of times Lee was able to drive Gerald around the zoo. At one point three little golden-headed lion tamarin monkeys climbed through the open car window and sat on Gerry's lap, to his intense delight and joy – after almost a year, ashen and haggard, he was back in the world of his beloved animals where he most truly belonged. 'The day before Christmas Eve,' she remembered, 'I was told he could come home for Christmas, which was wonderful. I got the guest-room ready for him, because there was no way he could make it up the stairs to the main bedroom – and then he came home. Jeremy was there to greet him at the manor and he helped me get Gerry through the front door and up the stairs to the flat, which was next to impossible. There was a Christmas tree to cheer him up and a lot of Christmas cards for him to read. I cooked some pigeons – his favourite – and we ate our Christmas dinner together in the dining-room, with candles and holly and everything, and Gerry ate a bit, though he was probably forcing it down, but he didn't have any alcohol, because he hadn't had a drop for months, he didn't fancy it any more. And then in the afternoon we went into the sitting-room and watched *Mary Poppins* on TV, and Gerry seemed to enjoy that, but he got very tired later and said he wanted to go back to bed.

'From this point forward Gerry began to get tireder and tireder and weaker and weaker, and after a few days I had our GP in and he reckoned Gerry was anaemic and fatigued. So on New Year's Eve we rang the hospital and said he had to come back. So he went back in, feeling weak, rotten and dehydrated – and he didn't come out.'

On 7 January 1995 Gerald Durrell celebrated his seventieth birthday. The occasion did not go unnoticed in the media. 'Happy birthday Gerald Durrell,' rejoiced the *Guardian*, 'seventy today and charismatic mega fauna, prolific raconteur and writer, flamboyant ruler of your Jersey Zoo for endangered animals. Your contribution to two generations' thinking about beasties and zoos has been immense.' Lee had organised a little bedside birthday party at the hospital for some of his oldest and closest friends. In spite of everything, Gerald had lived well, achieved much, carried on long after most people had hung up their hats, and finally notched up his three scores years and ten. It pleased him enormously that he had made it to his seventieth. It had been a target to aim for. A bottle of champagne was popped, and Gerald was given half a small glass. He took a few sips, then put it aside. By midday he was visibly tiring, and everyone prepared to leave. He had so much appreciated their coming, he said. It had been such a wonderful treat. Most of them he was never to see again.

Soon afterwards Gerald started going down. A week later the hospital telephoned Lee in the middle of the night. Gerald was delirious, they told her. His temperature had shot up stratospherically. He might not make it through the night. She drove down to St Helier as fast as the dark, narrow lanes of Jersey permitted. At the hospital she was given a bed in Gerald's room while a group of young doctors tried to concoct a cocktail of antibiotics to knock this latest emergency on the head. At four in the morning the antibiotics were finally administered intravenously, together with a strong dose of steroids.

Four hours later Gerald woke. As Lee could see, his eyes were bright, his mind was in order, the fever had gone, he was as happy as a lark. When Sarah Kennedy visited she was amazed at what she saw: 'The man I looked down on in his hospital bed was like Gerry as he must have been when he was a young man. He'd lost a tremendous amount of weight, so all the jowls and puffiness had gone. His skin had become totally clear and his eyes were an incredible brilliant blue, like the waters of Corfu. I could see how stunning he must have been when he was young. He really did look incredibly good at the end.' Gerry gave Sarah a big smile, and after she'd gone he half sat up in bed.

He was feeling great, he told Lee, and wanted to ring his sister. 'Marg,' he said when he got through, 'I'm feeling terrific. They've worked out a new course of drugs for me. I'm going to pull through.' Margaret recalled: 'He sounded just like the old Gerry. He had the old voice, the old light-heartedness, the old enthusiasm. It was as though he'd made a total recovery.' When Jeremy Mallinson went to see his old guru in the hospital he seemed almost his former self. 'When did you start working for me, Jeremy?' he asked. When Jeremy told him it was thirty-five years ago, he exclaimed: 'Thank God I only employed you on a temporary basis!'

Gerald still more or less refused to eat. Lee would spend hours trying to get him to suck soup through a straw or to take a few sips of a highly nutritious but horribly sweet medical milkshake, which he hated. He was now very weak and emaciated, and by Friday, 27 January, he was running a slight temperature. Dr Guyer asked him next day how he was feeling. 'Bloody awful,' Gerald replied. These were the last coherent words he ever uttered. Simon Hicks went to see him and came away near to tears. 'I was confronted for the first time with this hundred-year-old man,' he remembered. 'The most dreadful thing was that I couldn't actually see him, the real him, even when I looked in his eyes. Three-quarters of his spirit had gone. I just couldn't get near him – I could have wept. It was the end, really.'

Gerald was not speaking at all now. The nurse put some music on the record player for him – Mozart, Vivaldi, his favourites – but he was no longer listening; he had turned his face to the wall. On Sunday evening the nurse asked Lee whether she wanted to stay at the hospital for the night, but she said no, she'd been through this many times before, and went back to the lonely flat at the zoo. The countryside was dark and wintry, hardly a light anywhere. Black, lowering cloud swept in from the sea and hid the stars. The manor was empty and quiet as the grave when Lee got back. She had a drink, then went to bed, trying to shut it all out, but slept fitfully. At two in the morning the phone rang. It was the hospital. She ought to come down. There was a change happening.

By six or seven in the morning Gerry was virtually unconscious. Later the house doctor called Lee in. He was not going to make it, he told her. There was nothing that could be done. Gerald's GP, Jeremy Guyer, agreed. 'He couldn't have been kept going much longer. He was desperately ill and had shrunk to around a quarter of his original body weight. He was resigned to it. I'm quite sure he knew he was going to die when he came back to Jersey. He seemed to be quite happy about it. The septicaemia he went down with would have killed a healthy patient, let alone one in his condition.'

Lee rang Jeremy Mallinson, and he arrived at noon. 'They had stopped resuscitation,' she recalled. 'They were just sitting about, waiting. Jeremy and I talked about it and in the end we decided to let him go. Gerry had an oxygen mask over his face and his breath was very laboured. I could hear him struggling to breathe the oxygen in, and the gaps between his breathing grew longer and longer. I was sitting beside him, holding his hand. Jeremy was there with me in the room, and the nurse. Gerry's breathing got slower and weaker and eventually he stopped breathing altogether. It was over.'

Durrell's luck had finally run out – as, someday, somewhere, it was always bound to have done. A nurse fetched the house doctor, and he wrote the report there and then: death due to septicaemia.

Gerald Durrell died at about two o'clock on the afternoon of Monday, 30 January 1995. Within a few hours the Press Association had put out a news flash in two slugs a minute apart:

DEATH DURRELL. AUTHOR AND NATURALIST GERALD DURRELL, 70, DIED IN JERSEY GENERAL HOSPITAL TODAY ... DURRELL, WHO HAD A LIVER TRANSPLANT LAST YEAR, FOUNDED JERSEY ZOO. HIS WIFE LEE AND ZOO DIRECTOR JEREMY MALLINSON WERE AT HIS BED-SIDE. ENDS.

Already the press obituaries were being put together and film footage assembled for the early evening news broadcasts. It was a big story. The demise of a giant of his kind.

'I think it's a great mistake to feel that when your patient dies you have failed,' Dr Tibbs was to comment later. 'I don't think we failed. To me the success of the latter part of the battle to save Gerald Durrell was to get him back to Jersey, where he could celebrate Christmas, and have his birthday, and see his zoo and his animals again, say his goodbyes – a very important part of the dying process. So I think we gave him the opportunity of coming to terms with it and tying up loose ends and making a dignified exit.'

Gerald had always said he wanted to be cremated, but Lee decided that his close friends and family should say their goodbyes at the undertakers rather than the crematorium – it was more intimate, less industrial. So on the Thursday they foregathered in an undertakers' tiny parlour in a side street in St Helier. Sister Margaret, the last surviving member of the remarkable Durrell brood, came over from Bournemouth, and her son Gerry and granddaughter Tracy, and Larry's daughter Penny, and Lee's sister Hat from Memphis. They were joined by Jeremy and Odette Mallinson, John and Sylvia Hartley, Simon and Sarah Hicks, Tony and Maggie Allchurch, and Sam and Catha Weller. It was not a funeral. There was no priest, no formal service or prayers, no music.

'Lee had never believed Gerry was going to die,' Jeremy Mallinson recalled, 'so she wasn't quite sure what to do. But she knew what Gerry wouldn't have wanted, and she knew what she didn't want as well. So she evolved a very simple but terribly poignant farewell as she went along.' Standing there in the tiny funeral parlour, she asked if anyone wanted to say something – tell a story, anything they felt like – that would commemorate the passing of the man they had loved and followed. One by one they stood up, those who wanted to, and spoke a little. 'There were not many dry eyes in that room,' Lee remembered. 'The women were especially affected – but so were the boys.' Then Lee led them one by one or two by two into the side room, the tiny chapel of rest where Gerry's coffin lay. And there they said their last goodbyes.

The obituaries in the press and on television and radio were lengthy and fulsome. No one could have been left in any doubt that a great man had gone. Letters of grief and condolence poured in from around the world – from prime ministers and royals, celebrities and peasants, schoolchildren and total strangers who had been touched by the life of this man. Colleagues and friends paid tribute to a pioneering genius who was not only a colossus but a unique and idiosyncratic human being as well. Some of the tributes culled quotes from Gerald Durrell's own dicta, celebrating his vision of the miracle of life, the wonder of nature and the blindness and arrogance of man:

> A sparrow can be as interesting as a bird of paradise, the behaviour of a mouse as interesting as that of a tiger. Our planet is beautifully

intricate, brimming over with enigmas to be solved and riddles to be unravelled.

Many people think that conservation is just about saving fluffy animals – what they don't realise is that we're trying to prevent the human race from committing suicide . . . We have declared war on the biological world, the world that supports us . . . At the moment the human race is in the position of a man sawing off the tree branch he is sitting on.

Look at it this way. Anyone who has got any pleasure at all from living should try to put something back. Life is like a superlative meal and the world is the *maître d'hôtel*. What I'm doing is the equivalent of leaving a reasonable tip . . . I'm glad to be giving something back because I've been so extraordinarily lucky and had such great pleasure from it.

In the end, all things considered, he preferred the world of animals: 'They are so much more straightforward and honest. They have no sort of pretensions. They don't pretend they are God. They don't pretend they are intelligent, they don't invent nerve gas and above all they don't go to cocktail parties.'

A little more than a month later, on 9 March 1995, Gerald Durrell's ashes were laid to rest beneath a small marble plinth in a corner of the garden of Les Augrès Manor, that ancient and burnished pile of local granite where he had spent the last thirty-five years of his life, first with Jacquie and then with Lee, struggling to realise a dream and achieve a goal. It was a blustery, greying evening, with scudding clouds and a few shafts of sun and a hint of rain. The guests – family, friends, colleagues, staff, students from Les Noyers – gathered in loose clusters in front of the low little plinth that covered Gerald's ashes. Wrapped up against the sniping wind, they were serious, solemn, respectful, remembrance-full. Geoff Hamon, the Chairman of the Trust, spoke a few words of farewell. The General Curator, Quentin Bloxam, said a few more. As he spoke, the fitful cries of the lemurs came drifting into the courtyard on the eddying wind.

We are all indebted to this remarkable man who was so many years ahead of his time in realising the potential of captive breeding as a discipline for the protection of endangered species. We will all miss his humour and guiding hand, but we are all determined to continue to be one of the role models in the field of captive breeding. Our commitment to Gerald Durrell's philosophy is absolute . . .

Afterwards the people who had gathered there laid small bunches of spring flowers and heather around the plinth, and read the words inscribed on it, written almost ninety years before by an early American prophet of the conservation movement, William Beebe:

> The beauty and genius of a work of art may be reconceived, though its first material expression be destroyed; a vanishing harmony may yet again inspire the composer; but *when the last individual of a race of living things breathes no more, another heaven and another earth must pass before such a one can be again.*

Gerald Durrell was a man of the world and a man for all time and for all living things. And there was another part of this rich and rounded prodigy that could rightly be celebrated – his great gift for friendship, for generosity, for love and loving kindness, for honest laughter and good cheer – for in this part, as in all others, he was remarkable.

And so it was ended, and he was in another place, bequeathing his love for this one, entrusting it to our care. 'Now let me tell you something,' he had once said: it was his affirmation and credo, a prayer of a kind in celebration of a world he saw as endlessly wonderful and infinitely precious.

> I have seen a thousand sunsets and sunrises,
> on land where it floods forest and mountains with honey coloured light:
> I have seen a thousand moons . . .
> I have felt winds as tender and warm as a lover's breath;
> winds that carried the moist rich smell of a forest floor,
> the smell of a million flowers . . .
> I have known silence:
> the hot, drugged silence when everything is stilled by the eye of the sun;
> the silence when great music ends . . .

Now he has gone, but it remains.

Afterword

The memorial celebration was held in the great hall of the Natural History Museum in London – a cathedral to the world of animals and plants – on a hot and sultry evening in June 1995. More than a thousand people, public and guests, Trust members and fans, came to rejoice and give thanks for the life and work of Gerald Durrell. The queue stretched up Exhibition Road and past the Science Museum, and the audience was packed in round the great dinosaur skeleton in the hall and on the gothic galleries above.

Arranged and directed by one of Gerald's closest friends at the Trust, the celebration encompassed his entire life and work. There were speeches and photographs and clips of his films on a giant screen and readings from his writings and renderings of songs and music from Noël Coward and the Cameroons. Sir David Attenborough spoke of the Durrell magic, that had touched so many people's lives on a personal level because he was a crusader. Gerald had been a man before his time, he said, who had harboured a dream of owning a zoo – a special zoo whose main role was the survival of species. Princess Anne read out the message Gerald had addressed to future generations, exhorting them to treasure and honour the natural world and to cherish the earth's diversity of species – a message she herself had buried in a time capsule in the zoo grounds. From America Tom Lovejoy and Robert Rattner, Honorary Chairman and President of Wildlife Preservation Trust International, gave their own vivid recollections and reflections. The voices and the music echoed among the arches and cloisters and then died. Gerald had been given a big goodbye, and it was over.

Or was it? One morning in the early spring following Gerald's death I had walked with Lee through the grounds of the zoo he had founded on a wing and a prayer all those years ago. It was one of those plangent blue Channel Island mornings. The zoo was a haven of peace within a haven of peace, its leafy tranquillity only broken by an occasional heart-arresting jungle shriek or a collective brouhaha from the lemurs, an outburst full of sound and fury signifying territory.

I was a new boy then. I knew the broad ground-plan of the story but little of the details, and my casual encounters with man and beast around the zoo of Gerald Durrell's creation was an enlightening series of shocks and puzzles which grew curiouser and curiouser by the minute. Everywhere I looked I could see little bears cavorting, orang-utans climbing and swinging, lemurs dangling from the branches of an oak tree or tituping along the rope lines above the path, golden-headed lion tamarins skittering in and out of the camellia bushes, white owls staring, pink pigeons fluttering, tortoises lumbering, an aye-aye climbing a tree stump with infinite gradualness in its darkened enclosure. Everywhere I looked I observed seemingly contented, purposeful animal play and endeavour. Only the female snow leopard looked grumpy. 'It takes ten dumb animals to make a fur coat,' read the placard outside the creature's enclosure, indicating the cause of its endangeredness, 'but only one to wear it.'

I came to the enclosure for the lowland gorillas. The females and children were sitting quietly together, feeding and suckling and relating in an atmosphere of collective togetherness. The great white hope of the Jersey gorillas – the next big breeder – was pointed out to me. A hefty teenage male, he lay indolently sprawling on his back in an almost human posture of adolescent loafishness. A stranger came up to me.

'I hear you're writing Gerry's biography,' he said to me. 'I'm writing a biography too.'

This was a strange place for a literary coincidence, I thought. 'Oh, really? How interesting,' I said. 'Who of?'

'Jambo.'

'Jambo who?' I asked in my ignorance.

'Jambo,' he repeated. 'You know – our silverback gorilla. Gerry's opposite number, so to speak. Jambo the patriarch.'

A gorilla biography – it seemed par for this Alice in Wonderland grand tour. We passed another enclosure, and Lee called out as a keeper emerged from it.

'How'd it go?'

'Like a dream,' came the man's enthusiastic reply. 'She went into labour in the middle of the night. Absolutely no problem. A perfect delivery. Piece of cake.'

'What did she have?' asked Lee.

'A boy and a girl,' replied the keeper, unable to conceal his joy and pride, adding mysteriously and alarmingly: 'With perfect markings.'

Perfect markings? I had assumed the keeper had been talking about his wife and was delighting in the birth of twins, but I had a problem envisaging them the way he had described them.

'That was the spectacled-bear keeper,' Lee explained. 'One of the bears has just had babies.'

The birth of two offspring from an endangered species was reason enough for rejoicing. It was what Jersey Zoo and Trust were all about.

We came to an enclosure containing a small brown duck. It was frankly a dull little creature, one of Gerry's classic 'little brown jobs'. Sometimes it stood on one leg, and sometimes it stood on two. Otherwise it did nothing much, not even quack. But it was not here to divert the public on a wet afternoon. It was here to be saved from extinction, and what it looked like or what it did was not an issue. This unobtrusive creature was a Madagascar teal, the world's most obscure duck. Only a handful had ever been seen, but it was clear its numbers were steadily going down. Nothing was known about its breeding habits – the time of year, the kind of nest, on the ground or up a tree. No nest and no eggs had ever been found. The duck didn't seem to mind. This wasn't Madagascar, but it wasn't complaining. It had its own pond with nothing nasty lurking in it. There was no one with a shotgun or snare for miles. There was no one with a machete and a firebrand to destroy the leafy green bush that was its present habitat. The food was good and the natives were friendly.

It was fairly evident that every living thing in Jersey Zoo would go along with this. The animals were happy, active, and this side of extinction. Gerald Durrell the man was no more but his work lived on, and the reason for it – the embattled kingdom of living things – remained. And he had left behind an organisation and a team as dedicated to the cause and the mission as he. Lee had donned the mantle of Honorary Director of the Trust, and the Trust itself was soon to be rethought and restructured to face the challenges of the new millennium and given a new name – the Durrell Wildlife Conservation Trust – both in honour of its founder and in recognition of its worldwide commitments to animal conservation. Meanwhile its work would continue into the future, adapting as need be to new situations and new ideas.

Shortly after my trip to Gerald Durrell's zoo and Trust headquarters I visited the Mazet, the old converted farmhouse he had shared with Lee in Languedoc, and found his presence still so immanent and strong that it was as if he had just gone out for a stroll, and would be back soon. Later I returned to Corfu, staying with friends at the small coastal village of Kaminaki, not far from Kalami, while I researched the life and times, haunts and homes of the young Gerald and his family on the island. The season of the festival of the fireflies – that fantastic insect spectacle so vividly described in *My Family and Other Animals* – was long over. What happened at Kaminaki one stifling moonless night was therefore doubly odd.

I had been dining at the taverna on the beach with my friends, and stayed on after they left, engaged in a desultory conversation with strangers. By the time I started for home it was pitch-black, and I could not find the gap at the head of the beach that led to the ancient paved track to the house. As I wandered up and down, uncertain where to go, a tiny winking light, a curious, incessant, electric neon flash, suddenly appeared at chest height about three feet in front of me. I took a step towards it, and it backed away by the same distance, then hovered, winking steadily.

It was a firefly, I knew. But it was odd that it was around so late in the year, and so alone; and odder still that it should appear to be relating, or at least reacting, to a human being in this uncharacteristic way. I moved towards it again, and again it backed away by the same distance. And so we proceeded, the firefly always at chest height and three feet in front of me. I realised I had been led through the gap in the beach that I could not find, and that we were at the foot of the ancient track. Guided by the firefly I walked slowly up the invisible path, step by step in the total darkness.

Halfway up, the firefly stopped and hovered, winking vigorously, until I was almost abreast of it. Then it made a sharp turn of ninety degrees to the left and proceeded up another, shorter but steeper path, with me trustingly trudging behind. It stopped again, and I realised I was at the garden gate of the house where I ws staying. The firefly went over the gate, and I followed it across the unlit patio. The kitchen door was somewhere there in the dark, and the firefly flickered unerringly towards it. As I reached for the doorknob the firefly fluttered up and settled on the back of my hand, winking the while. I was home.

Was this normal? I asked myself. Were fireflies known to behave in this way towards *people*? I lifted my hand up to my face and peered closely at the wildly signalling minuscule organism. As I did so, I heard the voice of one of my friends, who, sitting silently in the dark, had witnessed everything: 'Good . . . *God!*' I blew gently on the firefly, and it rose, turned once in a flickering circle, flew off into the tops of the overhanging olive trees and vanished into the night.

'You realise what that was, don't you?' my friend said. He was a distinguished political journalist, and an eminently sane and sensible man. 'Gerald Durrell keeping an eye on you, lending a hand, helping you home. No question about it. I think I'd better have another Metaxa after *that*!'

Every Corfiot Greek I told the story to nodded dryly and said matter-of-factly, without a hint of surprise, 'Gerald Durrell.'

Gerald always believed that if he survived in a life after death it would be in some form of animal reincarnation. He had hoped it would be something fun – a soaring eagle, or a leaping dolphin – but perhaps a firefly would do at a pinch.

Make of this visitation what you will, there is no doubt that Gerald Durrell's spirit does live on in one way or another – in his books, in his zoo, in his ongoing mission, in the natural world he has left behind.

There have been six great waves of extinctions on earth during the millions of years of geological time. Extinction has always been a fact of life – the downside to existence, with evolution as the upside. 'One can't understand evolution, really, without understanding extinction,' noted American palaeontologist Niles Eldredge. 'And you can't understand extinction without first grasping ecology. Extinction is fundamentally a story of ecological collapse.'

We are in a period of ecological collapse right now, the consequence of habitat and species loss partly attributable to climate change and partly to the destructive activities of *Homo sapiens* (which in turn accelerate climate change). The predictions for future extinctions in our time are dire for both animals and plants – and perhaps for man himself, since man cannot escape the fate of the natural world, no matter how much he believes he can; like it or not, he remains part of the global ecosystem. It may be that in the long term the universe is implacably hostile to all life anyway. It may be that our planet and all its cargo are proceeding towards eventual extinction. It may be that in the shorter term all life proceeds according to the laws of evolution, through successive stages of extinction (from whatever causes) to universal oblivion. But as Gerald Durrell constantly reiterated throughout his adult life, that does not mean a man can stand idly by and watch it all happen without lifting a finger. With the millennium, perhaps, we will enter an age of ethics. Man can learn, as Gerald Durrell frequently pointed out; man can come to his senses, can change, can try to save the day. And thanks to the inspiration of people like him there are signs that, at the eleventh hour, this is beginning to happen; that we may one day hope to turn the tide of habitat-destruction and man-made extinction on earth.

That was Gerald Durrell's message, and that was Gerald Durrell's life mission. That message and that mission will be carried forward by those who succeed him.

The Durrell Wildlife Conservation Trust

As it enters the new millennium the Jersey Wildlife Preservation Trust has reviewed and renewed its mission. The vision of its founder, Gerald Durrell, has been enshrined in a new name, the Durrell Wildlife Conservation Trust, and in the simple and effective method that he began – and that his staff have refined over forty years – to save animals from extinction.

The world's problems and those of its wildlife stretch ahead and are likely to grow. The planet needs organisations like the Durrell Wildlife Conservation Trust to rescue and revive the most critically endangered species in sufficient habitat to survive whatever man-made crisis lies ahead.

If you would like to hear more about the work of the Durrell Wildlife Conservation Trust to save species from extinction, please write to the Trust at Les Augrès Manor, Trinity, Jersey JE3 5BP (telephone 01534 864666; fax 01534 865161; email jerseyzoo@durrell.org); or to Wildlife Preservation Trust Canada, 120 King Street, Guelph, Ontario N1E 4P8, Canada; or to Wildlife Preservation Trust International, 1520 Locust Street, Suite 704, Philadelphia PA 19102-4403, USA.

Sources

CHAPTER ONE: Landfall in Jamshedpur

Gordon Bowker, letter to the author, 15 October 1997
Gordon Bowker, *Through the Dark Labyrinth: A Biography of Lawrence Durrell*
Margaret Duncan (Durrell), interviews with Molly Briggs and Phyllis Coulson,
    January 1986, and with the author, 1995–98
Gerald Durrell, 'Autobiographical Fragments' (unpublished typescript, Jersey
    Archives)
Gerald Durrell, letter to a Mrs Seaward, October 1990
Jacquie Durrell, interview with the author, November 1995
Lawrence Durrell to Henry Miller, 27 January 1937
Nancy Durrell, 'Memoirs' (transcripts from tapes, c.1972)
David Hughes, *Himself and Other Animals*
Ian MacNiven, *Lawrence Durrell: A Biography*
Celia Yeo, Durrell Family Tree

CHAPTER TWO: 'The Most Ignorant Boy in the School'

Margaret Duncan (Durrell), interview with the author, 1995
Margaret Duncan (Durrell), interview with Molly Briggs and Phyllis Coulson,
    January 1986
Gerald Durrell, 'Autobiographical Fragments' (unpublished typescript, Jersey
    Archives)
Gerald Durrell, 'Lawrence Durrell' (typescript, c.1979, Jersey Archives)
Gerald Durrell, *My Family and Other Animals*
Lawrence Durrell to Henry Miller, 1937 (MacNiven Collection)
Lawrence Durrell (ed. Alan Thomas), *Spirit of Place*
Nancy Durrell, 'Memoirs' (transcripts from tapes, c.1972)
David Hughes, *Himself and Other Animals*
Dorothy Keep, interview with the author, summer 1996
Ian MacNiven, *Lawrence Durrell: A Biography*

CHAPTER THREE: The Gates of Paradise

The principal source for Gerald Durrell's life on Corfu remains *My Family and
Other Animals*. Though this has a number of shortcomings as biographical
source material - a tenuous chronology, an anecdotal approach, and some
tinkering with the literal truth – it remains very close to the spirit, and often the
letter, of his experience on the island as a boy, and his recollections of places,
landscapes and the natural history of Corfu are surprisingly exact. His later
accounts of his Corfu experience – *Birds, Beasts and Relatives* (1969), *Garden of*

the Gods (1978) and his unpublished autobiographical sketches – are essentially the mixture as before, albeit with a rather more tenuous grasp on fact, and do little to alter the basic narrative framework. Almost all of the main players in the island idyll are now dead, but a number have left memoirs of one sort or another, and these have provided valuable insights, elaborations and qualifications in the construction of this chapter.

Anne Barrowclough, *Daily Mail*, 19 November 1987

Margaret Duncan (Durrell), interview with the author, November 1997

Gerald Durrell, 'Autobiographical Fragments' (unpublished typescript, Jersey Archives)

Gerald Durrell, French TV interview

Gerald Durrell, 'Last Word', a tribute to Theo Stephanides, *JWPT Newsletter*, n.d.

Gerald Durrell, letter to Peter Barber-Fleming, BBC TV, 6 January 1987

Gerald Durrell, 'The Man of Animals' (manuscript, Corfu, c.1935, Jersey Archives)

Gerald Durrell, manuscript poem, Corfu, c.1935 (Durrell Archives, Manuscript Department, British Library)

Gerald Durrell, 'Script Notes' re 'My Family - 2nd Draft Scripts', sent to Joe Waters et al., BBC TV, 15 November 1986

Lawrence Durrell, 'Blue Thirst' (lecture at Caltech, Pasadena, Capra Press, Santa Barbara, 1975)

Lawrence Durrell, *Prospero's Cell*

Lawrence Durrell (ed. Alan Thomas), *Spirit of Place*

Nancy Durrell, 'Memoirs' (transcripts from tapes, c.1972)

Alex Emmett, interview with the author, 1998

Arthur Foss (with Alexia Mercouri and Marie Sanson), 'Theodore Stephanides', in *Greek Gazette* (1996)

David Hughes, *Himself and Other Animals*

Ian MacNiven, *Lawrence Durrell: A Biography*

Mary Stephanides to Peter Harrison, July and August 1998

Theo Stephanides, letter to Gerald Durrell, 3 November 1984 (Jersey Archives)

Theo Stephanides, *My Island Years*

Alan Thomas Collection of Durrell Family Papers (Manuscripts Department, British Library)

Alan Thomas, letter to Gerald Durrell, 11 October 1984

CHAPTER FOUR: The Garden of the Gods

All the Durrell villas and surrounding habitats on Corfu still exist today, though the Strawberry-Pink Villa has been much altered and extended.

Douglas Botting, Corfu field notes, June 1996

Gordon Bowker, *Through the Dark Labyrinth*

Geoffrey Carr, 'Memories of Corfu', in *The Corfiot*; and interview with the author, 1996

Menelaos Condos, interview with the author, June 1996

Margaret Duncan (Durrell), interviews with the author, 1995–1997

Gerald Durrell, 'An African Dialogue' in *Seven*, No. 5, Summer 1939 (Durrell Archives, Manuscript Department, British Library)

Gerald Durrell, *Birds, Beasts and Relatives*

Gerald Durrell, 'Death', in the *Booster*, Paris, November 1937

Gerald Durrell, foreword to *The Insect World of J. Henri Fabre* (Beacon Press, 1990)

Gerald Durrell, 'In the Theatre', in the *Booster*, Paris, October 1937

Gerald Durrell, interview with Michael Armstrong, February 1980

Gerald Durrell, taped conversation with John Burton, n.d.

Gerald Durrell, 'Script Notes' re 'My Family - 2nd Draft Scripts', sent to Joe Waters et al., BBC TV, 15 November 1986

Gerald Durrell, letter to Harriet McGeorge, c.1991

Gerald Durrell, *My Family and Other Animals*

Gerald Durrell, 'My Brother Larry', in *Twentieth Century Literature*, Vol. 33 no. 3, Hofstra University, 1997

Gerald Durrell, 'Night-Club' (typescript, c.1936, Durrell Archives, Manuscript Department, British Library)

Lawrence Durrell, letter to Henry Miller, March 1937 (MacNiven Collection)

Lawrence Durrell, letter to Ann Ridler, October 1939

Lawrence Durrell, 'A Landmark Gone', in *Orientations*, Vol. 1 No. 1 (Cairo, n.d.)

Lawrence Durrell (ed. Alan Thomas), *Spirit of Place*

Leslie Durrell, letter to Alan Thomas, 1936 (Durrell Archives, Manuscript Department, British Library)

Nancy Durrell, 'Memoirs' (transcripts from tapes, c.1972)

Tom Evans to Peter Harrison, July 1998

Peter Harrison, 'The Corfu Landscapes of Gerald Durrell', in *Landscape Review*, November 1996 and *The Corfiot*, August 1996

David Hughes, *Himself and Other Animals*

Lee Langley, 'The Other Mr Durrell', *Guardian*, 1 August 1970

Ian MacNiven, *Lawrence Durrell: A Biography*

Brian A. Maddock, notes and correspondence on the Durrell villas, June 1992 and February 1997

Tim Newell Price (School Archivist, Leighton Park School) to the author, July 1998

Mary Stephanides to Peter Harrison, August 1998

Alan Thomas, bibliography, in G.S. Fraser, *Lawrence Durrell*

CHAPTER FIVE: Gerald in Wartime

Margaret Duncan (Durrell), interview with the author, November 1997

Gerald Durrell, 'Autobiographical Fragments' (unpublished typescript, Jersey Archives)

Gerald Durrell, *Beasts in my Belfry*

Gerald Durrell, draft introduction to Lucy Pendar, *Whipsnade: My Africa* (2 August 1990, Jersey Archives)

Gerald Durrell, draft note for *Ark on the Move*
Gerald Durrell, interview with Michael Armstrong, February 1980
Gerald Durrell, taped conversation with John Burton, n.d.
Gerald Durrell, interview with Radiodiffusion Télévision Française, 1971
Gerald Durrell, 'Notes for an Autobiography' (typescript, 1994, Jersey Archives)
Gerald Durrell, 'A Transport of Terrapins', in *Fillets of Plaice* (1971)
Jacquie Durrell, interview with the author, November 1995
Lee Durrell, interview with the author, October 1996
David Hughes, *Himself and Other Animals*
Eileen McCarrol, 'Childhood in Corfu' (*Women's Weekly*, 7 November 1987)

CHAPTER SIX: Odd-Beast Boy

Jill Adams (*née* Johnson), interview with the author, July 1996
Robert Bendiner, *The Fall of the Wild: The Rise of the Zoo*
Gerald Durrell, 'Autobiographical Fragments' (unpublished typescript, Jersey Archives)
Gerald Durrell, *Beasts in my Belfry*
Gerald Durrell, draft note for *Ark on the Move*
Gerald Durrell, uncut draft of BBC radio talk *Vanishing Animals* (progamme five of series *Animal Attitudes*, 3 March 1958)
David Hughes, *Himself and Other Animals*
Peter Mathiessen, *Wildlife in America*
Lucy Pendar, *Whipsnade: My Africa*
Colin Tudge, *Last Animals at the Zoo*

CHAPTER SEVEN: Planning for Adventure

Ian Bevan, 'He brings them back alive', *John Bull*, 4 February 1950
Anthony Condos to the author and Peter Harrison, June and July 1998
Margaret Duncan (Durrell), interviews with the author, 1990, November and December 1997
Gerald Durrell, 'Autobiographical Fragments' (unpublished typescript, Jersey Archives)
Gerald Durrell, letter to Anthony Condos, 1 February 1989
Gerald Durrell, letter to Lawrence Durrell, 14 December 1954
Jacquie Durrell, interview with the author, November 1995
Lawrence Durrell to Henry Miller, 1947
Lee Durrell, interview with the author, October 1996
Margaret Durrell, *Whatever Happened to Margo?*
Lee Langley, 'The Other Mr Durrell', *Guardian*, 1 August 1970

CHAPTER EIGHT: To the Back of Beyond

Gerald Durrell, 'Cholmondeley', in the *Listener*, 28 September 1963
Gerald Durrell, *The Overloaded Ark*

Gerald Durrell, preface to Andrew Mitchell, *The Enchanted Canopy*
David Hughes, *Himself and Other Animals*

CHAPTER NINE: In the Land of the Fon

Sir David Attenborough, letter to the author, 5 April 1998
Bournemouth Echo, 'Off to Africa Wilds', January 1949
Bournemouth Echo, 'He's off to Darkest Africa', January 1949
Margaret Duncan (Durrell), interview with the author, December 1997
Gerald Durrell, *The Bafut Beagles*
Gerald Durrell, 'Cameroons Diary 1949–50'
Gerald Durrell to Richard Connif, *Geo*, May 1983
Gerald Durrell, letters to Louisa Durrell 6 February, 14 February, 8 March,
    28 April, 8 June 1949
Gerald Durrell, notes for lecture on animal collecting (Gerald Durrell Lecture File
    1954ff)
Gerald Durrell, notes for lecture at Royal Festival Hall, 13 November 1954
Gerald Durrell, *Snake Hole*, BBC Home Service, 12 July 1956
Gerald Durrell, taped conversation with John Burton, n.d.
Gerald Durrell, 'Ursula', in *Fillets of Plaice*
Peter Olney, interview with the author, July 1996
Ken Smith, letter to Leslie Durrell, 21 May 1949
Jean Stroud, 'Pit of Death', in *Look and Learn*, 2 December 1967

CHAPTER TEN: New Worlds to Conquer

The main source for the early days of the Gerald and Jacquie Durrell relationship
    is Jacquie Durrell's *Beasts in my Bed*
Sir David Attenborough to the author, 5 April 1998
Ian Bevan, 'He Brings them Back Alive', in *John Bull*, 4 February 1950
Gordon Bowker, *Through the Dark Labyrinth: A Biography of Lawrence Durrell*
Margaret Duncan (Durrell), interview with the author, November 1997
Gerald Durrell, 'Autobiographical Fragments' (unpublished typescript, Jersey
    Archives)
Gerald Durrell, letter to his bank, Bournemouth, c. summer 1958
Gerald Durrell, *Three Singles to Adventure*
Jacquie Durrell, interview with the author, November 1995
Jacquie Durrell to the author, September and October 97
Lee Durrell and Jeremy Mallinson to the author, July 1998
Margaret Durrell, *Whatever Happened to Margo?*
David Hughes, *Himself and Other Animals*

CHAPTER ELEVEN: Writing Man

Gerald Durrell, 'Cholmondeley, in the *Listener*, 28 November 1963
Gerald Durrell, interview with Michael Armstrong, February 1980
Gerald Durrell, 'Lawrence Durrell' in *Evening Standard*, 5 October 1961
Gerald Durrell, 'The Travel Bug is Stirring Again, *World Books Bulletin*,
    March 1956

Gerald Durrell, 'The Traveller as Writer', in *Books and Bookmen*, July 1956

Jacquie Durrell, *Beasts in my Bed*

Jacquie Durrell, 'For Always', magazine article, c.1962

Jacquie Durrell, interviews with the author, October 1995 and October 1997

Jacquie Durrell to the author, November 1995 and October 1997

Lawrence Durrell (ed. Alan Thomas), *Spirit of Place*

David Hughes, *Himself and Other Animals*

In Town Tonight, 1 August 1953 (BBC transcript)

Ian MacNiven (ed.), *The Durrell–Miller Letters*

Ian MacNiven and Harry T. Moore (eds), *Literary Lifelines: The Richard Aldington–Lawrence Durrell Correspondence*

Gavin Maxwell, 'The Technique of Travel Writing', National Book League, December 1960

Dr Alan Ogden, letters to the author, 18 and 20 October 1995

CHAPTER TWELVE: Of Beasts and Books

Carlos Selva Andrade, 'En el mundo heroico de la aventura científica', *Vea y Lea*, Buenos Aires, December 1953

David Attenborough, 'The Joys and Delights of Collecting', *World Books Bulletin*, February 1956

Evelyn D. Bangay in *Poetry Review*, January 1962

Alan Devoe, 'Fun with the Fon', *Saturday Review of Literature*, 8 January 1955

Gerald Durrell's archive of fan mail, Jersey Zoo

Gerald Durrell, *The Ark's Anniversary*

Gerald Durrell, cue sheets for Royal Festival Hall lecture, 13 November 1954

Gerald Durrell, *The Drunken Forest*

Gerald Durrell, letters to Lawrence Durrell, 20 October and 14 December 1954 (SIU)

Gerald Durrell, 'Zoo Article' (Jersey Zoo Archives)

Jacquie Durrell, *Beasts in my Bed*

Lawrence Durrell, *Bitter Lemons*

Lawrence Durrell (ed. Alan Thomas), *Spirit of Place*

Patrick Leigh Fermor, letter to the author, 23 October 1996

Ian MacNiven, *Lawrence Durrell: A Biography*

Rubi M. Rubens, 'Jacqueline y Gerald – dos nombres para una aventura', *El Hogar*, Buenos Aires, December 1953

W.J. Weatherby, 'The Durrell Brothers', *Guardian*, 6 May 1961

CHAPTER THIRTEEN: The Book of the Idyll

Gerald Durrell, 'Autobiographical Fragments' (unpublished typescript, Jersey Archives)

Gerald Durrell, 'A Bookman's Jottings', *Bookman*, October 1956

Gerald Durrell, 'Explanation re Corfu Book'(undated typescript filed with preliminary notes for *My Family and Other Animals*)

Gerald Durrell, interview with Michael Armstrong, February 1980

Gerald Durrell, taped conversation with John Burton, n.d.

Gerald Durrell, *My Family and Other Animals*
Jacquie Durrell, *Beasts in my Bed*
Jacquie Durrell, letter to the author, September 1997
Lawrence Durrell, 'Animal Collector's Family Rampage', *Books and Bookmen*,
    November 1956
Lawrence Durrell (ed. Alan Thomas), *Spirit of Place*
David Hughes, *Himself and Other Animals*
David Hughes, interview with the author, October 1995
Ian MacNiven and Harry T. Moore (eds), *Literary Lifelines: The Richard
    Aldington–Lawrence Durrell Correspondence*
Jane Lagoudis Pinchin, 'Sideways out of the House: Lawrence and Gerald
    Durrell', in *Blood Brothers: Siblings as Writers* (ed. Norman Kiele)
W.J. Weatherby, 'The Durrell Brothers', *Guardian*, 6 May 1961

CHAPTER FOURTEEN: Man and Nature

John Barber, 'Bring em Back Alive Golding is Home Again', *Bristol Evening
    Post*, 15 July 1957
Gordon Bowker, *Through the Dark Labyrinth: A Biography of Lawrence Durrell*
C.G. Bramwell, Conservator of Forests, letter to Forest Officer, Mamfe, 28
    January 1957
Commissioner of the Cameroons, Extract of Touring Notes – Mamfe Division,
    3 May 1957
Gerald Durrell, 'Bournemouth Zoo-Park' (typescript, 1956)
Gerald Durrell, draft article for *Reveille* magazine (typescript, 3 October 1957)
Gerald Durrell–Ivan Sanderson correspondence 1956/57 (Gerald Durrell
    Archives, Jersey Zoo)
Gerald Durrell, 'Man and Nature' (typed radio script, retitled *The Balance of
    Nature*, BBC German Service 29 August 1956)
Gerald Durrell, 'My Family did Really Exist', *World Books Bulletin*, 1957
Gerald Durrell, 'The Third Cameroon Expedition', in letter to Bob Morse, *Life*
    magazine, 9 November 1956
Gerald Durrell, *A Zoo in my Luggage*
Jacquie Durrell, *Beasts in my Bed*
Financial Times, 10 December 1956
Fon of Bafut, letter to Gerald Durrell, 25 January 1957 (original in JWPT
    archives, Jersey)
Peter Green, 'Five Gloriously Eccentric Years' (Reprint Society Broadsheet)
David Hughes, *Himself and Other Animals*
Melville's Choice (BBC Talks Department script, 2 December 1956)
Jane Lagoudis Pinchin, 'Sideways out of the House: Lawrence and Gerald
    Durrell', in *Blood Brothers: Siblings as Writers* (ed. Norman Kiele)
Sunday Express, 2 December 1956
Kenneth Young, 'A Boyhood in Paradise', *Daily Telegraph*, 12 October 1956

CHAPTER FIFTEEN: 'A Wonderful Place for a Zoo'

Jessie Forsyth Andrews, 'The Whole Creation – Or Only Part? Animals, Man and God', *Christian World*, 15 May 1958

Sir David Attenborough, 'Recollections of Gerald Durrell', *BBC Wildlife Magazine*, March 1995

Bournemouth Echo, July 1957, August 1958

David Clayton, 'Cholmondeley Steals the Show from Mr Durrell', *Evening Standard*, 9 April 1958

Gerald Durrell, Argentina 1959 papers (JWPT archives, Jersey)

Gerald Durrell, *The Ark's Anniversary*

Gerald Durrell, Broadcast File 1958 (JWPT archives, Jersey)

Gerald Durrell, Documents Relating to Proposed Zoo at Upton House, Poole, 9 October and 19 November 1957 (JWPT archives, Jersey)

Gerald Durrell, 'Down South' (typescript, c.1959)

Gerald Durrell, draft obituary of Sir Peter Scott, 2 July 1990

Gerald Durrell, *Encounters with Animals*

Gerald Durrell, 'How to Live with a Chimp, *Everybody's*, 31 May 1958

Gerald Durrell, letter to BBC Television Bristol, 12 August 1958

Gerald Durrell, letter to Mr J. Hiller, Town Hall, Poole, 9 October 1957

Gerald Durrell, 'Life with Chumley No. 3' (typescript, 19 October 1958)

Gerald Durrell, *Menagerie Manor*

Gerald Durrell in 'Mr Cholmondeley Came to Tea', *Exhibition News*, W.H. Smith Ltd, 14 August 1957

Gerald Durrell, 'My Life with a Chimp', *Everybody's*, 6 December 1958

Gerald Durrell, South America 1959 file (JWPT archives, Jersey)

Gerald Durrell, *The Whispering Land*

Gerald Durrell, 'The Wild Animal Preservation Trust – Preliminary Report' (Bournemouth, 1958)

Gerald Durrell, *A Zoo in my Luggage*

Jacquie Durrell, *Beasts in my Bed*

Jacquie Durrell to the author, 15 September 1997

Lawrence Durrell, letter to Henry Miller, 18 December 1957

Lawrence Durrell, letter to Henry Miller, February 1958

David Hughes, *Himself and Other Animals*

David Hughes, interview with the author, October 1995

Elspeth Huxley, *Peter Scott: Painter and Naturalist*

Ian MacNiven and Harry T. Moore (eds), *Literary Lifelines: The Richard Aldington–Lawrence Durrell Correspondence*

Dr Alan Ogden, letter to the author, 18 October 1995

Maurice Richardson, 'Animals Again', *Observer*, 20 April 1958

Tom Salmon, letter to the author, 4 December 1996

Peter Scott, letter to Gerald Durrell, 9 September 1958 (Jersey Archives)

Times Literary Supplement, autumn 1958

CHAPTER SIXTEEN: A Zoo is Born

Michael Armstrong, interview with the author, November 96
Michael Armstrong, Jersey Zoo Diary 1959
Sir David Attenborough, 'Recollections of Gerald Durrell', *BBC Wildlife Magazine*, March 1995
Douglas Botting, 'Bafut Beagles Hunt Again', *Daily Telegraph*, 28 October 1960
Gerald Breeze to the author, February 1998
Gerald Durrell, *The Ark's Anniversary*
Gerald Durrell, 'I Live in Jersey', *Homes and Gardens*, written 1 October 1960
Gerald Durrell, 'I Love Having my Own Zoo', *Weekend Magazine*, Canada, Vol.11, No.44, 1961
Gerald Durrell, 'Island Zoo', *Atlantic Monthly*, August 1961
Gerald Durrell, Jersey Zoo Log, 1959/60
Jacquie Durrell, *Beasts in my Bed*
Jacquie Durrell, interview with the author, November 1995
Jacquie Durrell to the author, 15 September 1997
Lord Jersey, letter to the author, 29 November 1996
Jeremy Mallinson and others in group discussion with the author at Jersey Zoo, November 1996
Leslie Norton, interview with the author, October 1997
Dr Alan Ogden, letter to the author, November 1995
Kenneth Smith, 'Jersey Zoological Park' (Jersey, March 1959)

CHAPTER SEVENTEEN: 'We're All Going to be Devoured'

Maria Craipeau and Jean Lattes, *Une Arche sans Tempêtes*
Gerald Durrell, *The Ark's Anniversary*
Gerald Durrell, 'Christmas at the Zoo' *Animals* magazine, 1963
Gerald Durrell, 'Dead as a Dodo', *Jersey* magazine, c.1967
Gerald Durrell, 'I Love Having my Own Zoo' *Weekend Magazine*, Canada, Vol.11, No.44, 1961
Gerald Durrell, 'Island Zoo', *Atlantic Monthly*, August 1961
Gerald Durrell, letter to Lawrence Durrell, c. October 1960 (Durrell Archives, Manuscript Department, British Library)
Gerald Durrell, letter to *Jersey Evening Post*, n.d.
Gerald Durrell, 'Summer in Corfu', *Punch*, 17 May 1961
Gerald Durrell, *Two in the Bush*
Jacquie Durrell, *Beasts in my Bed*
Jacquie Durrell, interview with the author, November 1995
Jacquie Durrell, letter to the author, 1 October 1995
Jacquie Durrell to the author, 24 January 1998
Ian MacNiven, *Lawrence Durrell: A Biography*
David Hughes, 'Gerald Durrell and Friends', *Harper's Bazaar*, March 1962
Christopher Parsons, address at memorial celebration, Natural History Museum, June 1995
Christopher Parsons, *True to Nature*

CHAPTER EIGHTEEN: Durrell's Ark

Maria Craipeau and Jean Lattes, *Une Arche sans Tempêtes*
Margaret Duncan (Durrell) in David Hughes, *Himself and Other Animals*
Margaret Duncan (Durrell) to the author, January 1998
Gerald Durrell, *Catch me a Colobus*
Gerald Durrell, *The Ark's Anniversary*
Gerald Durrell, draft obituary of Sir Peter Scott, 2 July 1990
Gerald Durrell, letter to J.F. Lipscomb, London Zoo, 20 June 1964
Gerald Durrell, letter to Alan and Ella Thomas, 1964 (Durrell Archives,
    Manuscript Department, British Library)
Gerald Durrell, *The Stationary Ark*
Jacquie Durrell, *Beasts in my Bed*
Jacquie Durrell, interview with the author, November 1995
Jacquie Durrell to the author, January and September 1997, January 1998
Louisa Durrell, letter to Lawrence and Claude Durrell, August 1963 (Durrell
    Archives, Manuscript Department, British Library)
Peter Grose, interview with the author, July 1996
John Hartley in group discussion with the author at Jersey Zoo, November 1996
John Hartley to the author, June 1998
Ian MacNiven, *Lawrence Durrell: A Biography*
Jeremy Mallinson, interview with the author, November 1995
Jeremy Mallinson, *Travels in Search of Endangered Species*
Christopher Parsons, *A Bull Called Marius*
Christopher Parsons, *True to Nature*
Catha Weller, interview with the author, November 1996

CHAPTER NINETEEN: Volcano Rabbits and the King of Corfu

BBC TV, *The Garden of the Gods*
Gerald Durrell, *The Ark's Anniversary*
Gerald Durrell, *Catch me a Colobus*
Gerald Durrell, 'Dead as a Dodo', c.1967
Gerald Durrell, letter to Leslie Durrell, 9 October 1967
Gerald Durrell, letter to International Union for the Conservation of Nature and
    Natural Resources, 20 July 1968
Gerald Durrell, letter to Alan and Shirley Thomas, 5 October 1966
Gerald Durrell, letters to Alan Thomas (Durrell Archives, Manuscript
    Department, British Library)
Jacquie Durrell to the author, 24 January 1998
Doreen Evans, interview with the author, July 1996
David Hughes, *Himself and Other Animals*
JWPT Newsletter, August 1969
Lee Langley, 'The Other Mr Durrell', *Guardian*, 1 August 1970
Christopher Parsons, *True to Nature*
Christopher Parsons, interview with the author, July 1996
Peggy Peel, *The Search for the Teporingo*, Australian Broadcasting Corporation,
    Melbourne, 1969

Marshall Pugh, 'Have You Lost the Sense of Wonderment?', *Daily Mail*, 23 February 1966
Peter Scott, letter to Gordon Bowker, 14 March 1997

CHAPTER TWENTY: Crack-Up

Gerald Durrell, 'The Antique World', National Magazine Co., 24 March 1972
Gerald Durrell, 'Christmas with Corals', *House & Garden* (USA), December 1971
Gerald Durrell, 'Directive to Sir Giles and Lady Guthrie' (typescript, n.d.)
Gerald Durrell in *JWPT Newsletter*, August 1969 and March 1970
Gerald Durrell, letter to Marie Aspioti, 7 May 1968
Gerald Durrell, letter to *Melbourne Age*, 3 June 1970
Gerald Durrell, letter to Alan Thomas, 6 February 1969
Gerald Durrell, letter to Alan and Ella Thomas, 27 May 1968
Gerald Durrell, memo to Sir Giles Guthrie, 19 June 1970
Gerald Durrell, typescript of article submitted to *Melbourne Herald*, 19 June 1970
Jacquie Durrell, *Beasts in my Bed*
Jacquie Durrell, interview with the author, October 1995
Jacquie Durrell to the author, 24 January 1998
Jacquie Durrell, quoted in *Melbourne Age*, 15 November 1969
Lawrence Durrell (ed. Alan Thomas), *Spirit of Place*
Peter Grose, interview with the author, July 1996
David Hughes, *Himself and Other Animals*

CHAPTER TWENTY-ONE: Pulling Through

John Burton, obituary of Gerald Durrell, *Guardian*, 31 January 1995
Gerald Durrell, letters to Lady Saranne Calthorpe, 27 June and 19 July 1971
Gerald Durrell, letter to Mr J.D. Cody, Collins Publishers, Melbourne, 22 March 1971
Gerald Durrell, letters to Lawrence Durrell, 19 November and 2 December 1971 (Durrell Archives, Manuscript Department, British Library)
Gerald Durrell, letter to Sir Giles Guthrie, 16 July 1971
Gerald Durrell, letter to Lord Jersey, 16 April 1971
Gerald Durrell, letter to Miss D. McAlpin, 18 March 1971
Gerald Durrell, letter and film outline to Christopher Parsons, 23 November 1970
Gerald Durrell, letter to Mai Zetterling, 19 June 1971
Gerald Durrell, manuscript notes for proposed cookbook (Jersey, n.d.)
Gerald Durrell, quoted in David Cobham, 'Animals are my Life', script for proposed TV programme, November 1975
Jacquie Durrell, letter to Lawrence Durrell, 21 October 1970
Jacquie Durrell to the author, 23 January and 21 February 1998
Peter Grose, interview with the author, July 1996
Sir Giles Guthrie, letter to Gerald Durrell, 14 June 1971
Lady Rhona Guthrie, interview with the author, October 1996

David Hughes, *Himself and Other Animals*

JWPT Report, 21 September 1970, and 'Memorandum', 24 September 1970

Jean Mohr, 'Durrell's Zoo', *World Health* (Lausanne), May 1968

Penny Nelson, 'We Must Own our Place of Work if the Zoo is to Survive', *Jersey Evening Post*, 12 February 1971

'Gerald Durrell OBE', *Oryx* (FFPS), vol. 29, 1995

Brian Park, in 'Memoirs of Gerald Durrell by Friends and Colleagues' (typescript, Jersey, 31 January 1995)

Christopher Parsons, *True to Nature*

Alan Thomas, letter to Gerald Durrell, 17 June 1970

Edward Whitley, 'The Man who Preferred Animals to People', *Daily Mail*, 31 January 1995

CHAPTER TWENTY-TWO: The Palace Revolution

HRH Princess Anne, in *Tribute to Gerald Durrell*, BBC South-West TV, 7 February 1995

Jean-Michel Damiani, letter to the author, 2 April 1972

Gerald Durrell, *The Ark's Anniversary*

Gerald Durrell, 'Forward', in R.W. Martin (ed.), *Breeding Endangered Species in Captivity*

Gerald Durrell, letters to Lawrence Durrell, December 1971

Gerald Durrell, letter to Sir William Haley, Jersey, 16 December 1972

Gerald Durrell, letter to Lord Jersey, 13 November 1972

Gerald Durrell, letter to B.K. Schramm, 14 December 1972

Gerald Durrell, letter to Alan Thomas, 31 May 1972

Gerald Durrell, in *JWPT Newsletter*, August 1972

Gerald Durrell, 'Memo to Trustees' Investigation Committee', 3 October 1972

Gerald Durrell, 'Progress Report 1963–72' (JWPT, c. January 1973)

Jacquie Durrell, interview with the author, October 1995

Jacquie Durrell to the author, 25 January 1998

Peter Grose, interview with the author, July 1996

Lady Rhona Guthrie, interview with the author, October 1996

Lord Jersey, letter to the author, 29 November 1996

Lord Jersey, letter to Lady Guthrie, 2 July 1991

'New Trustees Named by Jersey Wildlife Trust', *Jersey Evening Post*, 1 February 1973

Dr R.D. Martin, 'Gerald Durrell 1925–1995', *Biodiversity and Conservation*, no. 4, 1995

Dr R.D. Martin, interview with the author, November 1997

'Memorandum from the President of the Council of the JWPT', September 1971

Peggy Caird Peel, *International Conference on Endangered Species*, BBC External Services, 5 May 1972

Dr Reed, Director of National Zoological Park, Washington, quoted in JWPT memo 'Policy to be Stressed at the Scientific Advisory Committee Meeting, 1971'

CHAPTER TWENTY-THREE: Gerald in America

David Cobham to the author, 29 January and 16 February 1998
Fred Coleman, 'Zoo Dedicated to Animal Preservation', *Daily Press*, *Newport News*, Virginia, 30 January 1972
Gerald Durrell, *The Ark's Anniversary*
Gerald Durrell, quoted in David Cobham, 'Animals are my Life', script for proposed TV programme, November 1975
Gerald Durrell, *The Stationary Ark* (commentary typescript)
Jacquie Durrell, interview with the author, October 1995
Jacquie Durrell to the author, 23 January and 3 February 1998
David Hughes, interview with the author, October 1995
Thomas E. Lovejoy, 'Recollections of Gerald Durrell, *Dodo*, no. 31, 1995
Jeremy Lucas, 'Durrell and the Dodo' (unpublished ms, 1987)
Peter Olney, interview with the author, July 1996

CHAPTER TWENTY-FOUR: 'Two Very Lost People'

Isaiah Berlin, 'The Hedgehog and the Fox', in Henry Hardy and Aileen Kelly eds), *Russian Thinkers*
David Cobham to the author, January 1997 and February 1998
Margaret Duncan (Durrell) to the author, December 1997
Gerald Durrell, *The Ark's Anniversary*
Gerald Durrell, in *JWPT Newsletter*, no. 24, March 1975
Gerald Durrell, letters to Lawrence Durrell, 14 August 1976 and 7 April 1977
Gerald Durrell, letter to Shirley Thomas, 27 February 1976 (Durrell Archives, Manuscript Department, British Library)
Jacquie Durrell, interview with the author, October 1995
Jacquie Durrell to the author, January and October 1997, January and February 1998
W. Paterson Ferns to the author, 22 June 1998
John Hartley, interview with the author, October 1996
Simon Hicks, interview with the author, November 1996
David Hughes, *His Family and Other Animals*
David Hughes, interview with the author, October 1995
Judy Mackrell, interview with the author, June 1996
Jeremy Mallinson, interview with the author, October 1995
Jeremy Mallinson to the author, 29 June 1998
Peggy Peel, diary

CHAPTER TWENTY-FIVE: Love Story – Prelude

Aiken Standard, Aiken, South Carolina, 18 April 1977
Augusta Sunday Chronicle, 17 April 1977
Margaret Duncan (Durrell), interview with the author, 1996
Margaret Duncan (Durrell) to the author, January 1998
Gerald Durrell, *The Ark's Anniversary*
Lee Durrell, interview with the author, November 1995

Indira Gandhi, letter to Sir Peter Scott, 25 May 1976
JWPT Newsletter, Summer 1977
Alexandra Mayhew, interview with the author, July 1996
Alexandra Mayhew, letter to Mrs R. Mayhew, 18 March 1978
Alexandra Mayhew, 'Assam Diary' (ms, 1978)
Fiametta Rocco, 'How we Met', *Independent on Sunday*, 25 October 1992
Harcharn Singh, letter to Gerald Durrell, 22 March 1978

CHAPTER TWENTY-SIX: Love Story – Finale

Gerald Durrell to Margaret Duncan (Durrell), July 1978
Lawrence Durrell, letters to Henry Miller, 12 May 1978 and 6 January 1979
    (Ian MacNiven (ed.), *The Durrell–Miller Letters*)
Jane Gregory, 'Gerald Durrell and the Jersey Sanctuary', *Chicago Sun-Times*,
    September 1978

CHAPTER TWENTY-SEVEN: A Zoo with a View

Mark Abley, 'A Passionate Zoo Keeper and Other Animals', *Maclean's
    Magazine,* 1980
Tony Allchurch, interview with the author, 1997
Felicity Bryan, interview with the author, 1996
Joseph Campbell, *The Hero with a Thousand Faces*
Philip Coffey, interview with the author, 1997
Fleur Cowles, interview with the author, 1995
Fleur Cowles, 'Memories of Gerald Durrell' (typescript, 1995)
Margaret Duncan (Durrell), interview with the author, 1995
Gerald Durrell, *The Ark's Anniversary*
Gerald Durrell, interview on County Sound Radio, Guildford, and LBC, London,
    1985
Gerald Durrell, interview with *Indianapolis News*, 24 November 1979
Gerald Durrell, letter to Lawrence Durrell, 6 February 1978
Gerald Durrell, letter to Peter Grose, 6 April 1979
Gerald Durrell, letter to Dick Odgers, 3 June 1981
Gerald Durrell, *The Stationary Ark*
Gerald Durrell, taped conversation with John Burton, n.d.
Gerald Durrell, in 'The World Guide to the Best of Everything', *Highlife*
    magazine, 1979
Lee Durrell, interview with the author, October 1996
Peter Grose, letter to John Hartley, 12 December 1978
John Hartley, interview with the author, October 1996
Fred Hauptführer, 'Gerald Durrell, a Modern Noah', *People* magazine,
    1981
Simon Hicks, interview with the author, October 1996, and letter to the author,
    2 April 1998
David Hughes, *Himself and Other Animals*
International Crane Foundation, Baraboo, Wisconsin, telegram to the Japanese
    Government, via WPTI and JWPT, c.1979

Colin Jones, interview with the author
Jeremy Mallinson, interview with the author, November 1995
Dr R. D. Martin, interview with the author, November 1997
Dr Desmond Morris to the author, September 1996
Richard North, 'One Man and his Zoo', *Radio Times*, 5–11 July 1980
Peter Olney, interview with the author, July 1996
Robin Rumboll, interview with the author
Christopher Vogler, *The Winter's Journey*
Jenny Woolf, 'A Life in the Day of Gerald Durrell', *Sunday Times Magazine*,
    October 1983
Philip Ziegler, letter to Peter Grose, 5 March 1979
Lord Zuckerman, closing address to the second World Conference on Breeding
    Endangered Species in Captivity, in P.J.S. Olney (ed.), *1977 International
    Zoo Year Book*

CHAPTER TWENTY-EIGHT: Ark on the Move

Gerald Durrell, *Ark on the Move*
Gerald Durrell, *Golden Bats and Pink Pigeons*
Gerald Durrell, introduction to Alison Jolly and John Mack, *Madagascar: Crisis
    in Eden*
Gerald Durrell, letter to Hal and Harriet McGeorge, 20 July 1981
Gerald Durrell, 'Madagascar Notes' (transcripts from taped notes, 1981)
Gerald Durrell, 'The Mauritian Expedition', *JWPT Newsletter* no. 27, June 1976
W. Paterson Ferns to the author, 22 June 1998
Carl Jones to the author, 1996
Jeremy Mallinson, letter to Gerald Durrell, 7 August 1981
Dinah Sheridan, letter to Gerald Durrell, 19 July 1981
Theo Stephanides, letter to Gerald Durrell, 2 February 1982

CHAPTER TWENTY-NINE: The Amateur Naturalist

Lynne Barber, 'A Natural Gift' (*Independent on Sunday Magazine*, 1987)
Felicity Bryan, letter to Gerald Durrell, 15 July 1980
Richard Connif, 'Gerald Durrell', *Geo*, May 1983
'Durrell's Flora and Fauna', *Irish Times*, 13 November 1982
Gerald Durrell, *The Amateur Naturalist*
Gerald Durrell, 'Anthropomorphia' (ms, Jersey, c.1976)
Gerald Durrell, *The Ark's Anniversary*
Gerald Durrell, *How to Shoot an Amateur Naturalist*
Gerald Durrell, letters to Hal and Harriet McGeorge, 7 February and 31 March
    1983
Gerald Durrell, letter to Alexandra Mayhew, 15 September 1983
Gerald Durrell, letter to Alan Thomas, 26 May 1983
W. Paterson Ferns, letter to Gerald Durrell, 16 January 1984
Paula Harris (Quigley) to the author, April and May 1998
Simon Hicks, interview with the author, October 1996

Anne Hilton, 'A Must for Wildlife Beginners' (Trinidad and Tobago press review, n.d.)
'Madagascar Accord' *On the Edge*, spring 1983
Helen Paske, 'Animal Magnetism', *New Zealand Listener*, 12 January 1985
Joan Porter, interview with the author, November 1995
Peter Schirmer, *Talking of Books*, South African Broadcasting Corporation, 16 December 1982
Alan Thomas, letter to Gerald Durrell, 11 October 1984

CHAPTER THIRTY: To Russia with Lee

Gerald Durrell, *Durrell in Russia*
Gerald Durrell, 'Durrell in Russia' (thirteen television outlines, 1984)
Gerald Durrell, 'USSR Diary' (1994–95)
Gerald Durrell, 'Wildlife and Conservation in the USSR' (filming schedule, 1985)
Lee Durrell, interview with the author, November 1995
Lee Durrell, 'USSR Diary' (1994–95)
Nielsen-Ferns Productions, *Durrell in Russia* production document
'The Other Russians', *ROM Rotunda*, 25 November 1985

CHAPTER THIRTY-ONE: Grand Old Man

Jim Bawden, 'Modern Noah Saving Nature on Film', *Toronto Star*, 2 November 1986)
Book Buyer's Choice, April/May 1986
British Council, Yaounda, letter to Gerald Durrell, May 1990
Felicity Bryan, letters to Gerald Durrell, 19 June 1985 and 20 March 1987
John Burton, obituary of Gerald Durrell, *Independent*, 31 January 1995
Mike Cable, 'Growing up in the Garden of the Gods', *Radio Times*, 17 October 1987
Paul Donovan, 'The Pets of Paradise Isle', *Today*, 17 April 1987
Gerald Durrell, *The Ark's Anniversary*
Gerald Durrell, *The Aye-Aye and I*
Gerald Durrell, 'Happy with Larry', *Sunday Telegraph*, 21 April 1991
Gerald Durrell, taped conversation with John Burton, n.d.
Gerald Durrell, 'Introducing DICE', *On the Edge*, June 1990
Gerald Durrell, correspondence with the wife of the British Ambassador, Yaounda, May 1990 and August 1991
Gerald Durrell, letter to Hal and Harriet McGeorge, 21 January 1991
Gerald Durrell, letter to Mrs Adda Mayhew, 29 May 1987
Gerald Durrell, letter to Alan Thomas, 17 April 1991
Gerald Durrell's accountants' annual statements 1974–94 (Jersey Archives)
Lawrence Durrell, notebook, 1990
Lee Durrell, 'Brilliant Belize', *On the Edge*, March 1989
Sappho Durrell, journals (quoted in Ian MacNiven, *Lawrence Durrell*)
Simon Hicks, interview with the author, November 1995
Jersey Trust, 'Memories of Gerald Durrell by Friends and Colleagues', 31 January 1995

Eileen McCarroll, 'Childhood in Corfu', *Woman's Weekly*, 7 November 1987
Ian MacNiven, *Lawrence Durrell: A Biography*
Spike Milligan, letter to Gerald Durrell, 26 June 1987
Stephanie Nettell, 'A Slow Ride to Save the World,' *Guardian*, 4 November 1987
Justine Picardie, 'A Father's Shadow', *Independent*, 28 September 1991
Children at Piper's Corner School, Great Kingshill, Bucks, letters to Gerald Durrell, May 1984
Barbara Robson, 'The Darker Side of Durrell', *Sunday Telegraph*, 26 May 1991
Margaret Thatcher, letter to Gerald Durrell, 19 March 1986
Treasurer of the States of Jersey, letter to the President of the Tourism Committee, 1 May 1990
T.H. Watkins, 'Lights! Camera! Giraffes!' *Washington Post*, n.d.
Edward Whitley, 'My Family and Gerald Durrell, *Sunday Telegraph*, 5 February 1995
Edward Whitley, 'Unforgettable Gerald Durrell', *Reader's Digest*, July 1995

CHAPTER THIRTY-TWO: 'Details of my Hypochondria'

Jamie Ambrose, 'The Lady and the Tortoise, *The American*, 11 December 1992
Sharon Amos, 'Preservation Instinct', *Country Living*, January 1993
Sir David Attenborough, letter to the author, 4 April 1998
Margaret Duncan (Durrell), letter to a friend, 9 September 1990
Gerald Durrell, letter to David Jones, Director General, Zoological Society of London, 19 December 1991
Gerald Durrell, draft ms letter to John Knowles, Marwell Zoo, n.d.
Gerald Durrell, interview on County Sound Radio, Guildford, and LBC, London, 1985
Gerald Durrell, letter to Cyril Littlewood, 8 June 1993
Gerald Durrell, letter to *The Times*, 22 July 1992
Gerald Durrell, untitled draft typescript re Earth Summit and work of JWPT, 13 March 1992
David Hughes, *Himself and Other Animals*
Donald Dale Jackson in *The Smithsonian*, August 1993
Sarah Kennedy to the author, April 1998
Dr Desmond Morris to the author, 19 September 1996
'Sixth World Conference', *On the Edge*, May 1992

CHAPTER THIRTY-THREE: 'A Whole New Adventure'

'Animal Instinct', *Starweek* magazine, Canada, 25 January 1986
Sir David Attenborough, 'Let them come here', quoted in *On the Edge*, June 1994
Douglas Botting, *Gavin Maxwell: A Life*
Gerald Durrell, 'Autobiographical Fragments' (unpublished typescript, Jersey Archives)
Gerald Durrell, letters to Hal and Harriet McGeorge, 1992 and 1993
Jacquie Durrell, letter to Jeremy Mallinson, 31 March 1994
Lawrence Durrell, quoted in David Hughes, *Himself and Other Animals*

Lee Durrell, interview with the author, October 1996
Lee Durrell, letter to Françoise Kestsman, 28 November 1994
Margaret Duncan (Durrell), interview with the author, November 1997
'Gerald Durrell OBE' *On the Edge*, February 1995
Dr Jeremy Guyer, interview with the author
Paula and Jeremy Harris, interview with the author
Simon Hicks, interview with the author, November 1996
David Hughes, interview with the author, October 1995
Jeremy Mallinson, interview with the author, November 1997
Alexandra Mayhew, interview with the author, July 1996
Dr Guy O'Keeffe, interview with the author
Press Association news flash, 30 January 1995
Alun Rees, 'Maniac who Broke Heart of Durrell', *Daily Express*, 2 March 1995
Robin Rumboll, interview with the author
Dr Christopher Tibbs, interview with the author

BIBLIOGRAPHY
INDEX

Bibliography

Books by Gerald Durrell

The Overloaded Ark (Faber & Faber, 1953)
Three Singles to Adventure (Rupert Hart-Davis, 1954)
The Bafut Beagles (Rupert Hart-Davis, 1954)
The New Noah (Collins, 1955)
The Drunken Forest (Rupert Hart-Davis, 1956)
My Family and Other Animals (Rupert Hart-Davis, 1956)
Encounters with Animals (Rupert Hart-Davis, 1958)
A Zoo in my Luggage (Rupert Hart-Davis, 1960)
Look at Zoos (Hamish Hamilton, 1961)
The Whispering Land (Rupert Hart-Davis, 1961)
Island Zoo (Collins, 1962)
My Favourite Animal Stories (Lutterworth, 1962)
Menagerie Manor (Rupert Hart-Davis, 1964)
Two in the Bush (Collins, 1966)
The Donkey Rustlers (Collins, 1968)
Rosie is my Relative (Collins, 1968)
Birds, Beasts and Relatives (Collins, 1969)
Fillets of Plaice (Collins, 1971)
Catch me a Colobus (Collins, 1972)
Beasts in my Belfry (Collins, 1973)
The Talking Parcel (Collins, 1974)
The Stationary Ark (Collins, 1976)
Golden Bats and Pink Pigeons (Collins, 1977)
Garden of the Gods (Collins, 1978)
The Picnic and Suchlike Pandemonium (Collins, 1979)
The Mockery Bird (Collins, 1981)
The Amateur Naturalist (with Lee Durrell, Hamish Hamilton, 1982)
Ark on the Move (Collins, 1982)
How to Shoot an Amateur Naturalist (Collins, 1984)
Durrell in Russia (Macdonald, 1986)
The Fantastic Flying Journey (Conran Octopus, 1987)
The Fantastic Dinosaur Adventure (Conran Octopus, 1989)
The Ark's Anniversary (Collins, 1990)

Keeper (Michael O'Mara, 1990)
Marrying off Mother (HarperCollins, 1991)
Toby the Tortoise (Michael O'Mara, 1991)
The Aye-Aye and I (HarperCollins, 1992)
The Best of Gerald Durrell (edited by Lee Durrell, HarperCollins, 1996)

General

Bendiner, Robert, *The Fall of the Wild, the Rise of the Zoo* (Dutton, New York, 1981)

Bisson, Mike (ed.), *Jersey Zoo: The First Twenty-Five Years (Jersey Evening Post* Souvenir Publication, Jersey, 1964)

Bowker, Gordon, *Through the Dark Labyrinth: A Biography of Lawrence Durrell* (Sinclair-Stevenson, London, 1996)

Durrell, Jacquie, *Beasts in my Bed* (Collins, London, 1967)

Durrell, Jacquie, *Intimate Relations* (G. K. Hall, Boston, 1977)

Durrell, Lawrence, *Prospero's Cell* (Faber & Faber, London, 1945)

Durrell, Lawrence, *Bitter Lemons* (Faber & Faber, London, 1957)

Durrell, Lawrence, *Spirit of Place: Mediterranean Writings* (Faber & Faber, London, 1969)

Durrell, Lee, *State of the Ark* (Bodley Head, London, 1986. Foreword by Gerald Durrell)

Durrell, Margaret, *Whatever Happened to Margo?* (André Deutsch, London, 1995)

Eldredge, Niles, *Fossils: The Evolution and Extinction of Species* (Harry N. Abrams Inc., New York, 1991)

Evans, Peter, *Ourselves and Other Animals* (Pantheon Books, New York, 1987)

Hughes, David, *Himself and Other Animals: A Portrait of Gerald Durrell* (Hutchinson, London, 1997)

Huxley, Elizabeth, *Whipsnade: Captive Breeding for Survival* (1981)

Huxley, Elspeth, *Peter Scott: Painter and Naturalist* (Faber & Faber, London, 1995)

Jersey Wildlife Preservation Trust, *Before Another Song Ends* (Jersey, 1991)

Jersey Wildlife Preservation Trust, *The Wildlife Preservation Trust* (Jersey 1991)

Jersey Wildlife Preservation Trust, *The Wildlife Preservation Trusts* (Jersey, 1996)

Johnstone-Scott, Richard, *Jambo: A Gorilla's Story* (Michael O'Mara, London 1995)

Lucas, Jeremy, 'Durrell and the Dodo' (unpublished typescript, 1988)

MacNiven, Ian, *Lawrence Durrell: A Biography* (Faber & Faber, London, 1998)

MacNiven, Ian and Moore, Harry T., *Literary Lifelines: The Richard Aldington–Lawrence Durrell Correspondence* (Viking Press, New York, 1981)

MacNiven, Ian (ed.), *The Durrell–Miller Letters 1935–1980* (Faber & Faber, London, 1988)

Mallinson, Jeremy, *The Facts About a Zoo* (André Deutsch, London, 1980. Introduction by Gerald Durrell)

Mallinson, Jeremy, *Travels in Search of Endangered Species* (David & Charles, Newton Abbot, 1989. Foreword by Gerald Durrell)

Martin, R. D. (ed.), *Breeding Endangered Species in Captivity* (Academic Press, London, 1975. Foreword by Gerald Durrell)

Mathiessen, Peter, *Wildlife in America* (Viking Press, New York, 1964)

Olney, Peter (*et al.*), *Science for Conservation: Papers from the Sixth Zoo Breeding Conference* (London, 1991)

Osborn, Fairfield, *Our Plundered Planet* (New York, 1948)

Parsons, Christopher, *A Bull Called Marius* (BBC, London, 1971. Introduction by Gerald Durrell)

Parsons, Christopher, *True to Nature* (Patrick Stephens, Cambridge, 1982)

Pendar, Lucy, *Whipsnade: 'My Africa'* (The Book Castle, Dunstable, 1991. Introduction by Gerald Durrell)

Pinchin, Jane Lagoudis, 'Sideways out of the House: Lawrence and Gerald Durrell', in *Blood Brothers: Siblings as Writers* (ed. Norman Kiele, International Universities Press, New York, 1983)

Reader's Digest, *Protecting the Earth's Wild Animals* (London, 1997. Includes special illustrated condensation of Gerald Durrell's *The Aye-Aye and I*)

Stephanides, Theo, *Island Trails* (Macdonald, London, 1973. Introduction by Gerald Durrell)

Tudge, Colin, *Last Animals at the Zoo: How Mass Extinction can be Stopped* (Hutchinson, London, 1991)

Vandivert, Rita, *To the Rescue: Seven Heroes of Conservation* (Frederick Warne, New York, 1982. Includes Gerald Durrell)

Index